Artificial Intelligence

Springer
Berlin
Heidelberg
New York
Barcelona
Hong Kong
London
Milan
Paris
Singapore
Tokyo

K. R. Apt V. W. Marek
M. Truszczynski D. S. Warren (Eds.)

The Logic Programming Paradigm

A 25-Year Perspective

With 57 Figures

Springer

Prof. Krzysztof R. Apt
Stichting Mathematisch Centrum
Centrum voor Wiskunde en Informatica
Kruislaan 413
1098 SJ Amsterdam, The Netherlands
E-mail: apt@cwi.nl

Prof. Victor W. Marek
Prof. Mirek Truszczynski
University of Kentucky
Department of Computer Science
773 Anderson Hall
Lexington, KY 40506-0046, USA
E-mail: {marek, mirek} @cs.uky.edu

Prof. David S. Warren
University at Stony Brook
Computer Science Department
Stony Brook, NY 11794-4400, USA
E-mail: warren@cs.sunysb.edu

ACM Computing Classification (1998): D.1.6, D.1.3, F.3.2, F.4.1, H.2.3, I.2.3, I.2.11
ISBN-13:978-3-642-64249-4

Library of Congress Cataloging-in-Publication Data
The Logic programming paradigm: a 25-year perspective / K. Apt... [et al.].
p. cm. – (Artificial intelligence)
ISBN-13:978-3-642-64249-4 e-ISBN-13:978-3-642-60085-2
DOI: 10.1007/978-3-642-60085-2

1. Logic programming. I. Apt, Krzysztof R., 1949– .
II. Series: Artificial intelligence (Berlin, Germany)
QA76.63.L634 1999 005.1'15–dc21 98-18481 CIP

Softcover reprint of the hardcover 1st edition 1999

Cover design: Künkel+Lopka Werbeagentur, Heidelberg
Typesetting: Camera-ready by authors/editors
SPIN 10692061 45/3142 - 5 4 3 2 1 0 - Printed on acid-free paper

Preface

Historical Background

Logic programming was founded some 25 years ago. Its birth is usually associated with the seminal paper of Robert Kowalski [5] in which a computation mechanism was proposed that made it possible to use logical formulas as programs. About the same time this idea was realized by Alain Colmerauer and his team in a programming language, Prolog.

The creation of logic programming is the outcome of a long history that for most of its course ran within logic and only later inside computer science. For a proper historical perspective to this volume let us briefly retrace this history.

Logic programming is based on the syntax of first-order logic, which was originally proposed in the second half of the 19th century by Gottlob Frege and later modified to its current form by Giuseppe Peano and Bertrand Russell.

In the 1930s Kurt Gödel and Jacques Herbrand studied the notion of computatibility based on derivations. These works can be viewed as the origin of the "computation as deduction" paradigm. Additionally, Herbrand disscussed in his PhD thesis a set of rules for manipulating algebraic equations on terms that can be viewed now as a sketch of a unification algorithm.

Another thirty years passed before Alan Robinson published, in 1965, his seminal paper that lies at the foundations of the field of automated deduction. In this paper he introduced the resolution principle, the notion of unification and a unification algorithm.

Using the resolution method, one can prove theorems of first-order logic, but another step was needed to see how one could compute within this framework. In 1971 Kowalski and Kuehner introduced a limited form of resolution, called linear resolution. This finally formed the basis for Kowalski's subsequent proposal of what we now call SLD-resolution. This form of resolution is more restricted than the one proposed by Robinson in the sense that only clauses with a limited syntax are allowed. However, this restriction now has a side effect in that it produces a satisfying substitution, which can be viewed as the result of a computation.

A number of other ideas to realize the computation-as-deduction paradigm were proposed around the same time, notably by Cordell Green and Carl Hewitt, but Kowalski's proposal, probably because of its simplicity, elegance and versatility, became most succesful. In particular, the crucial insights of Alain Colmerauer on the programming side and David H. D. Warren on the implementation side made it possible to turn this approach to computing into a realistic approach to programming.

By now Prolog is standardized — see [3] and new books on Prolog and logic programming keep appearing, for instance [1] and [2].

Why This Volume

Logic programming is an unusual area of Computer Science in that it cuts across many fields that are themselves autonomous Computer Science areas. More specifically, chapters on it or its uses can be found in standard textbooks on programming languages such as [7] (see Chapter 8 "Logic Programming"), database systems such as [9] (see Chapter 3 "Logic as Data Model" that describes the datalog), compiler writing (see Chapter 4 "Compilation of Logic Programming Languages" in [10]), artificial intelligence (see, e.g., [8] in which all algorithms are implemented in Prolog), natural language processing (by employing Prolog, as in [4]), and more recently machine learning (see Chapter 10 "Learning Sets of Rules" in [6] that deals with inductive logic programming).

This richness of the logic programming paradigm can be attributed to the remarkable simplicity and conciseness of its syntax that, in its basic form, consists of Horn clause logic. The major discovery of Kowalski and Colmerauer 25 years ago was that this syntax is sufficient for computing. One of the first application areas of logic programming was natural language processing. Time has shown that this formalism can also be profitably used for a number of other purposes, for instance, knowledge representation, parallel computing, and machine learning. Further, various simple extensions made this formalism applicable for such diverse uses as database systems, formalization of commonsense reasoning, and constraint programming.

At the same time this omnipresence of logic programming is a sign of its weakness. In most of these areas logic programming has found a niche but did not become the main technology. In particular, in the case of software engineering the world seems to be ruled by the imperative programming paradigm, and the declarative programming paradigm embodied by logic programming and functional programming has not gained enough ground to be widely recognized by the industry.

On the other hand the number of industrial applications developed using the logic programming technology is steadily growing and is much larger than most of us realize. Originally, these applications have been developed using mainly Prolog. In more recent applications also constraint logic programming and inductive logic programming systems have been used.

These and related considerations about the current role of logic programming were behind the organization of a meeting in Shakertown, Kentucky, USA in April 1998.

Our idea was to review the state of the art in logic programming, to assess the situation in this field, and to clarify what progress has been made in it in recent years. We invited the leading researchers in all subareas of logic programming and asked them to review the field and to present promising future directions of research. In addition, we asked for input from colleagues from neighboring fields in order to put the situation within the logic programming field in an appropriate context. This led to the present volume that provides a unique perspective of this field, 25 years after its creation, a perspective that is broad in scope and rich in suggestions.

In fact, the articles here presented cover most of the areas of logic programming. Their emphasis is on the assessment of achievements in this field and on promising future directions.

Contributions

Contributions included in this book are organized according to their subject areas. The reader will find that, independently of their subjects, the papers can be classified into three main types. The first kind provides an assessment of a specific subfield of logic programming. The articles in this group deal with

- natural language processing, by Veronica Dahl,
- planning, by Vladimir Lifschitz,
- inductive logic programming, by Luc de Raedt,
- programming methodology, by Danny de Schreye and Marc Denecker, and
- concurrent logic programming, by Kazunori Ueda.

The contributions of the second kind offer some new lines of research by reassessing known ideas and concepts of logic programming and by shedding new light on their use. The articles in this group are by

- Krzysztof Apt and Marc Bezem, on an alternative approach to declarative programming,
- Howard Blair, Fred Dushin, David Jakel, Angel Rivera and Metin Sezgin, on relating logic programming to continuous mathematics,
- Marco Bozzano, Giorgio Delzanno, Maurizio Martelli, Viviana Mascardi and Floriano Zini, on the use of logic programming for rapid prototyping of multi-agent systems,
- Koichi Furukawa, on the use of inverse entailment in inductive logic programming,

- Manuel Hermenegildo, Germán Puebla and Francisco Bueno, on the use of abstract interpretations for program development,
- Gopal Gupta, on use of logic programming for program semantics and compilation,
- Michael Maher, on the addition of constraints to logical formalisms,
- Victor Marek and Mirek Truszczyński, on an alternative approach to logic programming via the use of stable models, and
- Carlo Zaniolo and Haixun Wang, on logic-based foundations for advanced database applications, such as data mining.

Finally, in the third type of contributions, the ideas originally conceived within logic programming are applied to areas that at first glance have nothing to do with it. These are contributions by

- Paul Tarau, on mobile agent programming,
- Jacques Cohen, on computational molecular biology, and
- Maarten van Emden, on numerical computing.

Additionally,

- Saumya Debray studies program optimization within a multi-language environment,

and, in a contribution from a neighbouring field,

- Philip Wadler provides some insights into the use of functional programming in industry.

We would like to take this opportunity to thank all the authors of the submitted papers for having agreed to contribute to this special issue and for their help in putting this volume together, and the referees for giving of their time and providing helpful reviews of the papers.

References

1. K. R. Apt. *From Logic Programming to Prolog.* Prentice-Hall, London, 1997.
2. W. F. Clocksin. *Clause and Effect.* Springer-Verlag, Berlin, 1997.
3. P. Deransart, A. Ed-Dbali, and L. Cervoni. *Prolog: The Standard.* Springer-Verlag, Berlin, 1996.
4. G. Gazdar and C. Mellish. *Natural Language Processing in PROLOG.* Addison-Wesley, 1989.
5. R.A. Kowalski. Predicate logic as a programming language. In *Proceedings IFIP'74*, pages 569–574. North-Holland, 1974.
6. T. M. Mitchell. *Machine Learning.* McGraw-Hill, 1997.
7. R. Sethi. *Programming Languages: Concepts and Constructs.* Addison-Wesley, 1989.

8. Y. Shoham. *Artificial Intelligence Techniques in Prolog.* Morgan Kaufmann, San Francisco, CA, 1994.
9. J.D. Ullman. *Principles of Database and Knowledge-base Systems, Volume I.* Principles of Computer Science Series. Computer Science Press, 1988.
10. R. Wilhelm and D. Maurer. *Compiler Design.* Addison-Wesley, 1995.

Amsterdam — *Krzysztof R. Apt*
Lexington, KY — *Victor W. Marek*
Lexington, KY — *Mirosław Truszczyński*
Stony Brook, NY — *David S. Warren*

Contents

Part I

Computing and Programming

1 Concurrent and Agent Programming

This chapter deals with logic programming approaches to multi-agent programming, mobile computing, and concurrent programming.

Multi-Agent Systems (MAS) can be defined as a set of autonomous, intelligent, and interacting entities that can flexibly cooperate to achieve a common goal or compete to satisfy "personal interests". This potentially makes them an ideal tool for Software Engineering, since it allow us to view a complex system abstracting from details. In particular, the MAS technology seems to be suitable for taking care of two aspects that are nowadays fundamental for new software products: *distribution* of computational entities and resources, and *integration* of different kinds of existing legacy software or data.

Bozzano, Delzanno, Martelli, Mascardi and **Zini** present an ongoing research project that uses logic programming (and in particular linear logic programming) and its techniques for executable specifications and rapid prototyping of Multi-Agent Systems. The MAS paradigm is a very rich one and the authors believe that logic programming will play a very effective role in this area, both as a tool to develop real applications and as a semantically well-founded language on which program analysis and proofs of properties could be based.

The paradigm shift towards networked, mobile, ubiquitous computing has brought a number of challenges which require new ways to deal with increasingly complex patterns of interaction: autonomous, reactive, and mobile computational entities are needed to take care of unforeseen problems. This led to the emergence of agent programs with increasingly sophisticated inference capabilities.

Tarau introduces Jinni, a new, lightweight, multi-threaded logic programming language, intended to be used as a flexible scripting tool for glueing together knowledge processing components and Java objects in networked client/server applications, as well as through applets over the Web. Its mobile code allows agents organized as multiple threads to move freely between local and remote sites. Networked Linda-style blackboards and a new coordination language, with the ability to express waiting and notification on complex conditions allow building synchronized multi-agent interactions with simple, reusable scripts. Code and data fetching over the Internet, and the ability to see HTML links as ordinary files, make Jinni appealing to application programmers, from inside and from outside the realm of logic programming.

Concurrent logic/constraint programming is a simple and elegant formalism of concurrency that can potentially address many important future applications including parallel, distributed, and intelligent systems. Its basic concept has been extremely stable and has allowed efficient implementations. However, its uniqueness makes this paradigm rather difficult to appreciate as it cannot be easily related to other programming paradigms.

Ueda discusses the relationship between concurrent logic/constraint programming and the remainder of logic programming and stresses the importance of understanding and enhancing the logic programming paradigm by an analytic approach. He also discusses the grand challenges that this paradigm shares with other formalisms of concurrency. They are: (1) a counterpart of λ-calculus in the field of concurrency, (2) a common platform for various non-sequential forms of computing, and (3) type systems that cover both logical and physical aspects of computation.

Logic Programming and Multi-Agent Systems: A Synergic Combination for Applications and Semantics

Marco Bozzano[1], Giorgio Delzanno[2], Maurizio Martelli[1], Viviana Mascardi[1], and Floriano Zini[1]

[1] D.I.S.I. - Università di Genova, via Dodecaneso 35, I-16146 Genova, Italy
[2] Max-Planck-Institut für Informatik, Im Stadtwald, Gebäude 46.1, D-66123 Saarbrücken, Germany

Summary. The paper presents an ongoing research project that uses Logic Programming, Linear Logic Programming, and their related techniques for executable specifications and rapid prototyping of Multi-Agent Systems. The MAS paradigm is an extremely rich one and we believe that Logic Programming will play a very effective role in this area, both as a tool for developing real applications and as a semantically well founded language for basing program analysis and proof of properties on.

1 Introduction

During the last few years *Multi-Agent Systems (MAS)* [WJ95,NN97] have certainly been one of the most debated approaches to software development. The main reason for this great interest is the intriguing way a software system is viewed in the MAS setting, i.e., as a set of autonomous, intelligent, and interacting entities that either cooperate to achieve a common goal or that compete to satisfy personal interests. MAS allow a *cognitive* vision of the system and provide the ability to abstract from details thus making them an ideal tool for *Software Engineering* [Pre94]. Furthermore, MAS technology is strictly related to two fundamental aspects of modern software products, i.e., *distribution* of computational entities and resources and *integration* of legacy software and data.

Given the high complexity of a MAS, it would be desirable to have a clear methodology supporting the whole development process, from the first informal requirement specification to the final implementation. In order to be applicable, this refinement process should preserve the correctness of the intermediate specifications w.r.t. the original requirements. An automatic tool supporting *formal* specification methods and providing *executable* specifications might greatly help verify correctness constraints when passing through the different refinement steps. It should allow the user to write, execute, and test specifications of agent behaviour, agent architecture, communication protocols, and interaction between agents. It should also support integration with existing software products and the automatic translation of the agent specification into existing programming languages.

To achieve this goal, an approach based on *Logic Programming (LP)* would be rather suitable for several reasons. First of all, LP is a powerful paradigm for rapid prototyping based on a very high-level syntax. As a consequence, the use of an LP-based formalism can provide a noteworthy reduction in software development time, a clear description of software functionalities, easy code maintenance and re-usability. Furthermore, the large amount of theoretical effort spent studying verification, analysis, and transformation of logic programs could be applied to develop automatic tools that validate the produced specification.

In this paper we present a framework that includes two different ways of applying LP-based technologies to the development of MAS. This is divided into two phases, supported by different specification and programming languages, both of which are based on the LP paradigm. In the preliminary phase, we use a high-level LP language to specify an application, to simulate the effect of a concurrent execution of the agents, and to check it for correctness. This phase is useful for the construction and validation of the conceptual structure of the system. In a subsequent phase, a "traditional" LP language, extended with communication primitives, is used to produce a more concrete software prototype, to be simulated and tested in a real distributed environment. The first phase concerns the study of a particular communication protocol between agents and the preliminary verification of the agents' behaviour in that context. The next phase provides an effective implementation of the communication protocol and of the agents' code, and faces the problem of the external software integration.

The paper is organized as follows. In the next section we present the main concepts underlying the MAS paradigm and we explain the choice of the LP languages that we use to develop MAS. Section 3 presents a general agent architecture, subsuming some existing models. Some ideas on how an LP-based specification language for this architecture could be structured are described in Section 4. Section 5 concerns a methodology for the specification of a MAS prototype, from informal requirements to implementation. It is applied on a simple toy example. Finally, Section 6 presents conclusions and future work.

2 Why and Which LP Languages for MAS Development?

Logic Programming, which in the 1980s had been identified as the best technology to implement knowledge intensive applications on highly parallel computer architectures, is today relegated to a secondary role in industrial software development. Languages like `C`, `C++`, and `Java` are undoubtedly more known and used than `Prolog`. Imperative languages are adopted for reasons of efficiency while object-orientation is today perceived as the possible new unifying paradigm for computing. However, efficiency is not always a real issue and extensions and integrations of LP with other paradigms fill the gaps of the first LP proposals. Moreover, some peculiarities of LP make it competitive or even better than imperative or object-oriented paradigms for facing particular kinds of applications. In particular, as remarked in [KS98,Wag97], LP is closely connected to the design and development of MAS. We will analyze which features make LP an ideal tool for specifying and prototyping MAS-based applications after having introduced the concepts of "agent" and "MAS".

2.1 A conceptual framework for agents and Multi-Agent Systems

The clearer and the more operationally usable the term "agent" is, the more generally accepted the definition of what an agent and a MAS are will be. At the moment there is no completely satisfactory definition of agent. However, the *weak definition of agency* [WJ95] is the most widely accepted among researchers. According to this definition an (artificial) agent is a computer system (both hardware or software) characterized by:

- *autonomy*: agents work largely independent of human intervention;
- *social ability*: agents communicate with each other, usually by means of some *agent communication language*;
- *reactivity*: agents perceive the external world, including other agents, and react to the incoming information accordingly;
- *pro-activeness*: agents are able to show goal-directed behaviour by taking the initiative to achieve their goals.

A "Multi-Agent System" is a collection of interacting agents which cooperate and coordinate with each other to achieve personal or common goals.

Agents usually need to symbolically represent the state of the world in which they are situated and thus are usually provided with an internal state to contain this piece of information. Beliefs and goals can be first order objects, explicitly represented in the state. In this case, according to [KS96], we mean *rational* agents. Otherwise, what the agents aim at is implicitly coded into the behaviour they are given.

From a practical applications point of view, the main types of agents [NN97] can be roughly classified as:

- *collaborative agents*: emphasize autonomy and cooperation; they are typically static and large and may have to negotiate to achieve acceptable agreements;
- *personal assistance agents*: support and provide pro-active assistance to users struggling with complex application programs;
- *mobile agents*: are software processes that can roam wide-area networks such as the world-wide web, interacting with foreign hosts, acting on behalf of their owner and returning 'home' having achieved their goals;

- *information agents*: are pro-active, dynamic, adaptive and cooperative information managers that manipulate or collate information from many distributed resources.

Even though some authors do define non-autonomous agents (see [LD95]), we believe that "computational" autonomy is a fundamental property for agents. It allows us to have *awake computational entities* in which a programmable *task control*, definable at the meta-level, can manipulate different kinds of behaviour. These kinds of behaviour are determined by the agent's features besides autonomy and social ability, thus resulting in various agent classes[1].

Reactive agents are characterized by behaviour determined by rules expressing what has to be done when external input is received. This input can be either a message from another agent or a signal coming from the *environment* and intercepted by the agent's sensors. Reactive agents do not have a symbolic representation of beliefs or goals and thus do not perform reasoning about them. This does not mean that a reactive agent does not have an internal state, but only that goal-oriented "intelligent" behaviour is an emergent property (see [Bro91]).

Pro-active agents exhibit active behaviour to achieve their goals. The difference with respect to reactive agents is that the actions the agent carries out are not directly driven by an external event (message or signal), but the agent can independently decide which action to perform. Also for this agent's class goals remain hard-wired into the behaviour of the agents and are not explicitly represented in their internal state.

On the other hand *rational* agents have an explicit knowledge base, encompassing beliefs and goals. Goal-oriented "intelligent" behaviour is explicitly "coded" into the agents (a typical example is [RG91]). An agent can usually exploit many different *plans* to achieve the goals that have been ascribed to it. A plan is chosen on the basis of the current beliefs and goals of the agent and can be dynamically modified if the beliefs and/or the goals change.

2.2 Logic Programming and Multi-Agent Systems.

A language for specification and programming of agents must be able to express the ideas underlying the concept of agent and to allow an easy modelling of them. The following observations naturally lead us to the choice of LP paradigms:

- *MAS execution*: the evolution of a MAS consists of non deterministic succession of events; from an abstract point of view an LP language is a non deterministic language in which computation occurs via a search process.

[1] The classification is not standard, but it is an attempt by the authors to identify some interesting classes of agents.

- *Meta-reasoning capabilities*: agents need to dynamically modify their behaviour so as to adapt it to changes in the environment. Thus, the possibility given by LP of viewing programs as data is very important in this setting. This feature is useful also for integrating external heterogeneous software; this is a fundamental aspect in MAS applications.
- *Rationality and reactiveness of agents*: the *declarative* and the *operational* interpretation of logic programs are strictly related to the main characteristics of agents, i.e., *rationality* and *reactiveness.* In fact, we can think of a *pure* logic program as the specification of the rational component of an agent and we can use the operational view of logic programs (e.g. left-to-right execution, use of non-logical predicates) to model the reactive behaviour of an agent. The adoption of LP for combining reactivity and rationality is carefully described in [KS96].

The above observations represent a good starting point to consider LP as a theoretical and practical foundation for the designing and development of MAS. However, as already remarked, traditional LP languages do not fulfill all requirements arising during the MAS development. In particular, though useful to specify a single agent (e.g. [KS98]), they do not provide facilities for modelling collections of distributed and communicating agents. In this paper we propose two extension in this sense:

- from a theoretical point of view, we will consider more powerful specification languages, namely linear logic programming languages;
- from a practical point of view we will propose new extensions of LP-based systems with features specific to the development of MAS.

Linear Logic Programming for MAS specification. Given the complexity of MAS, a good specification language should help specify many different operational aspects in a uniform and natural way. Extensions of Logic Programming based on Linear Logic seem particularly well-suited for this task. *Linear Logic* [Gir87] enriches the operational interpretation of classical logic in that formulas can be treated as resources. This idea has been incorporated in recent extensions of Logic Programming, the so-called *Linear Logic Programming (LLP) paradigm* [Mil95]. It has been successfully applied to formalize important programming aspects such as data management [HM94,BDM97], object-orientation [AP90,DM95,BDLM96], state-based computations [Chi95], and aspects of concurrency [Mil93,MMP96].

These features make LLP a suitable framework for specifying distributed systems and agent systems in particular. The notion of state in LLP has a natural correspondence with the notion of state and beliefs of an agent. The possibility of using resources during a computation is a natural means to support dynamic changes in the behaviour of an agent. Besides being very powerful specification languages, linear logic-based frameworks can also be used as programming languages as shown in [AP90,HM94,HPW96,Del97].

For our purposes, we will adopt the language $\mathcal{E}_{hhf}$ proposed in [Del97]. It is based on a particular subset of Forum [Mil96], a presentation of higher-order linear logic in terms of goal-driven proofs. $\mathcal{E}_{hhf}$ extends previous proposals like [AP90,HM94] and is defined in a *higher-order* setting, thus facilitating the development of applications based on meta-programming. In Sections 4 and 5 we briefly discuss the role of $\mathcal{E}_{hhf}$ in the specification methodology of our framework.

Logic Programming for MAS implementation. Even though it is executable, the LLP specification is too high level to produce a final agent-based software product. In fact, in writing an $\mathcal{E}_{hhf}$ MAS specification, some important issues must be neglected. For example, an interface between an $\mathcal{E}_{hhf}$ specification and existing software cannot be provided since this issue is abstracted away at the specification level and the integration of external modules and data is not supported by the language. Moreover, performance reasons suggest using a more efficient language than $\mathcal{E}_{hhf}$ for the actual implementation of a MAS prototype.

We are addressing these issues by means of CaseLP (*Complex Application Specification Environment based on Logic Programming* [MMZ97,MMZ98]), a prototyping tool for agent-based software realized in the Constraint Logic Programming language ECLiPSe [ACD+95]. Our tool provides an agent-oriented extension of ECLiPSe that is used to build a more concrete implementation of the MAS. Our implementation language has a number of programming features making the resulting prototype more efficient and easier to integrate with other technologies. CaseLP is described in Section 3, where it is analyzed as a simplified realization of a more general and flexible architecture.

3 A General Multi-Agent System Architecture

Agent architectures should be flexible enough to support the amalgamation of the different kinds of agents we have listed in Section 2 so as to give origin to *hybrid* agents with different degrees of reactivity, pro-activeness and rationality. Based on well-known agent architectures we propose a framework where reactive, pro-active and rational components are integrated, as shown in Figure 1. Dotted arrows represent the atomic actions that the various components can perform, while thin, continuous arrows represent the input that the components use to perform their actions. The environment, which is sensed through sensors and modified through effectors (the thick arrows at the top of the figure) is outside of the rectangle containing the agent's components. Interaction with other agents occurs via asynchronous point-to-point message passing. More precisely, the main components of an agent are:

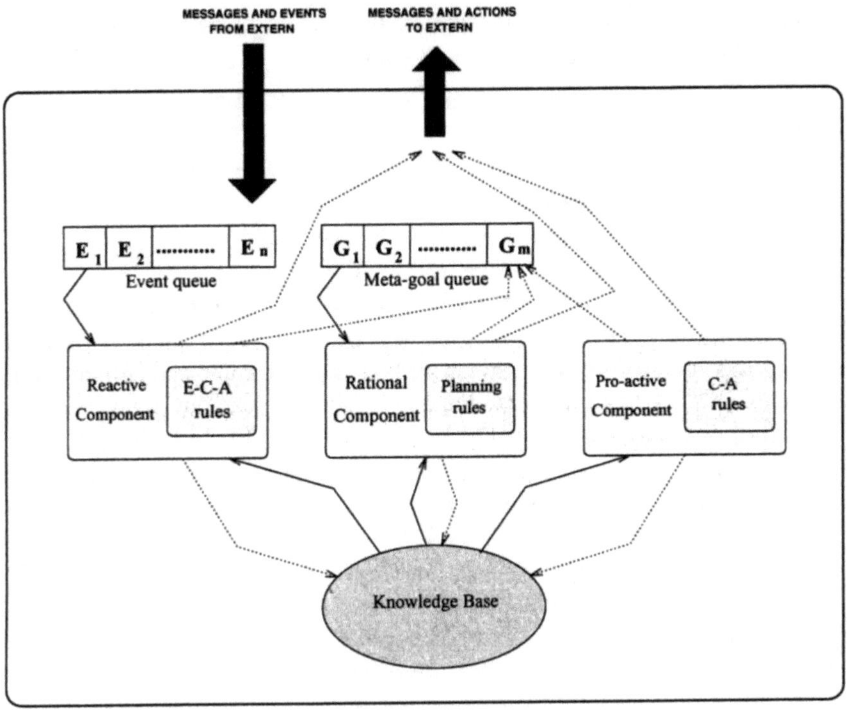

Fig. 1. The general architecture of an agent

The event queue. Events can be either "communication" or "perception" events. The former consist in the reception of messages coming from another agent, while the latter consist in the perception of the environment through sensors.

The meta-goal queue. An agent can respond to external stimuli or to state changes in a simple and immediate manner, but it can also respond in a more complex way by identifying a meta-goal which requires some sophisticated plan to be achieved. The meta-goals generated by the reactive and pro-active components are put into a meta-goal queue and are handled by the rational component, which can add meta-goals to the meta-goal queue as well. This happens, for example, when the rational component interrupts its execution and records a meta-goal describing what it has to do later.

The knowledge base. It reflects the beliefs of the agent at a given moment. It must be expressed in a language (such as first order logic ground facts) that the rational component is able to perform high level reasoning on. In the following we will refer to it as "state" or "knowledge base" indifferently.

The reactive component. It bases its behaviour on *event-condition-action* rules. The reaction cycle of this component is:

1. pick one event from the event queue and remove it;
2. check the current state;
3. according to the current event and the current state
   - update the state and/or
   - perform actions on the environment and/or
   - send messages to other agents and/or
   - put one or more meta-goals into the meta-goal queue.

The action of putting a meta-goal into the meta-goal queue is performed when the reaction to the event needs to be a complex task which requires some sort of reasoning. It represents a link between the reactive and the rational components.

The pro-active component. This component acts similarly to the reactive one, but does not take the event queue into account. Its behaviour is defined by a set of *condition-action* rules. The pro-action cycle is the same as the reactive component one, except for picking one event from the event queue and considering it during condition evaluation.

The rational component. This component applies some form of reasoning to achieve its current meta-goal. Its execution cycle is:

1. pick one meta-goal from the event queue and remove it;
2. check if the meta-goal still needs to be executed;
3. if it is, construct one or more plans to satisfy the meta-goal;
4. select a plan from the possible alternatives;
5. execute a certain number of atomic actions of the plan.

After the meta-goal has been chosen (step 1), a control is needed to verify if it must still be executed (step 2). In the agent's current situation, which is determined by its knowledge base content, performing the meta-goal may have become useless. After the agent's rational component has executed a certain number of atomic actions of the plan (step 5), the meta-level *task control* can decide to interrupt it. A meta-goal, representing the state of the plan execution, is then posted in the meta-goal queue to resume later on.

The execution of these three components is a question of the *task control* operating at the meta-level and regulating their interactions. The policy might vary from a very constrained sequential execution of the three activation cycles to a completely asynchronous one. In any case strategies to ensure the coherence of the state must be provided, together with some time-constrained evaluation method of the condition in event-condition-action and condition-action rules. This evaluation must not take too long, otherwise the advantage of the immediate action execution given by event-condition-action and condition-action rules is lost.

3.1 Four particular cases of the general architecture

The general architecture presented above should be expressive enough for most of the software agent applications and it is the final target of our ongoing research. Below some existing proposals related to this general abstract model are presented.

Schroeder and Wagner's Vivid Agents [SW].
Vivid agents are software controlled systems whose state comprises the mental components of knowledge, perceptions, tasks and intentions and whose behaviour is represented by means of action and reaction rules. The main functionalities of vivid agents regard handling perception and communication events via a perception system, updating and reasoning on a knowledge system, and representing and performing reactions and actions in order to react to events and to generate and execute plans.

It is easy to see that most of the features of the general agent architecture are present in Schroeder and Wagner's vivid agent. The pro-active behaviour is closely connected to the rational one and when there is no event in the event queue, the agent goes on executing the actions of the current plan. The vivid agents' reactive and rational components act concurrently by interleaving the plan execution with the reaction to incoming events. The two components work over two distinct copies of the knowledge base. Strategies are adopted to ensure the coherence of concurrent actions and the coherence between copies of the knowledge base.

Kowalski and Sadri's Unified Agent Architecture [KS96].
Kowalski and Sadri try to combine the rational and reactive behaviour of an agent by giving a complete proof reduction procedure based on the observation that in many cases it is possible to replace a goal G by an equivalent set of condition-action rules R. Moreover, they face the problem of controlling the reasoning process so that it works correctly with bounded resources. The resulting execution cycle is the following:

1. observe any input coming from the environment at time T;
2. record all input;
3. resume the proof procedure of the current goal statement by first propagating the input[2];
4. continue applying the proof procedure for a total of n inference steps;
5. select an atomic action respecting time constraints;
6. execute any such action and record the results.

This architecture and the more generic one described previously share the same aim of allowing an agent to be both reactive and rational. While in

[2] The *propagation of input* replaces the current goal statement with a simpler one, taking into account the observed input and the integrity constraints characterizing the agent's behaviour.

the general architecture the rational and reactive components are clearly separated, here they are collapsed into a single entity, whose behaviour is determined by the proof procedure and the resource bounding. The more the agent is reactive, the less it is rational, and vice versa. This probably means less flexibility of use, but easier implementation of the architecture.

Wooldridge's Computational Multi-Agent System [Woo92].
In this approach the behaviour of an agent is described by the following standard cycle:

1. interpret any message received;
2. update beliefs according to previous action and message interpretation;
3. derive deductive closure of belief set;
4. derive set of possible messages, choose one and send it;
5. derive set of possible actions, choose one and apply it.

Wooldridge defines two execution models for multi-agent systems: in the synchronous one all the agents in the system begin and complete an execution cycle together; in the more realistic asynchronous model, where execution is interleaved, at most one agent is allowed to act at any fixed point of time.

Wooldridge's architecture is a simplification of the general one. As in CaseLP described below, events are always communicative ones, and agents are reactive ones. They receive a message and react to it, without having an explicit representation of their goals and without adopting plans to achieve them.

Martelli, Mascardi and Zini's CaseLP [MMZ97,MMZ98].
CaseLP (*Complex Application Specification Environment based on Logic Programming*) is a prototyping and simulation environment for agent-based software applications developed at the Computer and Information Science Department of the University of Genova (Italy).

CaseLP agents communicate via point-to-point message passing, with messages written in KQML [MLF95]. There are two types of agents in the model: *logical agents*, which show capabilities of complex reasoning, and *interface agents* which only provide an interface between external modules[3] and the agents in the system. The agents share a common architecture whose main components are:

- an updatable set of facts, defining the *state* of the agent;
- a fixed set of rules, defining the *behaviour* of the agent;
- a *mail-box* for public messages and
- an *interpreter*.

[3] *External modules* are usually legacy passive service providers to be integrated into the MAS.

The interpreter is a peculiarity of interface agents. It translates the requests for services that are provided by external modules into the appropriate procedure call and translates the results back into a syntax comprehensible to all the agents in the system.

At the moment the system allows us to define *awake reactive agents*: every agent is activated at the beginning of the prototype execution and remains active until the end of the simulation. The behaviour of the agents consists in the following cycle:

1. pick one message from the mail-box and remove it;
2. select one rule whose head unifies with the current message;
3. prove the body of the rule.

The last step is carried out by means of the ECLiPSe interpreter. The atomic actions of updating the state and sending messages are carried out in the CaseLP setting by the *assert_state*, *retract_state* and *send* predicates which operate in a safe way.

Also CaseLP agents, like Wooldridge's, are reactive, still adopting goal reduction to find out what to do. The event queue is represented by the mail-box and contains only communicative events. Even though CaseLP is currently a simplification of the general architecture described above, it has the advantage of explicitly taking into account the integration of external software carried out by the interface agents.

CaseLP is an ongoing project that we plan to extend and improve on the basis of new and more demanding applications. However, the present implementation has already been successfully applied to some real-world case studies. Two of them were related to transportation and logistic problems [MMZ98]. One was developed in collaboration with *FS* (the Italian railways) and the other one was developed with Elsag Bailey, an international company which provides service automation. CaseLP was successfully adopted for a reverse engineering process in an application concerning the retrieval of medical information in distributed databases [Per98]. Finally, the combination of agent-oriented and constraint logic programming techniques has been used to solve the transaction management problem on a distributed database [MM].

4 A Multi-Agent System Specification Language

Logical languages have often been adopted to specify agents and Multi-Agent Systems [LLL+95,Rao96,MTF97]. In this section we propose the adoption of Linear Logic Programming as a high-level specification language, and list the reasons that make LLP a very suitable paradigm for these kinds of applications.

Agents combining reactive, pro-active and rational behaviour, such as the ones previously outlined, can be described in an LP setting by a tuple containing:

- the current state;
- the event and meta-goal queues;
- the event-condition-action rules driving the behaviour of the reactive component;
- the condition-action rules related to the pro-active component;
- the high level rules defining how the rational component constructs and executes plans.

We call this tuple a *configuration* of an agent. If we assume that the various rules defining the reactive, pro-active and rational behaviour do not change over time, they can be left out of the agent's configuration. The configuration of a MAS can simply be defined as the set of all the agents' configurations.

When an agent performs an action in a certain MAS configuration, the whole MAS reaches another configuration. If, for example, the action is sending a message, the receiver of the message will change its configuration since its event queue changes, thus leading to a MAS configuration change. A configuration change is called *transition*.

The execution of a MAS can be described as the sequence of the various configurations reached by the MAS. We can take all the configurations into consideration, but we can also concentrate on configurations that are reached after a complete execution cycle by a certain agent. This would involve many intermediate transitions, one for every atomic action performed by the agent. We could even consider only the configurations which are reached when every agent in the system has completed at least one cycle of execution. The granularity of the MAS execution changes according to what we are interested in observing.

4.1 The role of Linear Logic Programming

Linear Logic Programming allows us to characterize the form of computation previously outlined at a high level of abstraction. In fact, as briefly discussed in the introduction, LLP provides us with connectives to express *concurrency* and *synchronization* primitives. When combined with some representation of the agents, these primitives may be useful for simulating and testing a given MAS specification. In order to give an idea of the approach based on LLP, and in particular on the $\mathcal{E}_{hhf}$ fragment, it is necessary to outline what a linear logic program looks like.

The key point is to extend the syntax of *clauses* as defined in standard Logic Programming so as to provide *multi-conclusion* clauses. More precisely, $\mathcal{E}_{hhf}$-programs are collection of clauses of the form:

$$Cond \Rightarrow A_1 \parr \ldots \parr A_n \multimapinv Goal,$$

where the linear disjunction $A_1 \parr \ldots \parr A_n$ corresponds to the head of the clause (A_i's are atomic formulas), *Cond* is a goal representing the guard of the clause, and *Goal* is a goal representing the body of the clause. For the sake of the reader, we have limited our considerations to conditions defined by Horn programs.

The main peculiarity of such clauses is that the resources (formulas) they need in order to be applied are consumed right after their execution. In a sense multi-conclusion clauses resemble conditional multiset rewrite rules. Formally, given a program P and a multiset of atomic formulas Ω_0, a resolution step $\Omega_0 \rightarrow \Omega_1$ can be performed by applying a ground instance $C \Rightarrow A_1 \parr \ldots \parr A_n \multimapinv G$ of a clause in the program P, provided:

- the multiset Θ consisting of the atoms $A_1, \ldots, A_n$ is contained in Ω_0;
- the condition C is satisfied in P;
- Ω_1 is obtained by removing Θ from Ω_0 and by adding G to the resulting multiset.

In the $\mathcal{E}_{hhf}$-interpreter, instantiation is replaced by unification. At this point, since G may be a complex formula, the search rules (i.e., the logical rules of the connectives occurring in G) must be exhaustively applied in order to proceed.

Such derivations can be used to model the evolution of a collection of agents. For instance, let $Ag_1, \ldots, Ag_n$ be atomic formulas describing a collection of agents. The clause

$$Cond \Rightarrow (Ag_1 \parr \ldots \parr Ag_n \multimapinv Ag_1' \parr \ldots \parr Ag_n'),$$

describes the evolution of the state of the agents (e.g. Ag_i evolves in Ag_i') provided the condition $Cond$ is satisfied. New components can be added to the current state by using goal-formulas of the form $G_1 \parr G_2$. In fact, the goal $G_1 \parr G_2, \Delta$ simply reduces to G_1, G_2, Δ. This description, which is potentially non-terminating, can be used to observe the evolution of the simulated agent system, or, by using backward analysis, to detect potential violations of the specification requirements.

4.2 A syntax for the general architecture

For the sake of clarity, introducing an abstract, high-level and readable syntax to describe the behaviour of agents and to specify their different components (the reactive part, the pro-active one, and the rational one) will suffice.

As a matter of fact, the syntax we present has a direct mapping onto linear logic formulas, therefore the translation from the high-level language into linear logic clauses could be provided automatically through a compilation process. The only delicate point concerns the implementation of some kind of mechanism that guarantees the right interactions among the different components of an agent and among the agents in the system. At the moment, however, we have not committed ourselves to a particular model of task control, thus this mechanism has not been specified and the syntax we present below must simply be considered as an example[4].

We start the specification of the agents' components from the reactive part. This is specified through simple *event-condition-action* rules, which can be written as follows:

```
on event  event
check     st_query
update    st_update_list
perform   action_list
try       meta-goal_list
```

The meaning of each line is in agreement with the description in Section 3. In addition, sub-languages must be provided to describe events, state queries and updates, actions, and meta-goals. We do not deal with these issues here, but in Section 5.1 we do give an example. The syntax for the pro-active part is similar to the previous one except for the first line, which is not present since the pro-active component does not perceive external events. Lastly, the syntax for the rational component might look like

```
on goal   goal
check     st_query
generate  plan
```

A simple case-study. We consider a syntax for the case study which is explained in more detail in Section 5.1. The case study involves agents which show a *purely reactive* behaviour. In fact they simply react to incoming events by updating their state and generating new events depending on the current state. Events only include sending and receiving messages, and the communication protocol is based on asynchronous message passing: each agent may be thought of as owning a mailbox for incoming messages. In this case, we can specialize the syntax previously described for specifying the agents' behaviour.

```
on receiving  message
check         st_query
update        st_update_list
send          message_list
```

In the syntax above, *message* is an incoming message, *st_query* is a query on the current state, *st_update_list* is the list of state updates, and *message_list* is the list of new messages sent by the agent.

[4] The code of the examples given in the paper is available by anonymous ftp at the address `ftp://ftp.disi.unige.it/pub/person/BozzanoM/Terzo`.

Each message can be an "ask" (a service request sent to another agent) or a "reply" (a response sent for a given request). Accordingly, we will represent a message with a term like

$$\begin{aligned}type(&(\text{content}(C))\\&(\text{sender}(S)),\\&(\text{receiver}(\text{R})))\end{aligned}$$

where *type* may be *ask* or *reply*. We will also assume that every agent has a simple state consisting of ground facts, and a simple language for state modification based on the primitives *assert*(*Fact*) and *retract*(*Fact*).

5 Towards a Specification Methodology

In this section we analyze the different phases which make up the specification methodology of our framework, trying to outline the different contributions given to the development process by each phase. Our approach can be compared with the classical development cycle for software prototypes given in [Pre94].

1. **Identification of the set of agents and their interconnecting structure**. In this step the specification developer decides the static structure of the system and identifies the kind of agents the application requires. He/she also chooses the interconnection topology, i.e. which communication channels will be needed among them. This phase is quite informal, allowing different choices in the number and kind of agents required.
2. **Choice of the communication protocol among each pair of communicating agents**. This step consists in choosing the communication protocol between each pair of connected agents. As for the previous step, there is room for different choices, depending on what kind of information the agents need to exchange and on the synchronization mechanism.
3. **Specification of the behaviour of each agent in the system**. This step consists in specifying the behaviour of the agents, namely what each agent is able to do and how it performs its tasks. This is where Linear Logic Programming comes into play. This is the first phase that achieves some degree of formalization, by building an executable specification written in $\mathcal{E}_{hhf}$. It is important to notice that the whole process including steps 1 through 3 may be repeated more than once, either because the testing phase (step 4) reveals some flaws in the initial choices, or because the developer wishes to refine the specification by using a greater degree of granularity. The concept of *granularity* of a specification is fundamental. The developer often needs to study the execution of a Multi-Agent System at different levels of abstraction, progressively refining the specification as he/she is convinced of the design correctness. The $\mathcal{E}_{hhf}$ specification language seems to be quite suitable for this kind of design.

4. **Testing of the system.** This phase concerns testing the system in order to verify how much the prototype corresponds to the desired requirements. This may lead to changing, improving or refining the design. Using a logical language like $\mathcal{E}_{hhf}$ in this phase has great advantages since:
   - It is possible to evaluate a goal step by step, following the evolution of a particular system in detail. Various abstraction levels are possible, for instance observing only the messages exchanged between the agents, and/or observing the behaviour of a single agent, and so on.
   - Through *backtracking* it is possible to follow all the different evolutions of a given system, depending for example on the order of arrival of the various messages. It is therefore possible to simulate a distributed environment, where the order in which messages arrive may not correspond to the order in which they were sent.
   - It is possible to verify whether a particular computation may be carried out, or, more importantly, that *every* computation starting from a given configuration leads to a final state satisfying a given property, independently of the order of arrival of the messages and the order of execution by the agents. To this aim it suffices to run the desired computation together with a goal negating the desired property of the final state, and then to check whether the global goal fails.
   - It may be possible to employ standard techniques for proving program properties that have been developed in the logic programming context. Extending these techniques to the linear logic setting is part of our future work (see Section 6).
5. **Implementation of the prototype.** In this step each agent specification is firstly translated into executable code, then the MAS is built, creating a unique executable specification embedding all the defined agents. This step and the following one can be dealt with using CaseLP as a prototyping environment. CaseLP provides facilities for automatically translating an agent specification written in an extended logic language into an executable piece of code. It also allows the user to load these agents into a unique Multi-Agent System for further execution.
6. **Execution of the obtained prototype.** The last step tests the implementation choices, checking if the system behaves as expected. Any specification error or misbehaviour discovered in this step may imply a revision of the choices made in the first 3 steps. CaseLP allows us to initialize the mail-boxes of some agents with initial messages and then starting the MAS execution. In this phase CaseLP uses a round-robin scheduler which recursively activates each agent in the MAS. The activated agent inspects its mail-box looking for new messages and manages them according to the rules defining its reactive behaviour. When an agent has managed its messages, the scheduler passes to the following one. The scheduler activity stops when all the mail-boxes of the agents are empty. It is possible to monitor the execution of the system thanks to on-line and off-line text visualization of the exchanged messages. The CaseLP Visualizer [Ped98]

provides the user with an interface which allows him/her to initialize the system, integrate external software, start and monitor the execution in a user-friendly graphic fashion.

5.1 An Example: Student Data Retrieval

We present a very simple example in which agents, based on the CaseLP architecture, are described by the syntax presented at the end of Section 4. This will serve as an illustration of the specification methodology previously presented.

The problem. Suppose a user wants some information about students and marks of some courses at the University of Genova. The possible queries include the best, worst and average marks of each course, and the names of the students who got the marks. An external database contains this information. Three C procedures, *min*, *max* and *avg*, used to evaluate the minimum, maximum and average element of an integer array, could be linked to produce the final system.

This problem can be faced by developing a Multi-Agent System according to the given methodology. The third and fourth steps are described rather carefully, while the other ones are treated quite briefly. More details can be found in [MMZ98].

Step 1: identification of the set of agents and their interconnecting structure. An application of this type could be simulated using four agents: *user*, a logical agent which asks for information about the courses; *course information provider (cip)*, a logical agent which receives the user request and executes it; *mathematical function provider (mfp)*, an interface agent which is interfaced with the C procedures `min`, `max` and `avg`, and *course data provider (cdp)*, an interface agent which is interfaced with the database of University courses.

User is capable of sending requests to and receiving answers from *cip* which is the "core" of the system. It exchanges messages with both interface agents that are only able to communicate only with *cip*. Figure 2 depicts the structure of the MAS.

Step 2: choice of the communication protocol among each pair of communicating agents. Communication takes place via the protocol described at the end of Section 4. Each pair of agents communicate using asynchronous message passing, where a message can have *ask* or *reply* type.

Step 3: specification of the behaviour of each agent in the system. The behaviour of the agents can be explained in natural language as follows. *User* simulates an external user, asking questions to *cip* and receiving answers from it. *Cip* receives a request from the *user* and behaves on the basis of the

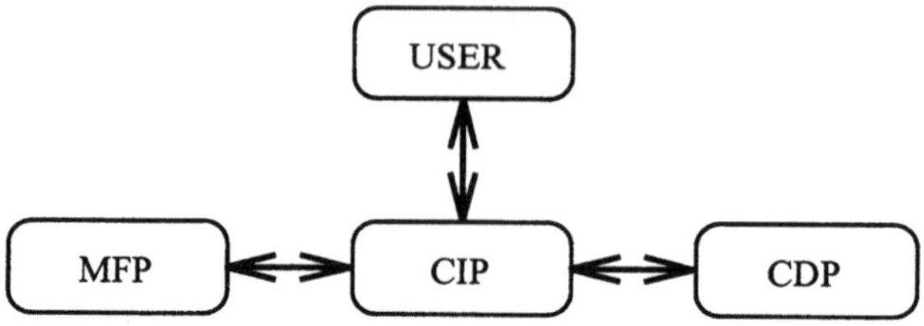

Fig. 2. Agents in the "Student data retrieval" example

type of request. If, for instance, *user* wants to know the best, worst, or average marks of a course, *cip* asks *cdp* to get the list of marks for that course. When the answer arrives, it asks *mfp* to evaluate the maximum, minimum or average value of the list. The result provided by *mfp* is then sent back to *user*.

This kind of behaviour by the *cip* agent is illustrated by the clauses in Figure 3, written according to the high-level syntax presented in Section 4. The first clause applies when *cip* receives a message requesting the best mark of a given course. This request is managed by sending a message to *cdp* asking for the list of marks for that particular course. In order to keep track of pending requests, the *cip* agent associates every request with a unique identifier and stores this piece of information in its internal state. The second clause applies when the corresponding reply from *cdp* arrives. By consulting its internal state, *cip* realizes that the request was to calculate the maximum mark of the list it received from *cdp*, therefore it contacts *mfp* to carry out this task. When the corresponding answer from *mfp* finally arrives, *cip* consults its internal state and forwards the result to S (third clause). The remaining clauses for *cip* and for the other agents in the system can be written similarly.

Remark. To get an idea of how a program written in this high-level syntax can be mapped into a linear logic program, we present the translation of the first clause of Figure 3. It must be recalled that a linear logic program is basically a collection of conditional multiset rewrite rules. The multi-conclusion clause for the considered rule is defined as follows:

Id1 is Id + 1 ⇒
  on_receiving(ask(content(best_mark(Course)),sender(S), receiver(cip))) ⅋
  ag(cip) ⅋ req_id(Id) ∘−
    ag(cip) ⅋ req_id(Id1) ⅋ associated(Id1,best_mark(Course),S)) ⅋
    send(ask(content(marks(Course,Id1)),sender(cip),receiver(cdp)).

The effect of such a clause is to *rewrite* the components of the current global state in agreement with the specification associated with the considered event.

Note that agents and events are represented by atomic formulas. The condition defined in the `check` part of the rule is handled in a special way. More precisely, the part of the condition which does not involve the global state (e.g. Id1 is Id+1) becomes a condition in the corresponding multi-conclusion

```
on receiving
   ask(content(best_mark(Course)), sender(S), receiver(cip))
check
   req_id(Id), Id1 is Id + 1
update
   retract(req_id(Id)), assert(req_id(Id1)),
   assert(associated(Id1, best_mark(Course),S))
send
   ask(content(marks(Course, Id1)), sender(cip), receiver(cdp)).

on receiving
   reply(content(marks(Mark_List,Course, Id)), sender(cdp), receiver(cip))
check
   associated(Id, best_mark(Course),S))
update

send
   ask(content(max(Mark_List,Id)), sender(cip), receiver(mfp)).

on receiving
   reply(content(max(Max,Id) sender(mfp), receiver(cip))
check
   associated(Id, best_mark(Course),S))
update
   retract(associated(Id, best_mark(Course),S))
send
   reply(content(best_mark(Course, Max)), sender(cip), receiver(S)).
```

Fig. 3. Code for *cip* using the abstract syntax for agents

rule, whereas, the part that involves the global state (e.g. req_id(Id)) becomes part of the head of the clause. In this way, req_id(Id) is automatically removed from the current state and substituted by req_id(Id1). The new information associated(..) and the new goal send(..) are asserted by simply including them in the body of the rule. The event `on_receiving` is generated as soon as an agent removes a message from its mailbox. We can specify this behaviour as follows:

$$\text{receive(Msg, Ag)} \parr \text{mailbox([Msg|T], Ag)} \parr \text{ag(Ag)} \multimapinv \\ \text{ag(Ag)} \parr \text{on\_receiving(Msg)} \parr \text{mailbox(T, Ag)}.$$

Again, note that the content of the mailbox is modified by rewriting the old list of messages into the new one.

The system is completely specified once the agents in the system and the initial state of each agent are specified. For instance, in the case of the *cip* agent, we have to specify what the initial value of *req_id* is. The prototype can then be tested starting from a particular configuration, i.e., a particular initialization of the agents' mail-boxes. Note that more than one agent can share the same behaviour. We should assume, for example, that more than one *cdp* agent is available to simulate a replicated database. In this case the behaviour is defined just once.

Another feature of this specification framework that we have previously insisted on is the possibility to refine the specification using different levels of abstraction. For instance, in this particular example it would be possible to firstly define the behaviour of the *cdp* agent in a very simple manner without implementing the actual mechanism which accomplishes a particular task. The set of clauses for this purpose would look like

```
on receiving
   ask(content(marks(course,Id)), sender(S), receiver(cdp))
send
   reply(content(marks(course, [28,30,...])), sender(cdp), receiver(S)).
```

for each *course* under consideration. Once the system has been tested and the interactions among the agents has been proved correct, the specification might be refined by describing the exact manner in which *cdp* accesses the database and finds an answer to a query.

Step 4: Testing the system. It is possible to test the system and verify its correctness with respect to the given requirements by executing the specification written in the previous step. To this aim, the $\mathcal{E}_{hhf}$ interpreter can be used to execute the code for this example. The user can set up an initial configuration, made up of some agents and some initialization messages, and follow how one computation proceeds. He/she can impose that the end of the computation correspond, for instance, to the situation in which all messages have been processed by the agents. He/she can then observe the final configuration, i.e. the agents and their corresponding states. Variable bindings, as usual in LP, can return values as well. For instance, it is possible to prove a goal like the following ("||" means concurrent execution):

```
ag cdp || ag cip || ag user || ag mfp ||
req_id cip 0 ||
send(ask(
   content (best_mark(data_base),Best),
   sender(user),
   receiver(cip)),cip)
```

The output of the simulation is the final configuration

```
ag cdp || ag cip || ag user || ag mfp ||
req_id cip 1
```

together with the variable binding *Best* = *30*.

The execution of a goal may be observed at various levels of granularity. The interpreter supports both a *trace* level, which allows us to observe low level details of the computation, and a *debug* level, which allows us to observe the interactions among the agents.

Another possibility is to exploit backtracking in order to follow *all* possible computations starting from a given configuration. By doing so a user can verify how the order in which the messages are exchanged affects the computation (this is crucial in distributed simulation). It is possible to verify whether a given property is satisfied *independently* of all possible orders of message exchanging and of all possible solutions for variable bindings. This is done by negating the property to be satisfied and proving that the corresponding goal necessarily fails. For instance, the failure of the following goal

```
(ag cdp || ag cip || ag user || ag mfp ||
req_id cip 0 ||
send(ask(
   content (best_mark(Course,Best),
   sender(user),
   receiver(cip)),cip)),
Best < 28.
```

proves that for *each* course the best mark is greater or equal to 28.

Step 5: Implementation of the prototype. In this step we use CaseLP to describe the agent behaviour by means of logical rules. Figure 4 shows some fragments of the *cip* agent code. The correspondence between this code and the first clause of Figure 3 is quite easy to see. `Activation` defines what the agent does when it is activated by the system scheduler i.e. it gets all the messages in its public mail-box. `Initial state` defines the initial state of the agent. `Behaviour` comprises the logic rule describing how to reply to a "best_mark" query.

In CaseLP implementation, *cdp* and *mfp* have been realized as *interface agents.* They share simple behaviour and are interfaced respectively to an ECLiPSe database and a C module via two different interpreters.

Step 6: Execution of the obtained prototype. CaseLP provides a tool (CaseLP Visualizer) that allows the user to load agents and external modules into the simulation environment and to visualize the execution of the MAS by means of a simple GUI. In our example the four agents, the ECLiPSe database and the C module are first loaded.

To start the simulation the mail-boxes of some agents are to be initialized, putting some messages into them. The CaseLP Visualizer provides an appropriate window for this aim, as illustrated in Figure 5.

```
Activation
   activate :- receive_all.

Initial state
   request_identifier(0).

Behaviour
   ask(content(best_mark(Course)), sender(S), receiver(cip)) :-
        req_id(Id), retract_state(req_id(Id)), Id1 is Id + 1,
        assert_state(req_id(Id1)),
        assert_state(associated(Id1, best_mark(Course), S)),
        send(ask( content(marks(Course, Id1)), sender(cip), receiver(cdp)), cdp)
```

Fig. 4. Code for *cip* in CaseLP

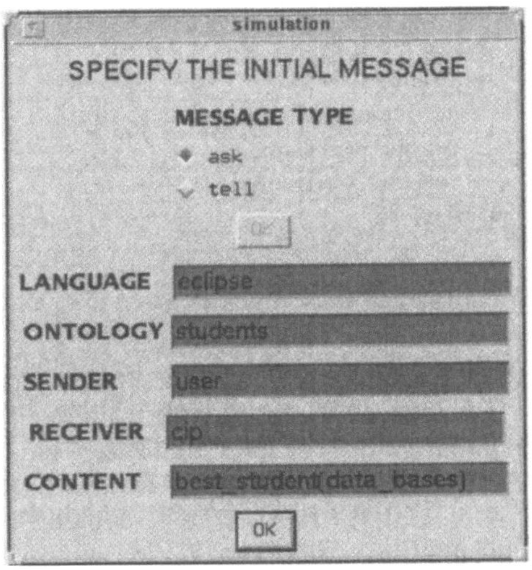

Fig. 5. CaseLP Visualizer: initialization window

While the execution is running, windows for each loaded agent appear on the screen. Information about state changes and exchanged messages is visualized for each agent. Figure 6 presents a snapshot of the MAS execution. After the execution has ended, it is possible to see a more detailed visualization of the occurred events, as illustrated in Figure 7. Exchanged messages and state updates are shown for each agent. Clicking on an event, it is possible to see more details, as shown in Figure 8. The figure represents an answer received by the agent *user*. Both the on-line and off-line visualization modalities provided by the CaseLP Visualizer are useful to monitor and verify the behaviour of the prototype, in order to check whether it behaves correctly.

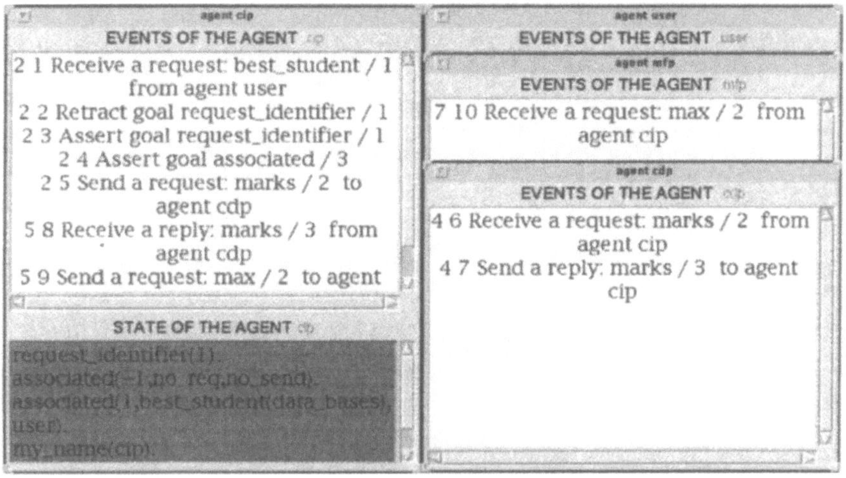

Fig. 6. CaseLP Visualizer: on-line visualization of execution

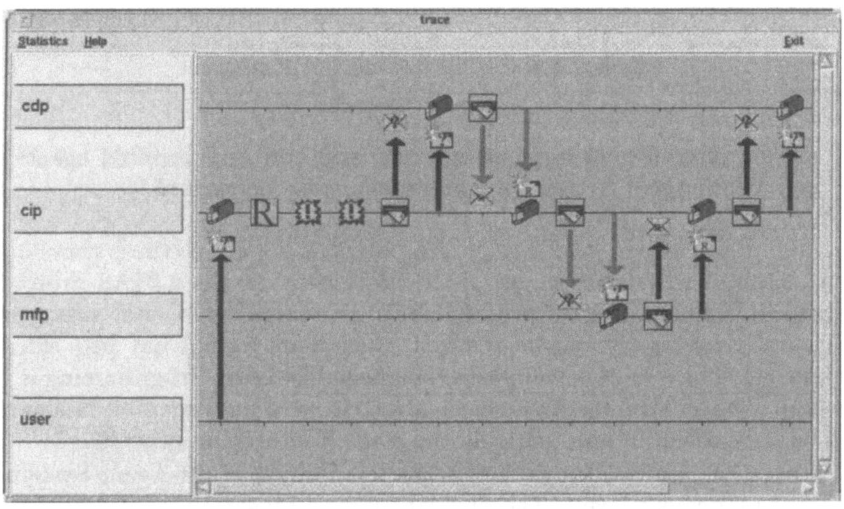

Fig. 7. CaseLP Visualizer: off-line tracing of execution

6 Conclusions and Future Work

In the paper *Agent Based Software Engineering* [Woo97], M. Wooldridge considers

> "the problem of building a Multi-Agent System as a software engineering enterprise [involving three main issues]: how agents might be specified; how these specifications might be refined or otherwise trans-

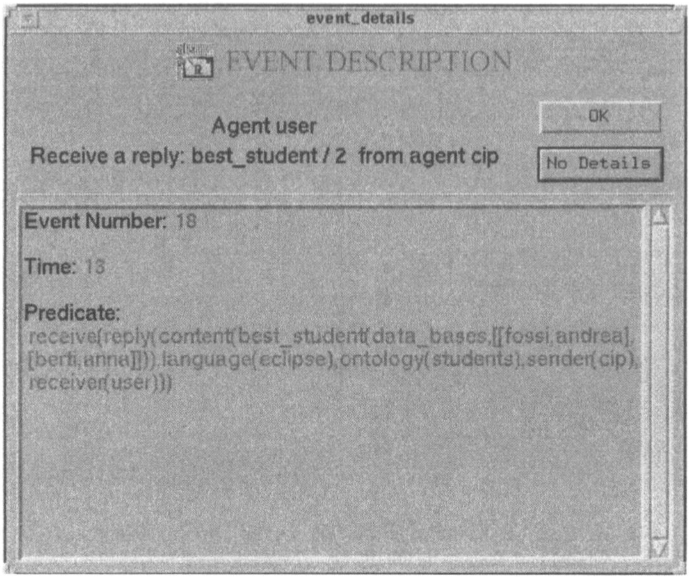

Fig. 8. CaseLP Visualizer: details of an event

formed into efficient implementations; and how implemented agents and Multi-Agent Systems might subsequently be verified."

The aim of our paper was to suggest a potential answer to these three questions, assuming that the target of the implementation is a MAS prototype instead of a final software product. In a prototype we do not need great efficiency, therefore it can be realized using more formal but less efficient technology. The role of a declarative language like Logic Programming is important. We can keep the first specification closer to implementation and this can be very useful in automatizing the whole prototyping process.

In fact, we use two logical languages to specify a Multi-Agent System at different refinement levels. The first language is Linear Logic Programming, suitable for an initial stage of the specification process. It can be easily used to describe the behaviour of systems where agents need to synchronize and run concurrently. An important aspect that is neglected in the LLP specification is the actual integration of external software. The behaviour of external modules is in fact simulated by LLP agents. We can directly execute the LLP abstract specification by means of the $\mathcal{E}_{hhf}$ interpreter and in this phase we can prove that the MAS is correct with respect to some original requirements expressed as a set of linear formulas.

The LLP specification is subsequently transformed into a more efficient LP program. Thanks to the meta-programming techniques that are easy to use in a logic programming paradigm, LP provides a tool for integrating existing external software modules in quite an easy, natural way. LP seems to be appropriate for a second phase of the specification and prototyping process, when the developer has an idea of the general mechanisms regulating the system under development and he/she wants to actually integrate some external modules. The LP specification is executed by means of the CaseLP prototyping environment. CaseLP allows us to follow what happens to the agents as if they were really distributed communicating entities. It gives the feeling of how MAS execution could go on by allowing us to change the initial conditions (the initial messages put into the mail-boxes before the simulation starts), and providing a certain nondeterminism by randomly delaying the messages sent by the agents. Moreover, it allows real integration of existing software, thus permitting the building of a system which is partly simulated and partly already implemented.

In this paper we have stressed the methodological aspects of building a MAS, rather than the analysis of an existing system. The ideal system, in fact, should support the MAS developer in all the steps pointed out in Section 5 and should allow the specification of reactive, pro-active and rational agents. Such a system would provide facilities for debugging the specification, for integrating external software modules and agents written in different languages, for supporting different communication protocols, and for checking properties at different levels. We could obtain this kind of system only by taking into account the different approaches we have outlined throughout this paper, and integrating them into a more general, multi-purpose system.

A proposal comes from the ARPEGGIO project, outlined in [DKM+]. ARPEGGIO *(Agent based Rapid Prototyping Environment Good for Global Information Organization)* aims to become a general open framework for the specification, rapid prototyping, and engineering of agent-based software. This framework will include contributions from the Department of Computer Science at the University of Maryland (USA) for aspects concerning the integration of multiple data sources and reasoning systems, from the Department of Computer Science at the University of Melbourne (Australia) for the work on animation of specifications, and from the Department of Computer and Information Science at the University of Genova (Italy) for the work on CaseLP and $\mathcal{E}_{hhf}$.

Lastly, an improvement in CaseLP and $\mathcal{E}_{hhf}$ functionalities is surely desirable. We could start by working on the following issues:

LLP specification. The efficiency and user-friendliness of the $\mathcal{E}_{hhf}$ interpreter for linear logic formulas could be improved. Furthermore, a tool for the automatic translation of a high level syntax, like the one of Section 4.2, into linear formulas and possibly into CaseLP clauses would be desirable.

Testing. It would be interesting to analyze how to extend standard LP testing techniques (symbolic model checking, partial evaluation, abstract interpretation) to support an automatic property verification of programs, and how to integrate these techniques with more traditional testing methods.

CaseLP implementation. We need to extend the range of languages/tools to which CaseLP can be interfaced. Currently we can integrate C, Tcl/Tk, the ECLiPSe Data and Knowledge Base and obviously ECLiPSe modules, but we would like to support other programming languages, thus providing a really *multi-language* specification tool.

System execution. In CaseLP we only simulate the distribution of the agents. We need a scheduler, and all the MAS execution runs over a single processor. We are studying how to actually distribute CaseLP agents over different machines, and are evaluating the use of CORBA [OHE97] for this purpose.

Acknowledgments

The authors would like to thank Valeria Perricone for the helpful contribution in improving the presentation of the paper. We also thank the anonymous referees for their useful comments.

References

[ACD+95] A. Abderrahamane, D. Chan, P. Dufresne, E. Falvey, H. Grant, A. Herold, G. Macartney, M. Meier, D. Miller, S. Mudambi, B. Perez, E. van Rossum, J. Schimpf, P. A. Tsahageas, and D. H. de Villeneuve. *ECLiPSe 3.5 User Manual.* European Computer Research Center, Munich, December 1995.

[AP90] J.M. Andreoli and R. Pareschi. Linear Objects: Logical Processes with Built-In Inheritance. In D.H. Warren and P.Szeredi, editors, *Proceedings of the 7th International Conference on Logic Programming*, pages 495–510. The MIT Press, Cambridge, MA, 1990.

[BDLM96] M. Bugliesi, G. Delzanno, L. Liquori, and M. Martelli. A Linear Logic Calculus of Objects. In *Proceedings of the Joint International Conference and Symposium on Logic Programming*, pages 67–81. The MIT Press, 1996.

[BDM97] M. Bozzano, G. Delzanno, and M. Martelli. A Linear Logic Specification of Chimera. In *Proceedings of DYNAMICS'97, a satellite workshop of ILPS '97*, 1997.

[Bro91] R. A. Brooks. Intelligence without representation. *Artificial Intelligence*, 47:139–159, 1991.

[Chi95] J. Chirimar. *Proof Theoretic Approach to Specification Languages.* PhD thesis, Department of Computer and Information Science, University of Pennsylvania, 1995.

[Del97] G. Delzanno. *Logic & Object-Oriented Programming in Linear Logic.* PhD thesis, Università of Pisa, Dipartimento di Informatica, March 1997.

[DKM+] P. Dart, E. Kazmierckaz, M. Martelli, V. Mascardi, L. Sterling, V.S. Subrahmanian, and F. Zini. Combining Logical Agents with Rapid Prototyping for Engineering Distributed Applications. Submitted to FASE'99.

[DM95] G. Delzanno and M. Martelli. Objects in Forum. In *Proceedings of the International Logic Programming Symposium*, pages 115–129. The MIT Press, 1995.

[Gir87] J.Y. Girard. Linear logic. *Theoretical Computer Science*, 50:1:1–102, 1987.

[HM94] J. Hodas and D. Miller. Logic Programming in a Fragment of Intuitionistic Linear Logic. *Information and Computation*, 110(2):327–365, 1994.

[HPW96] J. Harland, D. Pym, and M. Winikoff. Programming in Lygon: An overview. In M. Wirsing and M. Nivat, editors, *Algebraic Methodology and Software Technology*, volume 1101 of *Lecture Notes in Computer Science*, pages 391–405. Springer-Verlag, Munich, Germany, July 1996.

[KS96] R. Kowalski and F. Sadri. Towards a Unified Agent Architecture that Combines Rationality with Reactivity. In *Proc. of International Workshop on Logic in Databases*, San Miniato, Italy, 1996. Springer-Verlag.

[KS98] R. A. Kowalski and F. Sadri. From Logic Programming to Multi-agent Systems. Submitted to publication, 1998.

[LD95] M. Luck and M. D'Inverno. A Formal Framework for Agency and Autonomy. In *Proc. of the First International Conference on Multi-Agent Systems (ICMAS-95)*, pages 254–260, San Francisco, CA, June 1995.

[LLL+95] Y. Lesperance, H. Levesque, F. Lin, D. Marcu, R. Reiter, and R. B. Scherl. Foundations of a Logical Approach to Agent Programming. In M. Wooldridge, J. P. Müller, and M. Tambe, editors, *Intelligent Agents II*, pages 331–346. Springer-Verlag, 1995. LNAI 1037.

[Mil93] D. Miller. The π-calculus as a theory in linear logic: Preliminary results. In E. Lamma and P.Mello, editors, *Proceedings of the 1992 Workshop on Extension to Logic Programming*, volume 660 of *Lecture Notes in Computer Science*, pages 242–265. Springer-Verlag, Berlin, 1993.

[Mil95] D. Miller. Survey of Linear Logic Programming. *Computational Logic: The Newsletter of the European Network of Excellence in Computational Logic*, 2(2):63–67, 1995.

[Mil96] D. Miller. Forum: A Multiple-Conclusion Specification Logic. *Theoretical Computer Science*, 165(1):201–232, 1996.

[MLF95] J. Mayfield, Y. Labrou, and T. Finin. Evaluation of KQML as an Agent Communication Language. In M. Wooldridge, J. P. Müller, and M. Tambe, editors, *Intelligent Agents II*, pages 347–360. Springer-Verlag, 1995. LNAI 1037.

[MM] V. Mascardi and E. Merelli. Agent-Oriented and Constraint Technologies for Distributed Transaction Management. Submitted to IIA'99.

[MMP96] R. McDowell, D. Miller, and C. Palamidessi. Encoding transition systems in sequent calculus. *ENTCS*, 3, 1996.

[MMZ97] M. Martelli, V. Mascardi, and F. Zini. Applying logic programming to the specification of complex applications. *Mathematical Modeling and Scientific Computing*, 8, 1997. Proc. of *11th International Conference on Mathematical and Computer Modeling and Scientific Computing.*

[MMZ98] M. Martelli, V. Mascardi, and F. Zini. Towards Multi-Agent Software Prototyping. In H. S. Nwana and D. T. Ndumu, editors, *Proc. of The Third International Conference and Exhibition on The Practical Application of Intelligent Agents and Multi-Agent Technology (PAAM98)*, pages 331–354, London, UK, March 1998.

[MTF97] M. Mulder, J. Treur, and M. Fisher. Agent Modelling in METATEM and DESIRE. In *Intelligent Agents IV*. Springer-Verlag, 1997. LNAI 1365.

[NN97] D. T. Ndumu and H. S. Nwana. Research and development challenges for agent–based systems. *IEEE Proceedings of Software Engineering*, 144(1):2–10, February 1997.

[OHE97] R. Orfaly, D. Harkey, and J. Edwards. *Instant CORBA*. John Wiley and Sons, 1997.

[Ped98] M. De Pedrini. CaseLP Visualizer: un tool di visualizzazione per sistemi multi agente logici. Master's thesis, DISI – Università di Genova, Genova, Italy, 1998. In Italian.

[Per98] G. Persano. Gestione Distribuita di Informazioni Mediche Mediante Tecniche Multi-Agente. Master's thesis, DISI – Università di Genova, Genova, Italy, 1998. In Italian.

[Pre94] R. S. Pressman. *Software Engineering. A Practitioner's Approach.* McGraw–Hill International, UK, 3rd edition, 1994. European Edition. Adapted by D. Ince.

[Rao96] A. S. Rao. AgentSpeak(L): BDI Agents Speak Out in a Logical Computable Language. In W. Van de Velde and J. W. Perram, editors, *Agents Breaking Away*, pages 42–55. Springer-Verlag, 1996. LNAI 1038.

[RG91] A. Rao and R. Georgeff. Modeling Rational Agents within a BDI–Architecture. In R. Fikes and E. Sandewall, editors, *Proc. of Knowledge Representation and Reasoning (KR&R-91)*, pages 473–484, San Mateo, CA, 1991. Morgan Kaufmann Publishers.

[SW] M. Schroeder and G. Wagner. Vivid Agents: Theory, Architecture, and Applications. Submitted to the Journal of Logic and Computation.

[Wag97] G. Wagner. Artificial Agents and Logic Programming. In *Proc. of ICLP'97 Post Conference Workshop on Logic Programming and Multi-Agents*, pages 69–87, Leuven, Belgium, July 1997.

[WJ95] M. Wooldridge and N. R. Jennings. Intelligent agents: Theory and practice. *The Knowledge Engineering Review*, 10(2):115–152, 1995.

[Woo92] M. Wooldridge. *The Logical Model of Computational Multi–Agent Systems.* PhD thesis, Department of Computation, UMIST, Manchester, UK, October 1992.

[Woo97] M. Wooldridge. Agent–based software engineering. *IEE Proceedings of Software Engineering*, 144(1):26–37, February 1997.

Inference and Computation Mobility with Jinni

Paul Tarau

Department of Computer Science, University of North Texas, P.O. Box 311366, Denton, Texas 76203

Summary. We introduce Jinni (**J**ava **IN**ference engine and **N**etworked **I**nteractor), a lightweight, multi-threaded, logic programming language, intended to be used as a flexible scripting tool for gluing together knowledge processing components and Java objects in networked client/server applications, as well as through applets over the Web.

Mobile threads, implemented by capturing first order continuations in a compact data structure sent over the network, allow Jinni to interoperate with remote high performance BinProlog servers for CPU-intensive knowledge processing and with other Jinni components over the Internet.

These features make Jinni a perfect development platform for intelligent mobile agent systems.

Jinni is fully implemented and is being used in a growing number of industrial and academic projects. The latest version is available from
`http://www.binnetcorp.com/Jinni`

1 Introduction

The paradigm shift towards networked, mobile, ubiquitous computing has brought a number of challenges which require new ways to deal with increasingly complex patterns of interaction: autonomous, reactive, and mobile computational entities are needed to take care of unforeseen problems, to optimize the flow of communication, to offer a simplified and personalized view to end users. These requirements naturally lead towards the emergence of *agent programs* with increasingly sophisticated inference capabilities, as well as autonomy and self-reliance.

Jinni is a new, lightweight, logic programming language, intended to be used as a flexible scripting tool for gluing together knowledge processing components and Java objects in networked client/server applications and thin client environments. By supporting multiple threads, control mobility and inference processing, Jinni is well suited for the development of intelligent mobile agent programs.

Jinni supports multi-user synchronized transactions and interoperates with the latest version of BinProlog [16], a high performance, robust, multi-threaded Prolog system with ability to generate C/C++ code and stand alone executables.

For acronym lovers JINNI can be read as: **J**ava **IN**ference engine and **N**etworked **I**nteractor, although its wishmaker status (high level, dense, network ubiquitous, mobile, etc. agent programming language) is an equally good reason for its name.

2 The World of Jinni

Jinni is based on a simple **Things**, **Places**, **Agents** ontology, borrowed from MUDs and MOOs [14,1,3,9,20,15].

Things are represented as Prolog terms, basically trees of embedded records containing constants and variables to be further instantiated to other trees.

Places are processes running on various computers with at least one *server component* listening on a port and a blackboard component allowing synchronized multi-user Linda [6,10] transactions, remote predicate calls, and mobile code operations.

Agents are collections of threads executing a set of goals, possibly spread over a set of different **Places** and usually executing remote and local transactions in coordination with other **Agents**. Their state is distributed over the network of **Places** in the form of dynamic Prolog clauses and produced/consumed Linda facts[1]. Jinni does not provide a single abstract data type for agents or places because it is intended to be an infrastructure on top of which they are built in an application specific way. In a typical Jinni application, as crisp abstractions emerge through the development process, a hierarchy of Places and Agents is built. **Place** and **Agent** prototypes are clonable, support inheritance/sharing of **Things** and are easily editable/configurable using the visual tools of the underlying Java environments. Agent threads moving between places and agents moving as units can be supported. Places are used to abstract away language differences between processors, like for instance Jinni and BinProlog. They can contain the same or different code bases (contexts), depending on the application's requirements. As an extra feature, mobile code allows fast processing in Jinni by delegating heavy inference processing to high-performance BinProlog components.

3 Jinni as a Logic Programming Java Component

Jinni is implemented as a lightweight, *thin client* logic programming component, based as much as possible on fully portable, vendor and version independent Java code. Its main features come from this architectural choice:

- a trimmed down, simple, operatorless syntactic subset of Prolog,

[1] Jinni implements assert and retract in terms of non-blocking local Linda operations.

- pure Prolog (Horn Clause logic) with leftmost goal unfolding as inference rule,
- multiple asynchronous inference engines running on separate threads,
- a shared blackboard to communicate between engines using a simple Linda-style subscribe/publish (in/out in Linda jargon) coordination protocol, based on associative search,
- high level networking operations allowing code mobility [2,12,11,4,21,13] and remote execution,
- a straightforward Jinni-to-Java translator allowing packaging of Jinni programs as Java classes,
- the ability to load code directly from the Web and to show third party Web documents (text, graphics, multi-media) by controlling applet contexts in browsers,
- backtrackable assumptions [18,8] implemented through trailed, overridable undo actions, also supporting Assumption Grammars, a variant of extended DCGs.

Jinni's spartan return to (almost) pure Horn Clause logic does not mean it is necessarily a weaker language. Expressiveness of full Prolog is easily attained in Jinni by combining multiple engines. The magic is similar to just adding another stack to a Push Down Automaton: this morphs it into a Turing machine[2]! As we will show in section 5.1 control constructs like `if-then-else`, negation as failure, once/1, and operations like (eager or lazy) findall are easily expressed in terms of cooperating engines without using CUT or side effects. Engines give transparent access to the underlying Java threads and are used to implement local or remote, lazy or eager findall operations, negation as failure, if-then-else, etc. at source level. Inference engines running on separate threads can cooperate through either predicate calls or through an easy to use flavor of the Linda coordination protocol.

Remote or local dynamic database updates (with deterministic, synchronized transactions with immediate update semantics) make Jinni an extremely flexible Agent programming language. Jinni is designed on top of dynamic, fully garbage collectible data structures, to take advantage of Java's automatic memory management.

4 Basic Agent Programming with Jinni

Agents behaviors are implemented easily in terms of synchronized in/out Linda operations and mobile code. As an example of such functionality, we will describe the use of two simple chat agents, which are part of Jinni's standard library:

[2] Of course, Horn Clause logic is already Turing complete. What we mean here by expressiveness is just the informal concept of being able to express new constructs at source level in a natural way.

Window 1 : a reactive channel listener

```
?-listen(fun(_)).
```

Window 2 : a selective channel publisher

```
?-talk(fun(jokes)).
```

They implement a front end to Jinni's associative publish/subscribe abilities. The more general pattern `fun(_)` will reach all the users interested in instances of `fun/1`, in particular `fun(jokes)`. However, someone publishing on an unrelated channel e.g. with `?-talk(stocks(nasdaq))`. will not reach fun/1 listeners because stocks(nasdaq) and fun(jokes) channel patterns are not unifiable.

More realistic stock market agent's buy/sell components look as follows:

```
sell(Who,Stock,AskPrice):-
  % triggers a matching buy transaction
  notify_about(offer(Who,Stock,AskPrice)).

buy(Who,Stock,SellingPrice):-
  % runs as a background thread
  % in parallel with other buy operations
  bg(try_to_buy(Who,Stock,SellingPrice)).

try_to_buy(Me,Stock,LimitPrice):-
  % this thread connects to a server side constraint and waits
  % until the constraint is solved to true on the server
  % by a corresponding sell transaction
  wait_for(offer(You,Stock,YourPrice),[ % server side mobile code
    lesseq(YourPrice,LimitPrice),
    local_in(has(You,Stock)),
    local_in(capital(You,YourCapital)), % server side 'local' in/1
    local_in(capital(Me,MyCapital)),    % operations
    compute('-',MyCapital,YourPrice,MyNewCapital),
    compute('+',YourCapital,YourPrice,YourNewCapital),
    local_out(capital(You,YourNewCapital)),
    local_out(capital(Me,MyNewCapital)),
    local_out(has(Me,Stock))
  ]).
```

Note that this example also gives a glimpse on Jinni's multithreaded client/server design (background thread launching with `bg`), as well as its *server side constraint solving ability* (`wait_for, notify_about`). We will now describe these features and Jinni's architecture in more detail.

5 What's New in Jinni

5.1 Programming with Engines

Jinni inherits from BinProlog's design the ability to launch multiple Prolog engines having their own state. An engine can be seen as an abstract datatype which produces a (possibly infinite) stream of solutions as needed. To create a new engine, we use:

```
new_engine(Goal,AnswerTemplate,Handle)
```

Computation starts by calling `Goal` and producing, on demand, *instances* of `AnswerTemplate` The `Handle` is a unique Java Object denoting the engine, assigned to its own thread. It will be used, for instance, to ask answers, one at a time, or to kill the engine.

To get an answer from the engine we use:

```
ask_engine(Handle,Answer)
```

Note that Answer is an instance of the AnswerTemplate pattern passed at engine creation time, by `new_engine`. Each engine can be seen as having its own virtual garbage collection process. Engines backtrack independently using their (implicit) choice-point stack and trail during the computation of an answer. Once computed, an answer is copied from an engine to the master engine which initiated it. Extraction of answers from an engine is based on a *monitor object* which synchronizes the producer and the consumer of the answer.

When the stream of answers reaches its end, `ask_engine/2` will simply fail. The resolution process in an engine can be discarded at any time with `stop_engine/1`. This allows avoiding the cost of backtracking in the case when a single answer is needed. The following example in the Jinni distribution) shows how to extract one solution from an engine:

```
one_solution(X,G,R):-
  new_engine(G,X,E),
  ask_engine(E,Answer),
  stop_engine(E),eq(Answer,R).
```

Note that `new_engine/3` speculatively starts execution of Goal on a new thread and that either a term of the form **the(X)** or **no** is returned by `ask_answer`. Synchronization with this thread is performed when asking an answer, using a special monitor object. By extending the monitor `Answer` class, one can easily implement speculative execution allowing a bounded number of answers to be computed in advance (a form of OR-parallel execution). Note that answers are produced in standard Prolog (LD-resolution) order. This design choice is needed for improved predictability, keeping in mind that Jinni, as a multi-threaded environment, is already subject to more complex operational semantics.

It is quite surprising how simply all essential control constructs of Prolog can be built on top of this one_solution/3 primitive[3].

```
if(Cond,Then,Else):-
  one_solution(successful(Cond,Then),Cond,R),
  select_then_else(R,Cond,Then,Else).

select_then_else(the(successful(Cond,Then)),Cond,Then,_):-Then.
select_then_else(no,_,_,Else):-Else.

once(G):-one_solution(G,G,the(G)).

not(G):-one_solution(G,G,no).

copy_term(X,CX):-one_solution(X,true,the(CX)).

bg(Goal):-new_engine(Goal,_,_). % spawns a new background thread
```

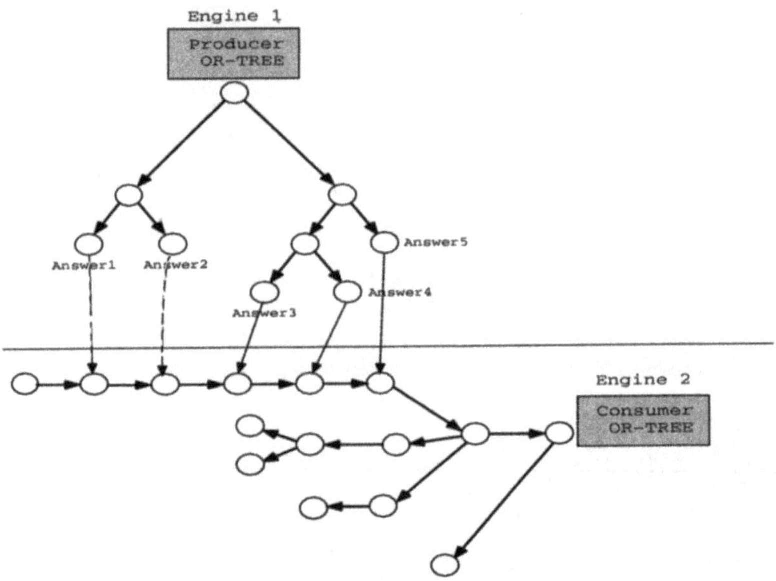

Fig. 1. Orthogonal Engines

Similarly, findall/3 is emulated easily by iterating over ask_engine/2 operations.

[3] In fact, for efficiency reasons, now Jinni has a `first_solution/3` builtin, which does not require a separate engine. It is implemented simply by throwing a special purpose *exception* when the first solution is found.

```
find_all(X,G,Xs):-
  new_engine(G,X,E),
  once(extract_answers(E,Xs)).

extract_answers(E,[X|Xs]):-
  ask_engine(E,the(X)),
  extract_answers(E,Xs).
extract_answers(_,[]).
```

Note that lazy variants of `findall` can be designed by introducing a stream-inspired concept of *lazy list*. This can be implemented by using a special JavaObject tail containing an Engine handle, which overrides default unification into a call to `ask_engine` to instantiate the tail to a new answer, if available, and to the empty list otherwise. To implement this functionality we would only have to extend Jinni's attributed variable class (AVar) with minimal new unification code.

Currently Jinni supports a programmer managed, *on demand* answer production through multiple *orthogonal*[4] *engines* (Fig. 1). We can see this programming pattern as the ability of an AND-branch of an engine to collect answers from multiple OR-branches of another engine. They give to the programmer the means to see the answers produced by an engine as a (lazy) data stream, and to control their production, in a way similar to Java's `Enumeration` interface.

In fact, by using orthogonal engines, a programmer does not really need to use findall and other similar predicates anymore - why accumulate answers eagerly on a list which will get scanned and decomposed again, when answers can be produced on demand? Still, encapsulating answers in lazy lists, can make their use even more transparent to Prolog programmers, as only one new construct

```
lazy_findall(AnswerTemplate, Goal, LazyAnswerList)
```

reusing a programmer's knowledge of `findall/3` would be needed.

5.2 Coordination and Remote Execution Mechanisms

Our networking constructs are built on top of the popular Linda [6,10,7] coordination framework, enhanced with unification based pattern matching, remote execution and a set of simple client-server components melted together into a scalable peer-to-peer layer, forming a 'web of interconnected worlds' (Fig 2):

```
out(X): puts X on the server
in(X):  waits until it can take an object matching X from the server
all(X,Xs): reads the list Xs matching X currently on the server
the(Pattern,Goal,Answer): starts a thread executing Goal on server
```

[4] We call them orthogonal (a geometric metaphor) as their execution proceeds independently.

The `all/2` operation, fetching the list of all matching terms is used instead of (cumbersome) backtracking for alternative solutions over the network. Note that the only blocking operation is `in/1`. Blocking `rd/1` is easily emulated in terms of `in/1` and `out/1`, while non-blocking `rd/1` is emulated with `all/2`. For expressiveness, the following derived operations are provided:

- `cout/1`, which puts a term on the blackboard only if none of is instances are present,
- `cin/1` which works like `in/1` but returns immediate failure if a matching term is absent
- `when/1` (a more efficient a non-blocking rd/1)

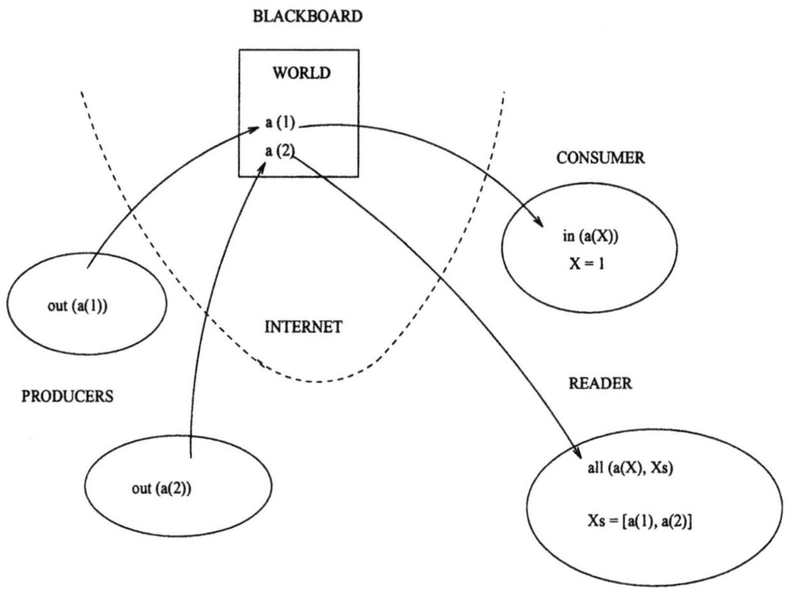

Fig. 2. Basic Linda operations

5.3 Server-side Constraint Solving

A natural extension to Linda is to use constraint solving for the selection of matching terms, instead of plain unification. This is implemented in Jinni through the use of 2 builtins:

Wait_for(Term,Constraint): waits for a Term such that Constraint is true on the server, and when this happens, it removes the result of the match from the server with an in/1 operation. Constraint is either a single goal or a list of goals [G1,G2,..,Gn] to be executed on the server.

Notify_about(Term): notifies the server to give this term to any blocked client which waits for it with a matching constraint i.e.

```
notify_about(stock_offer(nscp,29))
```

would trigger execution of a client having issued

```
wait_for(stock_offer(nscp,Price),less(Price,30)).
```

The use of server side constraint execution was in fact suggested by a real-life stock market application. In a client/server Linda interaction, triggering an atomic transaction when data verifying a simple arithmetic inequality becomes available, would be expensive. It would require repeatedly taking terms out of the blackboard, through expensive network transfers, and put them back unless the client can verify that a constraint holds. Our server side implementation checks a constraint only after a match occurs between new incoming data and the head of a suspended thread's constraint checking clause, i.e. a basic indexing mechanism is used to avoid useless computations. On the other hand, a mobile client thread can perform all the operations atomically on the server side, using local operations on the server, and come back with the results. The (simplified) server side fragment showing the implementation of `wait_for` and `notify_about` is as follows:

```
wait_for(Pattern,Constraint):-
  if(take_pattern(available_for(Pattern),Constraint),
     true,
     and(
      local_out(waiting_for(Pattern,Constraint)),
      local_in(holds_for(Pattern,Constraint))
     )
  ).

notify_about(Pattern):-
  if(take_pattern(waiting_for(Pattern,Constraint),Constraint),
     local_out(holds_for(Pattern,Constraint)),
     local_out(available_for(Pattern))
  ).

% takes the first matching Pattern for which Constraint holds
take_pattern(Pattern,Constraint):-
  local_all(Pattern,Ps),
  member(Pattern,Ps),
  Constraint,
  local_cin(Pattern,_).
```

Note that each time the head of the waiting clause matches incoming data, its body is (re)-executed. It would be interesting to explore use of *memoing* to reduce re-execution overhead. Although termination of constraint checking is left in the programmer's hand, only one thread is affected by a loop in the code, the server's integrity as such not being compromised. We think that improvement of implementation technology for server side constraint solving in a blackboard based framework rises some challenging open problems. Moreover, incorporating server-side symbolic constraint reducers (CLP, FD or interval based) can dramatically improve performance for large scale problems.

5.4 Mobile Code: for Expressiveness and for Acceleration

An obvious way to accelerate slow Prolog processing for a Java based system is through use of native (C/C++) methods. The simplest way to accelerate Jinni's Prolog processing is by including BinProlog through Java's JNI (as implemented in the latest version of our BinProlog/C/Java interface).

However, a more general scenario, also usable for applets not allowing native method invocations is the use of a *remote accelerator*. This is achieved transparently through the use of *mobile code*.

Code, State and Computation Mobility. The Oz 2.0 distributed programming proposal of [21] makes *object mobility* more transparent, although the mobile entity is still the *state* of the objects, not *live code*.

Mobility of *live code* is called *computation mobility* [5]. It requires interrupting execution, moving the state of a runtime system (stacks, for instance) from one site to another and then resuming execution. Clearly, for some languages, this can be hard or completely impossible to achieve.

General Magic's Telescript and Odissey [11] agent programming framework, IBM's Java based *aglets* [12] as well as Luca Cardelli's Oblique [2] have pioneered implementation technologies achieving *computation mobility*.

Jinni's Live Code Mobility. In the case of Jinni, computation mobility is used both as an *accelerator* and an *expressiveness lifting* device. A live thread will migrate from Jinni to a faster remote BinProlog engine, do some CPU intensive work and then come back with the results (or just sent back results, using Linda coordination). A very simple way to ensure atomicity and security of complex networked transactions is to have the agent code move to the site of the computation, follow existing security rules, access possibly large databases and come back with the results.

Jinni's mobile computation is a scaled down, simplified subset of BinProlog's mobile computation facilities. They are both based on the use of *first order continuations* i.e. encapsulated future computations, which can be easily suspended, moved over the network, and resumed at a different site. As continuations are first-order objects both in Jinni and BinProlog, the implementation is straightforward [17] and the two engines can interoperate transparently by simply moving computations from one to the other.

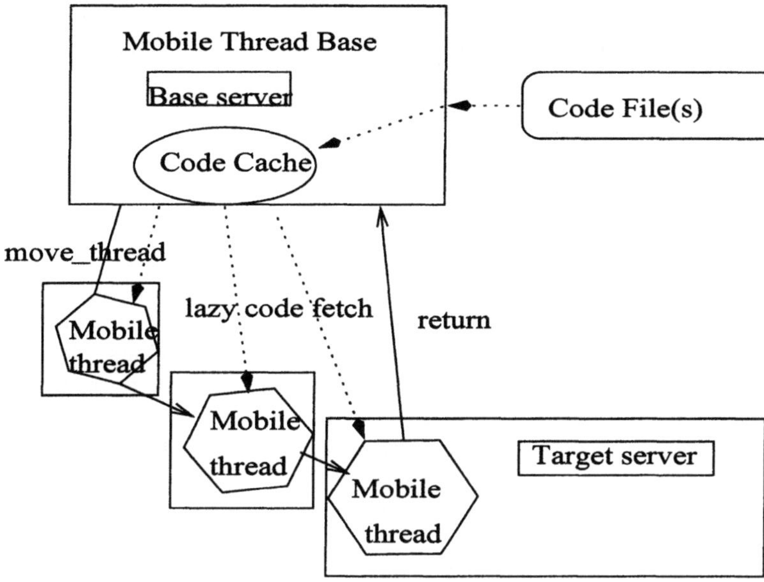

Fig. 3. Launching a mobile thread from its base

The target side waits in server mode. Once the continuation is received on the target side, the source might spawn a server thread as well, ready to execute code fetching and persistent database update requests from its mobile counterpart on the target side.

Fig. 3 shows the connections between a mobile thread and its base.

In the case of Jinni two simple **move/0** and **return/0** operations are used to transport computation to the server and back. The client simply waits until computation completes, when bindings for the first solution are propagated back:

```
Window 1: a mobile thread

?-there,move,println(on_server),member(X,[1,2,3]),
        return,println(back).
back
X=1;
no.

Window 2: a server

?-run_server.
on_server
```

In case return is absent, computation proceeds to the end of the transported continuation. Note that mobile computation is more expressive and more efficient than remote predicate calls as such. Basically, it *moves once*, and executes on the server *all future computations* of the current AND branch until a return instruction is hit, when it takes the remaining continuation and comes back. This can be seen by comparing real time execution speed for:

```
?-there,for(I,1,1000),run(println(I)),fail.

?-there,move,for(I,1,1000),println(I),fail.
```

While the first query uses `run/1` each time to send a remote task to the server, the second moves once the full computation to the server where it executes without further requiring network communications. Note that the `move/0, return/0` pair cut nondeterminism for the transported segment of the current continuation. This avoids having to transport state of the choice-point stack as well as implementation complexity of multiple answer returns and tedious distributed backtracking synchronization. Surprisingly, this is not a strong limitation, as the programmer can simply use something like:

```
?-there,move,findall(X,for(I,1,1000),Xs),return,member(X,Xs).
```

to emulate (finite!) nondeterministic remote execution, by collecting all solutions at the remote side and exploring them through (much more efficient) local backtracking after returning.

6 Jinni's Logical Engine

The inference rule of Jinni is called LD-resolution, consisting of repeatedly unfolding the leftmost goal in the body of the resolvent, seen as a clause with its head containing the answer pattern and its body the current state of the goal stack. It has the advantage of giving a more accurate description of Prolog's operational semantics than SLD-resolution.

With the notations of [19] each inference step is described as an algebraic clause composition operation $\oplus$ which unfolds the leftmost body-goal of the first argument.

Let A_0:-A_1,A_2,...,A_n and B_0:-B_1,...,B_m be two clauses (suppose $n > 0, m \geq 0$). We define

$$(A_0:\text{-}A_1,A_2,\ldots,A_n) \oplus (B_0:\text{-}B_1,\ldots,B_m) =$$
$$(A_0:\text{-}B_1,\ldots,B_m,A_2,\ldots,A_n)\theta$$

with θ = mgu(A_1,B_0). If the atoms A_1 and B_0 do not unify, the result of the composition is denoted as $\perp$. Furthermore, we consider A_0:-true,A_2,...,A_n to be equivalent to A_0:-A_2,...,A_n, and for any clause C, $\perp \oplus C = C \oplus \perp = \perp$. As usual, we assume that at least one operand has been renamed to a variant with variables standardized apart.

Jinni's main interpreter implements iteration of the $\oplus$ composition operation and backtracking over a set of clauses seen as a Java Enumeration type.

The implementation of Jinni's interpreter is minimalistic. A simple goal stack mechanism equivalent to BinProlog's *binarization* is used, giving full access to continuations as first order objects. The OR-stack is represented implicitly through the interpreter, with a Java Enumerations keeping the state of the current clause cursor and the top of trail cursor maintained directly as part of the state of a Java Stack object.

```
/**
  Main Jinni interpreter. Uses goal, which is part
  of the state of each program as a kind of goal-stack
  + current state of the computed answer substitution.
*/
private final void solve() throws OnceException {
  begin:
  for(;;) {
    goal=reduceBuiltins(goal); // loop over inline builtins
    if(goal.getBody() instanceof True) {
      if(first_only) throw new OnceException(goal);
      else { // send answer to controlling thread
        sendAnswer(goal);
        break begin;
      }
    }
    int oldTrailTop=trail.size();
    Clause reduced_goal=goal;

    // get set of clauses of current predicate
    Enumeration e=Init.bboard.toEnumerationFor(
      goal.getFirst().getKey());

    if(tracing>0) jtrace(reduced_goal,e);

    // backtrack over matching clauses
    while(e.hasMoreElements()) {
      Term T=(Term)e.nextElement();
      if(!(T instanceof Clause)) continue;

      // undo old bindings
      trail.unwind(oldTrailTop);

      // resolution step, over goal/resolvent of the form:
      // Answer:-G1,G2,...,Gn.

      goal=T.toClause().unfold_with_goal(reduced_goal,trail);
      if(null==goal) continue;
```

```
        if(!e.hasMoreElements()) {
           continue begin; // Last Call Optimization
        }
        solve(); // recursive call
      } // end of backtrack
      break begin;
    }
  }
```

We plan to accelerate Jinni by partially evaluating this interpreter to a Prolog-to-Java translator, along the lines of the jProlog[5] compiler co-developed with Bart Demoen.

7 A Meta-circular Interpreter for Jinni

The Prolog subset supported by Jinni has been designed with the idea of supporting program transformations and meta-interpretation.

In particular, in the absence of CUT, building a meta-interpreter which interprets itself according to the semantics of the object language is fairly easy. The following interpreter is *meta-circular* i.e. it has the property that `solve(solve(G))` computes the same answers as `solve(G)` or `G`, for any Jinni goal.

```
% meta-circular interpreter

solve(G):-
  once(reduce(G,NewG)),
  NewG.

% reflective reducer
% the simplest such beast is, of course: reduce(X,X).

reduce(G,G):-is_builtin(G).
reduce(',',(A,B),',',(solve(A),solve(B))).
reduce(G,',',(clause(G,Gs),solve(Gs))).
```

Note that reflection through a metacall to `NewG` is used in `solve/1`, after the `reduce/2` step is performed. Reflection is also apparent on builtins and, as it is usual with Prolog meta-interpreters, backtracking through clause/2 is reflected from the meta-language into the object language directly. The reader might ask why our meta-interpreter is different from the usual one. The answer is simple: if-then-else logic in the absence of CUT would make the naively adapted Prolog meta-interpreter unpleasantly complex.

[5] Available at: `http://www.cs.unt.edu/~tarau/`

8 Mutual Agent/Host Security: the *Bring Your Own Wine* Principle

Jinni has currently a `login + password` mechanism for all remote operations, including mobile code. However, the combination of meta-interpretation and computation mobility opens the door for experimenting with novel security mechanisms.

Let us consider the (open) problem of mutually protecting a mobile agent from its (possibly malicious) host as well as the host from the (possibly malicious) agent. Protecting the host from the agent is basically simple and well known. It is achieved through building a *sandbox* around the code interpreter as in Java. The sandbox can filter (usually statically) the instruction set, ensuring, for instance, that local file operations are forbidden.

However, protecting the agent from injection of a malicious continuation from the host, to be executed after its return is basically an open problem.

We will sketch here a solution dealing with both problems.

It is known that (most) language interpreters are Turing-equivalent computational mechanisms, i.e. it is not statically decidable what they will do during their execution. For instance, we cannot statically predict if such an interpreter will halt or not on arbitrary code.

The main idea is very simple: *a mobile agent will bring its own (Turing equivalent) interpreter*[6], give it to the host for static checking of sandbox compliance. Note that a sufficient condition for an interpreter to be sandbox compliant is that it *does not use reflection* and *it only calls itself or builtins provided by the sandbox.* Clearly, this can be statically checked, and ensures protection of the host against a malicious agent[7]. Protecting the mobile agent who brought its own meta-interpreter is clearly simpler than running over an unknown/statically unpredictable interpreter provided by the host. Moreover, in the presence of first order continuations, the agent can check properties of future computations before actually executing potentially malicious code[8]. Note that by bringing its Turing-equivalent interpreter, the agent can make sure that its own security checking mechanisms cannot be statically detected by the host. Clearly, supposing the contrary would imply that a malicious host would also solve the halting problem.

---

[6] It is inspired by the technique some restaurants in Canada apply to wine to avoid paying expensive licensing fees: they ask you to bring your own. Subtle side effects on the customers mind are therefore also their own responsibility.

[7] In multi-threaded systems like Jinni, non-termination based resource attacks are not an issue, as the interpreter can be made to run on its own thread and therefore it cannot block the host's server mechanism.

[8] In fact, in the case of Jinni's mobile code, the returning continuation is unified with the one left home, as the natural way to propagate bindings computed remotely. As far as the continuation contains no metacalls or clause database operations, no malicious actions as such can be attached by the visited host

9 Application Domains

Jinni's client and server scripting abilities are intended to support platform and vendor independent Prolog-to-Java and Prolog-to-Prolog bidirectional connection over the net and to accelerate integration of the effective inference technologies developed the last 20 years in the field of Logic Programming in mainstream Internet products.

The next iteration is likely to bring a simple, plain English scripting language to be compiled to Jinni, along the lines of the LogiMOO prototype, with speech recognizer/synthesizer based I/O. A connection between Jinni and its Microsoft Agent counterpart *Genie* are among the high priority tasks likely to be left to the growing community of Jinni co-developers[9].

Among the potential targets for Jinni based products: lightweight rule based programs assisting customers of Java-enabled appliances, from Web based TVs to mobile cell phones and car computers, all requiring knowledge components to adjust to increasingly sophisticated user expectations.

A stock market simulator is currently on the way to be implemented based on Jinni, featuring user programmable intelligent agents. It is planned to be connected to real world Internet based stock trade services.

Jinni's key features are currently being ported to BinProlog, which will support a similar multi-threading and networking model and at considerably higher engine performance, while transparently interoperating with Jinni through mobile code, remote predicate calls and Linda transactions.

10 Conclusion

The Jinni project shows that Logic Programming languages are well suited as the basic glue so much needed for elegant and cost efficient Internet programming. The ability to compress so much functionality in such a tiny package shows that building logic programming components to be integrated in emerging tools like Java might be the most practical way towards mainstream recognition and widespread use of Logic Programming technology. Jinni's emphasis on functionality and expressiveness over performance, as well as its use of integrated multi-threading and networking, hint towards the priorities we consider important for future Logic Programming language design.

Acknowledgments

We thank for support from NSERC (grants OGP0107411), the Université de Moncton, Louisiana Tech University as well as from E-COM Inc. and the

[9] Jinni's sustained growth is insured through a relatively unconventional *bazaar* style development process, similar to Linux and more recently Netscape client products.

Radiance Group Inc. Special thanks go to Koen De Bosschere, Phil Cohen, Veronica Dahl, Bart Demoen, Ed Freeman, Don Garrett, Armin Minkler, Stephen Rochefort, and Yu Zhang for fruitful interaction related to the design, implementation, and testing of Jinni. We also thank an anonymous referee for his salient comments helping to significantly improve the presentation of this paper.

References

1. The Avalon MUD. `http://www.avalon-rpg.com/`.
2. K. A. Bharat and L. Cardelli. Migratory applications. In *Proceedings of the 8th Annual ACM Symposium on User Interface Software and Technology*, Nov. 1995. `http://gatekeeper.dec.com/pub/DEC/SRC/research-reports/abstracts/src-rr-138.html`.
3. BlackSun. CyberGate. `http://www.blaxxun.com/`.
4. L. Cardelli. Mobile ambients. Technical report, Microsoft, 1998. `http://www.research.microsoft.com/users/adg/Research/Ambit/default.html`
5. L. Cardelli. Mobile Computation. In J. Vitek and C. Tschudin, editors, *Mobile Object Systems – Towards the Programmable Internet*, pages 3–6. Springer-Verlag, LNCS 1228, 1997.
6. N. Carriero and D. Gelernter. Linda in context. *CACM*, 32(4):444–458, 1989.
7. S. Castellani and P. Ciancarini. Enhancing Coordination and Modularity Mechanisms for a Languag e with Objects-as-Multisets. In P. Ciancarini and C. Hankin, editors, *Proc. 1st Int. Conf. on Coordination Models and Languages*, volume 1061 of *LNCS*, pages 89–106, Cesena, Italy, April 1996. Springer-Verlag.
8. V. Dahl, P. Tarau, and R. Li. Assumption Grammars for Processing Natural Language. In L. Naish, editor, *Proceedings of the Fourteenth International Conference on Logic Programming*, pages 256–270, MIT press, 1997.
9. K. De Bosschere, D. Perron, and P. Tarau. LogiMOO: Prolog Technology for Virtual Worlds. In *Proceedings of PAP'96*, pages 51–64, London, Apr. 1996.
10. K. De Bosschere and P. Tarau. Blackboard-based Extensions in Prolog. *Software – Practice and Experience*, 26(1):49–69, Jan. 1996.
11. GeneralMagicInc. Odissey. 1997. `http://www.genmagic.com/agents`.
12. IBM. Aglets. `http://www.trl.ibm.co.jp/aglets`.
13. E. Jul, H. Levy, N. Hutchinson, and A. Black. Fine-Grained Mobility in the Emerald System. *ACM Transactions on Computer Systems*, 6(1):109–133, February 1988.
14. T. Meyer, D. Blair, and S. Hader. WAXweb: a MOO-based collaborative hypermedia system for WWW. *Computer Networks and ISDN Systems*, 28(1/2):77–84, 1995.
15. P. Tarau. Logic Programming and Virtual Worlds. In *Proceedings of INAP96*, Tokyo, Nov. 1996. Keynote address.
16. P. Tarau. BinProlog 7.0 Professional Edition: Advanced BinProlog Programming and Extensions Guide. Technical report, BinNet Corp., 1998. Available from `http://www.binnetcorp.com/BinProlog/www`.
17. P. Tarau and V. Dahl. Mobile Threads through First Order Continuations. In *Proceedings of APPAI-GULP-PRODE'98*, Coruna, Spain, July 1998.

18. P. Tarau, V. Dahl, and A. Fall. Backtrackable State with Linear Affine Implication and Assumption Grammars. In J. Jaffar and R. H. Yap, editors, *Concurrency and Parallelism, Programming, Networking, and Security*, Lecture Notes in Computer Science 1179, pages 53–64, Singapore, Dec. 1996. Springer-Verlag.
19. P. Tarau and K. De Bosschere. Memoing with Abstract Answers and Delphi Lemmas. In Y. Deville, editor, *Logic Program Synthesis and Transformation*, Workshops in Computing, Springer-Verlag, pages 196–209, Louvain-la-Neuve, July 1993.
20. P. Tarau and K. De Bosschere. Virtual World Brokerage with BinProlog and Netscape. In P. Tarau, A. Davison, K. De Bosschere, and M. Hermenegildo, editors, *Proceedings of the 1st Workshop on Logic Programming Tools for INTERNET Applications*, JICSLP'96, Bonn, Sept. 1996. `http://clement.info.umoncton.ca/~lpnet`.
21. P. Van Roy, S. Haridi, and P. Brand. Using mobility to make transparent distribution practical. 1997, manuscript.

Appendix: A Quick Introduction to Jinni

Getting Started

Using Jinni Through an Applet: The latest version of Jinni is available as an applet at:

```
http://www.binnetcorp.com/Jinni
```

After entering a query like:

```
append(Xs,Ys,[1,2,3]).
```

the applet will display the results in its Prolog console style lower window.

Using Jinni in Command Line Mode: Consulting a new program

```
?-[<myprog>].
```

will read in memory the file `<myprog>.pro` program replacing similarly named predicates with new ones. It is actually a shorthand for reconsult/1. To accumulate clause for similarly named predicates, use consult/1. The shorthand

```
?-co.
```

will reconsult again the last reconsulted file.

Client/server Interaction: To try out Jinni's client/server abilities, open 3 shell windows:

```
Window 1

java  Jinni
..............
?-run_server.


Window 2

?-there.
?-in(a(X)).


Window 3

?-there.
?-out(a(hello)).
```

When entering the out command in Window 3 you will see activity in Window 2. Through the server in Window 1, Window 3 has communicated the word "hello" returned as a result of the in query in Window 2!

Bi-directional Jinni / BinProlog Talk

As client, Jinni talks to BinProlog servers with `out`, `cin` and `all` commands and with `the(Answer, Goal, Result)` or `all(Answer, Goal, Results)` remote execution queries. To try this out, start an unrestricted BinProlog server with:

```
?-trust.
```

BinProlog's `trust/0` starts a password protected server, willing to accept remote predicate calls and mobile code. BinProlog's default *run_server/0* only accepts a *limited set* (mostly Linda operations - a form of *sandbox* security). As a server, Jinni understands out, all, cin, rd, in commands coming from BinProlog clients and uses multiple threads to synchronize them as well as `the(Answer,Goal,Result)` or `all(Answer,Goal,ListOfResults)` remote execution queries. The most natural use is a Java server embedded into a larger application which communicates with Prolog clients. Jinni-aware BinProlog clients or servers are available from

```
http://www.binnetcorp.com/BinProlog
```

Secure operations can be performed using Jinni's and BinProlog login and password facilities. Both Jinni and BinProlog support computation mobility.

The **move/0** command transport execution from **Jinni** client to a **BinProlog** server for accelerated execution. For instance the Jinni command:

```
?-there,move,for(I,1,1000),write(I),nl,fail.
```

would trigger execution in the much faster BinProlog server where the 1000 numbers will be printed out.

Remote exection is deterministic and restricted to a segment of the current AND-continuation. The command:

```
?-there,move,findall(I,for(I,1,10),Is),return,member(I,Is).
```

will return the values for **Is** computed on the **Jinni** server, which can be explored, after **return/0**, through local backtracking by **member/2**, on the client side. This combination of move-findall-return-member shows that implementing code mobility as deterministic remote execution of a segment of the current AND-branch does not limit its expressiveness.

Concurrent Logic/Constraint Programming: The Next 10 Years

Kazunori Ueda

Department of Information and Computer Science, Waseda University,
4-1, Okubo 3-chome, Shinjuku-ku, Tokyo 169-8555, Japan

Summary. Concurrent logic/constraint programming is a simple and elegant formalism of concurrency that can potentially address a lot of important future applications including parallel, distributed, and intelligent systems. Its basic concept has been extremely stable and has allowed efficient implementations. However, its uniqueness makes this paradigm rather difficult to appreciate. Many people consider concurrent logic/constraint programming to have rather little to do with the rest of logic programming. There is certainly a fundamental difference in the view of computation, but careful study of the differences will lead to the understanding and the enhancing of the whole logic programming paradigm by an *analytic approach*. As a model of concurrency, concurrent logic/constraint programming has its own challenges to share with other formalisms of concurrency as well. They are: (1) a counterpart of λ-calculus in the field of concurrency, (2) a common platform for various non-sequential forms of computing, and (3) type systems that cover both logical and physical aspects of computation.

1 Grand Challenges

It seems that concurrent logic programming and its generalization, concurrent constraint programming, are subfields of logic programming that are quite different from the other subfields and hence can confuse people both inside and outside the logic programming community.

While most subfields of logic programming are related to artificial intelligence in some way or other—agents, learning, constraints, knowledge bases, automated deduction, and so on—, concurrent logic/constraint programming is somewhat special in the sense that its principal connection is to concurrency.

Concurrency is a ubiquitous phenomenon both inside and outside computer systems, a phenomenon observed wherever there is more than one entity that may interact with each other. It is important for many reasons. Firstly, the phenomenon is so ubiquitous that we need a good theoretical and practical framework to deal with it. Secondly, it is concerned with the infrastructure of computing (the environment in which computer systems and programs interact with the rest of the world) as well as activities within computer systems, and as such the framework scales up. In other words, it is concerned with *computing in the large*, and accordingly, programming in the large. Thirdly, it encompasses various important forms of non-sequential computing including parallel, distributed, and mobile computing.

Bearing this in mind, I'd like to propose the Grand Challenges of concurrent logic/constraint programming.[1] The theoretical computer science community is struggling to find killer applications, but I would claim that, as far as concurrency is concerned, there are at least three important scientific challenges besides finding killer applications.

1. *A "λ-calculus" in the field of concurrency.* It is a real grand challenge to try to have a model of concurrency and communication which is as stable as λ-calculus for sequential computation.
   We have had many proposals of models of concurrency: Petri Nets [36], Actors [2], Communicating Sequential Processes [24], and many formalisms named X-calculus, X being Communicating Systems [29], π [30], Action [31], Join [17], Gamma [4], Ambient [6], and so on.
   Concurrent constraint programming [38] is another important model of concurrency, though, unfortunately, it is often overlooked in the concurrency community. I proposed Guarded Horn Clauses (GHC) as a simple concurrent logic *language*, but in its first paper I also claimed:

   > "We hope the simplicity of GHC will make it suitable for a parallel computation model as well as a programming language. The flexibility of GHC makes its efficient implementation difficult compared with CSP-like languages. However, a flexible language could be appropriately restricted in order to make simple programs run efficiently. On the other hand, it would be very difficult to extend a fast but inflexible language naturally." [51] (1985)

   One of the reasons why there are so many models is that there are various useful patterns of interaction, some of which are useful for high-level concurrent programming and others rather primitive. Here, a natural question arises as to whether we can find a lowest possible layer for modeling concurrency. I am not sure if people can agree upon a single common substrate, but still believe that the effort to have a simple and primitive framework (or a few of them) is very useful and will lead to higher respect of the field. Note that everybody respects λ-calculus but it still has a number of variants and some insist that it is not fully primitive (see, for example, [1]).

[1] Concurrent constraint programming can be viewed both as a generalization of concurrent logic programming and as a generalization of constraint logic programming. This article will focus on the former view since the challenges of concurrent constraint programming from the latter view should be more or less similar to those of constraint logic programming.

Needless to say, a stable calculus is a challenge but is not an ultimate goal. What we need next is a high-level programming language fully supported by a stable theory.

2. *Common platform for non-conventional computing.* The next challenge is to see if a common platform—the pair of a high-level concurrent language and an underlying theory—can be the base of various forms of non-conventional computing such as

   - parallel computing,
   - distributed/network computing,
   - real-time computing, and
   - mobile computing.

   Historically, they have been addressed by more or less different communities and cultures, but all these areas share the following property: unlike conventional sequential computing, programmers must be able to access and control the physical aspects of computation. At the same time, programmers don't want to be bothered by physical considerations in writing correct programs and porting them to different computing environments. These two requirements are referred to as *awareness* and *transparency* (of/from physical aspects).
   The fact that all these areas have to do with physical aspects means that they all have to do with concurrency. They all make sense in computing environments participated in by more than one physical entity such as 'sites' and 'devices'. This is why it is interesting to try to establish a novel unified platform for these diverse forms of non-conventional symbolic computing.

3. *Type systems and frameworks of analysis for both logical and physical properties.* The third grand challenge is a framework of static analysis to be built into concurrency frameworks. The first thing to be designed is a type system. Here I use the term "type system" in its broadest sense; that is, to have a type system means to:

   (a) design the notion of types, where the notion can be anything that is well-defined and useful either for programmers or for implementations,
   (b) define typing rules that connect the world of program text and the world of types, and
   (c) establish basic (and desirable) properties of well-typed programs such as subject reduction and strong normalization.

   So a type does not necessarily represent a set of possible values a syntactic construct can denote in the standard semantics; for instance, a mode (directionality of information flow) is thought of as a type in a broad sense.

As we know, types play extremely important roles in programming languages and calculi. The fundamental difference between types and other formalisms of program analysis (such as abstract interpretation) is that, although well-typedness imposes certain constraints on allowable programs, the notion of types is exposed to programmers. Accordingly, types should be accessible to programmers and should help them understand and debug their programs better.
These features of type systems are expected to play key roles in concurrent programming. A challenge here is to deal with physical as well as logical properties of programs in a way accessible to programmers.

I believe addressing these scientific challenges is as essential as building killer applications because, only with such endeavor, declarative languages and theory-driven approach can find their raison d'être.

2 Two Approaches to Addressing Novel Applications

It is natural to think that addressing novel applications requires a powerful programming language with various features. A popular approach to making a logic programming language more powerful is to generalize it or to integrate useful features into it. Constraint logic programming, inductive logic programming, higher-order logic programming, disjunctive logic programming, etc. are all such generalizations. Some extensions are better thought of as integration rather than generalization; examples are functional logic programming and multi-paradigm extensions such as Oz [46].

However, there is a totally different approach to a more powerful language, which I call an *analytic approach*. In an analytic approach, one tries to identify smaller fragments of logic programs (or of extensions of logic programs) with nice and useful properties that may lead to efficient implementation.

Note that what I mean by "powerful" here is not in terms of expressive power. By identifying possibly important fragments of a general framework and studying them carefully, one may able to establish new concepts with which one can understand the whole framework in more depth and detail. Also, one may find that some fragment allows far more efficient implementation. (A popular example where simplicity is the source of efficiency is the RISC architecture.) One may build programming tools that take advantage of the properties of fragments. They are a source of power because it may open up new application areas that could not be addressed by the general framework.

The above claim could be understood also from the following analogy: having a notion of Turing machines does not necessarily mean that we don't have to study pushdown or finite-state automata. They have their values in their own rights. Another example is the relationship between untyped and typed λ-calculi. Yet another obvious example is the identification of Horn sentences from full first-order formulae, without which the logic programming paradigm would not exist today. Examples of smaller fragments of logic programming languages that have been studied in depth are Datalog (no function symbols) and concurrent logic languages (no search in exchange of reactiveness).

The analytic approach is useful also when one attempts to generalize or integrate features. Integration will succeed only after the features to be integrated have been well understood and the interface between them has been carefully designed. A criterion of success is whether one can give clean semantics to the whole integrated framework as well as to each component. If the components interact only at the meta (or extralogical) level, the whole framework is considerably more complicated (in terms of semantics) than their components, which means the verification and manipulation of programs become considerably harder. This issue will be discussed in the next section.

3 Logic Programming vs. Concurrent Logic Programming

Concurrent logic programming was born from the study of concurrent execution of logic programs. It turned out to enjoy a number of nice properties both as a formalism and as a language for describing concurrency. In the logic programming community, however, concurrent logic programming has always been a source of controversy. Unfortunately, the controversy was by and large not very technical and did not lead to deeper understanding of the paradigms.

A typical view of concurrent logic programming has been:

$$\begin{aligned}\text{Concurrent LP} &= \text{LP} + \text{committed choice}\\ &= \text{LP} - \text{completeness}\end{aligned}$$

Although both the first and the second equations are not totally wrong, viewing committed choice simply as losing completeness is too superficial.

Committed choice or don't-care nondeterminism is an essential construct in modeling reactive computing and has been studied in depth in the concurrency community. It is essential because one must be able to model a process or an agent that performs *arbitration.* (For instance, a receptionist will serve whoever *(s)he thinks* comes first, rather than whoever comes first.) Semantically, it is much more than just discarding all but one of possible execution branches. All the subtleties lie in what events or information should be the basis of choice operations; in other words, the subtleties lie in the semantics of guard rather than the choice itself. The presence or absence of nondeterminism makes fundamental difference to the denotational semantics of concurrency (see [24] for example). When I was designing Guarded Horn Clauses, I believed don't-care nondeterminism was so essential that it was a bad idea to retain both don't-care nondeterminism and don't-know nondeterminism in a single model of computation.

Nevertheless, we also found in our experiences with concurrent logic languages that most of the predicates are deterministic and very few predicates perform arbitration—even though they change the whole semantical framework. Thus the aspect of arbitration is not to be overstated. A much more productive view of concurrent logic programming will accordingly be:

$$\begin{aligned}\text{Concurrent LP} &= \text{LP} + \text{directionality of dataflow}\\ &= \text{LP} + \text{embedded concurrency control}\end{aligned}$$

This is more productive because it emphasizes the aspect of dataflow synchronization, an important construct also in logic programming without committed choice. Examples where dataflow synchronization plays important roles include delaying, coroutining, sound negation-as-failure, and the Andorra principle [37]. Dataflow-centered view of the execution logic programs best captures the essence of concurrent logic/constraint programs, as became clear from the ***ask* + *tell*** formulation advocated by Saraswat [38].

Another reason why the above view is more productive is that it addresses mode systems that prescribe the directionality of dataflow. Mode systems are attracting more interest in various subfields of logic programming because

- it shares with type systems many good properties from which both programmers and implementations can benefit, and
- many (if not all) predicates we write have a single intended mode of use, and there are a lot of situations where this fact can be exploited in interesting ways.

For example, Mercury [47] takes full advantage of strong moding to yield very efficient code.[2] Inductive logic programming benefits from moding in reducing search space [32]. Concurrent logic/constraint programming benefits enormously from strong moding both in implementation and programming [61,63,13,3], and I strongly believe that

$$\text{Moded Concurrent LP} = \text{ask} + \text{tell} + \text{strong moding}$$

is one of the most flexible realistic models of concurrency.

It is vital to see that ordinary logic programming and concurrent logic programming are targeted at different scopes. What logic programming is concerned with include knowledge representation, reasoning, search, etc., while concurrent logic programming aims at a simple programming and theoretical model of concurrency and communication. Accordingly, concurrent logic languages should aim at general-purpose algorithmic languages which can potentially act as coordinators of more application-specific logic languages.

[2] Note, however, that the mode system of Mercury is very different from the mode system of Moded Flat GHC discussed in this paper; the former deals with the change of instantiatedness, which is a temporal property, while the latter deals with polarity, which is a non-temporal property [63].

Since the conception of concurrent logic programming, how to reconcile two essential features in parallel knowledge information systems, search and reactiveness, has been one of the most difficult problems. The two paradigms could be integrated but should be done with utmost care. The solution adopted in PARLOG [14] was to use all-solutions predicates (à la `findall` in Prolog) to interface between the world of don't-know nondeterminism and the world of don't-care nondeterminism. The key issue here is how to gather multiple solutions obtained from different binding environments into a single data structure. Whether the all-solutions construct can be given clean, declarative meaning and whether it allows efficient implementation depend on the program and the goal for which solutions are to be collected [33,55]. Roughly speaking, the requirement has to do with the proper treatment of logical variables. Existing all-solutions predicates in Prolog involve the copying of solutions, exhibiting *impedance mismatch*.[3]

Moding seems to play an important role here; we conjecture that all-solutions predicates can be given simple, object-level semantics if the program and the goal are well-moded under an appropriate mode system similar to the mode system for Moded Flat GHC [61].

Another example where moding played an important role in essentially the same way is the First Order Compiler [41], a compiler from a class of full first-order formulae into definite clauses.

The issue of clean interfacing arises in constraint logic programming systems also. In realistic applications of constraint satisfaction, it is often crucial that a constraint solver can run concurrently with its caller so that the latter be able to observe and control the behavior of the former incrementally. However, language constructs for doing so are yet to be refined.

4 An Application Domain: Parallel/Network Programming

Where should concurrent logic/constraint programming languages find promising applications? I believe that the most important areas to address are parallel and network applications for a number of reasons:

1. Even "modern" languages like Obliq and Java feature rather classical concurrency constructs such as monitors and explicit locking. In more traditional languages like C or Fortran, parallel/network programming

[3] Oz features *computation spaces* (the pair of a local constraint store and a set of processes working on the store) as first-class citizens, with which encapsulated search can be programmed as higher-order combinators [45]. This approach is certainly cleaner in that a set of solutions is represented using (procedures returning) computation spaces instead of copied terms. In an analytic approach, however, we are interested in identifying a class of programs and goals for which a set of solutions can be represented without using higher-order constructs.

is achieved with APIs such as MPI, Unix sockets, and POSIX threads. These constructs are all low-level compared with synchronization based on dataflow and arbitration based on choice, and programming with APIs seems to be a step backwards from writing provably correct programs even though verification is not impossible.
2. Parallel computing and distributed computing are considerably more difficult than sequential computing. Good models and methodologies to build large applications quickly are desperately called for.
3. These areas are becoming increasingly popular in a strong trend towards large-scale global computing environments both for high-performance distributed computing [16] and for virtual network communities such as Virtual Places, Community Places and Matrix.[4]
4. These areas give us a good opportunity to demonstrate the power of small and yet "usable" languages with an appropriate level of abstraction. It seems essential to keep the languages simple enough—and much simpler than Java—to be amenable to theoretical treatment and to make them as easy to learn as possible. I anticipate that amenability to theoretical treatment, if well exploited, will be of enormous practical importance in these areas.

From a language point of view, the last point is the most challenging. Consider writing secure network applications with mobile code. This involves various requirements:

- Specification of *physical locations* (sites) where computation should take place.
- Reasoning about *resources*, such as time, stack and heap, that the computation may consume. Without it, downloaded code might make a so-called DoS (denial of service) attack by monopolizing computation resources.
- Security at various levels. Some of the high-level properties such as consistency of communication protocols can be guaranteed by typing and moding. Other high-level security issues may require more sophisticated analysis and verification. Low-level security could partly be left to Java's bytecode verifier if we use Java or Java bytecode as a target language.
- Transmission of various entities across possibly heterogeneous platforms. In addition to program code, linked data structures and symbols (usually given unique IDs locally on each site) are the main points of consideration in symbolic languages.

The requirements are so complicated and diverse that addressing them in an ad hoc way would result in a theoretically intractable language. It is an interesting and big challenge to obtain a language that allows and encourages formal reasoning about physical and logical properties of programs.

[4] Interestingly, the designers of Grid [16], Virtual Places, Community Places and Matrix have all worked actively on concurrent logic/constraint programming.

- 1983 Concurrent Prolog [42] and initial version of PARLOG [14]
- 1983-84 Big controversy (inside ICOT) on LP vs. concurrent LP for parallel knowledge information processing systems [44]
- 1985 First paper on GHC [51]
- 1985 GHC-to-Prolog compiler [52] used in our initial experiments
- 1985–86 GHC considered too general; subsetted to Flat GHC
- 1986 Prolog-to-GHC compiler performing exhaustive search [53]
- 1987 MRB (1-bit reference counting) scheme for Flat GHC [9]
- 1987 First parallel implementation of Flat GHC on Multi-PSI v1 (6 PEs) [25]
- 1987 ALPS [28] gave a logical interpretation of communication primitives
- 1987–1988 KL1 designed based on Flat GHC, the main extension being the *shoen* construct [57]
- 1988 Parallel implementation of KL1 on Multi-PSI v2 (64 PEs) [34]
- 1988 Strand [15] (evolved later into PCN [7] and CC++ [8])
- 1988 PIMOS operating system [10]
- 1988 Unfold/fold transformation and transaction-based semantics [54]
- 1989 Concurrent Constraint Programming [38]
- 1989 Controversy on atomic vs. eventual tell (Kahn's article in [44])
- 1989 MGTP (Model Generation Theorem Prover in KL1) project [19]

Fig. 1. GHC, KL1, and related events (Part I)

It may be a good idea for declarative language communities to share a set of (more concrete) challenges of the form "how can we program X in our formalisms?" to facilitate comparison between different paradigms. Instances of X may be:

- dynamic data structures (e.g., cyclic graphs; most declarative languages just ignore them, regrettably),
- live access counters of WWW pages,
- teleconferencing, and
- MUD (multi-user dungeon; text-based virtual reality).

5 Experiences with Guarded Horn Clauses and KL1

Although the progress has been admittedly slow, I am quite optimistic about the future of concurrent logic/constraint programming. My optimism is based on 15 years of our experiences with the paradigm since the initial stage of the Japanese Fifth Generation Computer Systems (FGCS) project. Figures 1–2 show the history of Guarded Horn Clauses (GHC) and KL1 as well as related events. The role and the history of the kernel language in the FGCS project are discussed in detail in my article in [44].

- 1989 Message-oriented implementation of Flat GHC [58]
- 1990 Mode systems for Flat GHC [58]
- 1990 Structural operational semantics for Flat GHC [59]
- 1990 Janus [39]
- 1991 Denotational semantics of CCP [40]
- 1991 AKL [26] (later evolved into Oz, Oz2, and Oz3)
- 1992 Parallel implementation of KL1 on PIM/m and PIM/p [48,23]
- 1992 Various parallel applications written in KL1, including OS, biology, CAD, legal reasoning, automated deduction, etc. [11,22,35]
- 1992 Message-oriented parallel implementation of Moded Flat GHC [60]
- 1992 KLIC (KL1-to-C compiler) designed [12]
- 1992 MGTP solved an open problem (IJCAI'93 award) [20]
- 1994 Proof system for CCP [5]
- 1994 Moded Flat GHC formulated in detail [61]
- 1994 ToonTalk, a visual CCP language [27]
- 1995 Constraint-based mode systems put into practice [63]
- 1996 klint, a mode analyzer for KL1 programs
- 1996 Strong moding applied to constraint-based error diagnosis [13]
- 1997 kima, a diagnoser of ill-moded programs
- 1997 KLIEG, a visual version of KL1 and its programming environment [50]
- 1997 Strong moding applied to constraint-based error correction [3]

Fig. 2. GHC, KL1, and related events (Part II)

5.1 GHC as the Weakest Fragment of Concurrent Constraint Programming

After 13 years of research, heated discussions and programming experiences since the proposal of GHC, it turned out that this simplest fragment of concurrent constraint programming was surprisingly stable and versatile.

Let us see why it was so stable. GHC is thought of as the weakest Concurrent Constraint Language in the following senses: First, it features *ask* and *eventual tell* (i.e., publication of constraints *after* committed choice) but not *atomic tell* (publication *upon* committed choice). Second, its computation domain is a set of finite trees. Nevertheless, GHC as well as its ancestors featured fundamental constructs for a concurrent programming language from the very beginning:

- parallel composition,
- creation of local variables,
- nondeterministic (committed) choice,
- value passing, and
- data structures (trees, lists, etc.).

The last two points are in contrast with other models of concurrency such as CCS and (theoretical) CSP that primarily focused on atomic *events*. GHC was proposed primarily as a concurrent language, though it was intended to be a model as well (Section 1).

Furthermore, GHC as well as its ancestors had the following features from the beginning:

1. *Reconfigurable process structures.* Concurrent logic languages supported dynamic reconfiguration of interprocess communication channels and dynamic creation of processes. Most mathematical models of concurrency, on the other hand, did not feature reconfigurable process structures until π-calculus was proposed in late 1980's.
2. *Object (process) identity.* This is represented by logical variables (occurring as the arguments of processes) through which processes interact with each other. Although objects themselves are not first-class in GHC, the variables identifying processes can be passed around to change the logical configuration of processes. Hence the processes were effectively mobile exactly in the sense of mobile processes in π-calculus.
3. *Input/output completely within the basic framework.* The input/output primitives of "declarative" languages had generally been provided as marginal constructs and in a quite unsatisfactory manner. I thought the design of general-purpose languages should proceed in the opposite way *by taking the semantics of input/output constructs as a boundary condition of language design.* Concurrent logic programs are often thought of as less declarative than logic programs, but real-life concurrent logic programs projected to logic programs (by forgetting synchronization) are much more declarative than real-life Prolog programs.

Later on, several important features were added:

1. KL1 [57] featured the notion of physical locations, though in a primitive form, to allow programmers to describe load balancing of parallel computation.
2. The mode system [61] introduced the notion of (statically decidable) *read/write capabilities* or *polarities* into each variable occurrence and each position of (possibly nested) data structures. In well-moded programs, a write capability can be passed around but cannot be copied or discarded, while a read capability can be copied and discarded. Well-modedness can be established by constraint-based mode analysis which is essentially a unification problem over feature graphs.
3. Linearity analysis, which distinguishes between one-to-one and one-to-many communication [64], enabled compile-time garbage collection and turned out to play a key role in parallel/distributed symbolic computation. For instance, parallel operations on an array in shared memory can be done without any interference by splitting the array into pieces in-place, letting parallel processes operate on its own piece in-place, and then merging the resulting pieces in-place [62]. Both mode analysis and and linearity analysis support resource-conscious programming by being sensitive to the number of occurrences of variables.

5.2 Logical Variables as Communication Channels

Most of the outstanding features of concurrent logic/constraint languages come from the power and the flexibility of logical variables as communication channels. Logical variables support:

- data- and demand-driven communication,
- messages with reply boxes,
- first-class channels (encoded as lists or difference lists),
- replicable read-only data, and
- implicit redirection across sites.

It is surprising that all these features are supported by a single mechanism. This uniformity gives tremendous benefits to theoretical foundations and programming systems, since a single framework can cover all these features.

5.3 Evolution as Devolution

It is generally understood that concurrent logic programming evolved into concurrent constraint programming by ALPS's logical interpretation of communication primitives [28] and Saraswat's reformulation of concurrent logic programming as a framework of concurrency [38]. However, I have an impression that the role of concurrent constraint programming as a generalization of concurrent logic programming has been a bit different from the role of constraint logic programming as a generalization of logic programming. While constraint logic programming has found several useful domains and applications, the main contribution of concurrent constraint programming has been in the understanding of the essence of the framework and the promotion of the study of semantics. The set of useful general-purpose constraint systems (other than obvious ones such as finite trees, integers and floating-point numbers) for concurrent constraint programming is yet to be identified.

Indeed, the history of the practice of concurrent logic programming could be summarized as "evolution by devolution" [49]. As conjectured in [51] (quoted in Section 1), GHC as the weakest fragment of concurrent constraint programming (d)evolved first by disallowing nested guards (Flat GHC) and then by featuring a mode system. Virtually all programs now written in KL1 and run by KLIC [12] are well-moded, though KLIC currently does not support mode analysis. On the other hand, there are only a few constructs added to KL1: *shoen* (a Japanese word meaning 'manor') as a unit of observing and controlling computation, the `@node( )` construct for process migration, and priorities.

Strong moding has degenerated unification (a case of constraint solving) to assignment to a variable, but has made GHC a much securer concurrent language; that is, it guarantees that constraints to be published to a shared store (binding environment) are always consistent with the current store. Linearity analysis guarantees that some class of programs (including most sorting programs, for instance) can run without generating garbage. Both analyses are useful not only for efficient implementation but also for the precise analysis of computational cost, which is essential in real-time computing and network programming with mobile code. In this way, degeneration may find new applications which could not be addressed by more general languages.

Oz [46,21] has taken a totally different approach from GHC. It has incorporated a number of new constructs such as ports (a primitive for many-to-one communication), cells (containers of values that allow destructive update), computation space (encapsulated store, somewhat affected by nested guards of full GHC and KL1's *shoen*), higher-order, etc., and has moved from fine-grained to coarse-grained concurrency. It still encompasses a concurrent constraint language, but is now better viewed as a multi-paradigm language.

In contrast, I'd like to keep GHC a *pure* concurrent constraint language. (Moded Flat) GHC is quite a small fragment but it is yet to be seen what additional constructs are really necessary to make pure concurrent logic/constraint languages usable.

6 Some Failures and Problems

Although I'm optimistic about its future technically, concurrent logic/constraint programming has experienced a number of non-technical problems.

1. *Misleading names of the paradigms.* Concurrent logic languages are primarily *concurrent* programming languages though they retain the nice properties of logic programming wherever possible, such as soundness of proof procedures and declarative reading.[5] Unfortunately, concurrency is so unpopular in the logic programming community that concurrent logic programming often sounds like nothing more than an incomplete variant of logic programming. (An even worse name once used was *committed-choice languages.*)
   Concurrent constraint programming (languages) sounds better in this respect, but it has another problem. The conception of concurrent constraint programming is often said to date from ALPS, but this often results in the ignorance of its pre-history, the era of concurrent logic programming. *Concurrent logic languages are, by definition, (instances of) concurrent constraint languages.*[6]

---

[5] One may argue that whether a concurrent language retains nice properties of logic programming is not very important, but this is not true. This criterion worked as a strong guideline of language design and resulted in many desirable properties as a concurrent language.

[6] At an early stage, I had understood GHC computation in terms of the exchange of bindings between processes rather than a restricted proof procedure:

2. *Community problem.* Although concurrent constraint programming is an elegant formalism of concurrency, it was born from logic programming, a paradigm quite unpopular in the concurrency community and the community of concurrent programming. So, this important paradigm can very easily be forgotten by both the logic programming community and the communities of concurrency theory and concurrent programming!

3. *Shortage of communication with neighboring communities.* This is a very general tendency and unfortunately applies to various communities related to concurrency. There are many techniques independently invented in the functional programming community, the (concurrent) object-oriented programming community and the (concurrent) logic programming community. Declarative arrays, frameworks of program analysis, scheduling of fine-grained tasks, and distributed memory management are all such examples.

   A bit more technical reason why concurrent logic/constraint programming is still unpopular in the concurrency community at large may be that its formulation looks rather indirect—popular and mundane idioms of concurrent programming such as objects, messages, and channels are all encoded entities.

4. *Few research groups.* Except for research groups on semantics, there are only two active (virtual) groups working on languages and implementation; one is the group working on Oz and the other working on GHC/KL1. Many key people who founded the field "graduated" too early before the paradigm became well understood and ready to find interesting applications. However, a good news is that most of them are working on the potential applications of the paradigm discussed earlier in this article. This leaves us a challenge to bridge the gap between what the paradigm offers and what the applications require.

5. *Textbooks.* Good textbooks and tutorial materials are yet to be published. There are some on concurrent logic programming, such as Shapiro's survey [43], but a tutorial introduction to the semantical foundations is still awaited. It's time to recast important concepts and results scattered over technical papers and re-present them from the current perspective.

> "... it is quite natural to view a GHC program in terms of binding information and the agents that observe and generate it." "In general, a goal can be viewed as a process that observes input bindings and generates output bindings according to them. Observation and generation of bindings are the basis of computation and communication in our model." [56] (1986)

Of course, it was definitely after the proposal of concurrent constraint programming that binding- (constraint-) centered view became popular and the study of semantics made progress.

7 Conclusions

Concurrent logic/constraint programming has been a simple and extremely stable formalism of concurrency, and at the same time it has been a full-fledged programming language. It is unique among many other proposals of concurrency formalisms in that information, communication and synchronization are modeled in terms of constraints, a general and mathematically well-supported framework. It is unique also in that its minimal framework (with *ask*, *eventual tell*, parallel composition, guarded choice and scoping) is almost ready for practical programming. That is, there is little gap between theory (computational model) and practice (programming language). The stability of the core concurrent constraint programming with *ask* + *eventual tell* indicates that the logic programming community came up with something essential in early 1980's and noticed it in full in late 1980's.

There seems to be a feeling that concurrent logic/constraint programming has established an independent scientific discipline *outside* the logic programming paradigm. There is certainly a fundamental difference in how computation is viewed—one is on deduction while the other is on reactive agents. However, the fact that each paradigm features what the other does not have and the fact that they still share a lot of technicalities at less fundamental levels strongly indicate that they should benefit from each other. An interesting example of such bridging can be found in Constraint Handling Rules [18], a concurrent constraint language specifically designed for programming constraint systems.

Since concurrent constraint languages aim at general-purpose languages, they can benefit from static analysis more strongly than logic programming languages can. So I'd like to conclude this article by claiming that constraint-based static analysis can make concurrent constraint programming a simple, powerful, and safe language for

- parallel and high-performance computing,
- distributed and network computing, and
- real-time and mobile computing.

Its role in concurrent constraint programming is analogous to, but probably more than, the role of type systems in λ-calculus.

Acknowledgments

Comments and suggestions from anonymous referees were extremely useful in improving the paper. The title of the paper was adapted from the title of the Dagstuhl Seminar (No. 9741) on concurrent constraint programming held in October 1997.

References

1. Abadi, M., Cardelli, L., Curien, P.-L. and Lévy, J.-J., Explicit substitutions. *J. Functional Programming*, Vol. 1, No. 4 (1991), pp. 375–416.
2. Agha, G. A., *Actors: A Model of Concurrent Computation in Distributed Systems*. The MIT Press, Cambridge, MA, 1986.
3. Ajiro, Y., Ueda, K. and Cho, K., Error-correcting Source Code. In *Proc. Fourth Int. Conf. on Principles and Practice of Constraint Programming (CP98)*, LNCS 1520, Springer-Verlag, Berlin, 1998, pp. 40–54.
4. Banâtre, J.-P. and Le Métayer, D., The GAMMA Model and Its Discipline of Programming. *Science of Computer Programming*, Vol. 15, No. 1 (1990), pp. 55–77.
5. de Boer, F. S., Gabbrielli, M., Marchiori, E. and Palamidessi, C., Proving Concurrent Constraint Programs Correct. In *Conf. Record of the 21st ACM SIGPLAN-SIGACT Symp. on Principles of Programming Languages*, ACM Press, 1994, pp. 98–108.
6. Cardelli, L. and Gordon, A. D., Mobile Ambients. In *Foundations of Software Science and Computational Structures*, Maurice Nivat (ed.), LNCS 1378, Springer-Verlag, Berlin, 1998, pp. 140–155.
7. Chandy, K. M. and Taylor, S., *An Introduction to Parallel Programming*. Jones and Bartlett, Boston, 1992.
8. Chandy, K. M. and Kesselman, C., CC++: A Declarative Concurrent Object-Oriented Programming Notation. In *Research Directions in Concurrent Object-Oriented Programming*, Agha, G., Wegner, P. and Yonezawa, A. (eds.), The MIT Press, Cambridge, MA, 1993, pp. 281–313.
9. Chikayama, T. and Kimura, Y., Multiple Reference Management in Flat GHC. In *Proc. 4th Int. Conf. on Logic Programming (ICLP'87)*, The MIT Press, Cambridge, MA, 1987, pp. 276–293.
10. Chikayama, T., Sato, H. and Miyazaki, T., Overview of the Parallel Inference Machine Operating System (PIMOS). In *Proc. Int. Conf. on Fifth Generation Computer Systems 1988*, ICOT, Tokyo, 1988, pp. 230–251.
11. Chikayama, T., Operating System PIMOS and Kernel Language KL1. In *Proc. Int. Conf. on Fifth Generation Computer Systems 1992*, Ohmsha and IOS Press, Tokyo, 1992, pp. 73–88.
12. Chikayama, T., Fujise, T. and Sekita, D., A Portable and Efficient Implementation of KL1. In *Proc. 6th Int. Symp. on Programming Language Implementation and Logic Programming (PLILP'94)*, LNCS 844, Springer-Verlag, Berlin, 1994, pp. 25–39.
13. Cho, K. and Ueda, K., Diagnosing Non-Well-Moded Concurrent Logic Programs, In *Proc. 1996 Joint Int. Conf. and Symp. on Logic Programming (JICSLP'96)*, The MIT Press, Cambridge, MA, 1996, pp. 215–229.
14. Clark, K. L. and Gregory, S., PARLOG: Parallel Programming in Logic. *ACM. Trans. Prog. Lang. Syst.*, Vol. 8, No. 1 (1986), pp. 1–49.
15. Foster, I. and Taylor, S., Strand: a Practical Parallel Programming Tool. In *Proc. 1989 North American Conf. on Logic Programming (NACLP'89)*, The MIT Press, Cambridge, MA, 1989, pp. 497–512.
16. Foster, I. and Kesselman, C., *The Grid: Blueprint for a New Computing Infrastructure*. Morgan-Kaufmann, San Francisco, 1998.

17. Fournet, C., Gonthier, G. Lévy, J.-J., Maranget, L. and Rémy, D., A Calculus of Mobile Agents. In *Proc. 7th Int. Conf. on Concurrency Theory (CONCUR'96)*, LNCS 1119, Springer-Verlag, Berlin, 1996, pp. 406–421.
18. Frühwirth, T., Theory and Practice of Constraint Handling Rules. *J. Logic Programming*, Vol. 37, No. 1–3 (1998), pp. 95–138.
19. Fujita, H. and Hasegawa, R., A Model Generation Theorem Prover in KL1 Using a Ramified-Stack Algorithm. In *Proc. Eighth Int. Conf. on Logic Programming (ICLP'91)*, The MIT Press, Cambridge, MA, 1991, pp. 535–548.
20. Fujita, M., Slaney, J. and Bennett, F., Automatic Generation of Some Results in Finite Algebra. In *Proc. 13th Int. Joint Conf. on Artificial Intelligence (IJCAI'93)*, 1993, pp. 52–57.
21. Haridi, S., Van Roy, P., Brand, P. and Schulte, C., Programming Languages for Distributed Applications. *New Generation Computing*, Vol. 16, No. 3 (1998), pp. 223–261.
22. Hasegawa, R. and Fujita, M., Parallel Theorem Provers and Their Applications. In *Proc. Int. Conf. on Fifth Generation Computer Systems 1992*, Ohmsha and IOS Press, Tokyo, 1992, pp. 132–154.
23. Hirata, K., Yamamoto, R., Imai, A., Kawai, H., Hirano, K., Takagi, T., Taki, K., Nakase, A. and Rokusawa, K., Parallel and Distributed Implementation of Concurrent Logic Programming Language KL1. In *Proc. Int. Conf. on Fifth Generation Computer Systems 1992*, Ohmsha and IOS Press, Tokyo, 1992, pp. 436–459.
24. Hoare, C. A. R., *Communicating Sequential Processes*. Prentice-Hall International, London, 1985.
25. Ichiyoshi N., Miyazaki T. and Taki, K., A Distributed Implementation of Flat GHC on the Multi-PSI. In *Proc. 4th Int. Conf. on Logic Programming (ICLP'87)*, The MIT Press, Cambridge, MA, 1987, pp. 257–275.
26. Janson, S. and Haridi, S., Programming Paradigms of the Andorra Kernel Language. In *Proc. 1991 Int. Logic Programming Symp. (ILPS'91)*, The MIT Press, Cambridge, MA, 1991, pp. 167–183.
27. Kahn, K. M., ToonTalk—An Animated Programming Environment for Children. *J. Visual Languages and Computing*, Vol. 7, No. 2 (1996), pp. 197–217.
28. Maher, M. J., Logic Semantics for a Class of Committed-Choice Programs. In *Proc. Fourth Int. Conf. on Logic Programming (ICLP'87)*, The MIT Press, Cambridge, MA, 1987, pp. 858–876.
29. Milner, R., *Communication and Concurrency*. Prentice-Hall International, London, 1989.
30. Milner, R., Parrow, J. and Walker, D., A Calculus of Mobile Processes, I+II. *Information and Computation*, Vol. 100, No. 1 (1992), pp. 1–77.
31. Milner, R., Calculi for Interaction. *Acta Informatica*, Vol. 33, No. 8 (1996), pp. 707–737.
32. Muggleton, S., Inverse Entailment and Progol. *New Generation Computing*, Vol. 13 (1995), pp. 245–286.
33. Naish, L. All Solutions Predicates in Prolog. In *Proc. 1985 Symp. on Logic Programming (SLP'85)*, IEEE, 1985, pp. 73–77.
34. Nakajima K., Inamura Y., Rokusawa K., Ichiyoshi N. and Chikayama, T., Distributed Implementation of KL1 on the Multi-PSI/V2. In *Proc. Sixth Int. Conf. on Logic Programming (ICLP'89)*, The MIT Press, Cambridge, MA, 1989, pp. 436–451.

35. Nitta, K., Taki, K. and Ichiyoshi, N., Experimental Parallel Inference Software. In *Proc. Int. Conf. on Fifth Generation Computer Systems 1992*, Ohmsha and IOS Press, Tokyo, 1992, pp. 166–190.
36. Petri, C.A., Fundamentals of a Theory of Asynchronous Information Flow. In *Proc. IFIP Congress 62*, North-Holland Pub. Co., Amsterdam, 1962, pp.386–390.
37. Santos Costa V., Warren, D. H. D. and Yang, R., Andorra-I: A Parallel Prolog System that Transparently Exploits both And- and Or-Parallelism. In *Proc. Third ACM SIGPLAN Symp. on Principles & Practice of Parallel Programming (PPoPP'91)*, SIGPLAN Notices, Vol. 26, No. 7 (1991), pp. 83–93.
38. Saraswat, V. A. and Rinard, M., Concurrent Constraint Programming (Extended Abstract). In *Conf. Record of the Seventeenth Annual ACM Symp. on Principles of Programming Languages*, ACM Press, 1990, pp. 232–245.
39. Saraswat, V. A., Kahn, K. and Levy, J., Janus: A Step Towards Distributed Constraint Programming. In *Proc. 1990 North American Conference on Logic Programming (NACLP'90)*, The MIT Press, Cambridge, MA, 1990, pp. 431–446.
40. Saraswat, V. A., Rinard, M. C. and Panangaden, P., Semantic Foundations of Concurrent Constraint Programming. In *Conf. Record of the Eighteenth Annual ACM Symp. on Principles of Programming Languages*, ACM Press, 1991, pp. 333–352.
41. Sato, T. and Tamaki, H., First Order Compiler: A Deterministic Logic Program Synthesis Algorithm. *J. Symbolic Computation*, Vol. 8, No. 6 (1989), pp. 605–627.
42. Shapiro, E. Y., Concurrent Prolog: A Progress Report. *IEEE Computer*, Vol. 19, No. 8 (1986), pp. 44–58.
43. Shapiro, E., The Family of Concurrent Logic Programming Languages. *ACM Computing Surveys*, Vol. 21, No. 3 (1989), pp. 413–510.
44. Shapiro, E. Y., Warren, D. H. D., Fuchi, K., Kowalski, R. A., Furukawa, K., Ueda, K., Kahn, K. M., Chikayama, T. and Tick, E., The Fifth Generation Project: Personal Perspectives. *Comm. ACM*, Vol. 36, No. 3 (1993), pp. 46–103.
45. Schulte, C. and Smolka, G., Encapsulated Search for Higher-order Concurrent Constraint Programming. In *Proc. 1994 International Logic Programming Symp. (ILPS'94)*, The MIT Press, Cambridge, MA, 1994, pp. 505–520.
46. Smolka, G., The Oz Programming Model. In *Computer Science Today*, van Leeuven, J. (ed.), LNCS 1000, Springer-Verlag, Berlin, 1995, pp. 324–343.
47. Somogyi, Z., Henderson, F. and Conway, T., The Execution Algorithm of Mercury, An Efficient Purely Declarative Logic Programming Language. *J. Logic Programming*, Vol. 29, No. 1–3 (1996), pp. 17–64.
48. Taki, K., Parallel Inference Machine PIM. In *Proc. Int. Conf. on Fifth Generation Computer Systems 1992*, Ohmsha and IOS Press, Tokyo, 1992, pp. 50–72.
49. Tick, E. The Deevolution of Concurrent Logic Programming Languages. *J. Logic Programming*, Vol. 23, No. 2 (1995), pp. 89–123.
50. Toyoda, M., Shizuki, B., Takahashi, S., Matsuoka, S. and Shibayama, E., Supporting Design Patterns in a Visual Parallel Data-flow Programming Environment. In *Proc. IEEE Symp. on Visual Languages*, IEEE, 1997, pp. 76–83.
51. Ueda, K., Guarded Horn Clauses. ICOT Tech. Report TR-103, ICOT, Tokyo, 1985. Also in *Logic Programming '85*, Wada, E. (ed.), LNCS 221, Springer-Verlag, Berlin, 1986, pp. 168–179.

52. Ueda, K. and Chikayama, T., Concurrent Prolog Compiler on Top of Prolog. In *Proc. 1985 Symp. on Logic Programming (SLP'85)*, IEEE, 1985, pp. 119–126.
53. Ueda, K. Making Exhaustive Search Programs Deterministic. In *Proc. Third Int. Conf. on Logic Programming (ICLP'86)*, LNCS 225, Springer-Verlag, Berlin, 1986, pp. 270–282. Revised version in *New Generation Computing*, Vol. 5, No. 1 (1987), pp. 29–44.
54. Ueda, K. and Furukawa, K., Transformation Rules for GHC Programs. In *Proc. Int. Conf. on Fifth Generation Computer Systems 1988*, ICOT, Tokyo, 1988, pp. 582–591.
55. Ueda, K., Parallelism in Logic Programming. In *Information Processing 89, Proc. IFIP 11th World Computer Congress*, North-Holland/IFIP, 1989, pp. 957–964.
56. Ueda, K., Guarded Horn Clauses: A Parallel Logic Programming Language with the Concept of a Guard. ICOT Tech. Report TR-208, ICOT, Tokyo, 1986. Also in *Programming of Future Generation Computers*, Nivat, M. and Fuchi, K. (eds.), North-Holland, Amsterdam, 1988, pp. 441–456.
57. Ueda, K. and Chikayama, T. Design of the Kernel Language for the Parallel Inference Machine. *The Computer Journal*, Vol. 33, No. 6 (1990), pp. 494–500.
58. Ueda, K. and Morita, M., A New Implementation Technique for Flat GHC. In *Proc. Seventh Int. Conf. on Logic Programming (ICLP'90)*, The MIT Press, Cambridge, MA, 1990, pp. 3–17. Revised version in *New Generation Computing* [61].
59. Ueda, K., Designing a Concurrent Programming Language. In *Proc. InfoJapan'90*, Information Processing Society of Japan, Tokyo, 1990, pp. 87–94.
60. Ueda, K. and Morita, M., Message-Oriented Parallel Implementation of Moded Flat GHC. *New Generation Computing*, Vol. 11, No. 3–4 (1993), pp. 323–341.
61. Ueda, K. and Morita, M., Moded Flat GHC and Its Message-Oriented Implementation Technique. *New Generation Computing*, Vol. 13, No. 1 (1994), pp. 3–43.
62. Ueda, K., Moded Flat GHC for Data-Parallel Programming. In *Proc. FGCS'94 Workshop on Parallel Logic Programming*, ICOT, Tokyo, 1994, pp. 27–35.
63. Ueda, K., Experiences with Strong Moding in Concurrent Logic/Constraint Programming. In *Proc. Int. Workshop on Parallel Symbolic Languages and Systems (PSLS'95)*, LNCS 1068, Springer-Verlag, Berlin, 1996, pp. 134–153.
64. Ueda, K., Linearity Analysis of Concurrent Logic Programs. In preparation.

2 Program Analysis and Methodology

The contributions in this chapter deal with various aspects of programming in the logic programming style, notably program optimization, automatic program derivation, correctness, validation and debugging.

Declarative programming advocates that a program has a dual reading as a formula in some logic with a simple semantics. Declarative programs are therefore easier to understand, modify and verify. **Apt** and **Bezem** find that reliance of (constraint) logic programs on recursion considerably complicates their declarative reading.

Consequently they propose a simple and realistic approach to declarative programming that draws on the ideas of logic programming and constraint logic programming in which recursion is replaced by bounded iteration. It is obtained by assigning a computational meaning to first-order logic using a constructive interpretation of satisfiability w.r.t. a fixed but arbitrary interpretation. This yields a logical reconstruction of a large fragment of an implemented programming language Alma-0, a language that combines the advantages of imperative and logic programming.

Existing programming language implementation techniques exact significant performance penalties for the use of "good" approaches to program development, such as code reuse through the use and sharing of libraries, and the use of appropriate programming languages to implement different components of an application that have different computational behaviors. This inhibits productivity and adversely affects the cost and quality of software.

Debray describes an approach to overcome some of this performance penalty by carrying out program optimization at link time. The idea is to read in executable programs, where libraries have been linked in and differences between the source languages for different modules are irrelevant, and to apply various low-level optimizations—including some that are necessarily not applicable at compile time—to such programs. Experiments with an implemented system indicate that this approach can yield significant performance improvements, across a wide variety of programming languages, even for programs that have been subjected to a high degree of compile-time optimization.

Research in programming language semantics (such as denotational semantics) has been traditionally based on the λ-calculus.

Gupta proposes Horn logic (and eventually constraint logic) as an alternative notation for writing declarative denotational semantics. He then goes on to show how this Horn logical rendering of denotational semantics can be used for numerous practical purposes such as automatic derivation of sequential (and parallelizing) compilers, verification of software systems and real-time systems, semantic porting, etc.

As logic programming systems mature and larger applications are built, an increased need arises for advanced development and debugging environments. **Hermenegildo, Puebla**, and **Bueno** argue that current program analysis tools, which are generally based on "abstract interpretation," have matured to a point where they have very interesting and promising applications in the context of program validation and debugging.

They propose a framework for program validation and detection of errors based on an assertion language. Program validation and detection of errors is first performed statically by comparing (partial) specifications written in terms of assertions against information obtained from static analysis of the program. The results of this process are expressed using assertions, as well. Assertions (or parts of assertions) which cannot be verified statically are translated into run-time tests. They also report briefly on an implementation of the framework which generates and checks assertions for Prolog, CLP(R), and CLP(FD) programs. This implementation can treat properties such as types, modes, non-failure, determinacy, and computational cost. It processes modules separately, performing incremental analysis.

Formulas as Programs

Krzysztof R. Apt and Marc Bezem

CWI, P.O. Box 94079, 1090 GB Amsterdam, The Netherlands

Summary. We provide here a computational interpretation of first-order logic based on a constructive interpretation of satisfiability w.r.t. a fixed but arbitrary interpretation. In this approach the *formulas* themselves are *programs*. This contrasts with the so-called *formulas as types* approach in which the proofs of the formulas are typed terms that can be taken as programs. This view of computing is inspired by logic programming and constraint logic programming but differs from them in a number of crucial aspects.

Formulas as programs is argued to yield a realistic approach to programming that has been realized in the implemented programming language Alma-0 [ABPS98] that combines the advantages of imperative and logic programming. The work here reported can also be used to reason about the correctness of non-recursive Alma-0 programs that do not include destructive assignment.

1 Introduction

1.1 Logic Programming and Program Verification

The logic programming paradigm in its original form (see [Kow74]) is based on a computational interpretation of a subset of first-order logic that consists of Horn clauses. The proof theory and semantics for this subset has been well understood for some time already (see, e.g. [Llo87]).

However, the practice has quickly shown that this subset is too limited for programming purposes, so it was extended in a number of ways, notably by allowing negation. This led to a long and still inconclusive quest for extending the appropriate soundness and completeness results to logic programs that allow negation (see, e.g. [AB94]). To complicate the matters further, Prolog extends logic programming with negation by several features that are very operational in nature.

Constraint logic programming (see, e.g. [JL87]) overcomes some of Prolog's deficiencies, notably its clumsy handling of arithmetic, by extending the computing process from the (implicit) domain of terms to arbitrary structures.

Logic programming and constraint logic programming are two instances of declarative programming. According to declarative programming a program has a dual reading as a formula in a logic with a simple semantics.

One of the important advantages of declarative programming is that, thanks to the semantic interpretation, programs are easier to understand, modify and verify. In fact, the dual reading of a declarative program as a formula allows us to reason about its correctness by restricting our attention to a logical analysis of the corresponding formula. For each logical formalism such an analysis essentially boils down to the question whether the formula corresponding to the program is in an appropriate sense equivalent to the specification.[1]

However, in our opinion, we do not have at our disposal *simple* and *intuitive* methods that could be used to verify in a rigorous way realistic "pure" Prolog programs (i.e. those that are also logic programs) or constraint logic programs.

We believe that one of the reasons for this state of affairs is recursion, on which both logic programming and constraint logic programming rely. In fact, recursion is often less natural than iteration, which is a more basic concept. Further, recursion in combination with negation can naturally lead to programs that are not easily amenable to a formal analysis. Finally, recursion always introduces a possibility of divergence which explains why the study of termination is such an important topic in the case of logic programming (see, e.g., [DD94]).

1.2 First-order Logic as a Computing Mechanism

Obviously, without recursion logic programming and constraint logic programming are hopelessly inexpressive. However, as we show in this paper, it is still possible to construct a simple and realistic approach to declarative programming that draws on the ideas of these two formalisms and in which recursion is absent. This is done by providing a constructive interpretation of satisfiability of first-order formulas w.r.t. to a fixed but arbitrary interpretation. Iteration is realized by means of bounded quantification that is guaranteed to terminate.

More precisely, assuming a first-order language L, we introduce an effective, though incomplete, computation mechanism that approximates the satisfiability test in the following sense. Given an interpretation I for L and a formula $\phi(\bar{x})$ of L, assuming no abnormal termination in an error arises, this

[1] This can be made precise in the following way. Let $\bar{x}$ be the free variables of the specification ϕ_s, and $\bar{y}$ some auxiliary variables used in the program ϕ_p. Now correctness of the program with respect to the specification can be expressed by the sentence $\forall\bar{x}\ ((\exists\bar{y}\ \phi_p(\bar{x},\bar{y})) \rightarrow \phi_s(\bar{x}))$, to be valid under the fixed interpretation. This sentence ensures that all solutions found by the program indeed satisfy the specification. Note that, under this definition, a program corresponding to a false formula is vacuously "correct", because there are no solutions found. Therefore the stronger notion of correctness and completeness obtained by requiring also the converse implication above, and loosely phrased as "equivalence in an appropriate sense", is the more adequate one.

mechanism computes a witness $\bar{a}$ (that is, a vector of elements of the domain of I such that $\phi(\bar{a})$ holds in I) if $\phi(\bar{x})$ is satisfiable in I, and otherwise it reports a failure.

The possibility of abnormal termination in an error is unavoidable because effectiveness cannot be reconciled with the fact that for many first-order languages and interpretations, for example the language of Peano arithmetic and its standard interpretation, the set of true closed formulas is highly undecidable. As we wish to use this computation mechanism for executing formulas as programs, we spend here considerable effort at investigating the ways of limiting the occurrence of errors.

From the technical point of view our approach, called *formulas as programs*, is obtained by isolating a number of concepts and ideas present (often implicitly) in the logic programming and constraint logic programming framework, and reusing them in a simple and self-contained way. In fact, the proposed computation mechanism and a rigorous account of its formal properties rely only on the basics of first-order logic. This contrasts with the expositions of logic programming and constraint logic programming which require introduction of several concepts and auxiliary results (see for the latter e.g. [JMMS98]).

1.3 Computing Mechanism

Let us explain now the proposed computation mechanism by means of an example. Consider the formula

$$(x = 2 \lor x = 3) \land (y = x + 1 \lor 2 = y) \land (2 * x = 3 * y) \tag{1}$$

interpreted over the standard structure of natural numbers. Is it satisfiable? The answer is "yes": indeed, it suffices to assign 3 to x and 2 to y.

In fact, we can compute this valuation systematically by initially assigning 2 to x and first trying the assignment of the value of $x + 1$, so 3, to y. As for this choice of value for y the equality $2 * x = 3 * y$ does not hold, we are led to the second possibility, assignment of 2 to y. With this choice $2 * x = 3 * y$ does not hold either. So we need to assign 3 to x and, eventually, 2 to y.

The above informal argument can be extended to a systematic procedure that attempts to find a satisfying valuation for a large class of formulas.

1.4 Plan and Rationale of the Paper

This paper is organized as follows.

In Section 2 we provide a formal account of the proposed computation mechanism. In Section 3 we show that this approach is both correct (sound) and, in the absence of errors, complete. In the Appendix, Subsection 9.3, 9.4, we investigate ways of limiting the occurrence of errors for the case of negation and implication.

For programming purposes first-order logic has limited expressiveness, so we extend it in Section 4 by a number of features that are useful for programming. This involves sorts (i.e., types), use of arrays and bounded quantifiers. The resulting fragment is surprisingly expressive and the underlying computation mechanism allows us to interpret many formulas as highly non-trivial programs.

As already mentioned above, formulas as programs approach to computing here discussed is inspired by logic programming and constraint logic programming but differs from them in a number of ways.

For example, formula (1) cannot be interpreted as a logic programming query or run as a Prolog query. The reason is that the equality symbol in logic programming and Prolog stands for "is unifiable with" and the term $2 * x$ does not unify with $3 * y$. In case of Prolog a possible remedy is to replace in (1) specific occurrences of the equality symbol by Prolog's arithmetic equality "`=:=`" or by the Prolog evaluator operator `is`. The correct Prolog query that corresponds to formula (1) is then

```
(X = 2 ; X = 3), (Y is X+1 ; 2 = Y), 2*X =:= 3*Y.
```

(Recall that "`;`" stands in Prolog for disjunction and "`,`" for conjunction.) This is clearly much less readable than (1) as three different kinds of equality-like relations are used here.

A more detailed comparison with (constraint) logic programming and Prolog requires knowledge of the details of our approach and is postponed to Section 5. In principle, the formulas as programs approach is a variant of constraint logic programming in which both recursion and constraint handling procedures are absent, but the full first-order syntax is used. We also compare in Section 5 our formulas as programs approach with the formulas as types approach, also called the Curry-Howard-De Bruijn interpretation.

The formulas as programs approach to programming has been realized in the programming language Alma-0 [ABPS98] that extends imperative programming by features that support declarative programming. This shows that this approach, in contrast to logic programming and constraint logic programming, can easily be combined with imperative programming. So the introduced restrictions, such as lack of a constraint store, can be beneficial in practice. In Section 6 we summarize the main features of Alma-0.

The work reported here can be used to provide logical underpinnings for a fragment of Alma-0 that does not include destructive assignment or recursive procedures, and to reason about programs written in this fragment. We substantiate the latter claim by presenting in Section 7 the correctness proof of a purely declarative Alma-0 solution to the well-known non-trivial combinatorial problem of partitioning a rectangle into a given set of squares.

In conclusion, we provided here a realistic framework for declarative programming based on first-order logic and the traditional Tarskian semantics, which can be combined in a straightforward way with imperative programming.

2 Computation Mechanism

Consider an arbitrary first-order language with equality and an interpretation for it. We assume in particular a domain of discourse, and a fixed signature with a corresponding interpretation of its elements in the domain.

Definition 1 (valuation, assignment). A *valuation* is a finite mapping from variables to domain elements. Valuations will be denoted as single-valued sets of pairs x/d, where x is a variable and d a domain element. We use $\alpha, \alpha', \beta, \ldots$ for arbitrary valuations and call α' an *extension* of α when $\alpha \subseteq \alpha'$, that is, every assignment to a variable by α also occurs in α'. Further, ε denotes the empty valuation.

Let α be a valuation. A term t is *α-closed* if all variables of t get a value in α. In that case t^α denotes the *evaluation* of t under α in the domain. More generally, for any expression E the result of the replacement of each α-closed term t by t^α is denoted by E^α.

An α-assignment is an equation $s = t$ one side of which, say s, is a variable that is not α-closed and the other side, t, is an α-closed term. ⊠

In our setting, the only way to assign values to variables will be by evaluating an α-assignment as above. Given such an α-assignment, say $x = t$, we evaluate it by assigning to x the value t^α.

Definition 2 (formulas). In order to accommodate the definition of the operational semantics, the set of formulas has an inductive definition which may look a bit peculiar. First, universal quantification is absent since we have no operational interpretation for it. Second, every formula is taken to be a conjunction, with every conjunct (if any) either an atomic formula (in short: an *atom*), or a disjunction, conjunction or implication of formulas, a negation of a formula or an existentially quantified formula. The latter two unary constructors are assumed to bind stronger then the previous binary ones. The atoms include equations of the form $s = t$, with s and t terms.

For maximal clarity we give here an inductive definition of the set of formulas. In the operational semantics all conjunctions are taken to be right associative.

1. The empty conjunction $\square$ is a formula.
2. If ψ is a formula and A is an atom, then $A \wedge \psi$ is a formula.
3. If ψ, ϕ_1, ϕ_2 are formulas, then $(\phi_1 \vee \phi_2) \wedge \psi$ is a formula.
4. If ψ, ϕ_1, ϕ_2 are formulas, then $(\phi_1 \wedge \phi_2) \wedge \psi$ is a formula.
5. If ψ, ϕ_1, ϕ_2 are formulas, then $(\phi_1 \rightarrow \phi_2) \wedge \psi$ is a formula.
6. If ϕ, ψ are formulas, then $\neg\phi \wedge \psi$ is a formula.
7. If ϕ, ψ are formulas, then $\exists x\ \phi \wedge \psi$ is a formula. ⊠

Definition 3 (operational semantics). The operational semantics of a formula will be defined in terms of a tree $[\![\phi]\!]_\alpha$ depending on the formula ϕ and the (initial) valuation α. The root of $[\![\phi]\!]_\alpha$ is labelled with the pair

ϕ, α. All internal nodes of the tree $[\![\phi]\!]_\alpha$ are labelled with pairs consisting of a formula and a valuation. The leaves of the tree $[\![\phi]\!]_\alpha$ are labelled with either

- *error* (representing the occurrence of an error in this branch of the computation), or
- *fail* (representing logical failure of the computation), or
- a valuation (representing logical success of the computation and yielding values for the free variables of the formula that make the formula true). ⊠

It will be shown that valuations labelling success leaves are always extensions of the initial valuation. For a fixed formula, the operational semantics can be viewed as a function relating the initial valuation to the valuations labelling success leaves.

We can now define the computation tree $[\![\phi]\!]_\alpha$. The reader may consult first Fig. 1 to see such a tree for formula (1) and the empty valuation ε.

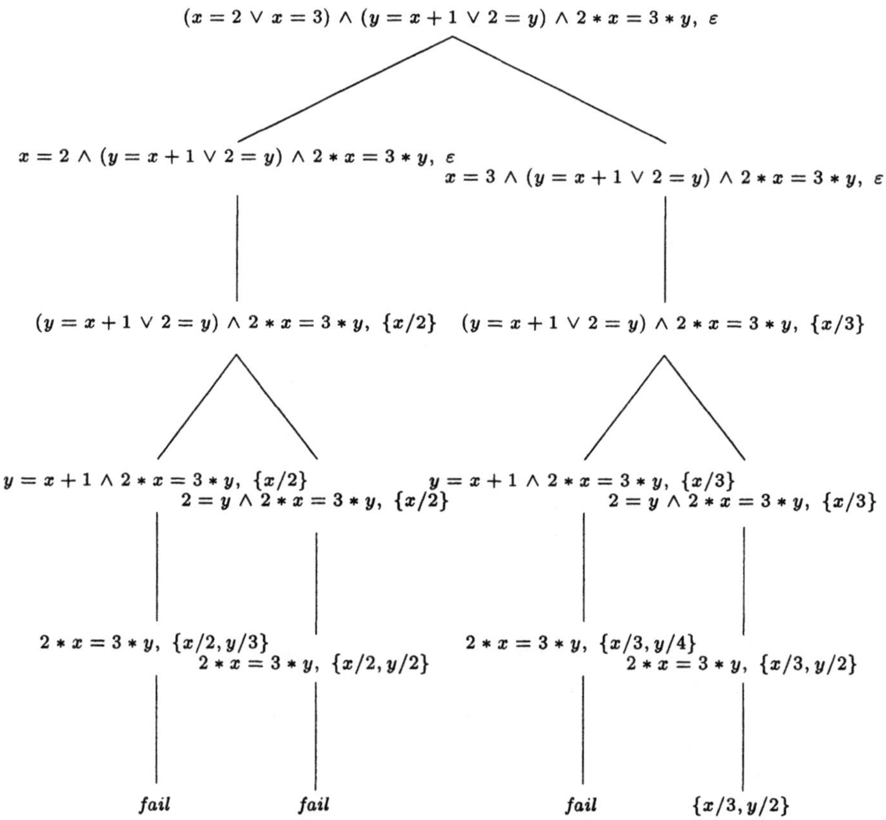

Fig. 1. The computation tree for formula (1) and valuation ε

Definition 4 (computation tree). The (computation) tree $[\![\phi]\!]_\alpha$ is defined by lexicographic induction on the pairs consisting of the *size* of the formula ϕ, and of the *size* of the formula ϕ_1 for which ϕ is of the form $\phi_1 \wedge \psi$, following the structure given by Definition 2.

1. For the empty conjunction we define $[\![\Box]\!]_\alpha$ to be the tree with the root that has a success leaf α as its son:

$$\Box,\ \alpha$$

$$\alpha$$

2. If ψ is a formula and A is an atom, then we distinguish four cases depending on the form of A. In all four cases $[\![A \wedge \psi]\!]_\alpha$ is a tree with a root of degree one.
   - Atom A is α-closed and true. Then the root of $[\![A \wedge \psi]\!]_\alpha$ has $[\![\psi]\!]_\alpha$ as its subtree:

$$A \wedge \psi,\ \alpha$$

$$[\![\psi]\!]_\alpha$$

   - Atom A is α-closed and false. Then the root of $[\![A \wedge \psi]\!]_\alpha$ has the failure leaf *fail* as its son:

$$A \wedge \psi,\ \alpha$$

fail

   - Atom A is not α-closed, but is not an α-assignment. Then the root of $[\![A \wedge \psi]\!]_\alpha$ has the *error* leaf as its son:

$$A \wedge \psi,\ \alpha$$

error

   - Atom A is an α-assignment $s = t$. Then either s or t is a variable which is not α-closed, say $s \equiv x$ with x not α-closed and t α-closed. Then the root of $[\![A \wedge \psi]\!]_\alpha$ has $[\![\psi]\!]_{\alpha'}$ as its subtree, where α' extends α with the pair x/t^α:

The symmetrical case is analogous.

3. If ψ, ϕ_1, ϕ_2 are formulas, then we put $[\![(\phi_1 \vee \phi_2) \wedge \psi]\!]_\alpha$ to be the tree with a root of degree two and with left and right subtrees $[\![\phi_1 \wedge \psi]\!]_\alpha$ and $[\![\phi_2 \wedge \psi]\!]_\alpha$, respectively:

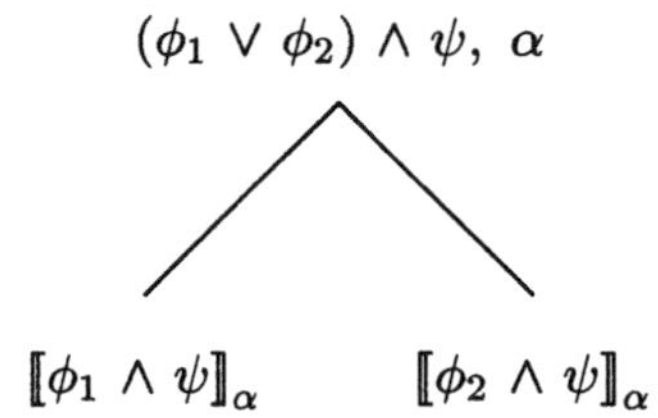

   Observe that $\phi_1 \wedge \psi$ and $\phi_2 \wedge \psi$ are smaller formulas than $(\phi_1 \vee \phi_2) \wedge \psi$ in the adopted lexicographic ordering.

4. If ψ, ϕ_1, ϕ_2 are formulas, then we put $[\![(\phi_1 \wedge \phi_2) \wedge \psi]\!]_\alpha$ to be the tree with a root of degree one and the tree $[\![\phi_1 \wedge (\phi_2 \wedge \psi)]\!]_\alpha$ as its subtree:

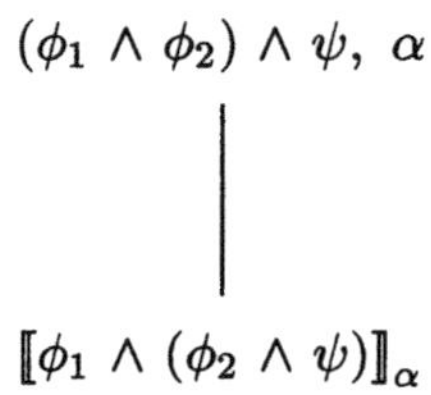

   This substantiates the association of conjunctions to the right as mentioned in Definition 2. Note that, again, the definition refers to lexicographically smaller formulas.

5. If ψ, ϕ_1, ϕ_2 are formulas, then we put $[\![(\phi_1 \to \phi_2) \wedge \psi]\!]_\alpha$ to be a tree with a root of degree one. We distinguish three cases.
   - Formula ϕ_1 is α-closed and $[\![\phi_1]\!]_\alpha$ contains only failure leaves. Then the root of $[\![(\phi_1 \to \phi_2) \wedge \psi]\!]_\alpha$ has $[\![\psi]\!]_\alpha$ as its subtree:

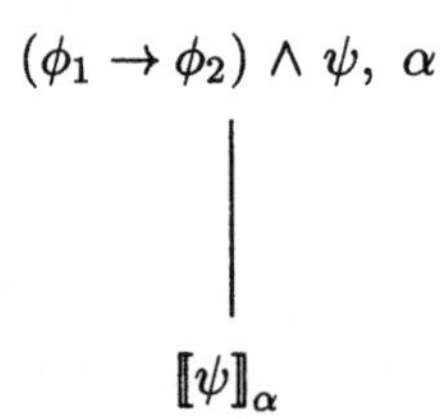

   - Formula ϕ_1 is α-closed and $[\![\phi_1]\!]_\alpha$ contains at least one success leaf. Then the root of $[\![(\phi_1 \to \phi_2) \wedge \psi]\!]_\alpha$ has $[\![\phi_2 \wedge \psi]\!]_\alpha$ as its subtree:

$$(\phi_1 \rightarrow \phi_2) \wedge \psi,\ \alpha$$

|

$$[\![\phi_2 \wedge \psi]\!]_\alpha$$

- In all other cases the root of $[\![(\phi_1 \rightarrow \phi_2) \wedge \psi]\!]_\alpha$ has the error leaf *error* as its son:

$$(\phi_1 \rightarrow \phi_2) \wedge \psi,\ \alpha$$

|

error

The above definition relies on the logical equivalence of $\phi_1 \rightarrow \phi_2$ and $\neg\phi_1 \vee \phi_1$, but avoids unnecessary branching in the computation tree that would be introduced by the disjunction. In the Appendix, Subsection 9.3, we explain how in the first case the condition that ϕ_1 is α-closed can be relaxed.

6. If ϕ, ψ are formulas, then to define $[\![\neg\phi \wedge \psi]\!]_\alpha$ we distinguish three cases with respect to ϕ. In all of them $[\![\neg\phi \wedge \psi]\!]_\alpha$ is a tree with a root of degree one.

- Formula ϕ is α-closed and $[\![\phi]\!]_\alpha$ contains only failure leaves. Then the root of $[\![\neg\phi \wedge \psi]\!]_\alpha$ has $[\![\psi]\!]_\alpha$ as its subtree:

$$\neg\phi \wedge \psi,\ \alpha$$

|

$$[\![\psi]\!]_\alpha$$

- Formula ϕ is α-closed and $[\![\phi]\!]_\alpha$ contains at least one success leaf. Then the root of $[\![\neg\phi \wedge \psi]\!]_\alpha$ has the failure leaf *fail* as its son:

$$\neg\phi \wedge \psi,\ \alpha$$

|

fail

- In all other cases the root of $[\![\neg\phi \wedge \psi]\!]_\alpha$ has the error leaf *error* as its son:

$$\neg\phi \wedge \psi,\ \alpha$$

$$|$$

error

There are basically two classes of formulas ϕ in this contingency: those that are not α-closed and those for which $[\![\phi]\!]_\alpha$ contains no success leaf and at least one error leaf. In Subsection 9.3 we give some examples of formulas in the first class and show how in some special cases their negation can still be evaluated in a sound way.

7. The case of $\exists x\ \phi \wedge \psi$ requires the usual care with bound variables to avoid name clashes. Let α be a valuation. First, we require that the variable x does not occur in the domain of α. Second, we require that the variable x does not occur in ψ. Both requirements are summarized by phrasing that x is *fresh* with respect to α and ψ. They can be met by appropriately renaming the bound variable x.
   With x fresh as above we define $[\![\exists x\ \phi \wedge \psi]\!]_\alpha$ to be the tree with a root of degree one and $[\![\phi \wedge \psi]\!]_\alpha$ as its subtree:

$$(\exists x \phi) \wedge \psi,\ \alpha$$

$$|$$

$$[\![\phi \wedge \psi]\!]_\alpha$$

   Thus the operational semantics of $\exists x\ \phi \wedge \psi$ is, apart from the root of degree one, identical to that of $\phi \wedge \psi$. This should not come as a surprise, as $\exists x\ \phi \wedge \psi$ is logically equivalent to $\exists x\ (\phi \wedge \psi)$ when x does not occur in ψ.
   Observe that success leaves of $[\![\phi \wedge \psi]\!]_\alpha$, and hence of $[\![\exists x\ \phi \wedge \psi]\!]_\alpha$, may or may not contain an assignment for x. For example, $\exists x\ x = 3 \wedge \psi$ yields an assignment for x, but $\exists x\ 3 = 3 \wedge \psi$ does not. In any case the assignment for x is not relevant for the formula as a whole, as the bound variable x is assumed to be fresh. In an alternative approach, the possible assignment for x could be deleted. ⊠

To apply the above computation mechanism to arbitrary first-order formulas we first replace all occurrences of a universal quantifier $\forall$ by $\neg\exists\neg$ and rename the bound variables so that no variable appears in a formula both bound and free.

Further, to minimize the possibility of generating errors it is useful to delete occurrences of double negations, that is, to replace every subformula of the form $\neg\neg\psi$ by ψ.

3 Soundness and Completeness

The computation mechanism defined in the previous section attempts to find a valuation that makes the original formula true if this formula is satisfiable, and otherwise it reports a failure. The lexicographic ordering used in Definition 3 guarantees that for any formula the computation tree is finite. In this section we prove correctness and completeness of this mechanism.

We start with an easy lemma which is helpful to keep track of valuations, followed by a definition.

Lemma 1. *For every formula ϕ and valuation α, $[\![\phi]\!]_\alpha$ contains only valuations extending α with pairs x/d, where x occurs free in ϕ or appears existentially quantified in ϕ. Moreover, if ϕ is α-closed then $[\![\phi]\!]_\alpha$ contains only valuations extending α with variables that appear existentially quantified in ϕ.*

Proof. By induction on the lexicographic ordering of formulas as given in Definition 4. ⊠

Definition 5 (status of computation tree). A computation tree is

- *successful* if it contains a success leaf,
- *failed* if it contains only failure leaves,
- *determined* if it is either successful or failed, that is, it either contains a success leaf or contains only failure leaves. ⊠

Note that according to this definition a successful tree can contain error leaves. This means that our error leaves differ from Prolog's run-time errors. In fact, in a top-down implementation of the proposed computation mechanism the depth-first search traversal of a computation tree should *not* abort but rather backtrack upon encounter of such a leaf and continue, if possible, in a search for a successful leaf.

We can now state the desired correctness result.

Theorem 1 (soundness). *Let ϕ be a formula and α a valuation.*

(i) If $[\![\phi]\!]_\alpha$ contains a success leaf labelled with α', then α' extends α and $\forall(\phi^{\alpha'})$ is true. (In particular $\exists(\phi^\alpha)$ is true in this case.)
(ii) If $[\![\phi]\!]_\alpha$ is failed, then $\exists(\phi^\alpha)$ is false.

Proof. See Appendix, Subsection 9.1. ⊠

The computation mechanism defined in Section 3 is obviously incomplete due to the possibility of errors. The following results states that, in the absence of errors, this mechanism is complete.

Theorem 2 (restricted completeness). *Let ϕ be a formula and α a valuation such that $[\![\phi]\!]_\alpha$ is determined.*

(i) Suppose that $\exists(\phi^\alpha)$ *is true. Then the tree* $[\![\phi]\!]_\alpha$ *is successful.*
(ii) Suppose that $\exists(\phi^\alpha)$ *is false. Then the tree* $[\![\phi]\!]_\alpha$ *is failed.*

Proof. See Appendix, Subsection 9.2. ⊠

Admittedly, the latter completeness result is very weak in the sense that any computation mechanism that satisfies the above soundness theorem also satisfies the restricted completeness theorem.

It is useful to point out that the computation mechanism of Section 2 used in the above theorems is by no means a simple counterpart of the provability relation of the first-order logic.

For the sake of further discussion let us say that two formulas ϕ and ψ are *equivalent* if

- the computation tree $[\![\phi]\!]_\varepsilon$ is successful iff the computation tree $[\![\psi]\!]_\varepsilon$ is successful and in that case both computation trees have the same set of successful leaves,
- $[\![\phi]\!]_\varepsilon$ is failed iff $[\![\psi]\!]_\varepsilon$ is failed.

Then $\phi \wedge \psi$ is not equivalent to $\psi \wedge \phi$ (consider $x = 0 \wedge x < 1$ and $x < 1 \wedge x = 0$) and $\neg(\phi \wedge \psi)$ is not equivalent to $\neg\phi \vee \neg\psi$ (consider $\neg(x = 0 \wedge x = 1)$ and $\neg(x = 0) \vee \neg(x = 1)$. In contrast, $\phi \vee \psi$ *is* equivalent to $\psi \vee \phi$.

We can summarize this treatment of the connectives by saying that we use a sequential conjunction and a parallel disjunction. The above notion of equivalence deviates from the usual one, for example de Morgan's Law is not valid.

A complete axiomatization of the equivalence relation induced by the computation mechanism of Section 2 is an interesting research topic.

4 Extensions

The language defined up to now is clearly too limited as a formalism for programming. Therefore we discuss a number of extensions of it that are convenient for programming purposes. These are: non-recursive procedures, sorts (i.e., types), arrays and bounded quantification.

4.1 Non-recursive Procedures

We consider here non-recursive procedures. These can easily be introduced in our framework using the well-known *extension by definition* mechanism (see, e.g., [Sho67, pages 57-58]).

More specifically, consider a first-order formula ψ with the free variables $x_1, \ldots, x_n$. Let p be a *new* n-ary relation symbol. Consider now the formula

$$p(x_1, \ldots, x_n) \leftrightarrow \psi$$

that we call the *definition* of p.

Suppose that, by iterating the above procedure, we have a collection P of definitions of relation symbols. We assume furthermore that the fixed but arbitrary interpretation has been extended with interpretations of the new relation symbols in such a way that all definitions in P become true. There is only one such extension for every initial interpretation.

Let ϕ be a formula in the extended first-order language, that is, with atoms $p(t_1, \ldots, t_n)$ from P included. We extend the computation mechanism $[\![\phi]\!]_\alpha$ of Section 2, by adding at the beginning of Clause 2 in Definition 4 the following item for handling atoms $p(t_1, \ldots, t_n)$ from P.

- Atom A is of the form $p(t_1, \ldots, t_n)$, where p is a defined relation symbol with the definition

  $$p(x_1, \ldots, x_n) \leftrightarrow \psi_p.$$

  Then the root of $[\![A \wedge \psi]\!]_\alpha$ has $[\![\psi_p\{x_1/t_1, \ldots, x_n/t_n\} \wedge \psi]\!]_\alpha$ as its subtree:

  $$A \wedge \psi,\ \alpha$$

  $$|$$

  $$[\![\psi_p\{x_1/t_1, \ldots, x_n/t_n\} \wedge \psi]\!]_\alpha$$

  Here $\psi_p\{x_1/t_1, \ldots, x_n/t_n\}$ stands for the result of substituting in ψ_p the free occurrences of the variables $x_1, \ldots, x_n$ by $t_1, \ldots, t_n$, respectively.

The proof of the termination of this extension of the computation mechanism introduced in Section 2 relies on a refinement of the lexicographic ordering used in Definition 4, taking into account the new atoms.

The above way of handling defined relation symbols obviously corresponds to the usual treatment of procedure calls in programming languages.

The soundness and completeness results can easily be extended to the case of declared relation symbols. In this version truth and falsity refer to the extended interpretation. So far for *non-recursive* procedures.

4.2 Sorts

In this subsection we introduce sorts (i.e., types). The extension of one-sorted to many-sorted first-order logic is standard. It requires a refinement of the notion of signature: arities are no longer just numbers, but have to specify the sorts of the arguments of the function and predicate symbols, as well as the sorts of the function values. Terms and atoms are well-formed only if the sorts of the arguments comply with the signature. In quantifying a variable, its sort should be made explicit (or should at least be clear from the context).

Interpretations for many-sorted first-order languages are obtained by assigning to each sort a non-empty domain and by assigning to each function symbol and each predicate symbol respectively an appropriate function and relation on these sorts.

Sorts can be used to model various basic data types occurring in programming practice: integers, booleans, characters, but also compound data types such as arrays.

4.3 Arrays

Arrays can be modeled as vectors or matrices, using projection functions that are given a *standard interpretation*. Given a sort for the indices (typically, a segment of integers or a product of segments) and a sort for the elements of the array, we add a sort for arrays of the corresponding type to the signature. We also add to the language *array variables*, or *arrays* for short, to be interpreted as arrays in the standard interpretation.

We use the letters a, b, c to denote arrays and to distinguish arrays from objects of other sorts. We write $a[t_1, \ldots, t_n]$ to denote the projection of the array a on the index $[t_1, \ldots, t_n]$, akin to the use of subscripted variables in programming languages. The standard interpretation of each projection function maps a given array and a given index to the correct element. Thus subscripted variables are simply terms. These terms are handled by means of an extension of the computation mechanism of Section 2.

A typical example of the use of such a term is the formula $a[0, 0] = 1$, which should be matched with the formula $x = 1$ in the sense that the evaluation of each equality can result in an assignment of the value 1 to a variable, either $a[0, 0]$ or x. So we view $a[0, 0]$ as a variable and not as a compound term.

To this end we extend a number of notions introduced in the previous section.

Definition 6. An *array valuation* is a finite mapping whose elements are of the form $a[d_1, \ldots, d_n]/d$, where a is an n-ary array symbol and $d_1, \ldots, d_n, d$ are domain elements. An *extended valuation* is a finite mapping that is a union of a valuation and an array valuation. ⊠

The idea is that an element $a[d_1, \ldots, d_n]/d$ of an array valuation assigns the value d to the (interpretation of) array a applied to the arguments $d_1, \ldots, d_n$. Then, if the terms $t_1, \ldots, t_n$ evaluate to the domain elements $d_1, \ldots, d_n$ respectively, the term $a[t_1, \ldots, t_n]$ evaluates to d. This simple inductive clause yields an extension of the notion of evaluation t^{α}, where α is an extended valuation, to terms t in the presence of arrays. The notions of an α-closed term and an α-assignment are now somewhat more complicated to define.

Definition 7. Consider an extended valuation α.

- A variable x is ***α-closed*** if for some d the pair x/d is an element of α.
- A term $f(t_1, \ldots, t_n)$, with f a function symbol, is ***α-closed*** if each term t_i is α-closed.
- A term $a[t_1, \ldots, t_n]$ is ***α-closed*** if each term t_i is α-closed and evaluates to a domain element d_i such that for some d the pair $a[d_1, \ldots, d_n]/d$ is an element of α.

An equation $s = t$ is an ***α-assignment*** if either

- one side of it, say s, is a variable that is not α-closed and the other, t, is an α-closed term, or
- one side of it, say s, is of the form $a[t_1, \ldots, t_n]$, where each t_i is α-closed but $a[t_1, \ldots, t_n]$ is not α-closed, and the other, t, is an α-closed term. ⊠

The idea is that an array a can be assigned a value at a selected position by evaluating an α-assignment $a[t_1, \ldots, t_n] = t$. Assuming the terms $t_1, \ldots, t_n, t$ are α-closed and evaluate respectively to $d_1, \ldots, d_n, d$, the evaluation of $a[t_1, \ldots, t_n] = t$ results in assigning the value d to the array a at the position $d_1, \ldots, d_n$.

With this extension of the notions of valuation and α-assignment we can now apply the computation mechanism of Section 2 to first-order formulas with arrays. The corresponding extensions of the soundness and completeness theorems of Section 3 remain valid.

4.4 Bounded Quantification

In this subsection we show how to extend the language with a form of bounded quantification that essentially amounts to the generalized conjunction and disjunction. We treat bounded quantification with respect to the integer numbers, but the approach can easily be generalized to data types with the same discrete and ordered structure as the integers.

Definition 8 (bounded quantification). Let α be a valuation and let $\phi(x)$ be a formula with x not occurring in the domain of α. Furthermore, let s, t be terms of integer type. We assume the set of formulas to be extended in such a way that also $\exists x \in [s..t]\ \phi(x)$ and $\forall x \in [s..t]\ \phi(x)$ are formulas. The computation trees of these formulas have a root of degree one and depend on s and t in the following way:

- If s or t is not α-closed, then the roots of both $[\![\exists x \in [s..t]\ \phi(x)]\!]_\alpha$ and $[\![\forall x \in [s..t]\ \phi(x)]\!]_\alpha$ have the error leaf *error* as its son.

- If s and t are α-closed and $s^\alpha > t^\alpha$, then the root of $[\![\exists x \in [s..t]\ \phi(x)]\!]_\alpha$ has the failure leaf *fail* as its son and the root of $[\![\forall x \in [s..t]\ \phi(x)]\!]_\alpha$ has a success leaf α as its son.
- If s and t are α-closed and $s^\alpha \leq t^\alpha$, then
  - the root of $[\![\exists x \in [s..t]\ \phi(x)]\!]_\alpha$ has $[\![\phi(x) \vee \exists y \in [s{+}1..t]\ \phi(y)]\!]_{\alpha\cup\{x/s^\alpha\}}$ as its subtree,
  - the root of $[\![\forall x \in [s..t]\ \phi(x)]\!]_\alpha$ has $[\![\phi(x) \wedge \forall y \in [s{+}1..t]\ \phi(y)]\!]_{\alpha\cup\{x/s^\alpha\}}$ as its subtree.

  In both cases y should be a fresh variable with respect to $\alpha, \phi(x)$ in order to avoid name clashes.

The soundness and completeness results can easily be extended to include bounded quantification. ⊠

5 Relation to Other Approaches

The work here discussed is related in many interesting ways to a number of seminal papers on logic, logic programming, and constraint logic programming.

5.1 Definition of Truth Compared to Formulas as Programs

First, it is instructive to compare our approach to the inductive definition of truth given in [Tar33]. This definition can be interpreted as an algorithm that, given a first-order language L, takes as input an interpretation I of L and a formula ϕ of L, and yields as output the answer to the question whether the universal closure of ϕ is true in I. This algorithm is not effective because of the way quantifiers are dealt with. This is unavoidable since truth is undecidable for many languages and interpretations, for instance Peano arithmetic and its standard model.

In the formulas as programs approach the initial problem is modified in that one asks for a constructive answer to the question whether a formula is satisfiable in an interpretation. The algorithm proposed here is effective at the cost of occasionally terminating abnormally in an error.

5.2 Relation to Logic Programming

Some forty years later, in his seminal paper [Kow74], Kowalski proposed to use first-order logic as a computation formalism. This led to logic programming. However, in spite of the paper's title, only a subset of first-order logic is used in his proposal, namely the one consisting of Horn clauses. This restriction was essential since what is now called SLD-resolution was used as the computation mechanism.

In the discussion we first concentrate on the syntax matters and then focus on the computation mechanism.

The restriction of logic programs and goals to Horn clauses was gradually lifted in [Cla78], by allowing negative literals in the goals and in clause bodies, in [LT84], by allowing arbitrary first-order formulas as goals and clause bodies, and in [LMR92] by allowing disjunctions in the clause heads. In each case the computation mechanism of SLD-resolution was suitably extended, either by introducing the negation as failure rule, or by means of transformation rules, or by generalizing so-called linear resolution.

From the syntactic point of view our approach is related to that of [LT84]. Appropriate transformation rules are used there to get rid of quantifiers, disjunctions and the applications of negation to non-atomic formulas. So these features of first-order logic are interpreted in an indirect way. It is useful to point out that the approach of [LT84] was implemented in the programming language Gödel of [HL94].

Further, it should be noted that bounded quantifiers and arrays were also studied in logic programming. In particular, they are used in the specification language Spill of [KM97] that allows us to write executable, typed, specifications in the logic programming style. Other related references are [Vor92], [BB93] and [Apt96].

So from the syntactic point of view our approach does not seem to differ from logic programming in an essential way. The difference becomes more apparent when we analyze in more detail the underlying computation mechanism.

To this end it is useful to recall that in logic programming the computing process takes place implicitly over the free algebra of all terms and the values are assigned to variables by means of unification. The first aspect can be modeled in the formulas as programs approach by choosing a *term interpretation*, so an interpretation the domain D of which consists of all terms and such that each n-ary function symbol f is mapped to a function f_D that assigns to elements (so terms) $t_1, \ldots, t_n$ of D the term $f(t_1, \ldots, t_n)$. With this choice our use of α-assignment boils down to an instance of matching which in turn is a special case of unification.

Unification in logic programming can be more clearly related to equality by means of the so-called homogenization process the purpose of which is to remove non-variable terms from the clauses heads. For instance,

```
append(x1,ys,z1) <- x1=[x|xs], z1=[x|zs], append(xs,ys,zs)
```

is a homogenized form of the more compact clause

```
append([x|xs],ys,[x|zs]) <- append(xs,ys,zs).
```

To interpret the equality in the right way the single clause

```
x = x <-
```

should then be added. This enforces the "is unifiable with" interpretation of equality. So the homogenization process reveals that logic programming relies on a more general interpretation of equality than the formulas as programs approach. It allows one to avoid generation of errors for all equality atoms.

In conclusion, from the computational point of view, the logic programming approach is at the same time a restriction of the formulas as programs approach to the term interpretations and a generalization of this approach in which all equality atoms can be safely evaluated.

5.3 Relation to Pure Prolog

By pure Prolog we mean here a subset of Prolog formed by the programs and goals that are Horn clauses.

Programming in Prolog and in its pure subset relies heavily on lists and recursion. As a result termination is one of the crucial issues. This led to an extensive study of methods that allow us to prove termination of logic and Prolog programs (see [DD94] for a survey of various approaches).

In contrast, our approach to programming is based on arrays and iteration that is realized by means of bounded quantification. These constructs are guaranteed to terminate. In fact, it is striking how far one can go in programming in this style without using recursion. If the reader is not convinced by the example given of Section 7 below, he/she is invited to consult other examples in [Vor92] and [ABPS98].

In the formulas as programs approach the absence of recursion makes it possible to analyze queries without explicit presence of procedures, by systematically replacing procedures by their bodies. This allows us to represent each program as a single query and then rely on the well-understood Tarskian semantics of first-order logic.

In the standard logic programming setting very few interesting programs can be represented in this way. In fact, as soon as recursion is used, a query has to be studied in the context of a program that defines the recursive procedures. As soon as negation is also present, a plethora of different semantics arises — see e.g. [AB94]. Finally, in the presence of recursion it is difficult to account for Prolog's selection rule in purely semantic terms.

5.4 Relation to Pure Prolog with Arithmetic

By pure Prolog with arithmetic we mean here an extension of pure Prolog by features that support arithmetic, so Prolog's arithmetic relations such as "=:=" and the Prolog evaluator operator `is`.

These features allow us to compute in the presence of arithmetic but in a clumsy way as witnessed by the example of formula (1) of Subsection 1.3 and its elaborated representation in Prolog in Subsection 1.4.

Additionally, a possibility of abnormal termination in an error arises. Indeed, both arithmetic relations and the `is` operator introduce a possibility of run-time errors, a phenomenon absent in pure Prolog. For instance, the query `X is Y` yields an error and so does `X =:= Y`.

In contrast, in the formulas as programs approach arithmetic can be simply modeled by adding the sorts of integers and of reals. The α-assignment then deals correctly with arithmetic expressions because it relies on automatic evaluation of terms. This yields a simpler and more uniform approach to arithmetic in which no new special relation symbols are needed.

5.5 Relation to Constraint Logic Programming

The abovementioned deficiencies of pure Prolog with arithmetic have been overcome in constraint logic programming, an approach to computing that generalizes logic programming. In what follows we concentrate on a specific approach, the generic scheme CLP(X) of [JL87] that generalizes pure Prolog by allowing constraints. In this scheme atoms are divided into those defined by means of clauses and those interpreted in a direct way. The latter ones are called constraints.

In CLP(X), as in our case, the computation is carried out over an arbitrary interpretation. At each step (instead of the unification test of logic programming and its application if it succeeds) satisfiability of the so far encountered constraints is tested. A computation is successful if the last query consists of constraints only.

There are two differences between the formulas as programs approach and the CLP(X) scheme. The first one has to do with the fact that in our approach full first-order logic is allowed, while in the latter — as in logic programming and pure Prolog — Horn clauses are used.

The second one concerns the way values are assigned. In our case the only way to assign values to variables is by means of an α-assignment, while in the CLP(X) scheme satisfiability of constraints guides the computation and output is identified with a set of constraints (that still have to be solved or normalized).

The CLP(X) approach to computing has been realized in a number of constraint logic programming languages, notably in the CLP($\mathcal{R}$) system of [JMSY92] that is an instance of the CLP(X) scheme with a two-sorted structure that consists of reals and terms. In this system formula (1) of Subsection 1.3 can be directly run as a query.

Once negation is added to the CLP(X) scheme (it is in fact present in CLP($\mathcal{R}$)), the extension of the CLP(X) syntax to full first-order logic could be achieved by using the approach [LT84] or by extending the computation mechanism along the lines of Section 2.

So, ignoring the use of the first-order logic syntax in the formulas as programs approach and the absence of (recursive) procedures that could be added to it, the main difference between this approach and the CLP(X) scheme has to do with the fact that in the former only very limited constraints are admitted, namely ground atoms and α-assignments. In fact, these are the only constraints that can be resolved directly.

So from this point of view the formulas as programs approach is less general than constraint logic programming, as embodied in the CLP(X) scheme.

However, this more limited approach does not rely on the satisfiability procedure for constraints (i.e., selected atomic formulas), or any of its approximations used in specific implementations. In fact, the formulas as programs approach attempts to clarify how far constraint logic programming approach can be used without any reliance on external procedures that deal with constraint solving or satisfiability.

5.6 Formulas as Programs Versus Formulas as Types

In the so-called *formulas as types* approach, also called the Curry-Howard-De Bruijn interpretation (see e.g. [TvD88]) (constructive) proofs of a formula are terms whose type is the formula in question. The type corresponding to a formula can thus be viewed as the (possibly empty) set of all proofs of the formula. Here 'proof' refers to an operational notion of proof, in which

- a proof of $\phi \vee \psi$ is either *left*(p) with p a proof of ϕ, or *right*(p) with p a proof of ψ;
- a proof of $\phi \wedge \psi$ is a pair $\langle p, q\rangle$ consisting of a proof p of ϕ and and a proof q of ψ;
- a proof of an implication $\phi \rightarrow \psi$ is a function that maps proofs of ϕ to proofs of ψ;
- a proof of $\forall x\ \phi(x)$ is a function that maps domain elements d to proofs of $\phi(d)$;
- a proof of $\exists x\ \phi(x)$ is of the form $ex(d, p)$ with domain element d a witness for the existential statement, and p a proof of $\phi(d)$.

Such proofs can be taken as programs. For example, a constructive proof of $\forall x\ \exists y\ \phi(x, y)$ is a function that maps d to an expression of the form $ex(e_d, p_d)$ with p_d a proof of $\phi(d, e_d)$. After extraction of the witness e_d the proof yields a program computing e_d from d.

The main difference between formulas as types and formulas as programs is that in the latter approach not the proofs of the formulas, but the formulas themselves have an operational interpretation. To illustrate this difference, consider the computation tree of formula (1) in Figure 1 with its proof:

$$ex(3, ex(2, \langle \mathit{right}(p_{3=3}), \langle \mathit{right}(p_{2=2}), p_{2*3=3*2}\rangle\rangle))$$

Here p_A is a proof of A, for each true closed atom A.

Observe that in the above proof the witnesses 3 and 2 for x and y, respectively, *have to be given beforehand*, whereas in our approach they are computed. In the formulas as programs approach the proofs are constructed in the successful branches of the computation tree and the computation is guided by the search for such a proof. Apart from differences in syntax, the reader will recognize the above proof in the successful branch of Figure 1.

Given the undecidability of the first-order logic, there is a price to be paid for formulas programs. It consists of the possibility of abnormal termination in an error.

6 Alma-0

We hope to have convinced the reader that the formulas as programs approach, though closely related to logic programming, differs from it in a number of crucial aspects.

This approach to programming has been realized in the implemented programming language Alma-0 [ABPS98]. A similar approach to programming has been taken in the 2LP language of [MT95]. 2LP (which stands for "logic programming and linear programming") uses C syntax and has been designed for constraint programming in the area of optimization.

Alma-0 is an extension of a subset of Modula-2 that includes nine new features inspired by the logic programming paradigm. We briefly recall those that are used in the sequel and refer to [ABPS98] for a detailed presentation.

- Boolean expressions can be used as statements and vice versa. A boolean expression that is used as a statement and evaluates to `FALSE` is identified with a *failure*.
- *Choice points* can be created by the non-deterministic statements `ORELSE` and `SOME`. The former is a dual of the statement composition and the latter is a dual of the `FOR` statement. Upon failure the control returns to the most recent choice point, possibly within a procedure body, and the computation resumes with the next branch in the state in which the previous branch was entered.
- The notion of *initialized* variable is introduced and the equality test is generalized to an assignment statement in case one side is an uninitialized variable and the other side an expression with known value.
- A new parameter passing mechanism, *call by mixed form*, denoted by the keyword `MIX`, is introduced for variables of simple type. It works as follows: If the actual parameter is a variable, then it is passed by variable. If the actual parameter is an expression that is not a variable, its value is computed and assigned to a new variable v (generated by the compiler): it is v that is then passed by variable. So in this case the call by mixed form boils down to call by value. Using this parameter mechanism we can pass both expressions with known values and uninitialized variables as actual parameters. This makes it possible to use a single procedure both for testing and computing.

For efficiency reasons the Alma-0 implementation does not realize faithfully the computation mechanism of Section 2 as far as the errors are concerned. First, an evaluation of an atom that is not α-closed and is not an α-assignment yields a run-time error. On the other hand, in the other two cases when the evaluation ends with the *error* leaf, in the statements `NOT S` and `IF S THEN T END`, the computation process of Alma-0 simply proceeds.

The rationale for this decision is that the use of insufficiently instantiated atoms in Alma-0 programs is to be discouraged whereas the catching of other two cases for errors would be computationally prohibitive. In this respect the implementation of Alma-0 follows the same compromise as the implementations of Prolog.

We now associate with each first-order formula ϕ an Alma-0 statement $\mathcal{T}(\phi)$. This is done by induction on the structure of the formula ϕ. The translation process is given in Table 1.

Formula	Alma-0 construct
A (atom)	A
$\phi_1 \vee \phi_2$	EITHER $\mathcal{T}(\phi_1)$ ORELSE $\mathcal{T}(\phi_2)$ END
$\phi_1 \wedge \phi_2$	$\mathcal{T}(\phi_1); \mathcal{T}(\phi_2)$
$\phi \rightarrow \psi$	IF $\mathcal{T}(\phi)$ THEN $\mathcal{T}(\psi)$ END
$\neg\phi$	NOT $\mathcal{T}(\phi)$

$\exists x \phi(x, \bar{y})$	p($\bar{y}$), where the procedure p is defined by
	PROCEDURE p(MIX $\bar{y}$: $\bar{\mathrm{T}}$);
	VAR x : T;
	BEGIN
	  $\mathcal{T}(\phi(x, \bar{y}))$
	END;
	where T is the type (sort) of the variable x and $\bar{\mathrm{T}}$ is the sequence of types of the variables in $\bar{y}$.

$\exists x \in [s..t]\phi$	SOME $x := s$ TO t DO $\mathcal{T}(\phi)$ END
$\forall x \in [s..t]\phi$	FOR $x := s$ TO t DO $\mathcal{T}(\phi)$ END

Table 1. Translation of formulas into Alma-0 statements.

This translation allows us to use in the sequel Alma-0 syntax to present specific formulas.

7 Example: Partitioning a Rectangle into Squares

To illustrate the Alma-0 programming style and the use of formulas as programs approach for program verification, we consider now the following variant of a problem from [Hon70, pages 46-60].

Squares in the rectangle. Partition an integer sized $nx \times ny$ rectangle into given squares $S_1, \ldots, S_m$ of integer sizes $s_1, \ldots, s_m$.

We develop a solution that, in contrast to the one given in [ABPS98], is purely declarative. To solve this problem we use a backtracking algorithm that fills in all the cells of the rectangle one by one, starting with the left upper cell and proceeding downward in the leftmost column, then the next column, and so on. The algorithm checks for each cell whether it is already covered by some square used to cover a previous cell. Given the order in which the cells are visited, it suffices to inspect the left neighbour cell and the upper neighbour cell (if these neighbours exist). This is done by the test

$$((1 < \texttt{i})\ \texttt{AND}\ (\texttt{i} < \texttt{RightEdge}[\texttt{i}-1,\texttt{j}]))\ \texttt{OR}$$
$$((1 < \texttt{j})\ \texttt{AND}\ (\texttt{j} < \texttt{LowerEdge}[\texttt{i},\texttt{j}-1])).$$

Here `[i,j]` is the index of the cell in question, and `RightEdge[i-1,j]` is the right edge of the square covering the left neighbour (`[i-1,j]`, provided `i > 1`), and `LowerEdge[i, j-1]` is the lower edge of the square covering the upper neighbour (`[i,j-1]`, provided `j > 1`). The cell under consideration is already covered if and only if the test succeeds. If it is not covered, then the algorithm looks for a square not yet used, which is placed with its top-left corner at `[i,j]` provided the square fits within the rectangle. The algorithm backtracks when none of the available squares can cover the cell under consideration without sticking out of the rectangle. See Figure 2.

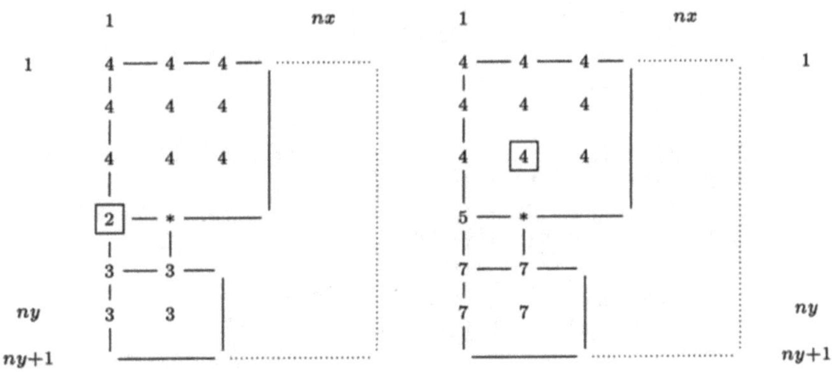

Fig. 2. Example of values of **RightEdge** (left diagram) and **LowerEdge** (right diagram), respectively. Entry $*$ is indexed by `[2,4]`. It is not covered already since neither $2 < \texttt{RightEdge}[1,4] = 2$ nor $4 < \texttt{LowerEdge}[2,3] = 4$.

In test (2) we used the **AND** and **OR** connectives instead of the ";" and **ORELSE** constructs for the following reason. In case all variables occurring in a test are instantiated, some optimizations are in order. For example, it is not necessary to backtrack within the test, disjunctions do not have to create choice points, and so on. The use of **AND** and **OR** enables the compiler to apply these optimizations.

Backtracking is implemented by a **SOME** statement that checks for each square whether it can be put to cover a given cell. The solution is returned via two arrays **posX** and **posY** such that for square S_k (of size `Sizes[k]`) `posX[k]`, `posY[k]` are the coordinates of its top-left corner.

The two equations `posX[k] = i` and `posY[k] = j` are used both to construct the solution and to prevent using an already placed square again at a different place.

The declaration of the variables `posX` and `posY` as `MIX` parameters allows us to use the program both to check a given solution or to complete a partial solution.

```
TYPE SquaresVector = ARRAY [1..M] OF INTEGER;

PROCEDURE Squares(Sizes:SquaresVector, MIX posX, posY:SquaresVector);

VAR RightEdge,LowerEdge: ARRAY [1..NX],[1..NY] OF INTEGER;
    i,i1, j,j1, k: INTEGER;

BEGIN
  FOR i := 1 TO NX DO
    FOR j := 1 TO NY DO
      IF NOT                          (* cell [i,j] already covered? *)
         (((1 < i) AND (i < RightEdge[i-1,j])) OR
         ((1 < j) AND (j < LowerEdge[i, j-1])))
      THEN
        SOME k := 1 TO M DO
          PosX[k] = i;
          PosY[k] = j;                        (* square k already used? *)
          Sizes[k] + i <= NX + 1;
          Sizes[k] + j <= NY + 1;                     (* square k fits? *)
          FOR i1 := 1 TO Sizes[k] DO
            FOR j1 := 1 TO Sizes[k] DO
              RightEdge[i+i1-1,j+j1-1] = i+Sizes[k];
              LowerEdge[i+i1-1,j+j1-1] = j+Sizes[k]
            END                          (* complete administration *)
          END
        END
      END
    END
  END
END Squares;
```

This program is declarative and consequently has a dual reading as the formula

$$\begin{aligned}&\forall i \in [1..nx]\ \forall j \in [1..ny]\\ &\neg(1 < i < \texttt{RightEdge}[i{-}1, j] \vee 1 < j < \texttt{LowerEdge}[i, j{-}1]) \rightarrow\\ &\exists k \in [1..m]\ \phi(i,j,k),\end{aligned}$$

where $\phi(i, j, k)$ is the formula

$$\texttt{PosX}[k] = i \land \texttt{PosY}[k] = j \land$$
$$\texttt{Sizes}[k]{+}i \leq nx{+}1 \land \texttt{Sizes}[k]{+}j \leq ny{+}1 \land \psi(i,j,k)$$

and $\psi(i,j,k)$ is the formula

$$\forall i' \in [1..\texttt{Sizes}(k)]\ \forall j' \in [1..\texttt{Sizes}(k)]$$
$$\texttt{RightEdge}[i{+}i'{-}1, j{+}j'{-}1] = i{+}\texttt{Sizes}[k] \land$$
$$\texttt{LowerEdge}[i{+}i'{-}1, j{+}j'{-}1] = j{+}\texttt{Sizes}[k]$$

This dual reading of the program entails over the standard interpretation the formula

$$\forall i \in [1..nx]\ \forall j \in [1..ny]\ \exists k \in [1..m]$$
$$\texttt{PosX}[k] \leq i < \texttt{PosX}[k]{+}\texttt{Sizes}[k] \leq nx{+}1 \land$$
$$\texttt{PosY}[k] \leq j < \texttt{PosY}[k]{+}\texttt{Sizes}[k] \leq ny{+}1 \qquad (2)$$

expressing that every cell is covered by a square. The entailment is not trivial, but can be made completely rigorous. The proof uses arithmetic, in particular induction on lexicographically ordered pairs (i,j). This entailment actually means that the program satisfies its specification, that is, if the computation is successful, then a partition is found (and can be read off from $\texttt{PosX}[k]$ and $\texttt{PosY}[k]$). The latter fact relies on the Soundness Theorem 1.

Conversely, assuming that the surfaces of the squares sum up exactly to the surface of the rectangle, the specification (2) entails the formula corresponding to the program, with suitable values for RightEdge, LowerEdge. Furthermore, the absence of errors can be established by lexicographic induction. This ensures that the computation tree is always determined. By the Completeness Theorem 2, one always gets an answer. If this answer is negative, that is, if the computation tree is failed, then by the Soundness Theorem 1 the formula corresponding to the program cannot be satisfied, and hence (2) cannot be satisfied.

8 Current and Future Work

The work here presented can be pursued in a number of directions. We listed here the ones that seem to us most natural.

Recursive procedures The extension of the treatment of non-recursive procedures in Subsection 4.1 to the case of recursive procedures is far from obvious. It requires an extension of the computation mechanism to one with possible non-terminating behaviour. This could be done along the lines of [AD94] where the SLDNF-resolution of logic programs with negation is presented in a top down, non-circular way.

Also, on the semantic level several choices arise, much like in the case of logic programming, and the corresponding soundness and completeness results that provide a match between the computation mechanism and semantics need to be reconsidered from scratch.

Constraints As already said in Subsection 5.5, the formulas as programs approach can be seen as a special case of constraint logic programming, though with a full first-order syntax. It is natural to extend our approach by allowing constraints, so arbitrary atoms that have no definition in the sense of Subsection 4.1. The addition of constraints will require on the computation mechanism level use of a constraint store and special built-in procedures that approximate the satisfiability test for conjunctions of constraints.

Automated Verification The correctness proof presented in Section 7 was carried out manually. It boils down to a proof of validity of an implication between two formulas, This proof is based on an lexicographic ordering so it should be possible to mechanize this proof. This would lead a fully mechanized correctness proof of the Alma-0 program considered there.

Relation to Dynamic Predicate Logic In [GS91] an alternative "input-output" semantics of first-order logic is provided. In this semantics both the connectives and the quantifiers obtain a different, dynamic, interpretation that better suits their use for natural language analysis. This semantic is highly nondeterministic due to its treatment of existential quantifiers and it does not take into account a possibility of errors.

It is natural to investigate the precise connection between this semantics and our formulas as programs approach. A colleague of us, Jan van Eijck, has recently undertook this study. Also, it would be useful to clarify to what extent our approach can be of use for linguistic analysis, both as a computation mechanism and as a means for capturing errors in discourse analysis.

Absence of abnormal termination Another natural line of research deals with the improvements of the computation mechanism in the sense of limiting the occurrence of errors while retaining soundness. In Appendix, Subsections 9.3 and 9.4 we consider two such possibilities but several other options arise. Also, it is useful to provide sufficient syntactic criteria that for a formula guarantee absence of abnormal termination. This work is naturally related to a research on verification of Alma-0 programs.

Acknowledgements

We would like to thank Jan van Eijck and David Scott Warren for a number of helpful suggestions.

References

[AB94] K. R. Apt and R. Bol. Logic programming and negation: a survey. *Journal of Logic Programming*, 19-20:9–71, 1994.

[ABPS98] K. R. Apt, J. Brunekreef, V. Partington, and A. Schaerf. Alma-0: An imperative language that supports declarative programming. *ACM Toplas*, 1998. In press. Available via `http://www.cwi.nl/~apt`.

[AD94] K. R. Apt and H. C. Doets. A new definition of SLDNF-resolution. *Journal of Logic Programming*, 18(2):177–190, 1994.

[Apt96] K. R. Apt. Arrays, bounded quantification and iteration in logic and constraint logic programming. *Science of Computer Programming*, 26(1-3):133–148, 1996.

[BB93] J. Barklund and J. Bevemyr. Prolog with arrays and bounded quantifications. In Andrei Voronkov, editor, *Logic Programming and Automated Reasoning—Proc. 4th Intl. Conf.*, LNCS 698, pages 28–39, Berlin, 1993. Springer-Verlag.

[Cla78] K. L. Clark. Negation as failure. In H. Gallaire and J. Minker, editors, *Logic and Databases*, pages 293–322. Plenum Press, New York, 1978.

[DD94] D. De Schreye and S. Decorte. Termination of logic programs: the never-ending story. *Journal of Logic Programming*, 19-20:199–260, 1994.

[GS91] J. Groenendijk and M. Stokhof. Dynamic predicate logic. *Linguistics and philosophy*, 14(2):39–101, 1991.

[HL94] P. M. Hill and J. W. Lloyd. *The Gödel Programming Language*. The MIT Press, 1994.

[Hon70] R. Honsberger. *Ingenuity in Mathematics*. Random House, Inc., New York, 1970.

[JL87] Joxan Jaffar and Jean-Louis Lassez. Constraint Logic Programming. In *POPL'87: Proceedings 14th ACM Symposium on Principles of Programming Languages*, pages 111–119. ACM, 1987.

[JMMS98] J. Jaffar, M.J. Maher, K. Marriott, and P. Stuckey. The semantics of constraint logic programs. *Journal of Logic Programming*, 37(1-3):1–46, 1998.

[JMSY92] Joxan Jaffar, Spiro Michayov, Peter Stuckey, and Roland Yap. The CLP($\mathcal{R}$) language and system. *ACM Transactions on Programming Languages and Systems*, 14(3):339–395, July 1992.

[KM97] F. Kluźniak and M. Miłkowska. Spill: A logic language for writing testable requirements specifications. *Science of Computer Programming*, 28(2 & 3):193–223, 1997.

[Kow74] R.A. Kowalski. Predicate logic as a programming language. In *Proceedings IFIP'74*, pages 569–574. North-Holland, 1974.

[Llo87] J. W. Lloyd. *Foundations of Logic Programming*. Springer-Verlag, Berlin, second edition, 1987.

[LMR92] J. Lobo, J. Minker, and A. Rajasekar. *Foundations of Disjunctive Logic Programming*. The MIT Press, 1992.

[LT84] J. W. Lloyd and R. W. Topor. Making Prolog more expressive. *Journal of Logic Programming*, 1:225–240, 1984.

[MT95] K. McAloon and C. Tretkoff. 2LP: Linear programming and logic programming. In P. Van Hentenryck and V. Saraswat, editors, *Principles and Practice of Constraint Programming*, pages 101–116. MIT Press, 1995.

[Sho67] J. R. Shoenfield. *Mathematical Logic.* Addison-Wesley, Reading, Massachusetts, 1967.

[Tar33] A. Tarski. *Pojęcie prawdy w językach nauk dedukcyjnych.* Towarzystwo Naukowe Warszawskie, Warszawa, 1933. In Polish. English version appeared in A. Tarski, *Logic, semantics, metamathematics: papers from 1923 to 1938*, Oxford, Clarendon, 1956.

[TvD88] A. S. Troelstra and D. van Dalen. *Constructivism in Mathematics.* Studies in Logic and the Foundations of Mathematics. North-Holland Publ. Co., Amsterdam, 1988. Two vols.

[Vor92] A. Voronkov. Logic programming with bounded quantifiers. In A. Voronkov, editor, *Logic Programming and Automated Reasoning—Proc. 2nd Russian Conference on Logic Programming*, LNCS 592, pages 486–514, Berlin, 1992. Springer-Verlag.

9 Appendix

9.1 Proof of the Soundness Theorem 1

The proof proceeds by induction on the lexicographic ordering on formulas which is defined in Definition 4. We carefully go through all inductive cases.

1. The case of the empty conjunction is trivial.
2. The first three of the four cases concerning atom A are obvious. It remains to deal with the last case, where atom A is an α-assignment $s = t$. Then either s or t is a variable which is not α-closed, say $s \equiv x$ with x not α-closed and t α-closed. The symmetrical case is analogous. The tree $[\![x = t \wedge \psi]\!]_\alpha$ is, apart from the root of degree one, identical to $[\![\psi]\!]_{\alpha\cup\{x/t^\alpha\}}$.
   If $[\![\psi]\!]_{\alpha\cup\{x/t^\alpha\}}$ contains a success leaf labelled by β, then by the induction hypothesis $\forall(\psi^\beta)$ is true. Since t is α-closed and β extends $\alpha \cup \{x/t^\alpha\}$, we have $(x = t)^\beta \equiv (x^\beta = t^\beta) \equiv (t^\alpha = t^\alpha)$. The last formula is true, so also $\forall((x = t \wedge \psi)^\beta)$ is true.
   If $[\![\psi]\!]_{\alpha\cup\{x/t^\alpha\}}$ is failed, then by the induction hypothesis $\exists(\psi^{\alpha\cup\{x/t^\alpha\}})$ is false. Note again that t is α-closed and let $x, x_1, \ldots, x_n$ be all the free variables of ψ that are not in the domain of α. (If $n = 0$ or if x does not occur in ψ, then the argument is even simpler.) Then we have $\exists((x = t \wedge \psi)^\alpha) \equiv \exists x, x_1, \ldots, x_n\ (x = t^\alpha \wedge \psi^\alpha(x, x_1, \ldots, x_n))$, which is logically equivalent to $\exists x_1, \ldots, x_n\ \psi^\alpha(t^\alpha, x_1, \ldots, x_n)) \equiv \exists(\psi^{\alpha\cup\{x/t^\alpha\}})$. It follows that $\exists((x = t \wedge \psi)^\alpha)$ is also false.
3. The case of $(\phi_1 \vee \phi_2) \wedge \psi$ uses the distributive law and the induction hypothesis applied to the the lexicographically smaller formulas $\phi_1 \wedge \psi$ and $\phi_2 \wedge \psi$.
4. The case of $(\phi_1 \wedge \phi_2) \wedge \psi$ uses the associativity of conjunction and the induction hypothesis applied to the the lexicographically smaller formulas ϕ_1 and $\phi_2 \wedge \psi$.

5. The case of $(\phi_1 \rightarrow \phi_2) \wedge \psi$ uses the logical equivalence of $\phi_1 \rightarrow \phi_2$ and $\neg\phi_1 \vee \phi_2$. If formula ϕ_1 is α-closed and $[\![\phi]\!]_\alpha$ is failed, then the argument is similar to the corresponding case of $\neg\phi \wedge \psi$ in the next case. The other case can be dealt with by applying the induction hypothesis to $\phi_1 \wedge (\phi_2 \wedge \psi)$.
6. For $\neg\phi \wedge \psi$ we distinguish three cases with respect to ϕ.
   - Formula ϕ is α-closed and $[\![\phi]\!]_\alpha$ is failed. Then, by the induction hypothesis, $\exists(\phi^\alpha)$ is false, so $\forall(\neg\phi^\alpha)$ is true. Since $[\![\neg\phi \wedge \psi]\!]_\alpha$ is, apart from the root of degree one, identical to $[\![\psi]\!]_\alpha$, we apply the induction hypothesis to ψ. If $[\![\psi]\!]_\alpha$ is failed, then $\exists(\psi^\alpha)$ is false, and hence $\exists((\neg\phi \wedge \psi)^\alpha)$ is false. If $[\![\psi]\!]_\alpha$ contains a success leaf β then β extends α and $\forall(\psi^\beta)$ is true. Note that $\forall(\neg\phi^\alpha)$ implies $\forall(\neg\phi^\gamma)$, for any γ extending α, *even if ϕ is not α-closed.* It follows that $\forall((\neg\phi \wedge \psi)^\beta)$ is true. Observe that we did not use the fact that ϕ is α-closed. So the proof remains valid under the first relaxation described in Subsection 9.3.
   - Formula ϕ is α-closed and $[\![\phi]\!]_\alpha$ contains at least one success leaf, labelled by an extension β of α. The tree $[\![\neg\phi \wedge \psi]\!]_\alpha$ consists of a root and a failure leaf in this case, so we have to show that $\exists((\neg\phi \wedge \psi)^\alpha)$ is false. By the induction hypothesis, $\forall(\phi^\beta)$ is true, and hence $\forall(\phi^\alpha)$ is true, as β is an extension of α and ϕ is α-closed. *This implication also holds if ϕ is not α-closed, provided that β does not contain any pair x/d where x is free in ϕ^α.* Consequently, $\exists(\neg\phi^\alpha)$ is false and hence also $\exists((\neg\phi \wedge \psi)^\alpha)$ is false. Observe that the proof remains valid under the second relaxation described in Subsection 9.3.
   - In all other cases there is nothing to prove as $[\![\neg\phi \wedge \psi]\!]_\alpha$ has then only error leaves.
7. For the case $\exists x\, \phi \wedge \psi$, assume that x is fresh with respect to ψ and some valuation α. It is convenient to make the possible occurrence of x in ϕ explicit by writing $\phi(x)$ for ϕ. Recall that apart form the root of degree one $[\![\exists x\, \phi(x) \wedge \psi]\!]_\alpha$ is identical to $[\![\phi(x) \wedge \psi]\!]_\alpha$.
   Assume $[\![\phi(x) \wedge \psi]\!]_\alpha$ contains a success leaf labelled by β. By applying the induction hypothesis to the lexicographically smaller formula $\phi(x) \wedge \psi$ we get that $\forall((\phi(x) \wedge \psi)^\beta)$ is true. It follows that $\forall((\exists x\, \phi(x) \wedge \psi)^\beta)$ is true. Some minor technicalities have been left to the reader here: the case in which x does not occur in the domain of β has to be settled by applying $(\forall x\, \phi(x)) \rightarrow (\exists x\, \phi(x))$ and not by inferring $\exists x\, \phi(x)$ from $\phi(x^\beta)$.
   Assume $[\![\phi(x) \wedge \psi]\!]_\alpha$ is failed. Then, again by the induction hypothesis, $\exists((\phi(x) \wedge \psi)^\alpha)$ is false. Since x does occur neither in α, nor in ψ, it follows that $\exists((\exists x\, \phi(x) \wedge \psi)^\alpha)$ is false. ⊠

9.2 Proof of the Restricted Completeness Theorem 2

(i) Suppose by contradiction that $[\![\phi]\!]_\alpha$ is not successful. Since this tree is determined, it is failed. By the Soundness Theorem 1 $\exists(\phi^\alpha)$ is false which is a contradiction.

(ii) Suppose by contradiction that $[\![\phi]\!]_\alpha$ is not failed. Since this tree is determined, it is successful. By the Soundness Theorem 1 for some β that extends α we have that $\forall(\phi^\beta)$ is true. This is a contradiction since the falsity of $\exists(\phi^\alpha)$ is equivalent to the truth $\forall(\neg\phi^\alpha)$ that implies the truth of $\forall(\neg\phi^\beta)$. ⊠

9.3 More Liberal Negation

In this subsection we show how in Definition 4 the restriction "ϕ is α-closed" in the case of the tree $[\![\neg\phi \wedge \psi]\!]_\alpha$ can be relaxed without losing soundness. There are basically two such relaxations.

First, observe by means of example that $\neg(0 = 1 \wedge x = y)$ is true, independent of the values of x and y. This observation can be generalized as follows. If $[\![\phi]\!]_\alpha$ is failed, then $[\![\neg\phi \wedge \psi]\!]_\alpha$ can be defined as the tree with a root of degree one and $[\![\psi]\!]_\alpha$ as its subtree, *even if ϕ is not α-closed.* In the proof of the Soundness Theorem we already accommodated for this relaxation, see Subsection 9.1.

Second, observe that the dual phenomenon also exists: $\neg(0 = 0 \vee x = y)$ is false, independent of the values of x and y. More generally, if $[\![\phi]\!]_\alpha$ contains a success leaf β not containing any pair x/d with x free in ϕ^α, then $[\![\neg\phi \wedge \psi]\!]_\alpha$ can be defined as the tree with a root of degree one and a failure leaf as its son, *even if ϕ is not α-closed.*

9.4 More Liberal Implication

The first and the second relaxation above can be both applied to the computation tree $[\![(\phi_1 \rightarrow \phi_2) \wedge \psi]\!]_\alpha$, the first to the case in which the tree $[\![\phi_1]\!]_\alpha$ is failed, and the second to the case in which the tree $[\![\phi_1]\!]_\alpha$ contains a success leaf not containing any pair x/d with x free in ϕ_1^α.

There are several other ways to liberalize implication. The aim is to be more complete, that is, to yield more determined computation trees (without losing soundness, of course).

As a first example, consider the following computation tree:

$$(0 = 1 \rightarrow x = 0) \wedge x < 1,\ \varepsilon$$

$$|$$

$$x < 1,\ \varepsilon$$

$$|$$

error

This computation tree is not determined. In contrast, using the equivalence of $\phi_1 \to \phi_2$ and $\neg\phi_1 \vee \phi_2$, we get the following computation tree which is determined, as it contains a success leaf $\{x/0\}$:

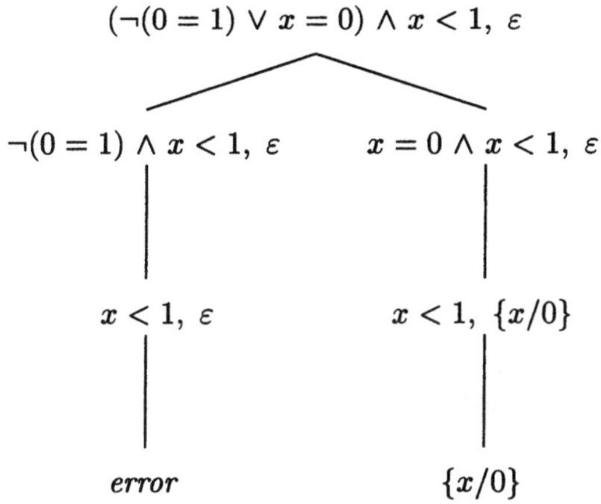

The above example shows that $\neg\phi_1 \vee \phi_2$ can be "more complete" than $\phi_1 \to \phi_2$, although in some cases the disjunction involves unnecessary branching in the computation tree. As an example of the latter phenomenon, compare the computation trees for $(0 = 1 \to 0 = 0) \wedge \psi$ and $(\neg(0 = 1) \vee 0 = 0) \wedge \psi$:

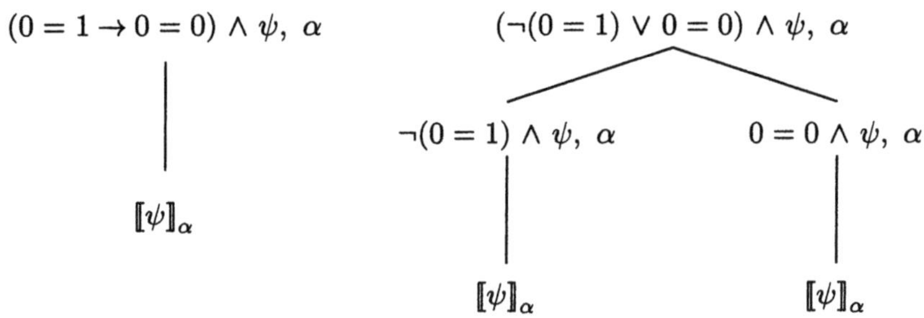

As a second example, consider the computation tree $[\![(x = 0 \to x < 1]\!]_\varepsilon$, which is not determined since $x = 0$ is not ε-closed:

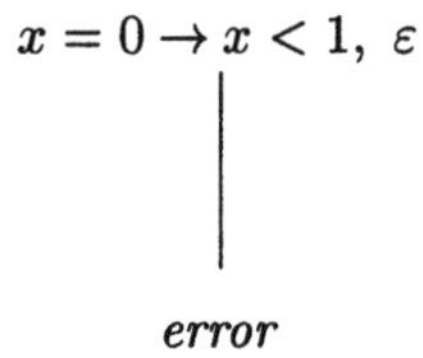

One would like to have this tree succeed with $\{x/0\}$. (The fact that $\{x/1\}$ is also a solution is beyond the scope of our method, since $[\![\neg(x = 0)]\!]_\varepsilon$ is not determined.) For this the equivalence of $\phi_1 \to \phi_2$ and $\neg\phi_1 \vee \phi_2$ does not help, as the computation tree $[\![\neg(x = 0) \vee x < 1]\!]_\varepsilon$ is not determined either:

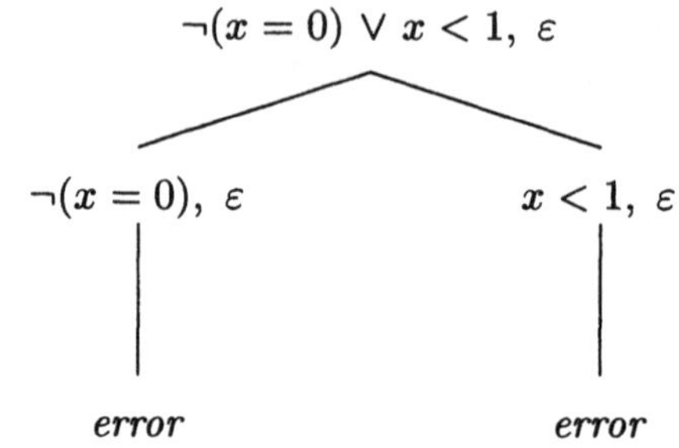

Note that the left subtree ends with *error* since $[\![x = 0]\!]$ succeeds with $\{x/0\}$. Liberal negation does not help us any further here.

In order to have $[\![(x = 0 \to x < 1]\!]_\varepsilon$ succeed it is necessary to transfer the valuation of the success leaf of the antecedent, i.e. $\{x/0\}$, to the consequent. Thus we are tempted to consider $\neg\phi_1 \vee (\phi_1 \wedge \phi_2)$ as a more useful logical equivalent of $\phi_1 \to \phi_2$ than $\neg\phi_1 \vee \phi_2$. The conjunction $\phi_1 \wedge \phi_2$ has the desired effect on the transfer of valuations. Indeed the following computation tree is successful:

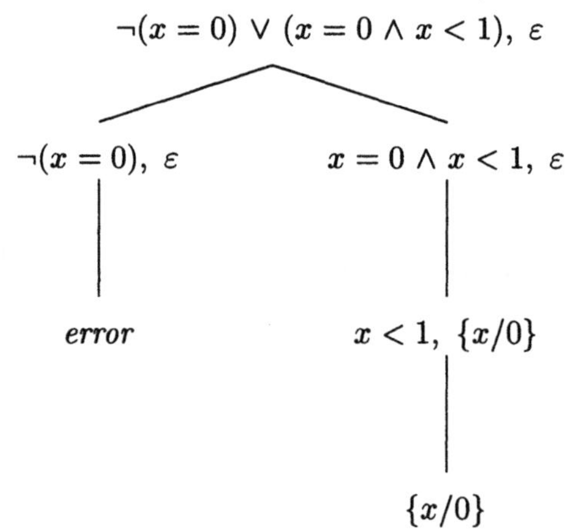

The combination of $\neg\phi_1 \vee (\phi_1 \wedge \phi_2)$ for $\phi_1 \to \phi_2$ with liberal negation yields the following computation tree for $[\![((x = 0 \wedge x = 1) \to 0 = 1) \wedge \psi]\!]_\varepsilon$:

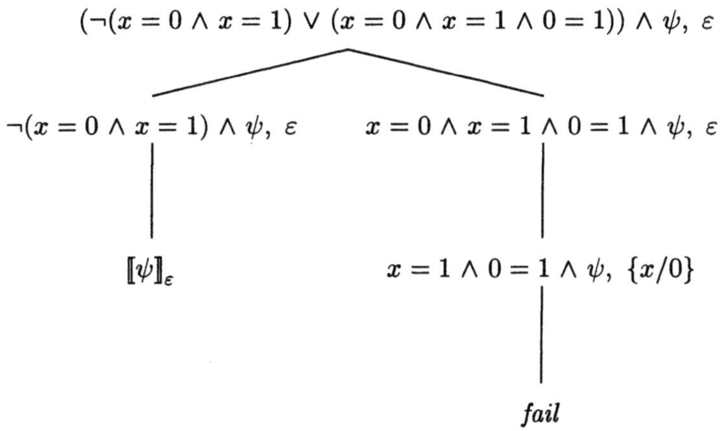

Note that the "guard" $x = 0 \land x = 1$ prevents $[\![\psi]\!]_\varepsilon$ to be computed twice, even if we replace $0 = 1$ by $0 = 0$.

On the other hand, this guard also prevents successful computations, such as in $[\![((x = 0 \land x = 1) \to x = 0) \land x < 1]\!]_\varepsilon$, where the solution $\{x/0\}$ is missed when $\neg\phi_1 \lor (\phi_1 \land \phi_2)$ is used instead of $\neg\phi_1 \lor \phi_2$ for $\phi_1 \to \phi_2$.

The above example shows that $\neg\phi_1 \lor (\phi_1 \land \phi_2)$ is not always "more complete" than $\neg\phi_1 \lor \phi_2$. Thus we are led to consider $\neg\phi_1 \lor \phi_2 \lor (\phi_1 \land \phi_2)$ as a third logical equivalent of $\phi_1 \to \phi_2$, in an attempt to collect all the successes of $\neg\phi_1 \lor \phi_2$ and $\neg\phi_1 \lor (\phi_1 \land \phi_2)$. Indeed this works for the successes, but not for the failures, as the following delicate example shows.

Consider $[\![\phi_1 \to \phi_2]\!]_\varepsilon$ with $0 = 0 \lor x < 1$ for ϕ_1 and $0 = 1$ for ϕ_2. Then both $[\![\neg\phi_1]\!]_\varepsilon$ and $[\![\phi_2]\!]_\varepsilon$ are failed, but $[\![\phi_1 \land \phi_2]\!]_\varepsilon$ has an error leaf due to the disjunct $x < 1$. This means that $[\![\neg\phi_1 \lor \phi_2]\!]_\varepsilon$ is failed, whereas neither $[\![\neg\phi_1 \lor (\phi_1 \land \phi_2)]\!]_\varepsilon$ nor $[\![\neg\phi_1 \lor \phi_2 \lor (\phi_1 \land \phi_2)]\!]_\varepsilon$ is determined.

From the above we can draw the following conclusions:

- Liberal negation is always an improvement for implication;
- For finding successes, use $\phi_1 \to \phi_2 \equiv \neg\phi_1 \lor \phi_2 \lor (\phi_1 \land \phi_2)$;
- For failures, use $\phi_1 \to \phi_2 \equiv \neg\phi_1 \lor \phi_2$.

Link-time Optimization of Multi-Language Programs

Saumya Debray

Department of Computer Science, The University of Arizona, Tucson, AZ 85721, USA

Summary. Different programming languages have different strengths and weaknesses, and typically are suited for different application domains. Because of this, for many applications, using a single programming language to implement all aspects of the program may not be the best or most effective way to build the application. However, current language implementation technology does not make it easy to construct good multi-language programs: in particular, there is usually a nontrivial performance overhead associated with the use of multiple languages. This article discusses the use of link-time optimizations on machine-executable files to reduce such overheads.

1 Introduction

The traditional model of compilation usually limits the scope of analysis and optimization to individual procedures, or possibly to modules. This model for code optimization does not take things as far as they could be taken, in two respects. The first is that code involving calls to library routines, or to functions defined in separately compiled modules, cannot be effectively optimized; this is unfortunate, because one expects programmers to rely more and more on code reuse through libraries as the complexity of software systems grows. The second, and more important, problem is that a compiler can only analyze and optimize code written in the language it is designed to compile. Consider an application that investigates the synthesis of chemical compounds using a top-level Prolog program to direct a search of a space of reaction sequences, and Fortran routines to compute reaction rates and yields for individual reactions, in order to determine whether a particular reaction sequence is practically useful (such an application was part of a recent project in the Chemistry department at the University of Arizona). With the traditional model of compilation, illustrated in Figure 1, analyses and optimizations will not be able to cross the barrier between program modules written in different languages. For example, it seems unlikely that current technology would allow Fortran routines in such an application to be inlined into the Prolog code, or allow context information to be propagated across language boundaries during interprocedural analysis of a Prolog procedure calling a Fortran routine. (Foreign function interfaces may allow an application to glue together components written in other languages, but they typically do little to allow information to be propagated between such components; moreover, foreign function interfaces in most systems are typically geared toward a particular underlying "host language" rather than allowing arbitrary mixing of modules written in different languages.)

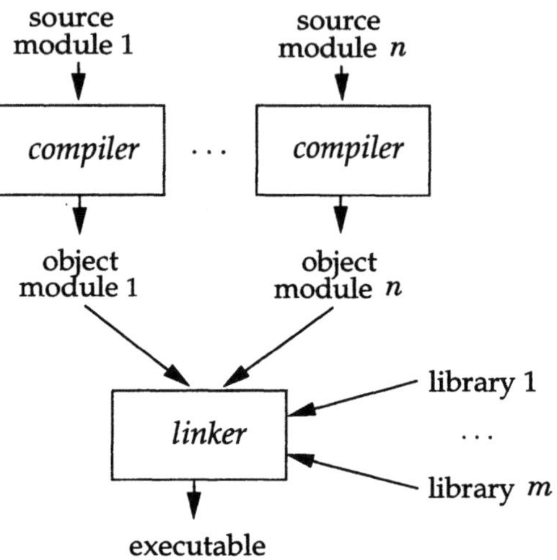

Fig. 1. The standard model of compilation and linking

In my opinion, the issue is especially pertinent to logic programming languages because I believe that many "real" applications are not, and will not be, written as monolithic, monolingual entities. As illustrated by the chemical synthesis application mentioned above, complex applications involve many different kinds of processing, which are typically best implemented in different languages; they may be integrated into a program either explicitly, in the form of program modules coded in different languages, or implicitly via libraries, but the fact remains that program units written in different languages will have to be composed into a whole. Since different languages typically have different features, e.g., in terms of control flow, data representation, or exception handling, interfaces between program modules in different languages typically incur some overhead. If this overhead is high—as it very often is—the programmer is effectively punished for using a conceptually good approach. This may, in turn, limit the range of languages he is willing to consider when writing an application.

A possible solution is to carry out optimization when the *entire* program—library calls and all—is available for inspection: that is, at link time, as illustrated in Figure 2. This is not intended as a replacement to traditional compiler optimizations, since a compiler for a particular language can generally be expected to have high-level semantic information about the constructs of

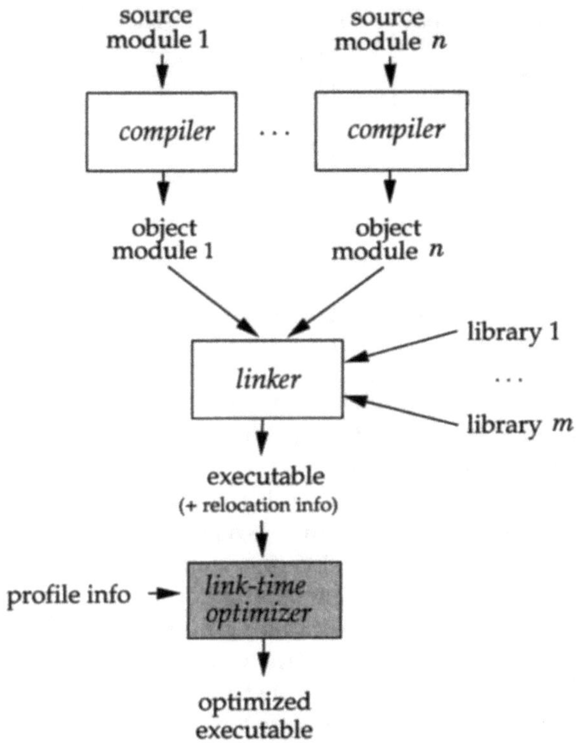

Fig. 2. Link-time code optimization

that language that are lost, or obscured, on compilation to executable code. Instead, our model is that link-time optimization supplements traditional compiler optimizations: each program module is optimized as far as possible by the appropriate compiler; following this, when the different modules and libraries are linked together to construct an executable, another round of optimization is carried out.

This article describes our experiences with link-time code optimization, for a variety of different languages, using a link-time optimizer called `alto` ("a link-time optimizer") that we have built for the DEC Alpha architecture. Apart from a variety of more or less "conventional" optimizations, `alto` implements several optimizations, or variations on optimizations, that are geared specifically towards programs that are rich in function calls—in particular, recursion—and indirect jumps (resulting, e.g., from tail call optimization). Experiments indicate that significant performance improvements are possible using link-time optimization, across a wide spectrum of languages, even for code generated using powerful optimizing compilers.

Program	*Language*	*Lines*	*Basic Blocks*	*Instructions*
compress	C	1420	4,425	18,489
hydro2d	Fortran	4292	26,048	115,957
boyer	Scheme	568	24,506	114,006
chat	Prolog	1183	29,970	109,273

Fig. 3. Scaling problems in executable code

2 Challenges in Link Time Optimization

We encountered two main challenges in constructing a link-time optimizer: the first is that of scale, the second is the difficulty of extracting semantic information from executable code.

The problem of scale has to do with the fact that executable programs are significantly larger than their source-level counterparts. This is illustrated in Figure 3 for programs in four different source languages: it can be seen that source programs that are a few hundred or a few thousand lines in size expand to executable programs containing tens or hundreds of thousands of machine instructions. There are two reasons for this. The first is that a high-level programming language construct that expresses a higher-level abstraction will typically require multiple lower-level constructs—in our case, machine instructions—to realize it. The second is that by the time we get to executable code, implementation-level components that are typically invisible at the source level, such as debuggers or garbage collectors, have been added in, together with any other library code that may be necessary.

The second significant problem is that machine code usually has much less semantic information than source code, which makes it much more difficult to discover control flow or data flow information. As an example, even for simple first-order programs, determining the extent of a jump table in an executable file, and hence the possible targets of the code derived from a `case` or `switch` statement, can be difficult when dealing with executables; at the source level, by contrast, the corresponding problem is straightforward. Furthermore, compiler analyses are typically carried out on representations of source programs in terms of source language constructs, disregarding "nasty" features such as pointer arithmetic and out-of-bounds array accesses. At the level of executable code, on the other hand, all we have are the nasty features. Nontrivial pointer arithmetic is ubiquitous, both for ordinary address computations and for manipulating tagged pointers. If the number of arguments to a function is large enough, some of the arguments may have to be passed on the stack. In such a case, the arguments passed on the stack will typically reside at the top of the caller's stack frame, and the callee will "reach into" the caller's frame to access them: this is nothing but an out-of-bounds array reference.

Matters are made worse by the interaction between these two problems. One might imagine, for example, that it might be possible to compensate for the lack of semantic information in executable code by using highly sophisticated and precise program analysis techniques. Unfortunately, this is usually not a practical option because of the large size of most executable programs. The result is that, in order to be practically usable, we are sometimes forced to resort to simple algorithms or rely on specific code idioms (e.g., to determine which register is being used as the stack pointer). This, in turn, can cause us to miss some optimizations in some situations.

An important issue that arises when a system relies on specific code idioms is that of the treatment of programs that do not follow such idioms. To our knowledge, at this time the only fundamental assumption that `alto` makes about input programs is that they do not carry out address arithmetic with code addresses (address arithmetic involving data addresses is not a problem). The reason for this is that the optimizing transformations carried out by `alto` almost inevitably result in changes to code addresses, and this can cause the program to behave incorrectly if it carries out nontrivial arithmetic involving such addresses. It should be noted that this assumption is not particular to `alto`, but is fundamental to most tools that rewrite executable files, e.g., instrumentation tools such as *pixie* and *atom*. Because of this assumption, it turns out that the current version of `alto` is unable to process executables generated by some functional language implementations, such as Objective Caml [13]. For other idioms, `alto` generally checks to identify program components that do not adhere to the conventions and idioms it recognizes, e.g., with regard to aliasing behavior on the runtime stack, treatment of callee-saved registers, etc. Such code is treated in a safe but conservative way, which is to say that they may not be optimized as much as those that do follow the idioms `alto` recognizes.

3 System Organization

The execution of `alto` can be divided into five phases. In the first phase, an executable file (containing relocation information for its objects) is read in, and an initial, somewhat conservative, inter-procedural control flow graph is constructed. In the second phase, a suite of analyses and optimizations is then applied iteratively to the program. The activities during this phase can be broadly divided into three categories:

Simplification : Program code is simplified in three ways: dead and unreachable code is eliminated; operations are normalized, so that different ways of expressing the same operation (e.g., clearing a register) are rewritten, where possible, to use the same operation; and no-ops, typically inserted for scheduling and alignment purposes, are eliminated to reduce clutter.

Analysis : A number of analyses are carried out during this phase, including register liveness analysis, constant propagation, and jump table analysis.

Optimization : Optimizations carried out during this phase include standard compiler optimizations such as peephole optimization, branch forwarding, copy propagation, and code motion out of loops; machine-level optimizations such as elimination of unnecessary register saves and restores at function call boundaries; architecture-specific optimizations such as the use of conditional move instructions to simplify control flow; as well as improvements to the control flow graph based on the results of jump table analysis.

This is followed by a function inlining phase. The fourth phase repeats the optimizations carried out in the second phase to the code resulting from inlining. The final phase carries out profile-directed code layout [12], instruction scheduling, and insertion of no-ops for alignment purposes, after which the code is written out.

4 Program Optimization

The optimizations carried out by `alto` are typically guided by information about the program's execution profile as well as the availability of machine level resources such as registers and cache. Interactions between these optimizations often have synergistic effects that can lead to unexpected improvements in the code. Here we discuss a few of the most important optimizations used.

4.1 Inlining

Traditionally, compilers for high level languages such as Prolog carry out inlining at, or close to, the level of the source program. At this level, the primary benefits of inlining come from specializing and simplifying the inlined procedure, e.g., by evaluating conditionals and pruning away code that becomes unreachable. Control of code growth during inlining, when implemented, is usually carried out via syntax-driven techniques, ranging from simple syntax-directed estimates of the size of the callee [2,3,11] to more refined estimates based on the residual size of the callee after specializing it to the call site under consideration [17].

At link time, by contrast, it is reasonable to expect that considerable amounts of inlining have already been carried out by the compiler. This means that it seems unlikely that link-time inlining will give rise to large amounts of code simplification and pruning, though some code simplification might occur due to the propagation of constant arguments into library routines or because of inlining across source-level language boundaries. On the other hand, more accurate information is available about object code size, making it easier to consider the effects of inlining on the instruction cache utilization of a program.

The motivations for carrying out inlining within `alto` are primarily to reduce or eliminate various overheads associated with procedure calls. This is especially important because, as mentioned earlier, existing compiler technology cannot be relied upon to do a good job of reducing or eliminating such overheads for a call from a procedure written in one language to one written in another. Code growth due to inlining is controlled in `alto` as follows: a function is inlined into a call site only if at least one of the following conditions holds:

(*i*) the call site under consideration is the only call site for that function;
(*ii*) the body of the called function is small enough that there is no net increase in code size after it has been inlined; or
(*iii*) the call site is "hot," i.e., has a sufficiently high execution count, and (`alto`'s estimate of) the cache footprint of the resulting code does not exceed the size of the instruction cache.

Inlining in the presence of higher order functions has typically been accomplished using sophisticated control flow analyses [11]. We believe that such analyses are too expensive to be practical at the level of machine code. Instead, we use a simple profile-guided inlining technique we call *guarded inlining* to achieve similar results. The basic idea behind this transformation is very simple. Suppose we have an indirect function call whose target we are unable to resolve. We use profiling to identify the frequencies of the various targets at each such indirect call. Suppose that the most frequent target is a function f at address $addr_0$. With guarded inlining, we insert code to test whether the target address is $addr_0$: if this is the case, execution drops through into the inlined code for f; otherwise, an indirect function call occurs, as before. It's not too difficult to see, in fact, that in general the transformation can be adapted to any indirect branch. This mechanism allows us to get the benefits of inlining even for call sites that can, in fact, have multiple possible targets, in contrast to schemes that require control flow analysis to identify a unique target for a call site before inlining can take place [11].

4.2 Memory Access Optimizations

We use an intra-basic-block transformation we call *register forwarding* to reduce the number of unnecessary loads from memory. The opportunity for this optimization arises because, in the course of other optimizations such as the elimination of unreachable code, register reassignment and elimination of unnecessary register saves and restores at function boundaries, etc., `alto` is able to free up registers that can then be reused for other purposes. In the simplest case, a register $\mathtt{r}_a$ is stored to a memory location $addr_0$, and a register $\mathtt{r}_b$ subsequently loaded from that address, with no redefinition of

$\mathtt{r}_a$ in between. In this case, assuming that we can verify that the contents of location $addr_0$ have also not been modified, register forwarding replaces the load operation by a register-to-register move from $\mathtt{r}_a$:

```
store ra, addr0                 store ra, addr0
...                  ⇒          ...
load rb, addr0                  move ra, rb
```

In general, register $\mathtt{r}_a$ may be modified after it has been stored to location $addr_0$ but before $\mathtt{r}_b$ is loaded from that location. In this case (again assuming that location $addr_0$ can be guaranteed to not have been modified), if there is a free register $\mathtt{r}_{tmp}$, it can be used to save the original value of $\mathtt{r}_a$ before $\mathtt{r}_a$ is modified, and eventually moved over to $\mathtt{r}_b$.

In order to guarantee that the memory location $addr_0$ is not modified between the initial store of $\mathtt{r}_a$ to it and the subsequent load into $\mathtt{r}_b$, we verify that any intervening stores to memory write to locations other than $addr_0$. For this, we use a slight generalization of a technique called *instruction inspection*, commonly used in compile-time instruction schedulers. we first carry out interprocedural constant propagation to identify references to global addresses. The memory disambiguation analysis then proceeds as follows: two memory reference instructions i_1 and i_2 in a basic block can be guaranteed to not refer to the same memory location if one of the following holds:

1. one of the instructions uses a register known to point to the stack and the other uses a register known to point to a global address; or
2. i_1 and i_2 use addresses computed into registers r_1 and r_2 respectively, and there are two (possibly empty) chains of instructions whose effects are to compute the value $c_1 + \mathit{contents\_of}(r_0)$ into register r_1 and $c_2 + \mathit{contents\_of}(r_0)$ into r_2, for some register r_0, such that the two chains do not use different definitions of r_0 in the basic block under consideration, and $c_1 \neq c_2$.

4.3 Unreachable Code Elimination

In compilers, unreachable code—i.e., code that will never be executed—typically arises due to user constructs (such as debugging statements that are turned off by setting a flag) or as a result of other optimizations, and is usually detected and eliminated using intra-procedural analysis. By contrast, unreachable code that is detected at link time usually has very different origins: most of it is due to the inclusion of irrelevant library routines, together with some code that can be identified as unreachable due to the propagation of actual parameter values into a function. In either case, link-time identification of unreachable code is fundamentally interprocedural in nature.

Even though unreachable code can never be executed, its elimination is desirable for a number of reasons:

1. It reduces the amount of code that the link-time optimizer needs to process, and can lead to significant improvements in the amount of time and memory used.
2. It can enable optimizations that otherwise might not have been enabled, such as bringing two basic blocks closer together, allowing for more efficient control transfer instructions to be used, or allowing for a more precise liveness analysis which might trigger several other optimizations.
3. The elimination of unreachable code can reduce the amount of "cache pollution" by unreachable code that is loaded into the cache when nearby reachable code is executed. This, in turn, can improve the overall cache behavior of the program.

Unreachable code analysis involves a straightforward depth-first traversal of the control flow graph, and is performed as soon as the control flow graph of the program has been computed. Initially, all basic blocks are marked as dead, and then basic blocks are marked reachable if they can be reached by another block that is reachable. The entry point of the program is always reachable. This analysis also makes use of context information as a basic block that follows a function call will be marked reachable if the corresponding call site is reachable, rather than the function that is called as the function could already be reachable due to a call from another call site.

For the set of benchmark programs we tested, on the average about 10% of the instructions were found to be unreachable. This is somewhat higher than the results of Srivastava, whose estimate of the amount of unreachable code in C and Fortran programs was about 4%–6% [16].

4.4 Code Layout

When `alto` creates the interprocedural control flow graph for a program, all unconditional branches are eliminated. The responsibity of the code layout phase is to arrange the basic blocks in the program into a linear sequence, reintroducing unconditional branches where necessary. There are three important issues that should be considered when determining the linear arrangement of basic blocks:

1. ***Branch mispredict penalties***: During the execution of a conditional branch, instructions are fetched from memory before the branch target has been determined in order to keep the instruction pipeline full and hide memory latencies. In order to do this, the CPU "predicts"—i.e., guesses—the target of the branch. If the guess is wrong, the instructions in the pipeline fetched from the incorrectly predicted target have to be discarded, and instructions from the actual target have to be fetched. The execution cost associated with an incorrect prediction is referred to as a branch mispredict penalty.
   Older processors often use static branch prediction schemes, e.g., where backward branches are predicted as taken and forward branches as not

taken. For such processors the benefit of a careful basic block layout is obvious. More modern CPUs, such as the Alpha 21164 used in our experiments, use history-based dynamic branch prediction schemes in the hardware, and result in code where branch misprediction penalties are much less sensitive to code layout. For this reason, `alto` does not consider this issue in determining code layout.

2. ***Control flow change penalty:*** Since instruction fetching precedes instruction decoding in the instruction pipeline, a change in control flow causes the fetch performed while decoding the instruction causing the control flow change to be wasted, thereby incurring a small performance penalty. Note that this is different from the branch mispredict penalty discussed above, since this penalty is incurred even for an unconditional branch, which can always be correctly predicted. A change in control flow also increases the possibility of a miss in the instruction cache. This suggests that for code layout, unconditional branches should be avoided where possible, and conditional branches should be oriented so that the fall-through path is more likely than the branch-taken path.
3. ***Instruction cache conflicts:*** Because modern CPUs are significantly faster than memory, delivering instructions to them is a major bottle neck. A high hit-rate of the instruction cache is therefore essential. Primary instruction caches typically are relatively small in size and have low associativity, in order to improve speed. This makes it advantageous to lay out the basic blocks in a program in such a way that frequently executed blocks are positioned close to each other, since this is less likely to lead to cache conflicts [12].

Alto implements two code layout schemes, one that exploits profiling information while the other does not. If no execution profile is available, `alto` attempts maintain the original code layout in the input program is preserved as closely as possible, and also to reduce the number of unconditional branches as far as possible. If profiling information is available, our primary goal is to reduce cache conflicts as far as possible. The code layout algorithm proceeds by grouping the basic blocks in a program into three sets: The *hot set* consists of the frequently executed blocks in the program; the *zero set* contains all the basic blocks that were never executed; and The *cold set* contains the remaining basic blocks. We then compute the layout separately for each set and concatenate the three resulting layouts to obtain the overall program layout. Our layout algorithm follows the (bottom-up positioning) approach of Pettis and Hansen [12], with minor modifications to address the problems identified by Calder and Grunwald [5].

The performance impact of profile-directed code layout is greatest in large programs where careful code organization is necessary to fully utilize the instruction cache. For many such programs, we see performance improvements of around 15% resulting from profile-directed code layout alone.

5 Performance Results

We did not have any explicitly multi-lingual programs, i.e., where different user modules were written in different languages. We therefore tested our link-time optimizer on programs written in a variety of different languages. In many cases, however, the resulting programs are effectively multi-lingual, e.g., as in the case of Prolog and Scheme programs where many of the libraries, as well as the runtime system, garbage collector, etc., are written in C. Note that in this situation, the Prolog or Scheme compiler will not be able to carry out optimizations such as inlining code from the runtime system into a point in the user program, while the C compiler that compiled the runtime system will not be able to tailor it to a particular Prolog or Scheme program; thus, at link-time we are able to exploit optimization opportunities that are not available at compile time.

The results of our experiments are shown in Tables 1—4. The timings were obtained on a lightly loaded DEC Alpha workstation with a 300 MHz Alpha 21164 processor with a split primary cache (8 Kbytes each of instruction and data cache), 96 Kbytes of on-chip secondary cache, 2 Mbytes of off-chip backup cache, and 512 Mbytes of main memory, running Digital Unix 4.0. The programs were compiled with a high level of optimization (see below); the resulting executables were instrumented using `pixie` to obtain an execution profile that was provided to `alto`, which was invoked with default switches together with a flag to use this profile information. The execution times for the original executables is given under the column labelled "Base" (T_{base}), while the times for the executables produced by `alto` are reported in the column labelled `alto` (T_{alto}). In each case, the execution time reported is the smallest time of 10 runs. The column labelled T_{alto}/T_{base} gives the improvement obtained from using `alto`.

5.1 C Programs

The benchmarks we used to test the effect of `alto` on C programs were the eight programs in the SPEC-95 integer benchmark suite: *compress*, a file compression program; *gcc*, a C compiler; *go*, a game playing program; *ijpeg*, a JPEG image compression program; *li*, a Lisp interpreter; *m88ksim*, a simulator for the Motorola 88100 microprocessor; *perl*, a Perl interpreter; and *vortex*, an object-oriented database program. The execution times reported are for the SPEC reference inputs; the profile inputs used were the SPEC training inputs. For processing by `alto`, the programs were compiled with the DEC C compiler V5.2-036 invoked as `cc -O4`, with linker options to retain relocation information and to produce statically linked executables. It can be seen, from Table 1, that for most programs tested, the use of `alto` led to significant improvements in performance, with an average improvement of over 17%.

Program	*Execution Time* (sec)		T_{alto}/T_{base}
	Base (T_{base})	alto (T_{alto})	
compress	280.46	263.57	0.940
gcc	266.93	221.91	0.831
go	342.77	319.35	0.932
ijpeg	338.18	327.32	0.968
li	314.79	261.65	0.831
m88ksim	325.91	221.90	0.681
perl	236.75	186.30	0.787
vortex	465.92	331.36	0.711
Geometric Mean:			0.829

Table 1. Performance results: C Programs

5.2 Fortran Programs

The Fortran benchmarks we used were the ten SPEC-95 floating point benchmarks: *applu* is a solver for certain kinds of partial differential equations; *apsi* solves for characteristics of atmospheric distribution of pollutants; *fpppp* is a quantum chemistry benchmark; *hydro2d* is an astrophysics application to compute galactic jets; *mgrid* is a multigrid solver for a three-dimensional potential field; *su2cor* is a quantum physics application that computes elementary particle masses; *swim* is a weather prediction program that solves shallow water equations; *tomcatv* is a vectorized mesh generation program; *turb3d* is a turbulence simulation program; and *wave5* is a simulation program to study plasma phenomena. The programs were compiled with the DEC Fortran compiler version 3.8, invoked as `f77 -O4`, with additional with linker options to retain relocation information and to produce statically linked executables. The performance numbers for these programs are reported in Table 2. The improvements in speed, averaging just under 4%, are the smallest of all the different languages we considered. We believe this is due to two factors: first, there was very little modularization in these programs—typically each benchmark would consist of one or two source files—and second, Fortran language restrictions, particularly with regard to aliasing through arguments to procedures, made it easier for the compiler to generate good code without having to resort to inter-procedural or inter-module analysis.

5.3 Scheme Programs

To evaluate `alto` on Scheme programs, we used Bigloo version 1.8, by Serrano [15]. Our experiments were run using nine commonly used Scheme benchmarks: *boyer*, a term-rewriting theorem prover; *conform* is a type checker, written by J. Miller; *dynamic*, an implementation of a tagging optimization algorithm for Scheme [8], applied to itself; *earley* is an implementation of

Program	Execution Time (sec)		T_{alto}/T_{base}
	Base (T_{base})	alto (T_{alto})	
applu	358.67	357.57	0.997
apsi	207.11	194.48	0.939
fpppp	457.32	418.23	0.914
hydro2d	440.29	425.89	0.967
mgrid	345.25	339.87	0.984
su2cor	225.05	216.99	0.964
swim	274.50	264.99	0.965
tomcatv	295.46	283.10	0.958
turb3d	349.77	336.24	0.961
wave5	230.12	223.69	0.972
Geometric Mean:			0.961

Table 2. Performance results: Fortran Programs

Earley's parsing algorithm, by Marc Feeley; *graphs*, a program that counts the number of directed graphs with a distinguished root and k vertices each having out-degree at most 2; *lattice* enumerates the lattice of maps between two lattices; *matrix* tests whether a given random matrix is maximal among all matrices of the same dimension obtainable via a set of simple transformations of the original matrix; *nucleic* is a floating-point intensive program to determine nucleic acid structure; and *scheme* is a Scheme interpreter by Marc Feeley. We considered only compiled systems, and restricted ourselves to compilers that translated Scheme programs to C code, because `alto` requires relocation information to reconstruct the control flow graph from an executable program, which means that the linker needs to be invoked with the appropriate flags that instruct it to not discard the relocation information; systems that compiled to C seemed to offer the simplest way to communicate the appropriate flags to the linker. The Bigloo compiler was invoked with the options `-O4 -unsafe -farithmetic -cgen`, except for the *nucleic* program, for which the options used were `-O3 -unsafesv -cgen`. The resulting C programs were compiled as described in Section 5.1. The profiling inputs used were the same as that used for the actual benchmarking.

Again, `alto` produces significant improvements for all of the benchmarks used, which achieve increases in speed ranging from 10% for *earley* to almost 28% for *nucleic*, with an average improvement of a little over 15%.

5.4 Prolog Programs

To evaluate `alto` on Prolog programs we used `wamcc` v2.21, by Codognet and Diaz [6]. The programs were compiled with the option `-fast_math`, and the resulting C code compiled using *gcc* version 2.7.2.2 at optimization level `-O2`, with additional flags to produce a statically linked executable and retain re-

Program	*Execution Time* (sec)		T_{alto}/T_{base}
	Base (T_{base})	`alto` (T_{alto})	
boyer	9.96	8.77	0.881
conform	3.79	3.11	0.821
dynamic	3.86	3.41	0.883
earley	8.42	7.58	0.900
graphs	11.98	9.86	0.823
lattice	18.59	16.35	0.880
matrix	21.42	18.09	0.845
nucleic	17.56	12.66	0.721
scheme	21.68	19.20	0.886
Geometric Mean:			0.847

Table 3. Performance results: Scheme Programs

location information. The resulting executables were profiled using the same inputs as were used for the actual benchmarking. We used eight benchmarks from the `wamcc` distribution: *boyer*, a term-rewriting theorem prover; *chat*, a small database with a natural language front end; *nand*, a logic synthesis program; *poly10*, a program for symbolic manipulation of polynomials; *reducer*, a combinator graph reduction program; *sendmore*, a cryptarithmetic puzzle; *tak*, a small, heavily recursive, program; and *zebra*, a logical puzzle based on constraints.

As can be seen from Table 4, `alto` produces significant performance improvements. The overall improvement is about 26% on the average, and several programs experience improvements exceeding 30%.

Program	*Execution Time* (sec)		T_{alto}/T_{base}
	Base (T_{base})	`alto` (T_{alto})	
boyer	23.33	16.05	0.688
chat	20.97	15.18	0.724
nand	20.79	14.31	0.688
poly10	20.99	14.13	0.673
reducer	19.05	13.82	0.725
sendmore	19.12	14.74	0.771
tak	21.00	18.79	0.895
zebra	22.26	16.95	0.761
Geometric Mean:			0.738

Table 4. Performance results: Prolog Programs

6 Discussion

The optimization of executable programs raises the question of whether or not the fact that the source modules for the application may have been written in different languages is still relevant at the level of machine language. It turns out that the dynamic low-level characteristics of programs *can* be very different, depending on the source languages they were written in. To some extent, this is a direct function of the sorts of application domain a language tends to be used for: for example, one would expect the proportion of floating point instructions executed in a representative suite of Fortran programs to far exceed that in a set of Prolog programs. It also depends greatly on source language features such as static vs. dynamic typing, garbage collection, etc. For example, our experiments comparing the Scheme programs considered in Section 5.3 with the C programs of Section 5.1 reveal significant low level differences:

- the proportion of memory operations in Scheme programs is 2.5 times larger than in C programs, presumably because of the use of dynamic data structures such as lists, which are harder to keep in registers, and due to garbage collection;
- the proportion of indirect jumps is three times higher in Scheme programs than in C code, due to the treatment of tail call optimization; and
- the proportion of conditional jumps in Scheme programs is close to double that in C programs, due at least in part to runtime dispatch operations on type tags.

Since Prolog is very similar to Scheme in terms of being a dynamically typed language with garbage collection and tail call optimization, we expect similar low level characteristics for Prolog programs as well. As another example of the influence of source language features on low level dynamic characteristics of programs, Calder and Grunwald find that C++ programs have a much higher proportion of indirect function calls than C programs, because of the way virtual function calls are implemented in C++ [4]. Such low-level differences have a profound effect on the kinds of information that are propagated, and the kinds of optimizations that are useful, during link-time optimization. Differences in the low-level characteristics of programs can also arise due to differences between compilers for the same source language, or because of different compilation options (e.g., for the optimization level) used for a particular compiler, though our experience suggests that programs compiled with different compilers, but subjected to comparable levels of optimization, tend to exhibit more or less similar low level characteristics. Link-time optimization can nevertheless be used to improve the performance of programs where different components may have been compiled with different compilers, e.g., the source programs with *gcc* but libraries with a vendor's in-house version of *cc*.

Another question, motivated by the difficulty of extracting semantic information from machine code, as discussed in Section 2, is whether it might be possible to carry out inter-module and inter-language optimizations by appropriately augmenting existing compiler technology. For example, one possibility, suggested by M. Hermenegildo [9], would be to have each different compiler used in a multi-lingual application generate interface files describing properties of the code it is compiling. These interface files could then be used to optimize the code that interacts with other compilation units, which might be other modules or possibly other components written in other languages. This idea is appealing because it allows optimization to take place at a level where semantic information has not been obscured by the translation to executable code, thereby making it possible to potentially achieve higher levels of optimization. A similar approach, though applied only to cross-module analysis and optimization for mono-lingual programs, has been used in the R^n programming environment [7]. The main problem with such an approach is that usually, the kinds of properties a compiler reasons about—and hence maintains information about in its data structures—are closely tied to the semantics of the source language it is compiling. For example, a compiler for an object-oriented language might be interested in aspects relating to inheritance and method dispatch, while one for a logic programming language might want to know about groundness and backtracking behavior. This suggests that devising a common set of properties of interest for compilers of different languages, and orchestrating the requisite degree of cooperation between them, may not be straightforward. It is also not clear whether such an approach would be able to accommodate optimizations such as inlining across language boundaries, or realize low level optimizations such as profile-directed code layout (Section 4.4). Nevertheless, the possibility of carrying out inter-language optimizations at a relatively high level is an intriguing one.

7 Conclusions

We believe that it is unrealistic to expect real application programs to be written entirely in logic programming languages. However, current implementation techniques incur a nontrivial performance penalty in crossing language boundaries. This penalty can be reduced by carrying out optimizations on executable code at link time. This article describes our experiences using `alto`, a link time optimizer for the DEC Alpha architecture that we have developed. Our experiments indicate that, for programs written in a variety of languages, `alto` is able to provide significant improvements in performance, even for programs that have been compiled with high levels of compile-time optimization.

Acknowledgements

The author is grateful to Manuel Hermenegildo for helpful comments on an earlier version of this paper. This work was supported in part by the National Science Foundation under grants CCR-9502826 and CCR 9711166.

References

1. A. V. Aho, R. Sethi and J. D. Ullman, *Compilers – Principles, Techniques and Tools*, Addison-Wesley, 1986.
2. J. M. Ashley, "The Effectiveness of Flow Analysis for Inlining", *Proc. 1997 SIGPLAN International Conference on Functional Programming*, June 1997, pp. 99–111.
3. M. Blume and A. W. Appel, "Lambda-splitting: A Higher-Order Approach to Cross-Module Optimizations", *Proc. 1997 SIGPLAN International Conference on Functional Programming*, June 1997, pp. 112–124.
4. B. Calder and D. Grunwald, "Reducing Indirect Function Call Overhead in C++ Programs", *Proc. 21st ACM Symposium on Principles of Programming Languages*, Jan. 1994, pp. 397–408.
5. B. Calder and D. Grunwald, "Reducing Branch Costs via Branch Alignment", *6th International Conference on Architectural Support for Programming Languages and Operating Systems*, October 1994, pp. 242–251.
6. P. Codognet and D. Diaz, "wamcc: Compiling Prolog to C", *Proc. Twelfth International Conference on Logic Programming*, June 1995, pp. 317–332. MIT Press.
7. K. D. Cooper, K. Kennedy, and L. Torczon, "The Impact of Interprocedural Analysis and Optimization on the Design of a Software Development Environment", Technical Report COMP TR84-6, Dept. of Computer Science, Rice University, Houston, Texas, 1984.
8. F. Henglein, "Global Tagging Optimization by Type Inference", *Proc. 1992 ACM Symposium on Lisp and Functional Programming*, pp. 205–215.
9. M. Hermenegildo, personal communication, Nov. 1998.
10. S. Jagannathan and A. Wright, "Effective Flow Analysis for Avoiding Run-Time Checks", *Proc. 1995 Static Analysis Symposium* (SAS '95), Sept. 1995.
11. S. Jagannathan and A. Wright, "Flow-directed Inlining", *Proc. SIGPLAN '96 Conference on Programming Language Design and Implementation*, May 1996, pp. 193–205.
12. K. Pettis and R. C. Hansen, "Profile-Guided Code Positioning", *Proc. SIGPLAN '90 Conference on Programming Language Design and Implementation*, June 1990, pp. 16–27.
13. X. Leroy, "The Effectiveness of Type-Based Unboxing", *Workshop on Types in Compilation '97*, Amsterdam, 1997.
14. V. Santhanam and D. Odnert, "Register Allocation across Procedure and Module Boundaries", *Proc. SIGPLAN '90 Conference on Programming Language Design and Implementation*, June 1990, pp. 28–39
15. M. Serrano and P. Weis, "Bigloo: a portable and optimizing compiler for strict functional languages" *Proc. Static Analysis Symposium (SAS '95)*, 1995, pp. 366–381.

16. A. Srivastava, "Unreachable Procedures in Object-Oriented Programming", *ACM Letters on Programming Languages and Systems* vol. 1 no. 4, Dec. 1992, pp. 355–364.
17. O. Waddell and R. K. Dybvig, "Fast and Effective Procedure Inlining", *Proc. 1997 Static Analysis Symposium* (SAS '97), Sept. 1997, pp. 35–52. Springer-Verlag LNCS vol. 1302.

Horn Logic Denotations and Their Applications

Gopal Gupta

Laboratory for Logic, Databases, and Advanced Programming,
Department of Computer Science, New Mexico State University,
Box 30001/CS, Las Cruces, New Mexico, USA 88003

Summary. In spite of decades of work, the practical impact of programming language semantics (denotational semantics) has been limited. Our thesis is that a major contributing factor to this lack of practical impact is the declarative notation used for expressing the semantics, namely, the λ-calculus. We propose to use Horn Logic (and eventually Constraint Logic) instead of the λ-calculus to express denotational semantics. This simple change leads to many practical applications, most notably to automatic program verification and automatic generation of compilers from semantics specifications. These Horn Logic denotations and their applications are discussed at length in this paper.

1 Introduction

There has been decades of work in programming language semantics, however, the practical impact of this area has been limited [40]. The reason is the different types of semantics that have been advocated—operational semantics, denotational semantics, and axiomatic semantics—that use different notations and that are designed for different types of users (language designers, implementors, programmers, etc.). Also, these different semantics are specified in a non-executable or only partially executable notation. Often, as Schmidt notes [40], formal semantics (especially denotational semantics) is mired in complex mathematics: "domain theory, intuitionistic type theory, category theory, linear logic, process algebra, continuation-passing style, or whatever" [40]. To quote him further: "formal semantics has fed upon increasing complexity of concepts and notation at the expense of *calculational clarity* ... General users desire semantics definitions with strong *calculational flavor*." We believe that this lack of "calculational flavor" has severely hindered the practical applications of programming language semantics. Schmidt offers the following challenge for researchers working in semantics:

> "A challenge for semantics writers is the following: design a calculational semantics for a significant subset of, say, Java, that can be learned and applied by first-year university students to debug their programs. Perhaps such a semantics will use graphical state and small-step transitions upon the state for its calculations, but

calculation upon program properties—that is, a variation on predicate transformer semantics—is also a possibility. In any case, it is crucial that the formulation be "mathematical" in the sense that denotational semantics was first termed mathematical: there must be an underlying consistent proof theory. And of course, the semantics should be some form of extension of BNF."

In this paper we present a simple solution to providing this "calculational clarity" to formal semantics. Our solution has all the characteristics that Schmidt requires a "popular" semantics to possess. Our simple solution [14] is to change the notation used for expressing denotational semantics: instead of the traditional λ-calculus, we propose to use *Horn Logic* (and eventually constraint logic [21]) as the language for specifying semantics. Horn logic is the basis of logic programming and the Prolog language [42]. By using Horn logic as the language for writing semantics, all three semantics—operational, denotational, and axiomatic—can be expressed in the same notation that is also executable, leading to myriad applications:

- Given that the syntax of a language, $\mathcal{L}$, can be expressed as a Definite Clause Grammar [42], the syntax of $\mathcal{L}$ can also be specified as a Horn Logic Program. Because the syntax and semantics of $\mathcal{L}$ are both expressed in Horn Logic, both are executable—the syntax specification yields a parser for $\mathcal{L}$, the semantics specification yields the back-end of an interpreter for $\mathcal{L}$.
- Given this executable syntax and semantics specification, various operational semantics for $\mathcal{L}$ can be obtained by choosing an appropriate Horn Logic selection function. Choosing an operational semantics yields an interpreter for $\mathcal{L}$ (according to that operational semantics).
- Partial evaluation of the interpreter (using a partial evaluator, such as Mixtus [36]) w.r.t. to a given program, $\mathcal{P}$ (written in $\mathcal{L}$), yields "compiled code" for $\mathcal{P}$. Provably correct compiled code is thus automatically obtained from the semantics specification.
- By using a bottom-up evaluation strategy (or a *tabling-based* evaluation strategy [6,37]), the fixpoint of the denotation of a program written in $\mathcal{L}$ can be computed and used for verification purposes.
- The postconditions and preconditions can be inserted in the program's Horn logical denotation and evaluated; by choosing a precondition carefully, and turning it into a *generator*, certain properties of interest of the program can be verified.
- By using evaluation engines other than Prolog, such as those that are tabling-based [6,37], and by choosing abstract semantics, abstract interpreters [10] for a language $\mathcal{L}$ can be automatically obtained from the abstract semantics specification of $\mathcal{L}$.
- By choosing a suitable semantic algebra, and using partial evaluation, abstract machines can be derived and studied for the language in question.

- A formal theory of *semantic porting* is also obtained. If a program written in a language $\mathcal{L}_1$ is to be ported to language $\mathcal{L}_2$, then the denotational semantics of $\mathcal{L}_1$ can be given in terms of $\mathcal{L}_2$. The interpreter obtained by using Horn logic for specifying the syntax (as a DCG) and semantics, is effectively a (formal, provably correct) language translation system.
- Our approach can be used for building executable software specifications. A software system can be thought of as an evaluator of its input language. The denotational semantics specification of this input language is a specification of the software system, and if this specification is executable (as is the case if Horn Logic is used), then a (rapid) prototype implementation of the software is obtained. The executable specification can be used for obtaining efficient implementation as well as for verification.
- Semantics of parallel languages is easily given, as logic programs naturally encapsulate parallelism. Additionally, parallelizing compilers can also be derived from *parallel semantics* of the language.
- By generalizing Horn Logic to Constraint Logic, more complex software systems, e.g., real-time systems, can be elegantly modeled and verified.

The two principal advantages of switching to Horn Logic are: (i) both the syntax and the semantics specification are executable, yielding an interpreter; and, (ii) The logical denotation of a program can also be used for verification. Most of the applications listed above follow from one of the two cases.

2 Logical Denotations

Denotational semantics [38,39,18] of a language has three components:

- *syntax*: specified as a context free grammar;
- *semantic algebra*: these are the basic domains along with associated operations; meaning of a program is expressed in terms of these basic domains.
- *valuation function*: these are mappings from patterns of parse trees and semantic algebras to values in the basic domains in the semantic algebra.

Traditional denotational definitions express syntax in the BNF format, and the semantic algebras and valuation function in the λ-calculus. However, a disadvantage of this approach is that while the semantic algebra and the valuation functions could be easily made executable, syntax checking and generation of parse trees cannot. A parser has to be written (or generated) to do syntax checking and generate parse trees. These parse trees will then be processed by the valuation functions to produce the program's denotation. These two phases constitute an interpreter for the language being defined. An interpreter for a language can be thought of as a specification of its operational semantics, however, using traditional notation (BNF and λ-calculus) it has to be obtained in a complex way.

The reason λ-calculus has been traditionally used for specifying the semantic algebras and valuation functions component of denotational semantics is because when it was first proposed by Scott, functional programming (with its formal basis in λ-calculus) was the only declarative formalism that was available. A declarative computational formalism is needed since the semantics is supposed to be mathematical (declarative), i.e., it should have a "consistent proof theory" [40]. However, today there is another declarative formalism that is available, namely, logic programming (with its formal basis in Horn logic, a subset of predicate logic). The additional advantage that logic programming possesses, among others, is that even syntax can be expressed in it at a very high level, and ***a parser for the language is immediately obtained from the syntax specification.*** Moreover, generation of parse trees requires a trivial extension to the syntax specification. (The parsing and parse tree generation facility of logic programming is described in almost every logic programming textbook, under the heading Definite Clause Grammars). The semantic algebras and valuation functions are also expressed in Horn logic programming quite easily, as relations (or predicates) subsume functions. The semantic algebra and valuation functions are executable, and can be used to obtain executable program denotation. A significant consequence of this is that the fixpoint of a program's denotation can be executed bottom-up (assuming that it is finite), which can then be used for verification. Thus, verification can also be done in the framework of Horn Logic.

Thus, given a language, both its syntax and semantics can be directly specified in logic programming. This specification is executable using any standard logic programming system. What is noteworthy is that different operational models will be obtained both for syntax checking and semantic evaluation by employing different execution strategies during logic program execution. For example, in the syntax phase, if left-to-right, Prolog style, execution rule is used, then recursive descent parsing is obtained. On the contrary, if a ***tabling-based*** [6] execution strategy is used then chart parsing is obtained, etc. Likewise, by using different evaluation rules for evaluating the semantic functions, strict evaluation, non-strict evaluation, etc. can be obtained. By using bottom-up or tabled evaluation, the fixpoint of a program's denotation can be computed, which can be used for verification and structured debugging of the program.

2.1 Discussion

Denotational semantics expressed in a Horn Logic notation is executable. So is denotational semantics expressed in the λ-calculus notation. However, Horn-logic expressed semantics allows for fixed points of programs to be computed much more intuitively, simply, and efficiently than, we believe, in the case of the λ-calculus. There is a whole body of literature and implemented systems (e.g., tabling based systems such as XSB [6]) for computing fixpoints of logic programs because of their applicability to deductive databases [37,25]. Due to this reason, semantics based verification (and program debugging) can be much more easily performed in the Horn Logic denotational framework than using the λ-calculus based denotational framework, as is shown later.

This becomes much more prominent when we generalize Horn Logic to Constraint Logic. This generalization makes specification and verification of very complex systems, e.g., real-time systems considerably easier [12] (it should be noted that the denotational specification and verification of real-time systems using the traditional λ-calculus approach will be quite cumbersome and complex).

One could argue that the denotation or mathematical meaning of a program (which denotational semantics attempts to captures) exists independently of the notation used for expressing it, just as integers exist independent of their representation (base 2, base 10, or whatever). Indeed denotations exist independent of the notation used, however, if we wish to use the denotation (meaning) of a program for some practical purpose, such as automatic derivation of efficient compiled code, verification of program properties, etc., then it has to be expressed symbolically in some form or the other for processing. *The symbolic notation in which the denotation is expressed will determine how easy or difficult this processing is going to be.* To complete the analogy with integers, the binary representation of integers is the most efficient form for realization on computers. Another analogy can be given from the field of Algorithms. In theory, an algorithm exists independently of the notation used to express it. However, in practice, an algorithm expressed in a high-level language is a lot easier to code, understand, and modify compared to one expressed in, say, an assembly language. Our thesis thus is that the notation used for expressing denotation has a tremendous impact on how many further (practical) uses it can be put to, and the ease with which it can be put to these uses.

Denotational semantics expressed as Horn Logic satisfies all the criteria laid out by Schmidt. Horn Logic has a consistent proof theory, and hence various automatic systems can be built for further processing Horn Logic Denotations, e.g., automatic generators of compiled code (including automatic generators of parallel compiled code), automatic program property verifiers, etc. The BNF spirit of denotational semantics is maintained since the meaning is still expressed as maps between parse tree patterns (abstract syntax) and "meaning spaces" (semantic algebras). A strong calculational flavor is present, as Horn Logic is executable, which permits both execution and verification.

Thus, given the Horn Logic Denotational Semantic of a language $\mathcal{L}$, the Horn Logic Denotation of a program written in $\mathcal{L}$ can be computed. This denotation is executable and can be put to many uses which include implementation (obtaining interpreters and compilers) and verification.

2.2 An Example of Logical Denotational Semantics

Consider a very simple subset of a Pascal like language that contains assignment statement, if-then-else, and while-do statement. To keep matters simple, assume that the only possible variable names allowed in the

```
Program ::= C.
C ::= C1;C2 |
      loop while B C endloop while |
      if B then C1 else C2 endif |
      I := E
E ::= N | Identifier | E1 + E2 |
      E1 - E2 | E1 * E2 | (E)
N ::= 0 | 1 | 2 | ... | 9
Identifier ::= w | x | y | z
```

Fig. 1: BNF grammar

program are w, x, y and z, and that the only data-type allowed is integers. Assume, again for simplicity, that constants appearing in the program are only 1 digit long. The context free grammar of this language is given in Figure 1. This BNF is easily transformed into a definite clause grammar (DCG) by a simple change in syntax [42] (plus removal of left-recursion, if a Prolog system is going to be used for its execution).

```
                    SYNTAX:
program(p(X)) --> comm(X), [.].
comm(X) --> comm1(X).
comm(comb(X,Y)) --> comm1(X),[;],comm(Y).
comm1(assign(I,E)) --> id(I),[:=],expn(E).
comm1(ce(X,Y,Z)) --> [if],expn(X),[then], comm(Y),
                          [else], comm(Z), [endif].
comm1(while(B,C)) --> [loop, while], bool(B),
                      comm(C), [endloop, while].
expn1(id(X)) --> id(X).
expn1(num(X)) --> n(X).
expn1(e(X)) --> ['('],expn(X),[')'].
expn(X) --> expn1(X).
expn(add(X,Y)) --> expn1(X),[+],expn(Y).
expn(sub(X,Y)) --> expn1(X),[-],expn(Y).
expn(multi(X,Y)) --> expn1(X),[*],expn(Y).
bool(equal(X,Y)) --> expn(X),[=],expn(Y).
bool(greater(X,Y)) --> expn(X),[>],expn(Y).
bool(less(X,Y)) --> expn(X),[<],expn(Y).
id(x) --> [w].          id(x) --> [x].
id(y) --> [y].          id(z) --> [z].
n(0) --> [0].           ....          n(9) --> [9].
```

Fig. 2: DCG for the BNF above

An extra argument has been added in which the parse-tree is synthesized. The DCG is a logic program, and when executed, a parser is automatically obtained. This parser parses a program in this simple language and produces a parse tree for it. This DCG is shown in Figure 2. Thus, the query to parse the program for computing the value of y^x and placing it in variable z:

```
?- program(P, [z,=,1,;, w,=,x,;,
               loop, while,w,>,0,
                  z,=,z,*,y,;, w,=,w,-,1,
```

```
                endloop, while], []).
```

will parse that program as syntactically correct, and produce the parse tree shown below:

```
P = p(comb(assign(z,num(1)),
    comb(assign(w,id(x)),while(
       greater(id(w),num(0)),
          comb(assign(z,multi(id(z),id(y))),
          assign(w,sub(id(w),num(1))))))))
```

The denotational semantics can be defined next, by expressing the semantic algebra and the valuation functions as logic programs. In the semantic definition, we assume that the input is initially found in variables x and y. The answer is computed and put in variable z. The semantic algebra consists simply of the store domain, realized as an association list of the form [(Id, Value) ...] with operations for creating, accessing, and updating the store, and is given below as a logic program:

```
SEMANTIC ALGEBRA 1:
initialize_store([]).
access(Id,[],0). %return 0 if uninitialized
access(Id,[(Id,Val)|_ ],Val).
access(Id,[_|R],Val) :- access(Id,R,Val).
update(Id,NewV,[],[(Id,NewV)]).
update(Id,NewV,[(Id,_)|R],[(Id,NewV)|R]).
update(Id,NewV,[P|R],[P|R1]) :- update(Id,NewV,R,R1).
```

Next, the valuation functions, that impart meaning to the language are specified, again as logic programs. These valuation functions, or valuation predicates, relate the current store, a parse tree pattern whose meaning is to be specified, and the new store that results on executing the program fragment specified by the parse tree pattern. These valuation predicates are shown in Figure 3; the very first valuation predicate takes the two input values, that are placed in the store locations corresponding to x and y. Once the syntax, semantic algebras, and valuation functions are defined as a logic program, an interpreter is immediately obtained. Now for both parsing and interpreting the program, define the logic program in Figure 4. The predicate main in Figure 4 is the denotation of the exponentiation program.

If the above syntax and semantics rules are loaded in a logic programming system and the query ?- main(5,2,A) for computing the value of 2^5 posed, then the value of A will be computed as 32. Notice that switching to logic programming for specifying denotational semantics results in a complete interpreter. Additionally, the fixpoint of this denotation can be computed and used, for example, for verification and debugging purposes (see later).

```
prog_eval(p(Comm), Val_x, Val_y, Output) :- initialize_store(Store),
      update(x, Val_x, Store, Mst), update(y, Val_y, Mst, Nst),
      comm(Comm, Nst, Pst), access(z, Pst, Output).
comm(comb(C1, C2), Store, Outstore) :- comm(C1, Store, Nstore),
                         comm(C2, Nstore, Outstore).
comm(while(B, C), Store, Outstore) :-
        (bool(B, Store) -> comm(C, Store, Nstore),
           comm(while(B, C), Nstore, Outstore); Outstore=Store).
comm(ce(B, C1, C2), Store, Outstore) :- (bool(B, Store) ->
           comm(C1, Store, Outstore); comm(C2, Store, Outstore)).
comm(assign(I, E), Store, Outstore) :-
       expr(E, Store, Val), update(I, Val, Store, Outstore).
expr(add(E1, E2), Store, Result) :- expr(E1, Store, Val_E1),
       expr(E2, Store, Val_E2), Result is Val_E1+Val_E2.
expr(sub(E1, E2), Store, Result) :- expr(E1, Store, Val_E1),
               expr(E2, Store, Val_E2), Result is Val_E1-Val_E2.
expr(multi(E1, E2), Store, Result) :- expr(E1, Store, Val_E1),
               expr(E2, Store, Val_E2), Result is Val_E1*Val_E2.
expr(id(X), Store, Result) :- access(X, Store, Result).
expr(num(X), _, X).
bool(greater(E1, E2), Store) :- expr(E1, Store, Eval1),
             expr(E2, Store, Eval2), Eval1 > Eval2.
bool(less(E1, E2), Store) :- expr(E1, Store, Eval1),
             expr(E2, Store, Eval2), Eval1 < Eval2.
bool(equal(E1, E2), Store) :- expr(E1, Store, Eval),
             expr(E2, Store, Eval).
```

Fig. 3: Valuation Predicates (with Semantic Algebra 1)

```
main(ValX, ValY, A) :-
    program(P, [z,=,1,;, w,=,x,;,
                 loop, while,w,>,0,
                      z,=,z, *, y, ;,
                      w,=,w,-,1,
                 endloop,while], []),
    prog_eval(P,ValX,ValY,A).
```

Fig. 4: Program Denotation

In the semantics above, we assumed that the store is maintained as an association list (SEMANTIC ALGEBRA 1), which is passed around as an argument. This does not exactly model imperative languages in which the memory store is treated as a global entity. Given that logic programs can support global data structures through their database facility (the `assert` and `retract` built-ins [42]), it is better to model the store as a collection of dynamic facts manipulated using `assert` and `retract`. If we decide to adopt this point of view, *the only change that will take place will be in the store algebra*, which transforms to:

```
SEMANTIC ALGEBRA 2 (globalized):
access(Var,Val) :- (store(Var,Val) -> true; Val = 0).
update(Var,Val) :- retractall(store(Var,_)),
        assert(store(Var,Val)).
```

Now, both the input and the output store arguments can be eliminated in the semantic valuation predicates. While we do use impure features of logic programming in this globalized semantic algebra, it should be noted that these features are restricted to the semantic algebra only. The advantage, however, is that the store argument that threads through the definition of valuation predicates is eliminated.

2.3 Discussion

Note that in the denotational specification, the meaning of the while program was given recursively, rather than using the traditional fixpoint approach [38,39]. This recursive meaning of the while loop preserves the "calculational aspect" of our logical denotational semantics. If one is interested in computing the fix points, then one can compute the fixpoint for the whole program's denotation (rather than compute it for pieces of the program and mix it with the denotation as is done in traditional λ-calculus based approach). In fact, we'd argue that one feature that hinders the "calculational clarity" of traditional λ-calculus based denotational semantics is the mixing of fixpoints and regular functions. As a consequence, the resulting denotation is quite complex, and difficult to reason with and process automatically. Specifying the semantics of the `while` loop recursively will have advantages in automatic compilation, as we will see shortly.

Note also that our semantic definition on two occasions uses impure Prolog: (i) the if-then-else `(p->q;r)` of Prolog has a hidden cut; and the arithmetic built-in `is`. Regarding (i), in most languages (especially in languages we are most interested in, namely, imperative languages and domain specific languages) the condition `p` is deterministic (and, hence, the hidden cut is inconsequential). In such a case, a (bottom-up) declarative semantics can be given to `(p->q;r)`. Thus, for all practical purposes, the if-then-else is declarative, so that the mathematical nature of the logical denotational semantics is not lost. Regarding (ii), the `is/2` arithmetic operator is not declarative, however, if we switch to arithmetic constraints [21] (and constraint logical denotations) to express arithmetic, then this declarativeness is restored.

A concern that one might have is that traditional denotational definitions make extensive use of higher order functions, which do not fit logically in the framework of logic programming. However, it should be noted that higher order functions are not indispensable for expressing denotations (a language without higher order functions can express all computable functions). The use of higher-order functions just makes the denotations more compact. In fact, this compactness and terseness introduced due to higher-order functions sometimes leads to difficult-to-understand semantics specification. Also, the presence of higher-order functions makes automatic processing of denotations (for verification, or compiler generation) extremely difficult. Thus, even though logic programming does not support higher order functions/predicates logically, it is adequate for specifying denotational semantics [48], including continuation semantics. The effect of ***continuation semantics*** is easily achieved, for example, by keeping list of commands still to be executed as an argument of the valuation predicates [38,14].

The main advantage of denotational semantics is that there exist powerful proof rules for reasoning about program equality and program properties: the principal of extensionality and fixed-point induction [38]. It would appear that these would have to be abandoned on switching to Horn Clause Denotations. However, this is not true. The principle of extensionality and fixed point induction are independent of the notation used for coding the denotation. Two predicates are the same if their fixpoints are identical (if the fixpoints are identical then essentially, for every possible input combination both predicates evaluate to true, which is essentially the principal of extensionality). Likewise, fixpoint induction applies equally well to Horn Logic Denotations. The fixpoint semantics of Horn logic programs is expressed using the T_p operator [25] (which is essentially the same as the functionals used in defining fixpoints of functions). To prove a property $\mathcal{P}$ for a predicate p one will have to show that $\mathcal{P}$ holds for $T_p \uparrow 0$ (which is essentially equivalent to the base case of fixpoint induction where one has to show that the property holds for $\lambda n.\bot$), and then show that if $\mathcal{P}$ holds for $T_p \uparrow n$ then it also holds for $T_p \uparrow (n+1)$ (which essentially carries out the induction step of the fixpoint induction). The fixpoint theory of logic programs is an extensively researched subject in the deductive database and logic programming community [45,3,37,6]. Efficient fixpoint computation engines such as XSB exist [6], and have been used for verification and model checking [33].

It is possible that one could dismiss Horn Logic Denotations as "Prolog coded interpreters," however, the uses to which these "Prolog coded interpreters" can be put to are many. If nothing else, our work demonstrates how such a "Prolog coded interpreter" can be systematically derived using a denotational approach and easily used for facilitating the task of verification/debugging, automatically obtaining efficient implementation, compilation, abstract interpretation, interoperation, etc. In fact, use of denotational definitions for the purpose of proving properties of programs is virtually non-existent, though this is one area where denotational semantics should be extensively used. The use of semantics for automatically proving properties of programs is one major research direction our research hopes to highlight [12,15,33].

One could argue that Horn Logic Denotations really represents operational semantics and not (declarative) denotational semantics. Two points could be made regarding this argument: (i) *implementational denotational semantics* have been proposed in the past as a means of incorporating operational concepts into denotational semantics [32]. One could argue that implementational denotational semantics are best represented in Horn Logic. (ii) A Horn Logic specification is declarative, in that any selection function [25] can be chosen to evaluate a Horn logic program. As we will see, for some applications (e.g., compilation) SLD resolution is better suited, while for certain others (e.g., verification) bottom-up evaluation is more appropriate.

3 Provably Correct Compilation

We next show the first application of a program's logical denotation: automatic generation of compiled code using simple techniques such as partial evaluation. Producing a true compiler generator has been a long quest for researchers in compiler theory and programming language semantics. While research in parser generators is very mature, research in back-end generators is not. It is well known in partial evaluation [20] that compiled code for a program $\mathcal{P}$ written in language $\mathcal{L}$ can be obtained by partially evaluating $\mathcal{P}$ w.r.t. the interpreter for $\mathcal{L}$. We have already obtained an interpreter for the language from its denotational specification. Removal of the semantic algebra for the store from our definition, followed by partial evaluation of the interpreter w.r.t. the program for computing y^x, results in "compiled" code. Our goal is to treat the semantic algebra operations as primitives, and hide their implementation from the partial evaluator. Using the Mixtus partial evaluation system from SICS [36], the program that results after partially evaluating the query `?- main(5,2,A)` from the previous section (using SEMANTIC ALGEBRA 1) is shown in Figure 5.

```
main(5,2,A) :-
       initialize_store(B),
       update(a,5,B,C),
       update(b,2,C,D),
       update(z,1,D,E),
       access(x,E,F),
       update(w,F,E,G),
       commandwhile(G,H),
       access(z,H,A).
commandwhile(A,B) :-
      (access(w,A,C),
       0<C -> access(z,A,D),
          access(y,A,E),
          F is D*E,
          update(z,F,A,G),
          access(w,G,H),
          I is H-1,
          update(w,I,G,J),
          commandwhile(J,B)
        ; B=A ).
```

Fig. 5: Compiled code

The resulting program is very similar to compiled code. Essentially, a series of memory `access`, memory `update`, arithmetic and comparison operations are left, that correspond to `load`, `store`, arithmetic, and comparison operations of a machine language. The while-loop, whose meaning was expressed using recursion, will (always) partially evaluate to a *tail-recursive* program. These tail-recursive calls are easily converted to iterative structures using jumps. Note that the update and access operations are also parameterized on the store name (in contrast, load and store operations of any machine architecture do not take the whole store as an argument). This parameter can easily be eliminated through globalization [38] (in fact, if we rewrote our valuation predicates using the globalized SEMANTIC ALGEBRA 2, given earlier, and then partially evaluated the interpreter, the store arguments will disappear; Thus, one could use ALGEBRA 2 for compilation, and ALGEBRA 1 for other applications where declarative purity is important). Thus, compiled machine code is just a few simple transformation steps away, and provably correct compiled code is obtained simply and automatically. Note that we can be confident that compiled code is correct only if we can prove that the partial evaluator is correct; the correctness of the partial evaluator needs to be proven only once.

Logic programming languages have been widely regarded as highly suitable for building compilers. In [49] Warren shows how the various phases of a compiler writing can be implemented as logic programs. The discussion here goes one step further than Warren's ideas, and shows how a compiler can be obtained from a language specification with little effort. Automatic compilation via partial evaluation is perhaps most useful for obtaining compilers and experimenting with implementations of *domain specific languages* [9,31] (see later).

Partial evaluation can also be used to obtain *parallel* code from the *parallel semantics* of an imperative language (e.g., Fortran). For obtaining parallel code, Horn logic has to be generalized to Constraint Logic. The idea is that if a parallel semantic specification is given for the language, then parallel compiled code can be obtained from this semantics specification via partial evaluation. Parallelism in imperative languages (e.g., Fortran) arises when *independent* iterations of a DO-loop are executed in parallel. Checking for independence of iterations requires solving linear Diophantine equations [50]. Linear Diophantine equations are nothing but linear arithmetic constraints, and hence independence conditions are easily and straightforwardly expressed in the constraint logical denotational framework. Partial evaluation of this parallel semantics (e.g., using Mixtus [36]) yields parallel code. Note that the parallel code obtained is provably correct. Details can be found in [13].

```
program
integer length, width, area, i
integer dimension (100) arr
length = 12
width = 3
do i = 1,8
arr[2*i] =length+1
length = arr[i+1]
enddo
end program
```

Fig. 6: A Fortran Program

For illustration purposes, we partially evaluate (using Mixtus) the parallel semantics of a simple Fortran like language (that includes variable declarations, DO loops, and single dimensional arrays) with respect to the program above (Figure 6). The parallel compiled code obtained is shown below:

```
COMPILED CODE output by MIXTUS:
go1 :- create_store,
       update(length, 0),
       update(width, 0),
       update(area, 0),
       update(i, 0),
       update(length, 12),
       update(width, 3),
       execute_body1(1).
execute_body1(A) :-
          (A>8 -> true  ;
           par_begin(task1, task2),
            start_task(task1),
               ( A=7 ->
                   wait(4) ;
                   true ),
               ( A=5 ->
                   wait(3) ;
                   true ),
               ( A=3 ->
                   wait(2);
                   true ),
               access(length, B),
               C is B+1,
               D is 2*A,
               E is D,
               update_arr(arr, E, C),
               F is A,
               G is F+1,
               access_arr(arr, G, H),
               update(length, H),
               ( A=4 ->
                   signal(7) ;
                   true ),
               ( A=3 ->
                   signal(5) ;
                   true ),
               ( A=2 ->
                   signal(3) ;
                   true ),
            end_task(task1),
            start_task(task2),
              I is A+1,
              execute_body1(I),
```

```
                    end_task(task2),
                   par_end).
```

Due to lack of space, we only show the final generated code and not the actual parallel semantics. Observe how array dependences are captured as dependencies between loop iterations that synchronize using `wait` and `signal`. Note that `par_begin`, `par_end`, `signal`, `wait`, `end_task`, `start_task` are constructs introduced in the semantic algebra of the parallel semantics (not shown here). Note that `execute_body1` is a tail-recursive (parallel) function, and hence can be converted to an iterative loop. Note also that the code is obtained from a globalized parallel semantics (i.e., the parallel semantics uses SEMANTIC ALGEBRA 2); it does not have a memory argument threading through.

4 Program Denotation and Verification

Axiomatic semantics is perhaps the most well-researched technique for verifying properties of programs. Axiomatic semantics which is traditionally expressed in first order logic, can also be expressed in Horn logic (or at least quite a large subset of axiomatic semantics can be expressed), as Horn logic is a subset of first order logic. In Axiomatic Semantics [19] preconditions and postconditions are specified to express conditions under which a program is correct. The notation $(P)C(Q)$ states that if the predicate P is correct before execution of command C, then Q must be correct afterwards. The pre-conditions and post-conditions can be expressed in Horn logic. The post-conditions of a program are theorems with respect to the denotation of that program and the program's pre-conditions [38,39]. Given that the denotation is expressed in Horn logic, the pre-conditions can be incorporated into this denotation, and then the post-conditions can be executed as queries w.r.t this extended program denotation, effectively checking if these post-conditions are satisfied or not. In effect, *model checkers* [8] can be specified and generated automatically. By generalizing Horn logic to constraint logic, real-time systems can also be specified and implemented [12] and parallelizing compilers obtained [13].

One way to prove correctness is to show that given the set of all possible state-configurations, S, that can exist at the beginning of the command C, if P holds for a state-configuration $s \in S$, then Q holds for the state-configuration that results after executing the command C in s. If the denotation is a logic program, then it is possible to generate all possible state-configurations. However, the number of such state-configurations may be infinite. In such a case, the precondition P can be specified in such a way that it acts as a *finite* generator of all possible state-configurations. A model checker is thus obtained from this specification. This model checker can be thought of as a debugging aid, since a user can obtain a program's denotation, add preconditions to it and then pose queries to verify the properties that (s)he things should hold.

We next give an example. Consider the program for computing y^x, whose logical denotation was given earlier. If we were to add the preconditions and the postconditions to the programs, we will obtain the annotated program in Figure 7. In Figure 7, `I(x)` means `x` is an integer. We assume that a variable appearing in the precondition is an input variable, and cannot be modified in the program. If the preconditions `I(x)` and `I(y)` could be turned into generators for integer values of `x` and `y`, then we can verify the correctness of the postcondition for all possible `<x,y>` pairs. Theoretically, `I(x)` and `I(y)` will produce infinite number of values, making the number of `<x,y>` pairs that can serve as input to this program infinite. However, if the preconditions were such that the state-configuration satisfying them are finite in number (i.e., preconditions act as finite generators), then this verification can be automatically done by encoding the preconditions and the postconditions in Horn logic.

```
(I(x) & I(y) & y >= 0)
z := 1 ; w := x;
while w > 0 do
     z := z * y ;
     w := w - 1;
od
(z = y**x)
```

Fig. 7: Annotated Program

Suppose we modified our precondition to state that `x` and `y` are numbers between 0 and 10, then the postcondition `z = y**x` can be immediately verified. The verification is done, by encoding the preconditions as **`between(0,10,ValX)`**, **`between(0,10,ValY)`** that acts as a generator for **`ValX`** and **`ValY`**, which are the values with which the program is interpreted. The program is further augmented with the negation of the post-condition as shown (negation ensures that the entire search space is explored, a substitute for computing the fixpoint of the program):

```
?- between(0,10,VarX), between(0,10,VarY),     %precondition
   main(VarX,VarY,Out),                        %interpret the program
   Z is ValY**ValX, Out \== Z.                 %negated postcondition
```

where **`between`** is defined as:

```
between(I, J, I) :- I =< J.
between(I, J, K) :- I < J, I1 is I+1, between(I1, J, K).
```

The above query will fail, proving that if $0 \leq X, Y, \leq 10$, then indeed this program works correctly. Essentially, the logical denotation together with the precondition as (finite) generators provides an easy way of generating all possible program state-space sequences. The post-condition is verified for each such sequence. For large programs, the search space may be enormous. However, a little better efficiency can be achieved by partially evaluating the above query and then running the resulting program (essentially, checking for the post-condition on the compiled program).

The set of all possible state-space sequences for model-checking can also be generated by using a logic programming system based on bottom-up evaluation or on tabling. In this sense, our ideas provide a formal framework for deductive model-checking as espoused in [33]. Essentially, by using logical denotations, deductive model-checkers can be automatically specified and implemented.
Our approach also produces the insight, namely, that model checking is essentially constraint solving. Let's use the CLP(FD) [44] notation for the previous query[1]:

```
?- VarX :: [1..10], VaryY :: [1..10],  %preconditions.
   main(5,2,A),                        %call to the program
   Z = ValY**ValX, A =\= Z             %negated postcondition
   indomain(VarX), indomain(VarY).     %generators
```

This will lead to a considerably more efficiency of verification, since finite-domain constraint solving can explore the search space more efficiently [44].

While the example given may sound simple, the fact that we can verify certain properties (even though with certain restriction) is of considerable importance. It shows that a logical denotational semantics can be used for verifying and debugging program. Essentially, the Horn Logical denotation axiomatizes a program w.r.t. the semantics of the language the program is written in. This axiomatized program can then be used for verification. Indeed this is an answer to Schmidt's challenge that we "design a calculational semantics for a significant subset of, say, Java, that can be learned and applied by first-year university students to debug their programs."

When we generalize Horn Logic to Constraint Logic more interesting applications become possible. For example, real-time systems can be modeled and verified/debugged using our approach. A real-time system is essentially a recognizer of a sequence of timed-event. A sequence of timed-event is correct if the individual events occur in a certain order (syntactic correctness) and the time at which these events occur satisfy the time-constraints laid out by the real-time system specification (semantic correctness). The syntax and semantics of a real-time system can be specified using constraint logic denotations [12] (the key insight is that the specification of a real-time system is a semantic specification of its corresponding timed-language [12]). Essentially, the time constraints are modeled as constraints over real numbers [21]. The semantic algebra models the state, which consists of the global time (wall-clock time), the valuation predicates are maps from sequence of events to the global time. This constraint logical denotational specification is executable and can be used for verifying interesting properties of real-time systems, e.g., safety (for instance, if we design a real-time system for a railroad gate controller, we want to make sure that at the time a train is at the gate, the

[1] The notation `X::[1..10]` specifies the finite domain of variable `X` to be the set {1..10} [44].

gate can never be open). In the real-time system modeled, we don't exactly know when an event is actually going to occur, all we know is the relationship between the time at which different events took place. Thus, the exact time at which each event took place cannot be computed from the constraint logical denotation. However, the constraints laid out in the denotation together with constraints that the safety property enforces can be solved to check for their consistency (essentially, the constraints laid out by the real-time system should entail the constraints laid out by the properties to be verified, if the property indeed holds). More details of how the denotational approach has been applied to modeling, verification and debugging of real-time systems, can be found elsewhere [12]. We include a short example below.

Let us consider the following problem. An automatic controller is designed to handle a gate at a railroad crossing. The system is composed of three entities, a gate-controller, the gate itself, and the train (the example is adapted from [1]). The train is modeled by the *timed-automata* [1] shown in figure 8(i). It recognizes four different events: (i) `approach` denoting approach of the train to the gate; (ii) `in` denoting that the train is at the gate; (iii) `out` denoting that the train has just left the gate; and, (iv) `exit` denoting that the train has left the gate area. The controller is modeled by the timed-automata in figure 8(ii); it recognizes the `approach` and `exit` events described above, together with the two events: (i) `lower` denoting starting of the lowering of the gate; and, (ii) `raise` denoting starting of the raising of the gate.

Fig. 8. Train, Controller, and Gate automata

Finally, the gate is modeled by the timed-automata in figure 8(iii). Time constraints force the train to employ at most 5 units of time to cross the gate area, with a speed which should allow 2 units of time to the gate to lower before the arrival of the train. The controller should be able to react in less than one unit of time to the approach of the train, and the gate should employ no more than a unit of time to completely lower or raise the gate.
This real-time system can be specified using the denotational approach. Essentially, the correct sequence of events is captured by a context free grammar, while the timing constraints are captured as part of the semantics using constraints over reals. The complete denotational specification of the system in the figure is given below. Note that because we are dealing with an

automata, the syntax recognition is done by a transition table, and the timing constraints are attached to the transitions; Also, the semantic algebra we need is for modeling the global clocks and is also fused with the single specification; thus, the syntax and semantics phase are modeled in one single specification. However, if we were dealing with *timed push down automata* than we will have to have separate syntax and semantic phase [12].

```
train(s0,approach,s1,T1,T2,T3) :- T3 = T1.
train(s1,in,s2,T1,T2,T2) :- T1 - T2 > 2.
train(s2,out,s3,T1,T2,T2).
train(s3,exit,s0,T1,T2,T2) :- T1 - T2 < 5.
train(X,lower,X,T1,T2,T2).
train(X,down,X,T1,T2,T2).
train(X,raise,X,T1,T2,T2).
train(X,up,X,T1,T2,T2).
```

```
gate(s0,lower,s1,T1,T2,T1).
gate(s0,lower,s1,T1,T2,T1).
gate(s1,down,s2,T1,T2,T2)
      :- T1 - T2 < 1.
gate(s2,raise,s3,T1,T2,T1).
gate(s3,up,s0,T1,T2,T2)
      :- T1-T2 > 1, T1-T2 < 2.
gate(X,approach,X,T1,T2,T2).
gate(X,in,X,T1,T2,T2).
gate(X,out,X,T1,T2,T2).
gate(X,exit,X,T1,T2,T2).
```

```
cntl(s0,approach,s1,T1,T2,T1).
cntl(s1,lower,s2,T1,T2,T2)
         :- T1 - T2 = 1.
cntl(s2,exit,s3,T1,T2,T1).
cntl(s3,raise,s0,T1,T2,T2)
         :- T1-T2 < 1.
cntl(X,in,X,T1,T2,T2).
cntl(X,out,X,T1,T2,T2).
cntl(X,up,X,T1,T2,T2).
cntl(X,down,X,T1,T2,T2).
```

Once these executable specifications of the train, controller, and the gate is obtained, we need to compose them together, and give the semantics of the complete system. The semantics of the complete system is given as a list of $\langle \epsilon, \tau \rangle$ pair, where ϵ is an event and τ the time that event took place. This composition of the three systems is done in the specification below:

```
driver([],S0,S1,S2,T,T0,T1,T2,[]).
driver([X|S],S0,S1,S2,T,T0,T1,T2,[(X,T)|R]):-
   train(S0, X, S00, T, T0, T00),
   gate(S1, X, S10, T, T1, T10) ,
   cntl(S2, X, S20, T, T2, T20) , TA > T,
   driver(S,S00,S10,S20,TA,T00,T10,T20,R).
```

Once the composed system has been specified, we have an executable specification of the composite real-time system. Note that an implementation of the composite system can also be automatically derived through suitable transformations. Note that if the event stream is non-terminating, then the driver will execute forever. The driver terminates when the event stream terminates.

The composite specification can be used for verifying various global properties. For example, we may want to verify the safety property that when the train is at the gate, the gate is always closed. These properties are specified by the designer, and ensure correctness of the real-time system specification. We use the axiomatic semantics based framework discussed earlier to perform this verification. We use pre-conditions to put restrictions on the event list to ensure finiteness, and then the properties of interest (post-conditions) can be verified. The net effect obtained is that of (deductive) model-checking.

Thus, our queries to the program will be of the form:

```
pre_condition(X),
driver(X, ...),
not post_condition(X)
```

where `post_condition` is the verification condition, while `pre_condition` is the condition imposed on the input to ensure finiteness. This query should fail, if the `post_condition` holds true. The `pre_condition` should be such that it generates all sentences that satisfy it. For example, if we want to check that the event `in` (train is in) never occurs before event `down` (gate is down), then the pre-condition is that the `in` or the `down` events must occur between two `approach` events. This pre-condition can be expressed so that it can act as a generator of all possible strings that start with an `approach` and end in `approach`. Integrating this pre-condition in the driver we get:

```
driver(_,[],_,_,_,_,_,_,_,[]) :-
driver(N,[X|S],S0,S1,S2,T,T0,T1,T2,[(X,T)|R]) :-
     train(S0,X,S00,T,T0,T00),
     gate(S1,X,S10,T,T1,T10) ,
     contr(S2,X,S20,T,T2,T20) ,
     TA > T, (X = approach ->
                (N = 0 -> M = 1; Rest = []);
                 M = N),
     driver(M,S,S00,S10,S20,TA,T00,T10,T20,R).
```

The driver thus acts as a generator, generating all possible strings that begin with `approach` and end in `approach` and that will be accepted by the automata. Now a property can be verified by calling the driver with uninstantiated input, and checking that the negated property does not hold for every possible meaning of the automata. Suppose, we want to verify that when the train is at the crossing, the gate must be down. This boils down to the following fact: in every possible meaning of a single run of the real-time system, the event `down` must occur before the event `in`. The negated property will be that the event `in` occurs before `down`. Thus, the query:

```
?- driver(0,X,s0,s0,s0,0,0,0,0,R), append(A, [(down,_)|_], R),
        append(_, [(in,_)|_], A).
```

will fail when run on a constraint logic programming system (we used the CLP(R) [21] system). The **append** program is the standard logic program for appending two lists.

Likewise, if we want to verify that the gate will be down at least 4 units of time. That is, an up cannot follow down within 4 time units, then we pose the following query:

```
?- driver(0,s0,s0,s0,0,0,0,0,X,R), append(A, [f(up,T2) |_], R),
        append(_, [f(down,T1)|_], A), T2 - T1 < 4.
```

The above query will fail. Using our system one can also find out the minimum and the maximum amount of time the gate will be closed by posing the following query:

```
?- driver(0,s0,s0,s0,0,0,0,0,X,R), append(A, [f(up,T2) |_], R),
     append(_, [f(down,T1)|_], A), N < T2 - T1 < M, M > 0, N > 0.
```

We obtain the answer `M < 7, N > 1`. This tells us that the minimum time the gate will be down is 1 units, and the maximum time it will be down is 7 units. Other properties of the real-time system can similarly be tested. *The ability to compute values of unknowns is a distinct advantage of a logic programming based approach and is absent from most other approaches used for verifying real-time systems.*

A major weakness of our approach is that we have to make sure that the denotation of a program is finite. If it is not, then we have to impose pre-conditions that ensure this. A popular approach to verifying an infinite state system is to *abstract* it (so that it becomes finite) while making sure that enough information remains in the abstraction so that the property of interest can be verified. The technique of abstraction can be easily adapted in our logical denotational approach: (i) one can give an abstract (logical denotational) semantics for the language, and then run tests on the resulting abstract denotation obtained, using the approach described above. (ii) we can use abstract interpretation tools built for logic programming to abstract the concrete denotation and use that for verifying the properties; in fact, work is in progress in our group to use non-failure analysis of constraint logic programs [4] to verify properties of real-time systems (see also Section 7.2).

5 Specification, Implementation and Verification of DSL Programs

In this section we discuss how our logical, denotational approach can be applied to specification, implementation, and verification of software systems, especially to programs written in Domain Specific Languages. The intuition for using logical denotational semantics is the following: a software system that interacts with its outside world can be thought of as a system that processes programs written in its input language. An executable denotational specification of this input language is essentially an executable specification of the software system. Thus, if we use logical denotational semantics for writing the semantics of the input language of a software system, then indeed we obtain an executable specification of the software system. Many large software systems define some kind of input language that has to be used to interact with them and to use them. Such languages are called *domain specific languages* [31,9], and have been the focus of much attention recently. Using our approach, giving the semantics of a DSL, essentially, gives an executable specification of the software system implementing the DSL. What is more, efficient implementations can be derived for this DSL, by choosing the right abstraction for the semantic algebra, and partially evaluating a DSL program to operations in the semantic algebra. Finally, properties of the software system can be automatically verified, by adding preconditions and postconditions to the denotation of a DSL program and executing them, in the way described in the previous section. We illustrate this application of our logical denotational semantics through an example: we consider the input language (a DSL) of a file-editor, and show how giving the logical denotational semantics of this DSL yields an executable specification of the file editor, and how we can verify certain properties that a file-editor should satisfy (e.g., modifying one file doesn't change other files).

```
program(session(I,S)) --> [edit], id(I),
        [cr], sequence(S).
sequence(seq(quit)) --> [quit].
sequence(seq(C,S)) -->
        command(C), [cr], sequence(S).
command(command(newfile)) --> [newfile].
command(command(forward)) --> [moveforward].
command(command(backward)) --> [moveback].
command(command(insert(R))) -->
        [insert],record(R).
command(command(delete)) --> [delete].
id(identifier(a)) --> [a].
id(identifier(b)) --> [b].
id(identifier(c)) --> [c].
record(rec(0)) --> [0].
....
record(rec(9)) --> [9].
```

Fig. 9: DCG for the Command Language

Consider a simple file editor which supports commands for opening a file, inserting and deleting records, moving forward and backward in the file, and closing the file. A specification for this editor can be given by giving a denotational semantics of its input command language. The editor supports the following commands: edit I (open the file whose name is in identifier I), newfile (create an empty file), forward (move file pointer to next record), backward (move file pointer to previous record), insert(R) (insert record whose value is in identifier R), delete (delete the current record), and quit (quit the editor, saving the file in the file system). The syntax of the editor language is given as a DCG in Figure 9. Our example is adapted from [38]. The DCG is slightly extended, so that it produces a parse tree during the parsing process. For simplicity we assume that there are only three possible file names a, b, and c, and that the records inserted consist of single digit numbers. Note that cr stands for a carriage return, inserted between each editor command. The above DCG specification when loaded in a Prolog system, automatically produces a parser.

We next give the semantic algebras (Figure 10) for each of the domains involved: the file store (represented as an association list of file names and their contents) and an open file (represented as a pair of lists; the file pointer is assumed to be currently at the first record of the second list). The semantic algebra essentially defines the basic operations used by the semantic valuation functions for giving meanings of programs.

```
%Define Access and Update Operations
access(Id,[(I,File)|_],File).
access(Id,[(I,File)|Rest],File1) :-
        (I = Id -> File1 = File;
                  access(Id,Rest,File1)).
update(Id,File,[],[(Id,File)]).
update(Id,File,[(Id,_)|T],[(Id,File)|T]).
update(Id,File,[(I1,F1)|T],[(I1,F2)|NT]) :-
       (Id=I1 --> F2 = File, NT = T;
             F2 = F1, update(Id,File,T,NT).
%Operations on Open File representation
newfile(([],[])).
copyin(File,([],File)).
copyout((First,Second),File):-
         reverse(First,RevFirst),
         append(RevFirst,Second,File).
forwards((First,[X|Scnd]),([X|First],Scnd)).
forwards((First,[]),(First,[])).
backwards(([X|First],Scnd),(First,[X|Scnd])).
backwards(([],Scnd),([],Scnd)).
insert(A,(First,[]),(First,[A])).
insert(A,(First,[X|Y]),([X|First],[A|Y])).
delete((First,[_|Y]),(First,Y)).
delete((First,[]),(First,[])).
at_first_record(([],_)).
at_last_record((_,[])).
isempty(([],[])).
```

Fig. 10: Semantic Algebra for the File System

The semantic valuation predicates that give the meaning of each construct in the language are given next (Figure 11). These semantic functions are mappings from parse-tree patterns and a global state (the file system) to domains (file system, open files) that are used to describe meanings of programs. The above specification gives both the declarative and operational semantics of the editor, and as discussed earlier, can serve both as an implementation as well as be used for verification.

```
prog_val(session(identifier(I),S),FSIn,FSOut) :-
    access(I,FSIn,File), copyin(File,OpenFile),
    seq_val(S,OpenFile,NewOpenFile),
    copyout(NewOpenFile,OutFile),
    update(I,OutFile,FSIn,FSOut).
seq_val(seq(quit),InFile,InFile).
seq_val(seq(C,S),InFile,OutFile) :-
                comm_val(C,InFile,NewFile),
                seq_val(S,NewFile,OutFile).
comm_val(command(newfile),_,OutFile) :-
    newfile(OutFile).
comm_val(command(moveforward),InFile,OutFile) :-
    (isempty(InFile) -> OutFile = InFile;
     (at_last_record(InFile) -> OutFile=InFile;
                    forwards(InFile,OutFile))).
comm_val(command(moveback),InFile,OutFile) :-
    (isempty(InFile) -> InFile = OutFile;
         (at_first_record(InFile) ->
    InFile = OutFile; backwards(InFile,OutFile))).
comm_val(command(insert(R)),InFile,OutFile) :-
    record_val(R,RV), insert(RV,InFile,OutFile).
comm_val(command(delete),InFile,OutFile) :-
    (isempty(InFile) ->
     InFile = OutFile; delete(InFile,OutFile)).
record_val(R,R).
```

Fig. 11: Valuation Predicates

Using a logic programming system, the above specification can serve as an interpreter for the command language of the editor, and hence serves as an implementation of the editor. Thus, the above semantic definition is an executable specification of an editor. Although editors are interactive programs, for simplicity, we assume that the commands are given in batches (interactive programs can also be handled by modeling rest of the unknown commands through Prolog's unbound variables: we omit the discussion to keep the presentation simple). Thus, if the editor is invoked and a sequence of commands issued, then assuming that we start with an unspecified file system (modeled as the unbound variable, `Fin`), the resulting file system after executing all the editor commands can be obtained by posing the query:

```
?- Comms = [edit,a,cr,newfile,cr,insert,1,cr,insert,2,cr,delete,
   cr,moveback,cr,insert,4,cr,insert,5,cr,delete,cr,quit]),
   program(Tree,Comms,[]),     %produce parse tree
   prog_val(Tree,Fin,Fout).  %execute commands
```

The final resulting file-system will be:

```
Fout = [(a,[rec(1),rec(4)])| _B ].
```

The output shows that the final file systems contains the file a that contains 2 records, and the previously unknown input file system (represented by Prolog's anonymous variable _B, aliased to Fin). The key thing to note is that in our logical denotational framework, a specification is very easy to write as well as easy to modify. This is because of the declarative nature of the logic programming formalism used and its basis in denotational semantics. It is also easy to verify the specification, thanks to use of Horn Logic. Given the executable implementation of the file-editor, and a program in its command language (a DSL), we can partially evaluate it to obtain a more efficient implementation of the program. The result of partially evaluating the file-editor specification, w.r.t. previous command-language program, is shown in Figure 12. Partial evaluation translates the editor command language program to a series of instructions that call operations defined in the semantic algebra. This series of instructions look a lot like "compiled" code. More efficient implementations of the editor can be obtained by implementing these semantic algebra operations in an efficient way, e.g., using a more efficient language, e.g., C, C++, or Java, instead of using logic programming.

```
access(a, Fin, C),
copyin(C, _),
newfile(D),
insert(rec(1), D, E),
insert(rec(2), E, F),
( isempty(F) -> G=F
; delete(F, G)),
( isempty(G) -> H=G
; at_first_record(G) ->
      H=G
; backwards(G, H)),
insert(rec(4), H, I),
insert(rec(5), I, J),
( isempty(J) -> K=J
; delete(J, K)),
copyout(K, L),
update(a,L,Fin,Fout).
```

Fig. 12: Compiled code

Given that our specification is executable, we can run it to check its soundness and to test that it meets our expectations. Consider the specification of the file editor. Under the assumption that the file system is finite and that the pool of possible records is also finite, we can verify, for instance, that every editing session consisting of an insertion followed by a deletion leaves the original file unchanged, by posing the following query:

```
?- true,          %Null pre-condition
   program(A,[edit,X,cr,insert,Y,cr,delete,cr,quit],[]),
   prog_val(A,F,G),
   F ≠ G.        %negated post-condition
```

The above query states that for all possible files X and for all possible records Y that can be inserted, the resulting file-system is different from the original file system, and this query should fail, if indeed the result of one insertion and one deletion leaves the file system unchanged. The backtracking mechanism of logic programming goes through all possible values for variables `X` and `Y` (finiteness is hence important and was coded in the specification by limiting the range of file names and record values; alternatively, this finiteness could be enforced in the precondition) and finds that in every case `F = G` holds, and thus finally the whole query fails because the final call asserts that `F` $\neq$ `G`. More complex inferences are possible on this semantic definition. For example, we can verify that if an editing session is open for a certain file, then this editing session will affect no other file [15].

6 Semantic Porting

Logical denotations also provide a formal theory of *porting* or *language filtering*. Porting can involve migrating a software from one machine/operating system to another (e.g. moving an application from a Sun Sparc running Solaris to a PC running Linux), or migrating a system written in one notation to another on the same machine (e.g. porting a database written in Oracle SQL to IBM DB2). It is the latter type of porting, that we are interested in. Essentially, this type of porting involves development of a semantic translation system to translate programs written in a language $\mathcal{L}_s$ to another language $\mathcal{L}_t$ (such a system is called a *filter*). Specification of a filter can be seen as an exercise in semantics. Essentially, the meaning or semantics of the language $\mathcal{L}_s$ can be given in terms of the constructs of the language $\mathcal{L}_t$. This meaning consists of both syntax and semantics specifications. If these syntax and semantic specifications are executable, then the specification itself acts as a translation system, providing a provably correct filter. The task of specifying the filter from $\mathcal{L}_s$ to $\mathcal{L}_t$ consists of specifying the DCG grammar for $\mathcal{L}_s$ and the appropriate valuation predicates which are essentially maps from parse tree patterns of $\mathcal{L}_s$ to parse tree patterns of $\mathcal{L}_t$.

Consider the translation of *Braille Nemeth Math* [28], a Braille-based language notation for the blind, to LaTeX. To obtain such a translator one can specify the semantics of the Braille Nemeth Math notation (a formal language) in terms of LaTeX. (such a translator can help the sighted instructors in grading the assignment/papers of blind students since these students write answers to their homework in Nemeth Braille which the instructors can't read). We next give the specification of a filter for translating Braille Nemeth Math code used for expressing *polynomials with polynomial powers* to LaTeX. Polynomial powers means that each variable can be raised to another polynomial: for example, $x^{x^2+1} + 5$ (note that in Nemeth Braille this will be coded as `x^x^^2^+1"+5`; the number of `^` indicates the exponent level and `"` the base line expression, hence the Nemeth Braille expression language is not context free). Assume, for simplicity, that the only variable names allowed are `x`, `y`, and `z`. Consider the grammar for such polynomials that also produces parse trees. We first give the syntax of Nemeth Braille for polynomials with polynomial powers as a DCG, then we give the semantics of the parse trees produced in terms of LaTeX. The resulting specification is executable and provides the filter.

```
SYNTAX:
exp(e(X)) --> term(X).
exp(e(T,O,E)) --> term(T), op1(O), exp(E).
term(t(X)) --> digit(X).
term(t(X)) --> vari(X).
term(t(V,H,T)) --> vari(V), hats(H), term(T).
op1(op(H,+)) --> hats(H), [+].
op1(op('"',+)) --> ['"'], [+].
op1(op(+)) --> [+].
hats([^]) --> [^].
hats([^|L]) --> [^], hats(L).
vari(x) --> [x].  vari(y) --> [y].  vari(z) --> [z].
digit(0) --> [0].  digit(1) --> [1].  digit(2) --> [2].
digit(3) --> [3].  digit(4) --> [4].  digit(5) --> [5].
digit(6) --> [6].  digit(7) --> [7].  digit(8) --> [8].
digit(9) --> [9].

SEMANTICS:
sexp(e(X),INL,L) :- sterm(X,INL,ONL,L1),
                    getlist(ONL, Bl), append(L1,Bl,L).
sexp(e(T,O,E),NL,L) :- sterm(T,NL,OL, L1),
          sop(O,OL,NL1), Close_Braces is OL - NL1,
          getlist(Close_Braces, Bl), sexp(E,NL1,L2),
          append(L1,Bl,Lp), append(Lp,[+|L2],L).
sop(op(H,+),_,Ct) :- shats(H,Ct).
sop(op('"',+),_,0).
sop(op(+),CL,CL).
shats([^],1).
shats([^|L],Ct) :- shats(L,Ct1), Ct is Ct1+1.

sterm(t(X),OL,OL,[X]).
sterm(t(V,H,T),Ct, OL, [V,^,'{'|R]) :- Ct1 is Ct+1,
                    shats(H,Ct1), sterm(T,Ct1,OL,R).
getlist(0,[]).
getlist(N,['}'|L]) :- N > 0, N1 is N-1, getlist(N1,L).
```

The grammar for Braille Nemeth code is given as a DCG. Expressing it as a DCG results in a parser immediately. The parser also produces the parse trees for the Braille Nemeth code. The denotations (meaning) of Braille Nemeth code parse tree patterns are expressed as logic programs which are maps from Nemeth math parse trees and the global state (the exponent level) to LaTeX math (the LaTeX expression is assembled as a list of symbols; it will perhaps be better to produce a term representing the LaTeX expression). The resulting program acts as an automatic translation system from Braille Nemeth code to LaTeX.

Thus, if we load this program on a logic programming system and pose the query for translating x^x^^2^+5"+6 Braille Nemeth code to LaTeX, the answer obtained is shown below:

```
| ?- exp(T,[x,^,x,^,^,2,^,+,5,'"',+,6],[]),sexp(T,0,L).

L = [x,^,'{',x,^,'{',2,'}',+,5,'}',+,6],
T = e(t(x,[^],t(x,[^,^],t(2))),op([^],+),
                         e(t(5),op('"',+),e(t(6)))) ?
```

The answer in L corresponds to the LaTeX expression x^{x^{2}+5}+6} (i.e., $x^{x^2+5}+6$).

Note that semantic filtering gives us another way of building provably correct compilers: a compiler is a semantic filter from a source language to a target machine language [35]. Another application of the logical denotational semantics based semantic porting is in *interoperability* of databases: both the query programs and data defined under one type of database can be translated to programs and data of another different database.

7 Other Applications

7.1 Derivation of Abstract Machines

Our approach can also be used to derive and experiment with different abstract machines for a given language. This is based on the observation that compilation using partial evaluation can be done to whatever degree we wish. We could first define our semantics at a very high level by defining the semantic algebras at a very high level. Partial evaluation can then be used to compile programs to this abstract machine. This semantics could be further refined, by giving a finer level semantics for this high level semantic algebra. The program compiled to this higher level algebra, can be partially evaluated further with respect to the interpreter obtained for this lower level semantics, to obtain an even lower level compiled code. This can be repeated further (i.e., still finer semantics can be defined). For example, consider the definition of the Prolog language itself: the semantics of the language can be defined in such a way, that on partial evaluation WAM [47] like compiled code is obtained. However, we could further refine this semantics, so that, instead, on partial evaluation native code is obtained. This is indeed under investigation, and our approach is being applied to Prolog to automatically generate compilers that compile to both WAM as well as native code [16].

7.2 Specification of Abstract Interpreters

So far we have been specifying concrete semantics in our logical denotation. The semantics specified can also be abstract. The resulting logic program acts as an abstract interpreter. Program properties can be then be verified using the pre-condition/post-condition approach described earlier. To obtain abstract semantics one has to only specify abstractions for semantic algebras. Recall that a semantic algebra consists of a set along with operations that apply to the elements of this set. An abstract semantic algebra can be obtained by abstracting this set as well as the concrete operations on this set. The abstraction function should be properly chosen in accordance to the criterion laid out in [10]. Once the semantic algebra has been abstracted, the valuation function should be appropriately modified as well, essentially replacing the calls to concrete semantic algebra functions by abstract ones. If the abstracted semantic algebras are finite then one can guarantee that the abstract semantics of the language in question is also finite. This follows from the fact that valuation functions are maps from parse trees and semantic algebras to semantic algebras. If the semantic algebras are finite, then the co-domains of the valuation functions are also finite. From this it follows that given a program `P` written in the language being studied, the fixpoint of `P`'s abstract denotation will be finite. The abstract denotation can be used to verify properties of programs. We omit details due to lack of space [17].

This denotational semantics based approach to abstract interpretation gives a computational interpretation to observations such as those made by Schmidt, namely, that data-flow analysis is model-checking of the abstract interpreter [41]. The preceding ideas are related to automatic generation of abstract interpreters for Prolog [30] (though our approach can be applied to any arbitrary language).

Furthermore, given a program to be analyzed and the denotational abstract semantics of the language the program is written in, then the abstract interpreter can be partially evaluated w.r.t. program. The checking of program properties can be done on this ***abstract compiled code***. This approach provides a formal frameworks for efforts such as those where abstract compilers were developed to make the process of abstract interpretation based analysis faster [43]. It also automates the process of deriving abstract compiled code from the language specification.

We hope that our work on generating abstract interpreters from abstract semantics will spur research in use of abstract interpretation for program verification (most use so far has been for static analysis in order to obtain faster compiled code).

7.3 Using Existing Logic Programming Technology

Once the denotation of a program is obtained as a logic program, all the analysis tools that have been developed for logic programming can be applied to analyze the properties of the logical denotation. For example, abstract interpretation based analyzers can be applied to the compiled program to check if two operations are independent [2]. Program termination analyzers [24] can be applied to check if the program will terminate. Non-failure analysis [4] can be applied to check for non-failure of the logical denotation, etc. At present, analysis tools developed for constraint logic programming [2] are being applied to analyze the denotations of Fortran programs to detect parallelism (as an alternative to work presented in [13]), while non-failure analysis is being used to aid in verification of real-time systems.

8 Related Work

Work on programming language semantics has been ongoing for decades. However, use of programming language semantics for practical applications has been very limited, as Schmidt notes [40]. Most work in practical use of semantics has been in automatic derivation of sequential compilers. Many systems have been developed for automatically generating interpreters and compilers from semantics specification [27,46,11,29,22,5]. However, because the syntax is specified as a (non-executable) BNF and semantics is specified in the λ-calculus, this automatic generation process is very cumbersome. The lack of "calculational clarity" in the traditional denotational semantics notation is the main reason why application of semantics based approaches to practical problems has been hindered. In contrast, our logical denotation approach imparts the much needed "calculational view." In fact, this simple change of approach, we believe, can have considerable impact on applications and use of programming language semantics. Most of the applications of denotational semantics outlined in this paper (automatic generation of model checkers, language filters, sequential compilers, parallelizing compilers, abstract interpreters, etc.) are possible in the existing frameworks found in the literature, however, they are too cumbersome to realize and hence not explored.

Using Horn logic for expressing denotational semantics has been considered by Stepney [35], however, she does not realize the immense potential that this simple switch of notations brings about. Stepney is solely interested in obtaining provably correct compilers. However, this provably correct compiler is specified by the user in her approach and not automatically generated as in our framework. In Stepney's approach, the compiler is specified by giving the meanings of program constructs in terms of machine instructions (i.e., the valuation functions map parse trees to machine instructions). Consel has independently applied denotational semantics and partial evaluation to the specification and implementation of domain specific languages [9]. He does consider verification in the same work, but this verification has to be done manually via user supplied proofs. In contrast, in our framework, verification can be done automatically. Also, Fritzson has considered deriving data-parallel code from denotational specification of a language, but once again the procedures involved are quite complex and cumbersome [34]. Miller has proposed using operational semantics to derive efficient implementations [26], while we are interested in deriving abstract machines from denotational specifications. Satluri and Fleck [7] have considered using logic programs for specifying the semantic actions associated with production rules of an attribute grammar. They are mainly concerned with providing a Horn-logic based operational semantics, and do not consider declarative denotational semantics at all.

9 Conclusions

In this paper we presented a Horn logic and constraint based framework for denotational semantics. The switch to logic programming provides a "calculational flavor" to formal semantics, and leads to many interesting applications. The most interesting aspect of this framework is that denotational specification once written can be quickly debugged and verified as well as compiled code automatically obtained. Thus, denotational semantics becomes an experimental tool, that can be used by software writers and language designers to experiment with software design and language design respectively. At present, several practical applications of the ideas presented in the paper are being pursued [12,13,15,17,16,23] by the author's research group.

Acknowledgments

Thanks to Enrico Pontelli for his collaboration on several of the applications discussed in this paper, to Shameem Akhter and Enrico Pontelli for helping with coding of the examples, to Art Karshmer, Sandy Geiger, and Chris Weaver for bringing the Braille to LaTeX translation problem to my attention. Thanks to Pieter Hartel of Southampton University for bringing Stepney's work to my attention. Thanks also to students in my Programming Language Semantics class at New Mexico State on whom this logic programming approach to Denotational Semantics was first tried.

The author has been supported by NSF grants CCR 96-25358, CDA-9729848, EIA 98-10732, HRD 98-00209, HRD 96-28450, and INT 95-15256, and by a grant from the Fulbright Foundation.

References

1. R. Alur and D. Dill. The Theory of Timed Automata. *Theoretical Computer Science*, 126, 1994.
2. M. Garcia de la Banda, M. Hermenegildo, et al. Global Analysis of Constraint Logic Programs. In *ACM Trans. on Prog. Languages and Systems*, Vol. 18, Num. 5, pages 564-615, ACM, 1996.

3. S. K. Das. Deductive Databases and Logic Programming. Addison-Wesley. 1992.
4. S. Debray, P. Lopez-Garcia, and M. Hermenegildo. Non-failure Analysis for Logic Programs. In *International Conference on Logic Programming.* MIT Press, 1997.
5. D.F. Brown et al. ACTRESS: an action semantics directed compiler generator. In *Proc. 4th Int'l Conf. on Compiler Construction.* Springer LNCS 641, pp. 95-109. 1992.
6. W. Chen and D. S. Warren. Tabled Evaluation with Delaying for General Logic Programs, *In JACM 43(1):20-74.*
7. S. Satluri and A. C. Fleck. Semantic Specification using Logic Programs. In *Proc. N. American Conf. on Logic Programming* 1989, MIT Press. pp. 772-791.
8. E. M. Clark, E. A. Emerson, A. P. Sistla. Automatic Verification of finite-state Concurrent Systems Using Temporal Logic Specification. In *ACM TOPLAS*, 8(2), 1986.
9. C. Consel. Architecturing Software Using a Methodology for Language Development. In *Proc. 10th Int'l Symp. on Prog. Lang. Impl., Logics and Programs (PLILP)*, Sep. 1998, Springer LNCS 1490, pp. 170-194.
10. P. Cousot, R. Cousot, "Abstract Interpretation: A Unified Model for Static Analysis of Programs for Construction or Approximation of Fix-points," In *Conference Record of the 4th ACM POPL,* pp. 238-252, 1977.
11. Thierry Despeyroux. Executable specification of static semantics. In *Semantics of Data Types*, Springer LNCS 173. pp. 215-234. 1984.
12. G. Gupta, E. Pontelli. A Constraint-based Denotational Approach to Specification and Verification of Real-time Systems. In *Proc. IEEE Real-time Systems Symposium*, San Francisco, pp. 230-239. Dec. 1997.
13. G. Gupta, E. Pontelli, R. Felix-Cardenas, A. Lara, Automatic Derivation of a Provably Correct Parallelizing Compiler, *In Proceedings of International Conference on Parallel Processing*, IEEE Press, Aug, 1998, pp. 579-586.
14. G. Gupta. Horn Logic Denotations and Their Applications. Internal Memo. Jan 1995.
15. G. Gupta, E. Pontelli. Specification, Verification, Composition, and Interoperation of Complex Software Systems: A Logical Denotational Approach. Technical Report. New Mexico State University. Dec. 1997.
16. G. Gupta, E. Pontelli, H. Guo, L. Zhu. Automatic Generation of a WAM-compiler and a Native Code Compiler for Prolog. New Mexico State University. Working paper.
17. G. Gupta, E. Pontelli. Horn Logical Denotational Framework for Abstract Interpretation. New Mexico State University. Working paper.
18. C. Gunter. Programming Language Semantics. MIT Press. 1992.
19. C. A. R. Hoare. An Axiomatic Basis for Computer Programming. *Comm. of the ACM.* Vol. 12. pp. 576-580, 1969.
20. N. Jones. Introduction to Partial Evaluation. In *ACM Computing Surveys.* 28(3):480-503.
21. J. L. Lassez and J. Jaffar. Constraint logic programming. In *Proc. 14th ACM POPL*, 1987.
22. P. Lee. Realistic Compiler Generation. The MIT Press, Cambridge, MA, 1989.
23. A. Karshmer, G. Gupta, S. Geiger, C. Weaver. A Framework for Translation of Braille Nemeth Math to LaTeX: The MAVIS Project. In *Proc. ACM Conference on Assistive Technologies*, ACM Press, pp. 136-143, Mar. 1998.

24. N. Lindenstrauss, Y. Sagiv. Automatic Termination Analysis for Logic Programs. In *Proc. International Conference on Logic Programming*, 1997. pp. 63-77.
25. J.W. Lloyd. Foundations of Logic Programming. Springer Verlag. 2nd ed. 1987.
26. J. Hannan and D. Miller. From Operational Semantics to Abstract Machines. In *Proc. Lisp and Functional Programming Conference*, 1990.
27. P.D. Mosses. Compiler Generation using Denotational Semantics. In *Math. Foundations of Computer Science*, Springer LNCS 45, pages 436-441, 1976.
28. A. Nemeth. The Braille-Nemeth Math Code. American Printing House for the Blind. 1972 Revision. Louisville, Kentucky.
29. F. Nielson and H. R. Nielson. Two level semantics and code generation. *Theoretical Computer Science*, 56(1):59-133. 1988.
30. C. R. Ramakrishnan, S. Dawson, and D. Warren. Practical Program Analysis Using General Purpose Logic Programming Systems: A Case Study. In *Proc. ACM Conf. on Programming Language Design and Implementation*. 1996.
31. C. Ramming. Editor, *Proceedings of the Usenix Conference on Domain-Specific Languages*, October 1997, Santa Barbara, California, USA.
32. M. Raskovsky, Phil Collier. From Standard to Implementational Denotational Semantics. In *Semantics Directed Compiler Generation*. Lecture Notes in Computer Science 94. Springer Verlag. pp. 94-139.
33. Efficient Model Checking using Tabled Resolution. Y.S. Ramakrishnan, C.R. Ramakrishnan, I.V. Ramakrishnan et al. In *Proceedings of Computer Aided Verification (CAV'97)*. 1997.
34. J. Ringstrom, P. Fritzson, M. Pettersson. Generating an Efficient Compiler for a Data Parallel Language from a Denotational Specification. In Lecture Notes in Computer Science, Vol. 786, pp. 248-260. 1994.
35. S. Stepney. High Integrity Compilation. Prentice Hall. 1993.
36. D. Sahlin. An Automatic Partial Evaluator for Full Prolog. Ph.D. Thesis. 1994. Royal Institute of Technology, Sweden. (Software available from www.sics.se)
37. K. Sagonas, T. Swift, and D. S. Warren. XSB as an efficient deductive database engine. In *Proc. SIGMOD International Conf. on Management of Data*, 1994.
38. D. Schmidt. *Denotational Semantics: a Methodology for Language Development*. W.C. Brown Publishers, 1986.
39. D. Schmidt. Programming language semantics. In CRC Handbook of Computer Science, Allen Tucker, ed., CRC Press, Boca Raton, FL, 1996. Summary version, ACM Computing Surveys 28-1 (1996) 265-267.
40. D. Schmidt. On the Need for a Popular Formal Semantics. *Proc. ACM Conf. on Strategic Directions in Computing Research,* Cambridge, MA, June 1996. ACM SIGPLAN Notices 32-1 (1997) 115-116.
41. D. Schmidt. *Dataflow Analysis is Model Checking of an Abstract Interpreter*. In *Proc. ACM POPL'98*.
42. L. Sterling & S. Shapiro. The Art of Prolog. MIT Press, '94.
43. J. Tan and I-P. Lin. Compiling Dataflow Analysis of Logic Programs. In *Proc. ACM Conf. on Programming Language Design and Implementation*. SIGPLAN Notices, 27(7), 1992.
44. P. Van Hentenryck. *Constraint Handling in Prolog*. MIT Press, 1988.
45. S. Abiteboul, R. Hull, V. Vianu. Foundation of Databases. Addison-Wesley, 1995.
46. M. Wand. Semantics-directed Machine Architecture. In *ACM POPL*. pp. 234-241. 1982

47. D.H.D. Warren. An Abstract Instruction Set for Prolog. Tech. Note 309, SRI Int'l, '83.
48. D.H.D. Warren. Higher Order Extensions to Prolog: Are They Needed? *Machine Intell.*, 10:441-454.
49. D.H.D. Warren. Logic Programming for Compiler-writing. *Software Practice and Experience*, 10, pp. 97-125. 1979.
50. H. Zima, B. Chapman. *Supercompilers for Parallel and Vector Computers.* ACM Press, '91.

Using Global Analysis, Partial Specifications, and an Extensible Assertion Language for Program Validation and Debugging

Manuel Hermenegildo, Germán Puebla, and Francisco Bueno

Department of Computer Science, Technical University of Madrid (UPM), Spain

Summary. We present a framework for the application of abstract interpretation as an aid during program development, rather than in the more traditional application of program optimization. Program validation and detection of errors is first performed statically by comparing (partial) specifications written in terms of assertions against information obtained from static analysis of the program. The results of this process are expressed in the user assertion language. Assertions (or parts of assertions) which cannot be verified statically are translated into run-time tests. The framework allows the use of assertions to be optional. It also allows using very general properties in assertions, beyond the predefined set understandable by the static analyzer and including properties defined by means of user programs. We also report briefly on an implementation of the framework. The resulting tool generates and checks assertions for Prolog, CLP(R), and CHIP/CLP(fd) programs, and integrates compile-time and run-time checking in a uniform way. The tool allows using properties such as types, modes, non-failure, determinacy, and computational cost, and can treat modules separately, performing incremental analysis. In practice, this modularity allows detecting statically bugs in user programs even if they do not contain any assertions.

1 Introduction

As (constraint) logic programming systems mature further and larger applications are built, an increased need arises for advanced development and debugging environments. Such environments will likely comprise a variety of co-existing tools ranging from declarative debuggers to execution visualizers (see, for example, [1,22,21] for a more comprehensive discussion of tools and possible debugging scenarios). In this paper we concentrate our attention on the particular issue of program validation and debugging via direct static and/or dynamic checking of user-provided *assertions* [18,19,8,6,36,2]. Classical examples of assertions are the type declarations used in languages such as Gödel [30] or Mercury [42] (and in traditional functional languages). But here, and encouraged by the capabilities of the currently available abstract interpreters, we depart in several ways from the traditional approaches.

We start by recalling some classical definitions (see, e.g., [10]) in program validation and debugging. Given a program P, we denote by $\mathcal{I}$ the *intended semantics* for P, i.e., the specification for P. We denote by $[\![P]\!]$ the *actual semantics* of the current implementation of program P. Note that we do not preclude the use of one semantics or another. The semantics may be declarative or operational, and, in the latter case, include such things as errors, undefined predicates, and so on. The particular semantics must indeed capture the observables one wants to validate.[1] Let us consider for simplicity a set-based semantics. We say that

- P is *partially correct* with respect to $\mathcal{I}$ iff $[\![P]\!] \subseteq \mathcal{I}$.
- P is *complete* with respect to $\mathcal{I}$ iff $\mathcal{I} \subseteq [\![P]\!]$.
- P is *incorrect* with respect to $\mathcal{I}$ iff $[\![P]\!] \not\subseteq \mathcal{I}$.
- P is *incomplete* with respect to $\mathcal{I}$ iff $\mathcal{I} \not\subseteq [\![P]\!]$.

Performing these validation tasks can result in the validation of P with respect to $\mathcal{I}$, i.e., proving that P is partially correct and/or complete with respect to $\mathcal{I}$, or in the detection of incorrectness and/or incompleteness *symptoms*, which would flag the existence of errors in P, and in which case a process of diagnosis should be started to locate such errors.

There are many ways in which the validation task can be performed [3,4,17,23,44]. In general, direct application of the previous definitions is not practical for different reasons. First, providing the entire and exact intended semantics $\mathcal{I}$ may be a tedious task. Also, the actual semantics $[\![P]\!]$ of P may be an infinite object and it is often more convenient to use approximations of it. In the framework we propose, as in most existing debugging frameworks, we concentrate on *partial correctness* [2] debugging, i.e., we try to detect incorrectness symptoms or to prove that they do not exist.

We assume that the starting point for correctness validation and debugging is a set of user-provided assertions. In order to distinguish this kind of assertions from others which will be introduced below, we call them `check` assertions, since the system aims at checking them. At the same time, we would like our system to be as general as possible. First, we would like the assertions to be *optional*: specifications may be given only for some parts of the program and even for those parts the information given may be incomplete. For example, assertions may be given for only some procedures or program points, and for a given predicate we may perhaps have the type of one argument, the mode of another, and no information on other arguments. Also, we are interested in supporting assertions which are much more general than traditional type declarations, and such that it may be statically *undecidable* whether they hold or not for a given program. Finally, we would like the system to *generate* assertions, especially for parts of the program for

[1] This is precisely one of our motivations for developing a framework capable of integrating different tools (possibly based on different semantics).

[2] For brevity, we will usually write correctness/incorrectness when referring to *partial* correctness/incorrectness.

which there are no `check` assertions. These assertions will have the status `true` and can be visually inspected by the user for checking correctness.[3]

As a consequence of our assumptions, the overall framework needs to deal throughout with approximations [10,15,28]. Thus, while the system can be complete with respect to statically decidable properties (e.g., certain type systems), it cannot be complete in general, and analysis may or may not be able to prove in general that a given assertion holds. The overall operation of the system will be sometimes imprecise but must always be *safe*. This means that all violations of assertions flagged by the system should indeed be violations, but perhaps there are assertions which the system cannot statically determine to hold or not. This means that the compiler cannot in general reject a program because it has not been able to prove that the complete specification holds. In order to limit the impact of this and at the same time detect as many errors as possible, we would like to design the framework and the assertion language in such a way that dynamic checking of assertions (run-time tests) is supported in addition to static checking. Furthermore, we would like to use, to the extent possible, the source language to perform such run-time tests, so that, at least conceptually, the addition of run-time tests to a program can be viewed as a source to source transformation.

Our approach is strongly motivated by the availability of powerful and mature static analyzers for (constraint) logic programs, generally based on abstract interpretation [15]. These analyzers have proved quite effective in statically *inferring* a wide range of program properties accurately and efficiently, for realistic programs (see, e.g., [29,34,12,24,25,31,8,9] and their references). Such properties can range from types and modes to determinacy, non-failure, computational cost, independence, or termination, to name a few. Traditionally the results of static analyses have been applied primarily to program optimization: parallelization, partial evaluation, low level code optimization, etc. However, here we are interested instead in the applications of static analysis in *program development* (see, e.g., [5,10,28]), and in particular in validation and error detection. Our objective is, along the lines suggested in [40], to combine program optimization and debugging into a generic integrated tool which uses multiple program analyses such as mode type, termination, cost, non-floundering, etc.

2 Overall Framework Architecture and Operation

Figure 1 depicts the overall architecture of the proposed framework. Hexagons represent the different tools involved and arrows indicate the communication paths among the different tools. It is a design objective of the framework that most of such communication be performed also in terms of assertions. This has the advantage that at any point in the debugging process the information

[3] Note however that if `check` assertions exist for such parts of the program, such checking is automated in the system by either compile-time or run-time checking.

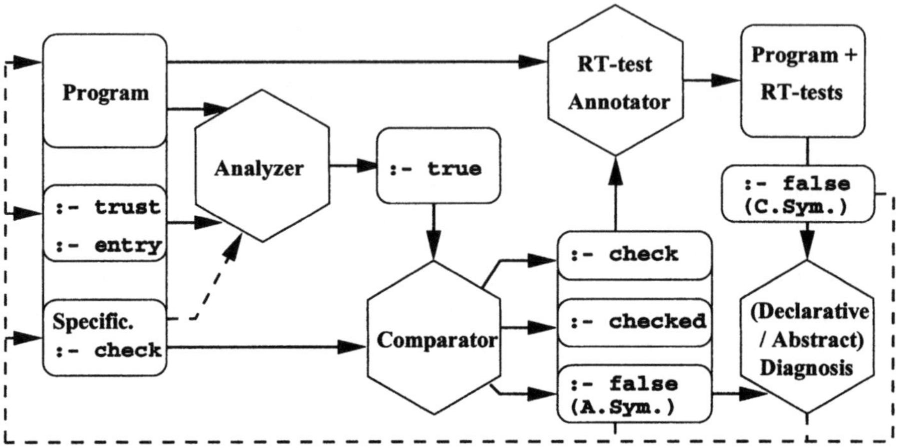

Fig. 1. A Combined Framework for Program Development and Debugging

is easily readable by the user. Also, rather than having different *assertion languages* for each tool, we propose the use of a common assertion language for all of them, since this facilitates the above mentioned communication among the different tools, enables easy reuse of information (i.e., once a property has been stated there is no need to repeat it for the different tools), and facilitates understanding of the intermediate results by the user, who only needs to learn a single assertion language. Note that not all tools need to be capable of dealing with all properties expressible in the assertion language. Rather, each tool only makes use of the part of the information given as assertions which the tool "understands." This is allowed in our framework by the approximation-based approach used throughout the system.

We now provide an overview of some of the characteristics of the assertion language used to describe the (partial) specification, we discuss how such assertions are used to perform run-time and compile-time program correctness validation and debugging, and we provide pointers to the rest of the paper, where each individual topic is discussed in more detail.

Check Assertions. As mentioned before, we assume that the user provides a set of assertions (the assertion language itself will be introduced in sections 3 and 4). All these assertions (and those which will be mentioned later) are written in the same syntax, with a prefix denoting their *status*. Because the user assertions are to be checked we say that such assertions have status "`check`" and refer to them as "`check` assertions" (see Figure 1).[4] The fact

[4] In addition, the user may optionally provide additional information to the analyzer by means of "`entry`" assertions (which describe the external calls to a module) and "`trust`" assertions (which provide abstract information on a predicate that the analyzer can use even if it cannot prove such information to be true) [8,36].

that an assertion has `check` status may be made explicit by prepending the `check` keyword to it, but `check` is the default assertion status and is therefore not required.

Intuitively, `check` assertions are just necessary conditions for the program to be correct. I.e., if they do not hold then the program is definitely incorrect. However, and as we do not require that `check` assertions encode a complete specification of P, the fact that all `check` assertions hold does not necessarily mean that the program is correct with respect to the semantics the user has in mind, much in the same way that a type correct program may produce incorrect results. Another way of looking at these assertions is as integrity constraints: if they do not hold then something is definitely wrong. Such assertions may be included in the program itself or provided separately.

We make a conceptual distinction between the notions of *property* and *assertion*. Properties are logic predicates, in the sense that the evaluation of each property either succeeds or fails (returns the value *true* or the value *false*). Properties are used to say that "X is a list of integers," "Y is ground," "p(X) does not fail," etc. The truth value of the assertion is that obtained by combining the truth values of the individual properties. Each individual assertion is constructed as a logic formula in a restricted syntax (to be described later) whose components are properties. The language of assertions we propose is structured around a relatively small and fixed set of (classes of) assertions, which will be discussed in more detail in Section 3. The use of one or another class of assertion will indicate in which sets of execution states the assertion is *applicable*, such as, for example: the success states or the call states of a predicate, the states corresponding to a program point between two clause body literals, the whole computation of a given call, etc. A program P is correct with respect to an assertion A if in all execution states reachable from valid input values for P either A is not applicable or the truth value of A is true. The assertion language leaves open the set of properties which may be used. The properties of interest may differ from one case to another and we allow the user to define such properties. There are two main kinds of properties: properties of execution states and properties of a computation. Such properties will be discussed in Section 4.

Run-time checking of assertions. The above mentioned assertions can then be checked at run-time, in the classical way, i.e., run-time tests will be added to the program which encode in some way the given assertions. In the proposed framework, this is performed by the run-time test *annotator* module in Figure 1. This module takes the program and the `check` assertions as input. We assume for now that the *comparator* module of Figure 1 simply passes the `check` assertions through. The transformation, discussed in Section 5, must be such that, whenever the transformed program is executed, the assertions are checked for the data actually being explored by the program during execution, and this is done at the execution points that the assertions refer to. If the checking of any of the assertions fails, this implies that the assertion is `false`. Thus, a concrete[5] incorrectness symptom has been detected and some kind of error message is given to the user. A procedure for localizing the cause of the error, such as standard or declarative diagnosis should be started.[6] *Correctness* of the transformation requires that the transformed program only produce an error if the specification is in fact violated.

Compile-time checking of assertions. Even though run-time checking can be very useful for detecting violations of specifications, it also has important drawbacks. First, run-time checking clearly introduces overhead into program execution. Also, it requires test cases, i.e., sample input data, which typically have an incomplete *coverage* of the program execution paths. Also, run-time checking cannot be used in general for proving that a program is correct with respect to an assertion, i.e., that the assertion is `checked`, as this would require testing the program with all possible input values, which is in general unrealistic.

Compile-time checking of assertions allows proving automatically at compile-time that (parts of) such assertions are implied by the program or, alternatively, that they hold for all possible program executions. This depends on the kind of properties in the assertions and the semantics used. In the case of declarative properties one can try to prove that they hold in the program model. For operational properties one will try to prove that they hold in all SLD trees. Modulo the semantics used, the whole process can also be viewed as computing at compile-time the results of run-time checking of assertions for all possible executions. Compile-time checking of assertions also allows proving that some assertions are violated without having to run the program.

As depicted in Figure 1, compile-time checking of assertions is performed in our framework by a *program analyzer* and an *assertion comparator.* The analyzer module is an abstract interpreter which automatically derives properties of the program. The kind of analysis performed may be selected by the user or determined automatically based on the properties used in the current `check` assertions. The derived properties are also expressed using assertions. They have the status "`true`," since they express properties which have been proved to hold. The `true` assertions are then compared against the given `check` assertions. The result might be that the assertion is validated or that it is proved not to hold. In the first case the corresponding assertions are rewritten as "`checked`" assertions; in the second case *abstract* symptoms are detected, the corresponding assertions are rewritten as "`false`" assertions, and error messages are presented to the user. Once again, diagnosis should be

[5] As opposed to *abstract* incorrectness symptoms, which are the ones detected by compile-time checking.

[6] It is out of the scope of this paper to discuss how program diagnosis should be performed. However, techniques such as declarative debugging [41,6,18,19], abstract debugging [13,14], or more traditional interactive debuggers [11,20] may be applied.

started, for example using abstract diagnosis [13,14], in order to detect the cause of the error. It is also possible that a (part of the) assertion cannot be proved nor disproved. In this case some assertions, or part of them, remain in `check` status, and possibly warning messages are presented to the user.

Note that it may also be interesting to implement analysis in a demand-driven way, so that information is inferred only for the program points which include assertions. The advantage of this approach is that it may be more efficient. However, three other considerations should be weighted against this. First, for many properties it is not possible to isolate the analysis of a given program point, and a global fixpoint has to be reached in any case, which requires analyzing at least the whole module involved. Also, the results of analysis are typically useful in other stages of compilation (e.g., to perform program specialization or other optimizations). Finally, in our experience bugs can often be detected by visual inspection of the assertions containing the information inferred by the analyzer, sometimes for program points which are "distant" from the user-provided `check` assertions. Compile-time checking is discussed further in Section 6.

3 The Assertion Language

Assertions may be used in different contexts and for different purposes. In run-time checking, assertions are traditionally used to express conditions which should hold at run-time. A usual example is to check that the value of a variable remains within a given range at a given program point. In declarative debugging [41], assertions have been used in order to replace the *oracle* by allowing the user expressing properties of the intended behaviour of the program [18,19,6]. Assertions can also be used to express properties about the program to be checked at compile-time. An example of this are type declarations (e.g., [30,42], functional languages, etc.), which have been shown to be useful in debugging. Assertions have also been used to provide information to an optimizer in order to perform additional optimizations during code generation (e.g., [42], which also implements checking). Assertions have also been proposed as a means of providing additional information to the analyzer, which it can use both to increase the precision of the information it infers and/or to perform additional optimizations during code generation [45,43,32,31]. Also, assertions can be used to represent analysis output in source form and for communication between different modules of the compiler which deal with analysis information [8].

The assertion language used in our framework has been designed with the aim of being useful in all the contexts mentioned above. With this objective in mind, we depart from previous proposals in allowing more general properties to be expressed. Each tool in each of the contexts will then use the properties which are relevant to it. Assertions are provided to specify the program points to which the properties are "attached." In this sense they

```
:- calls qsort(A,B) : list(A).                              % A1
:- success qsort(A,B) : list(A) => list(B).                 % A2
:- comp qsort(A,B) : (list(A),var(B)) + does_not_fail.      % A3

qsort([X|L],R) :-
        partition(L,X,L1,L2),
        qsort(L2,R2), qsort(L1,R1),
        append(R1,[X|R2],R).
qsort([],[]).
```

Fig. 2. An example predicate definition with assertions

work as schemas. Due to space limitations, we do not present here the complete assertion language, but rather we concentrate on a subset of it which suffices for illustrating the main concepts involved in compile-time and run-time checking of assertions. In particular, we will focus on *predicate assertions* rather than on *program point assertions.* Also for brevity, we will use only operational assertions, although the assertion language also includes declarative assertions (`inmodel`/`outmodel`). A more detailed description of the assertion language can be found in [36].

Predicate assertions relate properties to the invocations of a predicate. Three kinds of predicate assertions are provided; they relate properties to the execution states at the time of calling the predicate, at the time of its success, and to the whole of its computation. More than one predicate assertion (of the same or different kinds) may be given for the same predicate. In such a case, all of them should hold and composition of predicate assertions should be interpreted as their conjunction.

We first illustrate the use of this kind of assertions with an example. Figure 2 presents (part of) a CIAO [7] program which implements the *quick-sort* algorithm for sorting lists in ascending order. The predicate `qsort` is annotated with predicate assertions which express properties which the user expects to hold for the program.[7] Three assertions are given for predicate `qsort`: `A1`, `A2`, and `A3`, the meaning of which is explained below.

Assertions on Success States. They are similar in nature to the *postconditions* used in program verification. They can be expressed in our assertion language using the assertion schema '`:- success` *Pred* `=>` *Postcond.*' It should be interpreted as "for any call of the form *Pred* which succeeds, on success *Postcond*

[7] Both for convenience, i.e., so that the assertions concerning a predicate appear near its definition in the program text, and for historical reasons, i.e., mode declarations in Prolog or `entry` and `trust` declarations in PLAI [8] we write predicate assertions as directives. Depending on the tool different choices could be implemented, including for example putting assertions in separate files or incremental addition of assertions in an interactive environment.

should hold." For example, we can use the following assertion in order to require that the output of the procedure `qsort` for sorting lists be a list:

```
:- success qsort(A,B) => list(B).
```

Note that, in contrast to other programming paradigms, in (C)LP calls to a predicate may either succeed or fail. The postcondition stated in a `success` assertion only refers to successful executions.

Assertions Restricted to a Subset of the Calls. Sometimes we are interested in properties which refer not to all invocations of a predicate, but rather to a subset of them. With this aim we allow the addition of preconditions (*Precond*) to predicate assertions as follows: '*Pred* : *Precond*.' For example, `success` assertions can be restricted and we obtain an assertion of the form '`:- success` *Pred* : *Precond* => *Postcond*,' which should be interpreted as "for any call of the form *Pred* for which *Precond* holds, if the call succeeds then on success *Postcond* should also hold." Note that '`:- success` *Pred* => *Postcond*' is equivalent to '`:- success` *Pred* : `true` => *Postcond*.'

For example, the assertion `A2` in Figure 2 requires that if `qsort` is called with a list in the first argument position and the call succeeds, then on success the second argument position should also be a list.

Assertions on Call States. It is also possible to use assertions to describe properties about the calls for a predicate which may appear during program execution. This is useful for at least two reasons. If we perform *goal-dependent* analysis, a variation of `calls` assertions, namely `entry` assertions (see [8]), may be used for improving analysis information.[8] They can also be used to check whether any of the calls for the predicate is not in the expected set of calls (the "inadmissible" calls of [35]). An assertion of the kind '`:- calls` *Pred* : *Cond*' should be interpreted as "all calls of the form *Pred* should satisfy *Cond*." An example of this kind of assertion is `A1` in Figure 2 which expresses that in all calls to predicate `qsort` the first argument should be a list.

Assertions on the Computation of Predicates. Many properties which refer to the computation of the predicate, rather than the input-output behaviour, are not expressible with the assertions presented above. In particular, no property which refers to (a sequence of) intermediate states in the computation of the predicate can be easily expressed using `calls` and `success` predicate assertions only. Examples of properties of the computation which we may be interested in are: non-failure, termination, determinacy, non-suspension, non-floundering, etc. In our language this sort of properties are expressed by an assertion of the kind '`:- comp` *Pred* : *Precond* + *Comp-prop*,' which is interpreted as "for any call of the form *Pred* for which *Precond* holds,

[8] The `entry` (and `trust`) declarations are also instrumental in incremental modular analysis.

Comp-prop should also hold for the computation of *Pred*." Again, the field ': *Precond*' is optional. For example, `A3` in Figure 2 requires that all calls to predicate `qsort` with the first argument being a list and the second a variable do not fail.

4 Defining Properties

Whereas each kind of assertion indicates *when*, i.e., in which states or sequences of states, to check the given properties, the properties themselves define *what* to check. As mentioned before, properties are used to say things such as "X is a list of integers," "Y is ground," "p(X) does not fail," etc. and in our framework they are logic predicates, in the sense that the evaluation of each property either succeeds or fails. The failure or success of properties typically needs to be determined at the time when the assertions in which they appear are checked. As also mentioned previously, assertions can be checked both at compile-time and at run-time. In order to simplify the discussion, in this section we will concentrate exclusively on run-time checking (the role of properties during compile-time checking will be discussed in Section 6).

In order to make it possible to check a property at run-time, some *code* must exist somewhere in the system that performs this check. If the set of properties were fixed, the code to be used when performing the run-time tests could be contained in a predefined library. However, we would like to allow the user to define new, quite general properties. Since our properties are predicates, and we have assumed that our source language is a logic and/or constraint programming language (in which it is natural to define predicates and which typically offers extended meta-programming facilities), we choose to allow the user to *write the definitions of properties in the source language.* Writing the definition of a property in the source language has the advantage that in principle no special run-time support is then needed for checking properties at run-time, since it suffices to compile the predicate that defines the property with the rest of the program and simply call it at run-time in the appropriate places.[9]

A property may be a built-in predicate or constraint (such as `integer(X)` or `X>5`, and including extra-logical properties such as `var(X)`), an expression built using conjunctions of properties,[10] or, in principle, any predicate defined by the user, using the full underlying CLP language. As an example consider defining the predicate `sorted(B)` and using it as a postcondition to check that a more involved sorting algorithm such as `qsort(A,B)` produces correct results.

[9] Also, this allows using the standard program optimization tools (e.g., the program specializer) to avoid the run-time overhead of checking properties when they can be proven statically to hold.

[10] Although disjunctions are also supported, we restrict our attention to only conjunctions in our presentation.

However, while we would like to allow writing properties that are as general as allowed by the full source language syntax, some limitations are useful in practice. Essentially, we would not like the behaviour of the program to change in a fundamental way depending on whether the run-time tests are being performed or not. While we can tolerate a degradation in execution speed, turning on run-time checking should not introduce non-termination in a program which terminates without run-time checking. To this end, we require that the user ensure that the execution of properties terminate for any possible initial state. Also, checking a property should not change the answers computed by the program or produce unexpected side-effects. Regarding computed answers, in principle properties are not allowed to further instantiate their arguments or add new constraints.[11] Regarding side-effects, we require that the code defining the property does not perform input/output, add/delete clauses, etc. which may interfere with the program behaviour. It is the user's responsibility to only use predicates meeting these conditions as properties for run-time checking. The user is required to identify in a special way the predicates which he or she has determined to be legal properties. This is done by means of a declaration of the form "`:- prop` *`predicate/arity`*."[12]

Given the classes of assertions presented previously, there are two fundamental classes of properties. The properties used in the *Cond* of `calls` assertions, *Postcond* of `success` assertions, and *Precond* of `success` and `comp` assertions refer to a particular execution state and we refer to them as *properties of execution states.* The properties used in the *Comp-prop* part of `comp` assertions refer to a sequence of states and we refer to them as *properties of computations.*

4.1 Writing Properties of Execution States: Compatibility vs. Instantiation Properties

Consider a definition of the predicate `string_concat` which concatenates two character strings (we assume that strings are represented as lists of ASCII codes):

```
string_concat([],L,L).
string_concat([X|Xs],L,[X|NL]):- string_concat(Xs,L,NL).
```

Assume that we would like to state in an assertion that each argument "is a list of integers." However, we must decide which one of the following two

[11] However, the run-time checking scheme presented in Section 5 below guarantees that run-time checking is performed in an independent environment and thus will not modify computed answers.

[12] Nevertheless, the compiler performs some basic checks on properties and flags properties which can be detected with these checks to violate the required conditions.

possibilities we mean exactly: "the argument is *instantiated* to a list of integers" (let us call this property instantiated_to_intlist), or "if any part of the argument is instantiated, this instantiation must be compatible with it being a list of integers" (we will call this property compatible_with_intlist). For example, instantiated_to_intlist should succeed for calls with argument [] and [1,2], but should fail for X, [a,2], and [X,2]. In turn, compatible_with_intlist should succeed for calls with argument [], X, [1,2], and [X,2], but should fail for [X|1], [a,2], and 1. We refer to properties such as instantiated_to_intlist above as *instantiation properties* and to those such as compatible_with_intlist as *compatibility properties* (corresponding to the traditional notions of "instantiation types" and "compatibility types").

It turns out that both of these notions are quite useful in practice. In the example above, we probably would like to use compatible_with_intlist to state:

```
:- success string_concat(A,B,C) => ( compatible_with_intlist(A),
                                     compatible_with_intlist(B),
                                     compatible_with_intlist(C) ).
```

With this assertion, no error will be flagged for a call to string_concat such as string_concat([20],L,R), which on success produces the resulting atom string_concat([20],L,[20|L]), but a call string_concat([],a,R) would indeed flag an error.

On the other hand, and assuming that we are running on a Prolog system, we would probably like to use instantiated_to_intlist for sumlist as follows:

```
:- calls sumlist(L,N) : instantiated_to_intlist(L).

sumlist([],0).
sumlist([X|R],S) :- sumlist(R,PS), S is PS+X.
```

to describe the type of calls for which the program has been designed.

The property instantiated_to_intlist might be written as in the following (Prolog) definition:

```
:- prop instantiated_to_intlist/1.

instantiated_to_intlist(X) :-
       nonvar(X), instantiated_to_intlist_aux(X).

instantiated_to_intlist_aux([]).
instantiated_to_intlist_aux([X|T]) :-
       integer(X), instantiated_to_intlist(T).
```

(Recall that the Prolog builtin integer itself implements an instantiation check, failing if called with a variable as the argument.)

The property compatible_with_intlist might in turn be written as follows (also in Prolog):

```
:- prop compatible_with_intlist/1.

compatible_with_intlist(X) :- var(X).
compatible_with_intlist(X) :-
       nonvar(X), compatible_with_intlist_aux(X).

compatible_with_intlist_aux([]).
compatible_with_intlist_aux([X|T]) :-
       int(X), compatible_with_intlist(T).

int(X) :- var(X).
int(X) :- nonvar(X), integer(X).
```

Note that these predicates meet the criteria for being properties and thus the `prop` declaration is correct.

Ensuring that a property meets the criteria for "not affecting the computation" can sometimes make its coding somewhat tedious. In some ways, one would like to be able to write simply:

```
intlist([]).
intlist([X|R]) :- int(X), intlist(R).
```

but note that (independently of the definition of `int`) the definition above is not the correct instantiation check, since it would succeed for a call such as `intlist(X)`. In fact, it is not strictly correct as a compatibility property either, because, while it would fail or succeed as expected, it would perform instantiations (e.g., if called with `intlist(X)` it would bind `X` to `[]`). In practice, it is convenient to provide some run-time support to aid in this task.

As we will see in Section 5, the run-time support of the framework ensures that the execution of properties is performed in such a way that properties written as above can be used directly as instantiation checks. Thus, writing:

```
:- calls sumlist(L,N) : intlist(L).
```

has the desired effect. Also, the same properties can often be used as compatibility checks by writing them in the assertions as `compat(`*Property*`)` (which should be interpreted as "*Property* holds in the current execution state or it can be made to hold by adding bindings (or constraints) to the current execution state"). Thus, writing:

```
:- success string_concat(A,B,C) => ( compat(intlist(A)),
                                     compat(intlist(B)),
                                     compat(intlist(C)) ).
```

also has the desired effect. As a general rule, the properties that can be used directly for checking for compatibility should be *downwards closed*, i.e., once they hold they will keep on holding in every state accessible in forwards execution. There are certain predicates which are inherently *instantiation* checks and should not be used as *compatibility* properties nor appear in the definition of a property that is to be used with `compat`. Examples of such predicates (for Prolog) are `==`, `ground`, `nonvar`, `integer`, `atom`, `>`, etc. as they require a certain instantiation degree of their arguments in order to succeed.

4.2 Writing Properties of Computations

Properties which appear in `comp` assertions refer to the entire execution of the predicate that the assertion refers to. It is therefore assumed that one of its arguments (the first one) is precisely the given call to which the property refers. For example, in assertion `A3` of Figure 2 for `qsort(A,B)`, the property `does_not_fail` (no arguments) really means `does_not_fail(qsort(A,B))`. For this property, which should be interpreted as "execution of the predicate either succeeds at least once or loops," we can use the following predicate `does_not_fail` of arity 1 for run-time checking:

```
does_not_fail(Goal):-
      if( call(Goal),
          true,               %% then
          warning(Goal) ). %% else
```

where the `warning` predicate simply prints a warning message.

In this simple case, implementation of the predicate is not very difficult using the `if` builtin predicate present in many Prolog systems. However, it is not so easy to code predicates which check other properties of the computation and we may in general need to program a meta-interpreter for this purpose.

5 A Simple Run-time Checking Scheme

In this section we provide a possible scheme for translation of a program with assertions into code which will perform run-time checking. Our aim herein is not to provide the best possible transformation (nor the best definition of auxiliary predicates used by it), but rather to present simple examples with the objective of showing the feasibility of the implementation and hopefully clarifying the approach further. Simple definitions of the auxiliary predicates can be found in Appendix A.

Properties. In general, testing assertions at run-time implies checking whether the properties contained in them hold or not. If they hold, computation should continue as usual. If they do not hold, an error message should usually be issued to the user. We assume a predicate `check` which does the checking and raises errors where appropriate. The checking of the properties can be an *instantiation check* or a *compatibility check* (when the property to be checked is enclosed in an argument of a `compat` literal). Appendix A provides implementations of `check` for both kinds of properties.

Success Assertions. A possible translation scheme for `success` assertions into run-time tests is the following. Let $A(\texttt{p/n})$ represent the set of current assertions for predicate `p` of arity `n`. Let S be the set $\{Postcond$ s.t. '`:- success` $p(X1, ..., Xn)$ `=>` $Postcond$' $\in A(p/n)\}$. Then the translation is:

```
p(X1,...,Xn):- new_p(X1,...,Xn), check(S).
```

where `new_p` is a renaming of predicate `p`.

Let RS be the set $\{(Precond, Postcond)$ s.t. '`:- success` $p(X1, ..., Xn)$ `:` $Precond$ `=>` $Postcond$' $\in A(p/n)\}$. A possible translation scheme for `success` assertions with a precondition is as follows:

```
p(X1,...,Xn):-
        collect_valid_postc(RS,S),
        new_p(X1,...,Xn), check(S).
```

The predicate `collect_valid_postc/2` collects the postconditions of all pairs in `RS` such that the precondition holds.

Calls Assertions. A possible translation scheme for `calls` assertions into run-time tests follows. Let C be the set $\{Cond$ s.t. '`:- calls` $p(X1, ..., Xn)$ `:` $Cond$' $\in A(p/n)\}$. Then the translation is:

```
p(X1,...,Xn):-  check(C), new_p(X1,...,Xn).
```

Comp Assertions. Let RC be the set $\{(Prec, Comp\_prop)$ s.t. '`:- comp` $p(X1, ..., Xn)$ `:` $Prec$ `+` $Comp\_prop$' $\in A(p/n)\}$. Then, a possible translation scheme of `comp` assertions into run-time tests is as follows:

```
p(X1,...,Xn):-
        collect_valid_postc(RC,C),
        add_arg(C,new_p(X1,...,Xn),C1),
        ( C1 == [] ->
          call(new_p(X1,...,Xn)) %% then
        ; call_list(C1) ).       %% else
```

where the predicate `add_arg` adds the goal `new_p(X1,...,Xn)` as the first argument to any property of the computation, and `call_list` calls each goal in the argument list.

6 Compile-Time Checking

We now turn our attention to compile-time checking of assertions. As mentioned before, and motivated by the availability of practical global static analyzers supporting a number of abstract domains, our approach is to compare the information generated during global analysis with the `check` assertions present in the program. Because we typically support properties which are statically undecidable, the information available at compile-time will not always allow determining whether a given assertion will hold at run-time or not. This case may also arise because the analysis itself is not accurate enough. We accept the fact that the approach will be weaker *in general* than that offered by, e.g., *strong* type systems. On the other hand, the same results obtained with a strong type system can be achieved by selecting an analysis that uses the same type system as abstract domain and providing sufficient (type) assertions in the program.

Informally, the actual checking of the assertions at compile-time is performed as follows (precise details on how to reduce assertions at compile-time can be found in [37]). The properties which appear in the user-provided `check` assertions are compared one by one with the properties inferred by the analysis. An assertion is validated if all its properties are *implied* by the analysis results (preconditions require special consideration in this process). On the other hand, errors are detected if any property specified is *incompatible* with the analysis results. If it is not possible to prove nor to disprove an assertion, then such assertion is left as a `check` assertion, for which run-time checks might be generated. However, if some properties are implied but others cannot be proved nor disproved, the assertion as a whole can be *simplified*, in the sense of reducing the number of properties which have to be checked at run-time.

For example, assume that we have the following user-provided assertions:

```
:- check success p(X,Y) =>  (intlist(X),ground(Y)).
:- check comp    p(X,Y) +   (does_not_fail,terminates).
```

and that we are running a mode and non-failure analysis which has inferred the following information:

```
:- true success  p(X,Y) =>  (any(X),ground(Y)).
:- true comp     p(X,Y) +   does_not_fail.
```

Then, the user-provided assertions could be transformed into:

```
:- check success p(X,Y) => intlist(X).
:- check comp    p(X,Y) +  terminates.
```

With this compile-time simplification process in mind, we discuss further the nature of the properties which may appear in assertions and their treatment. In traditional systems which focus on compile-time checking (e.g., type systems), the properties allowed are usually restricted to those for which the available analyzer (e.g., the type checker) can decide whether they hold or not at compile-time. Conversely, in traditional systems which focus on run-time checking, usually only properties which are executable are considered. While most systems using assertions focus on either run-time or compile-time checking, in the framework we propose both techniques are combined. As a result, compile-time checking must be able to deal (at least safely) with properties that have perhaps been written with run-time checking in mind or for which no specific analysis is available. Conversely, the run-time checking machinery must also be able to deal correctly with properties that are primarily meant for compile-time checking.

Let us divide properties into classes *from the point of view of a given analysis*. First, we will call *native* properties those which are directly "understood" (abstracted) by this analysis. This is the case for example of properties like `ground` or `var` for a mode analysis, `does_not_fail` for a non-failure analysis, `terminates` for a termination analysis, or a predicate defining a (regular) type for a regular type analysis, etc. These native properties can be recognized when appearing in an assertion either by name (as with `ground`, `var`, etc.) or by syntax (e.g., for regular types [46,16], which in our case are defined by a regular logic program, and this can be recognized at compile-time).

If a property appearing in an assertion is native of an analysis then it is often possible to either prove it or disprove it, provided that the analysis is accurate enough and the "direction" of approximation performed by the analysis is the appropriate one [37,10] (this is the case for the properties `var` and `does_not_fail` in the example above). We say that the properties are *abstractly reducible* (to either true or false), or abstractly executable [39]. Note that, if the analysis is *precise* (in the sense that the abstract operations do not lose information beyond the abstraction implied by the abstraction function used [15]) and, obviously, terminates, then the native properties will be decidable in all cases. However, since there may in general be cases in which some such properties remain for run-time checking (and because in our framework the definitions of properties can be called from user programs) we require that there be an executable definition of all properties available in the system.

Note that there are properties which can be proved (or disproved) at compile-time by a given analyzer but for which no *accurate* definition can be written in the underlying language. An extreme example of this is the property `terminates`, for which it is obviously not possible to define a run-time test which will give a warning if it does not hold. For these properties, an *approximate* definition may be given, and this approximation should be correct in the usual sense that all errors flagged should be errors, but there may be errors that go unchecked. For example `terminates` may simply be over-approximated as `terminates(_).` which obviously succeeds for all terminating goals and therefore will not flag any terminating goals as non-terminating. However, the user should obviously not expect non-termination problems to be detected at run-time with this definition. In summary, it is not necessary that the executable definition of all properties be an exact implementation of a given property, but the user must provide, or import, some code for each property and understand and take into account the impact of approximation being performed in the property definition when using these properties in assertions.

Conversely, and again for a given analysis, there may be properties which are defined precisely and are perfectly executable at run-time, but which may not be *native* for that analysis. For them, the analysis may not be capable of obtaining an exact representation (abstraction). However, a useful approximation (usually an over-approximation) of such property can be obtained by *directly analyzing the code which defines the property.* As an example, consider the code for the property `intlist` as defined in Section 4. By simply analyzing this code the mode analyzer can abstract it (for its use as an *instantiation* property) as `ground`.

The fact that the resulting internal representation in the analyzer of a non-native property is itself an approximation must be taken into account. For example, if an over-approximation of the property definition is performed, as in the example above, and the analysis is itself an over-approximating analysis, an occurrence of the property in an assertion cannot be proved to hold. However, it can be proved that such property occurrence does `not` hold, if the information inferred by the analysis is *incompatible* with the internal representation of the property. In fact, in the example above it would be detected that the `intlist(X)` (i.e., `ground(X)`) requirement on success is incompatible with the inferred information `var(X)`, statically detecting the presence of an error.

In general, typical analyzers obtain over-approximations of properties, i.e., they succeed for a superset of the cases in which the exact property would succeed. However, for the case of properties in preconditions of `success` or `comp` assertions, under-approximations (i.e., the approximation succeeds for a subset of the cases in which the exact property would succeed) rather than over-approximations should be considered. Otherwise, the preconditions cannot be guaranteed to hold, and therefore it would not be possible in general to guarantee that the preconditioned assertion is applicable, since the exact precondition could possibly not be applicable, even though its approximation is implied by the analysis. More details on the use of approximations for program debugging can be found in [10,37].

7 A Sample Debugging Session with the CIAO System

We now illustrate some uses of the proposed framework by means of a sample session with `ciaopp`, the CIAO system preprocessor, which is currently a part of the programming environment of CIAO[13] [26], and which is directly based on the proposed approach.[14] `ciaopp` uses as analyzers both the LP and CLP

[13] The CIAO system is available at `http://www.clip.dia.fi.upm.es/Software/`.

[14] We have implemented the schema of Figure 1 as a *generic framework*. This genericity means that different instances of the tools involved in the schema can be incorporated in a straightforward way. Currently, two different experimental debugging environments have been developed using this framework: `ciaopp`, the CIAO system preprocessor, developed by UPM, and `fdtypes`, an assertion-based

versions of the PLAI abstract interpreter [34,9,25] and adaptations of Gallagher's type analysis [24], and works on a large number of abstract domains including moded types, definiteness, freeness, and grounding dependencies (as well as more complex properties, such as bounds on cost, determinacy, non-failure, etc., for Prolog programs).

We consider the program in Figure 3. Note that the program is a module. This helps performing precise global analysis. Also, note that properties can be defined in the module itself (e.g., `sorted_num_list`) or imported from other modules (e.g., `list`), and they can also be "builtins" (i.e., in modules loaded by default, such as `var`, `ground`, `num`, etc.). The `entry` declaration informs the analyzer that in all calls to `qsort`, the first argument will be a list of numbers and the second a free variable. This will aid goal-dependent analysis in order to obtain more accurate information. `A1` uses the parametric type `list(A, num)` which means that `A` is (or should be) a list of numbers. `A2` combines a mode property, `ground`, with a user-defined property, `sorted_num_list`. The code defining such property is included in the program in Figure 3. `A3` only contains mode properties while `A4` contains a combination of type and mode properties. Note that none of the assertions included in the program is compulsory and that properties natively understood by different analysis domains may be combined in the same assertion.

Using type and mode analysis, the assertions `A1` to `A4` are simplified at compile-time into:

```
:- checked calls qsort(A,B) : list(A,num).                          %A1
:- check success qsort(A,B) => sorted_num_list(B).                  %A2
:- false calls partition(A,B,C,D) : ground(A),ground(B).            %A3
:- checked success partition(A,B,C,D) => (list(C,num), ground(D)). %A4
```

Assertion `A3` has been detected to be false. This is a compile-time, or *abstract* incorrectness symptom, indicating that the program does not satisfy the specification given because the predicate `partition` will not be called in the right way. At this point diagnosis should start in order to detect the cause of the error. The obvious thing to do is to check the calls to `partition` and inspect their arguments. By doing this, the user could easily detect that in the definition of `qsort`, `partition` is called with the second and third arguments reversed. By correcting this bug we obtain the following definition of `qsort`:

---

type inferencing and checking tool developed by Pawel Pietrzak at the U. of Linköping, in collaboration with UPM. Also, an assertion-based preprocessor for PrologIV has been developed by Claude Lai of PrologIA extending the work of [44], which is based on the same overall design, but separately coded and using simpler analysis techniques. These three environments share the same source language (ISO-Prolog + finite domain constraints) and the same assertion language [36], so that source and output programs, possibly annotated with assertions and/or run-time tests can be easily exchanged. `fdtypes` has been interfaced by Cosytec with the CHIP system (adding a graphical user interface) and is currently under industrial evaluation.

```
:- module(qsort, [qsort/2], [assertions]).
:- use_module(library(lists),[list/2]).

:- entry qsort(A,B) : (list(A, num), var(B)).

:- calls qsort(A,B) : list(A, num).                            % A1
:- success qsort(A,B)  => (ground(B), sorted_num_list(B)). % A2

qsort([X|L],R) :-
        partition(L,L1,X,L2),
        qsort(L2,R2), qsort(L1,R1),
        append(R2,[X|R1],R).
qsort([],[]).

:- calls partition(A,B,C,D) : (ground(A), ground(B)).        % A3
:- success partition(A,B,C,D) => (list(C, num),ground(D)). % A4

partition([],_B,[],[]).
partition([e|R],C,[E|Left1],Right):-
        E < C, !, partition(R,C,Left1,Right).
partition([E|R],C,Left,[E|Right1]):-
        E >= C,   partition(R,C,Left,Right1).

append([],X,X).
append([H|X],Y,[H|Z]):- append(X,Y,Z).

:- prop sorted_num_list/1.

sorted_num_list([]).
sorted_num_list([X]):- number(X).
sorted_num_list([X,Y|Z]):-
        number(X), number(Y), X<Y, sorted_num_list([Y|Z]).
```

Fig. 3. A tentative qsort program

```
qsort([X|L],R) :-
        partition(L,X,L1,L2),
        qsort(L2,R2), qsort(L1,R1),
        append(R2,[X|R1],R).
qsort([],[]).
```

With this new version of the program, we proceed to perform compile-time checking of the assertions once more. While doing this we get an error message of the form:

```
ERROR (infer): Builtin predicate A < B at partition/4/2/1
is not called as expected:
```

```
called:   var(A) < ground(B)
expected: ground(A) < ground(B)
```

Where `partition/4/2/1` stands for the first literal in the second clause for predicate `partition/4`. This error has been detected by comparing the assertion `:- check calls A<B : ground(A), ground(B).` which is already included in `ciaopp` (see Section 8) with the mode information obtained by global analysis, which at the corresponding program point indicates that `E` is a free variable. By reconsidering the second clause of partition we can see that in the first argument of the head, there is an `e` which should be `E` instead. The corrected version of this clause is now:

```
partition([E|R],C,[E|Left1],Right):-
        E < C, !, partition(R,C,Left1,Right).
```

By performing compile-time checking on the updated program, the status of user assertions is as follows:

```
:- checked calls qsort(A,B) : list(A,num).                              %A1
:- check success qsort(A,B)  => sorted_num_list(B).                     %A2
:- checked calls partition(A,B,C,D) : ground(A),ground(B).              %A3
:- checked success partition(A,B,C,D) => (list(C,num),ground(D) ). %A4
```

No assertion is now detected to be false. Thus, we cannot conclude that the specification does not hold. Moreover, assertions `A1`, `A3`, and `A4` have been detected to hold in the program. However, `A2` has not been statically proved. We can see that it has been simplified, and this is because the mode analysis has determined that on success the second argument of `qsort` is ground, and thus this does not have to be checked at run-time. On the other hand the analyses used in our session (types and modes) do not provide enough information to prove that the output of `qsort` is a *sorted* list of numbers. While this property could be captured by including a more refined domain such as constrained types, it is interesting to see what happens with the analyses selected.[15]

Assuming that we stay with the analyses selected previously, the following step in the development process is to compile the program obtained above with the "generate run-time checks" option. In the current implementation of `ciaopp` we obtain the following code for predicate `qsort` (the code for `partition` and `append` remain the same as there is no other assertion left to check):

---

[15] Whether the property `sorted_num_list` holds in `A2` is not abstractly reducible to true with only (over approximations) of mode and regular type information. However, it may be possible to prove that it does *not* hold (another example of how properties which are not natively understood by the analysis can also be useful for detecting bugs at compile-time): while the regular type analysis cannot capture perfectly the property `sorted_num_list`, it can still approximate it (by analyzing the definition) as `list(B, num)`. If type analysis for the program were to generate a type for `B` not compatible with `list(B, num)`, then a definite error symptom could be detected.

```
qsort(A,B) :-
        new_qsort(A,B),
        postc([ qsort(C,D) : true => sorted(D) ], qsort(A,B)).

new_qsort([X|L],R) :-
        partition(L,X,L1,L2),
        qsort(L2,R2), qsort(L1,R1),
        append(R2,[X|R1],R).
new_qsort([],[]).

sorted_num_list([]).
sorted_num_list([_]).
sorted_num_list([X,Y|Z]):-
        X<Y, sorted_num_list([Y|Z]).
```

where `postc` is the library predicate in charge of checking postconditions of predicates – it accepts a list of assertions whose postcondition must be checked. The reason for using this predicate instead of `check` (which only receives the postcondition as argument), introduced in Section 5, is that if an error is detected, a more informative message can be printed than if only the postcondition responsible for the error is available.

Note also that the definition of predicate `sorted_num_list` has been optimized by the *abstract specializer* [38,39] by eliminating the `number` tests. This is possible by taking advantage of type analysis which tells us that on success the second argument of `qsort` is a list of numbers.[16]

If we run the program with run-time checks in order to sort, say, the list `[1,2]`, the CIAO system generates the following error message:

```
?- qsort([1,2],L).
ERROR: false success assertion for Goal qsort([1,2],[2,1])
Precondition: true  holds, but
Postcondition: sorted_num_list([2,1]) does not hold.

L = [2,1] ?
```

[16] Note that the availability of the abstract specializer allows an alternative implementation of the whole framework (also using both compile-time and run-time checking of assertions) by first generating in a naive way a program which performs run-time checking of all assertions and then applying the abstract specializer to this program. The resulting code would be similar to that obtained with the previous approach (first simplifying the assertions in a specialized module and then generating code for those which cannot be statically proved). `checked` assertions will result in run-time tests that are optimized away, false assertions will result in run-time tests that are transformed to `error`, etc. However, we have opted for the first alternative because we have found that it is easier for the user to understand things in terms of simplified assertions rather by looking at the run-time tests which remain in transformed code.

By observing this error message one can easily realize that there is some problem with `qsort`, as `[2,1]` is not the result of ordering `[1,2]` in ascending order. This is a (now, run-time) incorrectness symptom, which can be used as the starting point of diagnosis, using the previously mentioned declarative diagnosis techniques, standard debugging, etc. The result of such diagnosis should indicate that the call to `append` is the cause of the error and that the right definition of predicate `qsort` is the one in Figure 2.

8 Some Practical Hints on Debugging with Assertions

As mentioned before, one of the main features of the framework we present is that assertions are optional and can provide partial information. The fact that assertions are optional has important consequences on the ease of use and the practicality of the whole approach. An important drawback of many verification systems is the need for a relatively precise specification of the program. Writing such a specification is usually a tedious and not straightforward task. As a result users in practice often get discouraged and may decide not to use systems which require quite detailed specifications. In contrast, in our framework assertions can be written "on demand", perhaps adding them only for those program points and properties that the user wants to check in a given program. Clearly, as more (and more precise) assertions are added to a program, more bugs can potentially be detected automatically. Note that during the process of program development and debugging we will often turn our attention from some parts of the programs to others, and thus the set of assertions may change from one iteration to another.

The fact that assertions are optional obviously raises questions regarding issues such as, for which parts of the program should one write `check` assertions, what kinds of assertions should be used for a given objective, which kind of properties should be used in a given assertion, etc. Many of these questions are still open for research. Nevertheless, we can attempt to provide a few answers.

A point to note is that, from the point of view of their use in debugging, `calls` assertions are conceptually somewhat different from `success` and `comp` assertions. It is not of much use to introduce `success` and `comp` assertions during debugging for predicates which are known to be correct.[17] Introducing

[17] However, even if the predicate is known to be correct, such assertions can be very useful for other purposes. For example, the information in such assertions can be used to generate documentation automatically (see [27] for an example of such a tool, and most of the manuals in `http://www.clip.dia.fi.upm.es` for examples of the output produced by this tool). In addition, `true success` and `true comp` assertions can be used for describing *external* predicates, i.e., predicates for which no source code is available for the analyzer to process (such as WAM built-ins or predicates written in other languages). Also, `trust calls`, `trust success` and `trust comp` assertions can be useful for guiding the analysis [8].

		Types			*Modes*			*Aliasing*		
Prog	**Ps**	**Props**	**Infer**	**Simp**	**Props**	**Infer**	**Simp**	**Props**	**Infer**	**Simp**
ann	66	514	9.64	0.55	265	1.60	1.22	419	2.22	6.57
palin	6	28	0.56	0.19	15	0.18	0.02	22	0.21	0.02
progeom	10	58	0.70	0.65	56	0.08	0.06	57	0.06	0.06
queen	6	28	0.23	0.09	26	0.05	0.03	28	0.04	0.04
warplan	31	132	8.33	0.12	71	1.83	0.07	98	2.35	0.10

Fig. 4. Analysis/Checking Performance

`success` and `comp` assertions is in general most useful for *suspect* predicates. On the other hand, introducing `calls` assertions is a good idea even for correct predicates because the fact that a predicate is correct does not guarantee that it is called in the proper way in other parts of the program.

This observation has led us for example to introduce `check calls` assertions in the CIAO *libraries* for the predicates exported by such libraries. This includes all the system's built-in predicates. These assertions are then used by `ciaopp` during analysis of a *user program*, and this allows detecting bugs in such programs without having to add *any* assertions in them. These assertions use properties, including types and modes, which can be handled with good precision at compile-time by the analyses currently available in `ciaopp`. Our preliminary experience with this setup is very promising, as many calls to system predicates with incorrect types, modes, or even more complex properties are indeed detected at compile-time.

An important remark is that it is usually the case that different parts of the program are perceived by the user as having different levels of reliability [21]. For example, in order to detect a bug it is usually good practice to assume that library predicates are correct. For a tool to be successful, we believe that such different levels of reliability should somehow be reflected during the validation/debugging session so that the programmer's attention can concentrate on a particular part of the code. Otherwise the debugging task becomes unrealistic for real programs. This can be achieved in our framework by adding assertions for those predicates that attention is focussed on and by "removing" assertions for others which are no longer under consideration. One very sensible way of doing this is by using modules. Dividing a program into modules allows performing compile-time checking by focusing on a single module, while not judging the code in other modules, of which we are only aware of through a high-level description of the imported predicates (i.e., assertions for internal predicates of an imported module are effectively "turned off"). `ciaopp` allows modular debugging of programs and the description of imported predicates is once again done in terms of assertions. Such description can be provided by the user when the code for the imported module is not yet available or automatically generated using analysis information once it is available [8].

	With Run-time Checks					
	Types		*Modes*		*Aliasing*	
Prog	**Props**	**Slowdown**	**Props**	**Slowdown**	**Props**	**Slowdown**
ann	514	2.95	265	3.55	419	3.50
palin	28	15.0	15	6.00	22	9.00
progeom	58	104	56	65.0	57	66.0
queen	28	6.10	26	6.10	28	6.10
warplan	132	190	71	151	98	177

Fig. 5. Run-Time Checking Cost

9 A Preliminary Experimental Evaluation

The actual evaluation of the practical benefits of these tools is beyond the scope of this paper, but we are encouraged by our own experiences with the system (and the significant industrial interest in the prototype shown). It has certainly been observed during use by the system developers and a few early users that the environment can indeed detect some bugs much earlier in the program development process than with any previously available tools.

It is also not our current purpose to perform a detailed evaluation of the *performance* of the system. However, preliminary results also show that performance is reasonable. Figure 4 presents results for `ciaopp`, inferring *types* (using Gallagher's type analyzer [24]), *modes* (using a variant of the Sharing+Freeness domain [33]), and *variable aliasing* (using the standard Sharing+Freeness). Analysis times are relatively well understood for these domains. The assertion processing time (normalization, simplification, etc.) obviously depends on the number of assertions in the input program. Given the lack at this point of a standardized set of benchmarks including assertions, for our preliminary evaluation we have opted for a simple (and with obvious drawbacks, but at least repeatable) method of generating programs with assertions automatically: previous to our measurements, we have run the analyzer on each program, producing a program annotated with `true` assertions (which express the analysis results) for each predicate. We have then rewritten such assertions into `check` assertions, and used the resulting program again as input to the system. **Prog** is the program being debugged and **Ps** the number of predicates, and, thus, of assertions (analysis variants were collapsed into one per predicate) in the program. **Props** is the number of properties which appear in the program assertions. **Infer** the analysis time, and **Simp** the time taken by the comparator to simplify the input assertions. These times are relative to the time taken by the a standard Prolog compiler (the SICStus compiler, in this case) to compile the program without assertions. For example, a 2 for **Infer** means that analysis time is twice a normal Prolog compiler time for the benchmark.

Clearly, in our case all assertions should be proven to be checked statically and, indeed `ciaopp` does so. Figure 5 provides some data on the run-time cost of the assertions eliminated. It shows the slowdowns incurred when running the programs with the assertions relative to the running times of the original programs without assertions. **Prog** and **Props** are as before. Obviously, in our stylized case, when running the programs with assertions through `ciaopp` no slowdowns occur, since all run-time checks are eliminated.

Again, the purpose of presenting these results is just to give a flavor for the behavior of the system. Clearly, the results should be contrasted with those obtained in an exhaustive evaluation, using more realistic, user provided assertions, which is left as future work.

10 Discussion

Software development is a difficult and error-prone task. Automatic tools for aiding in validation and debugging of programs are of great importance, especially those which allow finding problems at compile-time. Type checking is without a doubt one of the most successful techniques for compile-time bug detection. Type systems can be regarded as simple assertion-based frameworks with a limited property language. These properties (i.e., the types) are defined using a restricted syntax which (in our terms) guarantees that the resulting expression is natively understood by the analyzer (generally just a checker, see below). In traditional strongly typed languages, type declarations must exist for each procedure and each declaration must be as accurate as possible. Then, an efficient type checking algorithm is used. If type checking succeeds, then the program is guaranteed to be type-correct. This avoids the need for run-time checking. The type checking algorithm is typically (quasi) decidable in the sense that if the program is type-correct then the algorithm is able to prove it. Thus, the traditional approach is to reject those programs which do not pass the type check as they are (almost surely) incorrect with respect to the given type declarations.

In spite of the above mentioned benefits of strongly typed systems, there are many situations in which such a framework is too restrictive. Examples of this are when we do not wish to impose having assertions (e.g., type declarations) for all predicates (which would be unnatural for untyped languages), when the assertions are not as accurate as possible (for example, only some arguments are described), or, even more importantly, when we are interested in properties which are more general than types but for which we may not have a complete algorithm for checking them at compile-time. Nowadays, more and more powerful static analyzers are available which are capable of inferring non-trivial properties about programs, but which fall in the above category in that, unlike (traditional) types, these properties are in general not completely decidable at compile-time. Thus, such analyzers can only perform a safe approximation, i.e., if analysis concludes that the property holds, then it actually holds. However, analysis may not be able to conclude that certain property holds when it indeed holds, even if it understands this property "natively."

One of the main motivations for the framework we propose is to help automate as much as possible the validation and debugging of programs with respect to properties which lay out of traditional type-systems. Unless we do so, we cannot use in an automatic way the results offered of the large number of existing and very powerful analyzers which "only" approximate properties. Also, we believe that the approach we propose is arguably more suitable as an extension to untyped languages, such as Prolog and many instantiations of the CLP scheme.

Once we lift the requirement that properties be statically decidable we open up a different design space beyond that of classical type systems which offers much more flexibility than traditional strong type systems: assertions are optional, the user can define new properties, and the approach can deal with properties which type systems simply cannot handle. In order to achieve this, the framework has to correctly deal throughout with approximations. This extension is done knowingly at the expense of completeness, in the sense that there may be cases in which the program is correct with respect to the (partial) specification but we may not be able to prove it statically. However, this loss of completeness only occurs for the more general cases, since the traditional "complete" cases, such as decidable type systems also fall within the framework, in the form of a particular abstract domain.

Acknowledgments

This work has been supported in part by ESPRIT project DiSCiPl and CICYT project ELLA. The authors would also like to thank Saumya Debray, Lee Naish, Jan Małuszyński, Wlodek Drabent, and Pierre Deransart for many interesting discussions on assertions and assertion-based debugging, the anonymous referees for useful feedback on previous versions of the paper, Pawel Pietrzak for his adaptation of John Gallagher's type analysis for CLP($\mathcal{FD}$), and Abder Aggoun, Helmut Simonis, Eric Vetillard and Claude Lai for their feedback on the assertion language design.

References

1. A. Aggoun, F. Benhamou, F. Bueno, M. Carro, P. Deransart, W. Drabent, G. Ferrand, F. Goualard, M. Hermenegildo, C. Lai, J.Lloyd, J. Maluszynski, G. Puebla, and A. Tessier. CP Debugging Tools: Clarification of Functionalities and Selection of the Tools. Technical Report D.WP1.1.M1.1-2, DISCIPL Project, June 1997.
2. K. Apt, editor. *From Logic Programming to Prolog.* Prentice-Hall, Hemel Hempstead, Hertfordshire, England, 1997.
3. K. R. Apt and E. Marchiori. Reasoning about Prolog programs: from modes through types to assertions. *Formal Aspects of Computing*, 6(6):743–765, 1994.

4. K. R. Apt and D. Pedreschi. Reasoning about termination of pure PROLOG programs. *Information and Computation*, 1(106):109–157, 1993.
5. F. Bourdoncle. Abstract debugging of higher-order imperative languages. In *Programming Languages Design and Implementation'93*, pages 46–55, 1993.
6. J. Boye, W. Drabent, and J. Małuszyński. Declarative diagnosis of constraint programs: an assertion-based approach. In *Proc. of the 3rd. Int'l Workshop on Automated Debugging–AADEBUG'97*, pages 123–141, Linkoping, Sweden, May 1997. U. of Linkoping Press.
7. F. Bueno. The CIAO Multiparadigm Compiler: A User's Manual. Technical Report CLIP8/95.0, Facultad de Informática, UPM, June 1995.
8. F. Bueno, D. Cabeza, M. Hermenegildo, and G. Puebla. Global Analysis of Standard Prolog Programs. In *European Symposium on Programming*, number 1058 in LNCS, pages 108–124, Sweden, April 1996. Springer-Verlag.
9. F. Bueno, M. García de la Banda, and M. Hermenegildo. Effectiveness of Abstract Interpretation in Automatic Parallelization: A Case Study in Logic Programming. *ACM Transactions on Programming Languages and Systems*, 1998. In Press.
10. F. Bueno, P. Deransart, W. Drabent, G. Ferrand, M. Hermenegildo, J. Maluszynski, and G. Puebla. On the Role of Semantic Approximations in Validation and Diagnosis of Constraint Logic Programs. In *Proc. of the 3rd. Int'l Workshop on Automated Debugging–AADEBUG'97*, pages 155–170, Linkoping, Sweden, May 1997. U. of Linkoping Press.
11. L. Byrd. Understanding the Control Flow of Prolog Programs. In S.-A. Tärnlund, editor, *Workshop on Logic Programming*, Debrecen, 1980.
12. B. Le Charlier and P. Van Hentenryck. Experimental Evaluation of a Generic Abstract Interpretation Algorithm for Prolog. *ACM Transactions on Programming Languages and Systems*, 16(1):35–101, 1994.
13. M. Comini, G. Levi, M. C. Meo, and G. Vitiello. Proving properties of logic programs by abstract diagnosis. In M. Dams, editor, *Analysis and Verification of Multiple-Agent Languages, 5th LOMAPS Workshop*, number 1192 in Lecture Notes in Computer Science, pages 22–50. Springer-Verlag, 1996.
14. M. Comini, G. Levi, and G. Vitiello. Abstract debugging of logic programs. In L. Fribourg and F. Turini, editors, *Proc. Logic Program Synthesis and Transformation and Metaprogramming in Logic 1994*, volume 883 of *Lecture Notes in Computer Science*, pages 440–450, Berlin, 1994. Springer-Verlag.
15. P. Cousot and R. Cousot. Abstract Interpretation: a Unified Lattice Model for Static Analysis of Programs by Construction or Approximation of Fixpoints. In *Fourth ACM Symposium on Principles of Programming Languages*, pages 238–252, 1977.
16. P.W. Dart and J. Zobel. A regular type language for logic programs. In F. Pfenning, editor, *Types in Logic Programming*, pages 157–187. MIT Press, 1992.
17. P. Deransart. Proof methods of declarative properties of definite programs. *Theoretical Computer Science*, 118:99–166, 1993.
18. W. Drabent, S. Nadjm-Tehrani, and J. Małuszyński. The Use of Assertions in Algorithmic Debugging. In *Proceedings of the Intl. Conf. on Fifth Generation Computer Systems*, pages 573–581, 1988.
19. W. Drabent, S. Nadjm-Tehrani, and J. Maluszynski. Algorithmic debugging with assertions. In H. Abramson and M.H.Rogers, editors, *Meta-programming in Logic Programming*, pages 501–522. MIT Press, 1989.

20. M. Ducassé. OPIUM - an advanced debugging system. In M. J. Comyn, G.; Fuchs, N.E.; Ratcliffe, editors, *Proceedings of the Second International Logic Programming Summer School on Logic Programming in Action (LPSS'92)*, volume 636 of *Lecture Notes in Computer Science* (subseries *LNAI*), pages 303–312. Springer Verlag, 1992.
21. M. Ducassé. A pragmatic survey of automated debugging. In Peter A. Fritzson, editor, *Automated and Algorithmic Debugging*, volume 749 of *Lecture Notes in Computer Science*, pages 1–15. Springer Verlag, May 1993.
22. M. Ducassé and J. Noyé. Logic programming environments: Dynamic program analysis and debugging. *Journal of Logic Programming*, 19,20:351–384, 1994.
23. G. Ferrand. Error diagnosis in logic programming. *J. Logic Programming*, 4:177–198, 1987.
24. J.P. Gallagher and D.A. de Waal. Fast and precise regular approximations of logic programs. In Pascal Van Hentenryck, editor, *Proceedings of the Eleventh International Conference on Logic Programming*, pages 599–613. The MIT Press, 1994.
25. M. García de la Banda, M. Hermenegildo, M. Bruynooghe, V. Dumortier, G. Janssens, and W. Simoens. Global Analysis of Constraint Logic Programs. *ACM Transactions on Programming Languages and Systems*, 18(5):564–615, 1996.
26. M. Hermenegildo, F. Bueno, D. Cabeza, M. García de la Banda, P. López, and G. Puebla. The CIAO Multi-Dialect Compiler and System: An Experimentation Workbench for Future (C)LP Systems. In *Parallelism and Implementation Technology for Logic and Constraint Logic Programming*. Nova Science, Commack, NY, USA, 1998.
27. M. Hermenegildo and The CLIP Group. `pl2texi`: An Automatic Documentation Generator for (C)LP – Reference Manual. The CIAO System Documentation Series – TR CLIP5/97.1, Facultad de Informática, UPM, August 1997.
28. M. Hermenegildo and The CLIP Group. Programming with Global Analysis. In *Proceedings of ILPS'97*, pages 49–52, Cambridge, MA, October 1997. MIT Press. (abstract of invited talk).
29. M. Hermenegildo, R. Warren, and S. K. Debray. Global Flow Analysis as a Practical Compilation Tool. *Journal of Logic Programming*, 13(4):349–367, August 1992.
30. P. Hill and J. Lloyd. *The Goedel Programming Language*. MIT Press, Cambridge MA, 1994.
31. A. Kelly, A. Macdonald, K. Marriott, P. Stuckey, and R. Yap. Effectiveness of optimizing compilation for CLP(R). In *Proceedings of Joint International Conference and Symposium on Logic Programming*, pages 37–51. MIT Press, 1996.
32. K. Marriott and P. Stuckey. The 3 R's of Optimizing Constraint Logic Programs: Refinement, Removal, and Reordering. In *19th. Annual ACM Conf. on Principles of Programming Languages*. ACM, 1992.
33. K. Muthukumar and M. Hermenegildo. Combined Determination of Sharing and Freeness of Program Variables Through Abstract Interpretation. In *1991 International Conference on Logic Programming*, pages 49–63. MIT Press, June 1991.

34. K. Muthukumar and M. Hermenegildo. Compile-time Derivation of Variable Dependency Using Abstract Interpretation. *Journal of Logic Programming*, 13(2/3):315–347, July 1992. Originally published as Technical Report FIM 59.1/IA/90, Computer Science Dept, Universidad Politecnica de Madrid, Spain, August 1990.
35. L. Naish. A three-valued declarative debugging scheme. In *8th Workshop on Logic Programming Environments*, July 1997. ICLP Post-Conference Workshop.
36. G. Puebla, F. Bueno, and M. Hermenegildo. An Assertion Language for Debugging of Constraint Logic Programs. In *Proceedings of the ILPS'97 Workshop on Tools and Environments for (Constraint) Logic Programming*, October 1997.
37. G. Puebla, F. Bueno, and M. Hermenegildo. A Framework for Assertion-based Debugging in Constraint Logic Programming. In *Proceedings of the JICSLP'98 Workshop on Types for CLP*, Manchester, UK, June 1998.
38. G. Puebla and M. Hermenegildo. Implementation of Multiple Specialization in Logic Programs. In *Proc. ACM SIGPLAN Symposium on Partial Evaluation and Semantics Based Program Manipulation*, pages 77–87. ACM Press, June 1995.
39. G. Puebla and M. Hermenegildo. Abstract Multiple Specialization and its Application to Program Parallelization. *Journal of Logic Programming. Special Issue on Synthesis, Transformation and Analysis of Logic Programs*, 1999. To appear.
40. D. De Schreye and M. Denecker. Assesment of some issues in CL-theory and program development, this volume, pp. 195–208.
41. E. Shapiro. *Algorithmic Program Debugging*. ACM Distiguished Dissertation. MIT Press, 1982.
42. Z. Somogyi, F. Henderson, and T. Conway. The execution algorithm of Mercury: an efficient purely declarative logic programming language. *JLP*, 29(1–3), October 1996.
43. P. Van Roy and A.M. Despain. High-Performace Logic Programming with the Aquarius Prolog Compiler. *IEEE Computer Magazine*, pages 54–68, January 1992.
44. E. Vetillard. *Utilisation de Declarations en Programmation Logique avec Constraintes*. PhD thesis, U. of Aix-Marseilles II, 1994.
45. R. Warren, M. Hermenegildo, and S. K. Debray. On the Practicality of Global Flow Analysis of Logic Programs. In *Fifth International Conference and Symposium on Logic Programming*, pages 684–699. MIT Press, August 1988.
46. E. Yardeni and E. Shapiro. A Type System for Logic Programs. *Concurrent Prolog: Collected Papers*, pages 211–244, 1987.

A Code for Run-time Checking

The following definition of predicate `check` can be used to check properties in assertions and raise errors if any property does not hold. We assume that conjunctions and sets are implemented by means of lists:

```
check([]).
check([Cond|Conds]):-
```

```
        not(inst_prop(Cond)),!, error(Cond), check(Conds).
check([_Cond|Conds]):-  check(Conds).
```

where the `error` predicate simply prints a message informing about an assertion which does not hold. Thus, unless otherwise stated by the user (by enclosing a property in a `compat` meta-call) the checking of each individual property is performed by means of the predicate `inst_prop`, which represents the *instantiation check* introduced in Section 4.1. As an example, a possible implementation (for Prolog) of the `inst_prop` check is:

```
inst_prop(Cond):-
       copy_term(Cond,NCond), call(NCond), variant(NCond,Cond).
```

where `variant` checks that its arguments are identical up to variable renaming. This guarantees that `NCond` has not been further instantiated during run-time checking, i.e., that `Cond` is not only compatible, but also *implied* by the calling substitution. In a CLP setting, the `inst_prop` check needs to test this implication (i.e., it is an *entailment* test).

Alternatively, if the property is to be checked for compatibility (i.e., it is enclosed in a `compat` meta-call), the corresponding test may be done by simply calling the property, allowing that the variables be further instantiated, i.e., that additional constraints be placed on the store. However, we do not want this possible further instantiation to be "propagated" to the rest of the execution. This can be ensured for example by using backtracking to undo things, e.g. (recalling that compatibility properties are wrapped around a `compat` meta-call):

```
compat(Cond):- not(not(Cond)).
```

The predicate `collect_valid_postc/2` used in checking assertions which have a precondition collects the postconditions of all pairs of pre and postconditions in its first argument such that the precondition holds. Note that those assertions whose precondition does not hold are directly discarded. A possible implementation of such predicate is given below:

```
collect_valid_postc([],[]).
collect_valid_postc([(Pre,Post)|Cs],PC):-
        not(not(inst_prop(Pre))),!,
        PC = [Post|PCs], collect_valid_postc(Cs,PCs).
collect_valid_postc([_|Cs],PC):-
        collect_valid_postc(Cs,PC).
```

The double negation by failure around `inst_prop(Pre)` is not strictly required. However it is introduced for reducing the memory-usage overhead introduced by run-time checking.

The predicate `add_arg` adds the goal in its second argument as the first argument to any property of the computation given in the list in the first argument. I.e.:

```
add_arg([],_,[]).
add_arg([C|Cs],Goal,[NC|NCs]):-
        C=..[F|Args], NC=..[F,Goal|Args], add_arg(Cs,Goal,NCs).
```

The predicate `call_list` calls each goal in the argument list:

```
call_list([]).
call_list([C|Cs]):- call(C), call_list(Cs).
```

Note that both `success` and `calls` assertions are in a sense special cases of `comp` assertions, since properties of call and success states can also be formalized as properties of the computation. For example consider the following predicates which could be used for checking `calls` and `success` properties at run-time:

```
calls(Goal,Prop):-
      ( call(Prop) ->
          true
      ;   error(Prop) ),
      call(Goal).
```

```
success(Goal,Prop):-
      call(Goal),
      ( call(Prop) ->
          true
      ;   error(Prop) ).
```

the assertion '`:- calls p(X) : ground(X)`' could be written '`:- comp p(X) + calls(ground(X)).`' Thus, an assertion language with only the `comp` predicate assertion would suffice. However, `calls` and `success` assertions appear very often in program debugging and their treatment (at least for run-time checking) is much simpler than that of the more general `comp` assertion. As a result, it is interesting to have a dedicated predicate assertion for them and only use `comp` assertions when the specification is not expressible as `calls` or `success` assertions.

3 Future of Declarative Programming

The contributions in this chapter provide an assessment of and comments on the future of two main approaches to declarative programming: logic programming and functional programming.

The area of theory and program development has received much attention in the field of logic programming and, more generally, in Computational Logic in the last decades. **De Schreye** and **Denecker** present a general assessment of this area.

They review different subareas of the computational logic theory and program development, including language implementation, program analysis and program transformation, and point out what they believe to be the main causes for success or failure. Then they discuss a novel view of the famous "Algorithm = Logic + Control" equation of Robert Kowalski, which played an important role in the theory and program development in the past. They conclude with comments on software engineering and promising future directions.

Declarative languages have been declared to have many advantages. But what is the evidence for these advantages? And if declarative languages are so wonderful, why aren't they more widely used? **Wadler** addresses these questions from the functional programming side of the declarative divide.

As evidence for the advantages of functional programming, Wadler cites six applications of functional programs, spanning theorem proving, telecommunications, genetic databases, database validation, expert systems, and multimedia networking. As to why they aren't more widely used, he lists a number of important inhibiting factors, and also mentions why some factors commonly thought to be inhibiting may not be. From this he draws morals as to how functional programmers might focus their attention in future. A coda reflects on the relation with logic programming.

Assessment of Some Issues in CL-Theory and Program Development

Danny De Schreye and Marc Denecker

Departement Computerwetenschappen, Katholieke Universiteit Leuven, Celestijnenlaan 200A, B-3001 Heverlee, Belgium

Summary. We make an assessment of the area of theory and program development in Computational Logic. We point out what we believe to be main causes for success or failure in this area. We revisit the "Algorithm = Logic + Control" equation of Kowalski and show how we believe it could be better understood and used. We indicate some promising directions for further work.

1 Introduction: on assessment

The area can be assessed with respect to different lines of objectives. The first is with respect to its achievements in fundamental or basic research. The second with respect to its impact on the software market.

1.1 Fundamental research

Again, one could distinguish between two lines of criteria. On the highest level, a very general criterion for the quality of basic research is *scientific elegance*. From two solutions to a same problem, criteria for fundamental research should select the one with the highest conceptual elegance. With respect to this, approaches to program and theory development in Computational Logic have performed exceptionally well.

However, an assessment could also be done with respect to the more specific long term objectives of this research area. These have often been stated by many different people of our community. As such, the line of thought for the long term objectives stated below is by no means original.

The motivations are rooted on two key observations. One is that software development is still very much a hand craft, in which each statement, each line of code, needs to understood in order to develop, adapt and maintain programs. The other observation is that, unlike other disciplines in engineering - such as chemical or mechanical engineering - there are very few formal mathematical foundations that can be exploited to support the software engineering process in a foundational and rigid way.

What is badly needed are techniques that bring software development from a hand craft to a scientifically supported, semi-automated process. In order to achieve this, since program development requires the understanding of each bit of code, the tools that provide the support for semi-automatization need to be semantics-based. In particular, we need formal, semantics-based tools for specification, analysis, verification and optimization of software.

This in turn imposes strong requirements on the programming languages for which such development can take place. In the context of programming languages with a very complex formal semantics, the realization of the mentioned semantics-based tools would be extremely difficult, if not impossible. Declarative languages, including Logic Programming languages, through their simple formal semantics, provide an ideal setting in which these long term objectives can be achieved.

1.2 Impact on the software market

Our perception of the software market is that it has two main characteristics that very much influence the potential impact of new technologies. The first of these is that the software market is inherently conservative, in the sense that it cannot, and should not, invest strongly in unstable technology. There are some exceptions to this. In particular, stand-alone applications, urgent problems for which no alternative solutions exist, or major-vendor supported hypes form such exceptions.

To clarify how this affects Computational Logic's impact in particular, we want to mention the example of the University Hospital at Leuven. Over the last 10 years, this very large hospital (with its several thousands of beds, one of the bigger world-wide) has been using Prolog as the basis for its information system, both for administrative and medical applications. As such, it has probably been one of the largest Prolog users in the world. Due to bankruptcy of their Prolog vendor, they were faced with the problem of finding a reasonably compatible Prolog at a reasonable price. This turned out to be difficult. So, considering the lack of guarantee on the stability of a potential new vendor (and the desire to move towards much more distributed and Internet based systems), they decided to move to Java. The example shows that our technology is insufficiently stable for companies to rely on it for their critical systems.

A second characteristic of the software market is that its demands on technology evolve very fast. Much faster than the speed at which basic research can produce solutions. In fact, computer science in general is much more driven by the demands imposed by industry than by previous progress achieved in fundamental research. As a result, few fundamental solutions to posed problems emerge sufficiently timely in order to be relevant, and most often ad-hoc partial solutions are preferred and become widely accepted.

At the Strategic meeting of the European Compulog Network of Excellence, held in Rome in the summer of 1997, a proposal was made to enhance the impact of Computational Logic on the software market by focusing on Internet-related research and applications (see [17]).

Although this is an interesting idea, we do see some problems with it. We do not believe that from the outside world Computational Logic is perceived as a paradigm which is specifically targeted towards (and suitable for) Internet development. Moreover, Computational Logic languages have definitely not been designed to deal with the specific issues, such as security, distributed programming, updates and component-based programming, that this application domain requires. Competing languages, like Java, do have specific support for these issues. As such, it is unclear whether it is realistic to believe that we can compete, and that Computation Logic will indeed acquire a part of this market.

1.3 Initial conclusions and overview

At least in Japan and Europe, Computational Logic has had the status of a minor hype around 1990. In Europe in particular, the Esprit research program funded quite a few projects, both in basic research and in R & D. Note that Esprit is a framework for industry-related research and therefore its funding of Computational Logic necessarily expresses industrial interest. In retrospect, one could criticize a majority of these projects for having focussed too much on basic research issues, while devoting less attention to the more practically relevant issues. Still, there have been important breakthroughs in the areas of Constraint Logic Programming and Inductive Logic Programming, with specific niches of application domains. In general, restricted to the area of program and theory development, the promises made by this area seemed to be too long-term to keep the interest from the outside world vivid.

In the remainder of the paper, we assess different areas related to theory and program development in Computational Logic. In particular: language implementation, program analysis and program transformation. We then discuss a novel view on the famous 'Algorithm = Logic + Control' equation of Robert Kowalski ([11]), which played an important role in theory and program development in the past. We then briefly comment on software engineering (or the lack of it in Computational Logic) and conclude with some promising future directions.

2 Implementation, analysis and transformation

2.1 Implementation

Within Logic Programming, language implementation has possibly been one of the most successful areas (see [20]). Around the beginning of the eighties, this area achieved highly efficient, industrial quality implementations for standard Prolog. Later, in the beginning of the nineties, similar results were obtained for Prolog augmented with delaying execution mechanisms ([16]), and by the end of the nineties, also for several extensions with constraint solving ([9]). Quoting Bart Demoen, industrial quality, efficient implementations can be expected for further extensions, including tabulation (see e.g. [26]) and abduction ([10]), in the coming years.

Another exponent of the work in this area is the success of Mercury (see [24]), where due to certain language restrictions and program declarations an efficiency comparable to C (and sometimes better) is obtained. Yet another, be it indirect success, is that some of the implementation techniques developed for Prolog, specifically on the level of memory management and garbage collection, were adopted in the implementation of Java (actually, even some of the implementors were imported).

A main strong point that boosted the achievements in this area is that language vendors actually invested in it. This is in contrast to some other areas of work, where no such support was given. We will return to this point below. A main weak point is that we never reached a highly efficient, industrial quality public domain Prolog. Having such a 'standard' Prolog available would have very much facilitated and boosted the work on the development of tools. It would have allowed much easier evaluation, comparison, integration and cross-fertilization between various techniques, which are all of the utmost importance in order to lift the techniques to wide-scale usability.

2.2 Analysis and transformation

In this section, we briefly assess achievements of Computational Logic in such areas as abstract interpretation, assertion-based analysis, termination analysis, unfold/fold transformation, partial evaluation and deduction, and program specialization in general. We refer to the tenth anniversary issue of the Journal of Logic Programming ([3]) for surveys on these areas. On the whole, the work in these areas has delivered much high quality basic research. Also, many good prototype systems have been developed. However, very few of these prototypes have been integrated into industrial quality Logic Programming languages.

What have been the bottlenecks for achieving such integrations ? A first and important one are the non-declarative features of Prolog. Although the very existence of a practical, efficiently implemented programming language, such as Prolog, has been of the utmost importance for our community, many powerful semantics-based analysis and optimization techniques that were developed for pure logic programs failed to scale up well for full Prolog. In some cases, the extensions to full Prolog became extremely messy and lost all the elegance of their "pure" counterpart. In most cases, the extended techniques simply lost most of their precision and power, failing to accurately treat the non-declarative features.

Similar bottlenecks turned up in the context of extending techniques from definite programs to normal ones, and from left-to-right SLD-resolution to the treatment of more complex computation mechanisms, e.g. those dealing with delay mechanisms (e.g. [16]) and constraint solvers (e.g. [9,18]). In both of these cases, somewhat similar to the extension to full Prolog, the cause of the bottleneck is the increased complexity of the semantics. This refers back to the statement in the introduction, that languages with a simple semantics are essential to make the development of semantics-based development tools feasible.

The semantics of logic programs with negation has been a matter of discussion and controversy for a long time. Although most issues have been resolved ([1]), the resulting preferred semantics are by no means simple. As a result, the percentage of works on program development that restrict the attention to definite programs is extremely high. Moreover, depending on the specific sub area, those techniques that do treat negation often only provide weak results for negative goals. For instance, most partial deduction methods only allow unfolding of negative literals when these are ground at specialization time (which is very restrictive due to the very nature of partial deduction).

In the context of more involved computation mechanisms, including delay mechanisms and constraint solvers, the increased complexity is on the level of the procedural semantics. Here again it turned out to be very hard to scale up techniques to these more complex semantics, while preserving elegance *and* precision. For instance, termination analysis under coroutining computation rules has taken much work and has produced fairly weak results. Similarly, abstract interpretation of constraint logic programs tends to loose a lot of precision.

Another reason for the lack of integration of development techniques in industrial quality systems is the weak position of the vendors. In contrast to the area of language implementation, vendors have not been able to support the research community in the integration of development tools into their systems.

A final bottleneck is that, at least for some of the subareas, there has been insufficient implementation oriented work in this area. In part this is due to a strong interest in theoretical issues, which is present in many areas in our field. Another important cause is that requirements for publications on implementation oriented work seem to be demanding a larger workload than for theoretical work. Most often, the implementations alone already require a substantial amount of work. In addition, requirements on detailed experimentations and comparisons with other approaches leads to an unbalance between the workloads attached to publication on practical versus theoretical work. This seems unreasonable. A change in attitude of the referees and editors is desirable to undo this.

2.3 The need for integrated development tools

Several semantics-based development techniques require similar types of information as input. Modes, types, data- and program flow patterns are of use for different verification and optimization techniques. This suggests that work should aim at developing integrated analysis/verification/optimization tools, in which the same information could be exploited in different ways.

At the very least, this would solve efficiency problems, relaxing the precision/efficiency trade-off.

Developments in this direction have been started in the last few years in different contexts. For instance, integration of abstract interpretation in termination analysis and in program specialization has received increasing attention. An integrated analysis tool, linked to an optimization tool, is under development in Madrid ([8,19]). Also, in the Mercury language, various types of information, partly declared, partly inferred, are combined in a powerful way to do both optimization and verification ([24]).

Taking this a step further, it has been suggested by Maurice Bruynooghe to further integrate these tools in a programming language specific editor. On the lowest level, the editor could support syntactic verification. Combined with incremental analysis, it could provide semantic verification. On top of that, based on the results of analysis, interactive, semi-automated optimization could be performed. In the context of open-box constraint logic programming, this could be enhanced even further. Today's open-box CLP languages ([18]) offer very rich control declaration languages. Combined and integrated with editing, analysis, verification and optimization support, such flexible control declaration languages could provide development tools that are in many ways similar to powerful program synthesis systems, such as the KIDS system of D. Smith ([23]).

3 "Algorithm = Logic + Control" revisited

The "Algorithm = Logic + Control" equation of [11] has motivated much work related to program development, especially in the context of program transformation and synthesis. In recent years, Robert Kowalski has revisited the equation, expressing that one should stress much more the procedural reading of logic programs, while reducing the emphasis on the declarative (in particular, the model theoretical) one ([13]).

As an initial response to that, we cannot help wondering why Logic Programming would be better at expressing procedures than procedural programming languages themselves. In some cases, in which the procedures are given in terms of natural language sentences (such as in legal reasoning applications), logic programs could indeed be the more natural way to encode such procedures. In many other cases though, such as in expressing algorithms, procedural languages seem to be more fit. This observation is backed up by many in our community. It suffices to inspect the literature to check how algorithms are typically represented in Logic Programming publications. The preferred language tends to be a Pascal-like one. Only in exceptional cases, when the author wants to illustrate his Prolog code for some algorithm, a Logic Programming style specification is used.

In this section, we want to revisit the equation from a different angle. We want to point out how the equation has led to problems in the design of logic programs in the past, especially in the context of software engineering criteria, and we want to indicate some directions for solutions.

3.1 A Pandora box called A = L + C

Let us first restrict the control, *C*, to SLD(NF)-resolution and afterward extend the discussion to more complex computation mechanisms. In this restrictive context, $A = L + C$ has created the conviction (or illusion) that we can simply represent a problem domain using declarative Horn clauses, after which SLD(NF) can generate solutions to particular queries. Practice has shown that this only works for very simple problems. As soon as a problem needs the traversal of larger search spaces, or needs other problem solving techniques than mere deduction, the declarative, Horn clause based approach is insufficient.

One may justly argue that the above statement seems to be contradicted by the many (pure) Prolog applications that have been developed in practice. Even most of the applications developed using the non-pure features of Prolog could probably also have been developed successfully without these non-pure features, at the expense of some efficiency.

The problem is that the Prolog programming used in such applications may be declarative in the formal mathematical sense (meaning: having a clear model-theoretical semantics), but it is *not* declarative with respect to the criteria that a software engineering methodology would impose.

In particular, successful larger Prolog applications are based on *term-based programming*. In term-based programming, the knowledge on the problem domain is not coded in atoms and clauses, but using terms. These terms are then grouped into lists, which actually represent theories of knowledge. Finally, Horn clauses are used to define new problem solvers, richer than SLD(NF)-resolution, which manipulate the theories encoded in the lists and which themselves are executed under SLD(NF).

As such, in term-based programming, the basis of the development is an equation $A = L' + C$, where L' is not the logic of the problem domain, but a logic defining some other execution mechanism, richer than SLD(NF), together with the original knowledge grouped into lists.

Now, the reason why this can be referred to as a Pandora box, is that in this representation, the knowledge on the problem domain does not appear as a first class citizen in the representation. The domain knowledge is buried inside lists, hidden inside procedures in *L'*. As a result, none of the usual requirements of software engineering, like re-usability, maintenance, etc. of that knowledge is achieved. If several applications are developed based on the same knowledge domain, each program will store and manipulate its own copy of the same data, with the usual disadvantages of duplication resulting from that.

Of course, a simple way to solve this is to encode the logic *L* in a separate theory, and to write a meta-program, *M*, such that execution of *L* under *M* under SLD(NF) is the same as executing L' under SLD(NF). In the resulting equation, $A = L + M + C$, the domain knowledge is now explicitly represented and accessible. Partial evaluation of L and M could then yield L' again, which could be considered as a more efficient, lower level implementation.

3.2 "AlgorithmS = Logic + ControlS"

The discussion above reveals a deeper conflict between the view of knowledge (or software) engineering on the one hand, with the traditional view of Logic Programming on the other hand. In knowledge engineering it is considered vital to have the knowledge base designed independently from the problem solving strategies used. Moreover, this implicitly assumes that a variety of different problem solvers can act on the same knowledge, since it is practically impossible to have one single solver that can (efficiently) solve a variety of problems on that same knowledge. In particular, one might provide deductive, abductive, inductive, constraint based, model generator based and simulator solvers, all available in the same environment and acting on the same knowledge base to solve different problems.

In Logic Programming, the traditional view has been to have one specific procedural interpretation, based on SLD(NF)-resolution, to solve all types of queries. The very name of "Logic Programming" reflects its focus on a fixed procedural interpretation for the given logic formulas, as the notion of "programming" can only exist if the execution model is known (and taking into account) in the development of the programs.

Some people have tried to bridge the gap between these two views by promoting program synthesis and transformation as a means to derive efficient programs from purely declarative specifications. Although this work has had some successes (see e.g. [5,6]), it is commonly believed that optimally efficient algorithms cannot be derived automatically from specifications. Note that the KIDS system ([23]) is not a counter example to this statement, since this system requires interaction with the programmer.

Turning back to the aspect of having a variety of different solvers available for solving different problems concerning a same knowledge base, it is interesting to note that this is exactly what the evolution on execution models for logic programs has been achieving over the last decennium. The introduction of delays, of various types of constraint solvers, in particular the open-box constraint solvers which provide an entire spectrum of different solvers combined in one, of tabulation ([26,21]), of model generation ([14]), of abductive ([10]) and inductive solvers ([15]), already provide a rich problem solving toolkit to support the knowledge engineering approach. However, as far as we know, current systems do not integrate a significant number of the above solvers into one powerful development system. We will return to this issue in the conclusions.

All the above suggest a new equation, "AlgorithmS = Logic + ControlS", that stands as a basis for Computational Logic theory and program development for the beginning of the next century. According to this equation, the logic of a problem domain is modeled in a theory L, which is reused for every possible problem one aims to solve within the domain. Depending on the nature of the specific problem at hand, an appropriate problem solver is selected, giving rise to a corresponding algorithm. The selection of the solver may be a hard task, especially when the variety of available techniques continues to increase. In addition, the resulting algorithms may be further optimized through analysis and specialization. If the knowledge base needs to be modified, the selection of the appropriate solvers may need to be revised and the optimization phase will definitely need to be reexecuted.

Whether within this picture there is still room or need for a (manual) implementation phase would depend on the complexity of the application. With the above approach we have only boosted the complexity of the type of problems which we can solve in a naive $A = L + C$ way. Undoubtably, this will not exactly get us quick-sort from a naive generate-and-test-sort specification (although, by selecting the appropriate constraint-based pruning and enumeration techniques, additionally optimized through specialization, we might get something which is close enough for our purpose!). So, in some very time-critical applications, an implementation phase will be needed. In such a phase, the logic L would still need to be remodeled to a logic L', more suitable for the particular problem. However,

1. the logic L should remain central in the system, as a basis for future modifications and reuse, while L' is only considered as a low level implementation for the specific problem,
2. the implementation step from L to L' should be very well documented, so that future maintenance, restarting from L is not endangered.

In [4], Alan Bundy gives a different critical evaluation of the "Logic = Algorithm + Control" equation. Similar to the discussion above, he also argues that, in general, a naive use of the equation can be lead to unacceptably inefficient programs. Different from us, he argues to extend the expressivity of the logic and to use program synthesis methods to transform richer logical specifications into efficient Horn programs. We believe that this is a valid alternative, but that, most likely, human interventions will continue to be required to guide such synthesis methods.

Also related is [12], where Robert Kowalski argues that Logic Programming needs to be extended with abduction and meta level reasoning to be able to use logic for all aspects of computation. The extension with meta level reasoning is in agreement with our concluding comments in Section 3.1. We see the extension with abduction as just one example of the many additional computation mechanisms that would be useful to increase the problem solving power of standard Logic Programming.

3.3 Software engineering

One issue that has not been raised above is how to design the logic L. We are not aware of the existence of a methodology for analysis and design in the context Computational Logic. On the other hand, Object-oriented analysis and Object-oriented design provide methodologies that are by now widely accepted in software engineering practice.

To our surprise, we noticed that in some of the approaches to OO-analysis (e.g. [2]), one of the main claims on the benefits of the approaches is that they provide *fully declarative specifications* of the analyzed problem domains. What is meant here is that the domains are entirely described in terms of objects, attributes and constraints.

It seems extremely important to connect Computational Logic theory and program development to such methodologies for analysis and design. Considering the declarative nature of some of these approaches, a push-button conversion between the OO-based representations and their logic counterpart should be very feasible.

4 Conclusions: future directions

4.1 Integration

Over the years, work in Logic Programming has spread out into a large number of increasingly less connected subareas. Some of the most prominent are formal semantics, non-monotonic reasoning, language implementation, program analysis, program synthesis and transformation, constraint logic programming, concurrent logic programming, functional-logic programming, abductive logic programming, inductive logic programming, deductive databases, natural language and logic programming, internet related developments and multi-agent related developments. For many of these areas, recent new research contributions often provide further extensions to techniques, methods, implementations and theory which already reached a high degree of refinement and specialization in the past. As a result, it often takes considerable expertise in a specific sub area to appreciate the significance of new contributions. This in turn has motivated the different subareas to organize their own specialized meetings, workshops and conferences, disconnecting from the main general conferences in the field.

Very much work remains to be done on integrating the key results obtained in these different subareas. By way of example, constraint logic programming has achieved impressive results on certain classes of problems. On the other hand, tabulation, more recently introduced in the area of deductive databases, also achieves very efficient problem solving on a variety of problems. As far as we know, the integration of constraint solving with tabulation, and their combined potential for applications, has not been studied at all.

One could produce a very long list of technological and theoretic achievements in Computational Logic, similar as in the example above, that have received considerable attention in isolation, but none in the context of other achievements. As a result, current Logic Programming languages only incorporate a fraction of the knowledge representation and problem solving power that the field produced in its various subareas over the last decennium. Also, formal theories only clarify the semantics and properties of isolated fragments of the full richness of the paradigm.

It is likely that many of the established techniques and results from separate subareas simply cannot be fruitfully and elegantly combined. But in many cases, the question of whether integration is feasible and useful has not received proper attention.

We believe that such integration activities are very important for the future of the field. In the areas involved with program and theory development in particular, they are crucial to obtain the long term objectives, as expressed in the introduction.

Of course, these problems are hard. They require a broad background, including expertise from different subareas. As such, they require a strong involvement from senior researchers in the field, and/or tight cooperation between different research teams.

At K.U.Leuven, a new research project entitled "LP+: a second generation Logic Programming language" was recently started to address some of these integration issues. It includes aspects on integration of knowledge representation in open theories, abduction, constraint solving, tabulation, efficient implementation, program and theory development techniques, efficient integrity checking and learning. We refer to [22] for an overview.

4.2 Computational Logic as a research vehicle for Computer Science

Another interesting direction for future research in Computational Logic lies in exploring the possibilities of porting and applying tools and techniques developed in Computational Logic to other programming paradigms. In the past, insufficient attention was given to applicability of methods and techniques outside the field. In particular, due to the powerful language features in the paradigm, such as unification, resolution and backtracking, certain problems, like for instance program optimization and analysis, are viewed upon differently from the Logic Programming perspective than from the perspective of languages with less powerful constructs. This sometimes leads to the development of richer techniques in Logic Programming, of which the applicability is not necessarily restricted to Logic Programming.

A typical example is positive supercompilation. Supercompilation ([25]) is a program transformation technique developed for functional programming languages, which extends partial evaluation. It is based on *driving* instead of reduction, where (in positive supercompilation) driving essentially generalizes matching to unification, introducing non-determinism in the unfolding. It has been shown in [7], that positive supercompilation is exactly the result of applying partial deduction to functional programs. As a side effect, the complex issue of how to control positive supercompilation could be resolved by importing results from Logic Programming on the control of partial deduction.

The example is by no means a stand-alone case. Other examples are for instance the way in which the apparently very different transformation techniques of *tupling* and *deforestation* in Functional Programming become very similar by moving from a functional to a relational representation. Yet another example, in the context of language implementation, is how memory management techniques for Prolog were adapted to the implementation of Java.

Aside from the powerful language features, applying techniques developed in Computational Logic to other paradigms is also very much facilitated by the fact that logic programs are so well suited for manipulating programs as data.

Acknowledgements

We shamelessly stole ideas from Bart Demoen on the assessment of language implementation, and from Maurice Bruynooghe on future directions for development tools. We are grateful to them for being nice victims. We thank Robert Kowalski, David S. Warren, Maurizio Martelli, Lee Naish and an anonymous referee for many interesting comments. We thank Wim Vanhoof for encouragements. We thank the organizers of the Shakertown meeting for their initiative. Danny De Schreye is a senior research associate of the Flemish Fund for Scientific Research (FWO). Marc Denecker is supported by GOA "LP+: a second generation Logic Programming language" and by FWO "Knowledge representation and reasoning in Open Logic Programming".

References

1. K.R. Apt and R.N. Bol. Logic Programming and negation: a survey. *The Journal of Logic Programming*, 19–20:9–72, 1994.
2. S. Van Baelen, J. Lewi, and E. Steegmans. Constraints in object-oriented analysis and design. In B. Magnusson, B. Meyer, J.-M. Nerson, and J.-F. Perrot, editors, *Technology of Object-Oriented Languages and Systems TOOLS 13*, pages 185–199. Prentice-Hall, 1994.
3. M. Bruynooghe, S. Debray, M. Hermenegildo, and M. Maher, editors. *The Journal of Logic Programming, Tenth Anniversary Issue, Vol. 19/20.* Elsevier Science Publishers, 1994.

4. A. Bundy. A broader interpretation of Logic in Logic Programming. In K. Bowen and R. Kowalski, editors, *Proceedings of the fifth International Conference and Symposium on Logic Programming*, pages 1624–1648. MIT-press, 1988.
5. Y. Deville. *Logic Programming: Systematic Program Development.* Addison-Wesley, 1990.
6. Y. Deville and K.-K. Lau. Logic program synthesis. *The Journal of Logic Programming*, 19–20:321–350, 1994.
7. R. Glueck and M. H. Soerensen. Partial deduction and driving are equivalent. In M. Hermenegildo and J. Penjam, editors, *Programming Languages: Implementations, Logics and Programs*, pages 165–181. Springer-Verlag, Lecture Notes in Computer Science, Volume 844, 1994.
8. M. Hermenegildo, G. Puebla, and F. Bueno. Using global analysis, partial specifications, and an extensible assertion language for program validation and debugging. This volume.
9. J. Jaffar and M. Maher. Constraint Logic Programming: a survey. *The Journal of Logic Programming*, 19–20:503–582, 1994.
10. A. C. Kakas, R. Kowalski, and F. Toni. The role of abduction in Logic Programming. In D. Gabbay, C.J. Hogger, and J.A. Robinson, editors, *Handbook of Logic in Artificial Intelligence and Logic Programming 5*, pages 235–324. Oxford University Press, 1998.
11. R.A. Kowalski. Algorithm = logic + control. *Communications of the ACM*, 22:424–431, 1979.
12. R.A. Kowalski. Problems and promises of Computational Logic. In J.W. Lloyd, editor, *Symposium on Computational Logic*, pages 1–36. Springer-Verlag, 1990.
13. R.A. Kowalski. Logic without model theory. In D. Gabbay, editor, *What is a Logical System?* Oxford University Press, 1995.
14. R. Manthey and F. Bry. A hyperresolution-based proof procedure and its implementation in Prolog. In *Proceedings of the 11th German Workshop on Artificial Intelligence*, pages 221–230, 1987.
15. S. Muggleton and L. De Raedt. Inductive Logic Programming: theory and methods. *The Journal of Logic Programming*, 19–20:629–680, 1994.
16. L. Naish. Automating control for logic programs. *The Journal of Logic Programming*, 2(3):167–183, 1985.
17. D. Pearce. Report on the CLN strategic planning workshop, Rome, June 20-21. Technical report, Compulog Network of Excellence, available at http://www.cs.ucy.ac.cy/compulog/newpage5.htm, 1997.
18. T. Le Provost and M. Wallace. Constraint satisfaction over the CLP scheme. *The Journal of Logic Programming, Special Issue on Constraint Logic Programming*, 16(3–4):319–359, 1993.
19. G. Puebla and M. Hermenegildo. Abstract multiple specialization and its application to program parallelization. *Journal of Logic Programming. Special Issue on Synthesis, Transformation and Analysis of Logic Programs*, 1999. To appear.
20. Peter Van Roy. The wonder years of sequential Prolog implementation. *The Journal of Logic Programming*, 19–20:395–442, 1994.
21. Konstantinos Sagonas, Terrance Swift, and David S. Warren. XSB as an efficient deductive database engine. In *Proceedings of the ACM SIGMOD International Conference on the Management of Data*, pages 442–453, Minneapolis, Minnesota, May 1994. ACM Press.

22. D. De Schreye, M. Bruynooghe, B. Demoen, M. Denecker, B. Martens, G. Janssens, L. De Raedt, S. Decorte, M. Leuschel, and K. Sagonas. Lp+: a second generation Logic Programming language. Technical report, Department of Computer Science, K.U.Leuven, available from ftp.cs.kuleuven.ac.be as /pub/dtai/project.ps, 1997.
23. D. A. Smith. Synthesis in the KIDS system. In Y. Deville, editor, *Proceedings of the Third International Workshop on Logic Program Synthesis and Transformation.* 1993.
24. Zoltan Somogyi, Fergus Henderson, and Thomas Conway. The execution algorithm of Mercury, an efficient purely declarative Logic Programming language. *The Journal of Logic Programming*, 29(1–3):17–64, October-December 1996.
25. V. F. Turchin. The concept of a super compiler. *ACM Transactions on Programming Languages and Systems*, 8(3):292–325, 1986.
26. David S. Warren. Memoing for logic programs. *Communications of the ACM*, 35(3):93–111, March 1992.

How Enterprises Use Functional Languages, and Why They Don't

Philip Wadler

Bell Labs, Lucent Technologies, 600 Mountain Ave, Room 2T-402, Murray Hill, NJ 07974-0636, USA

Summary. Logic programming and functional programming row in the same boat. Methods used to achieve success with one often transpose to the other, and both face similar obstacles. Here I offer a compendium of success stories for functional programs, followed by a list of obstacles to more widespread use of functional programming, in the belief that much of this experience is relevant to logic programmers. This material first appeared as columns in ACM SIGPLAN Notices [29,30]. The final section contains a few remarks specific to the relations between functional and logic programming.

1 An Angry Half Dozen

"Have you used it in anger yet?"

The time is a dozen years ago, the place is Oxford, and my fellow postdoc has just scrutinized my new bike. He's admired the chrome, checked the gears, noted the Kryptonite lock. Now he wants to know if I've used it to serious purpose. Gleaming chrome is well and good, but will it run you through the woods?

"Have you used it in anger yet?"

Seeing that my topic is functional languages, you may have just asked the same question, though perhaps in different words. You've scrutinized functional languages. You've admired the elegance of lambda calculus, checked the benchmarks from the compilers, noted the security provided by strong typing. Now you want to know if they have been used to serious purpose. Mathematical elegance is well and good, but will it run that mission-critical system?

Here are a half-dozen exemplars of functional programs used in anger.

1.0 Compilers

This one's a freebie. I won't count it toward the six, as it is obvious and incestuous.

Most compilers for functional languages are implemented in the language they compile. The Standard ML of New Jersey compiler (SML/NJ) is about 130K lines of Standard ML. The Glasgow Haskell compiler is about 90K lines of Haskell. Caml, another dialect of ML, is implemented in Caml. Erlang is implemented in Erlang, and some versions of Scheme in Scheme.

In some corners, functional languages bear a reputation for gross inefficiency, but this reputation is out of date. Code quality ranges from a shade better than C to an order of magnitude worse, with the typical case hovering at a factor of two or so slower. One example is the Pseudoknot benchmark, based on an application that uses backtracking search to determine three-dimensional protein structure. A large number of functional languages were benchmarked against this program, the best running two to three times slower than the equivalent C [15].

The functional community splits into two camps. Lazy languages evaluate arguments on demand, and so require highly disciplined use of side effects; strict languages evaluate arguments eagerly, but make it easier to exploit side effects. Haskell, Miranda, and Clean are lazy; Standard ML, Caml, Erlang, and Scheme are strict. Over the past few years there has been remarkable convergence between the two communities, and the Pseudoknot tests show lazy and strict languages have comparable performance.

Most functional languages now provide some means of interworking with programs written in C or other imperative languages. Interworking is straightforward for a strict language, but trickier for a lazy language. A key advance of recent years, achieved by a pleasing interplay of theory and practice, is to obtain interworking for lazy languages via such abstract concepts as monads and linear logic [28,23]. Profiling systems for functional languages have also improved vastly, and the usual code-measure-improve cycle is now routinely applied to improve the time and space behaviour of functional programs [26]. However, there are still few good debuggers for functional languages.

1.1 HOL and Isabelle

Hewlett-Packard's Runway multiprocessor bus underlies the architecture of the HP 9000 line of servers and multiprocessors. Hewlett-Packard applied the HOL (Higher-Order Logic) theorem prover to verify liveness properties of the arbitration protocols in Runway. Verification was achieved by a hybrid of theorem-proving in HOL and model-checking in SMV. This approach uncovered errors that had not been revealed by several months of simulation [6].

The Defense Science and Technology Organization, a branch of the Department of Defense in Salisbury, South Australia, is applying the Isabelle theorem prover to verify arming conditions for missile decoys. A graphical front-end has been added to Isabelle for this purpose, humorously called DOVE (Design-Oriented Verification and Evaluation) [21].

Both HOL and Isabelle are implemented in Standard ML. Standard ML is a descendant of ML, the *meta* *l*anguage of the ground-breaking LCF theorem prover. LCF in turn is an ancestor of both HOL and Isabelle. This circle reflects the intertwined history of theorem provers and functional languages [12,22,13].

ML/LCF exploited two central features of functional languages, higher-order functions and types. A proof tactic was a function taking a goal formula to be proved and returning a list of subgoals paired with a justification. A justification, in turn, was a function from proofs of the subgoals to a proof of the goal. A tactical was a function that combined small tactics into larger tactics. The type system was a great boon in managing the resulting tangle of functions, where some functions accept functions as arguments, and some of these return functions as results. Further, the type discipline ensured soundness, since values of the abstract data type "theorem" could only be created by a specified set of functions, each one of which corresponded to an inference rule of the logic. The type system Robin Milner devised for ML remains a cornerstone of work in functional languages.

HOL and Isabelle are just two of the many theorem provers that draw on the ideas developed in LCF, just as Standard ML is only one of the many languages that draw on the ideas developed in ML. Among others, Coq is implemented in Caml, Veritas in Miranda, Yarrow in Haskell, and Alf, Elf, and Lego in Standard ML again. An upcoming issue of the *Journal of Functional Programming* is devoted to the interplay between functional languages and theorem provers. Most theorem provers are written in functional languages, with the exception of a few systems written in Lisp (the granddaddy of functional languages).

1.2 Erlang

Ericsson's Mobility Server is marketed in twelve countries. Among other things, it controls some mobile phones for the European Parliament in Strasbourg. The Mobility Server is one of a range of Ericsson products implemented using Erlang, a functional language designed by Ericsson for telecommunications applications. At last count, Ericsson marketed eight products based on Erlang [1].

Ericsson has a separate division, Erlang Systems, that handles marketing, training, and consulting for Erlang. Over one thousand Ericsson employees have attended Erlang course and over five hundred are currently involved in product development using Erlang. The Mobility Server contains hundreds of thousands of lines of Erlang code, and products written in Erlang have earned Ericsson millions of kronor.

You might guess Erlang stands for "Ericsson Language", but actually it is named for A. K. Erlang, a Danish mathematician who also lent his name to a unit of bandwidth. (A phone system designed to bear 0.33 erlang will work even if one-third of its phones are in use at the same time.)

Erlang is dynamically typed in the same sense as Lisp, Scheme, or Smalltalk, which makes it one of the few modern languages to eschew ML's heritage of static typing. The basic data types are integers (with arbitrary precision, so overflow is not a problem), floats, atoms, tuples, lists, and process identifiers.

Primitives allow one to spawn a process, send a message to a process, or receive a message. Any data value may be sent as a message, and processes may be located on any machine. Erlang uses compression techniques to minimize the bandwidth required to transmit a value. Thus it is both trivial and efficient to send, say, a tree from one machine to another. Compare this with the work required in a language such as C, C++, or Java, where one must separately establish a connection, serialize the tree for transmission, and apply compression. To support robust systems, one process can register to receive a message if another process fails.

Ever since Guy Steele's pioneering work on Scheme, tail-recursion has been a mainstay of functional languages, and it is put to good use in Erlang. A server in Erlang is typically written as a small function, with arguments representing the state of the server. The function body receives a message, performs the computation it requests, sends back the result, and makes a tail-call with parameters representing the new state. Finite state machines are easily represented: just have one function for each state, with state transitions represented by tail calls. The daunting tasks of changing running code on the fly is solved by a surprisingly simple use of higher-order functions and tail-calls: design the server to receive a message containing a new function for the server, which is applied with a tail-call; a new variable can be added to the server state by a tail-call to a function with an added parameter.

Functional programmers often claim that the use of higher-order functions promotes reuse. The classic examples are the *map* and *fold* functions, which encapsulate common forms of list traversal, and just need to be instantiated with an action to perform for each element. Most, but not quite all, list processing can be easily expressed in terms of these functions. The Erlang experience suggests this notion of reuse scales up to support concurrent client-server architectures. A set of libraries encapsulate common server requirements, and just need to be instantiated with the action to be performed for each request. Most, but not quite all, required servers can be easily expressed in terms of these libraries.

Erlang bears a striking resemblance to another modern phenomenon, Java. Like Java, Erlang (along with all other functional languages) uses heap allocation and garbage collection, and ensures safe execution that never corrupts memory. Like Java, Erlang comes with a library that provides functionality independent of a particular operating system. Like Java, Erlang compiles to a virtual machine, ensuring portability across a wide range of architectures. And like Java, Erlang achieved its first success based on interpreters for the virtual machine, with faster compilers an afterthought.

Erlang succeeded not just because it was a good language design, but because its designers took the right steps to promote its growth. They evolved the language in tandem with its applications, worked closely with developers, and provided documentation, courses, hot-lines, and consultants. A foreign-language interface was essential to allow interworking with existing software in C. Users were often attracted to Erlang by the availability of tools and packages, such as an interface compiler for the ASN.1 exchange standard, and a real-time highly-reliable distributed database system called Mnesia, both implemented entirely in Erlang.

1.3 Pdiff

If you've ever made a long-distance phone call in the US, you've probably used a Lucent 5ESS phone switch. Each 5ESS contains an embedded, relational database to maintain information about customers, network topology, rates, features such as call waiting, and so on. The database is complex, containing nearly a thousand relations, and there are tens of thousands of consistency constraints (also called *population rules*) that the data must satisfy [11,7].

As new features are added to the switch, new transactions are required; for instance, one may need a new transaction to register a customer for call waiting. Each transaction should be *safe* in that it should leave the database in a consistent state. Ensuring safety was difficult and error prone, especially since the constraints were embedded in C programs that audit the database for consistency, and transactions were performed by other C programs.

The first step was to introduce PRL (Population Rule Language) to describe constraints and transactions. This marked a vast improvement over the use of C, but left the problem of determining for each transaction what conditions must be satisfied to ensure safety.

The next step was to introduce Pdiff (PRL differentiator). The input to Pdiff is the safety constraint for the database and an unsafe transaction, both written in PRL. Pdiff computes what condition must hold in advance of the transaction to ensure the database is consistent afterward. (This is similar to Dijkstra's computation of the weakest precondition that must hold in advance of a command to ensure a given predicate holds afterward.) Additional steps simplify this condition on the assumption that the database is consistent before the transaction. The output is a safe transaction in PRL, which checks all the necessary constraints for validity before allowing any change to the database.

Pdiff consists of about 30K lines of code written in Standard ML, written by researchers at Bell Labs. Pdiff improves the quality and reliability of switches, reduces the time to deploy new features, and has saved Lucent millions of dollars in development costs.

The Pdiff history reveals some problems of using a functional language in practice. When the time came to hand off maintenance of Pdiff to the 5ESS staff, no internal candidate could be found for the role. Developers prefer to have C++ or Java on their resume, and balk at languages perceived as "weird". Eventually a physicist looking to change fields was hired for the purpose. An opportunity was missed when the 5ESS team considered using

Standard ML to write the PRL compiler. Since Standard ML wasn't available for their machine (an Amdahl), they used C++ instead.

1.4 CPL/Kleisli

In April 1993, a workshop organized by the US Department of Energy considered the database requirements of the Human Genome Project. An appendix of the workshop report listed twelve queries that would be difficult or impossible to answer with current database systems, because they require combining information from two or more databases in disparate formats [8].

All twelve of these queries have been answered using CPL/Kleisli. CPL (Collection Programming Language) is a high-level language for formulating queries. Kleisli, the system that implements CPL, translates CPL into SQL for querying relational databases, or runs the queries against data in ASN.1, ACE, or other formats. CPL/Kleisli is in active use at the Philadelphia Center for Chromosome 22 and at the BioInformatics Centre of the Institute for Systems Science in Singapore [4].

Functional programming plays two roles here: CPL is a functional language, and Kleisli is written in Standard ML. The basic data types of CPL are sets, bags, lists, and records. The first three of these may be processed using a comprehension notation familiar to mathematicians and functional programmers. For instance, a mathematician may write $\{x^2 \mid x \in Nat, x < 10\}$ for the set of squares of natural numbers less than ten. Similarly, the CPL query

```
{ [ Name = p.Name, Mgr = d.Mgr ] |
  \p <- Emp, \d <- Dept,
  p.DNum = d.DNum }
```

returns a set of records pairing employees with their managers. The comprehension notation is reminiscent of SQL, where one may write

```
SELECT Name = p.Name, Mgr = d.Mgr
FROM Emp p, Dept d
WHERE p.DNum = d.DNum
```

for the same query. But CPL allows sets, bags, lists, and records to be arbitrarily nested, whereas SQL can only process "flat" relations, consisting of sets of records. The extra nesting in CPL helps one formulate queries for databases that don't fit the relational model. CPL also allows sums (similar to variant records in Pascal, and the datatypes used in most functional languages), making it easy to process data with alternative formats, such as books and journals in a bibliographic database.

A standard technique in functional programming is to apply mathematical laws to transform an elegant but slow program into an efficient equivalent. This technique is applied to good effect in CPL/Kleisli. The standard laws for transforming comprehensions can be viewed as generalizing well-known optimizations for relational algebra. For instance, a CPL query may depend on two relational databases held on different servers. The Kleisli optimizer will transform this into two SQL queries to be sent to the servers (performing as much work as possible locally at the server), and a remaining CPL program at the query site to combine the results. Lazy evaluation and concurrency allow SQL computation at the database sites and CPL processing at the query site to overlap.

CPL/Kleisli also exploits record subtyping. In the example above, `Emp` represents employees by a set of records. Each record must contain a `Name` and `DNum` field, but may contain other fields as well. The type system that permits this flexibility and the technique for implementing it efficiently were both adopted directly from research in the functional community.

1.5 Natural Expert

Every flight through Orly and Roissy airports in Paris is processed by an expert system called Ivanhoe, which generates invoices and explanations for the services used. Ivanhoe is written in Natural Expert, an expert system shell, formerly marketed by the German firm Software AG [18].

Polygram in France controls about one-third of the European market for CDs and cassettes. The Colisage expert system plans packing schedules to minimize empty space and routes to minimize numbers of stops (somewhat like simultaneously solving the Bin Packing and Traveling Salesman problems). Colisage was originally written in a production rule system called GURU, but was ported to Natural Expert when the GURU version proved hard to maintain. Polygram praised the Natural Expert system as shorter and easier to maintain.

Dozens of other applications have been programmed in Natural Expert, including a management support system, a system for assessing bank loans, a tool to plan hospital menus, and a natural-language front end to a database.

Natural Expert integrates an entity-attribute database management system with NEL (Natural Expert Language), a higher-order, statically typed, lazy functional language, roughly similar to Haskell.

One of the selling points of Natural Expert is its user environment. The database is used not only to manipulate user data, but also to store the NEL program itself, which is structured as a number of rules. The database records what rules refer to what other rules, aiding program maintenance. A simple hypertext facility lets the reader jump from use of a rule or attribute to its definition.

The result returned from a database access is typically a list of entity indexes. Lazy evaluation processes entities one at a time, reducing the amount of store required. This is important, because Natural Expert runs on mainframes. Surprisingly, mainframes often provide fewer resources than a personal computer: Natural Expert typically uses only 80K for the heap, and even then some clients complain it is too large.

Traditionally, lazy languages disallow side effects, because the order in which the effects occur would be difficult to predict. NEL, however, permits one use of side effects, a primitive that prints a given question on a terminal and returns the answer typed by the user. Questions are printed in an arbitrary order, but that's no problem for this domain. More importantly, thanks to lazy evaluation, a question is asked at most once, and only if it's relevant to the task at hand. Expert systems people call this "backwards chaining".

Training is key to industrial use of any system. Natural Expert is taught in a one-week course, which includes polymorphic types and higher-order functions. Typically, students grumble about all the compile-time error messages generated by the unfamiliar type system, but are pleased to discover that once a program passes the compiler it often runs correctly on the first try. Nonetheless, clients still point to lack of familiarity with functional languages as a bar to wider acceptance.

Although many of the applications built with Natural Expert are successful and in current use, sales of the system generated insufficient revenue, and Software AG has dropped it as a product.

1.6 Ensemble

Ensemble is a library of protocols that can be used to quickly build distributed applications. Ensemble is in daily use at Cornell to coordinate sharing of keys in a secure network, and to support a distributed CD audio storage and playback service. A number of commercial concerns have begun projects with Ensemble, including BBN, Lockheed Martin, and Microsoft [16].

Ensemble protocol stacks typically have ten or more layers. Highly-layered stacks are flexible, but can be slow. Ensemble regains speed by a series of optimizations. The protocol designer segments the code in each the layer, marking common cases. It is a simple matter (currently performed by hand, but easily automated) to trace which segments execute together, and collect these into optimized *trace handlers*. They also cache information to minimize header size and reorder computations to preserve latency. The result is a win-win architecture, offering both modularity and performance.

Ensemble is written entirely in Objective Caml, a dialect of ML. Ensemble beats the performance of its predecessor, Horus, by a wide margin, even though Horus is written in C. To quote the designers, "The use of ML does mean that our current implementation of Ensemble is somewhat slower than it could be, but this has been more than made up for by the ability to rapidly experiment with structural changes, and thereby increase performance through improved design rather than through long hours of hand-coding the entire system in C" [16].

The designers took care to restrict the use of features of ML they deemed expensive. Higher-order functions are used only in stylized ways that can be compiled efficiently. Exception handling and garbage-collected objects are avoided in the trace handlers. To squeeze the most out of Ensemble, a final step is to translate the trace handlers (which constitute only a small part of the code) into C by hand. This achieves a further improvement of about a factor of two.

A related effort is the Fox Project at Carnegie-Mellon University, which first demonstrated that systems software can be written in functional languages. You can access the FoxNet Web Server at `foxnet.cs.cmu.edu`. The HTTPD server, the TCP/IP stack, and everything down to the driver protocol is implemented in the Fox variant of Standard ML [3].

Ensemble has produced the fastest product of its kind, while the Fox Project stack runs at speeds varying from 8% faster to 100% slower than commercial implementations. However, this is comparing apples with oranges: Ensemble gains speed by experimenting with new protocols, while Fox measures its achievements against the fixed target of the TCP/IP protocol.

The Fox Project was an important precursor to Ensemble, in that it demonstrated functional languages could be used to build systems programs with reasonable performance. Nonetheless, in my opinion Ensemble marks a more important milestone for functional programming: FoxNet was created by researchers primarily interested in languages, while Ensemble was created by researchers primarily interested in networking.

1.7 Conclusions

So there you have it, six instances of functional languages used *in anger*. Or rather more than six, depending on how you count.

Perhaps some disclaimers are in order. I'm one of the designers of Haskell. Glasgow Haskell is due to my former colleagues, SML/NJ is due to my current colleagues, HOL is largely due to another former colleague, and Pdiff is due to other current colleagues. I consulted for Ericsson on the design of a type system for Erlang. CPL/Kleisli is partly based on my research into comprehensions. So I may be biased.

The list of applications given here is far from exhaustive. I've omitted Microsoft's Fran animation library for Haskell [9], Lufthansa's combination of a simple functional language with partial evaluation to speed up crew scheduling [2], Hewlett Packard's ECDL network control language, the Lolita natural language understanding system, and Mitre's speech recognition system, to name a few. Some of these are listed at a web page for Functional Programming in the Real World [31].

2 Why No One Uses Functional Languages

As we have just seen, to say that no one uses functional languages is an exaggeration. Calls to the European Parliament are routed by programs written in Erlang, virtual CDs are distributed on Cornell's network via Ensemble, real CDs are shipped by Polygram in Europe via Natural Expert.

Still ... I work at Bell Labs, where C and C++ were invented. Compared to users of C, "no one" is a tolerably accurate count of the users of functional languages.

Advocates of functional languages claim they produce an order of magnitude improvement in productivity. Experiments don't always verify that figure — sometimes they show an improvement of only a factor of four. Still, code that's four times as short, four times as quick to write, or four times easier to maintain is not to be sniffed at. So why aren't functional languages more widely used?

2.1 Reasons

Here is a list of some of the factors that inhibit adoption of functional languages. I'll note some research aimed at ameliorating these factors, but make no pretense of completeness.

Most of these factors remain serious impediments for most systems. Notable exceptions are Ericsson's Erlang (`www.erlang.se`) and Harlequin's ML Works (`www.harlequin.com`), two industrial-grade systems with extensive user environments and support.

Compatibility. Computing has matured to the point where systems are often assembled from components rather than built from scratch. Many of these components are written in C or C++, so a foreign function interface to C is essential, and interfaces to other languages can be useful.

The isolationist nature of functional languages is beginning to give way to a spirit of open interchange. Serious implementations now routinely provide interfaces to C, and sometimes other languages. As mentioned above, this is straightforward for strict languages, and recent advances with monads and linear logic has made it possible for lazy languages.

Conquering isolationism is a task for everyone, not just functional programmers. The computing industry is now beginning to deploy standards, such as CORBA and COM, that support the construction of software from reusable components. Recent work allows any Haskell program to be packaged as a COM component, and any COM component to be called from Haskell [24]. Among other applications, this allows Haskell to be used as a scripting language for Microsoft's Internet Explorer web browser. My colleagues at Lucent are currently applying similar ideas to the SML/NJ compiler.

Libraries. The fashionable idea of software reuse has been around for ages in the form of software libraries. A good library can make or break a language. Users are attracted to Tcl primarily on the strength of the Tk graphics library. Much of the attractiveness of Java has little to do with the language itself, but with the associated libraries for graphics, networking, databases, telephony, and enterprise servers. (Much of the unattractiveness of Java is due to those same libraries.)

Considerable effort has been extended on developing graphic user interface libraries for functional languages. Haskell boasts a plethora: Fudgets, Gadgets, Haggis, and Hugs Tk. SML/NJ has two, eXene and SML Tk. The SML language comes with a powerful module system, which makes flexible libraries easier to construct. One example of such a library is ML RISC, a retargetable back end that has been used for SML and C compilers and has been adopted to a number of architectures [10].

Portability and installation. I have heard of numerous projects where C won out over a functional language, not because C runs faster (although often it does), but because the hegemony of C guarantees that it is widely portable. As mentioned above, Lucent researchers would have preferred to build the PRL database language using SML, but chose C++ because SML was not available on the Amdahl mainframe they used.

On the other hand, abstract machines are a popular implementation technique, for both functional languages and for Java, in part because writing an emulator for the machine in C makes it is easy to port to a wide variety of architectures. The Hugs interpreter for Haskell is written in C, and fairly easy to port.

Even when a functional language has been ported to the machine and operating system at hand, it may not be easy to install. While Hugs is easy to install (one mouse click on my Windows box), installing the Glasgow Haskell compiler is something of an adventure (I've so far failed to install it on my local Irix machine).

Availability. Large projects are understandably reluctant to commit to a language unless it comes with a guarantee of continuing support. A few functional languages are available commercially: Research Software markets Miranda, ISL markets Poplog/SML, Harlequin markets ML Works, and Ericsson has a division devoted to support of Erlang. Nonetheless, for many functional languages, it remains difficult to ensure a stable source and reliable support.

An additional problem arises because functional languages are often under active development, creating tension between the needs of stability and research. The Haskell community is attempting to resolve these by defining Standard Haskell, a version of the language that will remain stable and supported while other versions of Haskell continue to evolve [17].

Footprint. Following the Lisp tradition, many functional language implementations offer a read-eval-print loop. While convenient, it is also essential to provide some way to convert a functional program into a stand-alone application program, that can be invoked directly without the intervention of a read-eval-print loop. Most systems now offer this. However, these systems often incorporate the entire runtime package for the library, and thus have unacceptably large memory footprints. An ability to develop compact stand-alone applications is essential.

Tools. To be usable, a language system must be accompanied by a debugger and a profiler. Just as with interlanguage working, designing such tools is straightforward for strict languages, but trickier for lazy languages. However, there are few debuggers or profilers even for strict languages, perhaps because constructing them is not perceived as research. That is a shame, since such tools are sorely needed, and there remains much of interest to learn about their construction and use.

Constructing debuggers and profilers for lazy languages is recognized as difficult. Fortunately, there have been great strides in profiler research, and most implementations of Haskell are now accompanied by usable time and space profiling tools. But the slow rate of progress on debuggers for lazy languages makes us researchers look, well, lazy.

At a larger scale, one wants integrated development environments and software engineering methodologies. Building an integrated development environment is a lot of work with little research content, so it is not surprising that this has attracted little attention. But there is plenty of interesting work to be done in applying software methodologies to functional languages, and it is disappointing that there is virtually no effort in this area.

Training. To programmers practiced in C, C++, or Java, functional programs look odd. It takes a while to come to grips with writing `f(x,y)` as `f x y`. Curried food and curried functions are both acquired tastes.

Programmers practiced in imperative languages are used to a certain style of programming. For a given task, the imperative solution may leap immediately to mind or be found in a handy textbook, while a comparable functional solution may require considerable effort to find (though once found it may be more elegant). And while many problems do have efficient functional solutions, there remain some tough nuts for which the best known solutions are imperative in style. Some functional languages lessen these problems by providing an escape to imperative style: SML includes updateable references as a basic data type, and Haskell provides them via monads [20].

The training problem is not intractable. Software AG found they could train industrial programmers to use Natural Expert in a one-week course that included lazy evaluation, polymorphic types, and higher-order functions. Typically, students were miffed when the compiler would repeatedly reject programs for type errors, but pleasantly surprised when their programs finally passed the type checker and ran correctly on the first try [18].

Popularity. If a manager chooses to use a functional language for a project and the project fails, then he or she is out on a limb with little support. If a manager chooses C++ and the project fails, then he or she has the defense that the same thing has happened to everyone else.

Though management problems are a significant barrier, the flipside is a significant opportunity: a large project that is in trouble may be willing to consider switching to a functional language because the increase in productivity may get them out of a jam. An effective way in can be to offer to prototype the solution in a functional language, and once the prototype is running show how to scale it to a full solution.

No less than managers, employees, too, have their worries. Experience with C++ or Java will buff up your resume nicely, while Haskell or SML will do you little good. Recall, for instance, that no developer could be found to maintain Lucent's Pdiff system, written in SML, so a physicist looking to switch fields was hired (as mentioned in Section 1.3).

2.2 Non-reasons

Having listed many good reasons why people avoid functional languages, let me now rebut two pieces of common cant as to why people don't use functional languages to which I do not subscribe.

Performance. A decade ago people might have reasonably rejected functional languages for poor performance, but these days the performance of functional languages is often within the same ballpark as C. Performance can vary widely, but for the symbolic manipulation to which functional languages are well suited, a rough estimate of within a factor of two of C seems fair.

More important, experience shows that performance that rivals C is not a requirement for success. Java has become enormously successful with performance significantly short of C. Tcl/Tk, Perl, and Visual Basic all rose to prominence with implementations that are interpreted. In the functional world, Erlang achieved its success as an interpreted language, and the Hugs interpreter for Haskell is more widely used than the Glasgow Haskell compiler.

One has languages with high performance that are not widely used, and languages with middling performance that are widely used. Performance is sometimes an issue, but it is rare for it to be the deciding factor. It is imprudent to expect that all we need do is make functional languages run blindingly fast in order for them to become immensely popular.

"They don't get it". Functional programming is beautiful, a joy to behold. Once someone understands functional programming, he or she will switch to it immediately. The masses that stick with outmoded imperative and object-oriented programming do so out of blind prejudice. They just don't get it.

The above paragraph echoes beliefs deeply held by many researchers. But the long list in the preceding section should make it clear that it may be possible to be attracted by functional programming, but still find it unusable.

For instance, here is a posting to the Haskell mailing list.

> I have been trying to learn Haskell and have been impressed with both its elegance and the way it allows me to write code that works on the first try (or two). However, I am not a researcher. I do commercial software development and need some documentation and stability. [19]

Mailing lists related to functional languages are rife with requests for foreign function interfaces, libraries, and tools.

Doubtless, there are prejudiced individuals out there, accustomed to C and its variants and dismissive of alternatives. But many out there do "get it", and eschew functional programming for other reasons.

2.3 Lessons

To summarize, there are a large number of factors that hinder the widespread adoption of functional languages. To be widely used, a language should support interlanguage working, possess extensive libraries, be highly portable, have a stable and easy to install implementation, come with debuggers and profilers, be accompanied by training courses, and have a good track record on previous projects. It helps if the implementation is efficient, but this is not an absolute requirement. Potential users may find the language attractive, but reject it because of some or all of the preceding factors. Here are the lessons I draw from this exercise.

Killer App. The factors listed constitute a significant barrier to use of functional languages, but not an absolute barrier. A user will forego many conveniences if given a compelling reason to do so. Tcl/Tk and Perl rose to prominence without benefit of debuggers or profilers.

Some researchers hope that the high-level nature of functional languages will prove compelling on its own, but experience to date suggests this hope is misplaced. Instead, experience shows that users will be drawn to a language if it lets them conveniently do something that otherwise is difficult to achieve. Like other new technologies, functional languages must seek their killer app.

Each of the "angry half-dozen" exploits some strength of functional languages. Telecommunications developers are drawn to Erlang by its support for concurrency and distribution; the latter is tied directly to the fact that functional data, being immutable, is well suited for transmission across a network. Creators of theorem provers are drawn to ML by its support for symbolic computations. Geneticists are drawn to CPL/Kleisli because its type system supports access to heterogeneous databases, and because the mathematical properties of functional languages can be exploited in query optimization. Expert system developers are drawn to Natural Expert because lazy evaluation resembles reasoning by backward chaining, and because lazy evaluation enables a space-efficient interface to databases.

Top-notch functional programming research is often tied to applications. Carnegie-Mellon grounds its functional programming work in the Fox project.

Chalmers researchers have close relations with Carlstedt and Logikkonsult, and among other things have applied partial evaluation to airline scheduling. Glasgow teamed up with York to produce a whole book of applications. The Oregon Graduate Institute is teaming up with Intel to look at hardware design. Yale researchers have applied functional programming to music performance and natural language understanding, and are teaming up with Microsoft to look at animation. However, most of this research has not centered around application libraries or packages that might attract significant user communities.

Applications have unexplored depths. Jump in, the water's fine!

Research emphasis. Despite the applications work listed above, functional programming researchers place far more emphasis on developing systems than on applying those systems. Further, the bulk of effort is devoted to language design, program analysis, and the construction of optimizing compilers, with far less to debuggers, profilers, and software engineering tools and methodologies.

Shifts in research emphasis may require shifts in the reward structure. As Kuhn noted in *The Structure of Scientific Revolutions*, the mainstream of academic work consists of incremental contributions to existing paradigms. Within functional programming, the mainstream is program analysis and compiler development. Leaders in the field need to move into the new areas of tools and applications, and conferences and journals need to explicitly welcome contributions in these areas. To aid a paradigm shift, a field may set out new criteria for judging work in new areas.

As I write, Gopal Gupta is organizing PADL 99, the First International Conference on Practical Aspects of Declarative Languages [14]. And Simon Peyton Jones and myself have just completed an editorial for the *Journal of Functional Programming* welcoming papers on functional programming practice and experience, and setting out the criteria we apply to judge them [25].

A modest proposal. Even a modest implementation of a functional language should provide a foreign function interface, a debugger, and a profiler. By this measure, I know of only a few modest implementations of functional languages, including Ericsson's Erlang, Harlequin's ML Works, and INRIA's CAML.

Andrew Tolmach and Andrew Appel devised an ingenious debugger for the SML/NJ implementation [27], but as the implementation evolved the debugger was not maintained, and there is no debugger available for the current release of SML/NJ.

There is a tension between building useful systems and extending the frontiers of research, and functional language researchers can pride themselves on having found the resources to build some excellent systems. We now need to take the next step, and ensure these systems include essential interfaces and tools. We should no longer settle for implementations that are not even modest.

Hope. This long list of reasons why no one uses functional languages may look depressing, but I prefer to look on the bright side. People do not reject functional languages because of stupidity, rather they reject them for a variety of good reasons. Stupidity is famously resistant to attack — these other problems are something we can tackle.

3 Functional and Logic Programming

There are many overlaps between logic programming and functional programming, and some intriguing differences.

I argued above that a "killer app" is essential for success. While functional languages have had moderate successes in a few areas, they have only become perceived as the language of choice in one fairly narrow area: theorem provers. On the other hand, logic programming languages have three "killer apps" where they have achieved widespread success: deductive databases, artificial intelligence, and constraint programming.

Arguably, this is why one can point to hundreds of industrial applications of logic programming (I saw one list with nearly one thousand entries), whereas equivalent applications of functional programming number in the dozens.

Unfortunately, in both the functional and logic camps, rather than play to our strengths we try to be all things to all people. With the exception of the original ML, which aimed squarely at theorem proving (and where its descendants have dominated that area), relatively few functional or logic languages aim at conquering one application area. Instead, advocates promote functional and logic languages as general purpose, good for whatever ails you. Perhaps a more specific emollient is in order. Designers of logic languages might have an easier job filling this prescription than those of functional languages, as logic languages already have a better track record with "killer apps".

The name *declarative* was coined to cover both functional and logic programming, recognizing that they have much in common. Despite this, the two communities meet together rarely, having separate conferences and journals.

One area of overlap is the attempt to build languages that combine the features of functional and logic languages. Most of the attempts in this direction seem to come from members of the logic programming community. There have been some technically strong achievements in this area, but as yet no "killer app" has emerged.

As mentioned above, Gopal Gupta is organizing PADL 99, the First International Conference on Practical Aspects of Declarative Languages. This aims to draw together two communities that should interact more, and to focus their attention on applications — a double win!

Acknowledgements

My thanks to Brian Kernighan, Doug McIlroy, and Jon Riecke for comments on earlier versions of this paper, and to all those who listened to and commented on my talks on this topic. Special thanks to the organizers, Krzysztof Apt, David Warren, Vitek Marek and Mirek Truszczyński, and the participants of the workshop on the Logic Programming Paradigm held in Shakertown, Kentucky, a great group from whom I learned a great deal.

References

1. Joe Armstrong. The development of Erlang. *ACM SIGPLAN International Conference on Functional Programming*, June 1997; *SIGPLAN Notices* 32(8):196–203, August 1997. Also see the Erlang page:
`http://www.erlang.se`
2. Lennart Augustsson. Partial evaluation in aircraft crew planning. *ACM SIGPLAN Symposium on Partial Evaluation and Semantics-Based Program Manipulation*, June 1997; *SIGPLAN Notices* 32(12):127–136, December 1997.
3. Edoardo Biagioni, Robert Harper, Peter Lee, and Brian G. Milnes. Signatures for a network protocol stack: A systems application of Standard ML. *ACM Conference on Lisp and Functional Programming*, 1994. Also see the Fox Project page:
`http://foxnet.cs.cmu.edu`
4. P. Buneman, S. B. Davidson, K. Hart, C. Overton, and L. Wong. A Data Transformation System for Biological Data Sources. *Proceedings of 21st International Conference on Very Large Data Bases*, Zurich, Switzerland, September 1995. Also see the Kleisli page:
`http://sdmc.iss.nus.sg/kleisli/MoreInfo.html`
5. P. Buneman, L. Libkin, D. Suciu, V. Tannen, and L. Wong. Comprehension Syntax. *ACM SIGMOD Record* 23(1):87-96, March 1994. (Invited paper.)
6. Albert J. Camilleri. A hybrid approach to verifying liveness in a symmetric multiprocessor. *10'th International Conference on Theorem Proving in Higher-Order Logics*, Elsa Gunter and Amy Felty, editors, Murray Hill, New Jersey, August 1997. Lecture Notes in Computer Science 1275, Springer Verlag, 1997.
7. Sandra Corrico, Bryan Ewbank, Tim Griffin, John Meale, and Howard Trickey. A tool for developing safe and efficient database transactions. *XV International Switching Symposium of the World Telecommunications Congress*, pages 173–177, April 1995.
8. Robert J. Robbins, Editor. Report of the Invitational DOE Workshop on Genome Informatics, 26–27 April 1993.
`http://www.bis.med.jhmi.edu/Dan/DOE/whitepaper/contents.html`
9. Conal Elliot and Paul Hudak. Functional reactive animation. *ACM SIGPLAN International Conference on Functional Programming*, June 1997; *SIGPLAN Notices* 32(8):196–203, August 1997.
10. Lal George, MLRISC: Customizable and Reusable Code Generators, Bell Labs technical report, May 1997.
`www.cs.bell-labs.com/cm/cs/what/smlnj/doc/MLRISC/`

11. T. Griffin and H. Trickey, Integrity Maintenance in a Telecommunications Switch, *IEEE Data Engineering Bulletin*, Special Issue on Database Constraint Management, 17(2) : 43–46, 1994.
12. M. J. Gordon and T. F. Melham, editors. *Introduction to HOL: A theorem proving environment for higher-order logic.* Cambridge University Press, 1993. Also see the HOL page:
`http://www.dcs.glasgow.ac.uk/~tfm/fmt/hol.html`
13. M. Gordon, R. Milner, and C. Wadsworth. *Edinburgh LCF.* Lecture Notes in Computer Science, Vol. 78, Springer-Verlag, 1979.
14. Gopal Gupta, chair, First International Conference on Practical Aspects of Declarative Languages.
`http://www.cs.nsmsu.edu/~complog/conferences/padl99/`
15. Pieter Hartel, *et al.* Benchmarking implementations of functional languages with 'Pseudoknot', a float-intensive benchmark. *Journal of Functional Programming*, 6(4):621–656, July 1996.
16. Mark Hayden and Robbert vanRenesse. Optimizing Layered Communication Protocols. *Symposium on High Performance Distributed Computing*, Portland, Oregon, August 1997. Also see the Ensemble page:
`http://simon.cs.cornell.edu/Info/Projects/Ensemble/`
17. J. Hughes and S. Peyton Jones, editors, Standard Haskell.
`www.cs.chalmers.se/~rjmh/Haskell/`
18. Nigel W. O. Hutchison, Ute Neuhaus, Manfred Schmidt-Schauss, and Cordy Hall. Natural Expert: a commercial functional programming environment. *Journal of Functional Programming*, 7(2):163–182, March 1997.
19. S. Alexander Jacobson `alex@i2x.com`, letter to Haskell mailing list, 3 May 1998.
20. J. Launchbury and S. L. Peyton Jones, Lazy functional state threads. In *ACM Conference on Programming Language Design and Implementation*, Orlando, Florida, 1994.
21. M. A. Ozols, K. A. Eastaughffe, and A. Cant. DOVE: Design Oriented Verification and Evaluation. *Proceedings of AMAST 97*, M. Johnson, editor, Sydney, Australia. Lecture Notes in Computer Science 1349, Springer Verlag, 1997.
22. Lawrence C. Paulson. *Isabelle: A Generic Theorem Prover.* Springer-Verlag LNCS 828, 1994. Also see the Isabelle page:
`http://www.cl.cam.ac.uk/Research/HVG/Isabelle/`
23. Rinus Plasmeijer and Marko van Eekelen, Pure and efficient functional programming using the "unique" features of Clean. *ACM SIGPLAN Notices*, to appear.
24. Simon Peyton Jones, Erik Meijer, and Daan Leijen. Scripting COM components in Haskell. *IEEE Fifth International Conference on Software Reuse*, Vancouver, BC, June 1998.
`http://www.haskell.org/active/activehaskell.html`
25. Simon Peyton Jones and Philip Wadler. Editorial: Practice and experience papers, *Journal of Functional Programming*, May 1998. Also see the JFP page:
`http://www.dcs.glasgow.ac.uk/jfp/`
26. P. Sansom and S. Peyton Jones, Formally-based profiling for higher-order functional languages, *ACM Transactions on Programming Languages and Systems*, 19(1), January 1997.
27. Andrew Tolmach and Andrew Appel, A Debugger for Standard ML. *Journal of Functional Programming*, 5(2):155–200, April 1995.

28. Philip Wadler. How to declare an imperative. *ACM Computing Surveys*, 29(3):240–263, September 1997.
29. Philip Wadler, An angry half-dozen, *ACM SIGPLAN Notices* 33(2):25-30, February 1998. [N.B. Table of contents on the cover of this issue is wrong.]
30. Philip Wadler, Why no one uses functional languages, *ACM SIGPLAN Notices* 33, 1998.
31. Philip Wadler. Functional programming in the real world. `http://www.cs.bell-labs.com/~wadler/realword/`

4 Continuous Mathematics

This chapter offers two contributions that relate logic programming and constraint logic programming to continuous mathematics.

Computer science uses a variety of formalisms to represent different computational paradigms. A neglected but a huge set of tools is based on modern mathematical analysis, the commonplace tool of working applied mathematicians, physicists, and engineers. Neural networks and fuzzy logic are two successful areas through which continuous mathematics entered into computer science.

Blair, Dushin, Jakela, Rivera and **Sezgin** argue that logic programming could incorporate the best of these paradigms in a formalism that is *also* declarative, through direct generalizations of previously understood semantics into the setting of continuous-valued logic. They discuss some of the ways continuous-valued logic programming can be realized by regarding logic programs as continuous dynamical systems.

Numerical applications in logic programming have been approached in an indirect way, via the CLP(X) scheme. This scheme allows one to incorporate a theory for a specific domain into the basic logic programming paradigm. By selecting the reals as the domain, one obtains CLP(R).

Van Emden argues that it is not just implementation problems that prevent CLP(R) from fulfilling its potential of providing accurate numerical results as logical implications from high-level problem definitions. Although it is true that methods (using intervals) exist for obtaining true assertions about real-valued results by means of floating-point arithmetic, it is not clear how to interface these with CLP(R). Another problem is that the obvious translation of a numerical problem to logic only tells whether or not a solution exists.

Van Emden proposes to solve these problems by distinguishing between the *definition* of the numerical problem and an *interval description* of the solution. Both are combined in so-called ND/ID formulas that allow us to overcome the current limitations of CLP(R).

Continuous Models of Computation for Logic Programs: Importing Continuous Mathematics into Logic Programming's Algorithmic Foundations

Howard A. Blair*, Fred Dushin, David W. Jakel, Angel J. Rivera, and Metin Sezgin

Department of Electrical Engineering and Computer Science, Syracuse University, Syracuse, New York 13244-4100, USA

Summary. Logic programs may be construed as discrete-time and continuous-time dynamical systems with continuous states. Techniques for obtaining explicit formulations of such dynamical systems are presented and the computational performance of examples is presented. Extending 2-valued and n-valued logic to continuous-valued logic is shown to be unique, up to choosing the representations of the individual truth values as elements of a continuous field, provided that lowest degree polynomials are selected. In the case of 2-valued logic, the constraint that enables the uniqueness of the continualization is that the Jacobian matrices of the continualizations of the Boolean connectives have only affine entries. This property of the Jacobian matrix facilitates computation via gradient descent methods.

1 Orientation

This paper is lightly technical; proofs are omitted in favor of intuitive discussion. Some derivations of principal results are sketched.

The semantics of logic programs, in almost all of the versions that remain today as serious topics of research or as bases for implementation of logic programming systems, fundamentally rest on the notion of interpretation, or synonymously, *structure*, for a first-order language. Herbrand models are mere special cases, and far less special than usually supposed, since every structure for a first-order language L is elementarily equivalent to a quotient of an Herbrand model of a suitable extension of L, [BM98]. The semantics of intuitionistic logics, modal logics, and even multi-valued logics are engineered from this notion of structure. Many of these semantics have an associated operator analogous to the one-step consequence operator $\mathbf{T}_P$ originally studied by van Emden and Kowalski [vEK76]. Viewed through the associated operator (which partially incorporates the semantics of the program), a logic program P is a discrete-state, discrete-time dynamical system. If we move to a continuous-valued logic, then there are analogues of these familiar semantic alternatives. We will discuss the move to continuous-valued logics,

* Address correspondence to this author.

which we call *continualization*, below. Continuous-valued logic programs are *continuous-state*, discrete-time operators, when viewed through the various associated consequence operators that generalize those of the discrete case. The continualization methods that we discuss lead to not only continuous but also differentiable operators. From that property one can 1) associate continuous-state, *continuous-time* dynamical systems, 2) provide a model theory for them in continuous-valued logic, 3) embed classical logic into continuous-valued logic, and 4) obtain continuous-time dynamical systems *equivalent* to the programs one starts with in the sense that both systems have the same fixed points, i.e. models.

Various models of computation such as register machines, Turing machines, and the simple imperative programming language (*cf.* [Te94]) show that computation can be viewed in the following way: Imagine n natural number variables $X_1, \ldots, X_n$ initialized to an n-tuple of values. A relatively simple function iteratively updates these values until a relatively simple n-ary relation is satisfied. Then the answer is extracted, again in a simple way, such as projection out of the final n-tuple. More fundamentally, this point of view is embodied in Kleene Normal Form Theorem [Sh67]. We can repeat what we just said this way: any computation takes a token on a lattice point in an n-space $\mathbf{R}^n$ and repeatedly jumps it around on lattice points until it lands in a desired region of the space that is easy to recognize, and an answer is projected out of the point where the token ends up. So, there arises the possibility of moving the token around smoothly as time progresses continuously. Call such a process a *smooth computation.* A continuous-time dynamical system is just a set of rules for moving a token around smoothly. Our point of view is that simple dynamical systems based on low degree polynomials play the same role in smooth computation as normal logic programs play in discrete computation.

It is important to dispose of two misconceptions. First, on reflection, one might suppose that the claims of the previous paragraph were really straightforward since in extending a discrete operator to a continuous operator there is so much freedom that just about anything can be crafted. This is *not* so under very simple linear algebraic restrictions. Continualization of a 2-valued or multi-valued logic involves choosing elements of a continuous field to stand for the underlying discrete truth-values. What freedom there is in continualization is highly structured. Subject to a simple constraint, a continualization is unique up to a dependence only on the elements of the field chosen to represent the discrete truth-values. Different choices of truth-value representations in the field produce linearly isomorphic continualizations. Thus, different choices of truth-value representations amount to a change of basis in the continualization.

For all of the preceding remarks, it remains that there is of course residual arbitrariness in continualization. Our response to this arbitrariness is to reflect on the distinction between the Euclidean plane and the set of all pairs of real numbers $\mathbf{R} \times \mathbf{R}$. An arbitrary choice of coordinates is involved in identifying the two spaces that is not determined by any natural geometric considerations [Bo86]. When one reflects on the consequences of Descartes' [De37] arbitrary imposition of coordinates on the Euclidean plane, the overwhelming response to the residual arbitrariness in Descartes' move is: so what?

The second misconception that the authors have frequently encountered, particularly among those well-versed in "engineering mathematics", is that dynamical systems are a special, rather limited case of systems of differential equations. This also is not so. This paper is not the place to elucidate this claim. The members of a nearly all-encompassing class of first and higher-order differential equations are representable as dynamical systems; we refer the interested reader to Hubbard and West, [HW95], and Guckenheimer and Holmes, [GH83].

Plan of the paper: We will begin by stating our contention about the fruitful relationship between logic programs and dynamical systems, and speculate on the long-range gains to be expected from pursuing investigations in that direction, and then we will relate our ideas to other existing work. The continualization of 2− and n−valued logic will then be presented with a discussion about the uniqueness of the continualization, and we will conclude the section on continualization with comments on the relationship of our continuous truth values to fuzzy logic. We will then present an example of a continuous-time dynamical system corresponding to a propositional program and show how the system tracks into the $\{0, 1\}$-valued fixed points of the program. A second example involves a very small program which turns out to have remarkable discrete-time dynamics and from which every finite and infinite propositional program can be modularly built. We will conclude the paper with a program over a signature with seven propositional letters that produces the sudden emergence and sudden collapse of enormously complex limit cycles as the interpretation of its main connective in its clause bodies is continuously tuned. We exhibit this program primarily as an example of emergent phenomena in continuous-valued logic.

2 The Contention and a Caution

We are proposing a supplementary direction of research for logic programming to go in. There is no claim of exclusivity here. In fact, we believe it is essential to coordinate efforts in the direction we propose with all worthwhile programs of research in logic programming, and also nonmonotonic reasoning.

We contend that logic programs, equipped with any of a variety of semantics, are representable as discrete time continuous state dynamical systems. Datalog programs are subsequently translatable into finite dimensional continuous time dynamical systems as well. Translation of predicate programs with function symbols into continuous time dynamical systems is clearly possible, but here the mathematics is heavy going, involving linear operators on infinite dimensional vector spaces, if, as far as we can see at present, unnatural encodings are to be avoided. This is a beautiful and powerful area of exploration, but mostly premature at this time, we think, for logic programming purposes. Nevertheless, we mention in passing that the dynamical properties of logic programs acting on a Hilbert space is intriguing [Mu96].

Notions rooted in logic are usefully and naturally translatable into notions from continuous mathematics, and more importantly, from the perspective of computing with (formal) logic, we import for free the staggeringly enormous arsenal of mathematical technology available in connection with computing the trajectories of dynamical systems and understanding their structure.

The big question of course is how much of what is imported is actually useful for the purpose of computing with formal logic. We shall attempt to demonstrate in this paper that even the most elementary computational aspects of dynamical systems have immediate application for computing with formal logic. Computing (feasibly) with logic can be seen as effectively (and feasibly) finding models, which are, in turn, fixed points of a suitable operator. (The notion of models-as-fixed-points is a pivotal contribution of Reiter's which he exploited when introducing the notion of *extension* in default logic, [Re80].) Below, we will discuss an approach to computing supported and stable models of Datalog programs using dynamical systems.

The desired fixed points associated with a particular program or theory are usefully seen as fixed points of an associated dynamical system. With regard to this latter perspective, one may get a glimmer of the possibilities by perusing the *Fix Point Theory on the Web* site.[1]

Our grand contention raises a vitally important caution. Suppose (perhaps at this stage it is just a supposition) that our contention has merit. There arises the temptation to go into dynamical systems and fixed point theory looking for applications that will drive logic programs. The area is vast, providing years of mathematical research to enter upon. The opportunities abound for writing a multitude of papers, each one amounting to show how an approach to fixed point finding may be suitably adapted to computationally driving logic programs in this or that class. The adaptability of gradient descent methods to finding models is probably a large enough area for investigation to start a small research industry that could go on for several years. *Most of this activity would probably be a catastrophic dilution of effort in logic programming.* So, we advocate a more cautious approach: whatever fruitful trails exist in dynamical systems and fixed point theory for logic programming purposes, these trails are probably best explored by carefully judging their suitability for enhancing less exotic research programs in logic programming, and nonmonotonic reasoning. We mention in passing

[1] `http://www.math.utep.edu/Faculty/khamsi/fixedpoint/fpt.html`

that *our own* primary concerns with regard to continualization techniques at present lie in (1) program and model complexity and (2) belief revision.

3 Long-term Expectations

In this section we will briefly indicate a number of lines of investigation that can be supported by continualization techniques, and argue for the likely payoff from each area of research that we mention. At this stage in our presentation it is necessary to mention that in section 6 we will present an example of a continuous-time dynamical system that computes the supported models of a ground Datalog program via the most naive so-called *gradient descent* method, that of following continuous trajectories. (For a brief description of gradient descent and a picture illustrating trajectories, see section 6). The example is *not* intended to advocate that supported models be computed in such a manner. Rather, we illustrate the continuous-time approach in the way we do because it highlights in a simple way the idea of the *basin-of-attraction* of a fixed point along with *geometric intuition* for how the collection of these basins is structured. This idea is important in applying continualization in the areas of research that we indicate below. The purpose of the example also includes showing how continuous-time dynamical systems can be seen as conservative extensions, from a logical point of view, of ordinary logic programs based on 2-valued (as well as 3- or n-valued) logic. The range of techniques which may subsequently be brought to bear on the dynamical systems that arise is enormous.

Roughly, gradient-descent is concerned with finding global minima of functions. The problem may be thought of as finding the locations of least altitude on a surface which is the function's graph. One may hope to find such optima by guessing and then descending as rapidly as possible on the surface much as a skier may take the path of steepest descent to get to the bottom of the trail as rapidly as possible.

Transfer of neural net methods: Neural networks, whatever their shortcomings, still represent a significant success for artificial intelligence. Perceptrons, which can be seen as simple neural nets, were originally described by Minsky and Papert [MP69] in terms of gradient descent algorithms. Gradient descent methods play a huge role in training algorithms [WZ89], [MMR97], [AGPC90]. Logic programming enjoys an advantage over neural networks by being able to equip the object corresponding to the neural net, namely the program, with a declarative semantics. The lack of declarative semantics for neural nets is sometimes enthusiastically regarded as some mysterious virtue they possess, having acquired abilities through training algorithms that could not have been feasibly programmed. If we think of a logic program as standing in place of a neural net, the expressive power available in logic programming permits concise formulation of much more robust formal systems than can be *readily* given with a neural net. It is not that neural nets cannot be used in this way, it is just that, as "linguistic" formalisms, logic programming constitutes a much higher level language than do neural network formalisms.

Neural nets enjoy an advantage over logic programs in that they robustly employ techniques from continuous mathematics for adaptation and operation, and also for their design. We are seeking the best of both worlds by trying to import similar techniques from continuous mathematics into the much higher level formalism offered by logic programs.

Transfer of fuzzy control methods: There is much controversy about the scientific quality of fuzzy logic as a development in *logic* [Pa91]. Still, fuzzy control, with its apparent basis in fuzzy logic, represents an important success for the area, and is having a greater impact on industrial-strength applications than is logic programming. It is not enough to dismiss this success as simply the result of the relative abundance of opportunities in different sorts of application/problem areas. The observations that we made above about the advantages of neural nets over logic programming also hold regarding the advantage fuzzy logic and control has over logic programming. Perusal of the fuzzy control literature (for example [KGK94,Ma77,TS85,TKK91]) seems to indicate that (1) fuzzy logic and control offers higher level formalisms that come closer to logic programming than do neural networks, and (2) the use of continuous mathematical techniques is somewhat, at least typically if not in principle, less robust than is seen in neural networks. There seems to be a trade-off: as the semantics of the formalism becomes increasingly clear and declarative, continuous mathematics drops away. Our contention is that this is neither desirable, nor intrinsically necessary, rather being due to accidents of developmental history and the concerns of the area's practitioners.

Equality relations in fuzzy control [KGK94] come close to logic programs as a relatively high level formalism. However, there is no high-level fuzzy formalism comparable to logic programming languages. Fuzzy control is more of a tool-box of techniques at the area's present state of development. Much stands to be gained, if the techniques and capabilities of fuzzy control techniques can be formally amalgamated into logic programming. Moreover, there has been some work in the foundations of fuzzy logic that is interesting from the point of view of mathematical logic. Here again, with careful selection, logic programming stands to gain at its foundations by incorporating this work from fuzzy logic [Ha98].

Comparative program behavior: The fundamental problem that investigation into comparative program behavior treats is seen by asking, given two programs P_1 and P_2, how are their supported models related? It is possible to smoothly deform P_1 into P_2. The well-known one-step consequence operator $\mathbf{T}_P$ enables a program P to be regarded as a transformation on interpretations of the program whose supported models are the transformations' fixed points. As P_1 is deformed along various paths to P_2, what happens to its fixed points? It turns out that in some cases the fixed points of P_2 are obtainable from the fixed points of P_1 by such deformations, and sometimes not. When failure occurs, the reasons involve singularities and basin boundaries, but systematic organized knowledge of what is going on remains to be developed. One payoff from such techniques is that it is possible to very rapidly find the supported models of a program at the other end of various deformations from P after all of the hard work and time spent on computing P's supported models.

One need not only be concerned with the motion of supported models as programs are smoothly altered. Take for example a deductive database with an intentional program, i.e. a program, to which a variety of collections of facts, i.e. extensional parts, can be adjoined. A user might ask whether a simple ground goal G follows from the intentional program together with its current collection of facts. A deduction of G (or a refutation of $\neg G$) becomes a smooth trajectory of a suitable representation of this deductive database's intentional part as a dynamical system. An extensional part, i.e. a collection of facts, together with a goal, becomes a starting point for a trajectory. As the starting point changes, how do the trajectories change? If we knew robust answers to that question, we would expect to obtain short-cuts to query processing in many cases.

Hybrid systems as constraint programs: A constraint program clause can be described as having the form

$$A \leftarrow \Gamma : \varphi$$

where $A \leftarrow \Gamma$ is simply a normal program clause and φ is a *constraint* which, loosely, is just something which takes on a truth value in possible models of the program. A *model* of a constraint program is then an interpretation M in which, after replacing each constraint φ by its truth value ν in M, the resulting program has M as a model. In continuous-valued logic one needs to know how a continuous truth-value contributed by a constraint is to be combined with the rest of the clause. It becomes possible to parameterize the propositional connectives in the clause bodies by parameters that depend upon ν. In the case of 2-valued normal logic programs, in which the negative literals can be seen as constraints, the outcome of constraint evaluation has the effect of varying discretely among a range of Horn clause programs, as is seen in the Gelfond-Lifschitz transform [GL88]. Thus the outcome of evaluating various constraints in a guessed model in continuous-valued logic can have the effect of *tuning* the program continuously among a continuum of programs. In the final section of the paper we will see the how enormously complex behavior *emerges* from tuning continuous-valued programs.

One application is to a paradigmatic class of control problems. These control problems can be described as having two major components, classically described as the *plant* and the *controller*. The controller receives sensor data in the form of continuous values and has the problem of adjusting tunable parameters in the plant so as to cause the sensor values to stay within acceptable ranges. Thus the controller may be described as steering the plant. The controller has a theory, or *control-law* in order to perform the steering task. Every so often, say every 50 milliseconds, the plant process changes enough so that a new control-law has to be devised. The more important problem facing the controller is the latter task. Control-law revision is a discrete task. In effect, the controller has to revise a theory. However, in continuous-valued logic the revision might be accomplished by tuning the continuous-valued logical operations in the control-law using the outcome of constraint evaluation, where the constraint expresses a continuous-valued relationship among the sensor readings.

Belief revision and theory change: One approach to theory change involves the notion of contracting a theory so that it does not entail a particular proposition φ. Given a theory T, the contraction of T with respect to φ is a suitably chosen consistent subtheory T' of T that does not entail φ [AGM85]. The corresponding notion for dynamical systems can be developed as follows. A theory T can be identified with a class of models $\mathcal{M}$. A subtheory T' of T is then identifiable with a superclass of models $\mathcal{M}'$ of $\mathcal{M}$. The notion for dynamical systems corresponding to that of *model* is *fixed point*. Thus the contraction notion for dynamical systems corresponds to increasing the number of fixed points that avoid certain regions in the space of possible fixed points.

Random combinatorial search and complexity: The fixed points of a dynamical system have (possibly empty) *basins of attraction*. Given a combinatorial search problem such as to find a Hamiltonian circuit in a graph, we may represent the problem as one of finding a supported or a stable model of a logic program [MT99]; in turn as one of finding a fixed point of a dynamical system. Distinct solutions are represented as distinct models. If one guesses a solution then the dynamical system may or may not move the guess to an actual solution if any adjustment is necessary. If the guess is moved to an actual solution σ then the guess was in the basin of attraction of σ. Two questions arise: (1) Given a guess that is in the basin of attraction of a solution, how fast can the guess be adjusted to produce the actual solution? (2) How likely is the guess to be in the basin of attraction of some solution? The first question has to do with the *flow* of the system (this is a question about vector fields) and the second question has to do with the size of the basins. If progress toward an actual solution has a rate bounded above zero, and trajectories have bounded arc-length, then producing a solution from a good guess is a linear-time process. The size of the union of all basins of attraction then becomes a representation of the probability of guessing correctly modulo a linear-time adjustment. Knowledge about how to build programs with large basins of attraction when represented as dynamical systems would provide knowledge of how to program combinatorial search problems with *probabilistically* low run-times.

The ability to tune the connectives in a program also permits the tuning of structural complexity. Take for example finite ground programs all of whose clauses have the form

$$A \leftarrow B \mid C$$

where A, B and C are atoms and $\mid$ is a Boolean connective. The problem of deciding whether a supported model exists in which not every atom is false is NP-complete when $\mid$ is taken as NAND (i.e not-both), and n^3 (where n is the number of clauses) when $\mid$ is taken as XOR (exclusive-or). So consider the following heuristic for deciding an instance of the former problem (where $\mid$ is NAND): replace NAND by XOR, find the solutions of the latter (XOR) problem, and drag the solutions over to possible solutions for the former (NAND) problem by subjecting $\mid$ to a deformation from XOR to NAND. We have only limited experience with the heuristic, but we do know that something interesting happens in cases when it fails. Namely, it appears from computational experiments that solutions obtained on the XOR side of the problem get crunched together in a singularity as they are subjected to a smooth deformation towards NAND. The singularity's location indicates where a sudden sharp discontinuity in the complexity of the associated satisfiability problem takes place.

4 Relationship to Prior Work

To the best of our knowledge there is no prior work that explores continuous-time dynamical systems *as such* as a model of computation that directly relates dynamical systems to logic programs, although clearly, much work in neural networks bears on dynamical systems as a model of computation.

Related work of a different character that bears on logic programs as continuous-time dynamical systems is due to Robert Paige, [Pa94]. Paige's work uses sophisticated techniques of finite differencing to translate from one programming language (just as a test bed example, SETL2) to another (again, just as an example, C). With dynamical systems (discrete or continuous time) one can continuously deform one logic program to another. Our own investigations have not yet examined any detailed relationship between our own work and Paige's, but that there is a relationship is clear and acquiring a detailed understanding deserves serious attention.

Much of the original inspiration for our work comes from the work of Melvin Fitting both on metric methods [Fi94] and on bi-lattice semantics [Fi91]. The metric methods work views a program from a particular class of logic programs as a certain kind of discrete-time dynamical system called a contractive iterated function system [Ba93] to obtain a unique supported model (i.e. fixed point) of the program. The bi-lattice semantics permits continuous-valued logic.

In [BDH97] two of us explored the relationship between logic programs and cellular automata [Wo86,Wo94,TM87]. Cellular automata are easily continualized into continuous-time dynamical systems. Moreover, if one is concerned not only with models of programs, but also with the computational paths (trajectories) of programs, Horn clause programs are sufficient for simulating *covered* (i.e. no local variables in clause bodies) normal logic programs. The result is made precise and is contained as a theorem in [BDH97]. Previously in [B-H96] we reported on how covered normal logic programs could be seen as elements of a metric space of bounded almost everywhere continuous functions.

Another major development is the optimization modeling language *Numerica* [VHDJ98,VHLD97,VH97]. The language allows users to solve hard nonlinear optimization problems expressed as ordinary differential equations (what we call here a *continuous-time dynamical system*) by sophisticated interval analysis. We see a strong natural affinity between *Numerica* and our own work. *Numerica* is an exciting tool and it behoove us, or anyone, to take full advantage of it in work regarding dynamical systems.

In comparison with *Numerica*, we are proposing to use dynamical systems to literally drive logic programs viewed dually as programs and as theories in continuous-valued logic. In fact, viewed in this manner, dynamical systems based on low-degree polynomials play exactly the same role for computing with respect to continuous-valued logic as normal predicate logic programs play with respect to 2- and 3-valued logic. In other words, *running* a dynamical system (by which we mean generating a trajectory) is to do a deduction in continuous-valued logic, literally. The emphasis in *Numerica* is to deduce, via numerical analysis methods (specifically involving interval analysis), the optima of a dynamical system. Our emphasis is not on the optima per se, but rather on the trajectories. In an example which we will develop in the next section, we will determine supported models of normal logic programs by gradient descent, which of course involves the search for global optima. But, the real point of the example is to illustrate how to obtain non-trivial continuous-time dynamical systems which are essentially fixed-point equivalent to the discrete-time one-step consequence operator associated with a given normal logic program. By "non-trivial" in this context, we mean a system that can be specified without knowing where the fixed points were located before we started.

The Quantitative Rule Sets (QRS) of van Emden [vE86] and paraconsistent programs, as formulated by Subrahmanian and Kifer, [KS92] are related to our work, since both approaches, particularly the former, and optionally the latter, use continuous-valued logic. The main distinction between our work and this earlier work involving continuous-valued logic is that finite propositional QRS programs and the paraconsistent programs are not literally everywhere differentiable, most particularly at the boundaries precisely where the special case of classical two-valued logics are obtained. Our current notion of program, that involves continuous-valued logic, is differentiable everywhere. Continuous-valued logic programs that lack this property block the final step to a continuous-time dynamical system. However, much of van Emden's results on QRS's carry over to our programs anyway.

Tucker, Tapia and Bennett [TTB85] introduced notions of differential and integral for Boolean functions from $\{0,1\}^n$ to $\{0,1\}$. Our continualizations have differentials that do not agree with theirs, except, coincidentally, for conjunction. However, the Tucker-Tapia-Bennett partial derivative of material implication with respect to the hypothesis is constantly 0, i.e. false. The intuition behind this outcome alludes us. In our case the same partial derivative is signed and turns out to be -1 times the logical negation of the conclusion, indicating that if the conclusion is true, no change takes place in the truth of the implication as the hypothesis changes, and if the conclusion is false, then the implication undergoes change in the direction opposite to the change in the hypothesis. This is arguably more natural. Still, our motivation is fundamentally computational, not semantical. We are not too much concerned with the meaning of our continuous truth values. As we will demonstrate below, the dynamical systems are intended for computational purposes, and can easily filter out non-$\{0,1\}$-valued fixed points. At the end of our discussion of continualization we will point out the relationship of our continualizations to fuzzy logic. It is a good fit by happenstance. So whatever value the reader may put on T-norms and T-co-norms, our conjunction and disjunctions satisfy the T-norm and co-norm postulates [KGK94]. Indeed, our continualizations of conjunction and disjunction are coincidentally the most commonly occurring continuous representations of these connectives in fuzzy logic, when we choose 0 to represent *false* and 1 to represent *true.*

5 Continualizing Propositional Connectives

The reader may wish to skip to the example below; however the proof of the uniqueness of continualization with respect to lowest degree choices of polynomials is remarkable for its brevity. Begin with n-valued logic where the semantics of the k-ary propositional connectives are given by various functions of the type

$$\{v_1, \ldots, v_n\}^k \longrightarrow \{v_1, \ldots, v_n\}$$

where $\{v_1, \ldots, v_n\}$ is the set of truth values. Let $\mathcal{B} = \{v_1, \ldots, v_n\}$. Choose your favorite field $\mathcal{F}$ (presumably a continuous field, but at this stage that isn't necessary) such that $\mathcal{B}$ can be embedded one-to-one into $\mathcal{F}$. Embed $\mathcal{B}$ into $\mathcal{F}$ as you like and regard $\mathcal{B}$ as a subset of $\mathcal{F}$. Consider linear combinations with respect to $\mathcal{F}$ of all functions of the type $\mathcal{B}^k \longrightarrow \mathcal{F}$ under pointwise addition and scalar multiplication. The set of all such functions is itself a vector space over $\mathcal{F}$ of dimension n^k. Call this vector space V. Now, consider any collection of functions from $\mathcal{F}^k$ to $\mathcal{F}$ that forms a vector space U, also of dimension n^k, such that the restriction of the functions in U from $\mathcal{F}^k$ to $\mathcal{B}^k$ is a mapping *onto* V. Then the restriction mapping is a linear isomorphism from U to V, from which it follows that there are no non-trivial automorphisms of U that respect the restriction mapping. That is, using the functions in U there is at most one way to generalize the functions in V.

We now choose U. The method involves a special case of a technique known as Lagrangian interpolation, with which the reader need not be familiar. Let U be the vector space of polynomials of degree $n-1$ in each of k variables with coefficients in $\mathcal{F}$ and variables in $x_1, \ldots, x_k$. For example, if $\mathcal{F}$ is the reals and $n = k = 2$, then U is the vector space of polynomials of the form

$$\lambda_1 + \lambda_2 x_1 + \lambda_3 x_2 + \lambda_4 x_1 x_2$$

where $\lambda_1, \lambda_2, \lambda_3, \lambda_4$ are real numbers.

U is a vector space over $\mathcal{F}$ of dimension n^k. We have only to show that the restriction mapping is *onto* V. For this we have to show that for every function f in V there is a polynomial in U that agrees with f on $\{v_1, \ldots, v_n\}^k$. Define the n^k-many distinct polynomials

$$P_{i_1 \ldots i_k}(x_1, \ldots, x_k) = \Pi^n_{\substack{j=1\\ j\neq i_1}} (x_1 - v_j) \cdots \Pi^n_{\substack{j=1\\ j\neq i_k}} (x_k - v_j)$$

for each choice of $i_m = 1, \ldots, n$, $m = 1, \ldots, k$. Let

$$p_{i_1 \ldots i_k} = P_{i_1 \ldots i_k}(v_{i_1}, \ldots, v_{i_k}).$$

From the way $P_{i_1 \ldots i_k}$ is defined, it follows that

$$p_{i_1 \ldots i_k} \neq 0.$$

Then

$$p^{-1}_{i_1 \ldots i_k} P_{i_1 \ldots i_k}(v_{i_1}, \ldots, v_{i_k}) = 1$$

and

$$p^{-1}_{i_1 \ldots i_k} P_{i_1 \ldots i_k}(x_1, \ldots, x_k) = 0$$

whenever $(x_1, \ldots, x_k) \in \mathcal{B}^k - \{(v_{i_1}, \ldots, v_{i_k})\}$. It is in taking the reciprocal of $p_{i_1 \ldots i_k}$ that we needed a field, and not merely a ring.

Now, let $f \in V$ be given and let

$$Q_f(x_1, \ldots, x_k) = \Sigma^n_{i_1=1} \cdots \Sigma^n_{i_k=1} f(v_{i_1}, \ldots, v_{i_k}) p^{-1}_{i_1 \ldots i_k} P_{i_1 \ldots i_k}(x_1, \ldots, x_k)$$

Then,

$$Q_f(v_{i_1}, \ldots, v_{i_k}) = f(v_{i_1}, \ldots, v_{i_k})$$

for all $(v_{i_1}, \ldots, v_{i_k}) \in \{v_1, \ldots, v_n\}^k$. That is,

$$f = Q_f$$

on $\{v_1, \ldots, v_n\}^k$. So the restriction map from U to V is onto. Hence there is exactly one way to extend the functions of type

$$\{v_1, \ldots, v_n\}^k \longrightarrow \{v_1, \ldots, v_n\}$$

to polynomials over $\mathcal{F}$ of degree $n-1$ in each of k variables.

We call this construction the lowest degree polynomial *continualization* of n-valued logic over field $\mathcal{F}$, when $\mathcal{F}$ is the real or complex number field. We have just shown this continualization to be unique among possible lowest degree polynomials up to the representations in $\mathcal{F}$ of the truth values. Notice that changes in the choice of truth-value representations in the field amounts to a change of basis in U.

Notice also that if we continualized with not necessarily lowest degree polynomials, then the polynomials that continualize the standard basis of the vector space V are divisible by the polynomials in U that continualize those same standard basis elements, since these not necessarily lowest degree polynomials merely contain superfluous factors of the form $x_i - v$ where $v \in \{v_1, \ldots, v_n\}$. Thus the choice of the space of polynomials by which to continualize V is exceedingly limited by linear algebraic constraints.

Example: In the case of 2-valued logic, with truth values represented by 0 and 1, whether 0 corresponds to *false* or to *true* is immaterial to the continualization; instead, the correspondence of 0 with *false* or *true* determines the interpretation of the truth tables. For example, in the truth table below, suppose $b_1 = b_2 = b_3 = 0$ and $b_4 = 1$. Then the truth table defines conjunction if 0 represents *false*, and defines disjunction if 0 represents *true*.

Consider a function from $\{0,1\}^2$ to $\{0,1\}$ defined by the truth table

p q	$p \bullet q$
0 0	b_1
0 1	b_2
1 0	b_3
1 1	b_4

Then

$$\begin{aligned} p \bullet q &= b_1(1-p)(1-q) + b_2(1-p)q + b_3p(1-q) + b_4pq \\ &= \lambda_1 + \lambda_2 p + \lambda_3 q + \lambda_4 pq \end{aligned}$$

where

$$\begin{bmatrix} 1 & 0 & 0 & 0 \\ -1 & 0 & 1 & 0 \\ -1 & 1 & 0 & 0 \\ 1 & -1 & -1 & 1 \end{bmatrix} \begin{bmatrix} b_1 \\ b_2 \\ b_3 \\ b_4 \end{bmatrix} = \begin{bmatrix} \lambda_1 \\ \lambda_2 \\ \lambda_3 \\ \lambda_4 \end{bmatrix}.$$

Notice that by the uniqueness of the continualizing polynomial under the assumption that the exponents are bounded by 1, each of the Boolean sentence connectives, conjunction and disjunction, *must* be represented by one of the functions given by the two polynomials uv, $u+v-uv$, depending on whether 0 or 1 represents *false*. Also, in the case of unary Boolean functions, negation *must* be represented by the function given by $1-u$. The inverse of the above matrix gives the restriction mapping discussed in the derivation above, with respect to a fairly natural choice of bases.

The example shows that our lowest degree continualizations force on us the most typical choices for continualizing conjunction and disjunction in fuzzy logic. To the perhaps limited extent that one accepts the notion of fuzzy truth values, our truth values can be interpreted as having the same meaning, or lack of it, as fuzzy truth values have.

6 A Continuous-Time Example

In this section we will show by the development of an example how to represent a normal ground Datalog program, i.e. a finite propositional normal logic program, as a continuous-time dynamical system. We shall not, in this paper, be rigorously detailed with these dynamical systems. The example is the following:

$$\begin{aligned} a &\leftarrow \neg b, \neg c \\ b &\leftarrow \neg a, \neg d \\ c &\leftarrow d \\ d &\leftarrow c \end{aligned}$$

With respect to the usual 2-valued semantics, this program has three supported Herbrand models, i.e. fixed points: $\{a\}$, $\{b\}$, $\{c, d\}$. The first two are stable, the third is not. Our methods have thus far concentrated on finding supported, (i.e. fixed point) models of programs. For propositional programs, a supported model can be checked for stability in linear time. Thus, regarding programs that do not have many more supported models than stable models, efficiently finding supported models is a useful heuristic for finding stable models.

A continuous-time dynamical system is a system of simultaneous equations of the form

$$\begin{aligned} \tfrac{dx_1}{dt} &= f_1(t, x_1, \ldots, x_n) \\ &\vdots \\ \tfrac{dx_n}{dt} &= f_n(t, x_1, \ldots, x_n) \,. \end{aligned}$$

Assumptions on the f_i vary according to the purpose at hand. In our applications the f_i are polynomials, and occasionally trigonometric, or exponential. Hence integrability and differentiability follow painlessly. Intuitively, t is time, and the equations express how a point is moving as a function of time and current position. If the f_i are all independent of t, then the system is said to be *autonomous*.

Let *false* be represented by 0, and *true* by 1. By the continualization method of the previous section we obtain the following transformation, whose $\{0,1\}$-valued fixed points are precisely the supported models of our program:

$$T\begin{bmatrix} a \\ b \\ c \\ d \end{bmatrix} = \begin{bmatrix} 1-b-c+bc \\ 1-a-d+ad \\ d \\ c \end{bmatrix}.$$

Let $\mathbf{R}$ be the field of real numbers. As an operator on $\mathbf{R}^4$, T has fixed points along two curved lines that orthogonally intersect at the point $(a,b,c,d) = (\frac{1}{2},\frac{1}{2},0,0)$. Projected onto the a,b-plane, these lines are along the main diagonal $b = a$ and the orthogonal line $b = 1-a$. The $\{0,1\}$-valued fixed points are $(1,0,0,0)$, $(0,1,0,0)$ and $(0,0,1,1)$ as we expect from the program. We shall see how the continuous-time dynamical system representation finds these fixed points.

Let I be the identity operator on $\mathbf{R}^4$ and put $R = T - I$. The kernel of R, i.e. the subset of $\mathbf{R}^4$ that R maps to $(0,0,0,0)$, is precisely the set of fixed points of T. The kernel of R can be found by gradient-descent methods, among many others. Of course, the kernel can be found analytically on this simple example, but gradient-descent methods are more easily scalable.

We show how to express the dynamical system corresponding to gradient descent for finding the kernel of R, and show how to augment it to filter out unwanted fixed points.

The *differential* of R denoted by dR is given by the Jacobian matrix of R. This matrix is the matrix of partial derivatives of the component functions of R. Specifically, if we express R by

$$\begin{bmatrix} y_1 \\ y_2 \\ y_3 \\ y_4 \end{bmatrix} = \begin{bmatrix} 1-x_1-x_2-x_3+x_2x_3 \\ 1-x_1-x_2-x_4+x_1x_4 \\ x_4-x_3 \\ x_3-x_4 \end{bmatrix}$$

then

$$dR = \left[\frac{\partial y_i}{\partial x_j}\right]_{i=1,2,3,4}^{j=1,2,3,4}$$

(i indexes rows, j indexes columns) The partial derivatives all have the affine form

$$\frac{\partial y_i}{\partial x_j} = a_{ij} + b_{ij}x_{k_{ij}}.$$

in the case of 2-valued logic when we continualize by polynomials with degree 1 in each variable.

Specifically for our example,

$$dR = \begin{bmatrix} -1 & -1+x_3 & -1+x_2 & 0 \\ -1+x_4 & -1 & 0 & -1+x_1 \\ 0 & 0 & -1 & 1 \\ 0 & 0 & 1 & -1 \end{bmatrix}$$

A program can always be first normalized to an equivalent program in 2-valued logic that has at most two literals in the clause bodies. Programs in such a normal form will yield affine forms for the resulting partial derivatives. The differential is a linear function whose graph, in a suitably translated coordinate system, forms a hyperplane tangent to the graph of R.

The standard (Euclidean) norm of a point is its distance from the origin. We denote the norm of a point $\mathbf{x}$ in $\mathbf{R}^n$ by $||\mathbf{x}||$. Note that $T(\mathbf{x}) = \mathbf{x}$ iff $R(\mathbf{x}) = \mathbf{0}$ iff $||R(\mathbf{x})|| = 0$ iff $||R(\mathbf{x})||^2 = 0$. (Squaring maintains differentiability when the kernel of R is reached.) We will reach the kernel of R by moving on tangent hyperplanes to the graph of $||R||^2$ that produce the most rapid instantaneous decrease in $||R||^2$. The *gradient* of $||R||^2$ is a vector that lies in this tangent hyperplane in a direction corresponding to the most rapid instantaneous change in $||R||^2$ and is given by $(d||R||^2)^T$. It can be calculated that, as long as the Jacobian is defined for this square-norm function,

$$(d||R||^2)^T = 2(dR)^T R$$

(Superscript T denotes matrix transpose.) The matrices have been transposed here so that one obtains the differential of $||R||^2$ as a column vector.

An instantaneous movement of $\mathbf{x}$ is expressed by $d\mathbf{x}$. To obtain the fastest decrease in $||R||^2$ while remaining on its graph, one moves $\mathbf{x}$ according to

$$\frac{d\mathbf{x}}{dt} = -(d||R||^2)^T = -2(dR)^T R .$$

(When written out without matrix notation, the equations above will be seen to conform to our definition of autonomous continuous-time dynamical system.)

We would like the system to stop moving $\mathbf{x}$ exactly when $||R||^2$ reaches 0. In general, one expects a dynamical system like this to occasionally get stuck at so-called saddle points or local minima. By adding auxiliary variables to the system, one can prevent it from reaching fixed points except at global minima *because we already know in advance what the global minimum is,* although not *where* it is, namely when $||R||^2$ is 0. We will not go into detail on this last point. More interesting is how to prune out unwanted fixed points of the dynamical system. Consider

$$C(\mathbf{x}) = [(x_i(x_i - 1))]_{i=1,\ldots,n}$$

The associated dynamical system is given by

$$\frac{d\mathbf{x}}{dt} = -2(dC)^T C .$$

Almost all points moved by this dynamical system are attracted exclusively to the vertices of the unit n-cube. The only exception is the point at the center of the cube. The sum of one's original system with the $0,1$-attractor does the trick. (The reader should intuitively reflect that motion produced by the sum of differentials accumulates in general in a nonlinear way).

Finally, the dynamical system in which we are interested, is

$$\frac{d\mathbf{x}}{dt} = -2(dR)^T R - 2(dC)^T C\,.$$

This system is almost fixed-point equivalent to the original logic program. It happens to have a saddle point, that is, a fixed point where further descent is still immediately possible. (We leave it to the reader to guess where.) Saddle points and local minima can be observed through auxiliary variables to correspond to values of $\mathbf{x}$ where the global minimum has not yet been achieved. The values of the auxiliary variables can thus be kept changing, destroying any possibility of achieving a fixed point of the dynamical system unless $\mathbf{x}$ is at a $\{0,1\}$-valued zero of $||R||^2$. These $\{0,1\}$-valued zeros of $||R||^2$ correspond to the supported models of the original program from which R was derived. For this reason, let us call a $\{0,1\}$-valued zero of $||R||^2$ a *supported model* of the dynamical system $\frac{d\mathbf{x}}{dt} = -2(dR)^T R - 2(dC)^T C$. We do not expect to reach one of these supported models no matter where we start; it is enough to be able to start with a reasonable probability of being in the basin of attraction of one of them. Repeated trials raise the probability as high as we like. Of course precise analysis of such probabilistic approaches is required, but at this stage we are offering only computational evidence of the utility of the approach. One approach to a complexity analysis involves estimating the volumes of the basins of attraction of the supported models.

Let $\mathbf{x}(t)$ be the position of a point at time t as it is determined by the system together with the starting position $\mathbf{x}(0)$. The position at time t can be calculated by iterating

$$\mathbf{x}(t + \Delta t) := \mathbf{x}(t) + \frac{d\mathbf{x}}{dt}\Delta t$$

where Δt approximates dt. In our example $\Delta t = 0.001$.

The figure below indicates the performance of the system in our example. The curves, called *trajectories*, that the dynamical system follows, begin at various integer lattice points in $\mathbf{R}^4$ and track into one of the supported models. The figure shows the trace of these trajectories on the (a, b)-plane.

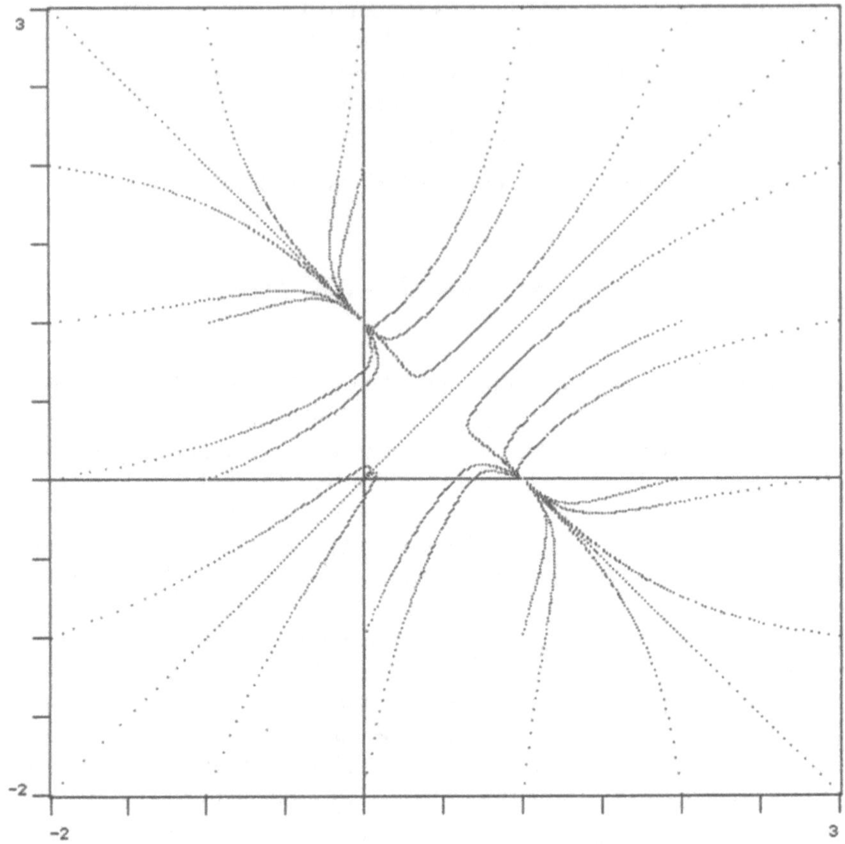

7 A Fundamental Discrete-time System

Consider the program

$$a \leftarrow \neg b$$
$$b \leftarrow \neg a$$

We take advantage of our 2-valued logic to re-express this program as the 2-valued equivalent

$$a \leftarrow b \,|\, b$$
$$b \leftarrow a \,|\, a$$

where the vertical bar indicates the NAND operation, i.e. not-both. As a discrete-time system with continuous states, we can express this program by

$$T \begin{bmatrix} a \\ b \end{bmatrix} = \begin{bmatrix} 1 - b^2 \\ 1 - a^2 \end{bmatrix}$$

T has four fixed points: $(1, 0)$, $(0, 1)$, $(-\phi, -\phi)$, and $(-\hat{\phi}, -\hat{\phi})$, where ϕ is the golden ratio, and $\hat{\phi}$ is $1 - \phi$. Iterating T, we can think of this process as taking place in discrete time steps. The convergence of the dynamical system is expressed by the following figure.

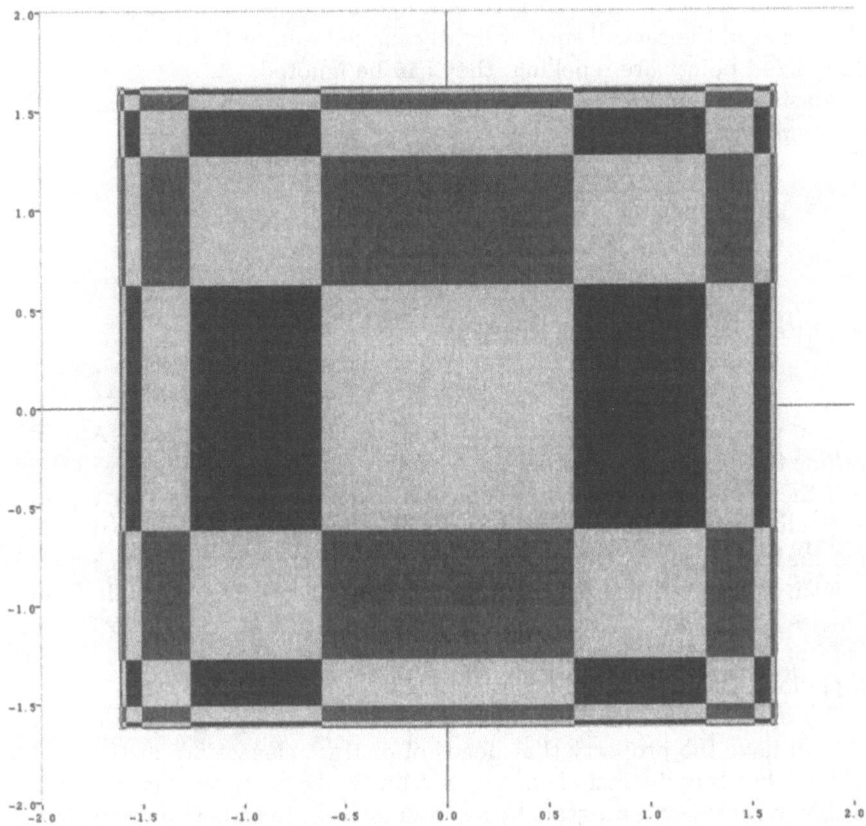

The checkerboard pattern within the figure consists of countably many rows and columns, increasingly squeezed into the figure as the outer boundary is approached. The sequence of squares on the diagonals does not decrease in area in geometric proportion as the sequence approaches the corners of the checkerboard; rather, the decrease is determined by the dynamical (i.e. iterative) properties of a certain degree-4 polynomial on the interval from 0 to the golden ratio. Starting points in the plane outside the shaded checkerboard figure lead to diverging iterations to infinity. Inside the figure, starting points in the central small interior square and in all regions depicted by the same light shade of grey, are attracted to a limit cycle oscillating between $(0, 0)$ and $(1, 1)$. Starting points in any of the rectangular areas bearing the same shade of grey as the rectangle containing the point $(1, 0)$ are attracted to $(1, 0)$, and similarly for $(0, 1)$. The remaining fixed points that involve the golden ratio are repelling; all sequences of iterations that do not start on them are repelled away from them. This is also true of the entire boundaries between rectangular patches, as well as the outer boundary; any sequence starting on or near them is repelled away from them. The fixed point $(-\phi, -\phi)$ is at the lower corner of the checkerboard figure, and $(-\hat{\phi}, -\hat{\phi})$ is at the upper right corner of the central smaller lightly shaded square. Since the non-$\{0,1\}$-valued fixed points are repelling, they can be ignored.

Consider the following propositional program, which we call an if-then-else *component.*

$$\begin{aligned} r &\leftarrow u \mid v \\ u &\leftarrow p \mid a \\ v &\leftarrow q \mid b \\ a &\leftarrow b \mid b \\ b &\leftarrow a \mid a\,. \end{aligned}$$

The pattern in this program expresses

$$r \leftarrow (\text{if } a \text{ then } p \text{ else } q)$$

Suppose one has a program in which these clauses are a part. Any *non-repelling* fixed point of the program, even if it is not $\{0,1\}$-valued, will satisfy the if-then-else interpretation. From this it follows that one can represent any (including infinite ones) propositional program in 2-valued logic with a program built from repeated uses of the component. By the term *represent* we mean that given a program P, we can find a program Q built from if-then-else components whose non-repelling fixed points restrict to the fixed points of P. (Thus the completion of Q is a conservative extension of the completion of P in 2-valued logic.)

The attentive reader may have noticed that the programs we treated so far all have the property that heads of distinct clauses are distinct. More generally, heads of distinct clauses do not unify. We point out that it is always possible to represent a program by a conservative extension to a program with this property, even when the initial program is infinite.

8 Emergent Phenomena from Tuning

We conclude the paper with an example of a program that produces emergent phenomena in continuous-valued logic as its main connective is tuned.

$$\begin{aligned} p_0 &\leftarrow p_6 \bullet p_1 \\ p_1 &\leftarrow p_0 \bullet p_2 \\ p_2 &\leftarrow p_1 \bullet p_3 \\ p_3 &\leftarrow p_2 \bullet p_4 \\ p_4 &\leftarrow p_3 \bullet p_5 \\ p_5 &\leftarrow p_4 \bullet p_6 \\ p_6 &\leftarrow p_5 \bullet p_0 \end{aligned}$$

The possible interpretations under consideration for the $p \bullet q$ connective are given by

$$\lambda_1 + \lambda_2 p + \lambda_3 q + \lambda_4 pq .$$

with the λ_i as real numbers. The space of these polynomials is of course linearly isomorphic to $\mathbf{R}^4$. We will vary the coefficients $(\lambda_1, \lambda_2, \lambda_3, \lambda_4)$ of these polynomials, and hence the interpretation of the connective $\bullet$, along a short line segment in $\mathbf{R}^4$ between the points $(a_1, a_1 + b_1, a_1 - b_1, b_1)$ and $(a_2, a_2 + b_2, a_2 - b_2, b_2)$, where

$$\begin{aligned} a_1 &= -0.6892 \\ b_1 &= 0.3446 \\ a_2 &= -0.6911 \\ b_2 &= 0.3456 \end{aligned}$$

In the figure that follows, the horizontal λ-axis from 0 to 1 is the line segment in $\mathbf{R}^4$ from $(a_1, a_1+b_1, a_1-b_1, b_1)$ to $(a_2, a_2+b_2, a_2-b_2, b_2)$. Thus, each value on the horizontal axis corresponds to an interpretation of $\bullet$. The vertical η-axis corresponds to the Euclidean norm of valuations. We will briefly explain this by considering just one point plotted in the figure.

There is a point $(\lambda, \eta) = (0.375, 4.7051)$ occurring on one of the fibers in the portion of the figure just to the left of center. The interpretation of the connective $\bullet$ is given by the polynomial

$$a + (a+b)p + (a-b)q + bpq$$

where

$$\begin{aligned} a &= (1-\lambda)a_1 + \lambda a_2 \\ b &= (1-\lambda)b_1 + \lambda b_2 \end{aligned}$$

where a_1, b_1, a_2 and b_2 are as above. Specifically, for the value $\lambda = 0.375$, the values of a and b are $a = -0.68991$ and $b = 0.34485$. The value $\eta = 4.7051$ is the Euclidean norm (the distance from the origin $(0,0,0,0,0,0,0)$) of the Herbrand interpretation (with continuous truth-values) given by $\mathbf{T}_P^{3197}(I_0)$ where $I_0(p_0) = 1$ and $I_0(p_1) \ldots = I_0(p_6) = 0$. That is, $I_0 = (1,0,0,0,0,0,0)$. (The reason we do not start the iteration at the origin of the space in this example is due to not wanting the truth value of every atom in the interpretations we reach to be equal). Specifically, the values of the atoms $p_0, \ldots p_6$ in $\mathbf{T}_P^{3197}(I_0)$ are given by

$$\begin{aligned} p_0 &= -1.1442045697971657 \\ p_1 &= -1.424646495185601 \\ p_2 &= -2.411334918922416 \\ p_3 &= -0.06419512110633097 \\ p_4 &= -2.3764341956984323 \\ p_5 &= -1.5553879344313004 \\ p_6 &= -2.2167841794959537 . \end{aligned}$$

What is the significance of the fact that this point (λ, η) occurs on this fiber? The fiber indicates an attracting limit cycle in the iteration of $\mathbf{T}_P$. The cycle has a period of 16. Only eight fibers are visible in the figure because the other eight are clustered in a similar figure corresponding to values with norms near 7 and are consequently off the top of the figure. Thus $\mathbf{T}_P$ is asymptotically converging to a limit cycle of period 16. Equivalently, the program corresponding to $\mathbf{T}_P^{16}$ has the valuation displayed above as a supported model. As the connective $\bullet$ is tuned continuously from left to right in the figure the model suddenly emerges out of somewhat chaotic iterative behavior at $\lambda = 0.197$, and appears to change continuously until it vanishes again at $\lambda = 0.542$. Actually, the structure of the fibers is collectively more complicated: there are three distinct values of λ where the eight fibers exchange places. This appears to be due to an irregular boundary of the basin of attraction around the fibers that captures the iteration of $\mathbf{T}_P$ at slightly different stages as the interpretation of $\bullet$ is tuned.

For each value on the horizontal axis, the program was iterated 2900 times beginning at $(1,0,0,0,0,0,0)$. If the norms of all of the valuations that result from an iteration are less then 64, then the iteration is deemed to not be diverging to infinity. A value on the vertical axis is the norm of a valuation. If the iteration is not diverging to infinity, then the norms of the next 300 iterations are plotted. The plots of every other iteration appear in the figure.

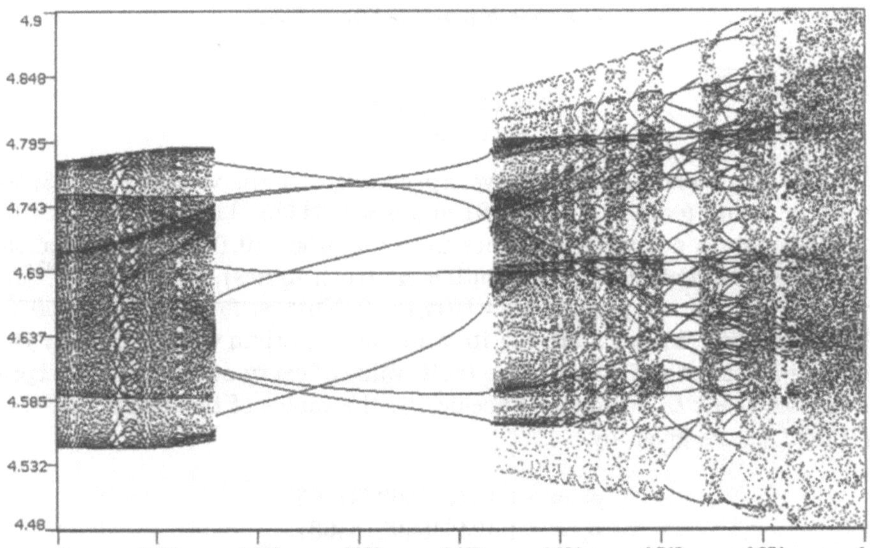

On the right-hand side of the figure the fibrous gaps are spreading out and becoming increasingly complex before somewhat abruptly disappearing as the cycle structure in the iterations vanishes.

Although beyond the scope of this paper, we know how to find the regions of the space of polynomials that give rise to this emergent complex behavior. The fact that models can be made to vary continuously as the program is tuned appears to facilitate the application to hybrid control discussed earlier and similar applications.

Acknowledgements

We thank Krzysztof R. Apt and Victor W. Marek for valuable suggestions for improving the paper, and we give special thanks to Jeffrey B. Remmel for his time and effort in protracted technical discussion on several of the application topics discussed here. We also thank Lisa Ahn, of the Bronx High School of Science, for her participation in the seminar in which several of the ideas were developed. That the restriction mapping in section 5 is a linear isomorphism was pointed out to us by H.F. Mattson, Jr.

References

[AGM85] Alchourrón, C.E., Gärdenfors, P. and Makinson, D. "On the Logic of Theory Change", *J. Symbolic Logic*, 50(2):510–530, 1985.

[AGPC90] Anderson, J.A., Gately, M.T., P.A. Penz and Collins, D.R. "Radar Signal Categorization Using a Neural Network", *Proceedings of the IEEE*, 78:1646–1657, 1990.

[Ba93] Barnesly, M. *Fractals Everywhere*, Academic Press, 1993.

[B-H96] Blair, H.A., Chidella, J., Dushin, F., Ferry, A. and Humenn, P. "A Continuum of Discrete Systems", *Annals of Mathematics and Artificial Intelligence*, 21(2-4):155–185, 1997.

[BDH97] Blair, H.A., Dushin, F., and Humenn, P. "Simulations Between Programs as Cellular Automata", in Jürgen Dix, Ulrich Furbach and Anil Nerode editors, *Logic Programming and Nonmonotonic Reasoning*, Proceedings of the 4th International Conference, Dagstuhl, Germany, volume 1265 of *Lecture Notes in Computer Science* (subseries *LNAI*), pp. 115–131. Springer-Verlag, 1997.

[BM98] Blair, H.A. and Marek, V.W. "Henkin Algebras with Applications to Default Logic", presented at NMR'98, Trento, Italy.

[Bo86] Boothby, W.M. *An Introduction to Differentiable Manifolds and Riemannian Geometry*, Academic Press, 1986.

[De37] Descartes, R. *La Géométrie*, 1637.

[vE86] van Emden, M. H. "Quantitative Deduction and Its Fixpoint Theory", *Journal of Logic Programming*, 3(1):37–53, 1986.

[vEK76] van Emden, M. H. and Kowalski, R. A. "The Semantics of Logic as a Programming Language", *JACM*, 23:733-742, 1976.

[Fi91] Fitting, M. "Bilattices and the Semantics of Logic Programming", *Journal of Logic Programming*, 11(1,2):91–116, 1991.

[Fi94] Fitting, M. "Metric methods, three examples and a theorem", *Journal of Logic Programming*, 21:113–127, 1994.

[GH83] Guckenheimer, J. and Holmes, P. *Nonlinear Oscillations, Dynamical Systems, and Bifurcations of Vector Fields*, Springer-Verlag Texts in Applied Mathematics, volume 42, 1983.

[GL88] Gelfond, M. and Lifschitz, V. "The Stable Model Semantics for Logic Programming", in Robert A. Kowalski, Kenneth A. Bowen, editors, *Logic Programming, Proceedings of the Fifth International Conference and Symposium*, Seattle, Washington, pp. 1070–1080, 1988.

[Ha98] Hajek, Petr. *Metamathematics of Fuzzy Logic: Trends in Logic, Vol. 4*, Kluwer, 1998.

[HW95] Hubbard, J.H. and West, B.H. *Differential Equations: A Dynamical Systems Approach, volumes I and II*, Springer-Verlag Texts in Applied Mathematics, volumes 5 and 18, 1995.

[KGK94] Kruse, R., Gebhardt, J. and Klawonn, F. *Foundations of Fuzzy Systems*, Wiley, 1994.

[KS92] Kifer, M. and Subrahmanian, V.S. "Theory of Generalized Annotated Logic Programming and its Applications", *Journal of Logic Programming*, 12(3,4):335–367, 1992.

[Ma77] Mamdani, E.H. "Application of Fuzzy Logic to Approximate Reasoning Using Linguistic Systems", *IEEE Transactions on Computers*, 26:1182–1191, 1977.

[MMR97] Mehrotra, K., Mohan, C.K. and Ranka, S. *Elements of Artificial Neural Networks*, MIT Press, 1997.

[MP69] Minsky, M. and Papert, S. *Perceptrons*, MIT Press, 1969.

[MT99] Marek, V.W. and Truszczyński, M. "Stable Logic Programming and an Alternative Logic Programming Paradigm", this volume, pp. 375–398.

[Mu96] Mundici, D. *Private communication.*

[Pa91] Parikh, R. *Private communication.*

[Pa94] Paige, R. "Viewing a Program Transformation System at Work", *Programming Language Implementation and Logic Programming*, Proceedings of the 6th International Symposium, PLILP'94, volume 844 of *Lecture Notes in Computer Science*, pp. 5–24, Springer-Verlag, 1994.

[Re80] Reiter, R. "A Logic for Default Reasoning", *Artificial Intelligence*, 13:81–132, 1980.

[Sh67] Shoenfield, J. R. *Mathematical Logic*, Addison-Wesley, 1967.

[Te94] Tennent, R. D. "Denotational Semantics", in *Handbook of Logic in Computer Science*, volume 3, pp. 168–324, Oxford University Press, 1994.

[TKK91] Takagi, H., Konda, T. and Kojima, Y. "Neural Networks Based on Approximate Reasoning Architecture", *Japanese Journal of Fuzzy Theory and Systems*, 3:63-74, 1991.

[TM87] Toffoli, T. and Margolis, N. *Cellular Automata Machines: a new environment for modeling*, MIT Press, 1987.

[TS85] Takagi, H. and Sugeno, M. "Fuzzy Identification of Systems and its Application to Modeling and Control", *IEEE Transactions on Systems, Man, and Cybernetics*, 15:116–132, 1985.

[TTB85] Tucker, T.H., Tapia, M.A. and Bennett, A.W., "Boolean Integral Calculus for Digital Systems", *IEEE Transactions on Computers*, c-34(1):78–81, 1985.

[VH97] Van Hentenryck, P. "Numerica: A Modeling Language for Global Optimization", *IJCAI97*.

[VHDJ98] Van Hentenryck, P., Deville, Y. and Janssen, M. "Consistency Techniques in Ordinary Differential Equations", *Proceedings of the Fourth International Conference on Principles and Practice of Constraint Programming*, Springer-Verlag, 1998.

[VHLD97] Van Hentenryck, P., Laurent, M. and Deville, Y. *Numerica: A Modeling Language for Global Optimization*, MIT Press, 1997.

[Wo86] Wolfram, S. *Theory and Applications of Cellular Automata*, World Scientific, 1986.

[Wo94] Wolfram, S. *Cellular Automata and Complexity*, Addison-Wesley, 1994.

[WZ89] Williams, R.J. and Zipser, D. "A Learning Algorithm for Continually Running Fully Recurrent Neural Networks", *Neural Computation*, 1:270-280, 1989.

The Logic Programming Paradigm in Numerical Computation

Maarten H. van Emden

Department of Computer Science, University of Victoria,
P.O. Box 3055, Victoria, B.C., V8W 3P6 Canada

Summary. Although CLP(**R**) is a promising application of the logic programming paradigm to numerical computation, it has not addressed what has long been known as "the pitfalls of [numerical] computation" [12]. These show that rounding errors induce a severe correctness problem wherever floating-point computation is used. Independently of logic programming, constraint processing has been applied to problems in terms of real-valued variables. By using the techniques of interval arithmetic, constraint processing can be regarded as a computer-generated proof that a certain real-valued solution lies in a narrow interval. In this paper we propose a method for interfacing this technique with CLP(**R**). This is done via a real-valued analogy of Apt's proof-theoretic framework for constraint processing.

1 Introduction

In the first flowering of the logic programming paradigm, a large part of computer science was identified as suitable territory for conquest. This ambitious program suffered a significant omission: numerical computation. In this paper we will argue that there are correctness problems of great practical importance in numerical computation and that logic programming is a promising method to solve these. In the rest of this introduction we will trace in historical order the various steps needed to go from conventional numerical computation to a logic programming system for numerical computation.

Via interval arithmetic to sound numerics. Correctness of numerical computation has not been fully addressed, either by the program verification community, or by logic programming. As we shall show below, this issue has also been ignored by mainstream numerical analysis. Only a distinct subculture, interval arithmetic, has taken seriously the possibility that users of numerical software might want guaranteed correct output.

In interval arithmetic one associates a set of reals with each real-valued unknown. Results of computations are given as membership of a set. This method is of practical value for two reasons:

1. The sets are restricted to closed, connected sets of reals such that its bounds, if any, are floating-point numbers. Such sets are called *intervals*. They are economically representable in computer memory, compared to other set representations.

2. Arithmetic is performed on intervals. As the result intervals can be computed by operations of a standard floating-point processor in such a way that correctness is preserved, the set operations are fast compared to most other set operations.

In this way numerical computations on standard floating-point processors can be interpreted as computer-generated proofs that a real-valued variable belongs to an interval that has a width near the limit imposed by the hardware. This method of ensuring correctness by combining intervals with modern floating-point hardware we call *sound numerics.*

Some proponents of interval arithmetic may not agree with the above re-description: other motivations and interpretations of interval arithmetic exist. However, its seems to us that sound numerics is the logical conclusion of a long development that started in the 1960s, even before Moore's landmark book [21].

Subsequent development of interval arithmetic. Upon its inception in the 1960s, interval arithmetic was warmly received in the numerical computation community. There are, however, several reasons why the initial enthusiasm turned into disparagement:

1. Dependencies between variables cause intervals to become disappointingly wide. For example, if the interval associated with x is $[0, 1]$, then the one associated with $x - x$ is $[-1, 1]$.
2. Result intervals were not always correct. To guard against improper rounding, a fudge factor was subtracted from computed lower bounds and added to computed upper bounds. This slowed down computation and was difficult to do correctly in all cases without undue loss of accuracy.
3. In the prevailing culture of computing, higher quality of results has only been acceptable in combination with higher performance. We still have to get used to the idea that higher quality may come at a cost.

As a result of these conditions, interval methods were rejected by mainstream numerical computation. Only after this early rejection some of the potential of interval arithmetic was realized.

As to point 1 above, the disappointingly large intervals turned out to be a non-issue. These are problematic in the restricted context of evaluation of expressions. But expression evaluation is a minor concern in numerical computation. An example of a major one is the solving of a nonlinear equation. Here interval arithmetic, in spite of the dependency problem, makes possible the Interval Newton method. This method is not merely a sound alternative to what is achieved more efficiently by conventional numerical computation. Interval Newton proves that no solutions exists outside certain narrow intervals; it also may prove that such an interval contains exactly one or at least one solution. Such results have not been obtained by conventional numerical computation.

As for point 2 above, the IEEE standard for floating-point arithmetic has made superfluous the use of fudge factors. Instead, one can efficiently control the rounding modes to ensure that result intervals contain all values they should contain with a minimum of information loss. However, the last details of its use in interval arithmetic are still an area of active research [16].

As for point 3 above, the rule that the fast drives out the good has rarely been violated. Only in niche applications such as Lisp and Prolog, has security and programming convenience been considered an adequate reward for loss of execution speed. The recent wide-spread acceptance of other interpreters such as those for Perl and Java may be a sign that Gresham's law is relaxing its grip on computing.

Thus there are three reasons for believing that interval methods are experiencing a reversal of misfortune. The advent of interval constraints is yet another one.

Interval constraints. Independently, Davis [9] and Cleary [7] arrived at a relational generalization of interval arithmetic, which is now known as *interval constraints.* Shortly after, Cleary's work was used in BNR Prolog [5,4] to obtain software that can be viewed in two different ways.

1. BNR Prolog as a version of Prolog where soundness is preserved for queries involving real numbers.
2. BNR Prolog as interval constraint system that happens to have Prolog as programming language front end.

Neither of these interpretations quite fits the logic programming paradigm: it is not clear how the decimals in the answer substitution make the answer a logical implication of the query. A step in this direction was taken by the CLP scheme.

CLP(**R**). The CLP scheme extends the scope of the logic programming paradigm in two ways. Semantically, it is an interface with theories that are important in applications, such as those for the integers, the reals, the regular expressions, and others. Operationally, it is an interface with important algorithms, such as Gaussian Elimination and Simplex.

Ironically, existing implementations of CLP(**R**) rely on conventional numerical computation. In this way the logic programming paradigm is compromised by the well-known pitfalls of floating-point computation. Forsythe [12] gave an early survey of the various ways in which the rounding errors of floating-point arithmetic can lead to nonsense output.

As illustration we restrict ourselves here to a particularly short and eloquent example, taken from Parker's paper [22]. Consider the recurrence relation

$$u_{k+1} = 111 - 1130/u_k + 3000/(u_k u_{k-1})$$

with initial values

$$u_0 = 2, u_1 = -4.$$

Computed results for u_{30}:

```
single precision  100.0000
double precision  100.00000000000
```

Parker reports that the value of u_{30} is between six and seven. As CLP(**R**) takes the results of floating-point computation at face value, one can "prove" anything by including computations such as these in the deduction.

What CLP(**R**) lacks are exactly the techniques of sound numerics.

Overview of this paper. Errors in numerical computation can arise from a variety of sources, most of which are of no concern to numerical analysis, as conventionally practiced. In the logic programming paradigm one is responsible for the entire span between program specification and computer output.

If numerical computation is to be included in the logic programming paradigm, then numerical problems need to be specified in logic. This seems virgin territory, even for a problem as simple as the one addressed in Section 2: solving a single equation with a real unknown.

In the remaining sections we briefly recapitulate CLP(**R**) and propose a proof-theoretic approach to providing a sound completion of this method.

2 Numerical Programs Need Verification

It is the aim of this paper to use logic programming to verify results obtained with numerical software. Before invoking the proposed tool, logic programming, let us consider what is required of *any* method of verification, whether logic programming or something else. The least one needs is a precise method for specifying the problem to be solved. Surprisingly, this turns out to be virgin territory. In this paper we consider the problem of formalizing a simple numerical problem: that of solving a single equation in a single unknown.

2.1 Specification of Equation-solving

In single-variable equation solving, the problem is to find a real x such that $f(x) = 0$, where f is a real-valued function of a real-valued argument.

The need to specify it in formal logic brings forward the question: "What does it mean to solve $f(x) = 0$?" Solutions in the mathematical sense are reals that typically have no finite representation in any conventional number system. The shortest description of such a real may well be: "The least (or the second largest, or whatever) x such that $f(x) = 0$". That shows that we do not necessarily want a *solution* of $f(x) = 0$. We just want *useful information* about the reals being defined by $f(x) = 0$. Preferably information that is finite in quantity, such as a solution being between two floating-point numbers that are sufficiently close together.

Given that it is the ambition of logic programming to cover the entire gap between specification and computer output, let us ask again: What does it mean to solve $f(x) = 0$? What can we expect as output? To start with, for a typical f, $f(\alpha) \neq 0$ for all double-length IEEE-standard-standard floating-point numbers α. Suppose that, untypically, there exists a floating-point number α such that $f(\alpha) = 0$. Then usually $f^{FP}(\alpha) \neq 0$, where f^{FP} is the algorithm's floating-point implementation of f. And if, peradventure, $f^{FP}(\alpha) = 0$, then it is likely that $f(\alpha) \neq 0$.

The Numerical Zero. Observations such as these will cause a numerical analyst to point out that it is an unspoken assumption that the purpose of computer software can at most be to find a *numerical* zero, which is any x such that $|f(x)| \leq \epsilon$ for a suitable $\epsilon > 0$.

However the idea of the Numerical Zero is only the first step. If one takes it too literally, one also runs into trouble. An algorithm for a Numerical Zero may be correct from the point of view of numerical analysis and still return an α such that $|f(\alpha)|$ is greater than ϵ.

After all, the algorithm finds that $|f^{FP}(\alpha)| \leq \epsilon'$, which is not inconsistent with $|f(\alpha)| > \epsilon$. There is usually a difference between $f(\alpha)$ and $f^{FP}(\alpha)$. The difference can be large if f^{FP} is ill-conditioned. Moreover, when ϵ is a nonzero power of ten, which happens a lot, then it is not equal to ϵ', which is a real with a finite binary representation. To make a long story short, there are plenty of possibilities for missing even such a realistic-sounding goal as the Numerical Zero.

Apart from these practical problems, there is a conceptual one. The obvious formalization of the Numerical Zero is $\exists x \in \mathcal{R}.\ |f(x)| \leq \epsilon$. This is subject to the same difficulty as before: The truth value of $\exists x \in \mathcal{R}.\ |f(x)| \leq \epsilon$ provides no information about the real that is asserted to exist. Such information is outside of the control of this formal specification and thus is prey to the well-known pitfalls of numerical computation.

Definition versus description. Thus we see that "solving $f(x) = 0$" is ambiguous. It could be interpreted as deciding whether $\{x \in \mathcal{R} \mid f(x) = 0\}$ is empty. This concerns the *definition* of a zero. It could also mean, in addition, providing useful information about such reals as may satisfy the definition. This is a matter of finding a useful *description* of the real number being defined.

The conceptual difficulties arising in formal specification of solving $f(x) = 0$ are removed by distinguishing between definition and description. The definition is involved in the problem *statement.* The description is the required *result.*

Logic is suited equally well for formal definitions as for formal descriptions. A formula F with a free variable x can serve either as a description or as a definition: any object substituted for x that makes F true, satisfies the definition or description.

We formalize the distinction between definition and description as follows. Suppose we have formulas A and B, both with free variable x, that represent a definition and description respectively. Formula $\forall x.(A \Rightarrow B)$ can be interpreted as saying that what B describes is defined by A. The implication is necessary because it is often the case that we cannot show conclusively by numerical methods that a solution exists. Thus we cannot expect always to be able to show that A is true (definition is satisfied) *and* B is true (this description applies). In general the best we can hope for is a proof that, *if* there is a solution (A is true), then it is described by B.

To be of practical interest, A and B need to have a certain form:

1. They have to have the same free variables, which we will denote by the n-tuple x.
2. A has to be what we call a *Numerical Definition*: a conjunction of atomic formulas built up out of the vocabulary of a theory of real numbers. That is, each atom is an equality or inequality between terms denoting reals. This restricted form facilitates implementation, yet is expressive enough for a wide variety of numerical problems.
3. B has to be what we call an *Interval Description.* We assume that what one wants to know about real numbers is how they relate to other real numbers that we can represent on a computer; in other words, floating-point numbers. Taking into account that a solution in general is a tuple of reals and that there is in general more than one solution, it is reasonable to make an interval description a disjunction of atomic formulas of the form $x \in b$ where x is a tuple of n variables and b is the Cartesian product of n floating-point intervals. This restricted form facilitates implementation, yet is expressive enough for a wide variety of numerical problems.

Thus, the general form is

$$\forall x \in \mathcal{R}^n.((A_1 \wedge \cdots \wedge A_k) \Rightarrow (x \in b_1 \vee \cdots \vee x \in b_n)).$$

We call this a *Numerical Definition/Interval Description sentence*, and abbreviate it to *ND/ID sentence.*

Not all descriptions are useful. They are the more useful the smaller n and the smaller, for given n, $b_1, \ldots, b_n$ are. An important case of n being as small as possible is $n = 0$. In that case the sentence states unconditionally that there are no solutions.

The conditionality of the ND/ID sentence seems disappointingly weak. If there is no solution, then the sentence can be true with *any* ID formula.

One should not lose sight of the fact that the ND/ID sentence states unconditionally that no solutions exist outside of the area designated by the ID formula.

Let us go back to the example of solving a single equation in a single unknown. In that case the ND/ID formula has the form

$$\forall x.(f(x) = 0 \Rightarrow (x \in [\alpha_1, \beta_1] \vee \cdots \vee x \in [\alpha_n, \beta_n])).$$

This formalization is suited to the limitations of numerical computation. If the solutions of $f(x) = 0$ are simple and well separated, then we can expect n to be equal to the number of zeroes and we can expect the intervals to be narrow. In pathological cases, any of the intervals can fail to contain a solution. This possibility cannot always be avoided because f may come so close to zero that the limited precision of the computer's arithmetic may fail to distinguish such a value of f from zero.

The constraint processing methods we consider in this paper have the property that at the location of such a false zero, the value of f is close to zero.

3 From Prolog to CLP(R)

One of the motivations of logic programming is that it yields results that are correct in the sense of being logically implied by the background knowledge. The role of the problem statement is to select that part of background knowledge that solves the problem. To play this role, the problem statement has to be expressed in logic.

Now that we have decided on a logic expression for numerical problems, let us see whether these can be solved in the logic programming paradigm. We start by tracing the development from Prolog [8], the first logic programming language.

Prolog has a subset that almost corresponds to a subset of first-order predicate logic in clausal form. The qualification is that most Prolog implementations omit the occurrence check in unification.

Exploiting the pure subset of Prolog was initially not a high priority among language designers and implementers. That defect has since been remedied by the language Gödel [17].

Pure Prolog realizes the following soundness result:

> If program P with query Q leads to success with substitution θ, then P logically implies $\forall x.(Q\theta)$, where x is the tuple of free variables in Q.

But the restrictions of pure Prolog are too severe to be of practical interest: data are restricted to trees based ultimately on symbolic constants.

3.1 Constraint Logic Programming

That we only get symbolic computation in Prolog is not surprising because the only computational step is goal reduction. There is no scope for software and hardware that implement any of the many powerful combinatorial and numerical algorithms that have been developed outside logic programming. The steps taken to overcome this limitation can be summarized under the term *constraint logic programming.*

In logic programming, all atoms in a condition are subject to goal reduction. In constraint logic programming an atom in a condition can be either a goal, to be treated by goal reduction as in logic programming, or a constraint. Constraints are not eliminated in the course of program execution. The conjunction of constraints is tested for consistency by extra-logical algorithms. A query, as generated during program execution, fails as soon as the conjunction of constraints is found to be inconsistent.

As in logic programming, execution terminates with success as soon as no goals remain in the query. In constraint logic programming there is typically in such a situation a nonempty conjunction of constraints. The answer is then conditional upon this residual conjunction. This describes the pioneering implementations of constraint logic programming: Prolog II and III.

The idea was formalized in the CLP scheme.

3.2 The CLP Scheme

The CLP scheme is based on the observation that in logic programming the Herbrand base can be replaced by any of many other semantic domains. For example, the reals. In this section we first review the CLP scheme as described in [18].

As the CLP scheme can be used with different semantic domains, it has as parameter a tuple $\langle \Sigma, \mathcal{D}, \mathcal{L}, \mathcal{T} \rangle$ describing the semantic domain, where Σ is a signature, $\mathcal{D}$ is a Σ-structure, $\mathcal{L}$ is a class of Σ-formulas, and $\mathcal{T}$ is a first-order Σ-theory. These components play the following roles. Σ determines the relations and functions that can occur in constraints. $\mathcal{D}$ is the structure over which computations are performed (for example the ordered field of the real numbers)[1]. $\mathcal{L}$ is the class of constraints that can be expressed. Finally, $\mathcal{T}$ axiomatizes properties of $\mathcal{D}$.

If a goal G has a successful derivation from program $\mathcal{P}$ with answer constraint C, then $\mathcal{P}, \mathcal{T} \models \forall[G \Leftarrow C]$. No substitution is applied to G because

[1] $\mathcal{D}$ is a structure (in the sense of model theory) consisting of a set D of values (the *carrier* of the structure) together with relations and functions over D as specified by the signature Σ. For example, the complete ordered field $\mathcal{R}$ has R, the set of real numbers, as carrier. The signature component of $\mathcal{R}$ specifies $\leq$ as relation, and $0, 1, +, -, \times, /$ as function symbols. The status of $=$ and $\neq$ varies between treatments: some include them in the signature; some regard them as part of logic.

in constraint logic programming unification is done by means of equations, which are part of the constraints.

Derivations in the CLP scheme are defined by means of *transitions* between states. A state is defined as a tuple $\langle A, C, S\rangle$ where A is a multiset of atoms and constraints and C and S are multisets of constraints[2]. Together C and S are called the *constraint store.* The constraints in C are called the *active constraints*; those in S the *passive constraints.*

The query Q corresponds to the initial state $\langle Q, \emptyset, \emptyset\rangle$. A successful derivation ends in a state of the form $\langle \emptyset, C, S\rangle$. The existence of such a derivation implies that

$$\mathcal{P}, \mathcal{T} \models \forall[(Q \Leftarrow (C \wedge S))]$$

The CLP scheme provides a framework for constraint store management by defining a derivation as a sequence of states such that each next state is obtained from the previous one by a transition.

There are four transitions:

1: Resolution

$$\langle A \cup \{a\}, C, S\rangle \rightarrow_r \langle A \cup B, C, S \cup \{s_1 = t_1, \ldots, s_n = t_n\}\rangle$$

if a is the atom selected out of $A \cup \{a\}$ by the computation rule, $h \leftarrow B$ is a rule of $\mathcal{P}$, renamed to new variables, and if $h = p(t_1, \ldots, t_n)$ and $a = p(s_1, \ldots, s_n)$.

$$\langle A \cup \{a\}, C, S\rangle \rightarrow_r \textit{fail}$$

if a is the atom selected by the computation rule, and for every rule $h \leftarrow B$ in $\mathcal{P}$, h and a have different predicate symbols.

2: Constraint Transfer

$$\langle A \cup \{c\}, C, S\rangle \rightarrow_c \langle A, C, S \cup \{c\}\rangle$$

if constraint c is selected by the computation rule.

3: Constraint Store Management

$$\langle A, C, S\rangle \rightarrow_i \langle A, C', S'\rangle$$

if $\langle C', S'\rangle$ is inferred from $\langle C, S\rangle$.

4: Consistency Test

$$\langle A, C, S\rangle \rightarrow_s \langle A, C, S\rangle$$

if C is consistent.

$$\langle A, C, S\rangle \rightarrow_s \textit{fail}$$

if C is inconsistent.

---

[2] We will often regard C and S as formulas. Then they are the conjunctions of the constraints they contain as multisets.

3.3 CLP(R)

How does CLP(**R**) fit into the CLP scheme? In the first place, the semantic domain that is a parameter in the CLP scheme is instantiated to a theory of the reals. In addition, the CLP scheme is customized by a constraint store management strategy. The active constraints are linear equations or inequalities. They are solved by, respectively, Gaussian elimination and Simplex. Hopefully, this results in additional variables being instantiated, so that some passive constraints become linear, so that they can be added to the active constraints. The aim is to remove all passive constraints this way.

Existing implementations of CLP(**R**) implement the algorithms to solve the generated equations in the same way as in conventional numerical analysis. As a result, rounding errors prevent CLP(**R**) answers from being logical consequences. Thus such implementations should not be considered logic programming systems, but numerical problem solvers to be compared with the like of MatLab. Such a comparison will give CLP(**R**) advantages such as the ability to handle certain nonlinear problems via its unique linearization scheme.

4 Sound CLP(R)

There are two methods for obtaining soundness with floating-point computation: interval arithmetic and interval constraints. The most straightforward way of protecting the soundness of CLP(**R**) is to implement its algorithms for Gaussian elimination and Simplex method in interval arithmetic. But it should be kept in mind that, in doing so, one is up against all the obstacles that have prevented, for three decades, a wide adoption of interval arithmetic. The experience has been that translating an algorithm that works well in conventional computation gives disappointingly large intervals if converted unchanged to interval arithmetic.

For this reason it is attractive achieve sound CLP(**R**) by means of interval constraints rather than interval arithmetic[3], as was proposed in [26]. In the present paper we supply some of the details that are missing in [26]. In supplying these details it turned out that the distinction in the CLP scheme between active and passive constraints is not useful. Thus we consider a simplified version of the scheme where there is only one type of constraint. We will not spell out in detail the transitions of the CLP scheme described in section 3.2 according to this simplification. Suffice it to say that the state $\langle A, C, S\rangle$ becomes $\langle A, C\rangle$ and that the constraint-store management transition is dropped.

[3] Why are large intervals no problem in interval constraints, which is otherwise so closely related to interval arithmetic? The explanation is not simple. But it is easy to convince oneself that it is so by considering the performance of Numerica [15] where superior time performance is obtained as well as very small intervals.

In CLP(**R**), the leaf nodes of the search tree for query G are distinguished by having an empty goal conjunction. Thus a leaf node contains only a constraint conjunction, say, C. Such a node represents the conditional answer $\forall x.(G\theta \Leftarrow C)$ (see footnote[4]). C is a conjunction of equalities or inequalities between terms denoting reals. This is general enough to cover many important problems of numerical computation.

Let us consider the case where C is a conjunction expressing an equation that would be written as $f(x) = 0$ in a conventional informal discussion. Do we just want to know whether the equation has a solution? If so, that information would allow us to improve the conditional answer $\forall x.(G\theta \Leftarrow C)$ to $\exists x.G\theta$. For example,

$$\forall x.(p(g(x)) \Leftarrow ((x+1)(x-1)=0))$$

would be "improved" to $\exists x.p(g(x))$ without a hint as to what such an x might be. It is reasonable to expect some useful information about the x that exists.

If this problem sounds familiar, it is because in section 2.1 we encountered the same puzzle when we were considering logic specification of equation-solving — at that time independently of the CLP scheme. In that section we concluded the need to distinguish between definition and description. We found that ND/ID sentences express both aspects. We saw that the conditionality of these formulas cannot always be avoided, so that they are useful as a generally applicable method for logically specifying numerical problems.

It is then clear what to do: to compute for every leaf node with constraint conjunction C an ND/ID formula where the ND part is C and where the ID part is as informative as we can make it. This desideratum often results in the ID part being the empty disjunction, i.e. the logical constant FALSE. In such a case $\neg\exists x.C$ has been proved and the leaf node can be omitted from the search tree. In case the ID part is not equivalent to FALSE, it is still possible that $\neg\exists x.C$. However, as we explain below, the method of interval constraints can make this combination of outcomes unlikely. Even then we still have valuable information: the contrapositive of the ND/ID formula guarantees that no solution to C exists outside the area described by the ID part.

5 Proving ND/ID Formulas

For a given constraint conjunction C we need to prove an ND/ID formula

$$\forall x.(C \Rightarrow (x \in b_1 \vee \cdots \vee x \in b_k))$$

[4] In the CLP scheme there are no explicit substitutions. Instead, equations are added to the constraint store; see the resolution transition in the description of CLP derivations. Although this has an attractive elegance, it has its advantages to be able to say that the constraint store specifies only the numerical problem to be solved. That is why we assume that substitutions are used in the same way as in the conventional way of describing SLD derivations [19].

where the ID part is as informative as possible.

We achieve this goal by means of interval constraints in a proof-theoretic framework inspired by that given by Apt [1] for constraints over discrete domains. Just as Apt's method is a proof-theoretic model for constraint processing over integers as pioneered in CHIP [10], so also his method can be used as a proof-theoretic model for interval constraints over the reals. We adapt Apt's inference rules to domains of reals and show how they can be used to prove useful ND/ID formulas.

5.1 CSPs

Apt's proof-theoretic framework defines Constraint Satisfaction Problems (CSPs) and formulates proof rules that derive from a given CSP one or more other ones. In our development of CSPs, we start with the part that is generally applicable. After that we continue with CSPRs, that is, CSPs intended for constraints over reals.

A CSP may be described as follows.

- Syntactically, a CSP is an expression of the form $C \Diamond D$ where C is a conjunction of atomic formulas having a tuple $x = (x_1, \ldots, x_n)$ of free variables. D is called the domain expression and has the form $x \in b$ where b is the Cartesian product of the domains of $x_1, \ldots, x_n$.
- The semantics of CSPs is determined by assigning to $C \Diamond D$ as meaning the first-order predicate logic sentence $\exists x.(C \wedge D)$. In any particular use of CSPs we assume an application-specific theory, for example a theory for the reals and for floating-point intervals. A CSP is *solvable* if its meaning is logically implied by the assumed application-specific theory.
- A CSP $C \Diamond (x \in b)$ is *failed* if b is empty.
- A *solution* of a CSP is a tuple τ such that $(C \wedge D)[x/\tau]$ (see footnote[5]) is a logical consequence of the assumed application-specific theory.
- Let C_1 and C_2 be CSPs with the same tuples of free variables. We say that C_1 *refines* C_2 if any solution of C_1 is a solution of C_2.

[5] The notation $(C \wedge D)[x/\tau]$ suggests that a domain element, that is, a nonsyntactic object, be substituted for a variable, which is a syntactic object. Taken literally, this is nonsense. However, there is sound intuition behind this nonsense, as proved by the fact that, if one handles this with care (see e.g. [11,13]), the desired result is achieved anyway.

Curiously, Shoenfield [25] tries to avoid the difficulty by assuming that there is a constant in the language for every domain element. As any reasonable language would have a countable set of names, axiomatization of a domain such as the reals seems to be ruled out.

5.2 CSPRs

So far CSPs in general. We continue by considering CSPRs: CSPs over the reals. Here the variables range over the reals. Hence the domains[6] are sets of reals. However, in the interest of practical computer implementation, not all sets of reals can occur as domain: only intervals of reals with floating-point numbers as bounds. These are intervals that are either unbounded (on one or on both sides) or bounded. Any bound that may occur in an interval is one of a finite set of real numbers that can be represented in the floating-point number format of a computer. Such reals are called "floating-point numbers". As the empty set is also counted as an interval, we have that the set of floating-point intervals is closed under intersection. Clearly, for any set S of reals there is a unique least floating-point interval (denoted $bx(S)$) containing S.

In CLP(**R**) we have assumed a conventional theory of the reals. It has equality and inequality as only predicate symbols. It has function symbols for addition, subtraction, multiplication, and division. In a CSP however, we assume that the constraint conjunction is based on a different vocabulary: no function symbols and two additional predicate symbols *sum* and *prod*. Their intended interpretation is such that $prod(x, y, z)$ iff z is the product of x and y, and similarly for $sum(x, y, z)$. Constraint conjunctions of CLP(**R**) can be translated to those of CSPR (usually introducing auxiliary variables) and vice versa. In practice it is desirable to use a theory of reals with additional symbols for commonly used functions such as exponentiation, logarithms, and trigonometric functions.

It is the task of the inference system for CSPRs to obtain a maximally informative ID expression for a given ND formula. We first discuss inference rules. In the section following the next, we present the inference system in which the rules are used.

Inference Rules. To obtain a maximally informative description, we need to make the domains for the variables small as possible. This can be done by inference rules that transform a CSP into a refinement of it. With every predicate (including at least equality, inequality, sum and product) there is associated a domain-reduction inference rule. We will only show a single example here.

Domain-reduction rule for the prod predicate. Let $C \diamond D_1$ be a CSP where C contains the atom $prod(x, y, z)$ and where the floating-point intervals X, Y, and Z are the projections of D_1 on x, y, and z. The domain-reduction rule for *prod* infers $C \diamond D_2$ from $C \diamond D_1$. D_2 is such that all its projections are

[6] "Domain" means universe of discourse in logic semantics and in the CLP scheme. In constraint processing it has a different meaning: set of values for a variable that are still possible at a certain stage of computation.

the same as the corresponding ones of D_1 except possibly for those on x, y, and z, which are shown in the table in Figure 1. The operations $*$ and $/$ on intervals are defined in interval arithmetic[7].

Projection on	D_1	D_2
x	X	$bx(X \cap (Z/Y))$
y	Y	$bx(Y \cap (Z/X))$
z	Z	$bx(Z \cap (X * Y))$

Fig. 1. Effect of domain-reduction inference rule for *prod* on intervals of CSPR

If domains were not restricted to floating-point intervals, then the projections of D_2 would simply be $X \cap (Z/Y)$, $Y \cap (Z/X)$, and $Z \cap (X * Y)$. In the interest of implementability we replace these sets by the smallest floating-point intervals containing them. This containment ensures the soundness of the inference rule.

The set $X * Y$ is typically not a floating-point interval, though it is a real interval. This is a mathematical way of saying that rounding errors are typically made when multiplying floating-point numbers. The set Z/Y may not even be a real interval. As inference rules have to yield intervals, these sets have to be converted to intervals. As inference rules have to be sound, the resulting intervals have to contain these sets. Hence the occurrence of the bx function in the table of Figure 1.

In the following we will repeatedly refer to Cartesian products of intervals. We will call such a product *box*.

Other domain-reduction rules There is a corresponding domain-reduction rule for the *sum* predicate, again based on interval arithmetic. In CSPR, every predicate comes with a domain-reduction rule. Hence also the equality and inequality predicates. These rules are not based on interval arithmetic.

The splitting rule A domain-reduction rule is a directly productive way of achieving our objective: by making a box smaller, it increases information about the location of solutions. But it may happen that no domain-reduction rule has an effect. In that case we turn to the splitting rule an inference rule that is not productive in that sense. It may be indirectly productive by producing CSPs on which domain-reduction rules do have an effect.

The splitting rule replaces $C\Diamond(x \in b)$ by $C\Diamond(x \in b_1)$ and $C\Diamond(x \in b_2)$ such that $b \subset (b_1 \cup b_2)$. We would like to have $b = (b_1 \cup b_2)$ and $b_1 \cap b_2 = \emptyset$, but the limited supply of floating-point intervals may only allow an approximation to this ideal. Both b_1 and b_2 are strictly smaller than b.

[7] Except that modifications are needed accommodate division by an interval containing zero. See [16].

We assume that any given CSPR comes with a *splitting strategy*, with as parameter a real number $\epsilon > 0$. The splitting strategy is a partial function on boxes that, if defined on a box b, yields two boxes b_1 and b_2 as described above, of at least approximately equal size.

Given a box b and such a splitting strategy as partial function, there is a uniquely determined binary tree with b as root where each non-leaf node x has as children the boxes that result from splitting x. The finiteness of the set of floating-point numbers, hence of intervals with floating-point numbers as bounds, hence of finite Cartesian products of such intervals, helps ensure that any splitting strategy's binary tree is finite.

An Inference Procedure. We describe an inference procedure for CSPRs that consists of constructing a search tree with an initial CSPR of the form $C\Diamond(x \in \mathcal{R}^n)$ as root and having as leaf nodes the CSPRs $C\Diamond(x \in b_1), \ldots,$ $C\Diamond(x \in b_k)$.

We first describe the auxiliary concepts. Then we present an algorithm to define the search tree of the inference system. This algorithm is only suitable for definition and is not intended for execution. Finally, we state what ND/ID sentence is proved by the inference procedure.

NC test. A CSP can be sometimes be shown to be unsolvable by showing that it fails to satisfy a Necessary Condition (hence "NC test") for solvability. This is useful because some necessary conditions can be tested with little computational effort. An example in a CSPR of the form $C\Diamond(x \in b)$ is to substitute the projections of b for the corresponding variables in C and then to evaluate C according to interval arithmetic. A necessary condition for solvability of $C\Diamond(x \in b)$ is that this evaluation comes out *true*. This is essentially the "Box(0) consistency" of Puget and Van Hentenryck [23].

Stabilization. Every CSP has a fixed repertoire of domain-reduction rules. When these are applied sufficiently many times, a limit CSP is reached that is invariant under all domain-reduction rules. The limit is independent of the order of applying these rules, provided the order is a *fair* one; for details see [20,26,2]. This process is also called *constraint propagation.*

For any given CSP, call it X, constraint propagation to the limit yields a uniquely determined stable CSP. Let us define the *stabilization operator* applied to X as the one that gives this uniquely determined stable CSP.

Search Tree. For given NC tests and splitting strategy, the search tree for a CSP is a binary tree of CSPs defined as follows.

1. Obtain the binary tree corresponding to the given CSP and splitting strategy.
2. In the resulting tree, apply to each node the NC tests. If the result is failure, mark the node F.

3. Apply the constraint propagation operator to each node not marked F. If the operator results in failure, then mark the node F.
4. **while** there exists a node N that is not marked F
   and that has two successors marked F
   do apply mark F to node N
5. **while** there exists a node N marked F
   do remove subtree rooted at N
6. **while** there exists a node N
   with two successors that are leaf nodes
   do remove these two leaf nodes

This algorithm only serves to facilitate the definition of the search tree. Any algorithm intended for execution will of course be much more efficient. The procedure *solve* of BNR Prolog [5] is a simple depth-first traversal of what our search tree would be if we had omitted the last step. Although *solve* is satisfactory in leaving out all failed nodes, it has the shortcoming of reporting adjacent non-failed nodes of what remains of the search tree according to our definition before the last step. This makes *solve* much less useful: it produces long listings of non-failed nodes that turn out to be replaceable by a single one. This is what the last step in our definitional algorithm improves upon.

What Does the Inference System Prove? The above inference system is intended to have the following

Property 1. Let $b_1, \ldots, b_k$ be the boxes at the leaf nodes of the search tree for a CSP of the form $C\Diamond(x \in \mathcal{R}^n)$. Then the ND/ID sentence $\forall x.(C \Rightarrow (b_1 \vee \cdots \vee b_k))$ is a logical consequence of the theory of reals in conjunction with the theory of floating-point numbers.

In principle the proof should be simple: the property claimed holds for the search tree after the first step in the definition algorithm. All that happens in the first step is splitting up the original search space $\mathcal{R}^n$ into sufficiently small boxes without loss of a single point. Each next step, if correctly implemented, removes parts of the search space that do not contain any solution.

An actual proof may, however, be a complex affair. It will have to depend not only on an axiomatization of the reals, but also on certain aspects of floating-point numbers.

6 Related Work

BNR Prolog [5] has combined Prolog with interval constraints. From the documentation available to us, it is a conventional Prolog where the unsound conventional floating-point arithmetic has been replaced by interval constraints.

For all we know, we may have been introducing Prolog IV. Whether or not that is the case is not easy to tell from the documentation [3] we have studied. The same holds for the Newton system [14]. For either system, presenting it explicitly as a sound CLP(**R**) may only be a formality.

The inference rules are modeled on those of Apt [1] for arithmetic constraints on integers. If his system is interfaced with the CLP scheme the same way CSPRs are in this paper, one would a get reconstruction of the CHIP system [10].

If Newton-like methods were used to enhance the NC tests and the constraint propagation in our inference system, the same search tree would be obtained as in Puget and Van Hentenryck [23]. In addition, they use Brouwer's fixpoint theorem to positively identify intervals containing at least one solution, or exactly one solution. Without such help from outside of the world of constraints one can only eliminate space as not containing any solution, so that answers are always conditional on there existing a solution.

Finally, there are the Russians. Many of the methods of interval constraints on reals were developed in Russia independently of work in the West under the name "subdefinite computation". Sources of pointers to this tradition are [24]. We do not know whether it has been determined who did what first in interval computation.

7 Conclusions

We have proposed to extend CLP(**R**) to a sound version by means interval constraints. As mechanism for interfacing the CLP scheme with interval constraint propagation, we proposed a version of Apt's proof-theoretic model for discrete constraint propagation. To do this, it was necessary to propose a logic specification of the example chosen, namely solving a single equation in a single variable. We conjectured that the ND/ID formulas introduced here will serve the same purpose in other numerical problems.

This work brings up a few related more general topics that we wish to discuss in the remainder of this section.

"Logic and numbers don't mix"? There is a widespread perception that logic, and therefore rigorous result verification, belong in the discrete world, which is disjoint from the world of continuous change where variables are real numbers. This perception has had several consequences. At the side of scientific modeling there has been a reluctance to state formally what it means for computer output to be an acceptable solution. At the side of program verification there has been a tendency to stay with discrete problems such as verification of protocols and hardware.

This work has shown that CLP(**R**) can be extended to a sound version. We hope that numerical analysts will find explicit and formal specification of numerical problems a welcome resolution of existing ambiguities.

Floating-point numbers, the untouchables of computer science. From a distance, floating-point numbers look like an acceptable surrogate for the reals. Close up they look horrible. There are only finitely many of them. Addition and multiplication, which should be associative, aren't. Multiplication, which should distribute over addition, doesn't.

Conventional numerical analysis has restricted its considerations to algorithms over the reals which are at best heuristic approximations to what happens during computer execution. Interval analysis has shown that with a modest improvement of floating-point hardware, such as achieved by the IEEE standard, one can extend mathematical reasoning to what is actually printed out on an actual computer.

The reluctance to face up to the discrepancies between reals and floating-point numbers has also infected logic programming: CLP(**R**) has ignored it. We have shown that via interval constraints, CLP(**R**) can be extended to cover the entire span from mathematical model in terms of reals at one end to computer output at the other end.

Numerical analysis as an independent science? Van Wijngaarden [27] was one of the few, before and after this 1966 publication, to deplore the ambiguous logical status of results in the conventional practice of numerical computation. As remedy he proposed to replace real analysis by a version more amenable to the idiosyncrasies of floating-point computation. He sketched an axiomatic re-foundation not only of numbers, but also of concepts of analysis such as limit, derivative and integral.

Even if such an ambitious enterprise turns out to be feasible, we doubt that mathematics will be enriched by it. The recent developments discussed in this paper show that it is perfectly practical to use computer hardware to derive true statements about reals that provide exactly the kind of information that engineers and scientists need.

All that was needed for this breakthrough was the following:

1. Use the familiar observation that every function f from a set S to a set T has a counterpart mapping the powerset of S to the powerset of T (the extension of f to the powerset [6]).
2. That most of what one wants to do with f can be done with its extension.
3. Computers, though hopeless at representing reals, are perfectly adequate for representing sets of reals. The limitation of the computer manifests itself in only being able to conveniently represent intervals bounded (if at all) by a floating-point number. Computations can be arranged so that rounding errors only make the set slightly larger. But the set of possible values still contains the true value of the real-valued unknown concerned.

This has been the approach taken by the Russians with their subdefinite computation [24].

Acknowledgements

Many thanks to Krzysztof Apt for initiatives, encouragement, and suggestions for improvement. The comments of the referee resulted in considerable further improvement. The Natural Science and Engineering Research Council of Canada provided research facilities.

References

1. K.R. Apt. A proof theoretic view of constraint programming. *Fundamenta Informaticae*, 33(3):263–293, 1998.
2. K.R. Apt. From chaotic iteration to constraint propagation. In *Proceedings of the 24th International Colloquium on Automata, Languages, and Programming (ICALP '97)*, 1997.
3. Frédéric Benhamou, Pascal Bouvier, Alain Colmerauer, Henri Garetta, Bruno Giletta, Jean-Luc Massat, Guy Alain Narboni, Stéphane N'Dong, Robert Pasero, Jean-François Pique, Touraïvane, Michel Van Caneghem, and Eric Vétillard. Le manuel de Prolog IV. Technical report, PrologIA, Parc Technologique de Luminy, Marseille, France, 1996.
4. Frédéric Benhamou and William J. Older. Applying interval arithmetic to real, integer, and Boolean constraints. *Journal of Logic Programming*, 32:1–24, 1997.
5. BNR. BNR Prolog user guide and reference manual. Version 3.1 for Macintosh, 1988.
6. N. Bourbaki. *Théorie des Ensembles (Fascicule de Résultats)*. Hermann, 1939.
7. J.G. Cleary. Logical arithmetic. *Future Computing Systems*, 2:125–149, 1987.
8. A. Colmerauer, H. Kanoui, R. Pasèro, and P. Roussel. Un système de communication homme-machine en français. Technical report, Groupe d'Intelligence Artificielle, Université d'Aix-Marseille II, 1972.
9. E. Davis. Constraint propagation with labels. *Artificial Intelligence*, 32:281–331, 1987.
10. M. Dincbas, P. Van Hentenryck, H. Simonis, A. Aggoun, T. Graf, and F. Berthier. The constraint programming language CHIP. In *Proc. Int. Conf. on Fifth Generation Computer Systems*, 1988.
11. H.B. Enderton. *A Mathematical Introduction to Logic*. Fletcher and Sons, Ltd, 1972.
12. George E. Forsythe. Pitfalls of computation, or why a math book isn't enough. *Amer. Math. Monthly*, 77:931–956, 1970.
13. Andrzej Grzegorczyk. *An Outline of Mathematical Logic: Fundamental Results and Notions Explained with All Details*. D. Reidel, 1974.
14. P. Van Hentenryck, L. Michel, and F. Benhamou. Newton: Constraint programming over nonlinear constraints. *Science of Computer Programming*, 1996.
15. Pascal Van Hentenryck, Laurent Michel, and Yves Deville. *Numerica: A Modeling Language for Global Optimization*. MIT Press, 1997.
16. T. Hickey, Q. Ju, and M. van Emden. Using the IEEE floating-point standard for implementing interval arithmetic. In preparation.
17. Patricia Hill and John Lloyd. *The Gödel Programming Language*. MIT Press, 1994.

18. Joxan Jaffar and Michael J. Maher. Constraint logic programming: A survey. *Journal of Logic Programming*, 19/20:503–582, 1994.
19. J.W. Lloyd. *Foundations of Logic Programming*. Springer-Verlag, 2nd edition, 1987.
20. Ugo Montanari and Francesca Rossi. Constraint relaxation may be perfect. *Artificial Intelligence*, 48:143–170, 1991.
21. Ramon E. Moore. *Interval Analysis*. Prentice-Hall, 1966.
22. D. Stott Parker. Monte Carlo arithmetic: an effective way to improve upon floating-point arithmetic. Technical Report CSD-970002, Computer Science Department, University of California at Los Angeles, 1997.
23. Jean-François Puget and Pascal Van Hentenryck. A constraint satisfaction approach to a circuit design problem. *Journal of Global Optimization*, 13(1), 1998.
24. Alexander L. Semenov. Solving optimization problems with help of the Unicalc solver. In R. Baker Kearfott and Vladik Kreinovich, editors, *Application of Interval Computations*, pages 211–224. Kluwer Academic Publishers, 1996.
25. Joseph R. Shoenfield. *Mathematical Logic*. Addison-Wesley, 1967.
26. M.H. van Emden. Value constraints in the CLP Scheme. *Constraints*, 2:163–183, 1997.
27. A. van Wijngaarden. Numerical analysis as an independent science. *BIT*, 6:66–81, 1966.

Part II

Knowledge Representation and Modeling

5 Constraints

Both contributions in this chapter deal with constraints. Constraint programming and logic programming represent different approaches to declarative programming but they have a common underpinning of relations. This facilitated the development of constraint logic programming.

Cohen argues that logic programming and its extensions such as constraint logic programming should play an important role in the very active area of computational molecular biology. This is because non-deterministic algorithms, constraints, optimizations, and learning from examples have proved to be valuable approaches in solving problems that are of interest to molecular biologists, geneticists, and biochemists.

He first presents a bird's-eye view of the field by describing the major phases of the translation of a DNA sequence into proteins. Various Chomsky-type grammars are presented to describe DNA constituents. Nondeterministic finite state grammars are effective in recognizing those constituents and can be used to generate directed acyclic graphs that concisely define all possible parses of a given string; these graphs can be efficiently traversed to determine the most likely parse satisfying pre-established constraints. Cohen also describes alternate methods that have been used to solve problems in biology including dynamic programming, inductive logic programming, and hidden Markov models.

Constraint logic programming is an example of an elegant and smooth incorporation of constraints into a logic formalism. Its development has sparked the embedding of constraints into several other logic languages.

Maher discusses the issues involved in the extension of logic formalisms to admit constraints. He briefly surveys existing work, from a range of disciplines, which combines constraints and logic formalisms. From this he identifies several common elements which can be used to guide further work in this area.

Computational Molecular Biology: A Promising Application Using LP and its Extensions

Jacques Cohen

Computer Science Department, Brandeis University, Waltham, MA 02254, USA

> *"Biology is so digital, and incredibly complicated, but incredibly useful ... I can't be as confident about computer science as I can about biology. Biology easily has 500 years of exciting problems to work on ..."*
>
> Donald Knuth in an interview given on Dec. 1993
> at the Computer Literacy Bookshops

Summary. The paper presents an introduction to some of the problems in computational molecular biology (CMB) viewed from a logic programming (LP) perspective. Non-deterministic formal grammars are presented to define biologically interesting subsequences of DNA. Also presented are compact representations of ambiguities by directed acyclic graphs. Various problems in CMB are discussed; their solutions using dynamic programming, hidden Markov models, and inductive logic programming are briefly described. It is believed that a study of these and related problems can contribute to provide a new impetus to LP research and its extensions.

1 Introduction

The purpose of this paper is to present a view of some of the current problems in molecular biology that – according to Donald Knuth's quote and my own belief – are of interest to the LP community. The paper will fulfill its goal if it can attract the attention of members of that community to this exciting new area.

My initiation to computational biology took place about five years ago when I was intrigued by a paper by David Searls on the linguistics of DNA [Searls]. In the past I have done research in languages and compilers. Searls' paper opened new vistas to me, by facilitating the understanding of key concepts in genetics that are akin to problems in parsing, compiling, and natural language processing (NLP).

A first step in enticing LP researchers and practitioners to the area of Computational Molecular Biology (CMB) is to point-out the similarities that exist between NLP and some of the CMB problems.

In NLP, or even in compiling, parsing is coupled with actions that give a meaning to a text being examined. Similarly, in one of the major problems in

Molecular Biology (MB), one wishes to first recognize, i.e., parse a sequence of letters representing DNA and then infer the proteins that are generated based on the recognition.

For the purposes of this paper it is convenient to assume that:

- DNA is a sequence using a terminal vocabulary {A,C,T,G}. The elements of this vocabulary are called nucleotides or bases.
- DNA can be initially viewed as a program "interpreted" by a complex biological machinery that generates proteins that are essential to sustaining life.

In addition, proteins are responsible for determining the characteristics of living organisms; biologists call these characteristics "function" and they can be as varied as those determining that an individual is blue-eyed, or that it contains abnormal (diseased) cells.

The above is admittedly a simplistic view of the problem. Further explanations and refinements about that view will appear in a companion article.

To achieve the goals of this paper as succinctly as possible, we will start by showing the discrete nature of MB. That will be followed by stating, using LP terminology, the major phases involved in "interpreting" the code given by DNA.

I will then concentrate on the description of ambiguous grammars capable of recognizing DNA components (subsequences) of biological interest. One of those components are subsequences of DNA that, for reasons that still remain unanswered, do not participate in the generation of proteins.

Having shown a particular major application of CMB, I will then briefly describe other CMB problems that I believe could be successfully solved using LP and its extensions. It should be stressed that the main application described in this paper can also be approached by other methods.

In the final remarks I summarize my views as to why LP and its extensions should play an important role in computational molecular biology. Essentially, the successes of LP in dealing with parsing, non-deterministic situations, inverse computations, coupled with the capabilities of Constraint LP in processing numerical problems, and the machine learning approach used in Inductive LP are assets that will likely play a significant role towards facilitating the solution of problems in CMB.

2 A Minimalist Introduction to DNA and Protein Generation

Figures 1 and 2 succinctly describe the major characteristics of DNA that are of interest to computational biologists. Basically, DNA is a double-stranded helicoidal arrangement of sequences involving four molecules called bases or nucleotides and represented by the letters A, T, C, and G.

• Cells' nuclei contain chromosomes.
• Chromosomes contain strands of DNA (Deoxyribose Nucleic Acid - see Glossary).
• DNA can be initially viewed as a variant of a straight-line "program" enabling the cell to produce aminoacids and their sequences - proteins - that are essential for continuing the life, cell reproduction and function.
• As a first approximation one can think of aminoacid generation as a "biological compiler or interpreter", contained within a cell, that translates DNA strings ("a program") into aminoacids, and subsequently into proteins. As a very rough initial approximation, one can think of DNA as a pseudo-source string and the resulting sequence of aminoacids (proteins) as a target string.

Fig. 1. Initial Approximate Model

DNA is capable of reproducing itself when a cell subdivides into two identical cells. In a simplified manner, suitable for the purposes of this paper, the generation of proteins from DNA proceeds in four phases (see Figure 3):

(1) One of the DNA strands is first *transcribed* into a similar sequence of nucleotides with a minor difference: the nucleotide U replaces the nucleotide T. That new single stranded sequence is called Pre-mRNA. (The "m" in mRNA stands for messenger.) The biological machinery performing the transcription is called *RNA Polymerase.*

(2) For reasons that remain unexplained, most of the elaborate cells (those containing a nucleus, and called eukariotic cells) also contain another biological machinery, called *Spliceosome* , that disregards certain subsequences of the Pre-mRNA and assemble the remaining ones into a sequence of nucleotides that are capable of triggering the generation of proteins. This second phase is called Splicing. Therefore, Pre-mRNA can be viewed as alternations of exons (sequences that contribute to the generation of proteins) and introns (sequences that do not contribute to the generation of proteins.) The result of the splicing is called mRNA and it is output outside the nucleus of the cell to the area called cytoplasm confined between the cell's nucleus and its external membrane.

(3) The mRNA is then processed by yet another complex biological machinery, called *Ribosomes*, that read triplets of nucleotides of the mRNA and generate sequences of aminoacids. This third phase, called *translation*, could be thought of as a table look-up.The triplets are called *Codons* and there are precisely 20 aminoacids that can be generated from the 64 possible triplets. The abbreviations for the 20 aminoacids and the (multiple) triplets that generate them are presented in Figure 4. That information is referred to by biologists as *Genetic Code.* Notice that there exist "flags" called stop-codons that halt the translation process. Ribosomes would humble any hardware or software designer: they operate in parallel reading and translating mRNA into the sequence of aminoacids.

• DNA is made of 4 bases (called nucleotides) One can initially think of DNA as strings using 4 letters A,C,G, and T.
• The complements of A, C, G, T are respectively T, G, C, A. The notion of complement is useful in cell reproduction and in biological computing.
• There is something like a BVM (Biological Virtual Machine.) Think of its code as consisting of triplets containing the letters A,C,G, and T. There are 4*4*4 = 64 such triplets, that biologists call Codons.
• There are exactly 20 aminoacids that are encoded by the 64 triplets. Therefore there is redundancy in the code, that is, several triplets generate the same aminoacid.

Fig. 2. The Discrete Nature of Molecular Biology

(4) The sequence of generated aminoacids then twists and folds to form given proteins. The number aminoacids needed to form a protein depends on the 3D configuration of the final protein. The process of achieving a final shape is called protein folding and is one of the major application areas in which computers can play an important role. The prediction of the 3D protein shape from a given sequence of aminoacids is still a very difficult computational problem whose solution has not yet reached the desired accuracy.

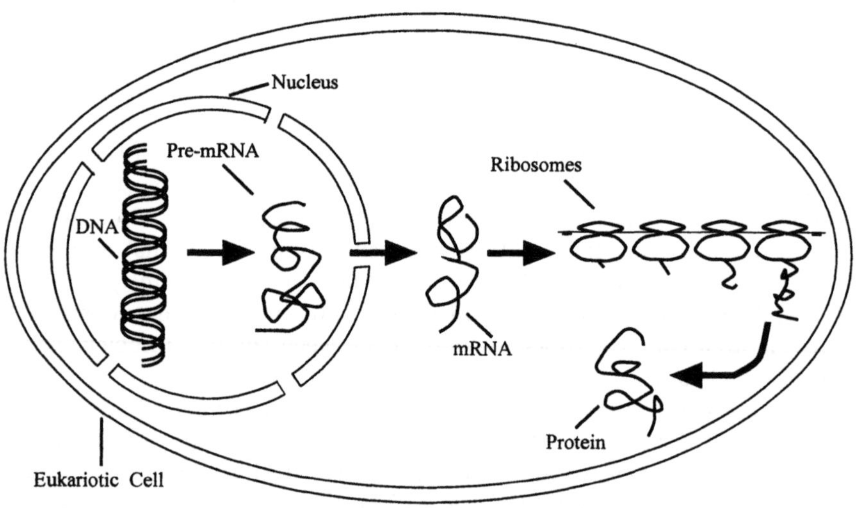

Fig. 3. Schematic Drawing of a Cell and the DNA-Protein Transformation

The entire process of transcription, splicing, aminoacid generation, and protein folding is schematically depicted in Figure 3. In the previous section

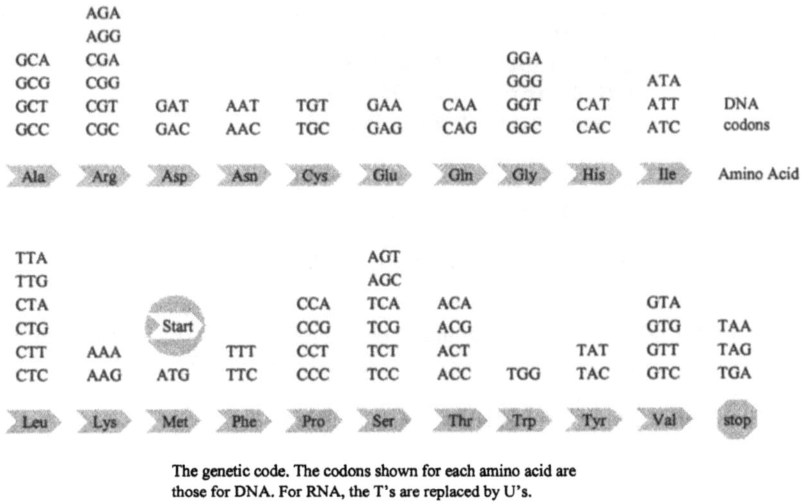

Fig. 4. The Genetic Code. Codons and the Aminoacids They Generate

I mentioned that DNA could be viewed as a straight-line program. Now that the entire transformation from DNA to proteins has been described, it is relevant to point out that once proteins are generated, they can interact with other proteins, with mRNA and with DNA.

There are proteins, produced by DNA, that will position themselves into various parts of the DNA and effect the process of transcription; they can actually prevent certain sequences of DNA to be transcribed into mRNA and eventually repress the production of other proteins.

Therefore the aforementioned view of a DNA as a straight-line program should include time-dependent conditionals. In other words, the biological program can indirectly modify itself and those modifications are time dependent and vary according to the stages of cell development.

Finally, notice that the above descriptions refer to 4 bases (or nucleotides), 20 aminoacids, and codons or triplets: this provides an initial justification for Knuth's phrase: "Biology is so digital, ..."

3 Top-Down Description of Protein Generation from DNA

We now present a short LP program sketching the various phases described in the previous section.

```
Protein_Generation (DNA, Proteins) :-
                Transcription (DNA, Pre_mRNA),
                RNA_Splicing (Pre_mRNA, M_RNA),
                Translation (M_RNA, Proteins).
.......
Translation (M_RNA, Proteins):-
                % Table look-up
                Generation (MRNA, Aminoacids),
                Combination (Aminoacids, Proteins).
```

Fig. 5. A Logic Program Sketching the Translation of DNA into Proteins

3.1 The Nature of Variables

The expression of the biological processes of transcription and translation by the above logic program allows us to introduce important concepts about typing in that program.

Let us denote the type of a parameter P by the couple P:τ in which τ is the type attributed to P. There are several variants of τ that are applicable to the variables in the clauses `Protein_Generation` and `Translation`.

The first of the possible types is that of "sequence of symbols", that could be represented by lists. Their elements could be bases (in the case of DNA, or of mRNA where T's are replaced by U's), aminoacids, or even proteins when specified by their names.

Generally, the type τ that exists in biological processes is that of *Geometry.* In the most general case, geometry is 3-Dimensional, i.e., atoms occupy positions in space and are linked among themselves by atomic bindings. (Biochemists and chemists have developed sophisticated data structures to represent molecules.) Tertiary structures are used to denote the molecules represented using 3D geometry.

Another form that is useful in studying the geometry of molecules is called *Secondary Structure.* That consists in distinguishing certain shapes like "helices" and "sheets" that are present in the 3D representation. A secondary structure could be represented in some kind of prefix form or term encompassing the elements described in sequences – e.g., helix($e_1, e_2, \ldots$), sheet($f_1, \ldots$).

Finally, *primary structures* are one-dimensional and representable by sequences of symbols or names. As it often happens in science, macro or micro analyses – corresponding to primary or tertiary structures – depend on the development of models capable of expressing realistically the phenomena being studied.

The most general problem that one could hope to solve in computational molecular biology is the one represented by the query:

```
?- Protein_Generation (DNA:3DGeometry, Protein:3DGeometry);
```

Notice that, as in most interesting logic programs, the input-output nature of the parameters is arbitrary. One could for example imagine an above query in which the first parameter is a variable and the second is bound to a given 3D protein structure. Thus the query should yield all the DNA component helices that could generate the specified protein. Such query enables us to have a good understanding of what is a *gene*: it is the portion of DNA – that may contain intron gaps – that is responsible for the generation of a given protein. To each gene there is one corresponding protein.

At present, we are far from being able to specify such queries, but that will hopefully change in the future. It would be already a substantial progress if one could execute:

```
?-Protein_Generation(DNA:Sequence,Proteins:Secondary-structure);
```

with the first parameter bound and the second unbound.

We now open a brief parenthesis to point out that pharmaceutical companies are interested in producing medication that may control a scarcity or abundance of certain proteins; that task may be accomplished by genetic means, by helping correct the genes responsible for malfunctions.

What makes this problem very difficult is that there are often several genes that are responsible for certain diseases. By studying the DNA of individuals and their families having rare diseases one may be more successful in pinning down the main responsible genes.

The plan for the next sections of this paper is to first present formal grammars that reflect the DNA components (introns and exons) such that the concatenation of the exons results in triplets whose translation generates one of the 20 aminoacids according to the information in Figure 4.

This is non-trivial mainly because a triplet may consist of one (or two) bases in the rightmost part of say, a left exon, followed by two (or one) bases in the leftmost part of the following exon. Therefore, the elimination of the introns has to be done so that the resulting concatenation of exons is a multiple of three. One can easily imagine that an incorrect splicing performed by the spliceosome may result in the production of an entirely different set of proteins.

4 Grammars Defining DNA Components

Consider the grammar rules:

$$\mathbf{S} \rightarrow E\ I\ S \mid E$$

defining alternations of **I**'s and **E**'s starting and ending with an **E** (e.g., **E I E I E**). The non-terminals **E** and **I** will stand respectively for exons and introns. If both **E** and **I** are sequences of the nucleotides (terminals represented by bold face small case letters), one has:

$$\mathbf{N} \rightarrow a \mid t \mid c \mid g \quad \text{and} \quad E \rightarrow N\ E \mid N \qquad I \rightarrow N\ I \mid N$$

Note that this grammar is highly ambiguous since any sequence of nucleotides can be parsed either as an exon or an intron.

Further notice that the grammar actually considers a single DNA strand, instead of Pre-mRNA. This is common practice, but the reader should keep in mind that the sequences being described should use a **u** instead of a **t**.

In what follows we sketch the development of a context-sensitive grammar of the type proposed by Searls in [Searls]. The purpose of that grammar is to mimic the fact that the triplets in the string representing the concatenation of all the **E**'s in the alternation **E I E I** ... **E** generate a sequence of aminoacids.

We start by replacing the rule **E** → **N E** | **N** by **E** → **A E** | **A** where the non-terminal **A** represents an aminoacid generated by a triplet of bases. For example, according to the genetic code table in Figure 4 the aminoacid *Tyrozine*, abbreviated using the non-terminal **Tyr** is generated by the triplets **tat** and **tag**. This corresponds to adding rules such as:

$$\mathbf{A} \rightarrow Ala \mid \ldots |Tyr| \ldots \quad \text{representing the twenty aminoacids,}$$

and the rules defining the corresponding triplets:

$$\mathbf{A}la \rightarrow gca \mid gcc \mid \ldots \qquad Tyr \rightarrow tat \mid tag \quad \text{etc.}$$

Now the context-sensitive rules are introduced to specify that elements of the triplets can "travel" in the DNA sequences. This is accomplished by rules such as:

$$\mathbf{a}E \rightarrow Ea \qquad tE \rightarrow Et \qquad cE \rightarrow Ec \qquad gE \rightarrow Eg$$

Further details can be added to the above grammar. For example, to represent sequences of aminoacids ending by stop codons one can replace the rule:

$$\mathbf{E} \rightarrow A\ E \mid A \quad \text{by} \quad E \rightarrow A\ E \mid H$$

where **H** represents a stop codon, i.e.:

$$\mathbf{H} \rightarrow taa \mid tag \mid tga$$

In a similar vein one can specify that introns are delimited by the couples **g***t* and **a***g*. Note that these markers are potential delimiters of introns but could even be parts of an exon.

The above context-sensitive grammar is mostly useful as a descriptive grammar. The resulting parsing complexity would preclude its practical use. One should keep in mind that even a context-free representation of DNA would not be feasible in practice to allow the recognition of the various exon-intron alternations; this is because general CFGs result in parsers with cubic complexity incapable of handling, in reasonable time, DNA strings containing tens of thousands of bases.

We now show that much simpler grammars (finite-state) can be developed to specify the same basic features namely alternations of exons and introns such that the combined length of the exons – when the introns are excised – is a multiple of 3. Note however that the grammar will still generate ambiguous strings. And that is not detrimental, since indeed there is indeed a multiplicity of possible parses. We will show later that it is possible to make efficient choices among all those parses.

The fact that exons are formed by triplets can be expressed by the rules

$$\begin{aligned}
\mathbf{E} &\to \mathbf{a}\ E_1 \mid c\ E_1 \mid g\ E_1 \mid t\ E_1 \\
\mathbf{E}_1 &\to \mathbf{a}\ E_2 \mid c\ E_2 \mid g\ E_2 \mid t\ E_2 \\
\mathbf{E}_2 &\to \mathbf{a}\ E \mid c\ E \mid g\ E \mid t\ E \mid a \mid c \mid g \mid t
\end{aligned}$$

The fact that introns are delimited by the markers **g***t* and **a***g* is expressed by:

$$\begin{aligned}
\mathbf{I} &\to \mathbf{g}\ I_1 \\
\mathbf{I}_1 &\to \mathbf{t}\ I_2 \\
\mathbf{I}_2 &\to \mathbf{a}\ I_2 \mid c\ I_2 \mid g\ I_2 \mid t\ I_2 \mid a\ I_3 \\
\mathbf{I}_3 &\to \mathbf{g}\ I_4 \qquad \text{and so on}
\end{aligned}$$

It is straightforward to combine the above rules in constructing the desired finite-state graph similar to the one that will be described in Section 9. Note that non-determinism is pervasive.

It would be a mistake to attempt transform the non-deterministic finite-state grammar into a deterministic one. One would have to pay the exponential time complexity for the transformation and, above all, one would loose expressiveness since the resulting parser would be unable to distinguish introns from exons. In Section 9, I will show how one can bypass this transformation by representing all the parses in a compact form and selecting one or a few of those parses using constraints.

Also it should be kept in mind that, for the particular application of detecting the sequences of exons and introns, one should rule out the usage of techniques like DCG's, since the actual DNA strings are very long and the pervasive non-determinism would make the parsing impractical from a complexity point of view.

5 Motivation for Introducing DAGs

Let us now consider another simple grammar capable of describing alternations of exons and introns. That highly ambiguous grammar has been suggested by Olivier Baby and is shown in Figure 6. Both introns and exons are sequences of bases but introns start with a marker **g***t* and end with the marker **ag**. The rules for the nonterminal <*left*> specify that the presence of an **gt** may signal an intron body, but it could also be a part of an exon. Similarly, the rules for the nonterminal <*right*> specify that the marker **ag** may or may not signal the end of an intron and the beginning of an exon.

<*gene*> ::= <*start_codon*><*gene_body*><*stop_codon*>
<*start_codon*> ::= **atg**
<*stop_codon*> ::= **taa** | **tag** | **tga**
<*gene_body*> ::= <*exon_body*><*left*> | <*exon_body*>
<*right*> ::= **ag**<*intron_body*><*right*> | **ag**<*exon_body*><*left*> | **ag**<*exon_body*>
<*left*> ::= **gt**<*intron_body*><*right*> | **gt**<*exon_body*><*left*> | **gt**<*exon_body*>
<*intron_body*> ::= <*base*>*
<*exon_body*> ::= <*base*>*
<*base*> ::= **a** | **c** | **g** | **t**

Fig 6. Regular Grammar Defining Alternations of Exons and Introns

Note that although the rules of the grammar are context-free, it would be easy to construct a non-deterministic finite-state grammar generating the same language. It is trivial to transform the grammar in Figure 6, into a set of DCG's capable of recognizing all possible alternations of introns and exons in a given DNA string. The tree of choices representing the execution of the DCG's is shown in Figure 7. The vertical string at the left of the figure is the input to the DCG's.

It is now possible to show that the tree in Figure 7 can be converted into a DAG. This is done using an approach that is similar to that used in Binary Decision Diagrams (BDDs.) Basically, one starts from the leaves of the tree and tries to repeatedly combine identical subtrees until a final minimal DAG is constructed. The result of such construction is shown in the DAG of Figure 8. It is seen that a zigzagging path between the left and right branches of the DAG represents a valid alternation of exons and introns. Furthermore, no valid alternations of introns and exons are missed (It should become clear now why Olivier Baby chose to name the nonterminals <*left*> and <*right*>.)

Unfortunately, the BDD like algorithm for constructing has exponential complexity. Even if more efficient BDD algorithms can be found for special cases, a better solution is possible. Consider the interesting question: given a non-deterministic finite-state grammar G, can one obtain the DAG directly from G in linear time? The answer is yes! And that construction is described in the following section.

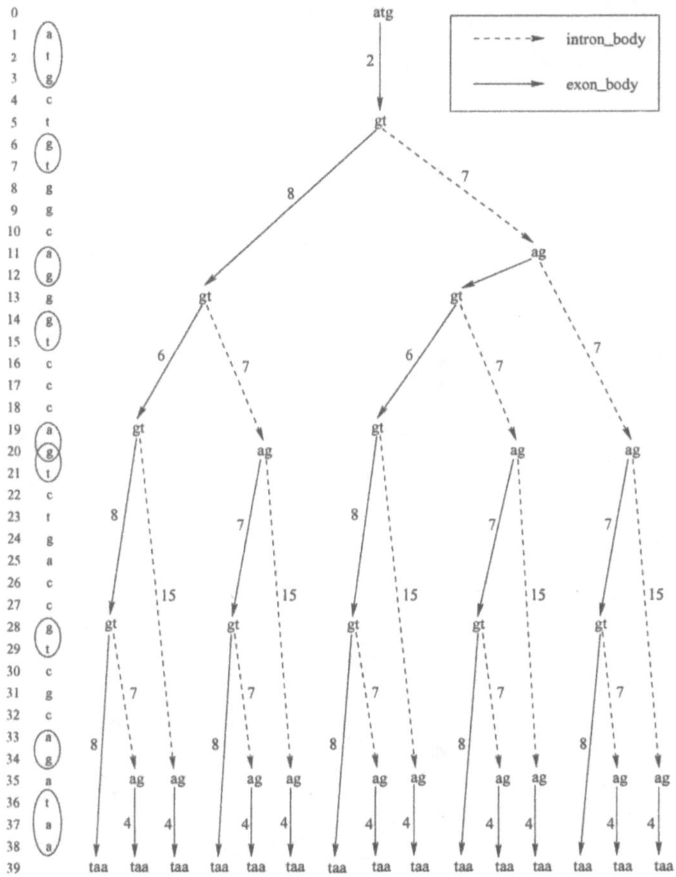

Fig. 7. Tree of Choices Obtained by Executing the DCG's Corresponding to the Grammar in Figure 6 (using the string shown at the left as input)

Note that even though the DAG construction has linear complexity, a simple listing of all the paths (interpretations or ambiguities) renders the complexity exponential.

Since this paper is directed to LP researchers, I cannot help mentioning the analogy of the above construction with the complexity of certain unification algorithms: they can be exponential, if care is not taken to recognize common subexpressions within terms. Another question worth asking is: can memoing be used to generate the DAG from the execution of DCG's? I do not believe so, and will be surprised if that turns out to be case and the construction could be achieved in linear time.

I also believe that it is an open problem to determine if there are subclasses of context-free languages for which the determination of all ambiguous

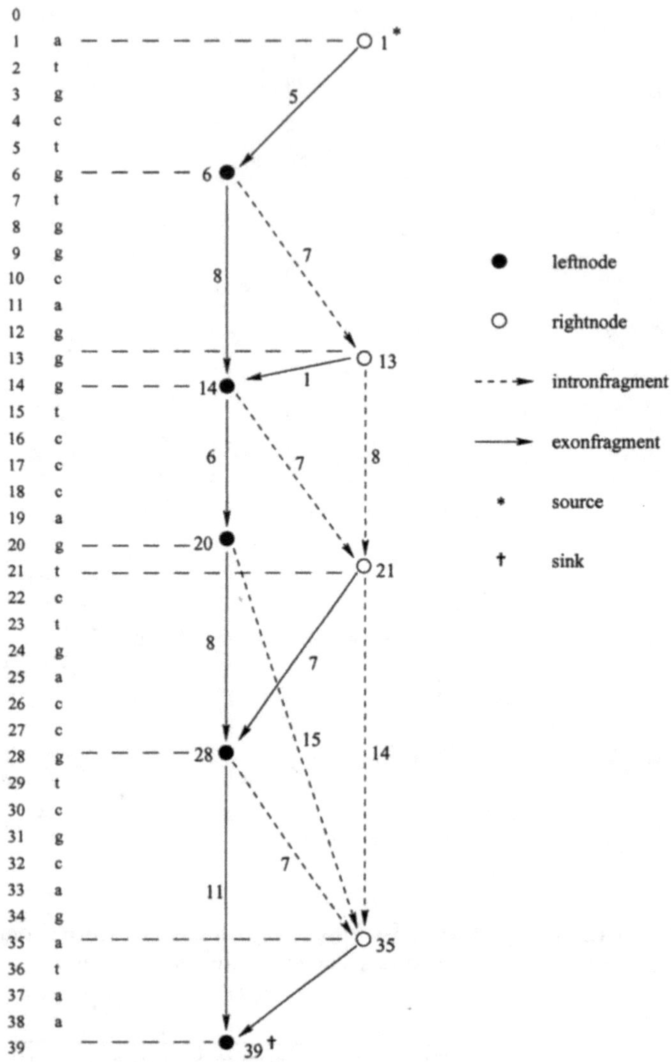

Fig. 8. DAG Representing all the Parses Described by the Tree in Figure 7

parses of a sentence can be expressed by a DAG whose construction can be performed in linear time.

6 Obtaining DAGs From NDFSA

It should be emphasized that the construction described in this section is similar to that known in speech recognition as the Viterbi algorithm (see [Durbin]). Viterbi-like algorithms are based on a preliminary learning- phase to determine probabilities that are subsequently used by dynamic programming techniques for optimizations. In contrast, the approach that follows, proposed by Olivier Baby and myself, aims at an entirely different (discrete) method of path selection without using probabilities or learning. Additional comments on Viterbi algorithms appear in Section 10.

Given a NDFSA with $|Q|$ states and an acceptable string s of length n, it is possible to generate, in $O(|Q|n)$ time and space, a Directed Acyclic Graph (DAG) whose paths

from the source node –corresponding to the initial state of the NDFSA–
to the sink node –corresponding to the final state of the NDFSA–

represent all the parses (ambiguities) in the string s being considered.

Note that there is no loss of generality in assuming that the NDFSA contains a unique initial and final states (which incidentally, could correspond to the same state).

The most convenient way to generate the DAG is to output onto a file the triplets $<x, y, z>$ specifying the transitions of a state (node) x to a state (node) z upon scanning a symbol y. Therefore the DAG is specified by a list of triplets.

The algorithm is briefly described as follows:

(0) Set the current state c to the initial state of the NDFSA. Also set as the current symbol t the first symbol of the string s.
(1) Consider the current state c of the NDFSA and the current symbol t in the input string. Output all the triplets $<c, t, c'>$ where c' are the states in the NDFSA that are reachable from c upon reading the symbol t.
(2) Readjust c and t by considering as new c's each of the previously generated c' and by considering as the new t the symbol following the previous t in the string s.
(3) Steps 2 and 3 are repeated until the final element of string s has been considered.

Since the string s is accepted by the given NDFSA, there will be a single final state reachable upon scanning the last element of s.

It should be noted that the above algorithm may generate triplets representing paths in the DAG that do not reach the unique final state of the NDFSA. It suffices to mention that, if desired, those paths can be eliminated (also in time $O(|Q|n)$) by having a backward pass that marks the nodes in the DAG that are reachable from the final sink node. The unmarked nodes and their edges can then be simply eliminated from the previous DAG yielding the final one.

7 Chromatic NDFSA and DAGs

The transformation of an NDFSA into its corresponding DAG can be extended to what Olivier Baby and I call *Chromatic* NDFSA. These are NDFSA whose transition edges are colored to denote parts of the recognition that need to be identified.

The DAG resulting from a chromatic NDFSA is referred to as a chromatic DAG in which the edges in the paths are colored according to the hues attributed to the chromatic NDFSA.

It will be seen that the purpose of the colors is to select subsequences of the string being parsed that correspond to paths of certain color passing through certain nodes. In the following subsection we give an example of a Chromatic NDFSA. In Section 9 we will provide a Chromatic NDFSA that can be used to detect alternations of introns and exons.

7.1 Example

Figure 9 shows a simple Chromatic NDFSA with two states, one symbol (a) and three colored edges. The example is taken from Olivier Baby's dissertation . Using English as the description language, the given NDFSA specifies that:

- Every red a is preceded by a green a,
- No blue a is preceded by a green a,
- No two consecutive green a's can occur,
- The sequence ends with a green a.

The Chromatic DAG corresponding to the NDFSA in accepting the string $a\ a\ a\ a$ is presented in Figure 9. The results of the forward and backward passes are also shown in that figure as well as the resulting 3 paths representing the 3 possible parses for the given string. Note that paths ending in state 0 have been eliminated in the backward pass since the final state is labeled 1.

8 Introducing "Criteria"

Let us now turn our attention to the short table and the diagram at the bottom of Figure 9. The table indicate the various appearances of the colors B (blue), G (green), and R (red) in the 3 valid parses for $a\ a\ a\ a$.

The diagram indicates the frequency distributions of each color as they vary with each symbol in the string. That diagram can also be constructed

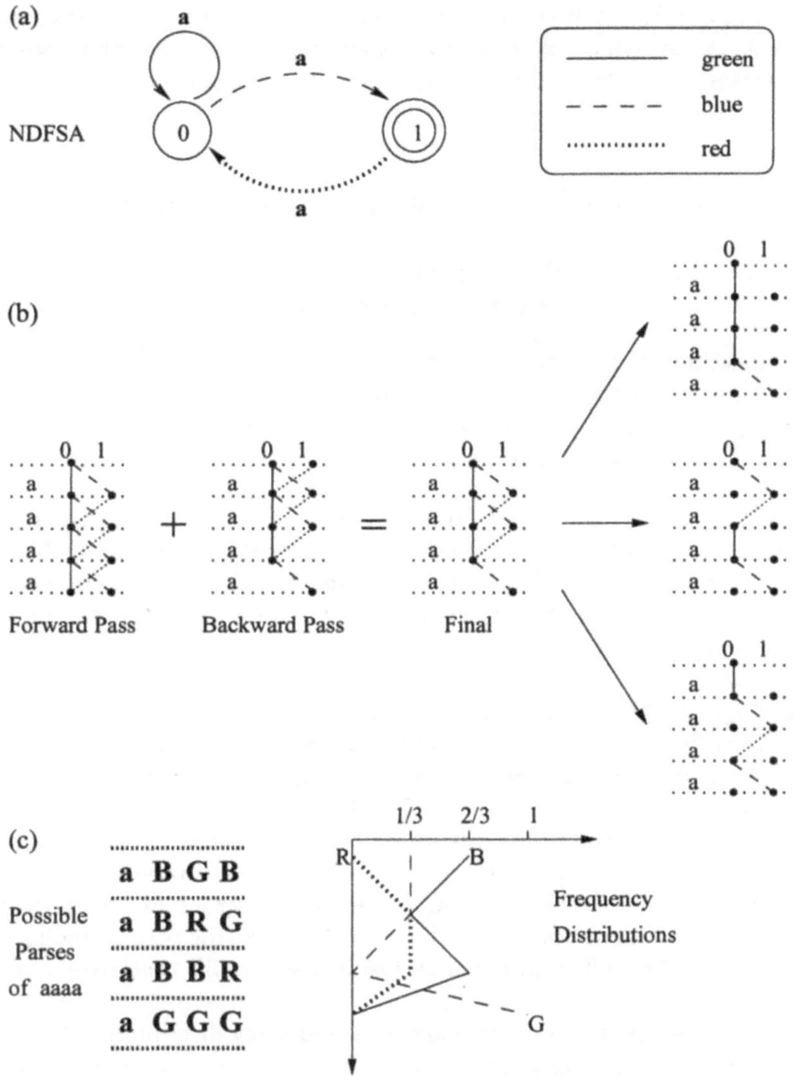

Fig. 9. An Example of a Chromatic NDFSA and its DAG

in linear time assuming that the number of states in the NDFSA is small compared to the length of the string being analyzed.

A criterion is defined as a user specified property relating to the frequency distribution diagram. For example a criterion may be:

> an a in the string $a\ a\ a\ a$ is considered to be red if its probability of being red in all possible parses is not null.

According to this criterion the second and third a's in the given string are red. The first and fourth a's do not satisfy that criteria. We have thus succeeded in detecting one subsequence satisfying the criteria and two others that do not.

9 Alternation of Introns and Exons Using NDFSA

Figure 10 depicts an NDFSA capable of differentiating alternations of exons and introns satisfying the following characteristics:

- The delimiters for introns are **g***t* and **a***g*.
- The combined length of the exons is a multiple of 3.
- An exon whose (individual) length is a multiple of 3 should not contain the stop codons **t***ga*, **t***aa*, or **t***ag*.

The first two features have already been explained. The third does not classify as a candidate for an exon a sequence containing stop codons (see Figure 4) if such sequence is itself a multiple of 3. Biologists call those sequences an *open reading frame* and an alternation of exons-introns containing such sequence should be disregarded.

A brief description of the NDFSA in Figure 10 is as follows. States 0, 1, 2 and 3 specify the triplicity of the combined length of exons, that may be interrupted by the introns detected by the markers **g***t* and **a***g*.

States 4, 5, and 8 screen out potential exons that contain stop codons. They are not accepted by the NDFSA. Figure 10 also shows the "colors" attributed to the edges. Basically exons are represented by solid edges and the dashed ones represent either introns or invalid alternations.

As described in Sections 6 and 7 one can construct in linear time the Chromatic DAG corresponding to the given NDFSA (the corresponding DAG is not shown.) The following criterion can be used to differentiate exons from introns:

"A base belongs to an intron only if its frequency distribution for being a potential exon is null." In other words, all the edges corresponding to a given base in the paths of the DAG defining valid alternations of exons-introns, are colored as introns.

This may seem like a very stiff requirement, but results using experimental data show that this criterion has a great accuracy in detecting potential introns. The results of using the given criterion for a particular sequence of yeast DNA are shown in Figure 11. In the case of yeast DNA, for which it is admittedly easier to detect the (sole) intron, the proposed approach has an accuracy approaching 99

The reader is referred to O. Baby's dissertation for detailed explanations of the results for the human genome, and comparisons with other methods of intron detection (`http://www.cs.brandeis.edu/~obaby`.) It should be

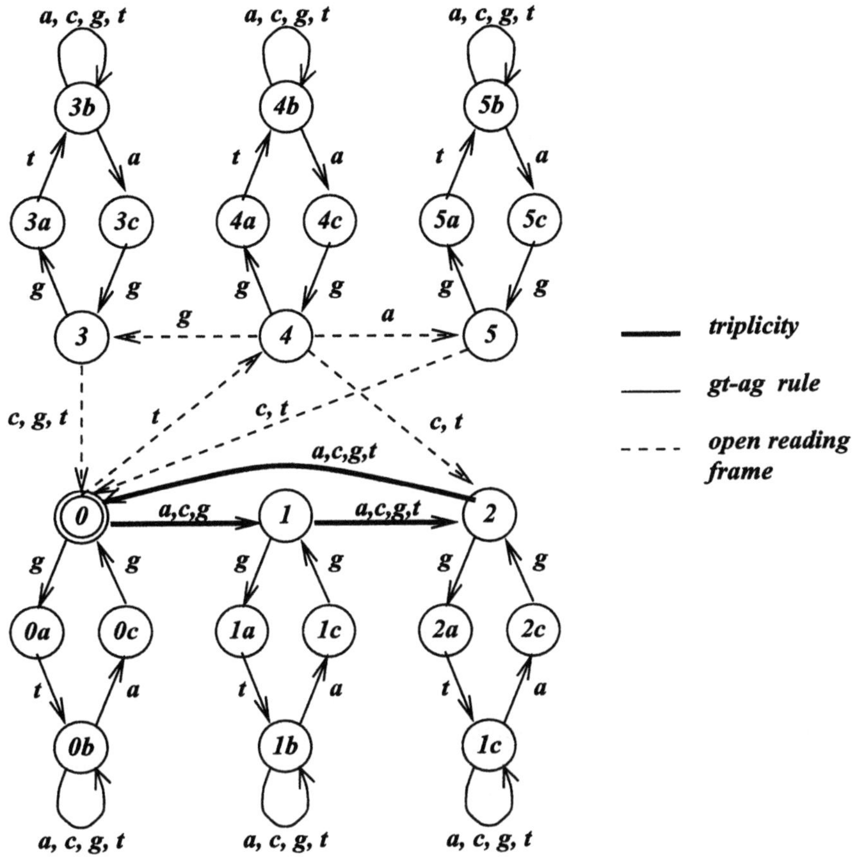

Fig. 10. NDFSA State-Graph Defining Alternations of Exons and Introns

emphasized that the results obtained by the described approach match those obtained by other methods.

It is quite possible that combinations of the proposed approach and ILP would yield even better results. In the case of ILP the user has to select the predicates that are relevant to a recognition and the present approach provides the inspiration to construct those predicates (see Section 10).

9.1 Constraints

The complexity of the algorithm described in Section 5 is $O(|Q|n)$ where $|Q|$ is the number of states in the NDFSA and n is the length of the string being analyzed. Assume one introduces constraints like:

- There should not be more than p bases in an exon or intron, or
- The total number of exons should not exceed q.

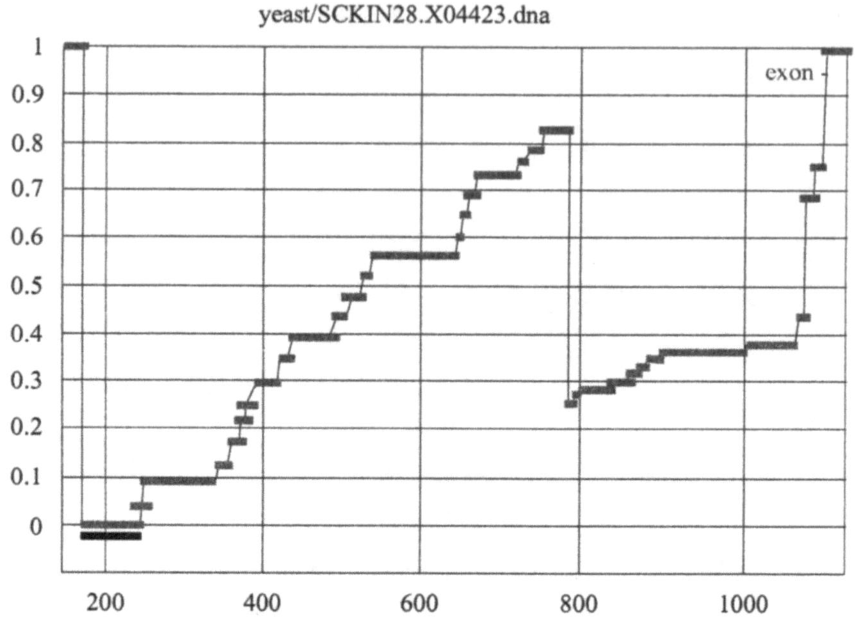

Fig. 11. Results Obtained for a Yeast DNA String. The abscissa represents the number of the bases in the string. The sole Intron corresponds to the subsequence having zero as ordinates (bases numbered 75 to 240). This is the only subsequence involving DAG paths through states that do not express Exons, according to the chromatic finite-state graph in Figure 10.

in which p and q may be fairly large integers. It should be apparent that a purist approach of expressing these constraints by NDFSA will require not only an automatic generation of the automaton but also will result in a very large number of states. This increases substantially the time and space complexities since it dramatically increases $|Q|$.

To bypass this predicament the designer should resort to adding these constraints not in the NDFSA, but while the DAG paths are computed. The reader will find out that the screening of the paths in the DAG that do not satisfy the above constraints can also be done in linear time with no additional space requirements.

10 Related Approaches

Dynamic Programming (DP) and Hidden Markov Models (HMMs) have probably been the most extensively used techniques in present day applications of Computational Molecular Biology including the exon-intron detection problem. In addition, Inductive Logic Programming (ILP) has been playing an increasingly important role in CMB. Both HMMs and ILP should be considered under the umbrella of machine learning methods. In this section I will briefly describe these techniques by means of examples.

In the so-called "Pairwise Alignment Problem" one considers two similar sequences S_1 and S_2 of symbols (nucleotides or aminoacids) and it is desired to establish an alignment, that is a positioning of the elements of S_1 and S_2 so that sequences of identical elements line up as much as possible. This accomplished by introducing the special symbol "-" indicating a valid displacement of elements in either S_1 or S_2.

The alignment problem is a combinatorial optimization in which one attempts to maximize a score function which (usually) considers a weight of +1 for the alignment of identical symbols, a weight of -1 for an alignment of different symbols, and a weight of -2 for the introduction of the "-" displacement. Essentially, one considers all possible pairs of successive symbols in S_1 and S_2 – including potential displacements using the "-" symbol – in either strings and computes the maximum score incurred by that configuration. The best final choice consists of considering sequences yielding those local maxima.

For example, if S_1 =GACGTA and S_2 =GATCGAA an alignment of total score +2 = 5 - 1 - 2 is accomplished by:

GA -CGTA
GATCGAA

Let us assume that the lengths of S_1 and S_2 are of the same magnitude n. The standard approach using DP consists of constructing an n by n matrix M in which the rows correspond to variants of S_1 (containing possible displacements) that are candidates for being considered in computing the optimal alignment. Similarly, the columns correspond to variants of S_2 that are also candidates for the optimal alignment.

The DP algorithm consists of two passes. The first computes the various total scores incurred by considering elements of S_1 and S_2 that are either identical, different or introduce displacements in either S_1 or S_2. Two embedded **for** - statements are used to perform this computation according to the paradigm of DP namely: a maximum is obtained by combining successive local maxima. These results are stored in the matrix M. The second pass inspects the constructed matrix M and selects – among several possible alignments – the ones that attain the maximum value. The time complexity of each of the passes is quadratic as well as the total space complexity. Although the second pass is capable of determining possible multiple solutions having the same total cost, only one is usually considered. DP is used in connection with HMM's to find the most likely parse when considering a number of possible ambiguous parses.

The easiest way to introduce HMM's is through stochastic grammars. These are Chomsky-type grammars in which one assigns probabilities π's for each α_i component of rules defining unions, such as: $\mathbf{N} \rightarrow \alpha_1 | \alpha_2 | \ldots | \alpha_n$.

The π's are such that their sum equals one for each rule defining the nonterminal **N**. The stochastic grammar model consists of determining experimentally (by learning techniques) the values of the π's by considering a large number of sample strings for which certain characteristics are known, and provided as input to the learning algorithm.

The analysis of a new problem consists of determining an outcome that is most likely, based on the probabilities π that have been determined by examining the large learning set. HMM's are simply stochastic regular (finite-state) grammars.

Consider for example, a non-deterministic situation as specified by the finite- state rules of an FSG defining transitions stemming from state **Q** upon recognizing the terminal **t**:

$$\mathbf{Q} \rightarrow t\ R \mid t\ U$$

The interesting case occurs when the FSG in question is ambiguous and a given string may be parsed in two or more ways. As seen previously, there is a one-to-one correspondence between a path in a DAG and a parse of a string generated by a given FSG. The term "hidden" in HMM refers to the fact that the transition from **Q** upon recognizing a symbol **t** is "unknown" or "hidden" and it is determined by establishing the probabilities π applicable to strings in the learning set for which the specific transitions to **R** or to **U** are known to apply.

Let us assume that, by virtue of the training set of strings, the first disjunct in the above rule defining **Q** is known to have a (high) probability p of success in specifying a path that correctly recognizes a given subsequence as having certain desired properties. The second disjunct has a (low) probability $(1 - p)$ and specifies another parse (or path in the DAG)

When confronted with a new sequence not in the training set, one can determine the DAG as in Section 6 and attribute probabilities of paths reaching a given node. Essentially, one computes the products of probabilities corresponding to the edges of a path. Then the previously explained dynamic programming approach becomes applicable, as follows.

First compute the subpaths having highest probability of reaching a given node in the DAG. One can record the pointer specifying the immediate predecessor(s) of the node providing the highest overall probability. In a second pass – just like that in the pairwise alignment problem – one determines the path of highest probability and therefore the most likely subsequence exhibiting properties similar to the strings presented in the training set. This determination of the most likely path in the DAG is known as the Viterbi algorithm. Viterbi used this approach in determining the most likely phonemes in speech recognition.

HMMs have been used in a variety of CMB problems including the determination of: protein secondary structure, the most likely alternation of introns and exons in pre-mRNA, and the pairwise or multiple alignment problems. In the case of protein secondary structure one determines the substrings corresponding to well-known substructures that commonly occur in the 3D shape of proteins (e.g., alpha-helices and beta-sheets)

The objective of Inductive Logic Programming is to determine a set of clauses C capable of discriminating certain characteristics of data, based on user-specified predicates P and a learning set indicating positive and negative instances of the data for which those characteristics are known.

For example, in a solution of the exon-intron problem using ILP, one would provide a set of learning examples made of DNA sequences for which the splice sites – the locations separating exons from introns – are known (the positive set); in addition one would specify other DNA sequences for which certain locations are known *not* to be splice sites (the negative set).

Furthermore, one would have to provide a number of predicates that the human problem-solver suspects to have an influence in the determination of the splice sites. That is where the ingenuity of the problem-solver plays a key role.

Consider for example, a predicate specifying a set of transition states in a finite-state automaton capable of discerning certain splice sites. Another predicate could specify triplicity, i.e., that the length of the combined exons should be a multiple of three. If a number of such predicates P are made available to an ILP processor, together with the positive an negative set of examples that processor attempts to find the combination of the Ps constituting clauses capable of recognizing splice sites.

11 Other Problems in Computational Molecular Biology

11.1 Protein Folding

Several approaches have been used to determine the shape of a sequence of aminoacids forming a protein (see [Creighton]). One which appears to be particularly amenable to a solution using LP consists of discretizing a 3D curve by considering it as formed by sequences of small linear segments each representing an edge of mini-cubes that are packed into a large cube. This is referred to as the lattice model.

A configuration of a protein can be approximated by considering the sequences of edges in 3D space that start from a vertex of the large cube and mimic the actual final shape of the protein (see Figure 12) The input to a protein folding problem is the sequence of aminoacids and the result is a sequence specifying each mini-cube edge that constitutes the final 3D curve.

A possible solution to this combinatorial problem is of the generate-and-test type, where the aim is to find the 3D curve that minimizes the total energy E which is a function of components of the aminoacids in the input sequence. It is possible that numeric computations using interval constraints could be used in the minimization of E.

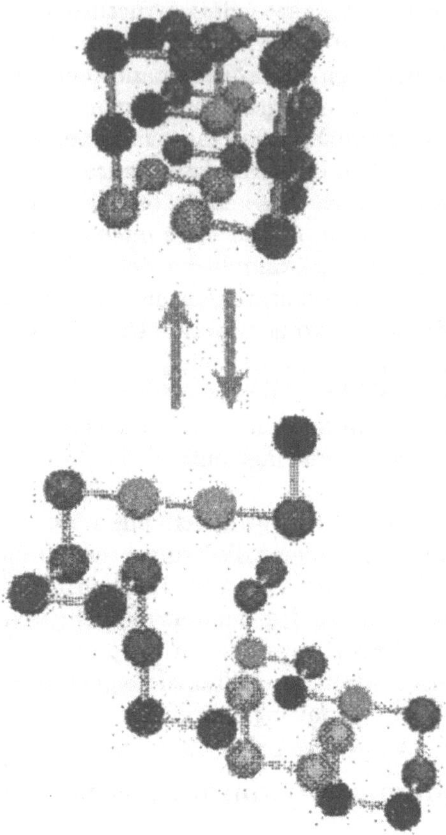

Fig. 12. Lattice Model of Protein Folding

11.2 Protein Secondary Structure Prediction

Inductive Logic Programming (IPL) has been successfully used to determine secondary structure of proteins defined by a sequence of aminoacids (see [Lavrac]). The approach consists of having a learning set for which one has available a sequence of aminoacids and the subsequences that correspond to an alpha-helix; this means that when the entire protein folds, the particular subsequence acquires the shape of a helix.

A recent paper by Turcotte, Muggleton and Sternberg [Turcotte] describes an ILP approach generating a logic program capable of detecting alpha and beta folding regions. Although the results are encouraging and match or may even surpass those obtained using other approaches, the accurate computer determination of 3-D protein shape still remains a challenging problem.

It should also be mentioned that DP and HMMs have been combined in attempting to solve protein-folding problems. First one uses HMMs (with the ancillary DP approach for determining most likely subsequences) to ascertain possible sites of subsequences corresponding to the alpha-helices and beta-sheets. The so-called protein threading approach consists of using DP (with given weights for the possible choices) so as to minimize the costs of combining sites describing the various components (alpha-helices, beta- sheets, and loops: the regions between those subcomponents). In that case constraints are imposed by specifying likely maximum and minimum distances between the components.

11.3 Secondary Structure of tRNA

Formal grammars, especially context-free, have been used to solve simplified versions of the protein folding problem aplicable to tRNA sequences. Before proteins are generated from mRNA there are strings of RNA material (called tRNA) that are used as a scaffolding for generating proteins from codons. An interesting problem is the determination of certain loops that are present in tRNA. Context-free grammars defining parentheses-type languages have been used to specify regions of tRNA that correspond to a certain type of folding.

The given sequence of nucleotides forming a tRNA string can then be parsed according to the grammar rules indicating subsequences that have certain geometrical properties. The proposed CFG's are highly ambiguous, and cubic complexity parsers have to be used. This problem resembles the one described in Section 9 for NDFSA and there may be DAG-like representations of parses that enable the choice of the most likely parse as it was done in the case of exon-intron detection. Stochastic context-free grammars (the counterpart of HMMs for CFGs) have also been utilized to solve this problem.

11.4 Phylogeny Trees

Note that the pairwise alignment problem for two sequences establishes a quantitative measure of similarity between those sequences. The determination of Phylogeny Trees of p sequences – nucleotides or aminoacids each representing a class of individuals – allows researchers to classify individuals according to evolutionary considerations.

Since DNA and proteins of all living organisms exhibit remarkable content similarities, phylogenic trees are useful in establishing relationships between different but similar species. The determination of phylogeny trees is performed by considering all different pairs of the p sequences and determining those that are most similar. They constitute the leaves of the first level subtrees. The resulting nodes (roots) are assumed to contain the characteristics of their children. The process of pairing these newly determined nodes continues as before, by constructing the most likely combined subtrees until a final tree is obtained.

12 Areas in CS That Are Applicable in Molecular Biology

Figure 13 lists some of the areas in computer science that have been used in the solving of molecular biology problems. An important topic is pattern matching and it appears under several guises. Pattern matching has been used to detect desirable sequences of nucleotides (e.g., determining splice sites separating coding and non-coding DNA regions.) Since insertions, deletions and even mutations often occur in nature, pattern matching associated with costs of insertions and deletions (called the *indel* problem) has acquired special significance. The previously mentioned alignment problem has been a fairly well studied problem in bioinformatics.

Pattern matching variants have been used to detect certain components of proteins. In that case a protein shape may be described by a polygonal line in 3D space. The problem becomes that of checking if a given short polygonal line (the pattern) can match parts of a longer polygonal line (the text) using rigid rotations and translations.

Probabilistic and statistical analyses are often used in determining the most probable splice sites separating exons from introns. Neural nets and – as mentioned earlier – HMM's have also been used for that purpose.

It should be apparent from the descriptions in the previous sections that there would be scores of 3D geometrical problems involved in protein folding and in drug design.

Large and complex data bases are already being used in the human genome project to store, retrieve and make comparisons of DNA sequences. Numerical analysis is also destined to play a role in dealing with problems in molecular biology. In particular, the new area of interval constraints has the potential of being used in the energy minimization computations in protein folding. Computer graphics techniques are essential in displaying complex 3D molecules. So are simulations of macromolecular behavior.

13 Some Comments About DNA Computing

Any general survey of computers and biology would be incomplete if no mention is made to biological computers. In what follows we briefly comment on how the complementary properties of nucleotides (A pairs with T and C pairs with G) can be used to perform hard combinatorial computations in a biology laboratory.

The key components of having DNA segments perform complex computations are:

- **Pattern Matching (PM) and approximate PM**
  - **Non-Deterministic Searches**
  - **Pattern Matching of Polygonal Lines in 3D**
- **Probabilistic Methods**
  - **Hidden Markov Models**
  - **Statistical Analysis**
  - **Signal Processing, Information Theory**
  - **Neural Nets, Genetic Algorithms**
- **Automata and Languages**
  - **Non-Determinism and Ambiguity**
- **Machine Learning,**
  - **Inductive Logic Programming**
- **Data Bases**
  - **Knowledge Representation**
  - **Data Mining**
- **3D Geometry Problems**
- **Simulations**
- **Computer Graphics**
- **Numerical and Symbolic Analysis**
  - **Energy Minimization**
- **Parallelism**

Fig. 13. Topics in CS related to Biology

(1) One can presently place an order to a genetic laboratory or company to provide (small) volumes of material in which practically all of the ingredients are copies of the same short sequence of single stranded nucleotides chosen by the customer. Using computer science terminology, one can order trillions of copies of single-stranded short strings containing a user selected combination of the letters A, C, G, T. This can be done for a relatively modest price, say a few tens of dollars.

(2) The attraction between the nucleotides C - G , and A - T is used to append two or more sequences of the genetic material described in (1). This is done in a lab by simply mixing the contents of two or more small test tubes containing genetic material.

(3) There exist laboratory manipulation techniques (e.g., gel electro-phoresis) that can screen the genetic material contained in a test tube and extract – from given sequences – subsequences containing a particular combination of nucleotides.This is the inverse operation of mixing the contents of two test tubes.

In reality the above steps can be complex. For example, caution has to exercised in selecting the initial genetic material, in carrying out the mixing and the screening, so that actual solutions of problems are obtained in suitable quantities to yield the desired results. These are obtained in a final test tube containing the appended and screened substrings that solve the problem.

The pioneer in the biological approach to computation is Leonard Adleman. He showed that small versions of an NP-complete problem can be solved using the above components. Specifically, Adleman solved the so-called Hamiltonian Path Problem (HPP) using the above techniques.

A very clear article by Adleman on the topic of DNA computing has recently appeared in *Scientific American.* That article is a highly recommended introduction to this fascinating new topic in which biology provides novel means for fast computation. Adleman's article covers in detail the techniques he used to solve the HPP.

Biological computers do not have the lightning speed of their hardwired counterparts. Biological reactions using the carefully planned attractions between nucleotides may take hours to complete. Nevertheless, they deal with a potentially exponential number of data and are processed in a massively parallel manner.

Another (NP-complete) problem that has attracted the attention of computer scientists is the satisfiability of boolean formulas. Its biological solution also consists of determining paths in graphs. It remains to be seen if the approach is feasible in practice to solve real problems involving graphs containing thousands of nodes and edges. Since the satisfiability problem is a basic one in logic, it is not impossible that biological computers may some day be used to solve logic problems.

Adleman's work opens new vistas to theoreticians and practitioners in computer science. A key theoretical aspect that has to be revised is that of complexity of computations. All the work done in complexity prior to Adleman's approach assumes that even massively parallel computations are carried out using a limited (polynomial) number of processors. For the first time in the history of computation one finds that, due to the bioware's enormous capacity for computation, there is a potentially exponential number of processing units.

14 Final Remarks

I hope to have shown through a brief birds-eye-view of the topic and also through some examples, the discrete and combinatorial nature of some of the relevant problems in molecular biology. LP and its extensions have shown to be wonderful tools in the solution of combinatorial problems, in natural language processing, in data base design, in machine learning (ILP) and more recently in numerical analysis, through the use of constraints. These areas are very germane to the work being done in computational molecular biology.

Every field seems to benefit from cross fertilization with another area: LP researchers might gain a renewed inspiration by exploring the problems it can solve in the realm of computational biology.

In doing so one must be realistic in viewing the differences between the two research cultures. As in mathematics, LP stresses abstractions, whereas biology requires a constant checking that a hypothesis should be confirmed by nature, using laboratory experiments.

Recent history has shown that the mathematical problems in computational biology have an inherent appeal, and there is a tendency for mathematically inclined researchers to develop abstractions and simplifications that are prone to neglect what happens in nature. On the other hand, current research in biology has a definite empirical component, and molecular biology laboratories usually seek to provide solutions to immediate problems that have practical and commercial value. Hopefully, the younger generation of computer scientists and biologists will be more likely to learn how to bridge these "cultural" gaps, by gaining a concurrent basic knowledge of both fields.

Finally, one should say a few words about evolution – the next most important area of study in molecular biology. DNA mutates due to environmental and reproductive processes, thus adding an extra dimension time – to the myriad of parameters in molecular biology that we have sketched in this paper.

Therefore, as Knuth pointed out, it is not unlikely that the next 500 years will occupy the attention of computer scientists and biologists to help decipher some of life's secrets. This is a task of enormous complexity that simply cannot be done without the tools perfected in decades of work in computer science.

Acknowledgements

It is with great pleasure that I acknowledge the help of Olivier Baby, a former doctoral student. I have learned a great deal of computational molecular biology by interacting with Olivier during the past four years. Many of the ideas expressed in this paper resulted from those interactions and some appear in detail in his dissertation. I also wish to express my thanks to the referee that provided a constructive review of the manuscript, and to Dr. Victor Marek and Zhuwen Li for the help in preparing this manuscript.

A Mini Glossary

Genome: Complete set of genetic information in a specific organism.

Gene: The basic unit of inheritance that controls a characteristic of living organisms. It can be considered as a substring of DNA that propagates that characteristic. Genes are present within the chromosomes residing in the cell.

DNA Deoxyribose Nucleic Acid: A large double-stranded molecule that contains, in coded form, all the information needed to generate proteins for living organisms. The coded information is a sequence of nucleotides.

Nucleotides: The individual components of DNA . They are one of the four bases A (Adenine), C (Cytosine) , G (Guanine), T (Thymine) These molecules have specific attractions to each other. An A is always attracted to a T and vice-versa. Similarly, a C is always attracted to a G. This dual attraction is the basis for DNA reproduction and biological computers.

Transcription: Synthesis of mRNA from a complementary DNA template.

mRNA - message Ribo Nucleic Acid: A single stranded molecule derived from the DNA. The transformation of DNA into mRNA involves two operations:

1. a one to one replacement of the base T by a U (Uracil), see **transcription**, and
2. the elimination of a sequence of bases (called Introns) whose presence in DNA remains a mystery and may be related to evolution, see **spliceosome.**

Introns do not participate in the generation of aminoacids and proteins. The elements of DNA that are translated into mRNA are called Exons and consist of a sequence of triplets called codons. The codons are later transcribed into aminoacids and proteins.

RNA Polymerase: Enzyme that synthesizes pre-mRNA from DNA.

Spliceosome: Biological machinery that detects and removes Introns in (pre-)mRNA and appends the resulting Exons which later code into aminoacids.

Splice-Sites: The junctions between exons from introns.

Translation: Synthesis of a protein from an mRNA template

Ribosomes: The protein-making machinery in the cell. This machinery can be considered as an actual "very intricate interpreter" that translates mRNA into aminoacids.

Genetic Code: Set of 64 codons (triplets) in DNA and the aminoacids they represent.

Aminoacids: Any of the 20 (water-soluble) organic molecules that are produced by the code in mRNA.

Protein: Molecules formed by a sequence of aminoacids (called polypeptides) and generated by a transcription of mRNA. The three-dimensional shape of proteins plays an important role in the physical stability of those molecules

Protein Folding: When proteins are dehydrated in the laboratory they acquire a linear form. Following rehydration proteins (almost) always return to their original 3D stable configuration. This is called protein folding and it plays an important role on the stability of the proteins that are generated for continuing life of cells and organisms.

References

Since this article is intended to facilitate an introduction to Computational Molecular Biology (CMB), many of the references listed below are not mentioned in the text. The following comments should help the reader in selecting the references of interest depending on his or her level of familiarity with the subject.

The list that follows includes URL's containing some of his articles. A good starting point for involvement in the field is to peruse through some of the URL's mentioned in the sequel.

The introductory paper by Lander, in the book edited by Lander and Waterman [Lander], is a very good general introduction relating the fields of Molecular Biology, Genetics, and Biochemistry.

The textbook by Setubal and Meidanis [Setubal] is a good introduction to computer scientists without prior knowledge of molecular biology. That text emphasizes computer science algorithms for sequence analysis using optimization techniques such as DP.

The book by Baldi and Brunak [Baldi] covers in detail the HMM approach to detecting subsequences of interest in DNA, RNA and proteins.

The recent book by Durbin *et al*, [Durbin] contains valuable information about alignments, HMMs, and Chomsky-type grammars. The text by Lavrac and Dzeroski [Lavrac] on Inductive Logic Programming contains a chapter where ILP is used to solve a protein folding problem. Finally, the recent monograph edited by Salzberg *et al* [Salzberg] contains a long chapter on protein-folding.

Among the introductory books dedicated exclusively to molecular biology (MB), the ones by Bailey [Bailey] , Berg and Singer [Berg], Freifelder and Malacinski [Freifelder] are highly recommended. Lewin [Lewin] is a treatise in that discipline. An amusing and very instructive paperback is *The Cartoon Guide to Genetics* by Gonnick and Wheelis [Gonnick]. It is in my choice as a starting point for the uninitiated reader.

The WWW offers a wealth of material on CMB, MB, and computing with DNA. The listed URL's include the highly recommended sites developed by the Department of Energy and a bioinformatics course at Stanford University directed to biologists and computer scientists, taught by Dr. Russ Altman.

Books on Computational Molecular Biology

[Baldi] Baldi,P., and Brunak, S., BioInformatics: The Machine Learning Approach, MIT Press, 1998.

[Setubal] Setubal, J., and Meidanis J., An Introduction to Computational Molecular Biology, PWS Publishing, 1997.

[Salzberg] Salzberg, S.L., Searls, D.B., Kasif, S., (editors), Computational Methods in Molecular Biology, Elsevier, 1998.

[Durbin] Durbin, R., Eddy, S., Krogh, A., and Mitchison, G., Biological Sequence Analysis, Cambridge University Press, 1998

[Lander] Lander, E.S., and Waterman, M.S.,(editors) Calculating the Secrets of Life, National Academy Press, 1995.

Waterman, M.S., Introduction to Computational Biology, Chapman & Hall, 1995.

Suhai, S., (editor) Theoretical and Computational Methods in Genome Research, Plenum Press, 1997.

Schulze-Kremer, S., Molecular BioInformatics: Algorithms and Applications, W. de Gruyter, Berlin-New York, 1996.

Gusfield, D., Algorithms on Strings, Trees and Sequences: Computer Science and Computational Biology, Cambridge University Press, 1997.

Hunter, L., (editor) Molecular Biology for Computer Scientists: Artificial Intelligence and Molecular Biology, MIT Press, 1993.

[Creighton] Creighton, T. E., (editor) Protein Folding, W.H. Freeman and Co, 1992.

Srinivasan, S., Homology Folding of Proteins, Springer-Verlag, 1998.

[Lavrac] Lavrac, N., and Dzeroski, S., Inductive Logic Programming, Ellis Norwood, 1994.

Muggleton, S. H., (editor) Inductive Logic Programming, Academic Press, 1992.

Books on Molecular Biology

[Gonick] Gonick, L. and Wheelis M., The Cartoon Guide to Genetics, Harper Perennial, 1991.

[Bailey] Bailey, J., Genetics and Evolution: The Molecules of Inheritance, Oxford University Press, New York, 1995.

[Berg] Berg, P., and Singer, M., Dealing with Genes: The language of heredity, University Science Books, Mill Valley, CA, 1992

Calladine, C.R., and Drew, H.R., Understanding DNA: The Molecule and How it Works, Second Edition, Academic Press, 1997.

[Lewin] Lewin, B., Genes VI, Oxford University Press, 1997

[Freifelder] Freifelder, D., and Malacinski, G.M., (editors), Essentials of Molecular Biology, Second Edition, Jones and Bartlett, 1993.

Articles

[Searls] Searls, D.B. The Linguistics of DNA, American Scientist, v, 80, pp 579-591, 1992.

[Turcotte] Turcotte, M., Muggleton, S.H., Sternberg, M.J.E., Application of Inductive Logic Programming to Discover Rules Governing the Three-Dimensional Topology of Protein Structure, in Lecture Notes in Computer Science 1446 (subseries LNAI), pp. 53–64, Springer-Verlag, 1998.

Hayes, B., The Invention of the Genetic Code, American Scientist, v 86, pp8-14

Holm, L and Sander, C., Mapping the Protein Universe, Science, v 273, pp 595-602, Aug. 1996.

Fickett, J.W., Finding Genes by Computer: The State of the Art, Trends in Genetic, v12, n8, pp 316-320, Aug. 1996.

Haseltine, W.A., Discovering Genes for New Medicines, Scientific American, pp 92-97, March 1997.
Kardar, M., Which Came First, Protein Sequence or Structure, Science, v273, p 610, Aug. 1996.

Journals

Science, Nature, Journal of Computational Biology, Computer Applications in BioSciences, Trends in Genetics, Journal of Mathematical Biology

Biological Computers

Adelman, L., Molecular Computations of Solutions to Combinatorial Problems, Science, v266, pp 1021-1024, 1994.
Adelman, L., Computing with DNA, Scientific American, August 1998, pp 54-61.
Gramss, T. et al , Non-Standard Computation, Wiley-VCH Publishers, 1998

Web Courses Worth Consulting:

Primer on Molecular Genetics from the U.S. Department of Energy
`http://www.ornl.gov/TechResources/Human_Genome/publicat/primer/intro.html`

Stanford Site A course on Bio Infórmatics offered by the Stanford Medical School and the CS Department
`http://smi-web.stanford.edu/projects/helix/mis214/`

The MIT Site on Introduction to Biology
`http://esg-www.mit.edu:8001/esgbio/chapters.html`

Yahoo Molecular Biology Page
`http://www.yahoo.com/Science/Biology/Molecular_Biology/`

University of Washington at Saint Louis
`http://www.ibc.wustl.edu/CMB/`

Searl's papers in WWW
`http://cbil.humgen.upenn.edu:80/~dsearls/papers`

Olivier Baby's Dissertation on Exon-Intron Recognition
`http://www.cs.brandeis.edu/~obaby`

Computing with DNA
`http://users.aol.com/ibrandt/dna_computer.html`

Adding Constraints to Logic-based Formalisms

Michael J. Maher

School of Computing and Information Technology, Griffith University,
Nathan 4111, Australia

Summary. Constraints are predefined relations with a special implementation mechanism. Logic formalisms provide specific reasoning facilities. We look at the effect of adding constraints to existing logic-based executable formalisms, focusing on the semantics of the combined formalisms. We find that in cases where this has been successful the operations of the formalism can be formulated logically and then extended easily to constraints. In many cases a disjunctive property of the constraints is reflected in the combined formalism, to the detriment of efficiency.

1 Introduction

Constraints are essentially relations among variables ranging over fixed domains. Since most logics incorporate predicate symbols – which are interpreted as relations – and variables, there is clearly a degree of compatibility between constraint- and logic-based formalisms. Indeed, in some sense both constraint programming and logic programming can be considered part of an umbrella relational programming paradigm.

On the other hand, there are differences between the aims of implementation and execution for constraint-based and logic-based formalisms. Logic-based formalisms have focussed on inferences of a generic form, often characterized in terms of logical consequence, which are independent of a domain of interpretation. In contrast, constraint-based formalisms have focussed on specific interpretations of the symbols they use and – in many cases – algorithms specific to these interpretations. Thus constraint solving is commonly specialized to particular domains whereas logic-based formalisms work from more generic rules of inference.

The preceding discussion does not provide the full story, of course. There has been a successful general-purpose approach to constraint solving via notions of consistency [35,56], and steady progress in developing specialized algorithms for logic formalisms to handle axiomatizations involving equality [51]. Nevertheless it is largely true that constraint solving assumes a fixed domain of values, whereas logic reasons over all possible domains.

It has become clear in recent years that the outcome of the combination of constraints and logic-based formalisms can be greater than the sum of the parts: the constraints field offers specialized algorithms and logic offers reasoning frameworks in which these algorithms can most easily be exploited. The common underlying relational language binds the two together.

In this paper we look at combining constraint reasoning with logic-based formalisms, focusing on the semantics of the combined formalisms. We survey much of the existing work on combined formalisms, and hope to outline some principles which can guide further combinations.

In the next two sections we introduce logical formalisms and constraints. We then outline some common and useful techniques for formalizing the combination of a logic formalism and a constraint domain. Then we review several situations where constraints and a logic formalism have been combined. Finally, we summarize some principles which can be drawn from the foregoing case studies.

2 Logic Formalisms

The mechanization of logic has developed over a long history. Work of Boole, Herbrand, Gentzen and Robinson – to mention only some highlights – has led to many successful implementations of logic-based systems. Most of this work has been in the realm of classical first-order predicate logic.

In classical logic the standard criteria of inference is soundness and completeness with respect to the *logical consequences* of a set of formulas – those statements that are true in all models of the original formulas. The importance of logical consequence comes from the unknown intended meaning of the non-logical symbols (constants, function symbols and predicate symbols). If the sentences S are true under the intended meaning of these symbols then the logical consequences of S are also true under the intended meaning. Thus correct conclusions are drawn, independent of intended meaning.

It is a property of classical logic that function symbols are not needed to achieve its full expressive power. However, through the use of "Skolem" functions, the problem of handling consequences of quantified formulas can be reduced to the problem of handling consequences of universally quantified formulas with function symbols. These function symbols can be interpreted arbitrarily as functions over a domain. However, Herbrand [16] showed that the problem of logical consequence reduces to a case where the function symbols have a certain fixed interpretation. That interpretation has become known as the Herbrand interpretation.

Definition 9. In a *Herbrand interpretation* the elements of the domain are terms, and a function applied to a sequence of terms produces a new term in the normal way of composition of terms.

Since the Herbrand interpretation is very syntactic in construction, symbols under this interpretation are sometimes said to be uninterpreted.

A sentence s is a *logical consequence* of a set of formulas S, written $S \models s$, if s is true in every model of S. Let $skolem(S)$ denote the Skolemization of the sentence s, that is, the unquantified formula with function symbols obtained by transforming the quantified formula s using the Skolemization process.

Theorem 1. *A set S of quantified formulas is unsatisfiable iff $skolem(S)$ is unsatisfiable iff $skolem(S)$ has no Herbrand model (i.e., has no model that is a Herbrand interpretation).*

Furthermore, only finitely many ground instances of $skolem(S)$ are necessary to demonstrate that $skolem(s)$ has no Herbrand model. This provides a basis for procedures that test whether S is unsatisfiable. A naive approach is to work directly with ground instances of formulas in $skolem(S)$, but that is generally intractable. Instead, reasoning can be done directly on the formulas in $skolem(S)$.

Indeed, each $f \in skolem(S)$ can be considered as representing the set of all its ground instances. Any propositional inference rule, for example

$$\text{From } A \text{ and } \neg A \vee B, \text{ infer } B$$

can be extended to such sets; from $p(t)$ and $\neg p(s) \vee q(u)$ instances of $q(u)$ can be inferred, but only those instances where t and s are equal. That is, we can infer $q(u)$ under the restriction that $t = s$. We express this by $q(u) \leftarrow t = s$. When we infer from formulas with restrictions we must conjoin the restrictions; thus from $p(t) \leftarrow e_1$ and $(\neg p(s) \vee q(u)) \leftarrow e_2$ we infer $q(u) \leftarrow e_1 \wedge e_2 \wedge t = s$

Moving from a propositional inference rule to a predicate logic rule in this way is called "lifting", and the literature contains many "lifting lemmas" showing that the predicate logic inference rule faithfully represents the propositional inference rule.

Herbrand outlined an algorithm [16] to simplify the equational restrictions, and Robinson independently proposed his unification algorithm [49]. Usually in the literature the restrictions generated by lifting are represented by the application of substitutions computed by a unification algorithm, following Robinson. However, it has become clear that unification can be seen as solving equational constraints in the Herbrand interpretation [16,28].

This approach to dealing with quantifiers (through Skolemization) and function symbols (through Herbrand interpretation and unification) has become almost universal. Herbrand's work might be thought of as the first addition of constraints to a logic formalism, since it involves a fixed domain of interpretation and a corresponding specialized equation solver. On the other hand, it was introduced as an implementation technique for logical consequence rather than as a new or extended formalism.

3 Constraints

Constraints are predefined relations over a predefined set of values. Given a signature Σ, describing the symbols to be used, the meaning of the constraints is given by a Σ-structure $\mathcal{D}$: the carrier of the structure is the set of values, and each symbol (constant, function or predicate) is mapped to an element, function or relation on $\mathcal{D}$. We assume that Σ contains the equality symbol $=$ which is interpreted as identity in the structure.

In principle, arbitrary formulas constructed from Σ, variables and logical symbols (such as $\wedge$, $\neg$ and $\exists$) might be used as constraints. However, in practice the class of formulas $\mathcal{L}$ that are permitted is usually restricted. For convenience of exposition it is generally assumed that $\mathcal{L}$ is closed under certain operations. The choice of closure conditions varies according to the situation in which the constraints are being used, but usually it is assumed that $\mathcal{L}$ is closed under variable renaming and conjunction of formulas. The closure conditions can be phrased as syntactic closures (e.g. if $c_1, c_2 \in \mathcal{L}$ then $c_1 \wedge c_2 \in \mathcal{L}$) or semantic closures (e.g. if $c_1, c_2 \in \mathcal{L}$ then $\exists c_3 \in \mathcal{L}$ such that $\mathcal{D} \models c_3 \leftrightarrow c_1 \wedge c_2$).

Given Σ, the pair $(\mathcal{D}, \mathcal{L})$ is called a *constraint domain.* We restrict our attention to non-trivial constraint domains, which contain a constraint that is neither universally true nor universally false. From a purely declarative perspective, a constraint domain specifies completely the syntax and semantics of constraints.

However, we will also need to consider the first-order theory of $\mathcal{D}$, which we denote by $T_\mathcal{D}$; $T_\mathcal{D}$ expresses all the first-order properties of $\mathcal{D}$. We have chosen to consider the complete first-order theory of $\mathcal{D}$ here, but in some situations [19,22] an incomplete subtheory is sufficient.

The Herbrand interpretation of a set of function symbols Γ can be considered a constraint domain $\mathcal{H}(\Gamma)$ (or simply $\mathcal{H}$ when Γ is not important). The set of values is the Γ-terms, the function symbols – as before – produce a new term from a sequence of terms, and there is only one predicate symbol, $=$. The first order theory of $\mathcal{H}(\Gamma)$ is Clark's equality theory [5] when Γ is infinite, and Clark's theory with an additional axiom when Γ is finite [41,37].

A second example of a constraint domain is $\mathcal{R}$, where the values are the real numbers, there are constants representing each rational number, functions $+$ and $-$, and relations $=$ and $\leq$ (all interpreted in the usual way).

In practice, single constraint domains are insufficient. Usually a constraint domain such as $\mathcal{R}$ is extended with Herbrand functions as in $\mathcal{H}$. The resulting constraint domain has as domain terms whose constants are either Herbrand constants or real numbers. In general, several constraint domains can be embedded in a single constraint domain. In what follows, we will not consider this internal structure of constraint domains.

An important property of constraint domains, if they have it, is an independence of constraints.

Definition 10. A constraint domain $(\mathcal{D}, \mathcal{L})$ has the *Independence of Negated Constraints* property (INC) if, for all constraints $c, c_1, \ldots, c_n \in \mathcal{L}$,

$$\mathcal{D} \models \tilde{\exists}\, c \wedge \neg c_1 \wedge \cdots \wedge \neg c_n \text{ iff } \mathcal{D} \models \tilde{\exists}\, c \wedge \neg c_i \text{ for } i = 1, \ldots, n.$$

or, equivalently,

$$\mathcal{D} \models c \rightarrow \bigvee_{i=1}^{n} c_i \text{ iff for some } j,\ \mathcal{D} \models c \rightarrow c_j.$$

INC was first formulated and proved by Colmerauer [6] for equations over infinite trees. A more general formulation and its consequences were developed in [29]. Both [29] and [39] have useful weakenings of INC.

The advantages of this property are that:

- testing the satisfiability of a conjunction of constraints and negated constraints reduces to a series of tests involving a single negated constraint,
- problems involving disjunction are simpler, since the disjunction of constraints is no more powerful than the collection of individual constraints.

Thus the INC, when it holds, greatly simplifies constraint solving. In particular, since testing disjunctive statements such as $\mathcal{D} \models c \rightarrow \bigvee_{i=1}^{n} c_i$ is co-NP-hard when INC does not hold [39], it can be the difference between a polynomial and an exponential algorithm.

The language of constraints $\mathcal{L}$ has a substantial effect on INC. Clearly, if $\mathcal{L}$ is closed under negation then $(\mathcal{D}, \mathcal{L})$ does not have INC. The Herbrand domain has INC when constraints are simply conjunctions of equations [28]. However, if $\mathcal{L}$ admits all existentially quantified conjunctions of equations then INC holds iff Σ is infinite [37].

While several constraint domains have INC, many interesting domains do not. Linear equations over the reals have INC, but when inequalities or multiplication are introduced, INC is lost (although a much weaker form of INC does hold [30]). Similarly, constraints over the integers do not have INC unless the language of constraints is severely restricted, for example, to lower bounds on variables.

Since logic formalisms typically only include function symbols that are treated in the Herbrand style, the problem of adding constraints to a logic formalism involves dealing with the extra complexity arising when the constraint domain no longer has INC.

To discuss operational aspects we need to consider the constraint solver. In general terms, a constraint solver is an oracle which can answer queries concerning constraints. Depending on the underlying formalism, different queries are important. For example, in constraint logic programming unsatisfiability is needed, whereas in concurrent constraint programming constraint entailment is most important. The term "constraint solver" is a misnomer: rarely are the constraints actually solved by a constraint solver.

To simplify the discussion, we will make some assumptions about constraint solvers. We will assume that each solver answers Boolean (that is true/false) queries about logical relations between constraints, and that every answer it gives is correct. Thus we are assuming a "black-box" solver that is sound. This overlooks "glass-box" solvers, such as the indexical constraints of [15], and stochastic solvers [55] which might give unsound answers. It also overlooks useful constraint manipulations such as constraint simplification. We will assume that a solver takes one primary constraint as an argument, although other constraints might be presented to the solver as part of the query.

A complete constraint solver is one that answers every query. In practice, many solvers do not answer all queries, for reasons that might involve computability, tractability, or simply pragmatics. Such solvers are incomplete, and may answer *true*, *false* or *unknown* (i.e. don't know). The behaviour of arbitrary incomplete constraint solvers can be very irregular, so we consider the following restrictions [22], which impose a degree of structure on the behaviour of incomplete solvers.

Let $\models s$ denote $\emptyset \models s$, $\exists_{-x} f$ denote the existential quantification of all variables in f *except* those in x, and let $\leq_Q$ be a class of quasi-orderings parameterized by Q that represents the "strength" of the answers to queries. A constraint solver $solv_Q$ for queries Q in constraint domain $(\mathcal{D}, \mathcal{L})$ is required to be:

logical: $solv_Q(c_1) = solv_Q(c_2)$ whenever $\models c_1 \leftrightarrow c_2$. That is if c_1 and c_2 are logically equivalent ***using no information*** about the constraint domain, then the solver answers the same for both.

monotonic: $solv_Q(c_1) \leq_Q solv_Q(c_2)$ whenever $\models c_1 \leftarrow \exists_{-vars(c_1)} c_2$. That is, whenever c_2 contains "more information" than c_1 the solver gives a stronger (or equal) answer on c_2.

To illustrate this framework, consider the query *unsat*, that asks whether the given constraint is unsatisfiable in $\mathcal{D}$. We define $\leq_{unsat}$ as follows: $true >_{unsat} false$, $true >_{unsat} unknown$ and $false \leq_{unsat} unknown$ and $unknown \leq_{unsat} false$. A complete constraint solver for *unsat* is monotonic. The appropriate quasi-ordering depends very much on the query Q. For example, for the query $imp(c')$, which asks whether the given constraint implies c', we define $true >_{imp(c')} unknown$ and $false >_{imp(c')} unknown$. A complete constraint solver for $imp(c')$ is monotonic.

Even with these restrictions on the behaviour of the constraint solver, the behaviour of a system with an incomplete solver can be difficult to predict since the declarative reading of the constraints may not be reflected by the behaviour of the solver. This is a source of difficulty in using constraints in logic formalisms.

4 Adding Constraints to Logic Formalisms

The notion of an interpretation for a logic formalism with constraints is largely determined by the notion of interpretation for the logic formalism and the constraint domain defining the constraints. In a straightforward approach, the interpretations suitable for the constrained logic formalism are simply those interpretations of the logic formalism in which the only individuals are those present in $\mathcal{D}$, and the meaning of the symbols in Σ is given by $\mathcal{D}$. In the case of classical logic, interpretations are those extensions of $\mathcal{D}$ which give meaning to the remaining symbols.

Potentially, we are addressing a wide range of logic-based formalisms, from subsets of classical logic to higher order logics and non-classical logics such as modal logics and linear logic. However, with this wide variety of logic formalisms there is little hope of extracting useful uniform techniques. The logic-based formalisms we will focus on are largely languages (or sub-languages) where there are few or no alternations of quantifiers. Usually variables are (perhaps implicitly) universally quantified.

If the logic formalism is simply universal (i.e. all formulas are of the form $\forall x_1 \forall x_2 \ldots \forall x_n\ \psi$ where ψ is a quantifier-free formula) we can make use of the constraints in a restricted way, inspired by Herbrand's technique. Essentially, we can treat ψ as a schema, representing the many propositional formulas obtained by replacing the variables by elements of $\mathcal{D}$ and treating the resulting instantiated atoms as propositions. Furthermore, we can use constraints to express restrictions, or subsets, of the set of all such propositional formulas. Thus $\psi \leftarrow c$ expresses the subset of formulas generated by valuations that satisfy c.

Using constraints in this way, any propositional inference rule in the logic formalism can be lifted to an inference rule for the constrained logic formalism. Propositional rules are based on the identity of propositions in different formulas. (For example, in an inference rule *from* A *and* $\neg A \vee B$ *infer* B the identity of the first formula and a sub-formula of the second is expressed by using the same proposition name for both.) This identity is lifted to an equality constraint, as it is with Herbrand's technique. In the lifted form of the above inference rule, from formulas $(\psi) \leftarrow c_1$ and $(\neg \rho \vee \phi) \leftarrow c_2$ we infer $(\phi) \leftarrow c_1 \wedge c_2 \wedge \phi = \rho$.

The inferred formula is of no use when the constraint is unsatisfiable (it represents the empty set of propositional formulas), so the ability to detect unsatisfiable constraints is required from a constraint solver.

Thus, by a direct extension of Herbrand's approach, constraints can be incorporated into both the model theory and inference mechanisms of a simply universal logical formalism.

Alternatively, we could allow constraints to be considered as just another kind of atom, so that constraints may appear wherever atoms may. From a semantic point of view, the resulting formulas might be meaningful, but this approach raises problems in adapting the inference rules. As an example, consider the addition of constraints in this way to definite clause logic programming. Formulas such as $c \leftarrow a_1, \ldots, a_n$ are meaningful, but resolution based on the head of this formula is not well-defined.

When the logic formalism permits alternation of quantifiers there are further difficulties in implementing the combined formalism. The Skolemization of formulas might still be valid (as in classical first-order logic, for example), but we cannot employ Herbrand's Theorem to simplify the reasoning we need to do. The reason is that the Skolem functions must be interpreted as functions over $\mathcal{D}$, rather than ranging over all domains, and the pre-defined meaning of the symbols in Σ can further restrict the possible interpretations of the Skolem functions. For example, the formula

$$\exists xy\ x + 1 = 2 \wedge y - 1 = 0 \wedge p(x) \wedge \neg p(y)$$

when Skolemized becomes

$$c_1 + 1 = 2 \wedge c_2 - 1 = 0 \wedge p(c_1) \wedge \neg p(c_2)$$

Clearly, a Herbrand interpretation of the constants will fail to recognize that $c_1 = c_2$.

If Skolemization is employed to implement the original logic formalism then we must abandon that implementation approach or develop a constraint solver that can also handle Skolem functions. (A simple case of the latter is investigated in [17].) In the case where both universal and existential quantifiers appear, but not in the same sentence (as in the above example), we can treat the resulting Skolem constants as variables subject to constraints.

Furthermore, in many non-classical logics Skolemization is not a valid transformation; the meaning of the Skolemized formula is different from the meaning of the original formula. (See [9] for a more careful statement of this point for modal logics.) In such cases, Skolemization cannot be used as a part of the implementation method.

Finally, we must note that, in most cases, consequence with respect to $\mathcal{D}$ cannot be captured by the inference rules over $\mathcal{D}$-schema. That is, the inference rules are not complete for consequences w.r.t. $\mathcal{D}$. This occurs because in general there are infinitary inferences that are valid in $\mathcal{D}$ but are not represented by the inference rules. For example, over the domain of natural numbers $\mathbb{N}$ with successor $+1$ the sentence $S : p(0) \wedge \forall x\ p(x) \rightarrow p(x+1)$ has as a consequence $\forall x\ p(x)$, but this cannot be derived finitely from the schematized inference rules. However, there is still hope if consequences are considered with respect to the first-order theory $T_{\mathcal{D}}$ of $\mathcal{D}$. In the example, $\forall x\ p(x)$ is not a consequence of S w.r.t. $T_{\mathbb{N}}$, since there is a non-standard model of $T_{\mathbb{N}}$ in which $\forall x\ p(x)$ is false.

If we wish to discard the assumption that all individuals are in $\mathcal{D}$ then a complication arises. The action of $\mathcal{D}$-interpreted functions and predicates on non-$\mathcal{D}$ individuals must be handled. (For example, should $\bullet + 0 = \bullet$ be true or false in the combined formalism when $\bullet$ is a non-$\mathbb{N}$ individual?) Perhaps a use of sorts can avoid this problem. Since such an approach has not been deeply pursued, to my knowledge, we will not explore it further.

5 Constraints in Logic Formalisms

We survey and discuss the addition of constraints to several logic formalisms. Although logic programming was the first logic formalism to which constraints, in the sense of this paper, were added [19], there was a significant precursor in automated reasoning [53]. For this reason, and because work on automated reasoning extends naturally the work of Herbrand. we begin the discussion with automated reasoning.

5.1 Automated Reasoning

Many of the comments of the previous section can be applied directly in the field of automated reasoning. A substantial part of this field addresses formulas in clausal form, which is a simply universal formalism. Thus, for example, the resolution inference rule [49] can be extended to admit constraints using Herbrand's technique.

However binary resolution alone is not complete. The propositional notation embeds the idempotence of disjunction: $A \vee A \vee B$ is simply represented as $A \vee B$. To account for this representation it is necessary to add the inference rule called factoring: from $p(s) \vee p(t) \vee B$ infer $p(s) \vee B$ under the restriction that $s = t$. A different extension of resolution that incorporates factoring is defined in [4].

Bürckert [4] showed his extended resolution is complete: a set of constrained clauses S has no model that is an extension of $\mathcal{D}$ iff there is a clause $false \leftarrow c$, where $\mathcal{D} \models \tilde{\exists}\, c$, that can be derived from S using the extended resolution[1].

Each derived constrained clause $A \leftarrow c'$ is of no interest if c' is unsatisfiable since it represents an empty set of propositional clauses; the constraint solving needed is a test for unsatisfiability. Simplification of c' is also useful. Notice that, in the event that the constraint solver is incomplete, constrained resolution can proceed when unsatisfiability of c' is *unknown* under the assumption that c' might be satisfiable. No unsound inferences are drawn, only uninteresting clauses. However, for the procedure to be complete, the constraint in the clause $false \leftarrow c$ must be shown to be satisfiable.

We can expect similar results for other inference rules that are complete under the Herbrand interpretation; very little of Bürckert's proof needs to change, since it is built on completeness at the propositional level and a lifting lemma.

5.2 Logic Programming

The addition of constraints to logic programming is the prototype for all additions of constraints to logic formalisms. This was proposed by Colmerauer and the semantic framework called the constraint logic programming (CLP) scheme was developed by Jaffar and Lassez [19]. The CLP scheme embodies both the straightforward extension of the model theory and the constrained schema approach to adding constraints to the language that were discussed in the previous section.

---

[1] The results of [4] are presented in a more general context.

To the extent that logic programming is based on Horn clauses the results for clausal reasoning carry over. A program consists of clauses written as rules, for example $p(x) \Leftarrow q(x,y), r(y)$. A goal, or query, is written $false \Leftarrow p(x), r(x)$. A program and goal is unsatisfiable exactly when the program implies that the body of the goal is satisfiable. SLD-resolution is complete, and can be extended with constraints in the same way as binary resolution. However, there is an important feature of logic programming that is not addressed in the previous section: the computation of answers[2].

If we interpret a goal $false \Leftarrow p(x), q(x)$ as a clause $\forall x\ \neg p(x) \vee \neg q(x)$ then we have trouble associating the variables in the goal with the variables in the answer constraints. Instead, we can negate the clause and Skolemize, producing $p(a) \wedge q(a)$, where a is a Skolem constant. Every occurrence of a in a constraint refers to the variable in the original goal. As discussed previously, we cannot treat a as a Herbrand constant; in fact, we will treat these Skolem constants as global variables that can be constrained.

With this treatment, SLD-resolution produces answers which are the accumulated constraints from each resolution step. The answers satisfy a stronger completeness property than the one above. For a program P and a query $q(x)$, SLD-resolution produces (possibly infinitely many) answers $c_1, c_2, \ldots$. These answers present exactly the meaning of the query, in the following sense:

$$P, \mathcal{D} \models q(x) \leftrightarrow \bigvee_{i=1}^{\infty} c_i$$

Thus, for any valuation v for x such that $q(v(x))$ is consistent with P and $\mathcal{D}$, there is an answer constraint that represents the valuation. Indeed,

$$\text{if} \quad P, \mathcal{D} \models q(x) \leftarrow c \quad \text{then} \quad \mathcal{D} \models c \rightarrow \bigvee_{i=1}^{\infty} c_i$$

However, in general we cannot establish – as we can in logic programming – that

$$P, \mathcal{D} \models c \rightarrow q \quad \text{iff} \quad \mathcal{D} \models c \rightarrow c_i \text{ for some answer } c_i$$

The program $\{q(x) \leftarrow x < 3; q(x) \leftarrow x \geq 3\}$ and goal $q(y)$ demonstrate this clearly. However, if we replace $\mathcal{D}$ by $T_{\mathcal{D}}$, the first-order theory of $\mathcal{D}$, then the infinite disjunction is reduced to a finite disjunction:

$$\text{if} \quad P, T_{\mathcal{D}} \models q(x) \leftarrow c \quad \text{then} \quad T_{\mathcal{D}} \models c \rightarrow \bigvee_{i=1}^{n} c_i$$

for some n, by a compactness argument [36]. If, further, $\mathcal{D}$ has INC then the disjunction can be eliminated altogether and we have

$$P, T_{\mathcal{D}} \models c \rightarrow q \quad \text{iff} \quad T_{\mathcal{D}} \models c \rightarrow c_i \text{ for some answer } c_i$$

[2] An answer is a constraint c such that $false \leftarrow c$ has been derived.

as is true in logic programming.

Also of interest in logic programming is finite failure: the exhaustive search of all SLD-derivations which terminates, in a finite time, without producing an answer. Provided execution is fair [22], the goals which finitely fail have a declarative characterization, and this characterization is preserved when constraints are added to the formalism:

$$P^*, T_{\mathcal{D}} \models \neg q \text{ iff fair execution of } q \text{ finitely fails}$$

Here P^* is the Clark-completion of P [5]. Since P^* contains embedded existential quantifiers, the extension of this result cannot be established with the techniques already discussed. The construction of [20] used to establish this result is specific to $T_{\mathcal{H}}$, but the construction of [59] is of a form that can be extended to other constraint domains. There are many other results that extend from logic programming to CLP, some only if the constraint domain satisfies a certain expressiveness property. See [22] for more details.

If the constraint solver is incomplete then potentially more answers will be found, although the extra answers will be vacuous – they will be unsatisfiable constraints that the solver cannot solve. Similarly, there might be some infinite executions that a complete solver would have failed. Thus, although completeness is retained with respect to answers, the characterization of finite failure is lost. It is shown in [22] that finite failure is well-defined for logical and monotonic constraint solvers, that is, failure does not depend on order of execution.

When negated atoms are permitted in the body of logic programming rules the situation is complicated. There are many proposed semantics for such rules (see [1]) and corresponding execution methods. Many of these semantics are formulated propositionally, so their extension to CLP is straightforward. Kunen's semantics [26] is not, but is possibly the most interesting since it is both declarative and computable. This semantics extends to CLP programs, as shown in [54].

General implementations of these semantics are not well advanced. Negation-as-failure[3] can be implemented in the same way as in logic programming [43], but to make this rule sound execution of such sub-goals should be delayed until the accumulated constraints determine a single value for each argument of q. Kunen's semantics can be implemented by constructive negation [54].

Implementations of negation intending to produce answers need to have a constraint solver capable of handling negated constraints. For example, a program $q(x, y) \Leftarrow x = y$ and a goal $\neg q(x, y)$ should produce the answer $x \neq y$. Similarly, existentially quantified constraints are also needed. Thus the appropriate constraint domain requires a constraint language closed under existential quantification and negation, and so will not have INC.

[3] Negation-as-failure can be expressed: to prove $\neg q$, demonstrate that execution of q finitely fails; if execution of q succeeds (gives an answer) then $\neg q$ fails.

In logic programming, as with most of the other formalisms we will discuss, there is already a constraint domain involved – the Herbrand domain. This simplifies the addition of constraints because we are simply replacing the Herbrand domain with another constraint domain. This replacement is discussed in detail in [38]. Briefly, unification problems become equational constraints; accumulated substitutions become accumulated constraints; unification is replaced by testing for unsatisfiability in $\mathcal{D}$; Clark's equality theory is replaced by $T_{\mathcal{D}}$; Herbrand models are replaced by $\mathcal{D}$-models; and groundedness of variables is replaced by determinedness.

The degree of compatibility between logic programming and its extension with constraints is remarkable. Taking Lloyd's book [32] as a guide, we find that most results and constructions easily extend to constraint logic programming. Extensions are not straightforward only in meta-programming, the use of a type theory to enumerate all Herbrand values, and in Lloyd's semantics for infinite executions. In each of these subjects there is reliance on properties of the Herbrand domain that are not first-order.

5.3 Concurrent Logic Programming

Although based on logic programming, concurrent logic programming languages [50] are focussed on concurrent programming, and a logical semantics has been of limited interest. The execution can be viewed as an incomplete proof procedure for logic programs because there is no search, and because there is an extra condition on the applicability of a rule which makes it possible for execution to halt without success or failure. However, this view distorts the focus on concurrent programming [58].

Of the many concurrent logic programming languages proposed, flat GHC [57] is the cleanest and simplest. In flat GHC, the extra condition on the applicability of a rule is that the atom $p(\tilde{s})$ to which the rule is applied must be an instance of the head $p(\tilde{t})$ of the rule. This rule enables a kind of dataflow synchronization of processes. The generalization of this condition to a constraint context is not obvious, but it turns out that $\tilde{s}$ is an instance of $\tilde{t}$ iff $\mathcal{H} \models \tilde{x} = \tilde{s} \rightarrow \exists \tilde{y}\ \tilde{x} = \tilde{t}$, where $\tilde{y}$ is the variables in $\tilde{t}$ and $\tilde{x}$ is new variables, not appearing in $\tilde{s}$ or $\tilde{t}$. As a result, these languages can be extended to incorporate constraints by allowing a "guard" constraint for each rule and phrasing the condition as implication of constraints [36].

The result is concurrent constraint programming, which has an elegant theory that subsumes concurrent logic programming [3]. A further generalization of such a language [11] has been used to define new constraints in terms of built-in constraints.

If the constraint solver is incomplete for $imp(c')$ queries then execution might deadlock even though, declaratively, execution could proceed. This, of course, makes it harder to program in the language. However, if the constraint solver is monotonic then once a guard is implied by the accumulated constraints, it will remain implied. This is certainly a convenient property to have, and one that motivated the original design of these languages.

5.4 Databases

Conventionally, the theory of relational databases has assumed that data values in relations are uninterpreted constants. In practice, query languages admit arithmetic tests on arithmetic data. Constraint databases have been introduced as a way to admit interpreted data values and to represent possibly infinite relations using constraints. Similarly, the theory of recursive queries and deductive databases has been formulated in terms of Datalog, in which there are only uninterpreted constants.

The extension from the logic formalism of (deductive) database data and queries to constraint databases (CDBs) follows the same path as previous cases. Indeed, first-order queries on databases are essentially a sub-case of automated reasoning and recursive queries are essentially a sub-case of logic programming. Thus facts in a CDB can be represented in the form $p(\tilde{x}) \leftarrow c$ and (recursive) queries can be represented by (recursive) rules with the same syntax as CLP. Some operations such as aggregation (which is not first-order) do not extend readily to constraints, in the sense that the query language is not closed unless further restrictions are made [27].

Despite close similarities with the previous formalisms, there are several operations that have greater relevance in a database context and have not been addressed above. Examples are testing whether a derived fact is subsumed by already-known facts and testing whether a query uniformly contains another (i.e. a query Q_2 produces a subset of the answers to Q_1, independent of the state of the database). In relational and deductive databases, facts are essentially tuples containing constants and variables, and testing for subsumption is straightforward and efficient. In CDBs, several facts can combine to subsume another fact. A derived fact $p(\tilde{x}) \leftarrow c$ is subsumed by existing facts $p(\tilde{x}) \leftarrow c_i$, $i = 1, ..., n$ exactly when $\mathcal{D} \models c \rightarrow \bigvee_{i=1}^{n} c_i$. In cases where $\mathcal{D}$ has INC this test reduces to a collection of tests $\mathcal{D} \models c \rightarrow c_i$, $i = 1, ..., n$.

When testing whether a conjunctive query Q_1 uniformly contains another Q_2 a similar disjunctive problem arises [25,24,38], which similarly simplifies when INC holds. For both these operations, the comparatively simpler definitions in the original formalism are special cases of the general definitions in which INC is exploited.

On the other hand, uniform containment of positive recursive queries is equivalent to $\mathcal{D} \models Q_1 \rightarrow Q_2$ for both Datalog and its extension with constraints [38]. However, this test is more complicated when $\mathcal{D}$ does not have INC. Other query optimization techniques, such as magic sets and selection pushing, apparently extend to constraints in a generic way [47,52], whether or not the constraint domain has INC.

The use of (domain) constraints in integrity constraints increases the flexibility of the integrity constraints, even when the data is purely relational (i.e.

without constraints). Three classes of integrity constraints: functional dependencies, equality-generating dependencies, and tuple-generating dependencies have been extended with constraints [2,39,40]. The corresponding algorithms to test for implication of dependencies reduce to the usual algorithms when constraints are omitted. As above, the algorithms are also simplified when INC holds.

5.5 Non-Monotonic Reasoning

Although many default reasoning techniques (e.g. default logic [48], circumscription [34]) can be applied to arbitrary formulas, they are most often applied to simply universal formulas. Other approaches (e.g. logic programs with negation under various semantics [12,13], defeasible logic [44]) consist only of simply universal formulas. Thus the approach of section 4 is applicable. Indeed, the semantic constructions for these logics carry over almost trivially to logics with constraints.

Even when constraints are not admitted in such logics, disequality constraint processing is necessary to compute consequences (unless formulas are immediately expanded to their propositional equivalents). For example, given the facts $p(x)$ and $\neg q(x,x)$, and the default rule *conclude* $r(x,y)$ *when* $p(x)$ *holds and* $q(x,y)$ *is consistent.* we should conclude $r(x,y) \leftarrow x \neq y$. Thus, as is the case with negation in logic programming, the constraint language needs to be closed under all logical connectives, as remarked in [8]. Hence INC will not hold in the constraint domain. For these languages the constraint solver must test for unsatisfiability, as pointed out in section 4.

Work on abductive reasoning [23] has extended abductive reasoning on logic programs to constraint logic programs. The approach is to treat constraints in the same way as abductive predicates – as conditions that are needed to derive a given goal. These conditions accumulate conjunctively. The test that the accumulated conditions are consistent involves (essentially) executing the conditions as a goal to the CLP program. Failure of the goal indicates inconsistency. The disjunctive behaviour that occurs when the constraint domain does not have INC is embedded in the backtracking behaviour of CLP.

5.6 Non-Classical Logics

The extension of non-classical logics by the incorporation of constraints is significantly more complicated than classical logic formalisms. Both the model theory and proof theory – if they exist – have greater variety and intricacy than their classical cousins.

In a possible-worlds approach to model theory we might want all worlds to have the same domain – the domain of $\mathcal{D}$. This is the most obvious extension as discussed in section 4. Furthermore, we would expect that that the symbols in Σ are rigid, denoting the same thing in every world. Such stipulations can have implications for properties of the combined formalism. For example, in modal logic they imply that quantification and necessitation commute [10]:

$$\forall x \,\square\, \psi \leftrightarrow \square\, \forall x\, \psi$$

The view of universally quantified formulas as constrained schemas of propositional rules justifies an execution similar to that in classical logic: every time two (or more) constrained formulas are "merged" or influence each other through the identification of two (or more) parts, the resulting formula(s) is constrained by the conjunction of the existing constraints and an equation relating each pair of terms that are to be identified.

This approach leaves the constraints somewhat outside the logic. To take an extreme case, conjunction of constraints is being performed, even if the logic formalism does not admit conjunction. Similarly, logical operators of the logic formalism are not being applied to the constraints. Whether this approach usefully combines the properties of the logic formalism and the constraints depends very much on the intended use of the combined formalism.

5.7 Non-logical Formalisms

It should not be forgotten that constraints have been added to formalisms that are not logical in nature. Language libraries such as Solver [18] embed constraint solving in non-logical programming languages. Similarly, rule systems have been extended with constraints [31]. Other constraint programming languages, like 2LP [33], are not presented in logical terms. In these cases, although the formalism itself is not logical, it seems that the ways in which the constraints are used remain logical [46], although it is not clear if it will remain so.

There has also been incorporation of constraints in formalisms that might be considered logical in nature, but have not been addressed by the foregoing. Instances include constraint functional programming [7] and constrained type systems [45].

6 Conclusion

The addition of constraints to logic formalisms permits the formalisms to address interpreted values in a direct way. Unfortunately, not all the properties of the formalism extend to the constrained formalism. Nevertheless, in the discussed case studies many of the properties have been preserved. This is particularly true of simply universal formulas.

In extending Herbrand-based logic formalisms to formalisms incorporating general constraints it seems that there is a general principle involved: if a property (or execution, or ...) of logic formalisms can be expressed purely logically (that is, without specific reference to the Herbrand universe – except as the domain of computation – or to the types of constraints used in $(\mathcal{H}, \mathcal{L})$, or to properties of $\mathcal{H}$ not implied by the first-order theory of $\mathcal{H}$), then that property extends to the constraint version of the formalism over domains which satisfy the Independence of Negated Constraints. For domains that do not satisfy INC, the extension may introduce disjunctions of constraints and operations that are co-NP-hard. When negation is involved, if only indirectly, the constraint domain must express negated constraints and INC will not hold.

One valuable consequence of adding constraints to a logic formalism is that a (generally) different perspective on the original formalism is revealed. In particular, clarity is often obtained, since the constraint perspective allows one to abstract away from the details of the execution of the formalism (such as unification and substitutions).

Constraints are predefined relations for which special implementation mechanisms are used. In this paper we have concentrated on the semantics of constraints and the effect of this semantics on the semantics of a logic-based formalism when they are combined, and not on the implementation mechanism. Although isolated works (for example [22]) have addressed the effects of the special implementation of constraints – such as incompleteness of the constraint solver – there is not yet a significant body of work on this issue. Thus a more detailed study which addresses such issues remains to be carried out.

Acknowledgements

I thank Krzysztof Apt for his comments on an early draft of this paper. This work was supported by the Australian Research Council under grant A49700519.

References

1. K.R. Apt and R. N. Bol, Logic Programming and Negation: A Survey, *Journal of Logic Programming*, 19/20, 9–71, 1994.
2. M. Baudinet, J. Chomicki and P. Wolper, Constraint-Generating Dependencies, in G. Gottlob and M.Y. Vardi (Eds.), *Database Theory – ICDT'95*, Lecture Notes in Computer Science 893, Springer-Verlag, 322–337, 1995.
3. F.S. de Boer and C. Palamidessi, From Concurrent Logic Programming to Concurrent Constraint Programming, in: *Advances in Logic Programming Theory*, Oxford University Press, 1994.
4. H-J. Bürckert, A Resolution Principle for Constrained Logics, *Artificial Intelligence* 66, 235–271, 1994.
5. K.L. Clark, Negation as Failure, in H. Gallaire and J. Minker (Eds.), *Logic and Databases*, Plenum Press, New York, 293–322, 1978.
6. A. Colmerauer, Equations and Inequations on Finite and Infinite Trees, *Proc. 2nd. Int. Conf. on Fifth Generation Computer Systems*, Tokyo, 85–99, 1984.

7. J. Darlington, Y. Guo and H. Pull, A New Perspective on Integrating Functional and Logic Languages, *Proc. Int. Conf. on Fifth Generation Computer Systems*, 682–693, Ohmsha, Tokyo, 1992.
8. J. Dix and F. Stolzenburg, A Framework to Incorporate Non-Monotonic Reasoning into Constraint Logic Programming, *Journal of Logic Programming 37*, 47–76, 1998.
9. M. Fitting, Modal Logic Should Say More Than It Does, in: J-L. Lassez and G. Plotkin (Eds.), *Computational Logic: Essays in Honor of Alan Robinson*, MIT Press, 113–135. 1991.
10. M. Fitting, Basic Modal Logic, in: *Handbook of Mathematical Logic and Logic Programming*, D. Gabbay (Ed.), Oxford University Press.
11. T. Frühwirth, Theory and Practice of Constraint Handling Rules, *Journal of Logic Programming 37*, 95–138, 1998.
12. A. van Gelder, K. Ross and J.S. Schlipf, Unfounded Sets and Well-Founded Semantics for General Logic Programs, *Journal of the ACM*, 38, 620–650, 1991.
13. M. Gelfond and V. Lifschitz, The Stable Model Semantics for Logic Programming, *Proc. 5th International Conference on Logic Programming*, 1070–1080, 1988.
14. P. van Hentenryck, *Constraint Satisfaction in Logic Programming*, MIT Press, 1989.
15. P. Van Hentenryck, V. Saraswat and Y. Deville, Design, Implementation and Evaluation of the Constraint Language `cc(FD)`, *Journal of Logic Programming 37*, 139–164, 1998.
16. J. Herbrand, Recherches sur la Théorie de la Démonstration, thesis, Université de Paris, 1930. In: *Ecrits Logiques de Jacques Herbrand*, PUF, Paris, 1968.
17. T. Hickey, Functional Constraints in CLP Languages, in: *Constraint Logic Programming: Selected Research*, F. Benhamou and A. Colmerauer (Eds.), MIT Press, 355–381, 1993.
18. ILOG, *ILOG Solver 4.2 Reference Manual*, 1998.
19. J. Jaffar and J-L. Lassez, Constraint Logic Programming, *Proc. 14th ACM Symposium on Principles of Programming Languages*, 111–119, 1987.
20. J. Jaffar, J-L. Lassez and J.W. Lloyd, Completeness of the Negation as Failure Rule, *Proc. IJCAI-83*, 500–506, 1983.
21. J. Jaffar and M.J. Maher, Constraint Logic Programming: A Survey, *Journal of Logic Programming 19/20*, 503–581, 1994.
22. J. Jaffar, M.J. Maher, K.G. Marriott and P.J. Stuckey, Semantics of Constraint Logic Programs, *Journal of Logic Programming*, 37, 1–46, 1998.
23. A. C. Kakas and A. Michael, Integrating Abductive and Constraint Logic Programming, *Proc. International Conference on Logic Programming*, 399-413, MIT Press, 1995.
24. P. Kanellakis, G. Kuper and P. Revesz, Constraint Query Languages, *Journal of Computer and System Sciences*, 51(1), 26–52, 1995.
25. A. Klug, On Conjunctive Queries Containing Inequalities, *Journal of the ACM* 35, 1, 146–160, 1988.
26. K. Kunen, Negation in Logic Programming, *Journal of Logic Programming*, 4, 289–308, 1987.
27. G. Kuper, Aggregation in Constraint Databases, *Proc. Workshop on Principles and Practice of Constraint Programming*, 166–173, 1993.

28. J-L. Lassez, M. Maher and K.G. Marriott, Unification Revisited, in: *Foundations of Deductive Databases and Logic Programming*, J. Minker (Ed), Morgan Kaufmann, 587–625, 1988.
29. J-L. Lassez and K. McAloon, A Constraint Sequent Calculus, *Proc. of 5th. Symp. on Logic in Computer Science*, 52–62, 1990.
30. J-L. Lassez and K. McAloon, A Canonical Form for Generalized Linear Constraints, *Journal of Symbolic Computation* 13, 1–24, 1992.
31. B. Liu and J. Jaffar, Using Constraints to Model Disjunctions in Rule Based Programming, *Proc. American National Conf. on Artificial Intelligence (AAAI)*, 1248–1255, 1996.
32. J.W. Lloyd, *Foundations of Logic Programming*, Springer-Verlag, Second Edition, 1987.
33. K. McAloon and C. Tretkoff, 2LP: A Logic Programming and Linear Programming System, Brooklyn College Computer Science Technical Report No 1989-21, 1989.
34. J.L. McCarthy, Circumscription - A Form of Non-Monotonic Reasoning, *Artificial Intelligence*, 13, 27–39, 1980.
35. A. Mackworth, Consistency in Networks of Relations, *Artificial Intelligence* 8(1), 99–118, 1977.
36. M.J. Maher, Logic Semantics for a Class of Committed-Choice Programs, *Proc. 4th International Conference on Logic Programming,* 858–876, 1987.
37. M.J. Maher, Complete Axiomatizations of the Algebras of Finite, Rational and Infinite Trees, *Proc. 3rd. Symp. Logic in Computer Science*, 348–357, 1988. Full version: IBM Research Report, T.J. Watson Research Center.
38. M.J. Maher, A Logic Programming View of CLP, *Proc. 10th International Conference on Logic Programming,* 737–753, 1993.
39. M.J. Maher, Constrained Dependencies, *Theoretical Computer Science 173,* 113–149, 1997.
40. M. Maher and D. Srivastava, Chasing Constrained Tuple-Generating Dependencies, *Proc. ACM Symposium on Principles of Database Systems*, 128–138, ACM Press, 1996.
41. A. Mal'cev, Axiomatizable Classes of Locally Free Algebras of Various Types, in: *The Metamathematics of Algebraic Systems: Collected Papers, 1936–1967*, Chapter 23, 262–281, 1971.
42. K. Marriott and P. Stuckey. *Programming with Constraints: An Introduction*, MIT Press, 1998.
43. L. Naish, *Negation and Control in PROLOG,* Lecture Notes in Computer Science 238, Springer-Verlag, 1986.
44. D. Nute, Defeasible Logic, in: *Handbook of Logic in Artificial Intelligence and Logic Programming, Vol. 3*, D.M. Gabbay, C.J. Hogger and J.A. Robinson (Eds.), Oxford University Press, 1994, 353–395.
45. M. Odersky, M. Sulzmann, M. Wehr, Type Inference with Constrained Types, *Theory and Practice of Object Systems*, to appear.
46. J.-F. Puget, Constraint Programming, *Proc. Joint Int. Conf. and Symp. on Logic Programming*, 3, MIT Press, 1996.
47. R. Ramakrishnan, Magic Templates: A Spellbinding Approach to Logic Programs, *Journal of Logic Programming*, 11, 189–216, 1991.
48. R. Reiter, A Logic for Default Reasoning, *Artificial Intelligence* 13, 81–132, 1980.

49. J. A. Robinson, A Machine-Oriented Logic Based on the Resolution Principle, *Journal of the ACM* 12(1), 23–41, 1965.
50. E. Shapiro, The Family of Concurrent Logic Programming Languages, *ACM Computing Surveys 21*, 412–510, 1989.
51. J. Siekmann, Unification Theory, *Journal of Symbolic Computation*, 7, 207–274, 1989.
52. D. Srivastava and R. Ramakrishnan, Pushing Constraint Selections, *Journal of Logic Programming*, 16, 361–414, 1993.
53. M. Stickel, Automated Deduction by Theory Resolution, *Journal of Automated Reasoning* 1, 333–355, 1984.
54. P. Stuckey, Negation and Constraint Logic Programming, *Information and Computation*, 118(1), 12–33, 1995.
55. P.J. Stuckey and V. Tam, Models for using Stochastic Constraint Solvers in Constraint Logic Programming, *Proc. Conf. on Programming Language Implementation and Logic Programming*, LNCS 1140, 423–437, 1996.
56. E. Tsang, *Foundations of Constraint Satisfaction*, Academic Press, 1993.
57. K. Ueda, Guarded Horn Clauses, *Proc. Japanese Logic Programming Conf.*, LNCS 221, 1985.
58. K. Ueda, Concurrent Logic/Constraint Programming: The Next 10 Years, this volume.
59. D.A. Wolfram, M.J. Maher and J.-L. Lassez, A Unified Treatment of Resolution Strategies for Logic Programs, *Proc. Second Int. Conf. on Logic Programming*, Uppsala, 263–276, 1984.

6 Machine Learning

The contributions in this chapter deal with *inductive logic programming*, which has been an active area of research since the early nineties. Inductive logic programming studies machine learning within the representations offered by computational logic and is considered as one of the more applicable subareas of computational logic.

De Raedt analyses the developments in inductive logic programming and gives special attention to the methodology that underlies it. To this end he provides a quantitative and qualitative study of the role of theory, techniques and applications in inductive logic programming. At the same time he analyses the relation of inductive logic programming to computational logic.

In inductive logic programming, background knowledge is used to learn new concepts in a supervised learning mode. *Inverse entailment* is one of the most promising methods for generating appropriate hypotheses that explain a given example w.r.t. a given background knowledge. It restricts hypotheses to single clauses and tries to compute the *most specific hypothesis* (MSH) entailed by all feasible single clause hypotheses. However, inverse entailment is known to be incomplete.

Furukawa studies inverse entailment and discusses new results based on the enhancement of MSH that make it complete in computing possible hypotheses. He also introduces a new branch of inductive logic programming that incorporates the idea of abduction.

A Perspective on Inductive Logic Programming

Luc De Raedt

Department of Computer Science, Katholieke Universiteit Leuven,
Celestijnenlaan 200A, B-3001 Heverlee, Belgium

Summary. The state-of-the-art in inductive logic programming is surveyed by analyzing the approach taken by this field over the past 8 years. The analysis investigates the roles of 1) logic programming and machine learning, 2) theory, techniques and applications, and 3) various technical problems addressed within inductive logic programming.

1 Introduction

The term inductive logic programming was first coined by Stephen Muggleton in 1990 [1]. Inductive logic programming is concerned with the study of inductive machine learning within the representations offered by computational logic. Since 1991, annual international workshops have been organized [2-8]. This paper is an attempt to analyze the developments within this field. Particular attention is devoted to the relation between inductive logic programming and its neighboring fields such as machine learning, computational logic and data mining, and to the role that theory, techniques and implementations, and applications play. The analysis clearly shows that inductive logic programming is a healthy field and it also points out a number of new challenges that it should address.

As with all essays of this kind, the reader should be aware that the perspective and analysis given is the author's one, and may not be generally accepted. Also, this essay is not meant as an introduction to the field of inductive logic programming. For such introductions, I refer to [9-11].

The paper is organized as follows: Section 2 situates inductive logic programming within machine learning and data mining; Section 3 analyzes the role of theory, techniques and applications in inductive logic programming; Section 4 investigates the relation of logic programming to inductive logic programming, and finally, Section 5 provides some directions for further research.

2 Inductive Logic Programming

The motivation for inductive logic programming comes from the field of machine learning [12]. Inductive learning techniques generalize specific observations into general laws. These laws can be used for explanatory or predictive purposes. Typically, one distinguishes two kinds of induction. Descriptive induction (Fig. 1a) starts from unclassified examples and induces a set of regularities these examples have in common. A typical application of descriptive induction is basket analysis where one analyzes the buying behavior of customers. Association rule discovery algorithms could e.g. discover that if customers buy sausage and mustard that there is a probability of 80 per cent that they will also buy beer. Typical systems that perform descriptive induction include Wrobel's MIDOS [20] and De Raedt and Dehaspe's Claudien [19]. Descriptive induction is used to gain insight into the properties that underly a given data set (without focusing too much on classification purposes).

Predictive induction (illustrated in Fig. 1b) starts from a set of observations or examples that are classified in two or more classes. The aim then is to find a hypothesis that classifies the examples in the correct class. Such hypotheses are then used for predicting the class of unclassified examples. A typical application is medical diagnosis where one starts from a set of patients (including symptoms and diagnosis) and aims at finding a hypothesis that will diagnose the patients starting from their symptoms. Typical systems that perform predictive induction include Quinlan's FOIL [17], Emde and Wettschereck's RIBL [18], Muggleton's Progol [16] and Blockeel' Tilde [21].

Within machine learning, predictive induction has received by far more attention than descriptive induction. The reason for this is that it is easy to evaluate. It is only with the advent of data mining that descriptive induction has become popular. The main problem with this form of induction is the interpretation of the results. Typical association rule discoverers would generate large numbers of regularities.

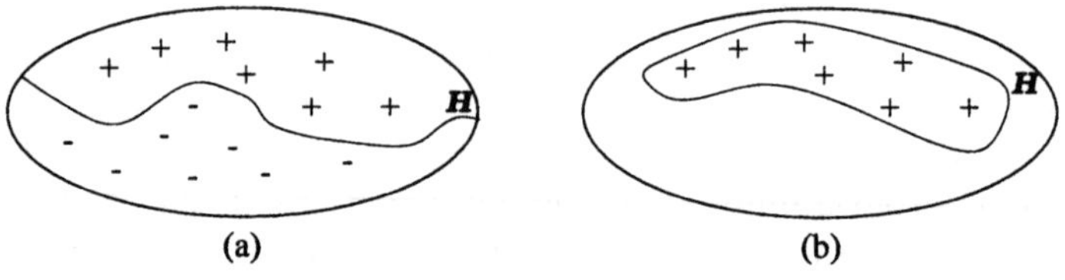

Fig. 1. Descriptive (a) versus Predictive Induction (b)

Data mining [13] and machine learning systems are often distinguished along other dimensions. Perhaps the most important dimension used is the representation. One then typically distinguishes propositional from first order representations. Propositional or attribute-value representations use a single table to represent the data set. Each example or observation then corresponds to a single tuple in a single relation. For all of the attributes the example then has one single value. On the other hand, relational learning and inductive logic programming employ first order structural representations. For instance, in the learning from interpretations setting an example corresponds to a set of facts. This generalizes attribute-value representations as examples now may consist of multiple tuples belonging to multiple tables. Because of the use of a more expressive representation inductive logic programming techniques are often computationally more expensive than their propositional counterparts. However, it is also the case that some applications (e.g. in biochemistry [22]) do require the richness of representation offered by inductive logic programming.

3 The Methodology of Inductive Logic Programming

From the very start of inductive logic programming (i.e. since the first workshop on inductive logic programming), the field has addressed three components: theory, techniques and implementations, and applications and experiments. The ideal view of inductive logic programming, often defended by its founder, Stephen Muggleton, is that the share of these three issues should be more or less equal. If so, there will be genuine interactions between theory, techniques and applications and one can talk of a healthy science.

At this point the question arises as to what extent the field has followed this standard. Some insight into possible answers for this question can be gained by investigating the past proceedings of the international inductive logic programming workshops and trying to quantify the shares of the three components. One possible quantification can be obtained by classifying all papers in one of the three categories of work depending on its main emphasis. Though such classifications are subjective by nature, the results of one such classification for the period 1991-1997 is given in Fig. 2.[1]

From these graphs there is no clear evolution of the shares of theory, techniques and applications. Nevertheless, the reader may notice that in all years all issues have been addressed to some extent. Perhaps the most important conclusion comes from summarizing over the considered years. The results are given in Table 1.

Theory	66	40%
Techniques	63	38.1%
Applications	36	21.9%

Table 1. Shares of theory, techniques and applications in number of papers and percentages in 1991-1997

From this table it follows that the shares of theory and techniques are more or less equal, whereas the share of applications is smaller but still very

[1] For instance, Ashwin Srinivasan classified fewer papers in the application category in his invited lecture at ILP-98.

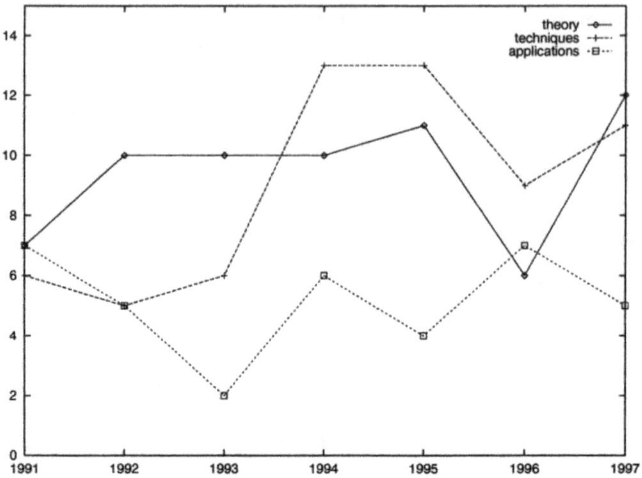

Fig. 2. Evolution of three categories of work in inductive logic programming during 1991-1997

significant (more than 20 %). In my opinion, this table shows why inductive logic programming is often perceived as a useful science[2]. One condition for achieving a good balance between the three components seems to be that there different criteria are used for different categories, especially for the application category. Within inductive logic programming workshops, it has always been an explicit policy to encourage application papers. Also, informal criteria used for such papers include: novelty of the application, new insights yielded in the application domain and also new insights into possibilities and limitations of inductive logic programming and its systems.

The balance between theory, techniques and applications also puts inductive logic programming on the same grounds as other successful areas of artificial intelligence such as constraint logic programming [15] and data mining [13].

Let us now investigate in some more detail these three categories of work in inductive logic programming.

3.1 Techniques and Implementations in Inductive Logic Programming

At present, several inductive logic programming systems are available in the public domain and are free for academic purposes (cf. MLnet's web-site at http://www.gmd.de/ml-archive). Well-known inductive logic programming systems include Progol [16], Foil [17], RIBL [18], Claudien [19], Tilde [21] and Midos [20].

[2] E.g., by David Cornwell, the project officer of the ESPRIT project on Inductive Logic Programming (1992-1995), who used this term in one of his reports.

Some of these systems (e.g. Progol, Midos, Tilde and Claudien) are being integrated and tested in commercial data mining systems such as Clementine (Integral Solutions Limited) and Kepler (Dialogis). Their implementation language is mostly C or Prolog. Due to difficulties with Prolog vendors and limitations of Prolog implementations there is a tendency to move towards C. Furthermore, as inductive logic programming is a non-classical Prolog application (due to the use of very large sets of grounds facts), inductive logic programming implementations could be significantly improved by using special purpose Prolog or Datalog implementations. In this way, inductive logic programming could benefit from the research results in deductive databases and Prolog technology. I consider this as one of the most important research directions for inductive logic programming because of the growing interest in and need to handle large data sets efficiently.

3.2 Applications of Inductive Logic Programming

Overviews of various applications of inductive logic programming can be found in e.g. [22]. Current application domains include: bio-chemistry, protein engineering, drug-design, natural language processing, finite element mesh design, satellite diagnosis, text classification, medicine, games, planning, software engineering, music analysis, software agents, information retrieval, ecology, traffic analysis and network management. An excellent example application is the mutagenicity domain [14]. This is an application with three important features: the hypotheses were generated by a general purpose inductive logic programming engine (Progol), the results were judged understandable by human experts, and new scientific insights in the application domain have been obtained (in particular, a new structural alert for mutagenic compounds was published in top-journals in the application domain). It should be mentioned that not all applications of inductive logic programming are of this kind. Indeed, different types of application papers can be distinguished. The first and most important class of applications (to which inductive logic programming owes much of its success) contains those applications for which new insights have been induced in the application domain (such as in the mutagenisis domain). This category has so far mostly been concerned with bio-chemistry, proteins, drugs, ecology and engineering. Another important class of application papers is concerned with applications that cannot easily be solved with classical attribute value learning systems. Such applications prove the need for inductive logic programming. Applications in this area include traffic analysis, natural language processing, information retrieval, ... The third class of application papers is exploratory and tries to prove that - in principle - inductive logic programming is applicable to a certain problem. Applications in this domain include music analysis, game-playing, and planning.

Finally, it should be mentioned that basically any paper about implementations or techniques in inductive logic programming should have an experimental section in order to validate the proposed techniques.

3.3 Theory of Inductive Logic Programming

The theoretical basis of inductive logic programming is grounded in computational learning theory [23] and computational logic.

Computational learning theory studies the convergence and complexity of learning using probability theory. Several authors have applied computational learning theory to inductive logic programming. A good overview can be found [24]. Despite this, most PAC-learning results for inductive logic programming are negative (mainly due to the polynomial complexity requirement) and hence a bit disappointing . Because of this the interest in this topic seems to have slightly decreased within inductive logic programming (but see [25,26] and [34] for some exciting new results).

Computational logic provides the basic representation formalisms, semantics and inference methods underlying inductive logic programming. Therefore one may wonder how much work within inductive logic programming is concerned with issues in computational logic. To this aim, I performed a quantitative analysis in the same style as for theory, implementations and applications. Again the papers of past international inductive logic programming workshops were classified. The aim was to understand how much work within inductive logic programming could be of relevance to or follows the same methodology or style as its parent field logic programming. This criterion was applied quite loosely. The results are illustrated in Fig. 3. The same caveat as before applies: this classification is by nature subjective.

The share of logic programming oriented work is more or less stable (with an exception in 1995): there is about 31 % of work related to logic programming. One conclusion that follows from this is that inductive logic programming is still closer to machine learning and data mining than to computational logic. Further insight can be obtained by investigating the topics studied in the intersection of inductive logic programming and computational logic. This is done in the next section.

4 The Relation Between Inductive Logic Programming and Logic Programming

4.1 An Analysis

The 31% of computational logic oriented work in inductive logic programming can be further classified according to the topic addressed. The most important results are shown in Table 2. The table clearly shows that the main issues are program synthesis and rules and frameworks for inductive inference. The

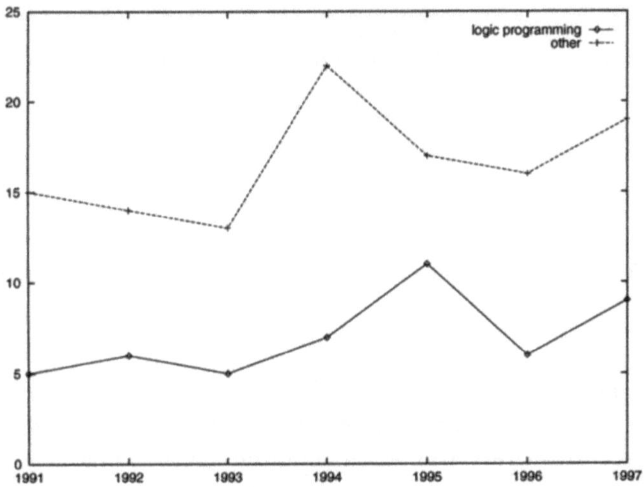

Fig. 3. The share of logic programming oriented work in inductive logic programming during 1991-1997

table also shows that there are several papers on issues that are not easily put under a common research topic. Let us briefly review all of these topics.

Inductive inference rules and operators are needed in order to generalize specific observations into general laws. They also determine the topology of the search space. Inductive inference operators are typically obtained by inverting deductive inference rules. If G $\models$ S, G is considered more general than S and S can be obtained from G by applying a sequence of deductive inference operators such as e.g. the resolution principle. On the other hand, G can be obtained by performing inductive inference, and thus by doing the inverse, that is by applying deductive inference rules in the inverse direction. This has led to various frameworks and operators for induction (cf. [9]). It is without any doubt the most important research topic in the theory of inductive logic programming. It is also the topic that has followed most closely the theory of logic programming. The vast majority of current inductive logic programming techniques is still based on Plotkin's framework for (-subsumption, developed in 1970. As this framework restricts S and G to single clauses, it is clear that there are still many unresolved questions and opportunities for research (e.g. about inverse implication or inverse resolution).

The second topic is program synthesis from examples, a topic that has been studied in computational logic since the seminal work of Ehud Shapiro [27]. However, despite vast amounts of work within inductive logic programming and beyond, program synthesis from examples alone proves to be a very hard task. The state-of-the-art is that inductive logic programming systems are able to induce the quicksort predicate from 7 examples if they already know sort and append. This is unlikely to be useful in practice and explains

Inference rules	16	30.8 %
Program Synthesis	12	23.1 %
Other issues	10	19.2 %
Negation	4	7.7 %
Constraint Logic Programming	4	7.7 %
Abduction	3	5.8 %
Implementation	3	5.8 %

Table 2. Different computational logic issues in inductive logic programming

why the interest in program synthesis [3] has decreased since 1995. This situation is unlikely to change in the near future. Because the scientific challenges (such as recursion) are similar in program synthesis as in grammar induction, the attention of the inductive logic programming community is shifting towards natural language processing. It is hoped that grammars are more constrained than logic programs and may therefore be easier to learn.

A third topic is negation. Semantics for negation has been a major topic of attention in computational logic. Nevertheless, within inductive logic programming this has not been a major research issue. This could be due to the difficulties to induce recursive programs. Without recursion, all semantics for negation basically coincide.

Constraint logic programming in combination with inductive logic programming has received some attention also in recent years.

There is quite some interest in the relation among abductive and inductive logic programming (cf. [28]). Also, abductive techniques can often be embedded within inductive ones. This is useful for instance for theory revision.

There is also some work on implementation issues of inductive logic programming (e.g. about how to integrate databases with inductive logic programming). Some of the other issues are concerned with different problem-settings (sometimes called semantics) for inductive logic programming, distances, meta-programming, ...

Finally, at present there is an increased interest in developing distance measures for inductive logic programming. As distances form the basis of several well-known propositional learning algorithms (such as k-nearest neighbor and k-means clustering), developing distances for inductive logic programming is a very important topic of research.

[3] Program synthesis was studied in the European ESPRIT project Inductive Logic Programming (1992-1995) but is not addressed in the follow-up project on Inductive Logic Programming II.

4.2 A Broader Perspective

Another perspective on the relation among induction and logic programming can be obtained by looking at the state-of-the-art in inductive logic programming with regard to applications and systems.

It is the case that some well-known systems (such as, e.g., FOIL [17]) basically employ a Datalog representation. Furthermore, most systems are limited to learning single non-recursive predicates. Those systems that do address recursion often have theoretical problems (such as correctness and termination), are inefficient, or else very much tuned towards program synthesis. These problems arise because if one learns multiple predicates or recursive predicates the search space explodes. When learning single predicates, each clause in a hypothesis can be considered independently of the other clauses. For recursive clauses or multiple predicate learning, the different clauses in a hypothesis are interdependent. Hence, the search proceeds at the hypothesis level (i.e., at the level of sets of clauses) instead of at single clauses.

Another reason for this is that in nearly all present applications of inductive logic programming no recursive rules have been found. To the best of my knowledge, so far there is only one recursive rule induced in a real-life application that has been discovered (in the finite-element mesh-design problem [29]).

As a consequence it is fair to say that to a large extent inductive logic programming uses logic programming representations and techniques from the early days (i.e., the seventies). One may wonder why this is so. I believe there are at least three possible explanations. First, some issues are still too difficult for inductive logic programming (such as recursion, negation and program synthesis). Second, there is the perception by some end-users of machine learning and data mining systems that inductive logic programming systems are harder to understand and less efficient than their propositional counterparts. Incorporating more advanced techniques from computational logic can only widen this gap. Finally, it may be that these more advanced techniques are not required in practice. Thus also from this point of view inductive logic programming is still closer to machine learning and data mining than to logic programming.

5 Research Directions for Inductive Logic Programming

In my opinion there are a number of important research directions for inductive logic programming.

First, in the intersection of computational logic and inductive logic programming, more research on inductive inference rules is needed. Related to this are distance measures.

Second, for what concerns scalability of inductive logic programming systems it is crucial to devise special purpose Datalog or Prolog systems tailored towards inductive logic programming. The key points where optimizations are possible are handling large sets of facts in main memory and counting operations (needed to test the coverage of generated hypotheses). For the above two issues, input from the computational logic community seems essential for achieving the goals.

Third, those problems that have proven very hard within program synthesis (such as recursion, theory revision and multiple predicate learning) may be easier to solve within grammar learning and natural language processing.

Fourth, more work is needed to make (inductive) logic programming and its engines more accessible to end-users. This should include intelligent human computer interfaces.

Finally, I would like to propose two other important research directions, which I am currently following. The first one aims at demonstrating that the methodology of and motivation for inductive logic programming not only applies to classification and description within machine learning, but to the whole of machine learning (and perhaps even artificial intelligence). In recent years, techniques have been developed to upgrade propositional clustering algorithms (e.g. [30]), instance-based learning [18], reinforcement learning [31], bayesian networks, ...

The other point is that a tight(er) integration between induction and logic programming can be obtained by following a similar approach as for constraint logic programming. Constraint logic programming essentially adds special primitives to existing logic programming languages such as Prolog, defines their semantics and continues with developing solvers for using the language. Within the data mining community a similar line of research has started to emerge [32]. The purpose is to embed data mining primitives in a declarative manner within database query languages. Given the research results of constraint logic programming, inductive logic programming and deductive databases, it seems natural to develop database mining query languages within computational logic. One such proposal was given by [33]. This approach to inductive logic programming would put the field on the same basis as constraint logic programming.

Acknowledgements

The author is supported by the Fund for Scientific Research, Flanders and by the ESPRIT project no. 20237 on Inductive Logic Programming II. He is grateful to Luc Dehaspe and Wim Van Laer for help with the figures and to the editors for encouraging him to write this paper.

References

1. Muggleton, S.: Inductive logic programming. New Generation Computing, Vol. 8:4, pp. 295-318, 1991.
2. Muggleton, S. (Ed.): Proceedings of the 1sst International Workshop on Inductive Logic Programming, Viano de Castelo, Portugal, 1991.
3. Muggleton, S. (Ed.): Proceedings of the 2nd International Workshop on Inductive Logic Programming, ICOT-Report, Japan, 1992.
4. Muggleton, S. (Ed.): Proceedings of the 3rd International Workshop on Inductive Logic Programming, Ljubjana, JSI-Report, 1993.
5. Wrobel, S. (Ed.): Proceedings of the 4th International Workshop on Inductive Logic Programming, Bad Honnef, Germany, GMD-Report, 1994.
6. De Raedt, L. (Ed.): Proceedings of the 5th International Workshop on Inductive Logic Programming, Leuven, Belgium, KUL-Report, 1995.
7. Muggleton, S. (Ed.): Proceedings of the 6th International Workshop on Inductive Logic Programming, Lecture Notes in Artificial Intelligence, Vol. 1314, Springer-Verlag, 1997.
8. Lavrac, N. and Dzeroski, S. (Eds): Proceedings of the 7th International Workshop on Inductive Logic Programming, Lecture Notes in Artificial Intelligence, Vol. 1297, Springer-Verlag, 1997.
9. Muggleton, S. and De Raedt, L.: Inductive logic programming: theory and methods, Journal of Logic Programming, Vol. 19-20, 1994.
10. De Raedt, L. (Ed.): Advances in inductive logic programming. IOS Press, 1996.
11. Nienhuys-Cheng, S.H. and de Wolf, R.: Foundations of inductive logic programming, Lecture Notes in Artificial Intelligence, Vol. 1228, Springer-Verlag, 1997.
12. Mitchell, T. Machine Learning, Mc Graw-Hill, 1997.
13. Fayyad, U. and Piatetsky-Shapiro, G. and Smyth, P. and Uthurusamy, R.(Eds.): Advances in Knowledge Discovery and Data Mining. MIT Press, 1996.
14. Srinivasan, A. and Muggleton, S.H. and Sternberg, M.J.E. and King, R.D.: Theories for mutagenicity: a study in first-order and feature-based induction. Artificial Intelligence, Vol. 85, pp. 277-299, 1995.
15. Jaffar, J. and Maher, M.: Constraint logic programming: a survey. Journal of Logic Programming, Vol. 19-20, 1994.
16. Muggleton, S.: Inverse entailment and Progol. New Generation Computing, Vol. 13:3/4, pp. 245-286, 1995.
17. Quinlan, J.R.: Learning logical definitions from relations. Machine Learning, Vol. 5, pp. 239-266, 1990.
18. Emde, W. and Wettschereck, D.: Relational instance based learning, in Saitta, L. (Ed.) Proceedings of the 13th International Conference on Machine Learning, Morgan Kaufmann, 1996.
19. De Raedt, L. and Dehaspe, L. Clausal Discovery. Machine Learning, Vol. 26, pp. 99-146, 1997.
20. Wrobel, S. An algorithm for multi-relational discovery of subgroups. In Komorowski, J. and Zytkow, J. (Eds.), Proceedings of the First European Symposium on Principles of Data Mining and Knowledge Discovery, Springer-Verlag, 1997.
21. Blockeel, H. and De Raedt, L.: Top-down induction of logical decision trees. Artificial Intelligence, Vol. 101:1/2, pp. 285-297, 1998.

22. Bratko, I. and Muggleton, S.: Applications of inductive logic programming, Communications of the ACM, Vol. 38, pp. 65-70, 1995.
23. Kearns, M. and Vazzirani, U.: An introduction to computational learning theory. MIT Press, 1994.
24. Cohen, W. and Page, C.D.: Polynomial Learnability and Inductive Logic Programming: Methods and Results. New Generation Computing, Vol. 13:3/4, pp. 369-409, 1995.
25. Khardon, R. Learning first order universal horn expressions. In Proceedings of the 11th International Conference on Computational Learning Theory, Morgan Kaufmann, 1998.
26. Chandra, R. and Tadepalli, P. Learning horn definitions using equivalence and membership queries. In Lavrac, N. and Dzeroski, S. (Eds.) Proceedings of the 7th International Workshop on Inductive Logic Programming, Lecture Notes in Artificial Intelligence, Vol. 1297, Springer-Verlag, 1997.
27. Shapiro, E.Y.: Algorithmic Program Debugging. The MIT Press, 1982.
28. Flach, P. and Kakas, T. (Eds.): Proceedings of the workshops on Abudction and Induction, 1996, 1997, 1998.
29. Dolsak, B. and Muggleton, S.: The application of inductive logic programming to finite-element mesh design. In Muggleton, S. (Ed.) Inductive Logic Programming, Academic Press, 1992.
30. Kirsten, M. and Wrobel, S.: Relational distance-based clustering. In Page, D. (Ed.) Proceedings of the 8th International Conference on Inductive Logic Programming, Lecture Notes in Artificial Intelligence, Vol. 1446, Springer-Verlag, 1998.
31. Dzeroski, S., De Raedt, L. and Blockeel, H.: Relational reinforcement learning, In Page, D. (Ed.) Proceedings of the 8th International Conference on Inductive Logic Programming, Lecture Notes in Artificial Intelligence, Vol. 1446, Springer-Verlag, 1998.
32. Imielinski, T. and Mannila, H.,: A database perspective on knowledge discovery. Communications of the ACM, Vol. 39, pp. 58-64, 1996.
33. De Raedt, L.: A relational database mining query language. In Plaza, J. and Calmet, J. (Eds.) In Artificial Intelligence and Symbolic Computation. Lecture Notes in Artificial Intelligence, Vol. 1476, Invited Paper, Springer-Verlag, 1998.
34. Muggleton, S.and Page, D. A learnability for universal representations, in Wrobel, S. (Ed.) Proceedings of the 4th International Workshop on Inductive Logic Programming, 1994.

From Deduction to Induction: Logical Perspective

Koichi Furukawa

Graduate School of Media and Governance, Keio University,
5322 Endo, Fujisawa, Kanagawa 252, JAPAN

Summary. This paper describes how Inductive Logic Programming is related to Logic Programming. It first introduces Model Inference System developed by Ehud Shapiro and then new Inductive Logic Programming technologies. It shows the technical progress from "subsumption" to "logical entailment" and insists the importance of utilizing "background knowledge." A new computational model for computing induction is presented. It is defined by an iteration consisting of the computation of the Most Specific Hypothesis (MSH) and search in a reduced concept lattice brought by the MSH. This computation model provides an efficient algorithm for computing induction in terms of deduction followed by an efficient search algorithm. This implies that the inversion of deduction can be solved rather efficiently when the problem is restricted to Horn clauses.

1 Introduction

Since the invention of Prolog, logic programming research has mainly been studying the logic of computation in terms of deduction and more particularly by resolution. It has been shown that SLDNF resolution acts as a main computational engine for the execution of Prolog. In a sense, a resolution step is regarded as a fundamental computation step in logic programming. There have been quite a few research and development efforts to investigate efficient execution in logic programming. Resolution step is now very efficient due to a very efficient compiling technique into Warren Abstract Machine.

On the other hand, induction has been thought to be very inefficient due to its too much nondeterminism. In order to show its computational complexity, let us briefly describe Shapiro's Model Inference System (MIS). MIS is a first-order-logic supervised learner based of enumeration, that is, it learns a concept describing given examples by enumerating possible hypotheses one by one and trying to find those which cover all positive examples and do not cover any negative examples. MIS enumerates hypotheses from general to specific by applying refinement operators to too general hypotheses to obtain more specific hypotheses. It succeeded in learning such simple Prolog programs as member, n_th and append. However, it could not learn, for example, quick sort. The reason why it could not learn quick sort is that we need extra predicates for partitioning and for appending lists to build quick sort.

A new school of inductive logic programming began its research activities when the First International Workshop on Inductive Logic Programming was held in Portugal in 1991. The most characteristic feature of the new ILP is its ability to utilize background knowledge. The logical framework of ILP can be described as follows: given background knowledge B, a set of positive example E which cannot be derived from B only, and a set of constraints I, the task of ILP is to find a hypothesis H satisfying $B \wedge H$ entails E while keeping the constraint I. Since B is an arbitrary First Order Theory, we can define it as an arbitrary Prolog program. This capability allows the learning task much simpler than those without background knowledge. This advantage has been proved by several real world examples done by the new ILP in the field of medicine, engineering, software engineering and so on.

Another characteristic of the new ILP school is that it adopts entailment rather than subsumption as its measure of generalization; that is, if a theory A entails a theory B, then A is considered to be more general than B. Since ILP is defined as entailment relation, it is more natural to adopt it as generalization measure than subsumption. Since subsumption is defined by subset relation and substitution, subsumption test can be performed rather efficiently than entailment test where we need a theorem prover.

From the view point of computational complexity, the challenge of the new ILP is to find an efficient algorithm to compute the inverse entailment: to find an appropriate hypothesis H which satisfies $B \wedge H$ entails E, or equivalently $B \wedge \neg E$ entails $\neg H$. The last expression suggests a possibility to compute H (or $\neg H$) in a deductive way.

In section 2, we define a procedure for inverse entailment. In section 3, we investigate the relationship between subsumption and entailment more carefully. In section 4, we introduce efforts to make inverse entailment complete under some condition. In section 5, we give a brief description on abductive inference in ILP. Finally, we conclude by giving future works to be done related to logic programming.

2 Inverse Entailment

In this section, we describe an algorithm for computing inverse entailment. It is defined by an iteration consisting of the computation of the Most Specific Hypothesis (MSH) and search in a reduced concept lattice brought by the MSH. We first give an informal definition of an algorithm for computing the most specific hypothesis given background knowledge and an example.

2.1 Computation of Most Specific Hypothesis

Given background knowledge B and a positive example E, let the most specific hypothesis be $MSH(B, E)$. We assume that the hypothesis consists of single clause. This assumption corresponds to so-called single fault assumption in fault diagnosis where we can fix the system by repairing the single fault. An important fact derived from this assumption is that the negation of a hypothesis becomes a conjunction of (Skolemized) ground facts. Therefore, we can compute the negation of the most specific hypothesis as a conjunction of all (positive and negative) literals which can be derived from $B \wedge \neg H$. Thus, we define the most specific hypothesis $MSH(B, E)$ as follows:

Definition 11. We denote the conjunction of all (positive and negative) ground literals which are true in all Herbrand models of $B \wedge \neg E$ by $\neg MSH(B, E)$.

As shown by Yamamoto [11], there are exceptional cases where MSH-(B, E) does not define the most specific hypothesis. This exceptional case is discussed later in Section 4.

However, the above definition is still valid in most cases and worth to analyze its characteristics further. From the definition, the problem for computing the negation of $MSH(B, E)$ is reduced to consequence finding problem. In some cases, there are infinitely many ground consequence literals. Therefore it is not feasible to compute all consequences. However, we can keep the computation process finite by restricting only those literals which can be deduced by a fixed deduction step. This restriction is known as *h-easiness*. Note that the resulting procedure is finite deductive computation.

2.2 Search in a Reduced Concept Lattice

The next step of the inverse entailment is to search an appropriate hypothesis in a reduced concept lattice defined by the MSH obtained in the last section. The concept lattice is defined as a subsumption lattice having $false$ as its top and $MSH(B, E)$ as its bottom. A simple search procedure is to search the lattice in a top down manner from its top toward to the bottom.

The subsumption lattice is dynamically built by applying refinement operators to a node of the current lattice. Refinement operators for subsumption lattice are 1. addition of a literal and 2. substitution to a variable. Note that the candidate literals for the addition are given as members of the MSH. Therefore, we can systematically generate all possible set of literals by generating all elements of the power set of the MSH. For the substitution part, what is given in MSH is the result of the substitution and therefore we need inverse substitution to those constants or variables in the MSH to make more general clauses. These computation can be done by a rather simple algorithm. The computational complexity of this generation is given as 2^N where N is the size of the MSH. This complexity seems very high but we can further reduce this by pruning nodes with higher score than known minimum score, for example.

Language biases are also used for pruning search. We use mode declaration for specifying restrictions of languages for defining predicates to be learnt. They specify predicates appearing in the body of the definition, argument types and input/output modes for each argument.

After generating a possible candidate clause, it is tested against other positive and negative examples. Those hypotheses covering more positive examples and less negative examples get higher score. In some cases, such as program synthesis, we do not allow any negative examples to be covered. The important thing is that the generated hypothesis must be simple enough compared to those individual facts covered by the hypothesis. Unless otherwise, there is no reason to replace the individual facts by the obtained hypothesis, which is too complicated. We measure the complexity of the hypothesis by the number of literals appearing in it. Should we have covered negative examples, we need to add their number to the complexity measure.

Cover check is done by testing whether an example is proved by background knowledge enhanced by the candidate hypothesis or not. For each candidate hypothesis, we need to perform cover checking for every remaining positive example and for every negative example. This test occupies the majority of the computation time in entire induction. It is crucial to decrease this computation time to improve the global efficiency of the induction task. Ozaki et al. [8] developed several algorithms to avoid duplicate computation within single hypothesis as well as among different hypotheses. The former optimization was achieved by adopting "magic set" technique (or equivalently OLDT resolution). The latter optimization was carried out by keeping proof results consisting of successful positive examples and their substitutions at each node of the subsumption lattice for later use after refining.

3 Subsumption and Entailment

In the last section, we approximated entailment test by subsumption test. Actually, this approximation is valid unless no self recursive computation occurs in the entailment proof. The next example gives the case when entailment holds though subsumption does not hold:

C_1:

$$nat(s(X)) \leftarrow nat(X)$$

C_2:

$$nat(s(s(X))) \leftarrow nat(X)$$

In this example, C_1 entails C_2 but does not subsume it. A corresponding ILP problem is as follows:

Example 1

$$\begin{cases} B_1 = int(0) \leftarrow \\ E_1 = int(s(s(0))) \leftarrow \\ H_1 = int(s(x)) \leftarrow int(x) \end{cases}$$

Then,

$$MSH(B_1, E_1) = int(s(s(0))) \leftarrow int(0).$$

In this example, H_1 is a correct hypothesis because it explains E_1 together with B_1. However, it cannot be computed from $MSH(B_1, E_1)$ using refinement under theta-subsumption because H1 does not theta-subsume MSH.

Note that this case provides users extra capability to give background knowledge and positive examples not only as an exact set of facts to fit the hypothesis but also as a set of related facts which would be interpolated to those facts with exact fit by applying the self recursion.

Muggleton [5] resolved this anomaly by introducing sub-saturants and flattening. Intuitively, this situation can be resolved by simply adding the interpolated literal $int(s(0))$ to $MSH(B_1, E_1)$. The introduction of sub- saturants achieves this. Roughly speaking, a sub-saturant of a given definite clause is a clause obtained by replacing the arguments in the head literal by those appearing in the body, keeping to avoid to have the same literal both in the head and in the body. The following theorem [5] guarantees the effectiveness of sub-saturants computation.

Theorem 1. *Let C and D be definite non-tautological clauses and $\mathcal{S}(D)$ be the sub-saturants of D. $C \models D$ only if there exists C' in $\mathcal{S}(D)$ such that $C \preceq C'$.*

What remains is the problem of cardinality of sub-saturant set. It is known that the cardinality is polynomially bounded if we restrict only function-free definite clause for the above D. However, it is quite simple to convert any clause into a function-free clause plus those clauses defining functions by flattening [5].

4 Completion of the Algorithm

Yamamoto gave yet another counter example for $MSH(B, E)$ not to be the most specific hypothesis. Let us show the example case:

Example 2

$$\begin{cases} B_2 = even(0) \leftarrow \\ \qquad\ even(s(x)) \leftarrow odd(x) \\ E_2 = odd(s(s(s(0)))) \leftarrow \\ H_2 = odd(s(x)) \leftarrow even(x) \end{cases}$$

Then,

$$MSH(B_2, E_2) = odd(s(s(s(0)))) \leftarrow even(0).$$

In this example, H_2 is a correct hypothesis because it explains E_2 together with B_2. However, it cannot be computed from $MSH(B_2, E_2)$ since $H_2 \models MSH(B_2, E_2)$ does not hold.

Yamamoto gave a description of the class of problems for which MSH-(B, E) becomes the most specific hypothesis correctly. He described the class in terms of SB-resolution defined by Plotkin [9]. The essential idea of the characterization is that the derived hypothesis cannot appear more than once in the proof of the example to be generalized (that is, the example used to derive $MSH(B,E)$). SB-resolution excludes such cases. Note that there is a strong similarity between the above two anomalies. In both cases, the derived hypotheses are used more than once in the proof.

Furukawa [1] gave another characteristics to the same class: background knowledge must not contain the example predicate in the body parts of their clauses. This avoids mutual recursion ranging between background knowledge and the hypothesis.

Recently Furukawa [2] and Muggleton [6] gave a complete algorithm by enhancing $MSH(B,E)$ for Horn clauses. For more general cases, no results are derived so far.

5 Abductive Inference in ILP

In ILP, it is implicitly assumed that the target predicate to be learnt is the same as that of examples. However, there is no such restriction in the logical setting of the ILP. Therefore it is possible to infer predicates other than that of examples. Let us consider the problem of guessing missing information in natural language processing. Suppose that we are given the following grammars and dictionary [3].

Example 3

$$\left\{\begin{array}{l} B_3 : s(X,Y) \leftarrow np(X,U), vp(U,V), np(V,Y) \\ \quad\quad vp(X,Y) \leftarrow v(X,Y) \\ \quad\quad np(X,Y) \leftarrow det(X,Z), noun(Z,Y) \\ \quad\quad det([the|X],X) \;\; n([man|X],X) \\ \quad\quad n([dog|X],X) \;\; v([hit|X],X) \\ \quad\quad adj([nasty|X],X) \\ E_3 : s([the, nasty, man, hit, the, dog], []) \\ H_3 : np(X,Y) \leftarrow det(X,U), adj(U,V), \\ \quad\quad\quad\quad\quad\quad noun(V,Y) \end{array}\right\}$$

The corresponding most specific hypothesis is given by:

$$\begin{array}{l} MSH(B_3,E_3) = \\ \quad s(A,B); np(A,C) \leftarrow det(A,D), adj(D,E), \\ \quad\quad\quad\quad\quad\quad\quad noun(E,C), vp(C,F), np(F,B) \end{array}$$

A possible generalization of this bottom clause is

$$H_3 : np(X,Y) \leftarrow det(X,U), adj(U,V), noun(V,Y)$$

Note that cover check for this hypothesis is done by trying to prove each positive example using background knowledge and this hypothesis. The only difference of this proof against the ordinal induction is that this hypothesis does not appear at the beginning but in the middle of the proof.

This capability enriches the usefulness of ILP because it allows us to learn not only rules but also missing facts in background knowledge.

6 Conclusion and Future Research Directions

In this paper, we presented the computation mechanism for realizing inductive inference. We showed that it can be decomposed to the computation of the most specific hypothesis and the search on the reduced subsumption lattice. The computation of the most specific hypothesis is reduced to consequence finding problem, which can be computed deductively. The reduction of the search space can be accomplished by introducing the bottom of the lattice as the most specific hypothesis and by introducing language bias. Many optimization techniques developed in logic programming field can be applied to bring further efficiency. The approximation of entailment by subsumption is recovered by sub-saturants-and-flattening techniques. Finally, $MSH(B, E)$ is extended to achieve its completeness when background knowledge is give as a set of Horn clauses.

An open problem for the completeness of inverse entailment is whether it would be complete for arbitrary clausal background theories.

The induction presented above is regarded as a supervised learning for obtaining classification rules to distinguish positive examples from negative ones. Since the rule is used to predict a class for unseen data, it is also called predictive learning. There is another category in ILP, called descriptive learning. The purpose of descriptive learning is to give description for the entire given data set. Since the technology for accomplishing descriptive learning is quite different from that of predictive learning, it might have seemed that there were no common framework. However, we can define the descriptive learning in terms of our basic logical framework of ILP: given background knowledge B, a set of positive example E which cannot be derived from B only, and a set of constraints I, the task of ILP is to find a hypothesis H satisfying $B \wedge H$ entails E while keeping the constraint I. In this framework, the descriptive learning corresponds to learn the constraint I rather than a hypothesis to explain examples. Descriptive learning is claimed to be more suitable for Data Mining.

There are several directions to extend ILP: 1. extension to disjunctive and non-monotonic logic, 2. extension to constraint logic programming, 3. extension to event calculus, and so on. The first extension would be interesting particularly in the field of law. The second extension is thought to be useful in real world application including arithmetic computations. For the third extension, an attempt to infer domain specific axioms needed to apply event calculus to each field.

Inductive and abductive inferences are quite natural inference types for human being. Abductive inference is often observed in daily life inference to make consistent. An alibi proves a suspect being not guilty. On the other hand, the lack of alibi strongly suggests the suspect being guilty. The latter inference is a kind of abduction. That is, the hypothesis that the suspect being guilty proves the lack of alibi, but not the other way around. Induction is in some sense more feasible than abduction because it contains the process of confirmation by explaining plural examples using the hypothesis. This process increases the feasibility of the hypothesis.

References

1. Furukawa, K., Murakami, T., Ueno, K., Ozaki, T. and Shimaze, K. On a Sufficient Condition for the Existence of Most Specific Hypothesis in Progol, Proc. of ILP-97, Lecture Notes in Artificial Intelligence 1297, Springer-Verlag, 157-164, 1997.
2. Furukawa, K. On the Completion of the Most Specific Hypothesis in Inverse Entailment for Mutual Recursion and Abductive ILP Setting, Proceedings of 32nd SIG-FAI, JSAI, March 1998 (in Japanese).
3. Moyle, S. and Muggleton, S. Learning Programs in the Event Calculus, Proc. of ILP-97, Lecture Notes in Artificial Intelligence 1297, Springer-Verlag, 205-212, 1997.
4. Muggleton, S. Inverting Implication, Proc. of ILP92, 19-39, ICOT Technical Memorandum: TM-1182, 1992.
5. Muggleton, S. Inverse Entailment and Progol, New Generation Computing, Vol.13, 245-286, 1995
6. Muggleton, S. Completing Inverse Entailments, Proc. of ILP98, Lecture Notes in Artificial Intelligence 1446, Springer-Verlag, pp. 245–249, 1998.
7. Murakami, T., Furukawa, K. and Ozaki, T. Realization of Abduction by Inverse Entailment and its Equivalence to Partial Deduction, Proceedings of 32nd SIG-FAI, JSAI, March 1998.
8. Ozaki, T., Furukawa, K., Murakami, T. and Ueno, K. Realizing Progol by Forward Reasoning, Proc. of ILP-97, Lecture Notes in Artificial Intelligence 1297, Springer-Verlag, 227-234, 1997.
9. Plotkin, G.D. Automatic Method of Inductive Inference, PhD thesis, Edinburgh University, 1971.
10. Yamamoto, A. Improving Theories for Inductive Logic Programming Systems with Ground Reduced Programs. Technical Report, Forschungsbericht AIDA-96-19 FG Intellektik FB Informatik TH Darmstadt, 1996.
11. Yamamoto, A. Which Hypotheses Can Be Found with Inverse Entailment? Proc. of ILP-97, Lecture Notes in Artificial Intelligence 1297, Springer-Verlag, 296-308, 1997.

7 Answer Set Programming

Recently, a new declarative computational paradigm, *answer set programming*, emerged from studies of stable model semantics of normal logic programs. This chapter presents the origins of this approach, contrasts it with standard logic programming, describes its key features, and demonstrates existence of important classes of applications.

The paper by **Lifschitz** is devoted to applications of answer set programming in planning and reasoning about action. The paper presents a logic programming perspective of these application areas, discusses some of the achievements of the field and describes challenges related to representing actions and to the design of planners.

More specifically, the paper discusses recent work on action languages and their translation into extended logic programming, on representing possible histories of an action domain by answer sets, on efficient implementations of the answer set semantics and their use for generating plans, and on causal logic and its relation to planning algorithms.

Stable model semantics was introduced to logic programming in the late 80s in an effort to provide an understanding of programs with negation. From the very beginning, however, there was a sense in the logic programming community that stable models did not fit into the paradigm of logic programming. **Marek and Truszczyński** reexamine the place and role of stable model semantics in logic programming and contrast it with a least Herbrand model approach to Horn programs.

The paper describes a computational formalism, *stable logic programming*, based on the syntax of $\text{DATALOG}^{\neg}$ and with semantics provided by stable models. The arguments presented in the paper, developed for the case of normal logic programs, clearly apply to extended logic programs and provide a foundation for the answer set programming. The authors argue that stable logic programming is well-attuned to problems in the class NP, has a well-defined domain of applications, and an emerging methodology of programming.

Action Languages, Answer Sets, and Planning

Vladimir Lifschitz

Department of Computer Sciences, University of Texas at Austin,
Austin, TX 78712, USA

Summary. This is a discussion of some of the achievements and challenges related to representing actions and the design of planners from the perspective of logic programming. We talk about recent work on action languages and translating them into logic programming, on representing possible histories of an action domain by answer sets, on efficient implementations of the answer set semantics and their use for generating plans, and on causal logic and its relation to planning algorithms. Recent progress in these areas may lead to the creation of planners which are based on the ideas of logic programming and combine the use of expressive action description languages with efficient computational procedures.

1 Introduction

This is a discussion of some of the achievements and challenges related to representing actions and the design of planners from the perspective of logic programming.

Describing the effects of actions and generating plans have been at the center of Artificial Intelligence research since the late fifties. In his classical paper *Programs with Common Sense*, John McCarthy [21] discusses the problem of planning his way to the airport, in which an initial state, described by the formula $at(I, desk)$, needs to be turned into a goal state that satisfies $at(I, airport)$. The goal can be achieved by executing first the action $go(desk, car, walking)$, and then $go(home, airport, driving)$. The effect of go is described by the axiom

$$did(go(x,y,z)) \supset at(I,y). \tag{1}$$

Other axioms tell us under what conditions it is possible to walk or drive from x to y; the possibility of executing an action a is denoted by $can(a)$.

More recently, work on representing changes caused by actions has been extended to causal dependencies that do not involve actions, including the cases when the cause and the effect are not even separated by a time interval—they obtain in the same state. If I have a watch on my wrist then $at(I, airport)$ is a cause for $at(watch, airport)$. There is no action or passage of time involved in this causal dependency; it is "static," unlike the "dynamic" dependency between going from x to y and being at y. Combinations of dynamic and static causal dependencies is what allows actions to have indirect effects, or "ramifications." When I go to the airport, $at(I, airport)$ is the direct effect of this action, and $at(watch, airport)$ is one of its many indirect effects.

Once an action domain is described by a formal theory, it may be possible to use a theorem prover for solving planning problems in this domain. The paper by Cordell Green entitled *Application of Theorem Proving to Problem Solving* [11] shows, for instance, how a resolution proof procedure can be used to solve the problem of getting a bunch of bananas hanging from the ceiling just beyond a monkey's reach. The answer literal method allows us to extract the value of the situation variable s from the proof of the formula

$$\exists s\, HAS(monkey, bananas, s)$$

found by this procedure. The value, which equals

$$\begin{array}{l} reach(monkey, bananas, \\ \quad climb(monkey, box, \\ \qquad move(monkey, box, under\text{-}bananas, s_0))), \end{array}$$

encodes a solution to the planning problem. Finding a plan by extracting a term from an existence proof is known as *deductive planning*.

The answer literal method was a precursor of logic programming, and it is not surprising that logic programming has always played an important role in research on describing the effects of actions and on planning.

One other reason why the study of causal dependencies is related to logic programming is that causation is noncontrapositive, just like rules in logic programs. We can say, for instance, that being underpaid usually causes a person to look for another job. But it is not true that the lack of interest in other jobs is usually a cause for being paid well. This is similar to the difference between the rules

$$p \leftarrow not\ q$$

and

$$q \leftarrow not\ p.$$

This formal similarity makes the if operator used in logic programming a better tool for formalizing causality than material implication with its contraposition property

$$\neg p \supset q \equiv \neg q \supset p.$$

Over the years, the early work referenced above has inspired many research projects and scores of papers and monographs. This note is not an attempt to survey all important ideas developed in this research. We concentrate here on a small fraction of these ideas, on just a few threads, and try to show how they interact with each other and what can be expected from them in the future.

2 Incomplete Information

Some examples of reasoning about actions involve the execution of an action in a state that is not completely described. Consider, for instance, three boxes A, B and C. Currently A is empty, but whether or not B and C are empty we are not told. Imagine now that an object is placed in box B. In the new state, A is empty and B is not; about C we still do not know.

In classical logic, the incompleteness of information corresponds to the use of incomplete theories. When the example above is formalized as a classical theory, the set of theorems of the theory might include formulas like

$$Empty(A,0),\ Empty(A,1),\ \neg Empty(B,1) \tag{2}$$

(the second argument of *Empty* represents time, and we assume here that the action in question is performed between the times 0 and 1); the formulas

$$Empty(B,0),\ Empty(C,0),\ Empty(C,1) \tag{3}$$

would be undecidable in the theory— neither these formulas nor their negations would be among the theorems. For traditional logic programming, on the other hand, representing incomplete information is a little bit of a problem. Given a ground atom like $Empty(C,1)$ as a query, a Prolog system can only give the answers *yes* and *no*; it has no way of telling us that the answer is unknown (other than by not terminating). In this sense, Prolog programs are similar to *complete* theories.

The issue of representing actions by logic programs in the absence of complete information was addressed in [9] using "extended" logic programs introduced in [8]. In addition to the negation as failure operator *not*, an extended program can use the second negation symbol $\neg$, taken from the vocabulary of classical logic. The head of an extended rule is not necessarily an atom; it can be also a negative literal $\neg A$. (In the theory of extended logic programs, the term "literal" is reserved for an atom possibly preceded by *classical* negation, not negation as failure.) In the body of a rule, both kinds of negation are allowed. For instance,

$$\neg p \leftarrow not\ p \tag{4}$$

and

$$p \leftarrow not\ \neg p \tag{5}$$

are extended rules. Rule (4), when included in a logic program Π, expresses, intuitively, that p is false if Π provides no evidence that p is true. It formalizes the "closed world assumption" for p. Rule (5) has the opposite meaning: p is true if Π provides no evidence that p is false.

The set of consequences of an extended program is a set of literals. This set may be incomplete—it may include, for instance, literals (2), but neither atoms (3) nor their negations.

3 Action Language $\mathcal{A}$

Many authors who write about representing action domains explain their ideas by showing how they apply to specific examples, such as the Yale Shooting scenario from [12] and its enhancements, or various versions of the blocks world. The method for representing actions in logic programming proposed in [9] is described there in a more systematic way: by defining a translation from an "action language" $\mathcal{A}$ into the language of extended logic programs.

Action languages are formal models of parts of the natural language that are used for talking about the effects of actions. The main elements of the language $\mathcal{A}$ are *effect propositions*

$$A \textbf{ causes } L \textbf{ if } F$$

where A is the name of an action, L is a literal, and F is a conjunction of literals (or, more generally, a propositional formula). The atoms occurring in L and F represent "propositional fluents," that is, conditions that may be true or false depending on the state of the world. The formula F is the precondition which guarantees that L would hold after executing A in a current state. To express that the execution of A causes L under all circumstances, we take the logical constant $\top$ ("true") as the precondition. For instance, the counterpart of (1) in the language $\mathcal{A}$ is

$$go(x, y, z) \textbf{ causes } at(I, y) \textbf{ if } \top \; .$$

The effect of action *Shoot* on fluent *Alive* from the Yale Shooting story can be described in $\mathcal{A}$ by the effect proposition

$$\textit{Shoot} \textbf{ causes } \neg \textit{Alive} \textbf{ if } \textit{Loaded} \; .$$

(Shooting is not assumed to affect the value of the fluent *Alive* unless the gun is loaded prior to the execution of the action.)

According to the semantics of $\mathcal{A}$, a set of effect propositions defines a *transition diagram*—a directed graph whose vertices correspond to states (functions from atoms to truth values) and whose edges are labeled by actions. For instance, the set consisting of one proposition

$$A \textbf{ causes } P \textbf{ if } Q \tag{6}$$

represents the transition diagram shown in Figure 1.

The vertical edge in the right part of the diagram shows that action A, executed in the state in which P is false and Q is true, would make P true, in accordance with the intuitive meaning of (6).

Note, on the other hand, that the two edges in the left part of the diagram are loops. According to the semantics of the language, the values of the fluents are not affected when A is executed in a state in which the precondition Q is

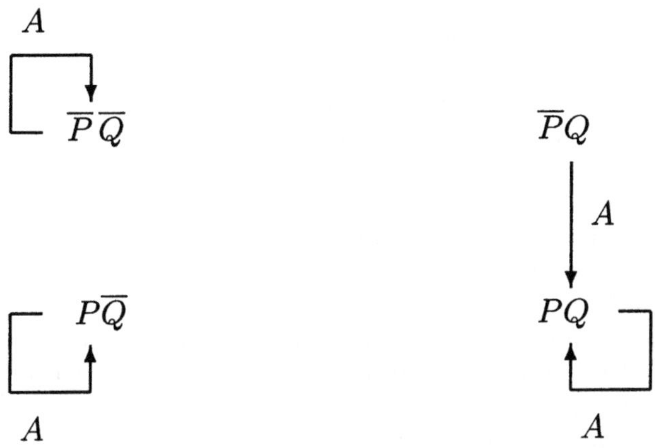

Fig. 1. Transition diagram for proposition (6)

not satisfied. In this sense, the semantics of $\mathcal{A}$ incorporates a solution to (a simple special case of) the frame problem.

The main theorem of [9] shows that the translation from $\mathcal{A}$ into the language of logic programming proposed in that paper is sound with respect to the semantics of $\mathcal{A}$.

4 Answer Sets and Histories

The set of consequences of an extended logic program is defined as the intersection of all "answer sets" (or "stable models") of the program. For instance, the program

$$\begin{array}{l} p \leftarrow not\ q \\ q \leftarrow not\ p \\ r \leftarrow p \\ r \leftarrow q \end{array} \qquad (7)$$

has two answer sets: $\{p, r\}$ and $\{q, r\}$; the only consequence of this program is r.

A program obtained by the translation process from [9] may have many answer sets, and the soundness theorem established in that paper makes no claims about individual answer sets for such a program. It only asserts that a literal which is a *consequence* of the program—that is to say, which belongs to *all* its answer sets—is true in the corresponding action domain.

Alternative translations from action languages to logic programming proposed in [3], [5] and [27] show that there may exist a close relationship between possible histories of an action domain (paths in its transition diagram) on the one hand, and individual answer sets for a logic program on the other. This idea has led Subrahmanian and Zaniolo [26] to the invention of a planning method which is based on logic programming but is different from deductive planning mentioned above. To find a plan that leads from a given initial condition to a given goal means to find a history corresponding to the execution of the plan, and this can be accomplished by finding an answer set for a corresponding logic program.

This method is an instance of what is now called *answer set programming*, or *stable model programming* [18]. It is also similar to *satisfiability planning* [13]—treating a planning problem as the problem of finding an interpretation satisfying a set of propositional formulas. Satisfiability planning has been successfully applied to some of the planning problems that are known to lead to serious computational difficulties in traditional planners [14]. The Subrahmanian-Zaniolo proposal is different in that they suggest using propositional logic programs under the answer set semantics instead of propositional theories.

The problem of finding an answer set for a propositional logic program and the problem of finding a satisfying interpretation for a set of propositional formulas are in the same complexity class: they are both NP-hard, just as the planning problem itself (assuming that the length of the plan is restricted by a polynomial). Using logic programs is an attractive idea because encoding action domains in logic programming may be easier than encoding them in classical propositional logic.

5 Computing Answer Sets

To implement the planning method from [26], we need an efficient system for computing answer sets. One such system, called SMODELS, is described in [23]. The current version of the system does not handle programs with classical negation, so that any answer set it computes is a set of atoms.

Given, for instance, the input file

```
p :- not q.
q :- not p.
r :- p.
r :- q.

compute all
```

as input, SMODELS will generate both answer sets for program (7). In the last line of the file, `all` can be replaced by a positive integer that shows how many answer sets we wish the system to compute. The user can also specify that the only answer sets to be generated are those that include, or do not include, a given atom (or given atoms). For instance, the directive

```
compute 1 {not p}
```

instructs the system to generate an answer set that does not include p.

As the designers of SMODELS indicate, their system is different from familiar logic programming systems in that it *does not perform query evaluation.* It treats a logic program as a constraint on a set of atoms, and generates the sets that satisfy this constraint.

When SMODELS is used to solve propositional satisfiability problems encoded in the language of logic programming, its performance is comparable to the performance of efficient propositional solvers [25].

The availability of this system made it possible for Dimopoulos, Nebel and Koehler [4] to conduct planning experiments using a method similar to the one proposed in [26]. They report that, for careful and compact encodings of planning problems, the performance of their method is comparable to that of efficient general-purpose planners.

Two other systems that can be used for planning in a similar way are DERES [1] and DLV [6] (Esra Erdem, personal communication).

6 Causal Reasoning

The methods for encoding action domains in logic programming proposed in [26] and [4] are not applicable in the presence of static causal dependencies. Consequently, as discussed in the introduction, they cannot be used when plans may include actions with indirect effects. To see how this limitation can be lifted, we need to consider some of the recent work on causal reasoning.

The theory we concentrate on in this section is proposed in [19] and generalized in [16]. Some of its roots are found in [7] and [17].

In this theory, we distinguish between claiming that a proposition is true and making the stronger assertion that there is a *cause* for it to be true. In the example from Section 2, for instance, about the formula $Empty(A, 0)$ we can only say that it is true, but about $\neg Empty(B, 1)$ we can also say that it is caused: its cause is that an object is placed in box B between times 0 and 1. The formula $Empty(A, 1)$ holds "by inertia," and here two views are possible: we can say that there is no cause for it (Lin's position) or that inertia is the cause (as McCain and Turner would say).

A *causal rule* is an expression of the form

$$F \leftarrow G \tag{8}$$

where F and G are formulas of classical logic. Intuitively, rule (8) expresses that F *is caused if* G *is true*. The dynamic causal dependency expressed in the introduction by formula (1) would be written in this language as

$$at(I, y, t+1) \leftarrow go(x, y, z, t)$$

(there is a cause for me to be at location y at time $t+1$ if I performed the action $go(x, y, z)$ during the unit time interval beginning at time t). Static causal dependencies can be represented by causal rules as well: the rule

$$at(watch, y, t) \leftarrow at(I, y, t)$$

says that whenever I am at a location y, there is a cause for my watch to be at y also.

Note that causal rules of the form

$$p \leftarrow p \tag{9}$$

are not trivial (although a rule of this form found in a logic program can be dropped without changing the meaning of the program, according to the answer set semantics). Causal rule (9) says that if p holds then there is a cause for this. Its role is similar to the role of the "inverse closed world assumption" (5) in a logic program.

Even though causal theories and logic programs have somewhat different properties, there exists a close relationship between them, and this relationship played an important role in the development of causal logic. The computational method for causal theories proposed in [19], called *literal completion*, is an elaboration of the completion method from [2] proposed as a semantics for negation as failure. Theorems relating causal theories to logic programs can be found in [7] and [28].

The system CCALC, written by Norman McCain at the University of Texas, performs reasoning about actions and planning for domains described by causal theories. It uses the process of literal completion to reduce these tasks to propositional reasoning problems, which are submitted to a propositional solver. Some information on its performance can be found in [20].

7 Action Language $\mathcal{C}$

In [10], ideas of causal logic are applied to the design of an action language that is considerably more expressive than $\mathcal{A}$. Among other things, the new language, called $\mathcal{C}$, allows us to represent static causal dependencies and to talk about the concurrent execution of actions.

In place of effect propositions of the language $\mathcal{A}$ (Section 3), $\mathcal{C}$ has proposition of two kinds: *static laws* of the form

$$\textbf{caused } F \textbf{ if } G \tag{10}$$

and *dynamic laws* of the form

$$\textbf{caused } F \textbf{ if } G \textbf{ after } H. \tag{11}$$

Here F and G are formulas whose atomic components represent fluents, as in the language $\mathcal{A}$. The formula H is of a more general kind: in addition to fluent symbols, it is allowed to contain the names of actions. Syntactically, action names are treated as atomic formulas; an assignment of truth values to action names represents the composite action which is executed by performing concurrently all elementary actions whose names are assigned the value *true*. If, for instance, the description of an action domain in $\mathcal{C}$ uses the action names A_1 and A_2 then it tells us about the effects of 4 composite actions: $A_1\overline{A_2}$ (performing A_1 only), $\overline{A_1}A_2$ (performing A_2 only), A_1A_2 (performing both actions concurrently) and $\overline{A_1}\,\overline{A_2}$ (doing nothing).

Direct effects of actions are described in $\mathcal{C}$ by dynamic laws (11) in which G is the logical constant $\top$. We will write such laws as

$$\textbf{caused } F \textbf{ after } H. \tag{12}$$

For instance, the counterpart of (6) in $\mathcal{C}$ is

$$\textbf{caused } P \textbf{ after } Q \wedge A. \tag{13}$$

The language $\mathcal{C}$ differs from $\mathcal{A}$ in that the idea of inertia is not incorporated into its semantics. If we want to assume that a certain fluent tends to keep the value it had before then an appropriate dynamic law needs to be postulated along with the laws describing the effects of actions. The expression

$$\textbf{inertial } F$$

stands for

$$\textbf{caused } F \textbf{ if } F \textbf{ after } F$$

(if F was true before and is true now then there is a cause for this). This elegant solution to the frame problem is due to McCain and Turner [19], who expressed it in the language of causal logic. Its advantage, in comparison with turning inertia into a "built-in" feature of the language, is that it gives the user freedom to decide which inertia assumptions are appropriate in each particular case.

For example, the formalization of the example from Section 3 in $\mathcal{C}$ includes, besides dynamic law (13), the inertia postulates

$$\begin{array}{l}\textbf{inertial } P\\ \textbf{inertial } \neg P\\ \textbf{inertial } Q\\ \textbf{inertial } \neg Q\end{array} \tag{14}$$

which we can abbreviate as

$$\textbf{inertial } P, \neg P, Q, \neg Q\ .$$

According to the semantics of $\mathcal{C}$, propositions (13) and (14) represent the transition diagram shown in Figure 2.

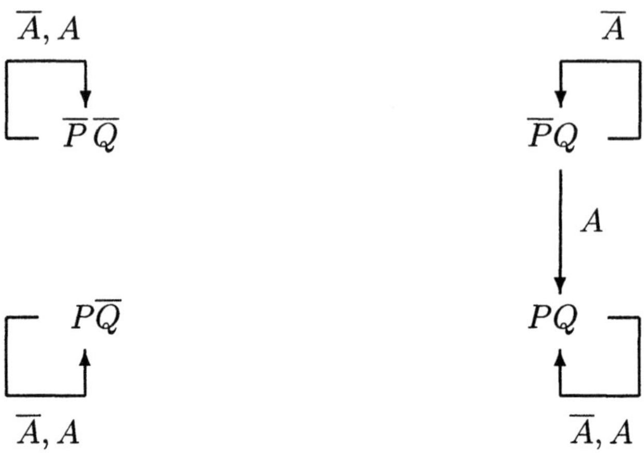

Fig. 2. Transition diagram for propositions (13), (14)

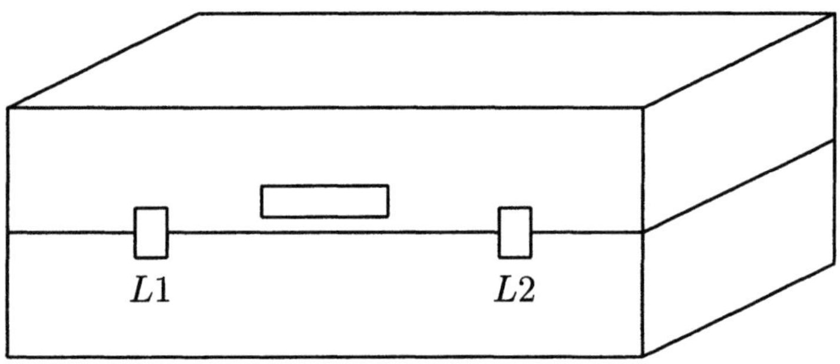

Fig. 3. Fangzhen Lin's suitcase

As an example of the use of static laws in $\mathcal{C}$, consider a suitcase with two latches (Figure 3) which is spring-loaded: it is open whenever both latches are up [17]. The suitcase is described in $\mathcal{C}$ by the propositions

$$\begin{array}{l} \textbf{caused } Up(l) \textbf{ after } \neg Up(l) \wedge Toggle(l) \\ \textbf{caused } \neg Up(l) \textbf{ after } Up(l) \wedge Toggle(l) \\ \textbf{caused } Open \textbf{ if } Up(L1) \wedge Up(L2) \\ \textbf{inertial } Up(l), \neg Up(l) \\ \textbf{inertial } Open, \neg Open \end{array} \tag{15}$$

($l \in \{L1, L2\}$). The third line is a static law.

According to the semantics of $\mathcal{C}$, assigning the value *true* to *Open* and the value *false* to both $Up(L1)$ and $Up(L2)$ does not give a possible state of this system, so that the transition diagram for (15) has only 7 vertices. Performing any action that makes $Up(L1) \wedge Up(L2)$ true has an indirect effect—it makes *Open* true also.

8 From $\mathcal{C}$ to Logic Programming

In this section, we restrict attention to the static laws (10) and dynamic laws (11) in which formula F is a literal and each of the formulas G, H is a conjunction of literals (or $\top$, which will be identified with the empty conjunction). All propositions from the two examples above satisfy this condition.

The problem of computing the transition diagram for a set of static and dynamic laws of this kind can be reduced to generating all answer sets for a logic program.

This logic program includes, besides the fluent names and action names, a copy P' of every fluent name P. The atoms P, P' represent the values of the fluent at the two vertices connected by an edge of the transition diagram.

The process of translating a set of static and dynamic laws into a logic program consists of three steps.

1. A static law

$$\textbf{caused } L_0 \textbf{ if } L_1 \wedge \cdots \wedge L_m$$

is turned into the pair of rules

$$\begin{array}{l} L_0 \leftarrow L_1, \ldots, L_m \ , \\ L'_0 \leftarrow not\ \overline{L'_1}, \ldots, not\ \overline{L'_m} \ . \end{array}$$

These rules express in the language of logic programming that the static law applies to both vertices connected by the edge. Note that each member $not\ \overline{L'_i}$ of the body of the second rule is obtained from the literal L'_i by putting the negation as failure operator in front of the complementary literal. The relation between L'_i and $not\ \overline{L'_i}$ is similar to the relation between the bodies of causal rule (9) and of logic programming rule (5) discussed in Section 6.

2. A dynamic law

$$\textbf{caused } L_0 \textbf{ if } L_1 \wedge \cdots \wedge L_m \textbf{ after } L_{m+1} \wedge \cdots \wedge L_n$$

is turned into the rule

$$L'_0 \leftarrow not\ \overline{L'_1}, \ldots, not\ \overline{L'_m}, L_{m+1}, \ldots, L_n \ .$$

3. For every action name A, we add the rules

$$\begin{array}{l} A \leftarrow not\ \neg A \ , \\ \neg A \leftarrow not\ A \ , \end{array}$$

and for every fluent name P the rules

$$\begin{array}{l} P \leftarrow not\ \neg P\ , \\ \neg P \leftarrow not\ P\ , \\ \leftarrow not\ P', not\ \neg P'\ . \end{array}$$

According to the answer set semantics, these rules require including one element of each complementary pair $\{A, \neg A\}$ and $\{P, \neg P\}$, and prohibit the answer sets that include neither P' nor $\neg P'$ for some fluent symbol P.

Results relating $\mathcal{C}$ to causal logic [10] and causal logic to logic programming [28] imply that the answer sets for the program formed in this way from a set of static and dynamic laws are in a 1–1 correspondence with the edges of the transition diagram corresponding to this set.

As an example, let us consider the program representing propositions (13) and (14). The rules of this program are

$$\begin{array}{l} P' \leftarrow Q, A \\ P' \leftarrow not\ \neg P', P \\ \neg P' \leftarrow not\ P', \neg P \\ Q' \leftarrow not\ \neg Q', Q \\ \neg Q' \leftarrow not\ Q', \neg Q \\ A \leftarrow not\ \neg A \\ \neg A \leftarrow not\ A \\ P \leftarrow not\ \neg P \\ \neg P \leftarrow not\ P \\ Q \leftarrow not\ \neg Q \\ \neg Q \leftarrow not\ Q \\ \leftarrow not\ P', not\ \neg P' \\ \leftarrow not\ Q', not\ \neg Q' \end{array} \qquad (16)$$

The answer sets

$$\begin{array}{l} \{ \neg P, \neg Q, \neg A, \neg P', \neg Q' \} \\ \{ \neg P, Q, \neg A, \neg P', Q' \} \\ \{ P, \neg Q, \neg A, P', \neg Q' \} \\ \{ P, Q, \neg A, P', Q' \} \\ \{ \neg P, \neg Q, A, \neg P', \neg Q' \} \\ \{ \neg P, Q, A, P', Q' \} \\ \{ P, \neg Q, A, P', \neg Q' \} \\ \{ P, Q, A, P', Q' \} \end{array}$$

for this program correspond to the edges of the diagram shown in Figure 2. For instance, the third line from the end corresponds to the vertical edge of the diagram, which begins at the vertex $\overline{P}Q$, is labeled A, and ends at PQ.

It is interesting to look at the logic programming counterpart of the dynamic laws that express inertia. Consider, for instance, the translation of the first of propositions (14) into logic programming, which is the second rule of (16). This rule says that P remains true after performing an action if there is no evidence that it becomes false. From the perspective of default logic, this is similar to the "frame default" proposed by Reiter [24] as a solution to the frame problem.

The two constraints at the end of (16) happen to be unnecessary, in the sense that removing them from the program would not affect its answer sets.

The logic programming representation of the static law from the suitcase example, expressed by the third line of (15), is the pair of rules

$$\begin{array}{l} Open \leftarrow Up(L1), Up(L2)\ , \\ Open' \leftarrow not\ \neg Up'(L1), not\ \neg Up'(L2)\ . \end{array}$$

Both occurrences of *not* $\neg$ in the body of the second rule can be actually dropped without changing the answer sets for the program. But there are cases when the presence of negation as failure in the translation of a static law is essential for the soundness of the translation relative to the semantics of $\mathcal{C}$.

9 Planning for Domains Described in $\mathcal{C}$

Now we can go back to the issue raised at the beginning of Section 6: the need to extend the planning method from [26] and [4] to action domains described using both dynamic and static causal dependencies.

Recall that the translation defined in the previous section turns a set of $\mathcal{C}$ propositions into a logic program whose answer sets represent the edges of the corresponding transition diagram. An easy modification of this translation allows us to represent paths of a fixed length n in this diagram; the original translation corresponds to $n = 1$. We may be able to solve planning problems for domains described in $\mathcal{C}$ by applying a program like SMODELS to the result of this translation.

As an example, consider the following planning problem that involves Lin's suitcase. Initially, both latches are down and the suitcase is closed. In a goal state that we want to achieve, the latches are down but the suitcase is open. If the concurrent execution of toggle actions is allowed then the problem can be solved in two steps: actions $Toggle(L1)$ and $Toggle(L2)$ are executed concurrently between times 0 and 1, and then again between times 1 and 2.

This problem can be submitted to SMODELS (version 1.10) as the input file shown in Figure 4. The first group of rules translates propositions (15) into logic programming. The time variables `T`, `T1` and the predicate `next` are used here in place of the distinction between P and P' in the translation from Section 8. The auxiliary predicates `nup` and `nopen` represent the classical negations of `up` and `open`; the need to use these predicates stems from the fact that the current version of SMODELS does not support classical negation. The two lines in the braces at the end of the input file describe the initial state and the goal of the planning problem.

```
up(L,T1) :- latch(L), next(T,T1), nup(L,T), toggle(L,T).
nup(L,T1) :- latch(L), next(T,T1), up(L,T), toggle(L,T).
open(T) :- up(l1,T), up(l2,T).
up(L,T1) :- latch(L), next(T,T1), up(L,T), not nup(L,T1).
nup(L,T1) :- latch(L), next(T,T1), nup(L,T), not up(L,T1).
open(T1) :- next(T,T1), open(T), not nopen(T1).
nopen(T1) :- next(T,T1), nopen(T), not open(T1).

toggle(L,T) :- latch(L), time(T), not last(T), not ntoggle(L,T).
ntoggle(L,T) :- latch(L), time(T), not last(T), not toggle(L,T).
up(L,0) :- latch(L), not nup(L,0).
nup(L,0) :- latch(L), not up(L,0).
open(0) :- not nopen(0).
nopen(0) :- not open(0).

latch(l1).  latch(l2).
time(0).  time(1).  time(2).
last(2).
next(0,1).  next(1,2).

compute 1 {
             not up(l1,0), not up(l2,0), not open(0),
             not up(l1,2), not up(l2,2), open(2)
           }
```

Fig. 4. Planning with SMODELS

In the output of SMODELS we read:

```
Stable Model: next(1,2) next(0,1) time(2) time(1) time(0)
latch(l2) latch(l1) nopen(0) nup(l2,0) toggle(l2,0)
toggle(l2,1) nup(l1,0) toggle(l1,0) toggle(l1,1) up(l2,1)
up(l1,1) nup(l2,2) nup(l1,2) open(1) open(2) last(2)
```

The elements of this answer set that contain the action name `toggle` represent a solution.

10 Topics for Future Work

One of the advantages of CCALC (Section 6) in comparison with the currently available versions of SMODELS, DLV and DERES (Section 5) is that its language is many-sorted and includes function symbols. These features are often convenient for describing action domains, and it would be good to add them to the other systems. In the presence of function symbols, the Herbrand universe can be infinite (although this is not necessarily the case for a many-sorted language), so that a program with function symbols may have infinite answer sets. In the context of answer set programming this is clearly unacceptable—all elements of an answer set need to be generated to produce a single solution to the problem! This difficulty can be resolved by imposing appropriate syntactic restrictions on the input.

Another difference between CCALC and the other three systems mentioned above is that it computes plans using a propositional solver, rather than methods specific for answer set programming. Logic programs whose answer sets correspond to plans, such as the one shown in Figure 4, are usually *tight*, which implies that the answer sets for such a program can be characterized by its completion formula (see [15], Section 3.2 and Corollary to Proposition 3.19). Thus the problem of finding an answer set for a tight program can be reduced to the problem of finding an interpretation that satisfies a certain formula of classical logic. (This is, in fact, how CCALC operates.) How does this method compare with the computational ideas of SMODELS and similar systems?

The planning methods discussed above, like satisfiability planning, are not applicable unless the given problem includes a complete characterization of the initial situation. It would be important to find ways to get around this limitation.

11 Conclusion

This paper is a sketch of several streams of ideas that interact in current research on actions and planning: action languages and translating them into logic programming; representing histories by answer sets; satisfiability planning; efficient implementations of the answer set semantics and their use for generating plans; causal logic and its relation to planning algorithms. In the course of this work, researchers have uncovered intriguing connections between the theoretical analysis of causal reasoning on the one hand, and the design of planners on the other.

In the years to come, we will see new advances both in methods for describing action domains and in implemented systems for computing answer sets. This may lead to the creation of planners which are based on the ideas of logic programming and combine the use of expressive action description languages with efficient computational procedures.

Acknowledgements

Many ideas of this paper have crystallized in the course of stimulating conversations with Michael Gelfond, Norman McCain and Hudson Turner. A talk on this subject was given at the Kentucky meeting on trends and directions in logic programming in April of 1998. I am grateful to the participants of the meeting for useful remarks and criticisms, and especially to Teodor Przymusinski who has presented a commentary on my talk and organized its discussion. This work was partially supported by National Science Foundation under grant IIS-9732744.

References

1. Pawel Cholewiński, Victor Marek, and Miroslaw Truszczyński. Default reasoning system DeReS. In *Principles of Knowledge Representation and Reasoning: Proc. of the Fifth Int'l Conference*, pages 518–528, 1996.
2. Keith Clark. Negation as failure. In Herve Gallaire and Jack Minker, editors, *Logic and Data Bases*, pages 293–322. Plenum Press, New York, 1978.
3. Mark Denecker and Danny De Schreye. Representing incomplete knowledge in abductive logic programming. In Dale Miller, editor, *Logic Programming: Proceedings of the 1993 Int'l Symposium*, pages 147–163, 1993.
4. Yannis Dimopoulos, Bernhard Nebel, and Jana Koehler. Encoding planning problems in non-monotonic logic programs. In *Proc. ECP-97*, 1997.
5. Phan Minh Dung. Representing actions in logic programming and its applications in database updates. In *Logic Programming: Proceedings of the Tenth Int'l Conf. on Logic Programming*, pages 222–238, 1993.
6. Thomas Eiter, Nicola Leone, Cristinel Mateis, Gerald Pfeifer, and Francesco Scarcello. The kr system DLV: Progress report, comparisons and benchmarks. In Anthony Cohn, Lenhart Schubert, and Stuart Shapiro, editors, *Proc. Sixth Int'l Conf. on Principles of Knowledge Representation and Reasoning*, pages 406–417, 1998.
7. Hector Geffner. Causal theories for nonmonotonic reasoning. In *Proc. AAAI-90*, pages 524–530, 1990.
8. Michael Gelfond and Vladimir Lifschitz. Classical negation in logic programs and disjunctive databases. *New Generation Computing*, 9:365–385, 1991.
9. Michael Gelfond and Vladimir Lifschitz. Representing action and change by logic programs. *Journal of Logic Programming*, 17:301–322, 1993.
10. Enrico Giunchiglia and Vladimir Lifschitz. An action language based on causal explanation: Preliminary report. In *Proc. AAAI-98*, pages 623–630, 1998.
11. Cordell Green. Application of theorem proving to problem solving. In *Proc. IJCAI*, pages 219–240, 1969.
12. Steve Hanks and Drew McDermott. Nonmonotonic logic and temporal projection. *Artificial Intelligence*, 33(3):379–412, 1987.
13. Henry Kautz and Bart Selman. Planning as satisfiability. In *Proc. ECAI-92*, pages 359–363, 1992.
14. Henry Kautz and Bart Selman. Pushing the envelope: planning, propositional logic and stochastic search. In *Proc. AAAI-96*, pages 1194–1201, 1996.
15. Vladimir Lifschitz. Foundations of logic programming. In Gerhard Brewka, editor, *Principles of Knowledge Representation*, pages 69–128. CSLI Publications, 1996.
16. Vladimir Lifschitz. On the logic of causal explanation. *Artificial Intelligence*, 96:451–465, 1997.
17. Fangzhen Lin. Embracing causality in specifying the indirect effects of actions. In *Proc. IJCAI-95*, pages 1985–1991, 1995.
18. Victor Marek and Mirosław Truszczyński. Stable models and an alternative logic programming paradigm, this volume, pp. 375–398.

19. Norman McCain and Hudson Turner. Causal theories of action and change. In *Proc. AAAI-97*, pages 460–465, 1997.
20. Norman McCain and Hudson Turner. Satisfiability planning with causal theories. In Anthony Cohn, Lenhart Schubert, and Stuart Shapiro, editors, *Proc. Sixth Int'l Conf. on Principles of Knowledge Representation and Reasoning*, pages 212–223, 1998.
21. John McCarthy. Programs with common sense. In *Proc. Teddington Conference on the Mechanization of Thought Processes*, pages 75–91, London, 1959. Her Majesty's Stationery Office. Reproduced in [22].
22. John McCarthy. *Formalizing Common Sense: Papers by John McCarthy.* Ablex, Norwood, NJ, 1990.
23. Ilkka Niemelä and Patrik Simons. Efficient implementation of the well-founded and stable model semantics. In *Proc. Joint Int'l Conf. and Symp. on Logic Programming*, pages 289–303, 1996.
24. Raymond Reiter. A logic for default reasoning. *Artificial Intelligence*, 13:81–132, 1980.
25. Patrik Simons. Towards constraint satisfaction through logic programs and the stable model semantics. Technical Report 47, Helsinki University of Technology, 1997.
26. V.S. Subrahmanian and Carlo Zaniolo. Relating stable models and AI planning domains. In *Proc. ICLP-95*, pp. 233-247, MIT Press, 1995.
27. Hudson Turner. Representing actions in logic programs and default theories: a situation calculus approach. *Journal of Logic Programming*, 31:245–298, 1997.
28. Hudson Turner. A logic of universal causation. *Artificial Intelligence.* To appear.

Stable Models and an Alternative Logic Programming Paradigm

Victor W. Marek and Mirosław Truszczyński

Department of Computer Science, University of Kentucky, Lexington, KY 40506-0046, USA

Summary. In this paper we reexamine the place and role of stable model semantics in logic programming and contrast it with a least Herbrand model approach to Horn programs. We demonstrate that inherent features of stable model semantics naturally lead to a logic programming system that offers an interesting alternative to more traditional logic programming styles of Horn logic programming, stratified logic programming and logic programming with well-founded semantics. The proposed approach is based on the interpretation of program clauses as constraints. In this setting, a program does not describe a single intended model, but a *family* of its *stable* models. These stable models encode solutions to the constraint satisfaction problem described by the program. Our approach imposes restrictions on the syntax of logic programs. In particular, function symbols are eliminated from the language. We argue that the resulting logic programming system is well-attuned to problems in the class NP, has a well-defined domain of applications, and an emerging methodology of programming. We point out that what makes the whole approach viable is recent progress in implementations of algorithms to compute stable models of propositional logic programs.

1 Introduction

Stable model semantics appeared on the logic programming scene in the late 80s in an effort to provide an understanding of programs with negation. Since it was first proposed by Gelfond and Lifschitz [GL88], it was regarded by logic programming community with a dose of reserve and unease. It was intuitively felt that the stable model semantics properly deals with negation and some formal evidence supporting this intuition was established. At the same time, the stable model semantics did not fit into a standard paradigm of logic programming languages. While standard approaches assign to a logic program a single "intended" model, stable model semantics assigns to a program a *family* (possibly empty) of "intended" models. Further, in the presence of function symbols, Horn logic programs can specify any recursively enumerable set, while stable model semantics increases the expressive power of logic programs well beyond currently acceptable notions of computability. Finally, the SLD-resolution, the true bread-and-butter of logic programmers and the heart of control mechanisms behind standard logic programming implementations, seems to be inappropriate for the stable model semantics.

As a consequence of these difficulties in reconciling the stable model semantics with a traditional paradigm of logic programming, the stable model semantics received relatively less attention from the logic programming community than other semantics proposed for programs with negation such as perfect model semantics for stratified programs and well-founded semantics.

In this paper we argue that rather than to try to resolve these inconsistencies and force stable model semantics into a standard logic programming mold (this effort most likely is doomed to failure), a change of view is required. Therefore, we propose a perspective on the stable model semantics that departs from several basic tenets of logic programming. At the same time, this perspective leads to a computational system very much in the general spirit of logic programming. The system is declarative, retains the separation of logic from control, has a well-defined domain of applications and emerging programming methodology. We refer to this version of logic programming as *stable logic programming* (or, SLP, for short).

There are several key elements to the view of the stable model semantics that we describe here. First, we restrict the syntax by disallowing function symbols. Thus, the syntax of SLP is the same as the syntax of DATALOG with negation. The restriction of the syntax has significant effect on the expressive power of programs. In particular, it curtails the ability to use recursion.

Second, we view a program as specifying a collection of models rather than a single model. Thus, SLP seems to be especially well suited for all these problems where solutions are subsets of some universe, as each solution can be modeled by a different stable model. Many combinatorial and constraint satisfaction problems fall into this category.

The restricted syntax (limiting the use of recursion) and the shift in the semantics (programs specify a collection of models rather than a single model), change the way in which we interpret and design programs. Programs are interpreted as constraints on objects of interest rather than recursive definitions of these objects. Even though often a single clause represents a constraint, in general, due to nonmonotonicity of the stable model semantics, constraints are modeled by groups of clauses (or, in the extreme case, an entire program). Hence, SLP requires a different approach to programming. Objects that in Horn logic programming would be represented as terms and defined recursively, in SLP are represented as different stable models and defined in terms of constraints.

Finally, although the SLP follows the basic logic programming tenet of "uniform control", the control used in SLP is different. Instead of SLD resolution used in Horn Logic programming, a backtracking search for stable models is used.

While (Horn) logic programming is well attuned to the concepts of Turing computability, recursively enumerable sets and partial recursive functions, SLP is related to a much more narrow class of problems. As we point out, all decision problems that are in NP can be solved within the paradigm of SLP. Moreover many (possibly all) search problems, whose decision versions are in NP, can be solved with SLP programs, too. While NP is much smaller than the class of r.e. sets, it still covers a wide collection of important computational problems including many combinatorial optimization and constraint satisfaction problems. This is one of the main reasons why we believe that SLP can evolve into a useful computational tool.

Recently, the idea of using logic programs with restricted syntax and nonstandard semantics was discussed in several papers. Niemelä [Nie98], in a closely related work, proposed function symbol-free logic programming with stable model semantics as a vehicle to process constraint satisfaction problem. Second, Cadoli and others [CP98], proposed the use of DATALOG programs *without* negation and with the semantics of parallel circumscription as a tool for solving decision problems in NP. The use of disjunctive logic programming as a knowledge representation system is discussed by Aravindan et al. [ADN97] and by Eiter et al. [ELM+97,ELM+98]. Finally, in [CMMT98] we study a similar use of default logic (a formalism extending SLP) as a programming environment for solving decision problems from the class Σ_2^P.

All these projects are supported by algorithms to process logic programs and by their implementations. Niemelä and Simons [NS95,NS96] developed a system, *smodels*, to compute stable models of logic programs. Algorithms to process DATALOG programs under parallel circumscription were presented in [CPSV98]. A disjunctive logic programming system `dlv` is described in [ELM+98]. Another implementation of disjunctive logic programming is discussed in [ADN97]. A system DeReS to process a wider class of programs – default theories – is described in [CMT96,CMMT98]. The emergence of implementations is the main reason why these alternative logic programming systems are becoming viable computational tools.

This paper is organized as follows. In the next section we provide a perspective of Horn logic programming, pointing to those of its features that are responsible for its expressivity. We discuss the effects of the negation operator in logic programming and show how it increases the expressivity beyond the currently accepted bounds. In Section 4 we formally introduce stable logic programming (SLP). Next, we study the expressive power of SLP, showing that the applicability of SLP is attuned to the class NP. In Section 6 we note the limitations in using recursion in SLP and show that SLP programs should be interpreted as descriptions of constraints. Consequently, the methodology of programming with SLP is different from that of ordinary logic programming. We discuss several examples and show how SLP programs that solve them can be developed. We discuss the issue of uniform control associated with SLP in Section 7. Conclusions and a "road map" for the future complete the paper.

2 Horn Logic Programming

The idea to use logic as a computational mechanism can be traced back to Herbrand's analysis of the effectivity of proofs in first-order logic [Her30]. In this work Herbrand discovered a *unification algorithm*, one of the basic constructions behind the present-day automated deduction and logic programming.

Transforming logic into a viable programming tool required two additional crucial steps. First of them was the introduction of the *resolution* rule by Robinson [Rob65] with unification as one of its key components. Over the years resolution was extensively studied [CL73,Lov78,MW88] and gained in stature as one of the most successful techniques of automated reasoning.

The second key step was to narrow down the focus of automated deduction to the class of *Horn theories* and even more specifically, to the class of *definite* Horn theories. A *definite Horn clause* is a formula of the form

$$q_1(\boldsymbol{t_1}) \wedge \ldots \wedge q_k(\boldsymbol{t_k}) \Rightarrow ct)$$

(written $p(t) \leftarrow q_1(\boldsymbol{t_1}), \ldots, q_k(\boldsymbol{t_k})$ by the logic programming community), where q_i and p are atoms of the language and $t, t_1, \ldots, t_k$ are terms (possibly with variables). A definite Horn theory (a *Horn logic program*) is a finite theory consisting of definite Horn clauses.

Each definite Horn theory P is consistent and possesses a least Herbrand model, $LM(P)$. This least model provides a natural and intuitive semantics for definite Horn theories and leads to a natural concept of computability. We say that a finite definite Horn theory P *specifies* (*computes*) a subset X of the *Herbrand universe* of P, $HU(P)$, if for some predicate symbol p occurring in P we have:

$$X = \{t \in HU(P) : p(t) \in LM(P)\}. \tag{1}$$

One of the fundamental results underlying the area of logic programming is that every recursively enumerable set can be specified by a definite Horn theory [Smu68,AN78]. This result shows that definite Horn theories are as expressive as Turing machines and precisely capture the concept of Church-Turing computability.

The area of logic programming was born in early 70s when it was realized that the elements of the set $\{t \in HU(P) : p(t) \in LM(P)\}$ can actually be *computed*. Namely, a special form of resolution, the *SLD-resolution* [Kow74,AvE82], and the so-called *lifting lemma* [Llo84] allow us to compute ground terms t (more generally, ground substitutions σ) such that $p(t)$ (or $p(\boldsymbol{X}\sigma)$) belongs to the least Herbrand model of a definite Horn theory.

Availability of this uniform control mechanism, SLD-resolution, is the key aspect of Horn logic programming. Horn programs, that is, definite Horn theories, need only to specify definitions and properties of objects and domains of interest. The programmer no longer needs to specify the exact way in which to perform the computation. The control is provided by the mechanism of the SLD resolution. This feature of logic programming, the separation of logic ("what" part) from control ("how" part), was and still remains one of the most attractive features of logic programming. It allows the programmers to focus only on the logic of the problem and frees them from the burden of specifying the control. Consequently, it carries with itself a promise of easier code development, facilitates modular design of software and eases the problems of program verification[1] [Kow79]. It is due to the separation of logic from control that logic programming is often classified as a *declarative* programming system.

Function symbols are critical for the Horn logic programming. The presence of function symbols in the language, especially of the list constructor $[\cdot|\cdot]$, allows the programmer to encode hereditarily finite higher-order objects as terms of the language. Consequently, logic program clauses can be used to describe recursive definitions of higher-order objects. Modeling the recursive definitions within logic programs is responsible for the expressive power of logic programming and became one of its most important and most common programming techniques.

The situation changes drastically if function symbols (in particular, $[\cdot|\cdot]$) are not available. This formalism was extensively studied as a possible query language by the database community and is known there as DATALOG (see, for instance, [Ull88]). Without function symbols in the language, the Herbrand universe of finite Horn programs is finite. Thus, the ability to represent higher-order objects in DATALOG is significantly restricted. Similarly, many recursive definitions can no longer be modeled by DATALOG clauses (those which describe how more complex objects of higher order can be constructed from simpler ones). Consequently, the expressive power of finite DATALOG programs is very limited. They can only express a proper subset of all polynomial-time computable queries [ACY91]. Thus, it is the presence of function symbols in the language that is responsible for the expressive power of Horn logic programming.

We will now summarize some of the key features of Horn logic programming.

1. The existence of a single intended model (a least Herbrand model) yields the semantics for Horn logic programs and the notion of computability. Horn programs compute extensions of predicates in the least model.
2. Function symbols in the language allow the programmer to encode higher-order objects as terms and represent recursive definitions of these objects by means of Horn clauses.
3. Horn programs can specify any recursively enumerable set. Thus, Horn logic programming precisely captures the commonly accepted notion of computability.

[1] This expectation did not entirely materialize. Peculiarities of logic programming implementations, including subtleties of search space pruning and its side effects resulted in a paradigm not easily accepted by real-life programmers.

4. Horn logic programming is declarative due to the separation of logic, represented by Horn programs, from uniform control, represented by the SLD resolution.

3 Negation in Logic Programming

As observed above, from the point of view of the expressive power, the Horn logic programming is as powerful as any programmer might want it to be — it captures recursively enumerable sets. However, as a declarative system, it was not quite satisfying. The ability to describe intuitive declarative specifications of objects to be computed was significantly hampered by disallowing the negation operator from the bodies of clauses. This was recognized very early on in the development of the field. In particular, the negation operator has been available in PROLOG since its creation [CKPR73] and extensions of Horn logic programming with negation in the bodies of program clauses were studied since mid 1970s.

In fact, the effort to extend Horn logic programming by allowing the negation operator in the bodies was among the strongest driving forces behind the development of the area in the past 25 years. The task is far from straightforward as adding negation implies that the existence of a unique least model (one of the fundamental features of the Horn logic programming paradigm) is no longer guaranteed.

Proposals to address the problem can be divided into two classes. Proposals of the first type attempt to salvage the notion of a *single* intended model at a cost of narrowing down the class of programs or weakening the semantics. Apt, Blair and Walker [ABW88] introduced the notion of *stratification*, a syntactic restriction on logic programs with negation. They assigned to each stratified program a single intended model, a *perfect model*. In another approach, van Gelder, Ross and Schlipf [VRS91] assigned to an *arbitrary* program a single intended 3-valued model, a *well-founded model*. These two proposals are still very much in the spirit of the Horn logic programming paradigm. Namely, in each of these approaches, a program specifies extensions of predicates in a single intended model — perfect or well-founded, respectively. Moreover, suitably modified versions of resolution were proposed as a uniform processing mechanisms [ADP95],[RRS+97].

However, both these approaches lead to problems with excessive expressive power. Apt and Blair [AB90] proved that stratified programs with finite number of strata specify precisely arithmetic sets. This means that they are expressive beyond what is at present considered computable. Since the well-founded model coincides with perfect model for stratified programs, the same result applies to well-founded semantics[2]. In fact, perfect models of locally stratified programs [Prz88] specify an even bigger class of sets — the class of

[2] In particular, the programmer that uses a logic programming environment based on the well-founded semantics (for instance XSB) must understand that some

hyperarithmetic sets [BMS95]. The same class of sets is specified by programs for which the well-founded model is total while, in general, well-founded semantics specifies the class of Π_1^1 sets [Sch95].

The common idea behind the proposals of the second type was to distinguish among all models of a program a *collection* of intended models rather than a single one. The class of *supported* models was introduced by Clark [Cla78] and, almost ten years later, Gelfond and Lifschitz [GL88] fine-tuned Clark's approach and defined the class of *stable* models as candidates for intended models of logic programs with negation.

Our goal in this paper is to present a perspective of logic programming with stable model semantics and, thus, from now on we will focus on stable models only. Let us briefly recall the definition of a stable model (for a detailed treatment, the reader is referred to [MT93]). Let P be a logic program and let P_g be the grounding of P. A subset M of the Herbrand base of P is a *stable model* of P, if M coincides with the least model of the *reduct* P_g^M of P_g with respect to M. The reduct P_g^M is the program obtained from P_g by removing from P_g all clauses containing in the body a literal of the form $\mathbf{not}(p)$, for some $p \in M$, and by removing literals of the form $\mathbf{not}(p)$ from all of the remaining clauses. Directly from this definition one can derive the following fundamental properties of stable models. First, every stable model of a logic program P is, indeed, a model of P. Furthermore, every stable model of P is a minimal model of P and a supported model of P. Finally, the family of stable models of a program forms an antichain.

The stable model semantics, from the day it was proposed, was the subject of some controversy. On one hand, it was commonly accepted that stable models provide the right semantics for logic programming with negation. There is an abundance of evidence to support this claim. For instance, it is known that the stable model semantics coincides with the least model semantics on definite Horn programs. For stratified logic programs it coincides with the perfect model semantics. Further, when the well-founded model is total, it defines a unique stable model [VRS91]. Finally, the well-founded model is the least three-valued stable model [Prz90]. In addition, as demonstrated in [MT89,BF91,Kam97], logic programming with the stable model semantics is closely related to default logic of Reiter [Rei80], a commonly accepted formalism for knowledge representation.

On the other hand, it was not clear how to reconcile the stable model semantics with the paradigm of Horn logic programming, as presented in Section 2. Three difficulties are: lack of a single intended model (the notion of specification given by (1) requires modifications), increase in the expressive power beyond the accepted limits of computability, and inadequacy of resolution-based control.

---

programs specify complex sets for which computation will not terminate. The non-termination occurs in Horn logic programming as well, but a more complex semantics adds an additional layer of complexity to programmer's task.

The first difficulty can, to some degree, be overcome by means of the so called *skeptical semantics.* Under this semantics, a ground atom is entailed by the program if it is true in *all* of its stable models. We say that a logic program with negation P *specifies* a subset X of $HU(P)$, if for some predicate symbol p occurring in P we have:

$$X = \{t \in HU(P): P \models_{skeptical} p(t)\}.$$

However, at this point, problems with the expressive power reappear. Indeed, stratified programs have unique stable model, thus skeptical semantics coincides with perfect model semantics for such programs. Consequently the results on the expressivity of perfect semantics for stratified programs apply in this situation. Moreover, the problem to decide the existence of a stable model of a finite logic program is Σ^1_1-complete, while the problem to decide the membership in all stable models is Π^1_1-complete [MNR94]. Thus, both problems are far beyond accepted notions of computability.

There is one additional complication. Due to the complexity, no form of resolution can be applicable in the general case of skeptical semantics, without drastic restrictions on the syntax of programs. Whereas in the case of well-founded semantics conditions limiting the complexity are known and resolution-based systems for well-founded semantics were developed [ADP95], [RRS+97], in the case of skeptical semantics such results have yet to be established.

4 Stable Logic Programming

The difficulty of fitting logic programming with stable model semantics into the paradigm of Horn logic programming, combined with an intuitive appeal of stable models, makes us believe that the place of stable model semantics in logic programming must be reexamined. To this end, we propose below an alternative paradigm to that of the Horn logic programming, a paradigm consistent with the properties of stable models. We will refer to it as *stable logic programming* (or, *SLP* for short).

While stable logic programming is in many aspects different from Horn logic programming, at the most general level it shares with it the key feature of separation of logic from control. Consequently, as other logic programming formalisms, stable logic programming is declarative. The programmer specifies the problem at hand as a logic program. This program is then processed by a uniform control mechanism, thus solving the original problem. The differences are in the syntax and semantics. These differences affect the control mechanism (it is no longer the SLD resolution), as well as the expressive power of stable logic programming and the corresponding programming methodology.

We will now specify stable model programming and discuss these differences in more detail. First, we will restrict the syntax since, as we saw earlier, without any restrictions the expressive power gets out of hand. Trivially, the negation operator must remain in the language (there is no need for the stable model semantics without it). The other major source of complexity, function symbols, must be eliminated, however. Indeed, even under a restriction of stratification, in the presence of both the negation operator and function symbols in the language, the complexity grows beyond the limits of computability [AB90]. Thus, in stable logic programming we adopt the language of logic programming that consists of denumerable collections of constant, variable and predicate symbols. In addition, we will allow for the negation operator to appear in the bodies of program clauses. Finite programs in this language will be referred to as *SLP programs.*

Due to the presence of negation, the existence of a least Herbrand model is no longer guaranteed. The semantics of SLP programs will be defined in terms of their stable models. Before we address this issue in more detail, let us observe that the formalism of finite function symbol-free logic programs with negation, was extensively studied by the database community. The formalism is often referred to as $DATALOG^{\neg}$ and several semantics for $DATALOG^{\neg}$ were studied. Stratified version of $DATALOG^{\neg}$ with perfect model semantics and with well-founded semantics received particular attention [AHV95]. At the same time, $DATALOG^{\neg}$ with stable model semantics has never drawn any significant interest in database community, mostly due to the fact that under the stable model semantics there is no guarantee of a single intended model that might be used to determine an answer to a query stated as a $DATALOG^{\neg}$ program. Skeptical stable semantics was not regarded as quite satisfactory either as the set of atoms entailed under this semantics is not a model of a $DATALOG^{\neg}$ query.

The lack of a single intended stable model, perceived as a problem by the logic programming and database communities, plays the key role in stable logic programming. Under the stable model semantics, a finite SLP program can be viewed as a specification of a *finite family of finite sets.* Let $SS(P)$ be the family of stable models of P. Now, we say that a finite SLP program P *specifies* a family of sets $\mathcal{X}$ if for some k-ary predicate p,

$$\mathcal{X} = \{\{(c_1, \ldots, c_k) \in HU(P): p(c_1, \ldots, c_k) \in M\}: \ M \text{ is } SS(P)\}. \qquad (2)$$

This notion of specification is the counterpart, in the case of SLP, to the notion of specification given by (1) in the case of Horn logic programming. It allows the programmer, without resorting to function symbols, to write logic programs that specify second-order objects which, in Horn logic programming, would be encoded by means of terms involving the $[\cdot|\cdot]$ operator. Thus, as we will state it more formally later, multiple intended models allow us to recover in SLP some of the expressive power of logic programming lost by eliminating function symbols from the language.

In addition, the notion of specification given by (2) suggests that SLP programs are very well suited to represent problems whose solutions are finite families of finite sets. For instance, a hamiltonian cycle in a directed graph is a set of edges, that is, a set of pairs of vertices. The collection of all hamiltonian cycles of a graph is then a collection of sets of pairs, that is an object of the form given by (2). In Section 6, we will exhibit explicit SLP programs that represent the hamiltonian cycle problem.

5 Expressive Power of SLP

Following Garey and Johnson [GJ79], we define a search problem, Π, to consist of a set of finite *instances*, D_Π. Further, for each instance $I \in D_\Pi$, there is a finite set $S_\Pi(I)$ of all *solutions* of Π for the instance I. An algorithm solves a search problem if for each instance $I \in D_\Pi$ it returns the answer "no" when $S_\Pi(I)$ is empty, and any solution $s \in S_\Pi(I)$, otherwise. Notice that all decision problems can be viewed as special search problems: for every instance I of a decision problem, define $S_\Pi(I) = \{\text{"yes"}\}$, if I is a "yes" instance of Π, and $S_\Pi(I) = \emptyset$, otherwise. Notice also that with each search problem one can associate a decision problem: given an instance $I \in D_\Pi$, decide whether $S_\Pi(I) = \emptyset$.

Several interesting search and decision problems can be associated with stable logic programming. Consider a finite SLP program P. Clearly, the Herbrand universe, the Herbrand base and the grounding of P are all finite. Consequently, stable models of P (if exist) are finite, too. It follows that the problem to compute, given a finite SLP program, its stable models is a search problem. An associated decision problem asks for the existence of stable models of a finite SLP program P. Other related decision problems ask whether a given element a of the Herbrand base $HB(P)$ belongs to some (or all) stable models of P.

To understand the expressive power of SLP, we need to study which search and decision problems can be reduced to search and decision problems associated with SLP. We will first consider the class of decision problems and restrict, for a moment, to propositional programs only. The following theorem [MT91] plays a key role in our discussion.

Theorem 1. *The problem to decide whether a finite propositional logic program has a stable model is NP-complete.*

Theorem 1 implies that for every decision problem Π in the class NP and for every instance $I \in D_\Pi$, there is a *propositional* program P^I_Π such that

(i) P^I_Π can be constructed in time polynomial in the size of I, and
(ii) Π has a solution for I if and only if P^I_Π has a stable model.

Thus, any decision problem Π in NP can be solved by a uniform control mechanism of deciding existence of stable models of logic programs. Given an instance I for which Π must be decided, one may encode Π and I as a propositional logic program P^I_Π (that can be constructed in time polynomial in the size of I) and decide whether I is a "yes" instance of Π by deciding whether P_Π^I has a stable model. Moreover, any decision problem that can be decided in this way is in NP.

Consider now a search problem Π. Assume that there is polynomial-time computable encoding assigning to every instance $I \in D_\Pi$ a propositional program P_Π^I. Assume also that there exists a polynomial-time computable function sol_Π defined on the set of pairs (I, M), where $I \in D_\Pi$ and M is a stable model of the program P_Π^I, such that the condition (i) and the following strengthening of the condition (ii) hold:

(iii) for every $I \in D_\Pi$, $sol_\Pi(I, \cdot)$ maps the set of stable models of P_Π^I *onto* $S_\Pi(I)$.

Search problems of this type can be solved in a similar way to the one described earlier for the case of decision problems. Given an instance $I \in D_\Pi$, one constructs the program P_Π^I, finds its stable model s, computes $sol_\Pi(I, s)$ (that is, decodes a solution to Π for I from the stable model s) and returns it as a solution to Π for I. If no stable model exists, the answer "no" is returned.

To the best of our knowledge, it is an open problem to characterize the class of search problems for which this approach can be used, that is, the class of search problems Π for which programs P_Π^I satisfying conditions (i) and (iii) can be found. We saw that all decision problems in the class NP can be solved in this way. Furthermore, all search problems whose associated decision problems are in NP, that we considered so far, also can be dealt with in this way (some of the encodings will be discussed later in the paper).

The approach presented above relies on encodings of decision and search problems as problems involving existence or computation of stable models of propositional programs. It is not entirely satisfactory as different programs P_Π^I are needed for each instance I of a problem or, to put it differently, the logic is not separated from data. We will now present yet another possible approach that takes advantage of variables in the language.

Consider a search problem Π. Assume that there exist:

(iv) an effective encoding edb_Π under which every instance $I \in D_\Pi$ is represented as a database under some, fixed for all instances from D_Π, relational database scheme,
(v) a *single* finite SLP program, P_Π, such that there is a polynomially computable function $sol_\Pi(\cdot, \cdot)$ such that for every $I \in D_\Pi$, $sol_\Pi(I, \cdot)$ maps the set of stable models of $edb_\Pi(I) \cup P_\Pi$ *onto* $S_\Pi(I)$.

Then, Π can be solved for an instance I by first constructing the program $edb_\Pi(I) \cup P_\Pi$, then by finding its stable model s and, finally, by reconstructing from s a solution $sol_\Pi^I(s)$.

This approach is more elegant and more in the spirit of standard programming. In this approach, P_Π can be regarded as a program (logic) for solving the problem Π, and the database $edb_\Pi(I)$ can be viewed as data. Thus, there is a clear separation of logic (uniform over all possible instances to the problem) and data (encodings of problem instances).

We say that a search problem can be *solved by a uniform SLP program* if there exist an encoding edb_Π and a program P_Π satisfying (iv) and (v). As in the case of two earlier approaches, the question is which search problems can be solved by a uniform SLP program. The following strengthening of Theorem 1 was first proved in [Sch95].

Theorem 2. *A decision problem can be solved by a uniform SLP program if and only if it is in the class NP.*

Thus, for decision problems we have a complete answer. The problem remains open for arbitrary search problems. Let us point out, though, that all search problems, whose associated decision problems are in NP, that we considered so far, can be so solved.

To summarize, due to the absence of function symbols, the expressive power of stable logic programming is restricted as compared to Horn logic programming. However, due to the use of negation and the stable model semantics, some of the lost expressive power is recovered. SLP can capture all decision problems in NP and many (perhaps all) search problems whose decision versions are in NP.

6 Recursion Versus Constraints

The restrictions in the syntax of SLP, the change in the semantics and, consequently, the change in the notion of specification (from (1) to (2)) requires a different approach to programming. Perhaps most importantly, the use of recursion is severely restricted. A limited version of recursion is still available. Namely, recursive definitions of predicates (or rather of sets that are their extensions) can be modeled by SLP clauses. For instance, the following SLP clauses define the transitive closure of a relation *rel*

$$tc(X,Y) \leftarrow rel(X,Y)$$
$$tc(X,Y) \leftarrow tc(X,Z), rel(Z,Y)$$

However, without function symbols to build terms representing higher-order objects, it is far from clear how a clause could capture such recursive definitions that specify how more complex objects are constructed from simpler ones. For instance, consider the following HLP program:

(clq1) $clique([X]) \leftarrow vertex(X)$
(clq2) $clique([Y|X]) \leftarrow clique(X), allconnected(Y,X)$

We assume here that the predicate $allconnected(Y,X)$ is defined so that to succeed precisely when vertex Y is connected by an edge to all vertices on list

X, and when X has no repetitions. The program consisting of the definition of *allconnected*, of clauses (clq1) and (clq2) and of the description of a graph G in terms of facts specifying the extensions of the predicates *vertex* and *edge*, computes all cliques in G. Notice that each time clause (clq2) is used in computation, it produces a longer list (more precisely, each iteration of the one-step operator associated with this program generates new ground terms that need to be included in the extension of the predicate *clique*. The capability of growing the set of available ground terms is both a strength and a weakness of HLP. It allows to code all hereditarily finite sets but, at the same time, makes it possible to write programs that do not terminate.

This phenomenon does not occur in SLP — the available constants are prescribed from the beginning and no new terms can be built of these constants as there are no function symbols that could accomplish this. At the same time, as we saw earlier, SLP is expressive enough to specify *some* higher-order objects. Namely, an SLP program specifies the collection of its stable models (or, as we defined in (2), collections of extensions of predicates in stable models). Clauses of the program do not represent recursive definitions of individual stable models but (often in groups) act as *constraints*. For instance, when considered in isolation, a ground clause

$$C = p \leftarrow q_1, \ldots, q_m, \mathbf{not}(r_1), \ldots, \mathbf{not}(r_n)$$

expresses the following constraint: at least one q_i does not belong to a putative stable model M, or at least one r_j belongs to M, or p belongs to M. In other words, M must be a model of the clause C treated as a propositional formula. Moreover, in a crucial difference with propositional logic, stable logic programming adds to this constraint also a preferred way to compute sets that satisfy it: in order to enforce the constraint, once all q_i are computed and none of r_j was established, p is added to the set rather than some q_i eliminated or some r_j added.

Here lies the key difference between Horn logic programming and stable logic programming. To specify a higher-order object in Horn logic programming, the programmer models the object as a term and represents in a program a recursive definition of the object. To specify a second-order object in SLP, the programmer thinks of the object as a stable model of a program and constructs the program by modeling a definition of the object expressed in terms of constraints. This feature makes SLP especially well suited to deal with constraint satisfaction problems, a point made in [Nie98].

An important issue raised by our discussion is how to represent constraints by SLP clauses. We will now present one such technique of adding *selection* clauses (in the case of default logic, this techniques is discussed in [CMMT98]).

Many applications specify objects of interest to a problem at hand by first specifying a general domain from which these objects have to be selected (the family of all subsets of a set, the family of all n-tuples over a given set, etc.)

and, then, by specifying additional conditions (constraints) these objects have to satisfy. In particular, constraint satisfaction problems are of this type.

Thus, to develop programs encoding solutions to such problems we might proceed in two steps. First, we develop an SLP program whose family of stable models encodes the general domain of candidate objects (all subsets, all sequences of length n, etc.). Next, we add to this program clauses representing constraints that must be enforced.

In many applications, involving subsets of some universe U, constraints are of the following form (here, A and B are two subsets of the same universe U):

$C(A,B)$ if a solution contains the set A, it must also contain at least one element from B (or, in other words, a solution must not contain the set A or must contain at least one element from the set B)

Assume that P is an SLP program whose stable models are subsets of U. Let $\mathcal{S}$ be a family of all stable models of P. To enforce the constraint $C(A,B)$ on sets in $\mathcal{S}$, that is, to construct a program whose stable models are exactly these stable models of P that satisfy $C(A,B)$, it is enough to add to P the clause (here $A = \{a_1,\ldots,a_k\}$ and $B = \{b_1,\ldots,b_m\}$):

$$k_{C(A,B)}: \qquad f \leftarrow a_1,\ldots,a_k, \mathbf{not}(b_1),\ldots,\mathbf{not}(b_m), \mathbf{not}(f)$$

where f is an atom not occurring in P. Formally, we have the following theorem[3].

Theorem 3. *Let P be a logic program and let $\mathcal{S}$ be the family of stable models of P. Then, for every constraint $C(A,B)$ where A and B are sets of atoms, M is a stable model of $P \cup \{k_{C(A,B)}\}$ if and only if $M \in \mathcal{S}$ and M satisfies $C(A,B)$.*

As a corollary from Theorem 3, it follows that conjunctions of constraints of type $C(A,B)$ (that is, formulas in the conjunctive normal form) can be enforced by SLP programs consisting of clauses $k_{C(A,B)}$, for each conjunct $C(A,B)$. Moreover, the size of this SLP program is linear in the size of the CNF formula.

Theorem 3 is only the first step towards a methodology of programming with SLP programs, since not all types of constraints can be represented by a single program clause. A *systematic* study of programming techniques appropriate in the case of SLP has not yet been conducted and is an important research topic. However, even the technique described above is quite powerful.

[3] A technique for enforcing constraints under supported model semantics of Clark was proposed by Lloyd and Topor in [LT84]. It is easy to see that their technique is applicable to stable model semantics as well. Theorem 3 is a particular case of Lloyd and Topor technique. We are grateful to Marc Denecker for bringing it to our attention.

We will now illustrate how it can be applied to encode several combinatorial problems.

First, we will revisit our "clique" problem. We assume that the graph is described by two lists of facts: $vertex(a)$ for all vertices a of the graph (we will denote the set of vertices by V), and $edge(a,b)$, for all edges $\{a,b\}$ of the graph. We denote these lists of facts by $edb_{clq}(G)$. To specify cliques by an SLP program, one first needs to write a program specifying all subsets of the set of vertices of a graph. This can be accomplished, for instance, by the following two clauses:

$$\begin{array}{ll}(\text{CLQ1}) & in(X) \leftarrow vertex(X), \mathbf{not}(out(X)) \\ (\text{CLQ2}) & out(X) \leftarrow vertex(X), \mathbf{not}(in(X))\end{array}$$

Stable models of the program consisting of clauses (CLQ1) and (CLQ2), and of facts $edb_{clq}(G)$ are of the form

$$edb_{clq}(G) \cup \{in(v): v \in K\} \cup \{out(v): v \notin K\},$$

where K is a subset of the vertex set. Thus, the stable models of this program are in one-to-one correspondence to all subsets of the vertex set and can be regarded as their representations.

Next, we need to select those stable models that represent sets satisfying the clique condition: any two vertices in a clique are connected by an edge. This condition may be expressed as a constraint of the type $C(A,B)$: if two vertices are in a clique then they are equal or they are connected with an edge. Thus, all these constraints (for all pairs of vertices) can be expressed by a single SLP clause:

$$\begin{array}{ll}(\text{CLQ3}) & f \leftarrow vertex(X), vertex(Y), in(X), in(Y), \mathbf{not}(X = Y), \\ & \quad \mathbf{not}(edge(X,Y)), \mathbf{not}(f)\end{array}$$

By Theorem 3, the program consisting of facts $edb_{clq}(G)$, and clauses (CLQ1) - (CLQ3) has as its stable models precisely those sets of the form $edb_{clq}(G) \cup \{in(v): v \in K\} \cup \{out(v): v \notin K\}$, for which K is a clique.

We will now further illustrate this approach by describing programs encoding the following problems:

1. Computing hamiltonian cycles in directed graphs,
2. Computing models of a propositional CNF formula,

For the first problem, we will need to represent directed graphs. Let G be a directed graph with the set of vertices V and with the set of directed edges E. We will represent G by the following facts: $vertex(a)$, for all vertices $a \in V$, $edge(a,b)$, for all *directed* edges $(a,b) \in E$, and $initialvtx(a0)$, for some vertex $a0 \in V$. We will denote this representation of G by $edb_{ham}(G)$.

Next consider the following clauses:

(HAM1) $in(V1, V2) \leftarrow edge(V1, V2), \mathbf{not}(out(V1, V2))$
(HAM2) $out(V1, V2) \leftarrow edge(V1, V2), \mathbf{not}(in(V1, V2))$

These two clauses, together with the set of facts $edb_{ham}(G)$ define an SLP program whose stable models are of the form

$$edb_{ham}(G) \cup \{in(a,b) : (a,b) \in A\} \cup \{out(a,b) : (a,b) \notin A\},$$

for some set of edges A. Thus, these stable models represent all subsets of the set of edges of G. Those sets of edges that are hamiltonian cycles satisfy the following additional constraints: (a) if two edges of the cycle end in the same vertex, then these edges are equal, and (b) if two edges of the cycle start in the same vertex then these edges are equal. By Theorem 3, these constraints can be enforced by adding the following two clauses:

(HAM3) $f \leftarrow in(V2, V1), in(V3, V1), \mathbf{not}(V2 = V3), \mathbf{not}(f)$
(HAM4) $f \leftarrow in(V1, V2), in(V1, V3), \mathbf{not}(V2 = V3), \mathbf{not}(f)$

The stable models of the so expanded program are of the form $edb_{ham}(G) \cup \{in(a,b) : (a,b) \in A\} \cup \{out(a,b) : (a,b) \notin A\}$, for some set of edges A spanning in G a set of vertex disjoint paths and cycles. Adding the following two clauses

(HAM5) $reached(V2) \leftarrow in(V1, V2), reached(V1)$
(HAM6) $reached(V2) \leftarrow in(V1, V2), initialvtx(V1)$

expands each of these stable models by the set of atoms $reached(a)$, for all these vertices a that can be reached from the vertex $a0$ by means of a nonempty sequence of edges that are "in" the model (note that we use this weaker notion of recursion that is still available in SLP). A stable model encodes a hamiltonian cycle if all vertices are reached. This constraint is enforced by the clause:

(HAM7) $f \leftarrow \mathbf{not}(reached(X)), \mathbf{not}(f)$

It follows that the program consisting of clauses (HAM1) - (HAM7) and of the facts in the set $edb_{ham}(G)$ has as its stable models the sets of the form

$$edb_{ham}(G) \cup \{reached(a) : a \in V\} \cup \{in(a,b) : (a,b) \in A\} \cup \{out(a,b) : (a,b) \notin A\},$$

for which A is the set of the edges of a hamiltonian cycle in G.

For the satisfiability problem, we need to represent CNF formulas. Consider a CNF formula φ with the set of clauses C and the set of variables V. The formula φ will be represented by several lists of facts: $var(a)$, for each $a \in V$, $clause(c)$, for each clause $c \in C$, $pos(c, v)$, for each variable v and clause c such that v appears positively in c, and $neg(c, v)$, for each variable v and clause c such that v appears negatively in c. This specification of a CNF formula φ will be denoted by $edb_{sat}(\varphi)$.

Consider now the following clauses:

$$\begin{array}{lll} \text{(SAT1)} & true(X) \leftarrow & var(X), \mathbf{not}(false(X)) \\ \text{(SAT2)} & false(X) \leftarrow & var(X), \mathbf{not}(true(X)) \end{array}$$

These two clauses generate all possible truth assignments to variables in V. More formally, the program consisting of $edb_{sat}(\varphi)$ and clauses (SAT1) and (SAT2) has as its stable models the sets of the form $edb_{sat}(\varphi) \cup \{true(v) : v \in U\} \cup \{false(v) : v \in V \setminus U\}$, where U is a subset of V. Thus, they represent the set of all valuations. The next two clauses

$$\begin{array}{ll} \text{(SAT3)} & sat(C) \leftarrow var(X), clause(C), true(X), pos(C,X) \\ \text{(SAT4)} & sat(C) \leftarrow var(X), clause(C), false(X), neg(C,X) \end{array}$$

simply define when a clause is satisfied and add to each stable model the set of clauses that are true in the valuation represented by this model. Formula φ is satisfiable if there is a valuation which makes all clauses true. This requirement can be enforced by adding the clause

$$\text{(SAT5)} \qquad f \leftarrow \quad clause(C), \mathbf{not}(sat(C)), \mathbf{not}(f)$$

It follows that M is a stable model of the program consisting of clauses (SAT1) - (SAT5) and of the facts in the set $edb_{sat}(\varphi)$ if and only if

$$M = edb_{sat}(\varphi) \cup \{sat(c) : c \in \mathcal{C}\} \cup \{true(v) : v \in U\} \cup \{false(v) : v \in V \setminus U\},$$

where $U \subseteq V$ is a (propositional) model of φ.

The encodings presented so far are *uniform*. That is, input data to a problem is encoded as a collection of facts and the constraints defining the problem as clauses (usually with variables) with the latter part not depending on a particular input. These two parts correspond well to the extensional and intensional components of a $DATALOG^{\neg}$ program. However, other encodings are also possible (and often easier to come up with).

To make the point, let us again consider the satisfiability problem. As before, consider a CNF formula φ with a set of variables V and a set of clauses $\mathcal{C}$. This time we will represent valuations as subsets of V. It turns out that there is a very simple propositional encoding of the satisfiability problem. First, note that the clauses

$$\begin{array}{ll} \text{(SAT}'\text{1)} & in(v) \leftarrow \mathbf{not}(out(v)) \\ \text{(SAT}'\text{2)} & out(v) \leftarrow \mathbf{not}(in(v)) \end{array}$$

(where in both (SAT′1) and (SAT′2) v ranges over V), specify all subsets of V. That is, the stable models of the program consisting of all clauses (SAT′1) and (SAT′2) are precisely the sets of the form $\{in(a) : a \in M\} \cup \{out(a) : a \in V \setminus M\}$, where M is a subset of V. Now, for each clause

$$c: \qquad \neg a_1 \vee \ldots \vee \neg a_k \vee b_1 \vee \ldots \vee b_m$$

of φ, add to the program the SLP clause

$$\text{(SAT}'3) \qquad f \leftarrow a_1, \ldots, a_k, \mathbf{not}(b_1), \ldots, \mathbf{not}(b_m), \mathbf{not}(f)$$

Since a set of atoms satisfies clause c if and only if it satisfies the constraint $C(\{a_1, \ldots, a_k\}, \{b_1, \ldots, b_m\})$, it follows that the program consisting of all clauses (SAT′1) - (SAT′3) has as its stable models sets of the form $\{in(a) : a \in M\} \cup \{out(a) : a \in V \setminus M\}$, where M is a model of φ.

Let us emphasize that the encodings discussed in this section are not unique. Two satisfiability encodings given here constitute but one example. Further, a different encoding of the hamiltonian cycle problem can be found in [Nie98] and more encodings (as propositional default theories and logic programs) for several combinatorial problems were given in [CMMT98]. These encodings may have different computational properties. In particular, the second encoding of satisfiability, even though it is not uniform and requires that a separate program be created for each satisfiability instance, may actually be better suited for processing. Thus, the issue of the programming methodology likely to result in programs whose stable models can be quickly computed is very important. It has not been studied yet but must receive significant attention if stable logic programming is to become a practical problem-solving tool.

7 Uniform Control in SLP

As we have seen in the earlier sections, SLP programs can specify a wide class of search and decision problems. In addition, they do so in a declarative fashion by modeling, in a direct way, constraints defining a problem at hand. Thus, SLP programs are well suited to represent the "logic" part in Kowalski's "algorithm = logic + control" phrase.

In order for the stable logic programming to serve as an effective computational problem solving tool (and not only as a knowledge representation formalism), we need to develop the other component of the Kowalski's equation — a *uniform control*. Since, in stable logic programming, problems are encoded by SLP programs and solutions correspond to stable models, this uniform control must consist of algorithms to process SLP programs and compute (or decide the existence of) their stable models.

Several such algorithms were proposed in the recent years. In particular, algorithms were proposed to decide the existence of stable models of a *propositional* logic program P, and to compute one (or all) stable models of P, if they exist. Algorithms that decide the membership of an atom in some or all stable models were also developed [NS96,CMT96,ELM+97,ADN97].

These algorithms employ a backtracking search through the space of all subsets of the Herbrand base of the program (the collection of all propositional letters that occur in the program). They also use a variety of search space pruning techniques. Some of these techniques rely on a generalization of the concept of stratification [CMT96]. Other methods use well-founded semantics in a way unit propagation is used in Davis-Putnam procedure for computing models of CNF formulas [NS96].

Notice that since there are no function symbols in the language of SLP, the Herbrand universe, the Herbrand base and the grounding of an *arbitrary* (that is, not necessarily propositional) finite SLP program are finite. There are straightforward algorithms to produce the (finite) ground version of a finite SLP program. More sophisticated algorithms, minimizing the size of the ground program while preserving the stable models, were proposed recently in [NS96,Cho96]. Thus, algorithms to compute stable models of finite propositional programs can be used with arbitrary finite SLP programs, too (and termination is guaranteed).

These algorithms led to implementations of several systems for processing SLP programs and for computing their stable models. Among them are *smodels* [NS95,NS96], DeReS [CMT96] and the system `dlv` described in [ELM+97]. Any of these systems can be used as a control mechanism for the stable logic programming environment and transforms SLP from a knowledge representation formalism into a computational programming tool.

Thus, in the transition from Horn logic programming to SLP not only the semantics and the methodology of programming changes. The control has to change, too. Instead of SLD resolution, the basis for the control mechanism of SLP is provided by backtracking search algorithms for search spaces of subsets of a given finite set (Herbrand base of a finite SLP program).

The stable logic programming became a viable proposal for a new logic programming system with recent advances in algorithms for computing stable models and subsequent implementations of these algorithms [NS96,CMT96], [ELM+97]. Even though comprehensive studies of these implementations have yet to be performed, available results provide reasons for optimism. For some classes of programs, systems such as *smodels* [NS96] and DeReS [CMT96] can successfully process programs with tens of thousands of clauses. In addition, as reported in [Nie98], *smodels* can successfully compete on a class of planning problems with special purpose planners (for more comprehensive discussion of applications of logic programming to planning see the paper by Lifschitz [Lif98] in this volume). It is clear that with the performance of the systems computing stable models improving, the attractiveness of SLP as a computational tool will grow.

Despite a significant progress and the existence of systems such as *smodels* and DeReS, much more work on algorithms for computing stable models is needed in order to obtain acceptable performance. There are several open problems such as development of new and more powerful pruning techniques and study of probabilistic algorithms for stable model computation.

8 Conclusions and Future Directions

In the paper we discussed the stable model semantics as the foundation of a computational logic programming system different from Horn logic programming. This system, the stable logic programming or SLP, shares with other logic programming systems their key feature: the separation of logic from control. However, despite the fact that the stable model semantics has its roots in the efforts to extend the principles of Horn logic programming to the case of programs with negation, the stable logic programming in several aspects differs significantly from standard logic programming systems.

1. In the SLP programs are assigned a collection of intended models rather than a single intended model as in Horn logic programming, stratified logic programming or logic programming with well-founded semantics.
2. Since there are no function symbols in the language, higher-order objects are represented in the SLP as stable models of programs rather than as ground terms of the Herbrand universe, as it is the case in Horn logic programming and other similar systems.
3. SLP programs are interpreted as sets of constraints on objects to be computed unlike in Horn logic programming where clauses model recursive definitions rather than constraints.
4. The control mechanism of SLP is no longer resolution-based. Instead, the uniform control of SLP consists of backtracking search algorithms for computing stable models of programs.
5. The SLP has lower expressive power than standard logic programming systems. While it may seem to be a limitation, the class of problems that can be solved in the SLP is still quite wide and includes all decision problems from NP and many search and constraint satisfaction problems of importance in artificial intelligence and operations research.

We believe that the perspective of stable logic programming presented in the paper certainly warrants further investigations. We will now outline several interesting research directions.

Let us start with the following fundamental question: why to use the stable logic programming and not simply propositional logic. Indeed, a finite collection of clauses (possibly with variables but not with function symbols) together with a finite collection of facts can be viewed as a representation of a finite propositional formula in the conjunctive normal form. Consequently, it can be viewed as an encoding of the family of models of this formula (in the same way in which an SLP program represents the family of its stable models - a key observation underlying stable model programming). Moreover, since propositional satisfiability problem is NP-complete, all decision problems in NP can be reduced in polynomial time to satisfiability testing. In view of the recent progress in algorithms for satisfiability testing [DABC96,SK93,SKC94], propositional logic deserves closer scrutiny as a knowledge representation mechanism. The work on applications of satisfiability algorithms to planning (see, for instance, [SK92]) further supports this contention.

Is there then a real need to resort to logic programming? This is a challenging open problem. We believe the answer is positive but cannot offer any rigorous argument in support of the claim. In our opinion, the advantage of stable logic programming stems from the following two properties of stable models. First, they are minimal. Thus, when dealing with optimization problems minimality comes for free with the stable model semantics. Second, they are *grounded* — facts are included in stable models only if they can be justified. Furthermore, a comparison between existing encodings of combinatorial problems shows that in many cases encodings in terms of logic programs are more concise than those in terms of satisfiability (possibly due to the groundedness property of stable models). In particular, we believe that the most concise encodings of the existence of a hamiltonian cycle problem as the problem of the existence of a stable model of a logic program are asymptotically more concise than similar encodings as the problem of the existence of a satisfying valuation of a CNF formula.

The contention of more concise representations available with SLP as compared to propositional encodings is based on experience rather than on a formal analysis. Developing a formal setting to compare stable logic programming with propositional logic and providing a rigorous account of advantages and disadvantages of both approaches are important general theoretical challenges.

The second important research direction is the development of a systematic study of the methodology for developing SLP programs. Some initial steps in this direction were presented in Section 6. There is a potential tradeoff here. On one hand, one of the most important objectives is ease of program development. On the other hand, we want our programs to run fast.

Third, despite the recent successes with implementing systems based on the stable model semantics, there is still much to be done. So far, performance studies for the existing systems have been rather ad hoc. More comprehensive experimental studies are needed that will give insights into the computational nature of stable models and will lead to faster algorithms. To support such studies one needs benchmarking systems. One step in this direction is TheoryBase, a system described in [CMMT95,CMMT98].

Next, the SLP seems to be especially well suited for dealing with constraint satisfaction problems. Thus, it is important to extend the language of the SLP so that important classes of constraints involving arithmetic operations and relations became easier to model. Possibility of incorporating the SLP into existing constraint solving systems is another important problem.

Finally, there is already evidence that the SLP can be a useful tool in solving planning problems [Nie98]. Studying applicability of the SLP paradigm to other classical problems of artificial intelligence and operations research may provide additional motivation to focusing on this approach and may gain badly needed recognition to logic programming.

Acknowledgements

The authors were partially supported by the NSF grants CDA-9502645 and IRI-9619233. The authors gratefully acknowledge comments of Howard Blair, Thomas Eiter, Vladimir Lifschitz and Ilkka Niemelä.

References

[ADP95] J.J. Alferes, C.V. Damásio and L.M. Pereira. A logic programming system for nonmonotonic reasoning. *Journal of Automated Reasoning*, 14:93–147, 1995.

[AB90] K. Apt and H.A. Blair. Arithmetical classification of perfect models of stratified programs. *Fundamenta Informaticae*, 12:1–17, 1990.

[ABW88] K. Apt, H.A. Blair, and A. Walker. Towards a theory of declarative knowledge. In J. Minker, editor, *Foundations of deductive databases and logic programming*, pages 89–142, Los Altos, CA, 1988. Morgan Kaufmann.

[ACY91] F. Afrati, S. Cosmodakis, and M. Yannakakis. On DATALOG vs. polynomial time. In *Proceedings of PODS'91*, pages 13–25, 1991.

[ADN97] C. Aravindan, J. Dix, and I. Niemelä. Dislop: Toward a disjunctive logic programming system. In *Proceedings of the 4th International Conference on Logic Programming and Nonmonotonic Reasoning*, pages 341–352, 1997. Springer LN in Computer Science 1265.

[AHV95] S. Abiteboul, R. Hull, and V. Vianu. *Foundations of Databases.* Addison-Wesley Publishing Company, 1995.

[AN78] H. Andreka and I. Nemeti. The generalized completeness of Horn predicate logic as a programming language. *Acta Cybernetica*, 4:3–10, 1978.

[AvE82] K.R. Apt and M.H. van Emden. Contributions to the theory of logic programming. *Journal of the ACM*, 29:841–862, 1982.

[BF91] N. Bidoit and C. Froidevaux. Negation by default and unstratifiable logic programs. *Theoretical Computer Science*, 78:85–112, 1991.

[BMS95] H.A. Blair, W. Marek, and J. Schlipf. The expressiveness of locally stratified programs. *Annals of Mathematics and Artificial Intelligence*, 15:209–229, 1995.

[Cho96] P. Cholewinski. *Automated reasoning with Default Logic.* PhD thesis, University of Kentucky, 1996. Ph.D. Thesis.

[CKPR73] A. Colmerauer, H. Kanoui, R. Pasero, and P. Roussel. Un système de communication homme-machine en français. Technical report, University of Marseille, 1973.

[CL73] C.-L. Chang and C.-T. Lee. *Symbolic Logic and Mechanical Theorem Proving.* Academic Press, 1973.

[Cla78] K.L. Clark. Negation as failure. In H. Gallaire and J. Minker, editors, *Logic and data bases*, pages 293–322. Plenum Press, 1978.

[CMMT95] P. Cholewiński, W. Marek, A. Mikitiuk, and M. Truszczyński. Experimenting with nonmonotonic reasoning. In *Proceedings of the 12th International Conference on Logic Programming*, pages 267–281. MIT Press, 1995.

[CMMT98] P. Cholewiński, W. Marek, A. Mikitiuk, and M. Truszczyński. Programming with default logic. Submitted for publication, 1998.

[CMT96] P. Cholewiński, W. Marek, and M. Truszczyński. Default reasoning system DeReS. In *Proceedings of KR-96*, pages 518–528. Morgan Kaufmann, 1996.

[CP98] M. Cadoli and L. Palipoli. Circumscribing datalog: expressive power and complexity. *Theoretical Computer Science*, 193:215–244, 1998.

[CPSV98] M. Cadoli, L. Palipoli, A. Schaerf, and D. Vasile. Np-spec: An executable specification language for solving all problems in np. Unpublished manuscript, 1998.

[DABC96] O. Dubois, P. Andre, Y. Boufkhad, and J. Carlier. Sat versus unsat. In *Cliques, Coloring and Satisfiability, Second DIMACS Implementation Challenge*, pages 415–436. American Mathematical Society, 1996.

[ELM+97] T. Eiter, N. Leone, C. Mateis, G. Pfeifer, and F. Scarcello. A deductive system for non-monotonic reasoning. In *Proceedings of the 4th International Conference on Logic Programming and Nonmonotonic Reasoning*, pages 363–374, 1997. Springer LN in Computer Science 1265.

[ELM+98] T. Eiter, N. Leone, C. Mateis, G. Pfeifer, and F. Scarcello. The KR System dlv: Progress Report, Comparisons, and Benchmarks. In *Proceedings Sixth International Conference on Principles of Knowledge Representation and Reasoning (KR-98)*, pages 406–417, June 2–4 1998.

[GJ79] M.R. Garey and D.S. Johnson. *Computers and intractability; a guide to the theory of NP-completeness.* W.H. Freeman, 1979.

[GL88] M. Gelfond and V. Lifschitz. The stable semantics for logic programs. In *Proceedings of the 5th International Symposium on Logic Programming*, pages 1070–1080, Cambridge, MA, 1988. MIT Press.

[Her30] J. Herbrand. *Recherches sur la théorie de la démonstrations.* PhD thesis, Paris, 1930.

[Kam97] M. Kaminski. A note on stable semantics for logic programs. *Artificial Intelligence Journal*, 96:467–479, 1997.

[Kow74] R. Kowalski. Predicate logic as a programming language. In *Proceedings of IFIP 74*, pages 569–574, Amsterdam, 1974. North Holland.

[Kow79] R. Kowalski. *Logic for Problem Solving.* North Holland, Amsterdam, 1979.

[Lif98] V. Lifschitz. Action languages, answer sets and planning. This volume.

[Llo84] J. Lloyd. *Foundations of logic programming.* Berlin: Springer-Verlag, 1984.

[Lov78] D. Loveland. *Automated Theorem Proving: A Logical Basis.* North Holland, 1978.

[LT84] J.W. Lloyd and R.W. Topor. Making prolog more expressive. *Journal of Logic Programming*, 1(3):225–240, 1984.

[MNR94] W. Marek, A. Nerode, and J. B. Remmel. The stable models of predicate logic programs. *Journal of Logic Programming*, 21(3):129–154, 1994.

[MT89] W. Marek and M. Truszczyński. Stable semantics for logic programs and default theories. In *Proceedings of the North American Conference on Logic Programming*, pages 243–256. MIT Press, 1989.

[MT91] W. Marek and M. Truszczyński. Autoepistemic logic. *Journal of the ACM*, 38:588–619, 1991.

[MT93] W. Marek and M. Truszczyński. *Nonmonotonic Logic – Context-Dependent Reasoning.* Series Artificial Intelligence, Springer-Verlag, 1993.

[MW88] D. Maier and D. S. Warren. *Computing with logic. Logic programming with Prolog.* The Benjamin/Cummings Publishing Company, Inc., 1988.

[Nie98] I. Niemelä. Logic programs with stable model semantics as a constraint programming paradigm. In *Proceedings of the Workshop on Computational Aspects of Nonmonotonic Reasoning*, pages 72–79, 1998.

[NS95] I. Niemelä and P. Simons. Evaluating an algorithm for default reasoning. In *Proceedings of the IJCAI-95 Workshop on Applications and Implementations of Nonmonotonic Reasoning Systems*, 1995.

[NS96] I. Niemelä and P. Simons. Efficient implementation of the well-founded and stable model semantics. In *Proceedings of JICSLP-96.* MIT Press, 1996.

[Prz88] T. Przymusiński. On the declarative semantics of deductive databases and logic programs. In *Foundations of deductive databases and logic programming*, pages 193–216, Los Altos, CA, 1988. Morgan Kaufmann.

[Prz90] T. Przymusinski. The Well-Founded Semantics Coincides With The Three-Valued Stable Semantics, *Fundamenta Informaticae*, 13:445–464, 1990.

[Rei80] R. Reiter. A logic for default reasoning. *Artificial Intelligence*, 13:81–132, 1980.

[Rob65] J.A. Robinson. Machine-oriented logic based on resolution principle. *Journal of the ACM*, 12:23–41, 1965.

[RRS+97] P. Rao, I.V. Ramskrishnan, K. Sagonas, T. Swift, D. S. Warren, and J. Freire. XSB: A system for efficiently computing well-founded semantics. In *Proceedings of LPNMR'97*, pages 430–440, Lecture Notes in Computer Science, 1265, Springer-Verlag, 1997.

[Sch95] J. Schlipf. The expressive powers of the logic programming semantics. *Journal of the Computer Systems and Science*, 51:64–86, 1995.

[SK92] B. Selman and H. A. Kautz. Planning as satisfiability. In *Proceedings of the 10th European Conference on Artificial Intelligence*, Vienna, Austria, 1992.

[SK93] B. Selman and H. Kautz. Domain-independent extensions to GSAT: Solving large structured satisfiability problems. In *Proceedings of IJCAI-93*, San Mateo, CA, Morgan Kaufmann, 1993.

[SKC94] B. Selman, H.A. Kautz, and B. Cohen. Noise strategies for improving local search. In *Proceedings of the Twelfth National Conference on Artificial Intelligence (AAAI-94)*, Seattle, USA, AAAI Press, 1994.

[Smu68] R.M. Smullyan. *First-Order Logic.* Springer-Verlag, 1968.

[Ull88] J.D. Ullman. *Principles of Database and Knowledge-Base Systems.* Computer Science Press, Rockville, MD, 1988.

[VRS91] A. Van Gelder, K.A. Ross, and J.S. Schlipf. Unfounded sets and well-founded semantics for general logic programs. *Journal of the ACM*, 38:620–650, 1991.

8 Database Systems

Query languages for relational databases, such as SQL, rely on logic for their semantics. The main objective of deductive database research is extending the expressive power of these languages to support reasoning, expert systems and other advanced applications. This line of research has produced techniques to efficiently support positive logic program evaluation via a bottom-up computation of least fixpoints. Then the notion of stratification was introduced to deal with nonmonotonic constructs such as negation and set aggregates. These advances were included in the new generation of commercial object/relational DB systems; thus SQL3 standards include support for stratified recursive queries.

Zaniolo and **Wang** revisit semantic and implementation issues for set aggregates, including user-defined aggregates. The characterization of aggregates by programs with nondeterministic choice constructs (which are known to have stable model semantics) yields the identification of a subclass of aggregates that are monotonic, and, thus, can be freely used in recursive programs. Several examples are given to illustrate the use of these aggregates in complex queries that are not supported well in either current SQL systems or Datalog prototypes. Finally, they describe efficient implementations of such user-defined aggregates in LDL++ and DB2.

Logic-Based User-Defined Aggregates for the Next Generation of Database Systems

Carlo Zaniolo and Haixun Wang

Computer Science Department, University of California at Los Angeles,
Los Angeles, CA 90095, USA

Summary. In this paper, we provide logic-based foundations for the extended aggregate constructs required by advanced database applications. In particular, we focus on data mining applications and show that they require user-defined aggregates extended with early returns. Thus, we propose a simple formalization of extended user-defined aggregates using the nondeterministic construct of choice. We obtain programs that have a formal semantics based on the concept of total stable models, but are also amenable to efficient implementation. Our formalization leads to a simple syntactic characterization of user-defined aggregates that are monotone with respect to set containment. Therefore, these aggregates can be freely used in recursive programs, and the fixpoints for such programs can be computed efficiently using the standard techniques of deductive databases. We describe the many new applications of user-defined aggregates, and their implementation for the logical data language $\mathcal{LDL}$++. Finally, we discuss the transfer of this technology to SQL databases.

1 Introduction

A new wave of database applications, particularly decision-support and data mining applications, are based on complex aggregates not supported by current DBMSs: in fact, SQL2 specifications only prescribe support for the five built-in aggregates of *sum, count, avg, max and min.* To remedy this problem, many vendors have moved to add new aggregates, such as data cubes [12] in their commercial releases. However, ad-hoc extensions by vendors are never enough, since data mining applications alone require a wide variety of new aggregate functions; moreover, other application domains, such as temporal reasoning and time-series analysis, require many new aggregates as well. A general solution consists in extending Database Management Systems (DBMSs) with *user-defined aggregates* (UDAs)—a functionality already provided, in Postgres [24] and SQL3 [19]. As we shall discuss later in the paper, however, the approaches followed by SQL3 and Postgres suffer from various limitations, which can be summarized as follows:

- Lack of declarative semantics, since the aggregates are defined via functions coded in a procedural language, and
- the aggregates so defined cannot express many of the aggregates used by data-mining applications (e.g., online aggregation), and cannot be used

in defining recursive predicates because of their nonmonotonic nature (in SQL3, negation and aggregates can only be used in stratified queries).

In this paper, we provide a simple and general solution to these problems as follows. In the next section, we discuss the different kinds aggregations required by new applications. In Section 3, we focus on the problems that current aggregates have in supporting these applications and, in Section 4, we propose user-defined aggregates for Datalog that express all the aggregates of interest. We also describe their efficient implementation in the extended $\mathcal{LDL}$++ system implemented at UCLA (Section 6). In Section 5, we propose a formal logic-based semantics for aggregates using the notion of stable models and nondeterministic choice. This semantics leads to a simple syntactic characterization of monotone aggregates, Section 7. Monotone aggregates can thus be used to support new applications, which are discussed in Section 8. The significance of these advances for SQL DBMSs is discussed in section 9.

2 New Applications Require New Aggregates

Our study of data mining and decision support applications suggest that data mining algorithms

- make heavy use of aggregates, but
- often employ them in forms that cannot be supported well or efficiently by SQL2.

Similar conclusions also apply to other advanced applications; however, data mining and decision support provide the best evidence of this general trend. As a first example, consider the data mining methods used for classification. For instance, say that we want to classify the value of PlayTennis as a 'Yes' or a 'No' given the following vector of attribute values

Outlook, Temperature, Humidity, Wind

and a training set such as that shown in Table 1.

The algorithm known as Boosted Bayesian Classifier [10] has proven to be the most effective at this task (in fact, it was the winner of the KDD'97 data mining competition). A *Naive Bayesian* [10] classifier makes probability-based predictions as follows. Let A_1, A_2, ..., A_k be attributes, with discrete values, used to predict a discrete class C. (For the example at hand, we have four prediction attributes, $k = 4$, and $C =$ 'PlayTennis'). For attribute values a_1 through a_k, the optimal prediction is the value c for which $Pr(C = c|A_1 = a_1 \wedge \ldots \wedge A_k = a_k)$ is maximal. By Bayes' rule, and assuming independence of the attributes, this means to classify a new tuple to the value of c that maximizes the product:

Outlook	Temp	Humidity	Wind	PlayTennis
Sunny	Hot	High	Weak	No
Sunny	Hot	High	Strong	No
Overcast	Hot	High	Weak	Yes
Rain	Mild	High	Weak	Yes
Rain	Cool	Normal	Weak	Yes
Rain	Cool	Normal	Strong	Yes
Overcast	Cool	Normal	Strong	No
Sunny	Mild	High	Weak	No
Sunny	Cool	Normal	Weak	Yes
Rain	Mild	Normal	Weak	Yes
Sunny	Mild	Normal	Strong	Yes
Overcast	Mild	High	Strong	Yes
Overcast	Hot	Normal	Weak	Yes
Rain	Mild	High	Strong	No

Table 1. Tennis

$$\prod_{j=1,\ldots,k} Pr(A_j = a_j | C = c)$$

But these probabilities can be estimated from the training set as follows:

$$Pr(A_j = a_j | C = c) = \frac{count(A_j = a_j \wedge C = c)}{count(C = c)}$$

The counts appearing in the numerator and denominator, above, can be easily computed using SQL aggregate queries. For instance, all the numerators values for the third column (the Wind column) can can be computed as follows:

```
SELECT Wind, PlayTennis, count(*)
FROM Tennis
GROUP BY Outlook, PlayTennis
```

For the training set of Table 1 this query returns:

```
(Weak, Yes, 6)
(Weak, No, 2)
(Strong, Yes, 3)
(Strong, No, 3)
```

Similar aggregate queries on the other three columns compute the remaining coefficients for the numerator, while the denominator can be evaluated by counting tuple grouped by PlayTennis. Then, the boosting step described in [29] can be implemented by simply increasing the weight of the misclassified tuples. In conclusion, this award-winning classification algorithm can be implemented well using the SQL count aggregate. This aggregate-based formulation is preferable to the original formulation given in [29] since it ensures scalability and performance on large training sets.

Count-like aggregates are also the linchpin of other classifiers, such as the one in [2] that will be discussed briefly in Section 8.

Associations. Many applications designed to discover associations make extensive use of count-like aggregates. For instance, consider the following example:

citizen(x,c), official_language(c,l) ⇒ speaks(x,l)

If citizen, official_language and speaks are stored as database relations, respectively named C, O and S, then the our confidence in the validity of this rule can be estimated as follows:

$$C_f = \frac{|(\pi_{1,3}C \bowtie O) \cap S|}{|(\pi_{1,3}C \bowtie O|} \tag{1}$$

The closer C_f is to 1, the stronger is our confidence in the validity of the rule. C_f can be computed by SQL queries using count.

In [29] we assume that we are given a database of relations and we describe a system to find implication rules, such as the one above, by searching for tables that satisfy some meta-level templates specified by the user. For instance, the transitive composition template applicable to our previous example is:

$$P(X,Y) \wedge Q(Y,Z) \Rightarrow R(X,Z)$$

where P, Q and R now stand for arbitrary database predicates. Then, the system search for the triplets P, Q and R of database relations for which C_f exceeds a given threshold, e.g., satisfies the condition $C_f > 0.8$. In [29], we described a system that uses the meta-level predicates of $\mathcal{LDL}$++ to perform such a search on a given database schema (using SQL's count aggregate on the underlying database).

In summary, some interesting association and classification methods can be implemented directly using the standard SQL2 aggregates. On the other hand, many complex and specialized aggregate computations used by other data mining algorithms cannot be expressed effectively using standard SQL2 aggregates. For instance, market data analysis represents one of the best known applications of association rules. The Apriori algorithm which is at core of this application searches for frequent items sets: i.e., it counts items and combination of items that are above a given threshold [2,3,5]. While this computation can be expressed using the SQL count aggregate, ensuring the efficiency of these queries represents much more of a challenge [27]. The same is true for a related class of queries called *iceberg queries* [11]. Also the classification algorithms discussed in [2] face similar problems—see discussion in Section 9.

In general, aggregate-like computations used in data mining algorithms cannot be implemented conveniently and efficiently using built-in SQL2 aggregates, or even employing SQL3's user-defined aggregates. We will now discuss their limitations and then propose an extended form of aggregate to overcome such limitations.

Online aggregation. The recently proposed concept of online aggregation finds many applications in data mining and OLAP algorithms [17]. A typical use of online aggregation is for estimating averages. Assuming that there is no skewing in the way the data is stored (or it is retrieved in ways that avoid skewing), the computation converges toward the final value after a relatively small portion of a large dataset is visited. Online aggregation provides a simple solution to this problem by the mechanism of *early returns*. By returning partial results, the online version of the aggregate allows the user to stop the computation as soon as convergence is reached within the desired degree of accuracy.

There are many situations where online aggregation is highly desirable; for instance, we can use it to speed-up the discovery of association rules, since C_f can be computed as the average value of a function f defined as follows: for each tuple contained in the denominator of Equation 1, f evaluates to one if the tuple is also contained in the numerator, and evaluates to zero otherwise. Thus, C_f can be evaluated using the following $\mathcal{LDL}$++ rule, where $\texttt{avg}\langle\texttt{W}\rangle$ in the head denotes that the aggregate **avg** is computed on the set of W-values satisfying the goals in the body of the rule:

$$\begin{aligned}\texttt{overlap}(\texttt{avg}\langle\texttt{W}\rangle) \leftarrow\ & \texttt{citizen}(\texttt{X},\texttt{Ct}), \texttt{official\_language}(\texttt{Ct},\texttt{L}),\\ & \texttt{if}(\texttt{speaks}(\texttt{X},\texttt{L})\ \texttt{then}\ \texttt{W} = 1\ \texttt{else}\ \texttt{W} = 0).\end{aligned}$$

Here, online aggregation can speed up the search dramatically, since the evaluation of most relation triplets can be dropped early if online average estimates are seen that fall well below the minimum threshold.

The ability of a computation to produce "early returns" is useful in many other situations besides online aggregation. For instance, to perform time-series analysis we need many different sorts of temporal aggregation, such as cumulative aggregation, and moving-window aggregation[21]. Thus, a user might request the running sum of sales, i.e., the running sum of the sales from a given time. This computation is facilitated by the fact that the data is normally stored sorted by time, as in Table 2. Then, for each new sale, the running sum simply adds the new amount to the running value and returns it as a partial result while continuing this one-pass computation. Thus the computation of a running sum is simple to express using the early-return mechanism of online aggregation. In SQL2, however, the running sum must be expressed as the sum of all sales up to the time of a given sale—a separate computation for each sale. SQL2 will also perform poorly in the computation of moving-window aggregate, where, e.g., we want to compute the average of last n sales, or the average of sales that took place during the last m days.

Year	Season	Month	Day	Year-Sales,	Season-Sales,	Month-Sales,	Day-Sales
1992	winter	feb	6	?	?	?	409
1992	winter	feb	26	?	648	648	239
1992	spring	mar	7	?	318	318	318
1992	summer	jun	23	?	?	394	394
1992	summer	jul	1	?	?	167	167
1992	summer	aug	22	?	?	?	176
1992	summer	aug	24	?	993	432	256
1992	fall	oct	13	?	?	?	481
1992	fall	oct	21	?	?	597	116
1992	fall	nov	11	2692	733	136	136

Table 2. Keeping track of Sales over Time

Another operation frequently used in OLAP and ROLAP applications is the computation of DataCubes [12]. A datacube is computed by *rolling-up* an aggregate over the different dimensions of data. In the temporal dimension, for instance, we might roll-up the sales by Year, Season, Month, and Day. In SQL2, we could find the daily sales by using group by Year, Season, Month, Day. and then find the monthly sales by group by Year, Season, Month, and so. This is quite wasteful since the computation of the monthly sales can be done in one pass over data that is temporally ordered. Therefore, many commercial DBMSs have now added special extensions for roll-up aggregates. However, it is easy to see that an early-return construct that supports online aggregation can also be used to compute roll-ups for data cubes. In fact, when the input changes from a day (month) to the next day (month), the aggregate value for the old day (month) can be returned while the aggregate computation for the new day (month) is restarted anew.

In summary, the ability of supporting early returns represents a critical extension that gives user-defined aggregates the ability to support a new wave of data-intensive applications, particularly data-mining applications. In the rest of the paper we develop the logic-based foundations for user-defined aggregates with and without early returns.

3 User-Defined Aggregates: the State of the Art

Postgres and SQL3. Postgres allows the user to specify aggregates in terms of state-transition functions [24,30]. The state functions sfuncl and sfunc2 compute the new state from the old state and the value of the new record. Finally, initcond is used to define the initial state of the aggregate, while finalfunc defines the computation to be performed at the end.

Postgres' idea of defining new aggregates by giving the functions for the initial state, the iteration state, and the final state has also influenced the SQL3 proposal. SQL3 prescribes that *iterative routines* should be used to define user-defined aggregates in some external language. In SQL3 [19], iterative routines consist of three parts:

- an *initialize routine* that gives an initial value to the aggregate
- an *iterate routine* yielding a new value for each new record in the table
- a *terminate routine* that returns the final value computed for the aggregate.

The $\mathcal{LDL}/\mathcal{LDL}$++ System The logical data language $\mathcal{LDL}$++, developed at MCC [9,33] supports user-defined aggregates. In $\mathcal{LDL}$++, an aggregate function f on a set S, can be introduced via the following inductive definition:

1. *Base*: the value $f(\{x\})$ on a singleton set must be defined in terms of x,
2. *Induction*: for any other set $S' = S \sqcup \{x\}$ the value of $f(S')$ must be defined in terms of $f(S)$ and x.

For instance, count and sum can be expressed as follows:

$Count$: $\mathsf{f}(\{\mathsf{x}\}) = 1$ *and* $\mathsf{f}(\mathsf{S}\sqcup \{\mathsf{x}\}) = \mathsf{f}(\mathsf{S}) + 1$
Sum : $\mathsf{f}(\{\mathsf{x}\}) = \mathsf{x}$ *and* $\mathsf{f}(\mathsf{S}\sqcup \{\mathsf{x}\}) = \mathsf{f}(\mathsf{S}) + \mathsf{x}$

In $\mathcal{LDL}$++, the computations pertaining to the base step and the induction step are expressed using, respectively, the predicates `single` and `multi`. Thus, `count` and `sum` could be expressed using the following rules:

For `count`:

```
single(count, Y, 1).
multi(count, Y, Old, New) ← New = Old + 1.
```

For `sum`:

```
single(sum, Y, Y).
multi(sum, Y, Old, New) ← New = Old + Y.
```

Once defined, the aggregates can be applied to concrete sets, or to virtual sets defined in the heads of rules. In this paper, we concentrate on the second situation, which syntactically, is denoted by pointed bracket pairs '⟨...⟩' in the head of a rule. For instance, to compute the number of employees in each department, we can write:

```
dept_size(D#, count⟨E#⟩) ← empl(E#, Sal, D#).
```

Here, ⟨`E#`⟩ denotes the set of `E#` *grouped by* the remaining columns in the head (i.e., grouped by `D#`). Thus `count⟨E#⟩` counts the employees for each department.

$\mathcal{LDL}$++ rule-based framework makes it easy to define new aggregates. For instance, to find the highest paid employees in each department along with their salaries we can write:

$$\texttt{top\_paid(D\#, maxpair}\langle\texttt{(E\#, Sal)}\rangle\texttt{)} \leftarrow \texttt{emp(E\#, Sal, D\#)}.$$

Here, `maxpair` denotes a new aggregate defined over sets of pairs (`E#, Sal`) grouped by `D#`. Now, `maxpair` can be defined by the user using the following rules:

```
single(maxpair, (E#, Sal), (E#, Sal)).
multi(maxpair, (E#, Sal), (Eold, Sold), (E#, Sal)) ←     Sal >= Sold.
multi(maxpair, (E#, Sal), (Eold, Sold), (Eold, Sold)) ← Sold >= Sal.
```

Observe that the two `multi` rules used to extract the maxima are not mutually exclusive. Thus, when a new employee is found with salary equal to the current max, both the new and old `E#, Sal` pairs are accepted as potential answers by our `maxpair` aggregate. Once defined, an aggregate can be used as any built-in aggregate. Thus, to derive the department with the max count of employees, we write:

$$\texttt{largest\_dept(maxpair}\langle\texttt{(D\#, Ecount)}\rangle\texttt{)} \leftarrow \texttt{dep\_size(D\#, Ecount)}.$$

Thus, in the application we want to preserve ties and return them in the result. Consider however the situation of a greedy algorithm, such as Prim's algorithm that generates a least cost spanning tree [16]. At each step of the computation, a least cost arc is added to the spanning tree being constructed—i.e., if several arcs share the same cost only one can be used—otherwise the final result is no longer a tree. This tie-breaking version of max-pair (actually of its dual min-pair), can be specified by simply replacing the ">=" condition in one of the two multi-maxpair rules above by ">". Thus the particular result returned by the aggregate depends on the order in which the the input data is processed (non-determinism).

These examples illustrate some of the properties needed in user-defined aggregates:

- Aggregates often take multiple fields (i.e., structured records) as an input, and return multiple fields for each record returned
- Aggregates often need to return multiple records (e.g., several employees sharing the same top salary in the department)
- Aggregates often return different results depending on the order in which the data is visited.

The newly proposed SQL3 standards, and the original version of $\mathcal{LDL}$++ developed at MCC, meet these basic requirements for user-defined aggregates; however they do not support early returns.

4 Aggregates with Early Returns

SQL3, Postgres, and the original version of $\mathcal{LDL}$++ developed at MCC cannot express important classes of aggregates, such as online aggregation or roll-ups for data cubing. This is due to the fact they not support early returns, since they assume that results are only produced at end of the computation. To remedy this limitation, at UCLA we have developed extensions of $\mathcal{LDL}$++ and SQL to support *early returns*, whereby partial results are produced during the computation of user-defined aggregates.

The extension of $\mathcal{LDL}$++ developed at UCLA supports the predicate `ereturn` along with `single` and `multi` previously discussed. Now, the user can define new online aggregates by simply writing rules for the situations where partial results must be returned during the on-going calculation of the aggregate. For instance, the following computation of averages produces a partial result every fifth element:

```
single(onl_avg, X, (X, 1)).
multi(onl_avg, X, (Sum, Count), (Sum + X, Count + 1)).
ereturn(onl_avg, X, (Sum, Count), Avg)   ← Count mod 5 = 0,
                                            Avg = Sum/Count.
```

The new version of $\mathcal{LDL}$++ also gives the user explicit control of final returns, using the predicate `freturn`. For instance to produce a final return for our `onl_avg`, without producing the same values as early returns, the user might write:

```
freturn(onl_avg, X, (Sum, Count), Avg) ← Count mod 5 ≠ 0,
                                          Avg = Sum/Count.
```

The new version of $\mathcal{LDL}$++ is upward-compatible with the old one: when the return rules are omitted the results are only returned at the end of the aggregate computation.

Although the early-return capability was specifically introduced to support online aggregation, we found that it enabled us to define a large number of new aggregates which would have been impossible (or prohibitively difficult and inefficient) to express without it. Take for instance our previous roll-ups example of Table 2. It is simple to code this by using the return rules to detect the changes in (`Year`, ..., `Day`) and returning the accumulated result for the columns which have changed and a question mark for the other columns. In fact, using user-defined aggregates extended with early returns, we implemented an assortment of complex aggregations including: online queries, median estimation, roll-up aggregates for data cubing, various temporal aggregates for time series, set-comparison aggregates, and Allen temporal operators [6]. Because of space limitation, we refer the reader to the detailed discussion, and live demo, in `http://www.cs.ucla.edu/ldl`.

We conjecture that user-defined aggregates so extended can support all aggregates that can naturally be computed in a single pass through the data. Aggregates, such as data cubes, where the computation requires several passes, can then be expressed by combining several user-defined aggregates.

The benefits of early returns extend beyond data mining applications. For instance, let us define a version of count, called mcount that returns the incremental count at each step:

```
single(mcount, Y, 1).
multi(mcount, Y, Old, New) ←    New = Old + 1.
ereturn(mcount, Y, Old, 1) ←    Old = nil, New = 1
ereturn(mcount, Y, Old, New) ← Old = nil, New = Old + 1.
```

The condition Old = nil is only satisfied when the first item in the set is found. Thus the first ereturn rule produces a value of 1 for mcount. The second rule returns all the values, $2, ..., n$ where n the actual cardinality of the set. At a first impression this aggregate might appear, strange and inefficient, but consider an actual example:

For instance the query "*Find all departments with more than 7 employees*" can be expressed using the following pairs of $\mathcal{LDL}$++ rules:

```
count_emp(D#, mcount⟨E#⟩) ← emp(E#, Sal, D#).
large_dept(D#) ←              count_emp(D#, Count), Count = 7.
small_dept(D#, Dname) ←       dept(D#, Dname), ¬large_dept(D#).
```

This example illustrates some of the benefits of online aggregation. Negated queries are subject to existential variable optimization; thus, $\mathcal{LDL}$++ stops searching for new employees in a department as soon as the threshold of 7 is reached. But the traditional count aggregate retrieves and count all employees in the department, no matter how high their number is.

Several authors have advocated extensions to predicate calculus with generalized existential quantifiers [18,14,32], to express a concept such as "*There exist at least seven employees*". This idea is naturally supported by new aggregate atleast⟨(K, X)⟩ that returns the value yes as soon as K Xs are counted. This aggregate of Boolean behavior can be defined as follows:

```
single(atleast, (K, Y), 1).
multi(atleast, (K, Y), Old, New) ←  Old < K, New = Old + 1.
ereturn(atleast, (K, Y), K1, yes) ← K1 = nil, K = 1.
ereturn(atleast, (K, Y), K1, yes) ← K1 ≠ nil, K1 + 1 = K.
```

Then, the previous queries searching for departments with more than 7 employees can simply be expressed as follows:

```
large_detp(D#) ← count_emp(D#, atleast⟨(3, E#)⟩)
```

Here, because of the condition $\mathtt{Old} < \mathtt{K}$ in the **multi** rule defining **atleast**, the search stops after seven employees, even for a positive goal, such as ?lrg_dpt(D#, yes), for which no existential optimization is performed.

Temporal queries provide a particularly fertile ground for the use of the new aggregates as demonstrated by the temporal extension of Datalog described in [6]. Another related domain is time-series analysis, where various kinds of computations that can be performed in a single pass through the data stream can be expressed using our extended aggregates. For instance, moving-window aggregates represent a type of computation that is performed frequently. In the following example we have sequences of closing prices for stocks, and we want to average the prices of IBM stocks over the last five days. Then we write the following $\mathcal{LDL}$++ program for which we defined the mw5avg aggregate:

```
p(mw5avg⟨A⟩) ← stock_closing('IBM', A).
```

```
single(mw5avg, Y, [Y]).
multi(mw5avg, Y0, OL, NL) ← if(OL = [Y1, Y2, Y3, Y4]
                              then L = [Y1, Y2, Y3]
                              else L = OL), NL = [Y0|L].

ereturn(mw5avg, Y0, [Y1, Y2, Y3, Y4], Avg) ←
                          Avg = (Y0 + Y1 + Y2 + Y3 + Y4)/5.
```

Therefore, the **return** rule, after five values have accumulated, returns their sum divided by 5; nothing is returned before that. The **multi** rule eliminates the least recent value from the list (but only after this has reached a length of five) and then adds the most recent value that becomes the head of the list.

5 Formal Semantics

The formal semantics of extended aggregates can be defined using the standard declarative semantics of Datalog, by simply viewing a program with aggregates as a short-hand for an expanded program without aggregates.

Take for instance, the following rule where we compute a new aggregate function myagr on a set of Y-values grouped by X:

$$r_1: \ \mathtt{p(X, myagr\langle Y\rangle) \leftarrow q(X, Y).}$$

The computation of a set aggregate requires the ability to enumerate the elements of the set one-by-one. For instance, if we make the assumption that the set elements are totally ordered, then we can visit them one-at-a-time in, say, ascending order. But such an assumption would violate the genericity principle [1], and still requires nonmonotonic constructs to visit the elements on-by-one, thus preventing the use of aggregates in recursive rules. A better solution consists in using `choice` [25,26] which can be freely used in recursive rules. In fact, positive programs with choice are equivalent to programs with negated goals which are guaranteed to have one or more total stable models [13].

Therefore, the first rewriting step for r_1 uses choice to produce a *chain* of results, rather than a set of results, from the body of r_1:

Ordering Rules:

```
next_r1(X,nil,nil) ← q(X,Y).
next_r1(X,Y1,Y2) ←   next_r1(X,_,Y1),q(X,Y2),
                     choice((X,Y1),(Y2)),choice((X,Y2),(Y1)).
```

Aggregates are computed by the following internal recursive predicate `cagr`:

`cagr` Rules

```
cagr(myagr,X,Y,New) ←   next_r1(X,nil,Y),Y ≠ nil,
                        single(myagr,Y,New),
cagr(myagr,X,Y2,New) ←  next_r1(X,Y1,Y2),cagr(myagr,X,Y1,Old),
                        multi(myagr,Y2,Old,New).
```

The recursive `cagr` rules implement the inductive definition of the UDA by calling on the `single` and `multi` predicates written by the user. Therefore, `single` is used once to initialize `cagr(myagr,X,Y,New)`, where `Y` denotes the first input value and `New` is value of the aggregate on a singleton set. Then, for each new input value, `Y2`, and `Old` (denoting the last partial value of the aggregate) are fed to the `multi` predicate, to be processed by the `multi` rules defined by the user and returned to head of the recursive `cagr` rule.

This general template defining aggregates is customized for each UDA by the user-supplied rules for `single`, `multi`, `ereturn` (for early returns), and `freturn` (for final returns):

Single, Multi, Early-Return, and Final-Return Rules

```
single(myagr,Y,New) ←              ...
multi(myagr,Y,Old,New) ←           ...
ereturn(myagr,Y,Old,Value) ←       ...
freturn(myagr,Y,Old,Value) ←       ...
```

Here, we have left the bodies of these rules unspecified, since no "special" restriction applies to them (except that they cannot use the predicate `p` being defined via the aggregate, nor any predicate mutually recursive with `p`).

The predicates `ereturn` and `freturn` are called by the yield rules that control what is to be returned:

Early-Yield Rule:

$$\begin{aligned}\texttt{p(X, AgrVal)} &\leftarrow \texttt{next\_r}_1\texttt{(X, nil, Y), Y} \neq \texttt{nil},\\ &\quad\ \texttt{ereturn(myagr, Y, nil, AgrVal)}.\\ \texttt{p(X, AgrVal)} &\leftarrow \texttt{next\_r}_1\texttt{(X, Y1, Y2), cagr(myagr, X, Y1, Old)},\\ &\quad\ \texttt{ereturn(myagr, Y2, Old, AgrVal)}.\end{aligned}$$

The first early-yield rule applies to the first value in the set, and the second one to all successive values. The values returned once all the values in the set have been visited is controlled by a final-yield rule:

Final-Yield Rule:

$$\begin{aligned}\texttt{p(X, AgrVal)} \leftarrow\ & \texttt{next\_r}_1\texttt{(X, \_, Y)}, \neg\texttt{next\_r}_1\texttt{(X, Y, \_)},\\ & \texttt{cagr(myagr, X, Y, Old)},\\ & \texttt{freturn(myagr, Y, Old, AgrVal)}.\end{aligned}$$

Therefore, the meaning of a program P containing a rule such as $\texttt{r}_1$, is simply the program P' obtained by replacing $\texttt{r}_1$ with the ordering rules, the cagr rules, the early-yield rules, and the final-yield rules, while leaving the remaining rules in P unchanged (including the user-supplied single, multi, early-return, and final-return rules). Now, *negation is only used in the final yield rule*. When the aggregate definition contains no final-return rule (i.e., only early return rules) then the final-yield rule can be eliminated and the remaining rules constitute a *positive choice program*; positive choice programs *define monotonic transformations* [15]. The monotonicity property is discussed in more details in the next section.

In summary, our powerful user-defined predicates are simply a syntactic short-hand requiring no semantic extensions to an enhanced Datalog language such as $\mathcal{LDL}$++. The use of special syntactic constructs, however, allows their direct implementation to achieve significant performance gains.

6 Monotonic Aggregation

The semantics of choice can be formally defined using the notion of stable model [13] . In fact, each program with choice can be rewritten into an equivalent program with negation which is guaranteed to have one or more total stable models [25]. Multiple canonical models tantamount to nondeterminism. Indeed, choice inherits the nondeterministic aspects of stable models [26], without suffering from any of the computational intractability problems of stable models. Programs with choice can be computed efficiently since choice defines a monotone transformation. For instance, consider the rule:

$$r_2 : \texttt{p(X, Y)} \leftarrow \texttt{q(X, Y), choice((X), (Y))}.$$

If P and Q respectively denote a set of p-atoms and q-atoms, the transformation defined by r_2 consists in selecting a maximal subset $P \subseteq Q$ such that the FD $X \to Y$ holds in P. This transformation is multivalued i.e., in general, more than one such maximal subset exits and, therefore, one must be selected arbitrarily—*nondeterministic semantics.*

A *nondeterministic mapping* from a domain D_1 to a range D_2 can be represented as a relation $\Pi(D_1, D_2)$. Then we can generalize the notion of monotonicity as follows:

Definition 12. *Monotonicity:* Let $\Pi(D_1, D_2)$ be a nondeterministic mapping, where D_1 and D_2 are domains partially ordered by $\geq_1$ and $\geq_2$, respectively. Then, Π is said to be monotone, when for each $(x, y) \in \Pi$ and every $x' \in D_1$ with $x' \geq_1 x$, there exists a $y' \geq_2 y$ such that $(x', y') \in \Pi$.

Let us now consider transformations defined by our rules. Their domains and range are Herbrand interpretations for the given program; thus, they are both ordered by the set-containment relation $\supseteq$. Then the transformation defined by rule r_2, above, is monotone: if P is a maximal subset of Q satisfying $X \to Y$, and $Q' \supset Q$, then we can construct P' by incrementally adding to P each tuple that does not conflict with X-values of tuples already in P. Then, $(P', Q') \in \Pi$.

Besides the transformation induced by a single rule with choice being monotone, the transformation induced by a positive program with choice is also monotone. This is for instance the case of the transformation induced by the recursive $\mathtt{next}_{\mathtt{r}_1}$ rules, which for each `X` construct a chain that defines a total ordering on the associated `Y`-values in `q(X, Y)`. The properties of positive programs with choice were discussed in [15], where as customary in deductive databases, a program P is viewed as consisting of two separate components: an extensional component, denoted *edb*(P), and an intensional one, denoted *idb*(P). Then the following result was proven in [15]:

Theorem 1. *Let P and P' be two positive choice programs where idb(P') = idb(P) and edb(P') $\supseteq$ edb(P). Then, if M is a choice model for P, then, there exists a choice model M' for P' such that $M' \supseteq M$.*

This theorem allows us to conclude that the recursive rules `next_r1(X, Y, Z)` define a monotone mapping from interpretations of `q(X, Y)` to interpretations of `next_r1(X, Y, Z)`. This mapping is nondeterministic since there are $n!$ orderings for each given set of cardinality n. (The monotonicity of the particular mapping established by the `next_r1(X, Y, Z)` rules can can also be verified directly, since an ordering on a set S can be extended to an ordering on a set $S' \supset S$ by simply attaching the elements of $S' - S$ to the end of the given ordering on S.)

Therefore, a program Q with user-defined aggregates consists of following parts:

1. The `cagr` computation rules

2. The $\texttt{next}_{\texttt{r}_1}$ rules defining the nondeterministic monotone ordering transformation
3. The **single**, **multi** and **ereturn**, and **freturn** rules written by the user
4. The early-yield rule,
5. All the remaining rules in the original program Q except r_1,
6. The final-yield rule.

The mapping $\Pi(2^{B_Q}, 2^{B_Q})$ defined by these six sets of rules will be called *the canonical mapping defined by Q*, denoted Π_Q. Assume now that the original program Q has no negated goal and no final-return rule. Then

- Since there is no *final-return* rule, the body of final-yield rule is never made true (enabled) and it can simply be dropped; then
- the remaining rules (i.e., those in points 1-5 above) are positive choice rules, and thus define a nondeterministic monotone mapping.

Therefore:

A UDA that does not have a final-return rule is monotone.

This observation provides a simple and elegant solution to the monotone aggregation problem that has been the subject of significant previous investigations [31,23].

Therefore, the fixpoint-based semantics and computation of positive logic programs can be extended to positive programs with monotone aggregates. We start with a rather obvious definition of the notion of fixpoint for multi-valued mappings:

Definition 13. *Fixpoint:* Let Π denote a mapping and let I be an element in the domain of Π. If $(I, I) \in \Pi$, then I will be called a *fixpoint* for Π.

Definition 14. A *computation* for Π is defined as a sequence

$$I_0, I_1, ..., I_n$$

where, $I_0 = \emptyset$, and for every j, $0 \leq j < n$, $(I_j, I_{j+1}) \in \Pi$ and $I_j \subseteq I_{j+1}$. Here, n can denote a positive integer or the symbol ω.

Definition 15. Let $\langle I_n \rangle$, $n \geq 0$, be a computation for Π. Then the (ω) limit for this computation is defined as follows:

$$lim_{n \geq 0} \langle I_n \rangle \;=\; \bigcup_{n<\omega} I_n$$

Consider now a program Q without negated goals where all the user-defined aggregates have no final-return rule: then Π_Q for this program is monotone. Therefore, *the ω-limit of a computation for such Π_Q is a fixpoint* *for Π_Q, and vice-versa.* Therefore positive programs with monotone aggregates extend the fixpoint semantics and computation of positive programs.

In conclusion, user-defined aggregates without a final-return rule can be used in positive programs without any restriction, since they have a fixpoint-based semantics that that is based on their stable model semantics. Moreover, bottom-up execution techniques of deductive databases, such as the seminaive fixpoint, remain valid for these programs. Indeed, monotone aggregates can be added to deductive database systems (and were added to $\mathcal{LDL}$++) with minimal effort.

7 Implementation of Extended Aggregates

The implementation of extended aggregates in $\mathcal{LDL}$++ aims at ensuring performance, and upward compatibility with the previous releases (thus, when no return rule is given by the user the system only returns the final result of the aggregate). In the implementation, we use an internal table to store the intermediate results of aggregation. The compilation of aggregate rules is simply a rewriting of these rules into rules without aggregates. Rewritten rules will have two built-in predicates, namely, **readTable** and **writeTable**, which retrieve rows from, and insert rows into, the internal table. The internal table is properly indexed on the group-by columns to speed-up the retrieval and insertion.

An aggregate rule has the following form:

$$\mathtt{p}(\mathtt{K_1}, \cdots, \mathtt{K_m}, \mathbf{aggr_1}\langle \mathtt{A_1}\rangle, \cdots, \mathbf{aggr_n}\langle \mathtt{A_n}\rangle) \leftarrow \mathtt{Rule\ Body}.$$

where $\mathtt{K_1}, \cdots, \mathtt{K_n}$ are group-by columns, $\mathbf{aggr_1}, \cdots, \mathbf{aggr_n}$ are either user defined aggregates or built-in aggregates, and $\mathtt{A_1}, \cdots, \mathtt{A_n}$ are the data the aggregation will be applied to. Both $\mathtt{A_i}$ and $\mathtt{K_i}$ should be bound by goals in the rule body.

The compiler rewrites the above rule into an internal rule as the one shown below; this rule is then linked with the **single**, **multi**, and **return** rules provided by the user. During interpretation, **readTable** is called, and get values from the rule body and from the internal table. The **Flag** argument in **readTable** tells the status of the reading. We have three possible situations:

- Flag=1 (Final State): **readTable** returns a final tuple from the table. Either (1) we have no more tuples from the data source, or (2) the last execution of the **multi** rule fails and either there are no group-by columns in the rule head or the group-by columns are all bound.
- Flag=2 (Initial State): This value is returned from **readTable** when the first tuple encountered with these $\mathtt{K_1}, \cdots, \mathtt{K_m}$ values; in this situation $\mathtt{Aold_1}, \cdots, \mathtt{Aold_n}$ are all `nil`. Then, the **single** rule will be evaluated and the result will be inserted into the table by **writeTable**.

- Flag=3 (Intermediate Recursive States): Here, **readTable** returns the old results which have the same group-by values as the current tuple. Old values are then combined with the current tuple via **multi** rules and the new result is put into the table by **writeTable**.

```
p(K1,···,Km,V1,···,Vn) ← readTable(K1,···,Km,A1,···,An,Aold1,···,Aoldn,Flag),
                          if (Flag = 1 then
                                freturn(aggr1,A1,Aold1,V1),
                                ...
                                freturn(aggrn,An,Aoldn,Vn)
                          else
                                if (Flag = 2 then
                                      single(aggr1,A1,Am1),
                                      ...
                                      single(aggrn,An,Amn)
                                else
                                      multi(aggr1,A1,Aold1,Am1),
                                      ...
                                      multi(aggrn,An,Aoldn,Amn)),
                                writeTable(K1,···,Km,Am1,···,Amn),
                                ereturn(aggr1,A1,Aold1,V1),
                                ...
                                ereturn(aggrn,An,Aoldn,Vn)).
```

8 Applications of Monotone Aggregation

Consider the following rule that uses the aggregate mcount, which returns the current count after each new value;

$$\texttt{q(mcount}\langle\texttt{X}\rangle\texttt{)} \leftarrow \texttt{p(X)}.$$

If p is a database predicate with $n \geq 1$ facts, then the rule returns $I_n = \{q(1), q(2), \ldots, q(n)\}$. If the original set of facts is increased to a new set of cardinality $m \geq n$, then, our rule returns: $I_m = \{q(1), q(2), \ldots, q(m)\}$, where $I_m \supseteq I_n$. *Therefore rules with* mcount *define a monotone deterministic mapping.*

All aggregates inductively defined using single, multi and early-return rules define monotone mappings. In general, these mapping are nondeterministic (unlike mcount). The examples which follow are based on those in [23], and show that, deterministic or otherwise, monotone aggregates provide a powerful and flexible tool for advanced applications.

Join the Party Some people will come to the party no matter what, and their names are stored in a sure(Person) relation. But others will join only after they know that at least K of their friends will be there. Here, `friend(A,B)` denotes that B views A as a friend.

```
willcome(P) ←                 sure(P).
willcome(P) ←                 c_friends(P,K), K >= 3.
c_friends(P,mcount⟨F⟩) ← willcome(F), friend(P,F).
```

Here, we have set $K = 3$ as the number of friends required for a person to come to the party. Consider now a computation of these rules on the following database.

```
sure(mark).
sure(tom).
sure(jane).

friend(jerry,mark).
friend(penny,mark).
friend(jerry,jane).
friend(penny,jane).
friend(jerry,penny).
friend(penny,tom).
```

Then, the basic seminaive computation yields:

```
willcome(mark).
willcome(tom).
willcome(jane).

c_friends(jerry,1).
c_friends(penny,1).
c_friends(jerry,2).
c_friends(penny,2).
c_friends(penny,3).

willcome(penny).

c_friends(jerry,3).

willcome(jerry).
```

This example illustrates how the standard seminaive computation [35] can be applied in conjunction with monotone user-defined aggregates.

The use of the aggregate `atleast` simplifies the computation of the previous query significantly. Our program now becomes:

```
wllcm(F,yes) ←                 sure(F).
wllcm(X,atleast⟨(3,F)⟩) ← wllcm(F,yes), friend(X,F).
```

Unlike in the previous formulation, where a new tuple `c_friends` is produced every time a new `friend` is found, a new `wllcm` tuple is here produced only when the threshold of 3 is crossed.

Next, we define `msum` and `mmin` that provide monotone extensions for `sum` and `min`. A `mmax` aggregate can be defined in a similar way. All these aggregates are monotonic and nondeterministic.

For `msum` we have:

```
single(msum, Y, Y).
multi(msum, Y, Old, New) ← New = Old + Y.
ereturn(msum, Y, Old, Z) ← if(Old ≠ nil then Z = Old + Y else Z = Y).
```

For `mmin` we have:

```
single(mmin, Y, Y).
multi(mmin, Y, Old, New) ← if(Y < Old then New = Y else New = Old).
ereturn(mmin, Y, Old, Y) ← if(Old ≠ nil then Y < Old).
```

Observe that we have also added conditions to limit the production of redundant returns.

Least-Distance Connections. For instance, given a graph `g(X, Y, C)` where `C` is the cost of an edge from node `X` to node `Y`, the least-cost path between any two nodes can be computed as follows:

```
ld(X, Y, mmin⟨C⟩) ←        g(X, Y, C).
ld(X, Y, mmin⟨C⟩) ←        ld(X, Z, C1), ld(Z, Y, C2), C = C1 + C2.
least_dist(X, Y, min⟨C⟩) ← ld(X, Z, C1).
```

This transitive-closure like computation adds a new arc `ld(X, Y, C)` provided that this then becomes the new least-cost arc between the nodes `X` and `Y`. The arcs so produced are then used in the next step of the seminaive computation. At the end of this fixpoint computation, the `least_dist` rule is used to select the least-cost arc between these two nodes, out of the succession of arcs of decreasing `C` values produced in the computation.

For a given graph, the values obtained during the computation of `ld` can vary depending on the order in which the arcs are considered. The final values in `least_dist`, however, are always the same (a nondeterministic computation producing a deterministic answer). In fact, the presence of the `least_dist` rule suggests that we might replace `mmin⟨C⟩` by simply `C` without changing the final result. However, in the situation where there are cycles of positive cost, our program terminates whereas the other will not. Also in a DAG, where longer paths correspond to higher costs, then our program performs significantly better than the other program.

Company Control. Another interesting example is transitive ownership and control of corporations. Say that `owns(C1, C2, Per)` denotes the percentage of shares that corporation C1 owns of corporation C2. Then, C1 controls C2 if it owns more than, say, 49% of its shares. In general, to decide whether C1 controls C3 we must also add the shares owned by corporations such as C2 that are controlled by C1. This yields the transitive control predicate defined as follows:

```
control(C, C) ←                  owns(C, _, _).
control(Onr, C) ←                twons(Onr, C, Per), Per > 49.
towns(Onr, C2, msum⟨Per⟩) ← contrl(Onr, C1), owns(C1, C2, Per).
```

Thus, every company controls itself, and a company C1 that has transitive ownership of more than 49% of C2's shares controls C2 . In the last rule, twons computes transitive ownership with the help of msum that adds up the shares of controlling companies. Observe that any pair (Onr, C2) is added at most once to control, thus the contribution of C1 to Onr's transitive ownership of C2 is only accounted once.

To further simplify the program and expedite the computation we can introduce a special aggregate as follows [1]:

```
single(sum49, Y, Y).
multi(sum49, Y, Old, Z) ←        Old < 49, Z = Old + Y.
ereturn(sum49, Y, Old, yes) ← if(Old = nil then Y > 49
                                  else Old + Y > 49).
```

Then the recursive rules become:

```
cntrl(Onr, C, yes) ←             owns(Onr, C, Per), Per > 49.
cntrl(Onr, C2, sum49⟨Per⟩) ← cntrl(Onr, C1), owns(C1, C2, Per).
```

Thus, the sum49 aggregate succeeds only when the 49% threshold is crossed during the summation. Here, the value of 49 was cast into the very definition of our aggregate. Alternatively, this value could be given as a parameter, as in the case of atleast.

Bill-of-Materials (BoM) Applications. BoM applications represent an important application area that requires aggregates in recursive rules. Say, for instance that psb(P1, P2, QT) denotes that P1 contains part P2 in quantity QT. We also have elementary parts that are purchasable for a price and will be delivered in a certain number of days: these are described by the relation basic(P, Price, Days). Then, the following program computes the cost of a part as the sum of the costs of the basic parts it contains.

```
part_cost(Part, 0, Cst) ←       basic(Part, Cst).
part_cost(Part, mcount⟨Sb⟩, msum⟨MCst⟩) ←
                    part_cost(Sb, ChC, Cst), prolfc(Sb, ChC),
                    psb(Part, Sb, Mult), MCst = Cst * Mult.
```

[1] The aggregate sum49 is deterministic.

Thus, the key condition in the body of the second rule is that a subpart `Sb` is counted in `part_cost` only when all `Sb`'s children have been counted. This occurs when the number of `Sb`'s children counted so far by `mcount` is equal to its total number of children in the `psb` graph. This last number is kept in the prolificity table, `prolfc`, which can be computed as follows:

```
prolfc(P1, count⟨P2⟩) ← psb(P1, P2, _).
prolfc(P1, 0) ←         basic(P1, _).
```

Also this BOM computation can be simplified and made more efficient using the `atleast` aggregate, yielding:

```
pcost(Part, yes, Cst) ←        basic(Part, MCst).
pcost(Part, atleast⟨(K, Sb)⟩, msum⟨Cst⟩) ←
                    pcost(Sb, yes, Cst), psb(Part, Sb, Mult),
                    prolfc(Part, K), MCst = Cst * Mult.
```

An improvement with respect to the previous formulation is that the `prolfc` relation is now used to qualify `Part` as they are counted in the the rule head.

The technique of counting the children could also be used with `least_dist` problem, above, if the underlying graph is acyclic. For cyclic graphs we must use the current formulation that exploits the property that extrema are unaffected by duplicates (idempotence).

9 Applications to SQL Databases

Encouraged by our success with $\mathcal{LDL}$++, we have designed and implemented a system called SQL-AG that supports SQL3 user-defined aggregates and actually extends it by supporting early returns. Then we explored the use of these new aggregates to express complex data mining algorithms, with encouraging results: complex algorithms, such as iceberg queries [11], and the SPRINT [2] algorithm enhanced with the PUBLIC [28] technique recently proposed for pruning, were quickly coded using special user defined aggregates

We have actually developed two versions of SQL-AG. The first is for Oracle DBMSs using P/SQL and is described in [4]. Here we describe the second system built on DB2 using user-defined scratch-pad functions. SQL-AG implements SQL3 specification for user defined aggregates on DB2. For example, a user can define an iterative routine for average as follows:

```
AGGREGATE FUNCTION myavg( IN NUMBER)
RETURNS NUMBER
STATE NumberPair
INITIALIZE average-init
ITERATE average-iterate
```

```
TERMINATE average-terminate
```

Here average-init, average-iterate and average-terminate are functions that the user will have to define in C. When the definition of an aggregate, such as myavg, is given, SQL-AG generates a C source file which defines the two user-defined functions, myavg() and myavg_groupby(), to implement the new aggregate. These two functions are then compiled and linked with DB2's library to support the new aggregate.

Once registered, user-defined aggregates can be used in SQL statements as if they are standard built-in aggregates (*sum, min, max, avg, count*). Take for instance the following SQL-AG query:

```
SELECT dept, myavg(salary)
FROM employee
GROUP BY dept
```

The SQL-AG system transforms the above query into the following equivalent query that is then execute on DB2:

```
SELECT dept, myavg(dept)
FROM employee
WHERE myavg_groupby(dept,salary)=0
GROUP BY dept
```

Thus, the function myavg_groupby is applied on very record for aggregation. This calls avg_multi and then updates the current values of state_type for dept that are kept in an hash table. Then myavg_groupby returns the value zero. DB2 applies the actual GROUP BY clause at the end of the scan. Thus, myavg(dept) in the select clause returns the results left in the hash table by the previous computation.

SQL-AG is quite general and efficient. Indeed, we have evaluated the efficiency of our implementation by coding builtins such as sum or avg in SQL-AG comparing performance. We tested performance of builtins computed in three different ways: (i) the original SQL builtin, (ii) the UDA running in fenced mode, and (iii) the UDA running in unfenced mode. User-defined aggregates running in fenced mode are almost 10 times slower than builtin aggregates. Unfenced UDAs are much better, since their performance is very close (10 percent above) that of the builtins. Thus the flexibility of supporting early returns is not bought at the price of lesser performance.

Aggregates with Early Returns. Online aggregation [17] exemplifies the new kind of column functions required by advanced applications, particularly data mining ones. For instance, the computation of averages often converges toward the final value after a small subset of input data is visited. Thus, it is desirable to produce "early returns" during the computation. Therefore, a new function called PRODUCE has been introduced in SQL-AG that will return values during the computation. For instance an online version of myavg can be defined as follows:

```
AGGREGATE FUNCTION online_avg( IN NUMBER)
RETURNS return_type
STATE number-pair
INITIALIZE online_avg_single
ITERATE online_avg_multi
PRODUCE online_avg_return
TERMINATE NOP
```

Here, the functions for INITIALIZE, ITERATE, are basically the same as those in myavg, and the newly introduced PRODUCE calls an online_avg_return function defined in C that returns a partial result every five new input values. This example illustrates a situation of particular significance, where is the situation where only early returns are used (i.e., TERMINATE is declared NOP or is missing) since *the aggregate function so defined is monotonic.* Thus, SQL3's limitation that queries must be stratified with respect to aggregates no longer applies. This allows us to support efficiently a host of applications that have been a problem for SQL. The following example [23] uses a monotonic count aggregate mcount defined in C, but behaving exactly as the `mcount` aggregate previously discussed for $\mathcal{LDL}$++.

Join the Party Some people will come to the party no matter what, and their names are stored in a sure(Pname) relation. But many other persons will join only after they know that at least 3 of their friends will be there. Here, friend(Pname, Fname) is a table denoting that Pname views Fname as a friend.

Example 1. Join the Party in SQL-AG

```
WITH wllcm(Name) AS
(  SELECT Pname FROM sure
UNION ALL
   SELECT f.PName
   FROM wllcm, friend f
   WHERE wllcm.Name = f.Fname
   GROUP BY f.PName
   HAVING mcount(f.Fname)=3
)
SELECT Name
FROM wllcm
```

SQL-AG implementation in DB2 of this query is shown below. Observe that we basically use the same translation as that of final returns in TERMINATE, modulo the absence of the GROUP BY clause. Thus, early returns from PRODUCE are returned immediately in the SELECT clause, rather than after the GROUP BY operation used for final returns.

Example 2. The DB2 implementation for the Join-the-Party Query

```
WITH wllcm(Name) AS
(  SELECT Pname FROM sure
UNION ALL
   SELECT f.PName
   FROM wllcm, friend f
   WHERE wllcm.Name = f.Fname
   AND mcount_groupby(f.Pname,f.Fname)=0
   AND mcount(f.Fname)=3
)
SELECT Name
FROM wllcm
```

10 Conclusions

In this paper, we have provided the logic-based foundations for the extended aggregate capability required by the next generation of database applications. In particular, we focused on data mining applications and showed that user-defined aggregates extended with early returns are critical to support a wide variety of applications ranging from online estimates to iceberg queries. Then, we proposed a simple formalization of our extended aggregates using programs with the nondeterministic construct of choice—a class of programs that combine total stable model semantics with efficient operational semantics. Furthermore, this formalization leads to a simple syntactic characterization of monotone user-defined aggregates. Since monotone aggregates can be used freely in recursive rules, complex queries and applications can now be expressed with simple programs amenable to efficient implementation.

Our results underscore the significance of logic in databases—a significance that was paramount in the original formulation of relational databases by Codd, but was much less so in more recent developments. In fact, in the thirty years that have passed since the introduction of the relational model, critics have often complained about the inability of relational databases to express critical queries, such as those required in BoM applications. The great work on recursion by deductive database researchers lead to the introduction of recursive queries in SQL3, but has not helped much with those queries. Indeed, most BoM queries require the computation of aggregates during the recursive traversal of the part/subpart graph; but, in SQL3, all queries must be stratified with respect to recursion and aggregates, and the same holds for most deductive database systems. Therefore, the aggregates-in-recursion challenge has been the focus of some of the best research work in the deductive database area [8,7,22,20,31,34,23]. Of particular interest, there is the work by Ross and Sagiv [23] who showed that, for each aggregate, a particular lattice can often be found, where this aggregate defines monotone transformations. The difficulty of automatically identifying such lattices [31] and deriving lattice-specific fixpoint computations prevented their implementation in actual systems. Given this background, our discovery of monotone aggregates that preserve the lattice and fixpoint computation techniques of positive programs represents an unexpected breakthrough.

References

1. Abiteboul S., Hull R. and Vianu V., *Foundations of Databases*, Addison Wesley, 1995.
2. R. Agrawal and R. Srikant, "Fast Algorithm for Mining Association Rules." In *Proceedings of the 20th VLDB Conference*, Santiago, Chile, 1994.
3. R. Agrawal and J.C. Shafer, "Parallel Mining of Association Rules: Design, Implementation and Experience", *IEEE Transactions on Knowledge and Data Engineering*, Vol.8, No. 6, Dec. 1996.
4. P. Barghava, "User-Defined Aggregates in Database Languages," MS Thesis, UCLA, 1998: `http://www.cs.ucla.edu/~czdemo/SQL-AG/`.
5. S. Brin, Rl Motwani, J. Ullman, and S. Tsur, "Dynamic Itemset: Counting and Implication Rules for Market Basket Data, *Proceedings ACM-SIGMOD Int. Conf on Management of Data*, May 1997.
6. C. X. Chen and C. Zaniolo, "Universal Temporal Data Languages," DDLP'98 Workshop, 1998.
7. M. P. Consens and A. O. Mendelzon, "Low Complexity Aggregation in Graphlog and Datalog," ICDT'90, 1990.
8. I. F. Cruz and T. S. Norvell, "Aggregative Closure: an Extension of Transitive Closure," *Proc.Fifth Int. Conference on Data Engineering*, pp. 384-389, 1989.
9. D. Chimenti, R. Gamboa, R. Krishnamurthy, S. Naqvi, S. Tsur, C. Zaniolo: The LDL System Prototype. *IEEE Transactions on Knowledge and Data Engineering* 2(1): 76-90 (1990)
10. Charles Elkan. "Boosting and Naive Bayesian Learning." Technical report no cs97-557, Dept. of Computer Science and Engineering, UCSD, September 1997.
11. M. Fang, N. Shivakumar, H. Garcia-Molina, R. Motawni, J. Ullman, "Computing Iceberg Queries Efficiently", *Proceedings of the 1998 VLDB Conference*, New York, NY, 1998.
12. J. Gray, A. Bosworth, H. Pirahesh, A. Layman. "Data Cube: A Relational Aggregation Operator Generalizing Group-By, Cross-Tab, and Sub-Total." *Proc. International Conference on Data Engineering*, 1996.
13. M. Gelfond and V. Lifschitz. The Stable Model Semantics for Logic Programming. *Proceedings of Joint International Conference and Symposium on Logic Programming*, pp. 1070–1080, Seattle, WA, 1988.
14. Gyssen, M., Van Gucht, D. and Badia, A., Query Languages with Generalized Quantifiers, in *Applications of Logic Databases*, R. Ramakrishan, Kluwer, 1995.
15. F. Gianotti, D. Pedreschi, and C. Zaniolo, "Semantics and Expressive Power of Non-Deterministic Constructs in Deductive Databases," *JCSS* to appear.
16. S. Greco and C. Zaniolo, "Greedy Algorithms in Datalog with Choice and Negation" *JICSLP'98*, Manchaster UK, June 16-19, 1998.

17. J. M. Hellerstein, P. J. Haas, and H. J. Wang. "Online Aggregation." *Proceedings of the 1997 ACM-SIGMOD Conference on Management of Data*, 249-256, ACM Press, 1997.
18. Hsu, P. Y. and Parker, D. S., Improving SQL with Generalized Quantifiers, *Procs Eleventh Intl. Conference on Data Engineering, 1995*, 398-305, IEEE Computer Society Press, 1995.
19. "Database Language SQL - Part 2: SQL/Foundation.", July 1996.
20. David B. Kemp and Peter J. Stuckey. "Semantics of logic programs with aggregates" *Proceedings of the 1991 International Symposium on Logic Programming*, pages 387–401, October 1991.
21. I. Motakis and C. Zaniolo, *Proceedings of the 1997 ACM-SIGMOD Conference on Management of Data*, 440-451, ACM Press, New York, 1997.
22. I. S. Mumick, H. Pirahesh, and R. Ramakrishan, "The magic of duplicates and aggregates," *VLDB 1990*, pp. 264-277, 1990.
23. K. A. Ross and Yehoshua Sagiv, "Monotonic Aggregation in Deductive Database", *JCSS*, 54(1), 79-97 (1997)
24. L. Rowe and M. Stonebraker. "The POSTGRES Data Model." *VLDB 1987*, 83-96, Morgan Kaufmann, 1987.
25. D. Saccà and C. Zaniolo. Stable models and non-determinism in logic programs with negation. *Proceedings of the Ninth ACM Symposium on Principles of Database Systems*, pages 205–217, 1990.
26. D. Saccà and C. Zaniolo. Deterministic and non-deterministic stable models. Journal of Logic and Computation, 7(5):555-579, October 1997.
27. S. Sarawagi, S. Thomas, R. Agrawal, "Integrating Association Rule Mining with Relational Database Systems: Alternatives and Implications," *Proceedings ACM-SIGMOD Int. Conf on Management of Data*, 343-354, ACM Press, 1999.
28. K. Shim and R. Rastogi, "PUBLIC: A Decision Tree Classifier that Integrates Building and Prun ing" *VLDB'98*, 405-415, Morgan Kaufmann, 1998.
29. W. Shen, K.Ong, B. Mitbander and C. Zaniolo, Metaqueries for Data Mining, Chapter 15 of *Advances in Knowledge Discovery and Data Mining*, U. M. Fayyad et al (eds.), 395-398, MIT Press, 1996.
30. M. Stonebraker, L. Rowe, and M. Hirohama. "The Implementation of POSTGRES." *IEEE Transactions on Knowledge and Data Engineering*, **2**(1), 145-152, March 1990.
31. A. Van Gelder. Foundations of Aggregations in Deductive Databases *Proc. of the Int. Conf. On Deductive and Object-Oriented databases DOOD'93*, 13-34 Springer Verlag, 1993.
32. Keenan, E. and Westertahl, D., Generalized Quantifiers in Linguistic and Logic, In *Generalized quantifiers in Natural Language*, van Benthem and ter Meulen (eds.) Foris Publications, 1985.
33. Carlo Zaniolo. "Design and Implementation of a Logic Based Language for Data Intensive Applications." *Proceeding of the International Conference on Logic Programming*, 1666-1687, MIT Press, 1988.
34. Carlo Zaniolo, N. Arni, and K. Ong. "Negation and Aggregates in Recursive Rules: the LDL++ Approach." *DOOD*, 204-221, 1993.
35. C. Zaniolo, S. Ceri et al., *Advanced Database Systems*, Morgan Kaufmann Publishers, 1997.

9 Natural Language Processing

Natural language processing was one of the first application areas of logic programming. **Dahl** argues that logic is in fact an inseparable part of language and therefore it plays an important role in natural language processing. She first examines families of formalisms from linguistics and computational linguistics, drawing their connections to logic. Next she discusses the pros and cons of logic programming as a general paradigm for language processing and considers which kinds of logic and logic programming features it would be desirable to include as standard for natural language applications.

Then she introduces Assumptive Logic Programming—logic programming augmented with linear, intuitionistic and timeless assumptions. She also briefly discusses a few of its recent applications, such as controlling virtual worlds and robots through natural language, extracting concepts from web documents, and generating VRML animations through English commands. Finally, she develops in some more detail the design of a novel application: creating databases through natural language discourse.

The Logic of Language

Veronica Dahl

Logic and Functional Programming Group, School of Computing Science, Simon Fraser University, Burnaby, B.C. Canada V5A 1S6

Summary. We argue that logic is an inseparable part of language and that it can play an important role in natural language processing. We first examine families of formalisms from linguistics and computational linguistics, drawing their connections to logic. Next we examine the pros and cons of logic programming as a general paradigm for language processing, and we consider which kinds of logic and logic programming features it would be desirable to include as standard in order to make natural language applications of logic programming more natural and easier to use. We then introduce Assumptive Logic Programming- that is, logic programming augmented with linear, intuitionistic and timeless assumptions. We briefly discuss a few of its recent applications, such as controlling virtual worlds and robots through natural language, extracting concepts from web documents, and generating VRML animations through English commands; and we develop in some more detail the design of a novel application: creating databases through natural language discourse.

Acknowledgement

To him to whom I owe everything [1].

1 Introduction

The above acknowledgement, translated from Claire Bretecher's comics, illustrates how important the subtleties of language are. The comic effect of its footnote is due to the violation of a presupposition of unicity that the singular pronoun "him" usually carries with it, and is only apparent after a (usually unconscious) process of inference that involves not only the statement itself, but also general knowledge of the world, social relationships, etc.

The ability to understand and produce language is so second-nature for humans, that it is easy to underestimate just how much inference and knowledge of the world must be spelled out for a computer to correctly produce and analyze seemingly simple utterances. In the talk that this article evolved from, I tried to answer David Scott Warren's question of where each of us was coming from. To me, the study of language and its automation is fascinating in itself, but also perhaps the most promising route towards my lifelong

[1] Saying this doesn't cost much, and it makes lots of people happy.

overall dream of somehow joining the humanistic and the formal sciences. My intuition is that if we can catch the soulful essences of humanistic disciplines and blend them a bit into our formal sciences, we might achieve a better balance in what I see as a divided world, where brain and spirituality have parted and gone their own separate, often misguided ways. Linguistics as a starting point offered the appeal of being highly formalized among the humanistic sciences, which made it amenable to treatment by a computer. Automatic deduction as a tool, in the form of logic programming, was becoming available just as I was starting along this path, and I have been in it ever since Alain Colmerauer introduced me to it [7].

Alas, in my overall dream I have failed miserably. I'm afraid the humanization of the formal sciences that many of us had in mind is turning, in our increasingly technified world, into a robotizing of the humanistic sciences instead. In the case of our discipline, this is partially due to our need to divide and conquer in order to have a chance at capturing so encompassing a phenomenon as language. But so many pieces have been cut out in the process, that the goal of coming back to the whole picture by integrating what we've learned has become more complex, and seems to keep moving further away.

Perhaps this is the history of most research overambitious goals setting the scene for more modest accomplishments that materialize as side effects. Yet however far from our intended destination we may land, these side effects are often interesting in themselves.

In this article, I advocate some kind of modest integration of the side effects obtained so far in the intersection of computational logic and natural language. I believe this integration should be grounded around real world applications - a perfectly feasible goal by now, and one which blends well with present needs out there, and should take into account the needs of language specialists who are not experts in LP or even in computing.

I first overview some basic problems of the study of language, as well as their solutions within logic programming and computational linguistics, focusing in how logic is central for solving these problems (this section contains some overlap with [10]). Next I speculate on which features of logic programming would constitute a computational linguist's wishlist. Finally, I advocate the use of several of these features, and propose what I think are promising lines of research re. contemporary applications, e.g. on robotics and virtual worlds, concept extraction from the web, generating VRML animations and database creation through speech.

2 Some Basic Problems in Natural Language Processing

The most studied problem in natural language processing is the parsing problem: given a grammar and a presumed sentence in the language defined by that grammar, obtain some representative structure(s) if the sentence is indeed in the language.

Whether for parsing or other NLP problems, such as generation, translation, concept extraction, etc, we need to capture an infinite number of sentences with a finite device such as a grammar. This implies the need for a concise, regularity-capturing description means, such as can be provided by logic programming.

Whatever tool we use, one inescapable problem is the ambiguity that plagues natural language, e.g., as manifest in:

- Preposition phrase attachment: A typical example is: "John saw the man in the park with a telescope", which is ambiguous for instance re who was in the park, and who had a telescope — the man or John?
- Coordinated sentences: E.g., does "I'd like to dance samba or rumba and merengue", mean samba or (rumba and merengue), or (samba or rumba) and merengue?
- Compound nouns: It is difficult to see which of the nouns are head nouns and which are modifiers. For instance, Gerald Gazdar and Chris Mellish identify no less than 42 distinct structural descriptions in the innocent-looking phrase: "Judiciary plea settlement account audit" [17], with just binary noun compounding. Many of these would not even occur to a human but must be carefully sorted through by a machine.

Another problem is that of avoiding overgeneration. During analysis this is often not crucial, assuming the sentences that are input are correct, but for synthesis we should not allow our grammar to produce more sentences than the correct ones.

Finally, we must provide a means for recognizing relationships between parts of the sentence that may be arbitrarily far away from each other, e.g. in order to relate a pronoun with the noun phrase it refers to, or in order to allow topicalization, as in

```
"Logic, we love"
"Logic, I know we love"
"Logic, I suspected he knew we love"
```

where the direct object of "love" has been displaced for emphatic effect, and can appear at an arbitrary distance from it.

3 The Omnipresence of Logic in Language

Deduction is needed for arriving at the correct meaning of even the simplest sentences, e.g., for:

- using pragmatic knowledge to glean implied meanings: For instance, a professor's indirect request for a student to close the classroom door might be "It's awfully noisy in here", accompanied perhaps with a look in the direction of the student closest to the door, but with not even a mention of doors. The student in question uses pragmatic knowledge and deduction in order to correctly interpret the statement.
- disambiguating through world knowledge inference: In the first of the following sentences, "cold" implicitly modifies "feet" as well as "hands", but this is not the case for the second sentence.

  ```
  She had cold hands and feet.
  She had cold hands and fever.
  ```

- long distance dependencies, e.g. for attaching pronouns to antecedents (e.g. "The cop caught Ann speeding. He gave her a ticket"), which sometimes involves as well deduction from world knowledge (e.g. "Ann was caught speeding. He gave her a ticket", where the antecedent of "he" is not even explicit in the discourse).

Of course, deduction is also useful for the parsing process itself, and logic grammars [1] can certainly be viewed as variants of logic programs. Further LP features which are interesting to natural language processing are: automatic rewriting, automatic unification (linguists have developed their own variants, as we shall see, known as Unification Based Formalisms), the notion of parsing or generation as an automatic side effect of grammar description, and the possibility of uniformity throughout which results from being able to use logic for practically all stages of development, from meaning representation to parsing methodology to evaluation of the meaning representations obtained. More recently, features such as the handling of hypotheses have added attractiveness to LP [18,42].

4 Linguistically Principled Approaches to Natural Language Processing

We can identify three important families of linguistically-principled approaches to natural language processing: unification-based (also known as constraint-based), logico-mathematical, and principles-and-parameters. This classification is far from universally agreed upon, being just our own modest attempt to organize the vast material in the literature around the language-processing-as-deduction axis. It is moreover not a clearly disjoint classification: some of the approaches described under a specific family also partake of some features of another family.

4.1 Unification-based Approaches

Unification in linguistic theories often refers to the combination of compatible feature structures rather than of first-order terms. Feature structures are representations of partial information made in terms of features or attributes and their values. A value can be either undefined (roughly corresponding to a variable in logic programming), or another feature structure. Unification combines two feature structures into another if the information conveyed in both is consistent. For instance, the unification of feature structures (1) and (2) below produces the new feature structure (3).

$$\begin{bmatrix} \text{agreement} : \boxed{1}\ [\text{number} : \text{singular}] \\ \text{subject} : [\text{agreement} : \boxed{1}] \end{bmatrix}$$

$$[\text{subject} : [\text{agreement} : [\text{person} : \text{third}]]]$$

$$\begin{bmatrix} \text{agreement} : \boxed{1} \begin{bmatrix} \text{number} : \text{singular} \\ \text{person} : \text{third} \end{bmatrix} \\ \text{subject} : [\text{agreement} : \boxed{1}] \end{bmatrix}$$

Shared information is marked by numeric labels rather than by shared variables. Thus, the value of the *agreement* feature of the subject is understood to be the same as that of the whole structure's agreement feature (i.e. the feature-value pair "number:singular"), because they share label (1). As in logic programming, the information flow is a two-way one (e.g., one of the structures unified contributes the value for the *number* feature, while the other one does so for *person*). But unlike logic programming, the handling of partial information does not necessitate explicit arguments or any other explicit position for the unknown information: it is simply omitted when not there, and added on when unification calls for its addition.

We next show a sample feature-based grammar fragment in which, for convenience, we use variables instead of labels, and we associate each syntactic category with the list of its feature-value pairs.

```
S -->     NP              VP
        [num:X,         [num:X]
        case:nom]

NP                -->     name
[num:X,                  [num:X,
case:Y]                  case:Y]

NP                -->    Pronoun
[num:X,                  [num:X,
```

```
case:Y]                  case:Y]

VP              -->       V
[num:X]                  [num:X,
                         subcat:1]

VP              -->       V              NP
[num:X]                   [num:X,       [case:acc]
                          subcat:2]

Name            -->  Maria               V               -->  laughs
[num:sing]                               [num:sing,
                                          subcat:1]

Pronoun         -->  them                V               -->  designs
[num:plu,                                [num:sing,
case:acc]                                 subcat:2]
```

With respect to this grammar, we can analyze the sentence "Maria designs them", for instance, with the direction of analysis, top-down or bottom-up, being irrelevant.

Because feature structures have a natural representation as graphs, the linguistic notion of unification is often that of *graph* unification.

A variety of unification-based formalisms has independently sprung from different fields – linguistics, computational linguistics, and artificial intelligence. This diversity resulted in a variety of names and definitions. Thus, the unification-based framework can also be found in the literature under the names of *constraint-based* or *information-based.*

Just as is the case with unification in logic programming, feature structure unification can be seen as a specific kind of constraint enforcement. Also as in logic programming, other methods for constraint enforcement are used as well. It has been shown that feature structures may be essentially interpreted as terms allowing freedom of order and number of the arguments (e.g. [28,5,22]).

Two representative approaches to Unification Based Grammars are Lexical Functional Grammar [4] and Generalized Phrase Structure Grammar [16].

4.2 Logico-Mathematical Approaches

Higher Order Logics. Intuitionistic and linear logic treatments of computational linguistics issues such as long-distance dependencies have been proposed for instance in [31,27,32,18,42], mostly within the general GPSG framework.

The relativization process, for instance, can be expressed in intuitionistic logic through the inference rule of implication introduction. Pareschi and

Miller [31] first proposed this rule to control when the empty noun-phrase is used.

For instance, the following rule for *relative* can be represented as follows in λ-Prolog (input and output string arguments, which logic grammars usually make invisible, need to be explicit in this formulation- they are noted with no commas):

```
relative (that::L1) L2 :-  (np Z Z) => s L1 L2.
```

The np clause stretching between the string Z and the same string Z (i.e., describing an empty np) is only available during the proof that there is a sentence between strings L1 and L2, within the proof that there is a relative clause between a string L1 fronted by "that" and a string L2. This prevents empty noun phrases from being generated outside relative clauses.

This approach, however, still admits incorrect sentences, the avoidance of which would involve cumbersome additions. In particular, the freely available rule of weakening, which allows unused assumptions to be simply discarded, results in relative clauses with no empty noun phrase (as in * the house [that Jack built the house]). Linear logic [18] has been proposed to remedy this problem, but it does not remedy other problems, involving both over- and undergeneration.

Categorial Grammars. The line of work starting with Lambek [24,25] and leading to modern categorial grammar [43,29,44], which has close relations with lambda-calculus and with non-commutative linear logic, is an important instance of the "parsing as deduction" paradigm. Categorial grammars are grammars in which information about all possible combinations of constituents is embedded in their categories. They are based on the idea that language expressions can be analyzed as the functional product of a functor applied to a suitable set of simpler argument expressions [30].

Categories are divided into *basic* and *derived.* Basic categories are just category symbols. Derived categories, noted A/B, where A and B are (simple or derived) categories, may be identified with functions which map expressions of category B into the set of expressions of category A. The concatenation of an expression E_1 of category A/B with an expression E_2 of category B is an expression of category A. When E_2 is expected at the left of the function rather than the right, the function is noted A\B.

For instance, if our basic categories are N and S, we can define the category for "likes" as the derived category (S\N)/N. Then if we attach the category N to the lexical items "Maria" and "Caitlin", we can analyze "Maria likes Caitlin" as an S, as follows:

```
Maria           likes          Caitlin
-----           --------       -------
  N             (S\N)/N           N
                ----------------------
                         S\N
--------------------------------------
                  S
```

Thus, a categorial grammar is defined by specifying the categories of basic expressions. The language generated by such a grammar is the closure of the set of basic expressions under functional product. Our ubiquitous example, long distance dependencies, can be analyzed as involving categories produced under a composition operator [36].

Since functions and arguments need not be restricted to those that have only syntactic properties, categorial grammars can be used to study the composition of grammatical expressions across a variety of domains: syntactic, semantic, phonological, etc.

Various extensions of categorial grammar have been proposed. Flexible categorial grammars, including rules for "type change" of expressions have been studied for instance in [43]. Ways of merging the categorial and the unification grammar framework have been studied for instance in [40,48].

4.3 Principle-and-Constraints Approaches

Approaches based on principles and constraints, such as Government-Binding, Barriers, and HPSG, move away from construction-specific and language-particular rules, replacing them by a small set of universally valid principles plus a set of language-specific constraints, from whose deductive interactions the necessary constructions follow.

Head-Driven Phrase Structure Grammar. Head-Driven Phrase Structure Grammar, or HPSG [33], is based on the intuition that each phrase contains a central word, called its lexical head, which determines many of the syntactic properties of that phrase (e.g. for a verb phrase, the verb; for a prepositional phrase, the preposition; etc.).

A sign such as the lexical sign *moon* can be described by a feature structure with attributes PHON (phonology), SYN (syntax) and SEM (semantics). Syntactic features are further classified as LOC (local) and BIND (binding).

Local features in general specify inherent syntactic properties of a sign (e.g. part of speech, inflection, case, etc.), and lexicality (whether a sign is lexical or phrasal). *Binding* features are non-local in the sense that they provide information about long distance dependencies.

Local syntactic features are further classified into *head features*, *subcategorization features* (SUBCAT) and *lexical features* (LEX). Head features specify syntactic properties that a lexical sign shares with its projections (i.e. the phrasal signs headed by a lexical sign). Subcategorization features express what kinds of phrasal signs the sign in question typically combines with (e.g. for *walk*, the SUBCAT list is $< NP$[NOM]$>$, indicating that *walk* must combine with a single NP in nominative case). LEX is a binary feature which distinguishes between lexical and non-lexical signs. Feature structures of non-lexical signs have a fourth attribute, daughters (DTRS), further described below. Binding features include SLASH, which provides information about gaps and their binding to an appropriate dislocated constituent (as in "Which principle did John believe _ had been discovered", in which "Which principle" must be bound to the gap, represented '_'); REL, which give information about unbound relative elements in the sign, and QUE, which performs the same function about interrogative elements.

HPSG-inspired approaches include Constraint Logic Grammars, or CLGs [3,13], which were inspired in the CLP paradigm [19], the Comprehensive Unification Formalism, or CUF [14], and CU-Prolog [39].

Chomskyan Approaches. Good introductions to Chomskyan theories can be found in [45,8]. Simplifying somewhat the presentation of van Riemsdijk and Williams [45], we can view the principal components of a GB grammar [6] as consisting of three rule systems and a set of modules which define well-formedness conditions on each of the following four levels of representation:

- D-structure or DS, which reflects the thematic structure of the utterance (basically, "who did what to whom");
- an intermediate level called S-structure, or SS, representing its surface grammatical structure, and related to D-structure by the displacement of NPs from their D-structure positions;
- logical form, or LF, in which meaning is most explicitly represented, and related to S-structure by the displacement of certain phrases;
- phonological form, or PF, where phonological properties are defined, and related to S-structure by a phonological mapping.

The modules act as conditions on rule application, or as well-formedness conditions on representations or on rules. Research joining Chomskyan theories and logic programming includes [35,20,9,11,34,21,2,12].

5 A Computational Linguist's Wishlist for Prolog

When invited to the talk from which this article evolved, I consulted several colleagues (Harvey Abramson, Hassan Ait-Kaci, Dan Fass, Mark Johnson, Michael McCord, Fred Popowich, David Scott Warren, Eric Villemonte de la Clergerie, Fernando Pereira, Randy Sharp) working or having worked on processing language through logic re. what Prolog features would be useful to them.

The most universally required feature was an improvement in efficiency, given that large natural language projects need to handle hundreds of thousands of rules. It was interesting in particular to learn why some researchers that had been previously fascinated with logic programming, and continued to be, resorted nevertheless to other implementation paradigms even though their design process continued to be logic-based. For instance, Michael McCord quoted a 20 fold speedup for his C versions of his translation system, LMT (personal communication, 1998).

Such concerns about efficiency are now partially out of date. Recent Prolog implementations do reduce the gap considerably (e.g. Mercury, BinProlog's logic grammars which compile to C), and they provide moreover the ability to generate C code and run it remotely over the web. These recent developments have not yet become sufficiently known, and the bad reputation that math and logic hold, as being difficult subjects, for the general public, makes procedural notations more familiar, and therefore more attractive, than logic-based syntax. Some of the concerns overtly related to efficiency might in fact have been tinted by this notational aversion. However, there does remain a gap between Prolog and say, C, in terms of combined speed, robustness and completeness. Bridging this gap should be a priority for the LP community.

Also important is the lack of reliable licensing. When a given Prolog company ceases to exist, for instance, contracts that depend on it suffer. It would seem that what we need is a commercially available, support-guaranteed, competitively efficient Prolog standard- and there is no technical reason why we could not have one.

The need for better environments was also mentioned, e.g. static tools for debugging large programs (as for untyped languages in general).

Transparent mechanisms to avoid left-recursion and recomputations are also desired. Presently, these are only available in experimental systems such as XSB (`http://www.cs.sunysb.edu/~sbprolog/ xsb-page.html`).

As Eric Villemonte de la Clergerie has pointed out, the practical development of systems based on Typed Feature Structures seem to require low level modifications of the current WAM model, given that structure copying mechanisms are not very efficient for them (because unification will build many temporary structures). Copying vs. sharing is also an issue for tabular based systems (e.g. for DyALog [46], which uses sharing, and for XSB, which gets the benefit of some sharing through its use of a trie data structure to represent its tables)- particularly when there are relatively large structures built that must be tabled. That situation might well arise when feature structures are required for complex sentences.

Other items in the wishlist include: the construction of packed parse forests (it is costly to construct and enumerate different trees); some simple way to change the parse strategy, which would be a nice complement to Prolog's strength for easy prototyping; some standard implementation of (typed) feature structures; the automation of some types of constraints which are natural to natural language processing (e.g. on strings, on trees); coroutining; more syntactic sugar such as a notation for optional or repeated constituents; higher order notations as those provided in Lambda Prolog or in Assumption Grammars; and empirical and statistical techniques (e. g. to account for preferences), for which good and efficient treatment of floating point numbers is needed.

Mark Johnson has suggested that the ultimate test for logic programming as the methodology of choice for natural language applications would be to show that it can describe some set of linguistic constructions faster and more accurately than any of the available alternatives. The idea of a grammar-writing contest at Computational Linguistic conferences, in the style of Bart Demoen's programming contests at the Logic Programming conferences, comes to mischievous mind...

6 What Fashion of the Day Are We Losing To?

The reasons why LP has not spread as much as it should have given its potential are diverse.

Fad plays a role, as in all areas of the new and quickly evolving discipline that Computing Sciences is. Cultural traditions also play a role, as is clear from the fact that in Europe logic programming is much more popular than in North America. We have also seen how partly misplaced concerns about efficiency have affected the use of logic programming. The LP community's focus on academic developments is also partly responsible. For instance, for natural language applications it would have been relatively easy to produce commercial prototypes impressive enough to make Prolog spread, albeit with no publishable value. But researchers typically shied away from these types of efforts- and given academia's emphasis on the publish-or-perish dictum, one can hardly blame them. This focus on academic developments probably strengthened, by the way, the average person's suspiciousness of logic as a high-brow, unwieldy creature.

Whatever the reason behind LP's popularity not being up-to-par with its promise, it is interesting to examine what competing frameworks are becoming more popular. One would think that competing artificial intelligence languages would be our main rival- but this is not the case. The main family of competitor AI languages, the functional family, with illustrious representatives such as Lisp and Haskell, suffers from the same lack of wordly success as does logic programming.

Would we then be losing ground to other quick prototyping languages? Wrong again. Most researchers with knowledge of Prolog who work in complex AI systems end up prototyping in Prolog, then implementing in ... C!

In such a context, the first answer on how to regain the natural language processing market could simply be: "Just you wait". Maintaining, say, large natural language processing systems written in C will eventually become a nightmare.

More actively, we can do the following:

- choose one of the recent, efficient Prolog versions as the standard one, and take steps towards guaranteeing support and no risk of licenses left dangling upon contracts which depended on them. This is easier said than done, since companies' view of what is secure involves five or six or more vendors all supplying compatible products, as for C++ for instance.
- judiciously incorporate features from the above section's wishlist into the chosen Prolog (some are easy to add, some are not);
- go out into the real industrial applications world. Having useful applications to show which can be reasonably updated will be invaluable when the realization hits that large C systems do not lend themselves to easy maintenance.

7 How Can Logic Programming Benefit from Regaining the Market?

In a Newsweek interview in March 1998, Bill Gates identified what in his opinion is the next step in making computers easier to use: whizzy computer graphics, voice-recognition software and natural language understanding so the computer can listen to you, voice synthesis so it can talk back to you, AI programs to guess what you really want.

Our position is that LP is the major promise for current ambitious plans such as those of Microsoft re. natural language communication with computers. The accessibility of speech related software of reasonable reliability has turned a series of interesting applications, such as speech guided computer use, into attainable goals. The advent of the web, while providing many nice new functionalities, has made it necessary to attack problems that were not as crucial earlier, such as concept extraction and semantic-based search. Logic programming, in our opinion, is one of the most promising tools for the achievement of the new goals. The time seems ripe to draw on the expertise of the excellent but scattered specialists in the field of Natural Language Understanding and Computational Logic, and to join forces in order to avoid duplication of efforts, and to get the best possible results. In fact, one such collaborative effort is under way, between the Americas and Europe.

We next describe recent research on one extension to logic programming which has proved useful for natural language applications, and we discuss how it can facilitate novel natural language processing applications with relative ease.

8 Assumptive Logic Programming and Grammars

Assumptive Logic Programs [37] are logic programs augmented with a) linear and intuitionistic implications scoped over the current continuation, and b) implicit multiple accumulators, useful in particular to make the input and output strings invisible when our program describes a grammar (in which case we talk of Assumption Grammars [42]). Hidden accumulators allow us to disregard the input and output string arguments, as in DCGs, but with no preprocessing requirement.

Here we shall only be concerned with (affine) linear and intuitionistic implications, respectively noted +X and *X. Affine linear logic is the kind in which assumptions need to be consumed at most once, rather than exactly once as in linear logic. The use of linear affine implication is exemplified in 11.3; in this section we shall only use intuitionistic implication. Both are consumed through the same notation, -X.

Terminal symbols will be noted as: `#word`.

We shall now illustrate how assumption grammars can deal with inter-sentential dependencies through the example of anaphora, in which a given noun phrase in a discourse is referred to in another sentence, e.g. through a pronoun. We refer to the noun phrase and the pronoun in question as entities which co-specify, since they both refer to the same individual of the universe.

As a discourse is processed, the information gleaned from the grammar and the noun phrases as they appear can be temporarily added as hypotheses ranging over the current continuation. Consulting this information, then, reduces to calling the predicate in which this information is stored.

We exemplify the hypothesizing part through the following noun phrase rules:

```
np(X,VP,VP):- proper_name(X),  -specifier(X).
np(X,VP,R):- det(X,NP,VP,R), noun(X-F,NP), *specifier(X-F).

pronoun(X-[masc,sing]):- #he.
pronoun(X-[fem,sing]):- #her.

anaphora(X):- pronoun(X).

noun(X-[fem,sing],woman(X)):- #woman.
```

The intuitionistic assumption, `*specifier(X)`, keeps in `X` the noun phrase's relevant information. In the case of a proper name, this is simply the constant representing it plus the agreement features gender and number; in the case of a quantified noun phrase, this is the variable introduced by the quantification, also accompanied by these agreement features.

Potential co-specifiers of an anaphora can then consume the most likely co-specifiers hypothesized (i.e., those agreeing in gender and number), through a third rule for noun phrase:

```
np(X,VP,VP):- anaphora(X), -specifier(X).
```

Using intuitionistic implication ensures that the same referent can be related to multiple pronouns (as in "Bill misbehaved, then he lied, then he launched an attack to deflect the public's attention", where both occurrences of "he" refer to "Bill").

9 Controlling Virtual Worlds and Robots Through Natural Language

Virtual and robotics worlds have special characteristics that can be exploited for implementing natural language control:

- they mostly employ imperative (subjectless) outermost sentences
- dynamic changes of the world are driven by natural language utterances
- formula production is inadequate: subformulas must be evaluated by consulting the world (e.g. "Craft a car, give it to Peter" must evaluate "it" to the new world object represented by the car that avatar crafted)

These features induce interesting interactions between the parser and the world description. We have experimented with the following applications of Assumption Grammars:

9.1 Generating VRML Animations Through Natural Language

This research, done in collaboration with Andrea Schiel and Paul Tarau (paper under preparation), presents a proof-of-concept internet-based agent programmed in BinProlog which receives a natural language description of a robot's goal in a blocks world, and generates the VRML animation of a sequence of actions by which the robot achieves the stated goal. It uses a partial order planner.

The interaction storyboard is as follows: The user types in an NL request via an HTML form, stating a desirable final state to be achieved. This is sent over the Internet to a BinProlog based CGI script working as a client connected to the multi-user World-State server. The NL statement is used to generate an expression of the goal as a conjunction of post-conditions to be achieved. The goal is passed to the planner module, also part of the CGI script. The plan materializes as a VRML animation, ending in a visual representation of the final state to be sent back as the result of the CGI script, as well as in an update of the WorldState database.

Our analyzer, based on Assumption Grammars, can deal with anaphora and multisentential input.

The results we prototyped for the blocks world can be transposed to other domains, by using domain-tailored planners and adapting the NL grammar to those specific domains. A more interesting extension is the development of a single agent to produce VRML animations from NL goals with respect to different applications of planning. This might be achieved by isolating the domain-specific knowledge into an application-oriented ontology; adapting a partial order planner to consult this ontology modularly; and likewise having the grammar examine the hierarchy of concepts in order to make sense of domain-oriented words.

9.2 Driving Robots Through Natural Language

A series of mini-robots commandable through natural language [41,26] moves in an enclosed room, avoiding obstacles through sensors. They know about time units, can detect features such as room temperature, humidity, etc., and can recharge themselves through sources of light positioned within the room.

We develop a logic system for the command language into which natural language commands translate and from which commands are executed. This high degree of formalization is currently believed necessary in robotics, and allows us in particular great economy: the syntax of our logic system is the representation language for commands, and its semantics is the high level execution specification, resulting in several calls to Prolog and C routines.

Natural language commands are of the form exemplified below:

- Go to the nearest source of light in ten minutes.
- Go to point P taking care that the temperature remains between X and Y degrees.
- Let robot A pass.
- Give X to robot B.
- Stop as soon as the humidity exceeds H.

Imperative sentences with an implicit subject, which are rare in other applications, are common here. Complements are typically slots to be filled in mostly by constants.

Our approach combines the two current main approaches in robotics: a high-level deductive engine generates an overall plan, while dynamically consulting low level, distributed robotics programs which interface dynamically with the robot's actions and related information.

9.3 LogiMOO — a Virtual World Consultable in Natural Language

We have developed a Bin-Prolog based virtual world running under Netscape and Explorer, called LogiMOO, with a multilingual and extensible natural language front end [38]. It allows communication between distant users in real time, hiding the complexities of the distributed communication model through the usual metaphors: places (starting from a default lobby), ports, ability to *move* or *teleport* from one place to another, a *wizard* resident on the server, *ownership* of objects, the ability to *transfer* ownership and a built-in notifier agent watching for messages as a background thread.

LogiMOO makes use of linear and intuitionistic assumption techniques, and is based on a set of embeddable logic programming components which interoperate with standard Web tools. Immediate evaluation of world knowledge by the parser yields representations which minimize the unknowns, allowing us to deal with advanced Natural Language constructs like anaphora and relativization efficiently. We take advantage of the simplicity of our controlled language to provide as well an easy adaptation to other natural languages than English, with English-like representations as a universal interlingua.

The peculiar features of the world to be consulted- a virtual world- induced novel parsing features which are interesting in themselves: flexible handling of dynamic knowledge, immediate evaluation of noun phrase representations, allowing us to be economic with representation itself, inference of some basic syntactic categories from the context, a treatment of nouns as proper nouns, easy extensibility within the same language as well as into other natural languages.

The Appendix shows a sample consultation session.

10 Concept Based Retrieval Through Natural Language

Another interesting application, now that the web creates the need for intelligent retrieval of texts, is to automate the classification among semantic lines of texts retrieved. Assumption Grammars have been proposed, in conjunction with other techniques from Artificial Intelligence and Databases (concept hierarchies, multi-layered databases and intelligent agents) for intelligently searching information pertaining to a specific industry on the web.

For instance, if we are within a forestry domain of interest, we can use a taxonomy of forestry-related concepts, which allows the search engine to specialize or generalize given concepts (e.g. going from "water" to "lakes", or vice versa), and to use the contextual information provided by forestry domains in order to avoid nonsensical answers. Search engines that base their search on keywords rather than semantics, in contrast, have been known to respond for instance to a query for documents related to "clear cuts near water" with "Complete poetical works from William Wordsworth", among a list of other equally wrong associations.

The next section will show our taxonomy encoding schemes in some detail, albeit for another application. One approach to concept-based retrieval through controlled natural language can be found in [47].

11 Database Initialization from Natural Language

If we agree that the next challenge for computers will be more human like communication, including visual, speech and natural language understanding components, we will, among other developments, need to provide a means to input information to the computer simply through natural language. Given that the database field is sufficiently formalized, and includes logic-based incarnations such as Datalog, it is tempting to think of exploring how we can go from language sentences (spoken or written) to the automatic creation of a database that represents the information in those sentences.

Of course, this is an whole new field of research with many interesting aspects to it. In this section we will first describe one possible approach for database creation from natural language, and then we will argue that a simple higher level extension of LP, timeless assumptions, greatly facilitates the task of going from discourse to databases. More research is needed to provide a thorough proof of concept.

11.1 Underlying Conventions

Let us examine what kinds of English descriptions we shall admit, and what kinds of representations for database relations should be extracted automatically from them.

The Natural Language Subset. Our subset of language consists of sentences in the active voice, where relation words (nouns, verbs and adjectives) correspond to database predicates, and their complements to arguments of these predicates. For instance, "John reads Ivanhoe to Mary" generates the Prolog assertion

reads(john,ivanhoe,mary).

Vocabulary reasonably common to all databases belongs to the static part of our system (e.g. articles, prepositions, common verbs such as "to be", etc.), and vocabulary specific to each application (e.g. proper names, nouns, verbs proper of the application, etc.) is entered at creation time, also through spoken language, with menu-driven help from the system.

In the interest of ease of prototyping, we shall first only use universal quantifiers (as in the clausal form of logic), whether explicit or implicit, and only the restrictive type of relative clauses (i.e., those of the form "(All) ... that...", where the properties described by the relative clause restrict the range of the variable introduced by the quantifier "all". Such relatives translate into additional predicates in the Horn clause's body, as in

```
People like cats that purr.
```

for which a possible translation is

```
like(P,C):- person(P), cat(C), purrs(C).
```

We will also generate predicates with compound names coming from a noun phrase's head noun and list of adjectives, rather than a new predicate for each adjective, as in:

```
Canadian citizens can apply for old age pensions.
   can_apply(C,P):- canadian_citizen(C), old_age_pension(P).
```

Synonyms can be recognized by the natural language analyzer, so that for instance "persons" can be used interchangeably with "people". It is easy to include alternative lexical definitions in the language processing module of our system, so that all words for a given concept, say "people" and "persons", translate into a single database relation name (say, "people"). Thus we can allow the flexibility of synonyms together with the programming convenience of having only one constant for each individual- no need for equality axioms and their related processing overhead.

Semantic Types. It is useful to have information about semantic types. For instance, we may have informed the database that people like animals, and may not have explicitly said that people like cats that purr. But if we knew that cats are animals, we could easily infer that people like cats and that they like cats that purr, given the appropriate query.

If we wanted to reject semantically anomalous input, much of this could be done through simply checking type compatibility between, say, the expected argument of a predicate, and its actual argument. For instance, if "imagine" requires a human subject, and appears in a sentence with a non-human subject, the user can be alerted of the anomaly and appropriate action can be taken. Variables can be typed when introduced by a natural language quantifier, and constants can be typed in the lexicon, when defining proper names. The notation used to represent a semantic type can reflect the relevant set inclusion relationships in the type hierarchy.

Much effort has been devoted to efficient encodings of type hierarchies. A recent survey and breakthrough results for logic programming are presented in [15]. These results can be easily transfered to a menu-driven module of our system which will question the user about a topmost class in the database's domain, its subsets, etc., and accordingly construct the class hierarchy encoded in such a way that set inclusion relationships are decidable with little more than unification. A visual representation of the type hierarchy thus constructed is under way, as feedback to the user.

Set-orientation. Our logic programming representation of a database should be set-oriented. That is, rather than having n clauses for representing a unary property that n individuals satisfy, we can have one clause for the entire set (e.g. biblical([adam,eve]). Database primitives for handling relations on sets are provided.

Intensionally as well as extensionally represented sets are allowed, in two ways. First, having semantic types associated to each variable and constant makes it possible to give intensional replies rather than calculating an extensionally represented set. For instance, we can reply "all birds" to the question of which birds fly if the database expresses that all entities of type bird fly, rather than checking the property of flying on each individual bird (assuming we even were to list all birds individually). We can even account for exceptions, e.g. by replying: "All birds except penguins". The user can always choose to request an extensional reply if the first, intensional answer is not enough.

Secondly, we have found it useful in some cases to represent sets of objects as a type and an associated cardinality (e.g., in a query such as "How many cars are in stock?", we do not really want to have a name for each of the cars, being only interested in the numbers of (indistinguishable) entities of type car.

Events In order to correctly relate information about the same event given in different sentences of a discourse, we translate n-ary relations into sets of binary ones linked by an event number. For instance, if we input the sentence:

"John gave Rover to Mary."

instead of generating the ternary relation:

```
gave(john,rover,mary)
```

the analyzer generates a representation that keeps track of the event, or information number within the discourse, through the three assertions[2]:

```
gave(1,who,john).
gave(1,what,rover).
gave(1,to,mary).
```

This method roughly corresponds to event logics, dating as far back as 1979 [23]. It provides us with a simple way to be flexible as to the number of arguments in a relation. Notice that the event number is not necessarily the same as the sentence number. If our next sentence is

```
"This happened in 1998"
```

[2] In fact, semantic types are also generated at language analysis stage, but we overlook them here for simplicity.

then the system needs to recognize the event described in the previous sentence as the one referred to by "this", and add the following clause to the database:

```
gave(1,when,1998).
```

In order for our natural language analyzer to be able to effect such translations, it needs information about semantic types of each argument of a relation. This is given in the lexicon, specifically in the definitions of nouns, verbs and adjectives, since these words typically correspond to predicates in a database. Lexical definitions for these can either be input once and for all for a given domain, or elicited from the user in menu-driven fashion. The latter option has the attraction of providing extensibility to the system, which can then admit new words into its vocabulary.

11.2 Notation Conventions

Type Declarations. The user can describe type hierarchies as the partial example below shows, or through a menu-driven questionnaire which will result in them.

```
type(being,[person,god,animal,inanimate]).
type(person,[man,woman]).
type(person,[doctor,patient,nurse,salesperson,teacher,
   driver,unemployed]).
type(inanimate,[vehicle,furniture,appliance,house,company]).
type(vehicle,[car,truck,motorbike]).

set(man,[adam,cain,abel]).
set(woman,[eve]).

generic(car).
```

The "type" definitions express that people, god, animal and inanimate are subtypes of being, that people are in turn classified either according to sex or to occupation, and so on. Subtypes must be disjoint, and must completely cover the type (i.e., the union of individuals in all subtypes of a type must be equal to the set of individuals of that type).

The "set" definitions represent leaf types in the hierarchy in extensional fashion.

The "generic" definitions represent leaf types in the hierarchy such that individuals are not to be distinguished from each other, but merely counted (as in "Renault sold 400 cars in 1997").

Type definitions are complemented internally and invisibly with the addition of a convenient representation for the type, and a description of how to reach, if possible, the specific elements of the type as well. For instance, the second type declaration above gets compiled into:

```
type(person,[X&person],Set):- type_union([man,woman],Set).
```

which uses the pre-defined predicate "type_union" to calculate the set of individuals in both subtypes. Of course, type_union eventually consults the "set" and "generic" definitions to give either extensional, intensional, or mixed replies to queries, as the user might require.

As we have seen, semantic types are also referred to by the system's natural language component. We examine how this works in the next section.

Relation Definitions. In this section we will use the n-ary representation of relationships for the sake of simplicity, but in fact all relations are compiled into the binary, event-focussed notation described before.

As we said, our relation-inducing words are nouns, verbs and adjectives. The system elicits type definitions from the user upon creating the domain-specific part of the lexicon. For instance "to live in" will induce a relation with two arguments: a person and a place, so one of the definitions for "lives" will declare it as a verb with an expected subject of type person and an expected complement of type "place" introduced by the preposition "in".

From the user's description of the type hierarchy, the system will be able to reconstruct the convenient representation of each type, so that the definition of the word "lives", for instance, ends up looking as follows:

```
verb(S-being&person&X,C-place&Y, prep(in),lives_in(S-X,C-Y)) :-
    #lives.
```

This rule expresses that the word "lives" is a verb, that it expects a subject represented S with type represented "X&person&being", as well as a complement represented C, introduced by the preposition "in", and with type represented as "Y&place&being". "&" is an operator in infix notation, meant to represent set inclusion relationships. For instance the above verb definition expresses that the subject's type is known to be of type "person" which is included in "being" (i.e., both a person and a being), and that further specification of the type is possible, by unification of the variable X with the representation of one of the subtypes of "person". Thus, if we are parsing the sentence

```
All doctors live in limbo.
```

our grammar rules are written such that the subject's representation, namely

```
Subject-doctor&person&being
```

must unify with the representation expected of the subject by the verb definition, namely

```
S-X&person&being
```

Failure to unify indicates semantic incompatibility, and results in the sentence's rejection and an error message. Successful unification may, as in the example above, further specify a given type ("person" becomes more precisely determined as "doctor").

So, a user's English description of database information results in the analyzer extracting type representations for the arguments of the relations induced by each noun, verb or adjective in a sentence, and using them to construct the database relation definitions that represent the information given in the sentence, e.g.

```
lives_in(S-doctor&person&being,limbo&place&being).
```

More complex relations compile similarly, e.g. the user's information in English that

```
People like cats that purr.
```

compiles into:

```
likes(P-X&person&being,C-Y&cat&animal&being):- purrs(C).
```

Notice that type information translates into type representations attached to the variables rather than into unary predicates on the right hand side.

11.3 Timeless Assumptions for Flexible Database Creation

When we create databases through natural language, we will likely use anaphora quite a bit. Alternative paraphrases of the same phrase should also be allowed.

To obtain this flexibility, we will also define, on top of the linear and intuitionistic assumptions we already have, another type called timeless assumptions, which will allow us to consume assumptions after they are made (as before), but also, when a program requires them to be consumed at a point in which they have not yet been made, they will be assumed to be "waiting" to be consumed, until they are actually made:

```
% Assumption:

% the assumption being made was expected
% by a previous consumption
=X:- -wait(X), !.
% if there is no previous expectation of X, assume it linearly
=X:- +X.
```

```
% Consumption:

% uses an assumption, and deletes it if linear
=-X:- -X, !.
% if the assumption has not yet been made,
% adds its expectation as an assumption
=-X:- +wait(X).
```

With these definitions it no longer matters whether an assumption is first made and then consumed, or first "consumed" (i.e., put in a waiting list until when it is actually made) and then made.

We can use timeless assumptions for instance to build a logic programmed database directly from:

```
The blue car stopped. Two people came out of it.
```

or:

```
Two people came out of it after the blue car stopped.
```

To cover both cases, we could timelessly assume an object of description D for each noun phrase represented by a variable X and with features F that appears in the discourse:

```
=object(X,F,D).
```

When encountering a pronoun with matching features F', in a sentence that further describes the referred object as D', replace the timeless assumption by one which adds D' to what is known of X:

```
=object(X,F,D&D').
```

Once the discourse ends, we can firm the assumption into a regular database clause.

12 Conclusion

We have studied the main problems in processing language, the main approaches to these problems both in logic programming and in computational linguistics, and the societal and practical reasons why the adoption of logic programming for natural language projects has not been as widespread as its real potential should have commanded. We have also proposed a line of action which includes striving for extended features useful to natural language and for an efficient, licence-reliable Prolog standard; and the need to focus for a while on software of not necessarily publishable value but impressive and practical. It is only through getting out there in the real world that the full potential of logic programming can be given the recognition it deserves.

We believe that natural language applications are at present privileged among all possible logic programming applications, given the new need for processing massive amounts of web data which are mostly expressed in natural language, the availability of fairly reliable speech recognition software, and the existing desire to provide more human-like means of communication with computers- a desire which was always there, but has only recently become an attainable goal.

With this article we hope to stimulate further efforts in this direction.

Acknowledgements

Thanks are due to Harvey Abramson, Hassan Ait-Kaci, Dan Fass, Mark Johnson, Michael McCord, Fred Popowich, David Scott Warren, Eric Villemonte de la Clergerie, Fernando Pereira, and Randy Sharp for useful comments on this article's first draft, and to the anonymous referees. This research was made possible by NSERC grant 611024.

Appendix: A Sample LogiMOO Consultation Session in Controlled English and Spanish

```
TEST: Go to the lobby. Look.
WORDS: [go,to,the,lobby,.,look,.]
SENTENCES: [go,to,the,lobby] [look]

==BEGIN COMMAND RESULTS==
you are in the  lobby
SUCCEEDING(go(lobby))
user(veronica,none,'http://localhost').
user(paul,none,'http://localhost').
login(paul).
online(veronica).
online(paul).
place(lobby).
place(office).
contains(lobby,veronica).
contains(lobby,paul).
SUCCEEDING(look)

==END COMMAND RESULTS==

TEST: Craft a cat. Where is the cat? Who has it?
WORDS: [craft,a,cat,.,where,is,the,cat,?,who,has,it,?]
SENTENCES: [craft,a,cat] [where,is,the,cat] [who,has,it]
```

```
==BEGIN COMMAND RESULTS==
SUCCEEDING(craft(cat))
cat is in lobby
SUCCEEDING(where(cat))
joe has cat
SUCCEEDING(who(has,cat))

==END COMMAND RESULTS==


TEST: Dig the bedroom. Go there. Dig a kitchen, open a port south
 to the kitchen, go there, open a port north to the bedroom. Go
 there. Craft a song-au. Give it to the Wizard.

==BEGIN COMMAND RESULTS==
SUCCEEDING(dig(bedroom))
you are in the  bedroom
SUCCEEDING(go(bedroom))
SUCCEEDING(dig(kitchen))
SUCCEEDING(open\_port(south,kitchen))
you are in the  kitchen
SUCCEEDING(go(kitchen))
SUCCEEDING(open\_port(north,bedroom))
you are in the  bedroom
SUCCEEDING(go(bedroom))
SUCCEEDING(craft(song.au))
logimoo:<joe>\# 'wizard:I give you song.au'
SUCCEEDING(give(wizard,song.au))

==END COMMAND RESULTS==


TEST: Craft a Gnu. Who has it? Where is it? Where am I?
WORDS: [craft,a,gnu,.,who,has,it,?,where,is,it,?,where,am,i,?]
SENTENCES: [craft,a,gnu] [who,has,it] [where,is,it] [where,am,i]

==BEGIN COMMAND RESULTS==
SUCCEEDING(craft(gnu))
joe has gnu
SUCCEEDING(who(has,gnu))
gnu is in bedroom
SUCCEEDING(where(gnu))
you are in the  bedroom
SUCCEEDING(whereami)

==END COMMAND RESULTS==
```

```
TEST: Give to the Wizard the Gnu that I crafted. Who has it?
WORDS: [give,to,the,wizard,the,gnu,that,i,crafted,.,who,has,it,?]
SENTENCES: [give,to,the,wizard,the,gnu,that,i,crafted] [who,has,it]

==BEGIN COMMAND RESULTS==
logimoo:<joe>\# 'wizard:I give you gnu'
SUCCEEDING(give(wizard,gnu))
wizard has gnu
SUCCEEDING(who(has,gnu))

==END COMMAND RESULTS==

TEST: construya un gato. donde esta el gato? quien tiene lo?
WORDS: [construya,un,gato,.,donde,esta,el,gato,?,quien,tiene,lo,?]
SENTENCES: [construya,un,gato] [donde,esta,el,gato] [quien,tiene,lo]

==BEGIN COMMAND RESULTS==
SUCCEEDING(craft(gato))
gato is in lobby
SUCCEEDING(where(gato))
veronica has gato
SUCCEEDING(who(has,gato))

==END COMMAND RESULTS==
```

References

1. H. Abramson and V. Dahl. *Logic Grammars.* Monograph, Symbolic Computation AI Series. Springer-Verlag, 1989.
2. Jamie Andrews, V. Dahl, and F. Popowich. A Relevance Logic Characterization of Static Discontinuity Grammars. Technical report, CSS/LCCR TR 91-12, Simon Fraser University, 1991.
3. S. Balari and G. B. Varile. CLG(n): Constraint Logic Grammars. In *Proc. International Conference on Computational Linguistics*, pages 1–6, 1990.
4. J. Bresnan. *The Mental Representation of Grammatical Relations.* MIT Press, 1982.
5. B. Carpenter. *The Logic of Typed Feature Structures – with Applications to Unification Grammars, Logic Programs and Constraint Resolution.* Cambridge University Press, 1992.
6. N. Chomsky. *Lectures on Government and Binding.* Foris Publications, 1981.
7. A. Colmerauer. *Metamorphosis Grammars*, volume 63, pages 133–189. Springer-Verlag, 1978.
8. E. A. Cowper. *A Concise Introduction to Syntactic Theory.* University of Chicago Press, 1992.
9. V. Dahl. Discontinuous Grammars. *Computational Intelligence*, 5(4):161–179, 1989.
10. V. Dahl. Natural Language Processing and Logic Programming. *Journal of Logic Programming*, 12(1):681–714, 1994.

11. V. Dahl and F. Popowich. Parsing and Generation with Static Discontinuity Grammars. *New Generation Computing*, 8(3):245–274, 1990.
12. V. Dahl, F. Popowich, and M. Rochemont. A Principled Characterization of Dislocated Phrases: Capturing Barriers with Static Discontinuity Grammars. *Linguistics and Philosophy*, 16:331–352, 1993.
13. L. Damas and G. B. Varile. CLG: A Grammar Formalism Based on Constraint Resolution. In Morgado, E. M. and Martins, J. P., editors, *Proc. EPIA 1989*, Lecture Notes in Artificial Intelligence 390, Springer-Verlag, 1989.
14. A. Eisele and J Dorre. *A Comprehensive Unification Formalism.* DYANA internal memo, Institut für Maschinelle Sprachverarbeitung, University of Stuttgart, 1990.
15. A. Fall. The Foundations of Taxonomic Encoding. *Computational Intelligence*, 14(4):1–45, 1998.
16. G. Gazdar, E. Klein, G.L. Pullum, and I Sag. *Generalized Phrase Structure Grammar.* Harvard University Press, Cambridge, MA., 1985.
17. G. Gazdar and C. Mellish. *Natural Language Processing in Prolog – An Introduction to Computational Linguistics.* Addison-Wesley, 1989.
18. J. Hodas. Specifying Filler-Gap Dependency Parsers in a Linear-Logic Programming Language. In Krzysztof Apt, editor, *Logic Programming Proceedings of the Joint International Conference and Symposium on Logic programming*, pages 622–636, MIT Press, 1992.
19. J. Jaffar and J.-L Lassez. Constraint Logic Programming. In *Proc. 14th ACM Symposium on Principles of Programming Languages*, pages 111–119, 1987.
20. M Johnson. Deductive Parsing with Multiple Levels of Representation. In *Proc. 1988 Conference of the Association for Computational Linguistics*, pages 241–248, 1988.
21. M Johnson. *Deductive Parsing: The Use of Knowledge of Language*, pages 39–64. Kluwer Academic Publishers, 1991.
22. M Johnson. Logic and Feature Structures. In *Proc. Twelfth International Joint Conference on Artificial Intelligence*, pages 992–992, 1991.
23. R.A. Kowalski. *Logic for Problem Solving.* North-Holland, 1979.
24. J Lambek. The Mathematics of Sentence Structure. *American Mathematical Monthly*, 65:154–169, 1958.
25. J Lambek. Multicategories Revisited. *Categories in Computer Science, Contemporary Mathematics*, 92:217–239, 1987.
26. Thomas M.C., Dahl V., and Fall A. Logic Planning in Robotics. In *Proceedings 1995 International Conference on Systems, Man and Cybernetics*, pages 1904–1908, 1995.
27. D.A. Miller and G Nadathur. Some Uses of Higher-order Logic in Computational Linguistics. In *Proceedings of the 24th Annual Meeting of the Association for Computational Linguistics*, pages 247–255, 1986.
28. M. Moens, J. Calder, E. Klein, M. Reape, and H Zeevat. *Expressing Generalizations in Unification-based Grammar Formalisms*, pages 174–181. European Association for Computational Linguistics 89, 1989.
29. M. Moortgat. *Categorial Investigations: Logical and Linguistic Aspects of the Lambek Calculus.* PhD thesis, University of Amsterdam, Amsterdam, The Netherlands, October 1988.
30. R. T. Oehrle, E. Bach, and D. Wheeler, editors. *Categorial Grammars and Natural Language Structure.* Reidel, 1988.

31. R. Pareschi and D Miller. *Extending Definite Clause Grammars with Scoping Constructs*, pages 373–389. Warren, David H. D. and Szeredi, P., editors, International Conference in Logic Programming, MIT Press, 1990.
32. F. C. N Pereira. *Semantic Interpretation as Higher-order Deduction.* In J. van Eijck, editor, Logics in AI, Proc. European Workshop JELIA '90, pages 78–96, Springer-Verlag, 1991.
33. C.J Pollard and I.A. Sag. Information-based Syntax and Semantics. Technical Report CSLI Notes 13, Center for the Study of Language and Information, Stanford, 1987.
34. E. P. Stabler. Representing Knowledge with Theories about Theories. *Journal of Logic Programming*, 9(1):105-138, 1990.
35. E.P. Jr. Stabler. Restricting Logic Grammars with Government-binding Theory. *Journal of Computational Linguistics*, 1987.
36. M. Steedman. Dependency and Coordination in the Grammar of Dutch and English. *Language*, 61:523–568, 1985.
37. Paul Tarau, Veronica Dahl, and Andrew Fall. Backtrackable State with Linear Affine Implication and Assumption Grammars. In Joxan Jaffar and Roland H.C. Yap, editors, *Concurrency and Parallelism, Programming, Networking, and Security*, Lecture Notes in Computer Science 1179, pages 53–64, Springer-Verlag, 1996.
38. Paul Tarau, Koen De Boschere, Veronica Dahl, and Stephen Rochefort. LogiMOO: an Extensible Multi-User Virtual World with Natural Language Control. accepted for publication in Journal of Logic Programming.
39. H. Tuda, Hasida K., and Sirai H. JPSG Parser on Constraint Logic Programming. In *Proceedings of the European Chapter of the Association for Computational Linguistics*, pages 95–102, 1989.
40. H. Uszkoreit. Categorial Unification Grammars. In *Proceedings International Conference on Computational Linguistics 86*, pages 187–194, 1986.
41. Dahl V., Fall A., and M. C. Thomas. Driving Robots through Natural Language. In *Proceedings 1995 International Conference on Systems, Man and Cybernetics*, 1995.
42. Dahl V., Tarau P., and Li R. Assumption Grammars for Processing Natural Language In Lee Naish, editor, *Proceedings International Conference on Logic Programming'97*, pages 256–270, MIT Press, 1997.
43. J. van Benthem. The Lambek Calculus. In R. T. Oehrle, E. Bach, and D. Wheeler, editors, *Categorial Grammars and Natural Language Structure*, Dordrecht, The Netherlands, 1988.
44. J. van Benthem. *Language in Action – Categories, Lambdas and Dynamic Logic*, volume 130 of *Studies in Logic and the Foundations of Mathematics.* North-Holland, 1991.
45. Henk van Riemsdijk and Edwin Williams. *Introduction to the Theory of Grammar.* MIT Press, 1986.
46. E. Villemonte de la Clergerie. *Automates à Piles et Programmation Dynamique. DyALog: Une application à la Programmation en Logique.* PhD thesis, INRIA, Paris, 1993.
47. Osmar Zaiane, Andrew Fall, Rochefort Stephen, Dahl Veronica, and Paul Tarau. On-line Resource Discovery Using Natural Language. In *Proceedings of RIAO'97*, pages 336–355, McGill University, Montreal, June 1997.
48. H. Zeevat, E. Klein, and J. Calder. Unification Categorial Grammar. In *Lingua e Stile*, volume 4, pages 499–527. Editrice il Mulino, 1991.

Springer Series
Artificial Intelligence

N. J. Nilsson: Principles of Artificial Intelligence. XV, 476 pages, 139 figs., 1982

J. H. Siekmann, G. Wrightson (Eds.): Automation of Reasoning 2. Classical Papers on Computational Logic 1967–1970. XXII, 638 pages, 1983

R. S. Michalski, J. G. Carbonell, T. M. Mitchell (Eds.): Machine Learning. An Artificial Intelligence Approach. XI, 572 pages, 1984

J. W. Lloyd: Foundations of Logic Programming. Second, extended edition. XII, 212 pages, 1987

N. Cercone, G. McCalla (Eds.): The Knowledge Frontier. Essays in the Representation of Knowledge. XXXV, 512 pages, 93 figs., 1987

G. Rayna: REDUCE. Software for Algebraic Computation. IX, 329 pages, 1987

L. Kanal, V. Kumar (Eds.): Search in Artificial Intelligence. X, 482 pages, 67 figs., 1988

H. Abramson, V. Dahl: Logic Grammars. XIV, 234 pages, 40 figs., 1989

P. Besnard: An Introduction to Default Logic. XI, 201 pages, 1989

A. Kobsa, W. Wahlster (Eds.): User Models in Dialog Systems. XI, 471 pages, 113 figs., 1989

Y. Peng, J. A. Reggia: Abductive Inference Models for Diagnostic Problem-Solving. XII, 284 pages, 25 figs., 1990

A. Bundy (Ed.): Catalogue of Artificial Intelligence Techniques. Fourth revised edition. XVI, 141 pages, 1997 (first three editions published in the series)

R. Kruse, E. Schwecke, J. Heinsohn: Uncertainty and Vagueness in Knowledge Based Systems. Numerical Methods. XI, 491 pages, 59 figs., 1991

Z. Michalewicz: Genetic Algorithms + Data Structures = Evolution Programs. Third, revised and extended edition. XX, 387 pages, 68 figs., 1996 (first edition published in the series)

V. W. Marek, M. Truszczyński: Nonmonotonic Logic. Context-Dependent Reasoning. XIII, 417 pages, 14 figs., 1993

V. S. Subrahmanian, S. Jajodia (Eds.): Multimedia Database Systems. XVI, 323 pages, 104 figs., 1996

Q. Yang: Intelligent Planning. XXII, 252 pages, 76 figs., 1997

J. Debenham: Knowledge Engineering. Unifying Knowledge Base and Database Design. XIV, 465 pages, 288 figs., 1998

H. J. Levesque, F. Pirri (Eds.): Logical Foundations for Cognitive Agents. Contributions in Honor of Ray Reiter. XII, 405 pages, 32 figs., 1999

K. R. Apt, V. W. Marek, M. Truszczynski, D. S. Warren (Eds.): The Logic Programming Paradigm. A 25-Year Perspective. XVI, 456 pages, 57 figs., 1999

MIX
Papier aus verantwortungsvollen Quellen
Paper from responsible sources
FSC® C105338

If you have any concerns about our products,
you can contact us on
ProductSafety@springernature.com

In case Publisher is established outside the EU,
the EU authorized representative is:
Springer Nature Customer Service Center GmbH
Europaplatz 3, 69115 Heidelberg, Germany

Printed by Libri Plureos GmbH
in Hamburg, Germany